AN ECONOMIC HISTORY

OF THE UNITED STATES

AN ECONOMIC HISTORY

OF THE UNITED STATES

———— SECOND EDITION ————

JAMES F. WILLIS AND MARTIN L. PRIMACK

San Jose State University

PRENTICE HALL

Englewood Cliffs, New Jersey 07632

Library of Congress Cataloging-in-Publication Data

Willis, James Frederick
  An economic history of the United States.

  Primack's name appears first on the earlier edition.
  Includes bibliographies and index.
  1. United States--Economic conditions. I. Primack,
  Martin L. II. Title.
HC103.W56   1989   330.973   88-23871
ISBN 0-13-224163-3

Editorial/production supervision
  and interior design: *Millicent Lambert*
Cover design: *Lundgren Graphics*
Manufacturing buyer: *Margaret Rizzi*

Cover art, "Industrial Composition" by Lewardowsky.
Courtesy of The Bettmann Archives, Inc.

 © 1989, 1980 by Prentice-Hall, Inc.
A Division of Simon & Schuster
Englewood Cliffs, New Jersey 07632

Printed in the United States of America
10 9 8 7 6 5 4 3 2 1

ISBN 0-13-224163-3

Prentice-Hall International (UK) Limited, *London*
Prentice-Hall of Australia Pty. Limited, *Sydney*
Prentice-Hall Canada Inc., *Toronto*
Prentice-Hall Hispanoamericana, S.A., *Mexico*
Prentice-Hall of India Private Limited, *New Delhi*
Prentice-Hall of Japan, Inc., *Tokyo*
Simon & Schuster Asia Pte. Ltd., *Singapore*
Editora Prentice-Hall do Brasil, Ltda., *Rio de Janeiro*

To Marianna and Jim, Jr.
In memory of my beloved wife, Marlene

CONTENTS

PREFACE

The twin themes of this book are *choice* and *change*. Together they will permit us to look at the evolutionary process by which America, originally an area with a small, if growing, economy, was transformed into a society that sits center stage among the world's nations. We seek to understand how its people come to enjoy a standard of living, including a variety of choices, that is probably the greatest ever known.

Our story, then, is one of economic development. It contains many questions and problems addressed by individuals, organizations, and governments. Of course, these questions and problems changed both in nature and in emphasis as the evolutionary processes worked to make a rural, often isolated, and largely independent society into one that is centralized and highly interdependent. Was this a smooth, continuous, and harmonious transformation? Hardly! The fascinating tale of the problems and debates surrounding changing economic institutions and practices, with their concomitant political and social effects, is the stuff of which this book is made.

If these remarks make it seem as though economic historians have concluded their research, that they now have a full explanation for our development process, the truth is far from it. Though there has been a vast amount of research on such issues as land, tariff, and immigration policies, monetary and fiscal policies, and the causes and effects of slavery—to name a few—our understanding is far from complete.

Still, there is, at any moment in time, in every area of study, a "state of the art." We attempt in this book to present a state-of-the-art economic history of the United States by summarizing the conclusions of research done until recently and by providing bibliographies at the end of each chapter that will enable readers to explore more fully the original research that forms the basis for the current synthesis that this test represents. Of course, even extensive bibliographies are selective rather than exhaustive. For students preparing an extended paper on a particular topic, however, the bibliographies should provide a useful point of departure.

HOW TO TELL THE STORY

There are two primary modes of exposition of economic history. The topical mode involves separately examining each particular topic, such as the influence of foreign trade on economic development. The chief advantage of this approach is that it permits a longer and more continuous view of historical change, which is particularly beneficial when examining a secular process such as economic development. The disadvantages of this approach are that it usually demands an exposition of great length and complexity and it isolates elements of historical change that are often interdependent. In other words, the topical mode of exposition gives the "long view" of history at the expense of the "big picture."

The second mode of exposition, the chronological, divides history into distinct time periods. This is the device that we adopt in this textbook because we believe it simplifies historical analysis and because it appeals to the natural human tendency to relate time and historical events. We do so with some misgivings, however, because the chronological convention seems to suggest that the process of economic development consists of a series of identifiable and distinct stages. While some historians have argued just that, we are unpersuaded. On the contrary, we believe that economics is a process of interdependent events that, while not likely to be smooth, is nonetheless continuous.

THE ECONOMICS OF ECONOMIC HISTORY

Economists interpret history through the use of tools of their trade, economic theory and quantitative methodology. Most of the research cited in this volume is cast in those terms. In other words, economic history is interpreted in much the same way as contemporary economic events. In all of this, it is well to bear in mind the difference between economic interpretation and economic determinism.

Economic interpretation involves employing economic theory and methodology to assay the economic causes and consequences of events. Human events, after all, can be interpreted from many different perspectives. An event such as the American Revolution, for example, can be interpreted as military history, diplomatic history, or political history. But a war can also be viewed as economic history, because it results partly from economic causes and has a series of economic consequences.

Scholars rarely engage in **economic determinism**, that is, interpret the history of human events in purely economic terms. As we shall see in subsequent chapters, a few, such as Charles Beard and Karl Marx (though not all present-day Marxists), have sought to view history as a progression of events in which people act almost exclusively on the basis of their economic self- interest or through adjusting to the changing economic reality. This notion of economic determinism is now almost totally rejected. Today economists are concerned with the interrelationships among political, social, cultural, and economic events. We will see some of these interactions, for example, when we observe how British political policies affected the economic position of the American colonies and how the economic position of the colonies affected their political relationship to Great Britain.

Because such interactions are extremely complex, this introductory section is devoted to explaining some basic ideas about economics and economic history. Most importantly, we'll explain how this book is organized and suggest an effective way to use it as a tool in your studies.

THEMES WITHIN THEMES

We stated earlier that the themes of this book are choice and change. These are very broad notions, not unlike the major melodic theme of your favorite musical composition. And, economic development has many subthemes that resemble minor melodic strains. In both cases, of course, they are "minor" only in relation to the grander strains of the major theme. We have chosen to emphasize several subthemes in this work. To begin, we believe that economic development in the United States is importantly a story about the creation of a market economy. As with all such economies, the system involved property rights as well as a means of assigning or transferring those rights. We shall trace the evolution of the nation, then, from the time of the original communal European settlements in North America through the various stages by which isolated markets evolved into their late-20th-century forms.

Another subtheme is the changing relationship between government and business in the United States. From earliest colonial times, government has played a significant role in the American economy, though never without controversy over its appropriateness as a facilitator of development and as a regulatory agent. We shall trace these controversies from the colonial period through early independence (including the famous Federalist debates) to the current debate about regulation and deregulation.

AN OVERVIEW OF THE BOOK

This book has a structure, an organizational plan, designed to provide maximum benefits to the reader. Each chapter contains the following outline or skeleton on which we flesh out the body of American economic history:

1. A clear statement of economic **theory**. In most chapters, we will set forth a theory or **model**. Recall that a model is a set of formal relationships between factors or forces. As such, it is an abstraction from, or a simplification of, the immensely complex reality of a period. Because economic reality is always too complex to be described fully, we build these abstractions in order to focus on key interrelationships.

2. The **data**. As economic events are recorded, they become data. Economists work with two general classes of data: **time series data** and **cross-sectional data**. Time series data show the occurrence of a particular kind of event at different points in time. The amount of cotton exported during each year between 1815 and 1860 is an example. Cross-sectional data show the occurrence of a particular event in different activities at the same point in time or over the same span of time. The rates of return on investment in agriculture, industry, and commerce in the period from 1900 to 1930 are an example. Throughout this book, you will encounter both kinds of data.

   Of course, in a broader sense the word *data* refers to all events or happenings that are observed and recorded, not simply those that are quantified or quantifiable. Many data, especially those of an institutional nature, are not amenable to either time series or cross-sectional quantification. Bear in mind, though, that when economists talk about data, they are generally referring to those quantified phenomena that can be used in testing various hypotheses or arguments within theories or models.

3. An **interpretation**. Theory and the data appropriately suggested by that theory to test hypotheses are the ingredients necessary to interpret and explain historical events and sequences of events. By using the data to test a hypothesis within the framework of a model, economic historians can determine whether to accept or reject that argument. Frequently this method permits the student of history to determine to what extent the occurrence of one event may be explained by the occurrence of another event or of several other events. Such a study might, for example, permit a student of the American colonial period to conclude that per capita income in the colonies would have been only 1 percent higher in the absence of British economic controls. A reasonable interpretation of this result might be that the British controls had little effect on colonial growth, that the colonies would not have grown appreciably more rapidly in the absence of those controls. A further possible interpretation might be that this indicates an absence of colonial "exploitation."

Such interpretations are the final products of economic history. You will notice that the interpretations are diverse; even for the same period, the explanation of cause-and-effect relationships will vary, depending on the model of historical assumptions employed and on the data used to test that model. As new interpretations are made, old interpretations are sometimes rejected. The rejection by more recent scholars of Charles Beard's economic interpretation of the formulation and adoption of the federal Constitution is an example.

4. **Glossary**. Economists, including economic historians, have a distinct language in which they communicate among themselves and with others. Terms such as *demand function, aggregate demand,* and *linearly homogeneous production function* have very precise meanings. All students of economics must attribute the same meaning to a term and use it correctly—unlike the world of Alice in Wonderland where it was said, "Words mean whatever I say they mean!" The same term may be used again many times throughout the book. If you are unfamiliar with a term, you can find its definition in the Glossary at the end of the book.

5. **Questions**. The questions at the end of each chapter provide an opportunity for self-evaluation and call attention to topics the reader should review before going on to the next chapter. When you have answered the questions correctly, you will have summarized the major elements and conclusions of the chapter and strengthened your understanding through effective repetition.

6. **Suggested Readings**. American historians have long said that they suffer from "an embarrassment of riches." The riches are the numerous research studies of virtually every period of our history. Although some unexplored areas remain open for fruitful study, the literature of United States economic history is extensive. Some of the most important studies are listed in the Suggested Readings at the end of each chapter. Citations to those studies are found in parenthesis throughout the chapters. For example, a reference within a chapter followed by a number on parenthesis (5) means that the citation to that author's work will be found as the fifth item in the Suggested Readings section at the end of the chapter. The list will enable you to read further into the subject area of the chapter and also to begin the reading for a research paper.

Keeping these points in mind as you read will enhance the contribution this book can make to your study of economic history.

Chapter 1

THE COLONIES BEFORE 1763

The expectation of substantially different economic as well as social, political, and religious conditions and opportunities was a strong force in bringing the European colonists to North America. In large measure, those expectations, particularly the ones regarding changed economic conditions, were fulfilled, although not always in the ways the early colonists anticipated. From the early seventeenth century to the end of the French and Indian War, we can observe in North America the evolution of an economy that reflects the peculiar economic conditions of the area and the evolution also of a set of economic ties to the European economies that reflects the specialized advantages of the two parts of the world.

What accounts for the relatively rapid growth of the North American colonies even before 1763? What caused the **production possibilities function** of the colonies, the relationship that shows the various combinations of output that full employment of a nation's resources (land, labor, capital, and entrepreneurship), using the best current technology, to shift outward? In graphical terms, what caused the **production possibilities curve,** the diagrammatic presentation of the production possibilities function, to shift to the right? Were the colonies an "empty land," with few resistances to **economic development,** waiting to be developed? The "empty land–staple export–leading sector" hypothesis about colonial growth provides some very useful insights into the reasons for the colonies' success. According to this hypothesis, it is the emergence of one or more leading export sectors that provides the stimulus to incorporate more and more of a society's resources into development-oriented uses. ·

As we shall see in looking at the individual colonies and geographic regions, staple exports played a very important role in colonial growth, especially in providing the funds with which to import scarce resources. The growth of leading sectors benefiting from demand increases clearly offset what might have been a tendency toward the unfavorable terms of trade that some commodity-exporting areas suffer in the early phases of economic development.

GROWTH AND DEVELOPMENT

Intensive and Extensive Growth

There are two dimensions to growth itself. When total output increases owing to the use of more resources (land, labor, capital, and entrepreneurship), **extensive growth** occurs. As land is cleared, as population grows, as more capital instruments are used, output of commodities and services increases. This type of growth tends to occur in almost all societies, although stagnation is possible, or even decline, if less good land is used, if population falls, or the like. Extensive growth usually involves little change in the composition of output; if the society has been producing basic food staples or textiles, it is likely to demand more of those items. Moreover, from the supply side, it is likely to go on producing them in the same ways or with the same techniques.

In contrast, **intensive growth** involves not only significant changes in the composition of output but also increasing output per capita. This means that the composition of output changes (usually to fewer basic agricultural goods and more semiprocessed and processed goods) and that there are more goods of all types available to be consumed. On the supply side, productivity (output per unit of input) grows because of changes in the techniques of production and/or in the composition of output. These productivity changes encourage increases in demand. This rise in demand itself may cause increases in productivity because it allows specialization to be increased and capital and land to be used more efficiently.

Finally, economic development is the end product of long-term intensive growth. As per capita income grows and as the mix of goods and services changes, structural change tends to occur. While it is impossible to specify the precise structural changes, a few illustrations will suffice. The distribution of income is likely to change, either because of changes in the pattern of ownership of resources and returns to resource owners, or because of changes in public subsidization of activities and transfer payments to individuals. Some would argue that population growth is likely to decline (beyond some point), that the age distribution of the population will change, that more social or publicly provided overhead capital will be added. Not all of these changes will necessarily occur in a particular country, but they illustrate the kinds of structural changes that seem likely to accompany intensive growth and transform it into a joint process of economic development.

The Staple Theory of Leading Sectors

Several historians have written about the importance of the production and export of staple commodities to economies in their early economic development. Perhaps the most important of these scholars is Harold A. Innis (15, 16), a Canadian economic historian whose arguments, while limited to Canada, have broader applicability.

Fundamentally, Innis's staple theory is one of a group of **leading sector theories,** which hypothesize the existence of a sector or sectors of the economy that create effects on intensive growth and development that spread, through demand and supply influences, to the rest of the economy (hence the term *spread effects*). Such sectors (for example, tobacco exports) literally lead the rest of the economy into processes of intensive growth and development. The Innis argument clearly, and perhaps only, applies to "empty lands," those in which a new economy (rather than an evolution from an old economic order) evolves.

The importance of staple exports, then, consists largely in the diversification effects of the exportation of one or more staple commodities on the creation and expansion of domestic markets. In turn, this market growth depends on the export-import patterns that exist between the staple-producing area and the rest of the trading world. The supply of staple exports will depend on the initial endowments (relative amounts of land, labor, and capital) and on the technology of producing the staple good or goods.

The combination of two things—initial endowments and the technology of staple production—will determine the input-output combinations, or the **production function,** of the staple-producing area and the substitutability of production factors. Given the production function and the size of the market for the staple export, there will be a derived set of demands for the factors of production, land, labor, and capital. Given the supplies of these three resources, this set of demands will determine their market incomes. The resultant pattern of production will create a distribution of market incomes, and thereby a size and pattern of domestic demand, together with the possibility of processing intermediate goods from the staple commodities.

An example will illustrate how this process tends to work in an "empty land" area. Let us suppose that the staple-producing area begins with certain initial endowments of land, labor, and capital and that there is an initial set of supply-demand relationships for the staple. For the sake of specificity, let us suppose that tobacco is the staple good and that there is an increase in the demand for tobacco. The demand increase will induce an increase in the quantity supplied, with immediate spread effects to the resource markets through increases in the demand for land, labor, capital, and entrepreneurship. These increases in demand will raise the incomes of some or all of the resource owners involved by increasing the quantity of those resources employed, or their prices, or both.

If land is the factor of production in relatively great supply, if that land is highly fertile, and if labor and capital can be readily imported (and, of course, if the society can produce entrepreneurs), then average incomes in the staple export society will rise substantially. The distribution of that income, together with the **marginal propensity to import**—the amount of increased income spent on imported goods—will determine the amount and the way in which the structure of demand changes. The **production function of the staple**—the function that shows the relationship between resource inputs and staple product output—may be such that the staple is produced on large plantations. If so, and if the incomes flow largely to a small group of people with a high marginal propensity to import, then the increase in demand for domestically produced products will be relatively small and there will be correspondingly small increases in the size of the domestic market. If the reverse occurs, that is, if the income increase is more widely spread among people with lower marginal propensities to import, then the spread effects on the domestic economy will be relatively great.

What will determine the ability of the staple economy to continue the process of growth and diversification? If it begins with a favorable land-labor ratio, it must be able to reallocate its own resources and to import relatively scarce factors, labor, and capital. The **empty land** is not one in which population is pressing on the means of subsistence, but one in which high soil fertility and a large supply of land attract (initially through immigration) a large number of people who anticipate relatively high real incomes. These resource supply factors permit the initial and continuing increases in product supply and counteract the tendency to increasing costs that is built into all production processes. At the same time, the income increases permit an economic diversification that has many benefits, including the relative price and income stability that is lacking in economies tied to a single staple export.

Clearly the entire process just outlined will only succeed in societies that are nontraditional, whose institutional structure permits and encourages entrepreneurs to reallocate resources in favor of productivity-increasing uses. This means that development must be seen not only as possible but also as desirable. "Creative entrepreneurship," to use a phrase of Joseph Schumpeter's, must be allowed to work. It must allocate the presumably large supplies of the abundant resource(s). It must also allocate the scarce resources presumably available through importation to produce new products and old products in new and more productive ways, to open new markets (including resource markets), and to distribute these products in new ways or to change the organization of industries.

Replacing and Learning from the Indian Economies

A major qualification to the staple theory's usefulness in explaining North America's development is its failure to encompass some of the area's peculiar advantages. It is important to remember that the colonists adapted to the resources they encountered and also found in those initial conditions certain favorable elements created by the Indian cultures. North America was not, after all, a completely empty land. Not only did the colonists learn of new crops, especially corn and tobacco, from the Indians, but they also learned much about cultivation, crop rotation (a practice they frequently ignored), and agricultural tools and fishing techniques. All economic development is a learning process. The eastern Indian tribes lived well, reflecting a relatively high level of productivity that was the result of long-term learning. It was no small advantage to the colonists to be able to avail themselves of the adaptive learning processes of several million indigenous people. The technological superiority of the colonists, especially in the uses of metals, made it possible for them ultimately to supplant the Indians. Ironically, though these technological advantages were few in number, they were extremely important in determining which of the two cultures and economies would become dominant in North America. The Europeans' slight technological edge, together with the Indians' lack of immunity to European diseases, virtually dictated the answer, in spite of an amazing adaptation by the North American Indians to European resources (including horses) and economic techniques. The colonists, seeking resources, pushed the Native Americans into less and less desirable land until they were indeed, from an economic view, facing an empty land.

Although with this important qualification the processes of development described in the model worked generally throughout the colonies, the specifics were different from place to place. Also, both the type and size of the spread effects (demand-supply effects on the rest of the economy) differed, not only from one colony to another but also, and more especially, from one area of the colonies to another.

Extensive Growth and the Dual Economy

One must keep in mind that the colonial economy also expanded through extensive growth of the noncash sector of a dual economy. Let us add the following specifications about relationships in this dualistic or two-sector economy. First, the cash sector of the colonial economy was tied to both internal and foreign trade on a fairly regular basis. But the barter sector was only infrequently and irregularly tied to internal, coastal, or overseas trade.

Second, the production processes of the cash sector involved higher capital-labor ratios than those in the barter sector. The latter were relatively labor and land intensive. Because of this, productivity was higher in the cash sector than in the barter sector.

Third, while the barter sector might grow through land clearing, population increases, and even the employment of some capital equipment, intensive growth—the increase in real per capita output—was tied to productivity increase and thus occurred largely in the cash sector. Specifically, the assumption is that as people moved from subsistence activities to urban cash activities, the loss in productivity and real income (for example, to women producing goods on subsistence farms) was more than offset by the increase in real goods produced by people working with more capital instruments. Unlike the dual economy of some underdeveloped nations such as Indonesia, which has a distinctly separate Western export sector as well as a traditional village economy, or the dual economy of Italy, which has a northern urban manufacturing-based economy and a southern agrarian economy, the market and noncash economies of the American colonies were intertwined in the same geographic regions and even within the same enterprise, viz., the family-size farm of New England.

The success of both extensive and intensive growth in the American colonies may be seen in the population growth data in Table 1.1. Several important facts are reflected in these population growth figures. Note that there was a very high rate of overall population growth. In each 30-year period from 1660 to 1780, colonial population more than doubled.* This was unquestionably one of the highest rates of population growth in the world at that time. In an empty land, it was a decided plus so far as expanding the labor force (extensive growth), restraining labor costs, and increasing the size of the market were concerned. It clearly shifted the production possibilities curve of the colonies to the right.

Neither the growth effects of the increase in staple exports, nor the increase in the noncash economy was evenly distributed through the colonies. This is a familiar effect in economic development; some areas or regions are better suited than others to take advantage of the original stimuli that an increase in staple exports creates. Thus we see in Table 1.1 that the relative populations (and market sizes) of the colonies changed substantially. Whereas in 1660 the New England colonies contained about 53 percent of total population (47,000 of 89,000), by 1780 that northernmost region contained only about 26 percent of the total population (714,000 of 2,726,000). At the same time, we should note that even New England's population grew 15-fold between 1660 and 1780, a growth that seems modest only by comparison with the 30-fold increase for all the colonies and 37-fold increase for the colonies from Delaware south to Georgia.

The extensive growth within the noncash economy was important throughout the 13 colonies. However, in this review of the individual economies, the main emphasis will be on the staple export aspects of growth.

The Southern Colonies

By 1720, Virginia was the most populous colony. Its growth depended very heavily on the increasing demand for tobacco, an increase that continued throughout the colonial period. Because the tobacco-growing techniques of the period rapidly depleted the soil, plantations after a few years simply moved on, clearing a new region farther inland and beginning the production cycle again. Although tobacco was grown commercially even on the frontier, high transportation costs imposed a severe limit on its supply from interior locations. Largely for this reason, the tobacco plantation system, with its spread effects, was concentrated along the Virginia–Maryland–Chesapeake Bay coast, and toward the end of the colonial period began to move south to North Carolina.

Although the Jamestown colony almost failed in its first year for lack of food and because of weather conditions, shortly afterward a remarkably successful export was developed. In 1616, a low-cost process for curing tobacco was developed

---

*Although it is outside the time dimension of this chapter, 1780 is included here to accommodate the 30-year comparisons.

Table 1.1. Population of the American Colonies, 1630–1780.

	1780	1750	1720	1690	1660	1630
Maine[a]	49,000	—	—	—	—	—
New Hampshire	88,000	28,000	9,000	4,000	2,000	—[b]
Vermont	48,000	—	—	—	—	—
Massachusetts	269,000	188,000	91,000	57,000	35,000	1,000
Rhode Island	53,000	33,000	12,000	4,000	2,000	—
Connecticut	207,000	111,000	59,000	22,000	8,000	—
SUBTOTAL	714,000	360,000	171,000	87,000	47,000	
New York	211,000	77,000	37,000	14,000	5,000	—[b]
New Jersey	140,000	71,000	30,000	8,000	—	—
Pennsylvania	327,000	120,000	31,000	11,000	—	—
SUBTOTAL	678,000	268,000	98,000	33,000	5,000	
Delaware	45,000	29,000	5,000	1,000	—[b]	—
Maryland	245,000	141,000	66,000	24,000	8,000	—
Virginia	538,000	231,000	88,000	53,000	27,000	3,000
North Carolina	270,000	73,000	21,000	7,000	1,000	—
South Carolina	180,000	64,000	17,000	4,000	—	—
Georgia	56,000	5,000	—	—	—	—
SUBTOTAL	1,334,000	543,000	197,000	89,000	36,000	
GRAND TOTAL	2,726,000	1,171,000	466,000	209,000	89,000	5,000

[a]Maine was included in Massachusetts until 1760.
[b]Less than 1,000.

SOURCE: Adapted from U.S. Bureau of the Census, *Historical Statistics of the United States, Colonial Times to 1957* (Washington, D.C.: U.S. Government Printing Office, 1960).

that permitted shipment to Europe. Although other export staples were developed later, the success of tobacco exports, in spite of the English king's strong feelings against the "noxious weed," is reflected in the growing importation of American tobacco by England from 1620 to 1760 (Table 1.2).

Table 1.2.   Imports of American Tobacco by England (including reexports).

YEAR	MILLIONS OF POUNDS	YEAR	MILLIONS OF POUNDS
1620	0.1	1730	41.0
1630	0.5	1740	41.0
1640	1.3	1755	64.0
1672	17.6	1760	85.0
1708	30.0		
1722	35.0		

SOURCE :   U.S. Bureau of the Census, *Historical Statistics of the United States, Colonial Times to 1957* (Washington, D.C.: U.S. Government Printing Office, 1960).

The data indicate that tobacco exports (imported by England for its consumption and also to be reexported to the European continent) grew over the entire period from 1620 to 1760, and especially rapidly from 1640 to 1672. Most of the tobacco market was in Europe, which meant, given overland transportation costs, that early tobacco plantations were located near the headwaters of rivers and their tributaries. The supply increases reflected in the data show that the creative entrepreneurship required for this staple product expansion was forthcoming.

These data suggest that tobacco, which was the first major export staple from the North American colonies, may well have been the area's first leading sector. Once the institutional restraints on entrepreneurial incentives were relaxed, resources were clearly allocated and reallocated toward growth in the staple export sector.* Still, the growing of tobacco was a very labor-intensive activity (the labor input per acre of land was about one-half a man-year). From early growth in seedbeds through the drying, grading, and packing, much labor was required. Since that was a factor in short supply, relatively high returns (reflecting tobacco's productivity) were required to attract immigrants to the South, especially the upper South during the early years of the colonies. The success of the market signal may be seen in the population growth figures in Table 1.1.

With labor the scarce resource and land the abundant one, free market forces would cause wage rates to increase. Without economies of scale, these higher wage rates would increase costs for larger than family-size units and reduce profits from southern export staples. Since there is little evidence that economies of scale existed for larger than family-size units, one might assume that the dominant size unit in southern staple production, especially tobacco, was the family farm.

---

*The principal such restraint was a prohibition against private land ownership and the pooling of output that had existed during the early "starvation years."

But here the importance of institutions, including legal ones, becomes relevant. Rather than use relatively high-cost free-wage labor, entrepreneurs with the financial capital to take advantage of the high returns from the cultivation and export of southern staples used the legal institutions of chattel slavery (permanent black slavery) and indentured servitude (temporary white slavery) to buy their labor. As Galenson (9) and Heavener (14) have shown, indentured servants were a significant part of the supply of imported labor until the middle of the eighteenth century. Both forms of legal slavery made it possible for large-scale units to dominate the production of southern staples.

One of the direct growth effects in South Carolina was the development of a port city and the service industries to facilitate the low-cost export of indigo and rice (see Table 1.3). South Carolina's premier city, Charleston, became the only large urban area in the South during the colonial period. By the time of the American Revolution, Charleston had 10,000 people, making it the fourth-largest city in the colonies, after New York (28,000), Philadelphia (22,000), and Boston (15,000).

Table 1.3. Rice Exported from Charleston (5-year averages).

YEARS	BARRELS
1716–1720	9,000
1721–1725	19,000
1726–1730	31,000
1731–1735	41,000
1736–1740	58,000
1741–1745	68,000
1746–1750	51,000
1751–1755	58,000
1756–1760	69,000

SOURCE : *Lewis Cecil Gray, History of Agriculture in the Southern United States to 1860*, Vol. 1 (Washington, D.C.: Carnegie Institution, 1933).

As with tobacco in the regions to the north, the high returns from rice and indigo could only be profitably exploited in large plantation-size units. Again, large-scale units could only be maintained through the use of a system of servitude.

The very rapid growth of North Carolina's population is more difficult to explain in terms of exporting staples and the growth effects of those activities. Until 1700, little of the area beyond the immediate coast or tidewater had been settled. It is apparent from Figure 1.1 that even by 1775 the colonial economy and society, especially that part engaged in commercial activities, was tied to deep-water shipment, which restricted the colonization of the far inland areas as a growth effect of staple exports. The tidewater area that was settled and that had been commercialized was an extension of the rice-growing agriculture to the south and the tobacco-growing agriculture to the north. Throughout the colonial period, North Carolina

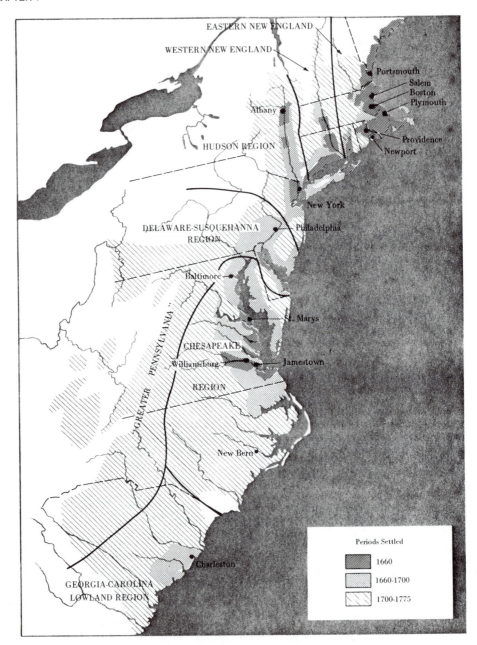

Figure 1.1. Colonial Settlement, 1607–1775.

SOURCE: Rowland Berthoff, *An Unsettled People: Social Order and Disorder in American History* (New York: Harper & Row, 1971), p. 25.

remained essentially a frontier area. Land availability and soil productivity were sufficiently high to afford a fairly substantial real income to those settlers who were drawn to its piedmont or interior areas (frequently from Virginia). The high transportation costs of overland shipment of goods, however, created a major barrier to the commercialization of these frontier areas. The major exception was the pine trees for their sap, which was made into naval stores, that is, turpentine, tar resin, and pitch. These products, highly valued for naval and merchant vessels, received subsidies from the British.

The Middle Colonies

The middle colonies (those from New York south to Maryland) enjoyed a substantial increase in population between 1660 and 1780. In 1780, the total population of New York, New Jersey, and Pennsylvania (the second most populous colony) was 678,000. The growth of agricultural exports, plus the spreading of primarily self-sufficient farming into the interior, especially in Pennsylvania, appears to explain most of that population increase and extensive growth.

Land that is not readily usable for commercial agriculture because of transportation costs is not truly a resource. The general agricultural advantage of the middle colonies was a large supply of land laced by a network of rivers and waterways. The combination of the two attracted large numbers of immigrants (including the so-called Scotch-Irish in the eighteenth century), especially to Pennsylvania.

Farming in the middle colonies was extensive; that is, it was land intensive, with relatively little capital or fertilizer used. This pattern is common to many agricultural areas in the early phases of economic development. Although it often depletes the soil at a rapid rate, it may well be a rational pattern in terms of the size, and growth in size, of the market and the relative prices of land, capital, and fertilizer.

The major exports developed in the middle colonies were wheat and flour (by far the two largest), corn, meat, lumber, flaxseed, and livestock. This pattern of exports became especially pronounced with the increase of exports to the West Indies and reexports of southern tobacco and other products (especially from Philadelphia) to England and the European continent. Philadelphia and New York City also provided an urban market for specialized agricultural goods as well as for the processed goods that urban laborers and merchants demanded.

One interesting question about the middle colonies in this era is why so much of the growth and its spread effects were concentrated in Pennsylvania, an area that became known as "the best poor man's country" because immigrants found that even a poor man could do well there. The basic reason was the availability of land. New York offered limited opportunities in the seventeenth century because of the constraints imposed by the old Dutch patroon system with its large landholdings and by Indian (Iroquois) control. New Jersey suffered from the political instability engendered by a long-standing dispute over its colonial charter and corresponding problems with land titles. William Penn's colony, however, had a relatively abundant amount of land, good river systems to transport bulky commodities such as wheat at a cost that allowed a net profit to growers and shippers, a political and religious climate that was favorable to creative enterpreneurship, and highly fertile land near the coast. The combination of these factors is probably enough to explain the relatively greater growth of Pennsylvania than of New York or New Jersey. The combination also probably explains why the spread effects within New York of the growth of its great port city (the largest in the colonies by the time of the Revolution) were more limited than they might have been with different land availability constraints.

The New England Colonies

Recall that in 1660 New England (from Maine to Connecticut) contained over half the population of the colonies. By 1780, the region had only slightly more than one-fourth of the population. The reason for the *relatively* slower growth of this region is that in a period when intensive growth and development depended so strongly on staple exports, New England had no such export commodity. Also, agricultural expansion was limited by the Indian lands to the west, French Canada to the north, and the more inhospitable climate toward what is now Maine.

New England encountered intermittent conflict throughout the seventeenth century. Even after the end of King Phillip's War in 1678, the conflicts were

Figure 1.2. An Early American Port. (Photo from the National Archives)

numerous, the losses high. Only in the eighteenth century did the frontier expansion resume; even then the pace was slow until the end of the French and Indian Wars in 1763. Nonetheless, the region did have certain natural advantages. The main endowment was a series of fine natural harbors. Fishing, fish processing, whaling, and shipbuilding became important economic activities. Indeed, shipbuilding, a manufacturing activity permitted and even encouraged under England's laws, became a leading sector. As such, it was an important source of the earnings that permitted the import not only of consumer goods but also of the capital that financed early colonial expansion.

New England's disadvantage during the colonial period was not that it had *no* exports. It exported fish, lumber, ships, whale oil, and many other products. But with the possible exception of shipping services, it simply did not have a single export staple (or combination of staples) whose market(s) grew rapidly because of European taste and preference, or because of income growth, or because they complemented the economic expansion of the continent. Even within the region, however, success was relative. Although Boston declined as a port relative to New York and Philadelphia (perhaps even to Charleston), it was a prosperous city. Newport, Rhode Island, also prospered, particularly through export and reexport of goods to the West Indies. The important point is that the leading sectors of the colonial economy were largely in the southern and middle colonies rather than in New England. The structure of European demand, the initial endowment of resources, and the relative advantage of the colonies all dictated that, through most of the colonial period, the impetus for intensive growth would be strongly concentrated geographically from Pennsylvania to South Carolina.

THE INSTITUTIONAL BACKGROUND

Although in real-income terms the colonies grew at a rate that was very rapid for their times, that rate would probably seem modest by more recent American experience. Nonetheless, their emergence as a growing society is unquestionable. In large measure, their ability to take advantage of favorable international market conditions, to supply staple exports to a growing European market, was attributable to favorable political, social, and **economic institutions**—including indentured servitude and even slavery. No matter how noxious the idea of self-imposed servitude limited in time by contract or of the imposed lifetime service of slavery is to twentieth-century minds and values, in colonial times these institutions provided a labor supply that was important to North America's development. We have already mentioned the early decisions to permit private ownership of land and to allow private appropriation of the profits (and losses) of engaging in economic activity. While it is difficult to quantify the effects of these decisions on economic development, they were undeniably important in terms of reallocating resources and achieving creative entrepreneurship.

However, efforts to inhibit reallocation of resources were undertaken. After the restoration of King Charles II, for example, the proprietors in South Carolina sought to create a feudal economy, with all its obstacles to resource reallocation (including a group of serfs tied to the land). In all instances, these efforts were rejected, a result not surprising among people who had fled such restrictions in Europe and who, confronted with readily available land (at least initially), refused to be tied to feudal baronies.

THE MARGINAL PROPENSITY TO IMPORT

Little is known in any systematic fashion about the colonists' marginal propensity to import. The marginal propensity to import depends on, among other factors, the distribution of income.

In the South, the slave plantation system in tobacco, indigo, and rice produced an unequal distribution of income. The plantation slave owners received a substantial portion of total income, not only in comparison with the slaves but also with small-scale family farmers. The northern colonies also had an unequal distribution of income mirroring the unequal command over resources, though perhaps the distribution was less skewed than in the South.

There were other factors that contributed to an unequal distribution of income, such as differences in abilities and skills, primogeniture, and differences in initial endowments. This skewed distribution may have increased the propensity to import because people with higher incomes tended to want European luxury manufactures. Clearly, though, the propensity to import was not so high that it prevented the development of unspecialized merchants, home manufacturers, and local financial sources. In other words, it was not high enough to impose a barrier to the diversification of the colonial economy.

THE COLONIES: UNDERDEVELOPED
OR WAITING TO BE DEVELOPED?

Although the staple theory provides insights into the development of the North American colonies from the early 1600s to 1763, it is probably not accurate to consider those colonies underdeveloped in the modern sense of that term. In many respects, the physical endowments of the region (the natural resource base) in relation to world market demand made the area not so much an "empty land" as one capable of being developed by a group with an institutional structure that could harness the demand signals, reallocate resources to their most productive uses, and provide staple exports that would provide the income basis for further economic expansion.

REVIEW OF ECONOMIC CONCEPTS: SOME
FUNDAMENTALS

Determining Prices

How are prices established in marketplaces? The following statement is familiar to almost everyone: Prices are determined by supply and demand. That statement is correct; indeed, it is definitional. But we must add one stipulation: So long as competitive conditions exist, the independent influences of supply and demand determine price.

Before we go further, we should define the term **competition.** Competition is the market form in which no buyer or seller is able to influence price. The market conditions necessary for competition to exist are:

1. *Absence of collusion.* No buyers and no sellers act together to influence price.
2. *Flexible prices.* Prices determined by supply and demand must be completely free to move up or down to whatever level is determined by the market.
3. *Free entry and exit.* Buyers and sellers must be free to enter and leave the market without nonmarket restrictions, and the market restrictions must make entry and exit relatively easy.

Finally, in order for supply and demand influences to be independent, the demand for a good must not depend on the incomes that are generated by the production of that good (a condition that would be violated, for example, in a mill town where employees were the principal customers of the mill and their demand depended on the incomes they received from the company).

What Is Demand? Since, by assumption, demand and supply are independent of each other in our market pricing model, let us examine each influence in turn before putting them together to form a theory of pricing.

The first fact to remember about demand is that it is a schedule of relationships. Specifically, **demand** is a schedule that indicates the quantity of a good that will be purchased at each of a set of prices in a particular time period.

What will such a schedule look like? Economists expect a picture of a demand schedule to look like the demand curve drawn in Figure 1.3. (Note that economists call such relationships *curves* even if they are linear.)

The second thing to remember about demand is the **law of demand,** which states that consumers will buy more of goods at (relatively) low prices than at (relatively) high prices. The downward-sloping demand curve in Figure 1.3 obeys this law. Note that as price falls (for example, from 5 to 4), the quantity of tobacco sold increases (from 9 to 10). The law of demand can be explained in terms of two effects that derive from price changes:

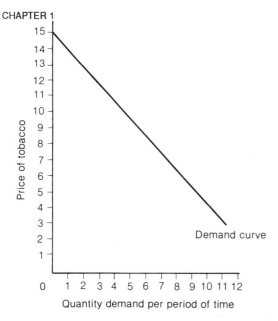

Figure 1.3. A Hypothetical Demand Curve for Colonial Tobacco.

1. The **substitution effect** of a price changes. As the price of a good falls, consumers tend to substitute that relatively cheaper good for other, now relatively more expensive goods. In Figure 1.3, as the price of tobacco falls, consumers tend to substitute that good for other (now) relatively more expensive goods (whose prices, by assumption, are unchanged).

2. The **income effect** of a price change. As the price of a good falls, the purchasing power or real income of a consumer is increased, and the consumer tends to buy more of that good. (For the time being, we'll ignore the exceptions to this effect and focus only on normal goods, those whose rate of consumption increases as purchasing power increases.)

Quantity Demanded and Demand Shifts The combination of these two effects, then, ordinarily produces a downward-sloping demand curve such as that shown in Figure 1.3. A demand curve is drawn on the assumption that the price of the good (measured on the vertical axis) is the independent variable, and the resulting quantity demanded (measured on the horizontal axis) is the dependent variable. Thus we say that—other things being equal—only a change in the price of a good can cause a change in the quantity demanded of that good. The qualification that other things must be equal is known as the ceteris paribus assumption.

The **ceteris paribus assumption** involves holding constant: (a) money income; (b) tastes and preferences; (c) prices of substitutes (goods whose consumption is a substitute for the good in question) and complements (goods consumed in conjunction with the good in question); (d) population, or the number of consumers; and (e) expectations about future prices. A change in any one of these factors (or any combination of them) will tend to cause a change in demand or a shift of the demand curve.

Figure 1.4 is useful for illustrating the difference between changes in demand and changes in quantity demanded. Along Demand Curve D_1, for example, changes in price occur from price = 15 to price = 3. Each of these price changes causes a change in quantity demanded (as price decreases, there is an increase in quantity demanded). Thus changes in quantity demanded are the same as movements along a particular demand curve. The movement from Demand Curve D_1 to Demand Curve D_2, however, is an increase in demand, or a shift of the demand curve. The movement from D_1 to D_2 may be the result of a change in any of the five shift factors identified earlier (for example, an increase in population).

The hypothetical demand curves in Figures 1.3 and 1.4 are market or industry demand curves; that is, they reflect the total demand for the product portrayed. Underlying any such demand curves are numerous individual demand curves. Market demand curves are the summation or adding up of individual demand curves (assuming no interdependencies among consumers). Since all consumers, by assumption, are affected by income and substitution effects, individual demand curves generally have the same downward-sloping configuration as the market curves we have shown.

What Is Supply?   Like demand, supply is a schedule of relationships. Supply is defined as the schedule showing the quantity of a good that a firm or various firms will offer for sale at each of a set of prices in a particular period of time.

Figure 1.4.   Changes in Demand and Changes in Quantity Demanded, for Colonial Tobacco.

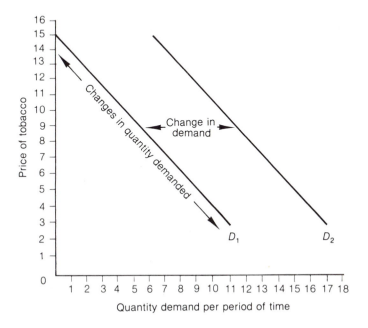

What will such a schedule or set of relationships look like? Economists expect the picture of a supply curve to resemble the supply curve in Figure 1.5. Note that the supply curve slopes up, to the right. The curve, in other words, reflects the **law of supply**—the hypothesis that firms supply more to the market at (relatively) higher prices than at (relatively) lower prices.

Why is the law of supply a generally valid and applicable principle? To answer this question, we must learn what determines supply. Supply basically depends on the costs of production, which, in turn, depend on the prices of resources employed in production and the productivity of those resources. Two market factors may cause the upward-sloping supply curve: (a) as the firm produces more, its costs may increase because it has to pay a higher price for each unit of a resource; (b) as the firm produces more, it will ultimately experience diminishing productivity from the additional resources it hires. This latter effect is known as the **law of diminishing returns:** As a firm hires successive equal increments of a variable resource and uses the resource in conjunction with a fixed resource (or resources), a point will be reached beyond which the additional units of the variable resource add less and less to output. As this happens, each additional unit of output costs more than the previous one (even at a constant resource price).

For either one or both of these reasons, profit-maximizing firms supplying tobacco to the market will supply more only as price rises. Since this is true for each firm, it is true for *all* firms, as the upward-sloping market supply curve in Figure 1.5 shows. Market supply curves, like market demand curves, are aggregates; they involve adding up the quantities supplied by each firm at each possible price (assuming there is no collusion or interdependencies between firms).

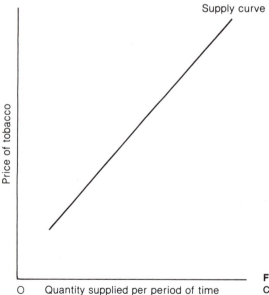

Supply curve

Price of tobacco

O   Quantity supplied per period of time

Figure 1.5. A Hypothetical Supply Curve, for Colonial Tobacco.

You have probably noticed the reappearance of the *ceteris paribus* assumption. In Figure 1.5, the only factors that changed were the price of the good (the independent variable) and the quantity supplied (the dependent variable). These are the factors that were held constant: (a) technology or techniques of production; (b) resource prices (if the firm does not buy resources at constant prices; that is, as a competitor); (c) prices of other products; (d) firms' expectations about future prices for their product; and (e) the number of firms. Changes in any one of these five factors could cause the change in supply reflected in the shift from S_1 to S_2 in Figure 1.6. Suppose, for example, that tobacco producers expected tobacco prices to fall in the future. This change in their price expectations might well cause producers to supply more tobacco at all prices in the present.

We have shown that the only factor that *can* cause a change in the quantity supplied of a good is a change in that good's price. The factors that can cause a change in supply include changing technology and changed expectations of future prices. The only factor that *cannot* cause a change in the supply of a good is a change in the price of that good.

The supply changes we have looked at were all due to changes in market factors, especially those affecting the costs of firms. Of course, cost changes can be imposed on firms by governments. Taxes, duties, regulations of one sort or another that raise the costs of firms—all can cause a reduced supply. In Figure 1.6, tobacco producers might have been willing to supply S_2 tobacco to a free market. If govern-

Figure 1.6. Changes in Supply and Changes in Quantity Supplied, for Colonial Tobacco.

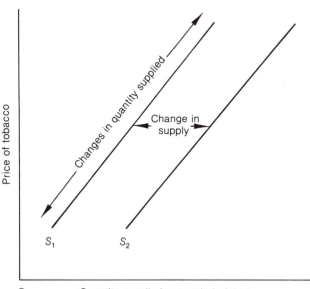

ments imposed import duties on that tobacco, or imposed cost-increasing regulations on the sellers of tobacco, then supply might have shifted to S_1.

Prices: Putting Supply and Demand Together We began this section by saying that prices are determined by supply and demand. Now let us see just how and why that is so. Figure 1.7 will be helpful in this regard. In the figure, we have drawn the demand curve for colonial tobacco from Figure 1.3 and the supply curve for that same product from Figure 1.5. What price will result, given D and S? It will be an **equilibrium price,** the central tendency of this market. Also, it will be a market-clearing price, one that eliminates both gluts and shortages.

In this instance, price will tend toward 8.2, where demand equals supply. Why this is so can be made evident by comparing the equilibrium price with disequilibrium prices, both those above 8.2 and those below 8.2. Consider the situation if the price were 10. At that price, consumers want to buy A, while suppliers offer to sell B. The difference (AB) is excess supply, or surplus or unintended accumulation of tobacco by producers. Since this is a competitive market, the information about excess supply or surplus is readily transmitted, and, in response, sellers offer lower and lower prices to eliminate the glut. Finally, prices will tend toward 8.2, at which point the quantity supplied (offered for sale) equals the quantity demanded.

Next, consider price = 6.4. At that price, consumers want to buy D while suppliers only want to offer C. The difference, CD, is excess demand, or a shortage. Knowing of this shortage and attempting to buy more, consumers begin to offer higher and higher prices. As a result, the price rises toward 8.2, where the shortage or excess demand is eliminated.

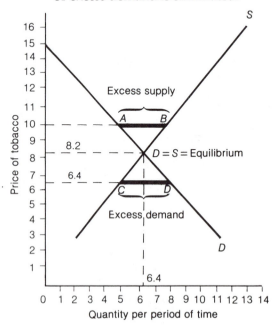

Figure 1.7. Pricing Colonial Tobacco.

Summing Up   We conclude that prices in competitive markets are established by the independent influences of supply and demand. These prices are equilibrium prices that tend to clear the markets; that is, they eliminate excess supply and excess demand.

Production Possibilities   A visual representation of intensive and extensive growth may be seen in the production possibilities curve, a curve showing the various combinations of output that full employment of a nation's resources and the best of current technology can produce. Such a curve is seen in Figure 1.8; *ABC* represents a frontier or the maximum attainable output with full employment of the colony's resources and the best technology at a given time. It is concave to the origin, to indicate that **opportunity cost** the amount of the one good given up to produce more of the other, rises; that is, as resources are reallocated from the production of one good to the production of the other (say, from growing tobacco to catching and processing fish), more and more of the one good (tobacco) must be given up to obtain a constantly increasing amount of the other (fish). This effect is also known as the law of diminishing returns. Curve *ABC*, then, is a frontier, the maximum output combination of the two goods attainable with a colony's limited resources as the colony attempts to meet the (assumed) unlimited wants of its people or to deal with the problem of scarcity.

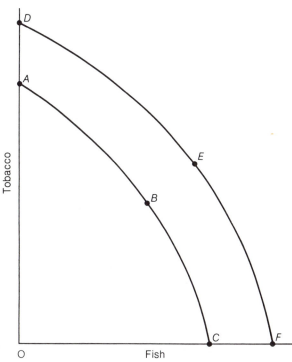

Figure 1.8. Hypothetical Production Possibilities Curves in a North American Colony for Tobacco and Fish.

Curve *DEF* represents a higher level of attainable combinations of the two goods. What can move a society such as the hypothetical colony from *ABC* to *DEF*? The answer is indicated in the aggregate production function. The shift may result from more resources, labor, and capital ($dR > 0$, $dL > 0$, $dK > 0$); if so, it is the result of extensive growth. Alternatively, the shift may result from increasing marginal productivity of resources (*MPL*, *MPK*, and *MPR* are growing), and this may be the effect of a positive T', or improving technology; if so, the shift is the result of intensive growth.

Economic Institutions

Economic development is the end product, the improvement in human welfare that results from the structural changes that accompany combined extensive and intensive growth. Therefore, it is vitally important to productivity growth that economic institutions—the organizational means through which economic decisions are made and implemented—enhance productivity growth. They may do so by reducing the impediments to an efficient allocation of resources and by exhausting the economies of scale that an evolving technology makes possible. The particular economic institutions established by a society bear directly on the fundamental questions that all economies must answer. If private ownership of the means of production, combined with legal enforcement of market-determined contractual arrangements, is a basic institutional feature, the answers to the questions *how* to produce, *what* to produce, *who* will receive the output, and what to provide for the future will be provided primarily by the market. A different set of institutional arrangements, such as public ownership and control, would result in other answers.

A society's institutions also affect the efficiency or costs of making economic decisions. One of the basic costs of decisions is **information cost,** the cost of obtaining the price information and technical information necessary to make rational decisions—those consistent with individual and group objectives. The other basic cost is **transactions cost,** the cost of effectuating exchanges between buyers and sellers. An efficient set of institutions minimizes these two kinds of costs for buyers and sellers. How close a society comes to achieving its greatest output significantly depends on the effectiveness or efficiency of its economic institutions.

QUESTIONS

1. What is the staple theory developed by Harold Innis, and to what type of countries does it apply?
2. What were the major economic differences between a cash economy and a noncash economy within the colonial dual economy?
3. What is the production function of a staple-producing area, and how does it relate to the demand for resources and the distribution of market incomes?

4. How does a high marginal propensity to import affect the spread effects of staple exports?

5. What is the importance of immigration to the success of the staple export-producing land? The importance of creative entrepreneurship?

6. In what ways did the southern colonies adapt to the initial resource conditions they encountered? What became the first great staple export of the upper South?

7. Why is it likely that spread effects of staple export increases will not be felt evenly throughout a nation or region or set of colonies?

8. Why did so many of the spread effects of staple export growth in the colonial period accrue to Virginia?

9. What caused South Carolina's dramatic population growth during the colonial period? What of North Carolina?

10. In what respects did the middle colonies differ in their economic growth from the South? What accounts for the relative concentration of spread effects in Pennsylvania among the middle colonies?

11. What caused New England to grow less rapidly during the colonial period than either the southern or middle colonies? What were the successful aspects of New England's growth?

12. In what respects were the institutional structures of the colonies favorable to staple export-led growth? To what should we attribute this institutional success?

13. Does it appear that the marginal propensity to import was a barrier to the diversification of the colonial economy? If it was not, what *was* the principal barrier?

14. Were the North American colonies an underdeveloped area or an empty land waiting to be developed?

15. What was the importance of the Indian heritage to the economic development of the colonies?

SUGGESTED READINGS

1. Alston, Lee J., and Marton Owen Shapiro. "Inheritance Laws Across the Colonies: Causes and Consequences." *Journal of Economic History, 44* (June 1984).

2. Anderson, Terry. "Wealth Estimates for the New England Colonies, 1650–1709." *Explanations in Economic History, 12* (1975).

3. Baldwin, Robert E. "Patterns of Development in Newly Settled Regions." *Manchester Schools of Economic and Social Studies, 24* (1956).

4. Bidwell, Percy W., and John I. Falconer. *History of Agriculture in the Northern United States, 1620–1860.* Washington, D.C.: Carnegie Institution, 1925.

5. Bruchey, Stuart. *The Colonial Merchant: Sources and Readings.* New York: Harcourt Brace Jovanovich, 1966.

6. Callender, Guy S. *Selections from the Economic History of the United States, 1765–1860.* Boston: Ginn, 1909.

7. Curtin, Philip. *The Atlantic Slave Trade: A Census.* Madison: University of Wisconsin Press, 1969.

8. Egnal, Marc. "The Economic Development of the Thirteen Continental Colonies, 1720 to 1775." *William and Mary Quarterly, 32*, (1975).

9. Galenson, David. "Immigration and the Colonial Labor System: An Analysis of Indenture." *Exploration in Economic History, 14* (October 1977).

10. Galenson, David. *White Servitude in Colonial America: An Economic Analysis.* New York: Cambridge University Press, 1981.

11. Galenson, David W. "The Rise and Fall of Indentured Servitude in the Americas: An Economic Analysis." *Journal of Economic History, 44* (March 1984).

12. Gray, Lewis Cecil. *History of Agriculture in the Southern United States to 1860.* Vol. 1. Washington, D.C.: Carnegie Institution, 1933.

13. Gunderson, Gerald. *A New Economic History of America.* New York: McGraw-Hill, 1976. Chap. 2, pp. 28–68.

14. Heavener, Robert. "Indentured Servitude: The Philadelphia Market, 1771–1773." *Journal of Economic History, 27* (September 1978).

15. Innis, Harold A. *The Cod Fisheries: The History of an International Economy.* Toronto: University of Toronto Press, 1940.

16. Innis, Harold A. *The Fur Trade in Canada: An Introduction to Canadian Economic History.* Toronto: University of Toronto Press, 1930.

17. Josephby, Alvin C. *The Indian Heritage of America.* New York: Knopf, 1968.

18. Land, Aubrey C. "The Tobacco Staple and the Planter's Problems: Technology, Labor and Crops." *Agricultural History, 43* (1969).

19. Potter, Jim. "The Growth of Population in America, 1700–1860." In *Population in History: Essays in Historical Demography,* ed. O. V. Glass and B. E. C. Eaversley. Chicago: Aldine, 1960.

20. Price, Jacob. "The Economic Growth of America and the European Market, 1697–1775." *Journal of Economic History, 24* (1964).

21. Rothenberg, Winifred B. "The Market and Massachusetts Farmers, 1750–1855." *Journal of Economic History, 41* (June 1981).

22. Watkins, M. H. "A Staple Theory of Economic Growth." *The Canadian Journal of Economics and Political Science 29* (May 1963).

Chapter 2

THE LATE COLONIAL ECONOMY, 1770

To illustrate the late colonial period processes of economic growth and development in the North American colonies, we shall focus on the year 1770. In our analysis of this era, we shall include the economic relationships between the North American colonies and Great Britain that are necessary to understand in order to answer the important question raised in Chapter 3: What effects did the complex economic controls imposed on the colonies by British mercantile policy have on colonial growth and welfare?

We will begin by looking at colonial agriculture, the sector that provided employment for perhaps 90 to 95 percent of the colonial population. Following that, we will outline the main features of commerce, both internal trade (that within and between the colonies) and overseas trade. Though it was only a small part of the economy, we will describe the manufacturing sector, placing special emphasis on the factors that limited its expansion. Finally, we will look at an area especially difficult to quantify, the "quality" of human economic behavior. Specifically, we will examine several factors that molded the "economic mind" of the American colonists.

COLONIAL AGRICULTURE

In all important respects, agriculture dominated the colonial economy. Although urban areas were becoming more important, only slightly more than 4 percent of the people lived in towns in 1770. Thus it was in agriculture that the vast majority of the population found their employment, income, and living environment around 1770, the period just before the American Revolution.

We have already seen that the production possibilities curve, which identifies the possible combinations of output of an economy, is determined by the supply of factors of production and the state of technology; it is drawn on the assumption that these factors of production are fully employed with the best technology. A fruitful approach to an analysis of colonial agriculture, therefore, is to examine the three factors of production—land, labor, and capital—and to analyze the state of technology with which they were employed. In addition, since the production possibility frontier can be affected by changes in productivity from sources other than technological change, it is appropriate to consider these forms of changing productivity also.

Land

Although land was abundant and almost anyone who wished to farm could buy land on easy terms, land ownership was not evenly divided and the pattern of land ownership varied from one colony to another. Changes in these patterns involved significant institutional change, although the institutional form differed greatly. In some areas, the family farm became dominant; in other areas, commercial plantations evolved. In New England, agriculture was dominated by small family-size farms concentrating on general-purpose agriculture. This pattern was probably due, at least in part, to the region's lack of an export crop that required larger size to gain **economies of scale** (reduced unit costs of the crop available with higher rates of production) or that commanded high enough returns to justify the employment of (high-wage) free labor or the costs of servile labor.

This is not to say that all landholding was decentralized. In New York, there were some large holdings owned by the descendants of the original Dutch settlers of New Amsterdam. When the British conquered this Dutch colony, they reaffirmed the existing pattern of ownership. In Pennsylvania, there were holdings larger than family size in the rich agricultural lands above and to the west of Philadelphia. Because of high land fertility in these areas, specialized wheat export farming was profitable. In the coastal areas of Maryland and Virginia around Chesapeake Bay, large tobacco plantations were flourishing. These plantations in the Piedmont area were based on the export demand for tobacco and the institution of slavery.

In North Carolina, on the other hand, small family-size farms were the rule. In South Carolina and Georgia, there were rice plantations along the coast and indigo plantations farther inland. Slaves were used as the labor force, and rice and indigo were important export crops. Rice production required large holdings and considerable capital investment in irrigation structures in order to achieve economies of scale.

In summary, then, there were the large landholdings of the Dutch patroons in New York, the commercial wheat-exporting farms in Bucks and Lancaster counties in Pennsylvania, the tobacco plantations around Chesapeake Bay in Maryland and Virginia, and the rice and indigo plantations of South Carolina and Georgia. Other areas in the North American colonies were characterized by relatively small-scale family farms devoted to general agriculture. It is important to remember that, despite the uneven distribution of land ownership, the supply of land was plentiful and, in the language of economists, there was relative ease of entry into agriculture during colonial times.

Labor

On a family-size farm, the family provided its own labor. But on the large commercial farms of Virginia, Maryland, South Carolina, Georgia, and Pennsylvania, the problem of finding a labor supply was crucial. While methods of providing that supply varied, the relative cheapness of land prevented a large supply of free labor from developing. Why work for someone else when you could farm your own land—unless, of course, you could earn much more as a wage laborer? And this was unlikely, given the high level of labor productivity associated with a nearly free good, land. However, a small supply of wage labor did exist. It consisted primarily of recent immigrants, young sons of small farmers, and former indentured servants. These groups often worked for wages for a time to accumulate the funds needed to buy their own land, which in many cases necessitated moving toward the frontier. In spite of laws that required individuals to work and even imprisoned those who refused, labor remained in relatively short supply to the end of the colonial period.

Because of the high wages resulting from this scarcity of wage labor, the large commercial farms resorted to unfree labor. At first they used indentured servants, primarily Englishmen, but also including indentured blacks. Indentured servants were sold into servitude for various lengths of time: usually four to seven years. Some whites voluntarily put themselves into bondage to pay for their transportation to the New World. Slavery became the other source of unfree labor. By the end of the seventeenth century, slaves brought from the West Indies and Africa to become strictly the property of their owners had replaced indentured labor to a marked degree in the tobacco areas of Virginia and Maryland and the indigo and rice areas of South Carolina and Georgia.

The lot of both chattel slaves and indentured servants was often harsh. As Philip Curten (5) has shown, blacks were taken from communities in West Africa where conditions of slavery were relatively mild or were captured by slave traders and involuntarily sold into slavery. Their journey to the American colonies, as well as to the West Indies and South America, was often accompanied by extreme hardship. They were usually chained down in cargo holes where overcrowded conditions, disease, and other dangers took a heavy toll in human lives. Nonetheless, the number of slaves grew rapidly, and by 1770, slaves constituted from one-third to almost two-thirds of the population in the southern colonies.

While many of the indentured servants sold themselves into temporary servitude for three to four years to pay their passage to the colonies, a significant portion consisted of criminals sold by the English courts into indentured servitude for as long as seven years. Philip Foner (8) maintains that these people were often worked more severely than black slaves because their owners sought to obtain as much work as they could out of them before their fixed term of servitude was up.

Indentured servitude was all but eliminated by the end of the Revolutionary War. Many states had passed laws ending the practice of indentured servitude during the war, and others conferred freedom on those who had fought in the Revolutionary armies. The end of indentured servitude was ensured after the war by a steady flow of immigrants, the refusal of courts to imprison people for failure to pay debts, and the development of much more efficient labor markets. In these markets, flexible contract-based wage agreements replaced indentured servitude entirely in the first two decades of the nineteenth century.

Capital

Major forms of capital formation in agriculture were the clearing of land for cultivation, the construction of necessary farm buildings, and, to a lesser degree, the accumulation of farm animals. The most important costs in constructing this capital were the labor costs provided by the farm family itself. Drawn out over a number of years, such labor was extremely costly, even though it did not involve substantial outlays of money. Martin Primack (21) has estimated that the cost of clearing one acre of forest in the eastern United States in 1860 was at least 35 days of labor. It was probably higher in the colonial period. The construction of farm buildings and other forms of agricultural capital also involved large outlays of labor most often contributed by the farm family itself.

For small-scale farming, very little cash was necessary, in part because land was cheap and easy terms were available. Much land was obtained through settling towns (as in New England), squatting (for example, in Pennsylvania), and grants for settling (for example, in Virginia). The few simple tools that were needed were made by the farmer himself or by the local blacksmith. The problem of money capital was much more critical for large-scale commercial agriculture. The amount of funds necessary for purchasing land was much greater. Animals, tools, and buildings required larger cash outlays; and labor costs, especially slave labor costs, which constituted capital outlays, were higher.

The three major sources of money capital were funds brought by the commercial settlers themselves on emigration from Great Britain and other European countries, reinvestment of profits, and foreign (British) investment. It should be noted that while the third source, British investment, may have been significant for individual investments, it was not for total investment. As Shephard and Walton (24) and Shepherd and Williamson (25) have shown, the colonies' balance of trade (exports minus imports) was roughly zero. In view of this, there could have been no net foreign investment in the colonies. Many of the plantations of the southern colonies were established by the younger sons of moderately well-to-do families from England who arrived in the New World with funds and often land grants. Other plantations were started with meager resources but proved profitable, and some of these profits (it is impossible to estimate how much) were reinvested in the plantations.

The earliest British investments in the colonies were channeled through special monopoly corporations. These corporations, chartered by the king, had exclusive rights to engage in activities in certain areas. An important example was the Virginia Company, which founded and supported the Jamestown and Virginia settlements. Although their efforts to realize profits for their investors failed uniformly, these companies succeeded in providing the basic support needed by a number of colonies in their early years.

By the mid-seventeenth century, corporate support of the colonies had been replaced by a web of commercial credit extended by British merchants in exchange for the planters' crops. These merchants would extend credit to a planter for supplies, equipment, consumer goods, and, especially, slaves. Seldom did a planter find his crop sufficient to repay the debt.

Agricultural Productivity

The colonial period was spread over 168 years, from the founding of Jamestown in 1607 to the American Revolution in 1775. Most writers assume that there was very little change in agricultural productivity during the period; that is, that output per unit of input did not increase appreciably. If one only looks at the tools and equipment and techniques used, this would seem to be true. Technological improvement was, in effect, nonexistent. Agricultural innovations developed in Britain in the eighteenth century had not reached the North American continent by 1775. There were, however, three factors that may have contributed to increased productivity between 1607 and 1760: increased knowledge of how to farm in the New World, more and more favorable land-labor ratios, and opportunities for specialization permitted by increases in market sizes that resulted from rising population and exports.

The advantages of increased knowledge of an agricultural area are obvious. Every geographic area differs in climatic conditions (such as temperature and rainfall), kinds of soil, and soil conditions (drainage and so on). All of these factors create a certain set of optimal agricultural practices because they affect decisions about the kinds of crops grown, planting time, cultivation, and harvesting time. Farmers need time to acquire the knowledge necessary for developing a new agricultural area up to its highest productive potential. The rate of increase in output resulting from increased knowledge diminished as colonial farmers approached the optimum set of agricultural product mix and practices, but as new areas were settled, this learning process was repeated.

Increases in productivity through more favorable land-labor ratios are more complex. For a given technology, there is a certain combination of land and labor that will produce the lowest cost per unit of agricultural output. In the colonies, land (other than already cleared land taken from the Indians) had to be cleared of trees. Therefore, the settler started with an amount of cleared or improved land that was too small to produce lowest costs. As more land was cleared, the land-labor ratio moved toward the optimal (low-cost) ratio, and the productivity increase resulted in decreased costs.

But once again, in the more settled areas, this source of productivity increase diminished as a more efficient combination of land and labor was achieved. As settlers moved into the frontier, the process was repeated. We assume that increases in productivity in the new areas were more than enough to offset the declines in productivity caused by losses in soil fertility in the settled areas.

It is the size of the market that determines the degree to which any producer can specialize his labor. The greater the opportunity for specialization, the higher the potential for increased productivity. Therefore, as the urban populations slowly increased, so did the demand for agricultural products around these small but growing urban areas. Farmers specialized more in dairy products, vegetable crops, poultry, and other animal products. International trade also stimulated specialization. Thus specialized areas appeared for tobacco in Virginia and Maryland, for indigo and rice in South Carolina and Georgia, and for grain in eastern Pennsylvania.

To summarize briefly, productivity increases in colonial agriculture were not obtained primarily through technological development or through the introduction of new crops. Rather, productivity increased through the dynamics of a developing economy in an empty land.

Self-Sufficiency

We have argued that high internal transportation costs and other factors limited both the amount of internal commerce and the distances over which trade took place. Nonetheless, internal trade was important in the colonies because very few farms—only those in the most inaccessible frontier areas—were completely self-sufficient. Prior to 1770, most settlements were located along river systems leading to the sea. Maintaining a settlement far from these rivers was made difficult by high overland transportation costs. A system of general stores sprang up on the frontiers, however, connecting frontier agriculture to the port cities by rivers. Even the more remote settlers were served by wandering peddlers who traded with the general store. One sees in this the slow but inexorable extension of the market economy to the shifting frontier of the American economy.

Besides articles of consumption, farmers needed gunpowder, iron, and iron products. In exchange, they sold crops, livestock, and, in frontier areas, furs. After clearing land, farmers reduced the trees to pearl and potash for sale. Despite commercial contacts, however, a substantial amount of home manufacturing provided a degree of self-sufficiency on even the largest and most accessible plantations.

The commercial nexus was obvious in the grain farms of Pennsylvania, in the tobacco plantations of Virginia and Maryland, and in the indigo and rice plantations of South Carolina and Georgia. But even here self-sufficiency and its corollary, home manufacture, were highly developed. Corn, wheat, vegetables, and animal products were produced to feed both the slave population and the owner and his family. Clothing, furniture, and farm tools also were widely produced on the plantation.

In brief, both the totally commercial farm and the totally self-sufficient farm were rare. In terms of dualism, few of the colonists (except those on the isolated frontier) were totally within the noncash economy, and few were totally within the cash economy. The substantial majority were, with varying degrees of intensity, producing within both the cash and noncash economies.

As market demand increased and specialization advanced, especially in manufacturing, self-sufficiency declined. In agriculture, farmers found it more profitable to concentrate their resources on market production and buy more of their consumption goods in the market rather than to produce them at home. Intensive growth was quickened as resources shifted from nonmarket to market production. But the pace of this process did not quicken greatly until the 1830s, and thus must be reserved for a later chapter.

COLONIAL MANUFACTURING

Before 1770, manufacturing for sale in the North American colonies was rudimentary and employed only a small percentage of the total labor force. Industry was severely hampered by two main factors: relative factor endowments, especially scarce and therefore costly labor; and the limited demand that resulted from a small market constrained by high internal transportation costs.

First, the easy availability of land continually siphoned off the potential wage-earning labor force from manufacturing. This short supply of labor resulted in high wages and therefore high production costs. Thus the colonies' comparative advantage rested largely in land-intensive (agricultural) activities rather than in relatively capital- and labor-intensive (manufacturing) activities.

A characteristic, if not a limiting, factor in the development of manufacturing in the colonies was the relatively inexperienced management and simplistic technology. The industrial labor force consisted primarily of artisans working with simple tools in small establishments. They had little experience with the processes and industries that were developing in the home country. Although the industrial revolution had barely begun in England by 1770, England had undergone a process of quickening development in a wide variety of industries over the preceding 200 years. These developments had not yet reached the colonies. But if colonial technology was not as productive as England's, it was nevertheless appropriate to the demands created by a much smaller market. One should not, therefore, consider the relatively unsophisticated colonial technology as an important limiting factor in manufacturing development.

The most severe limitation on manufacturing development was simply the size of markets. The colonies had few manufacturing export markets because there were few goods in which they enjoyed a comparative advantage over British manufacturers.

Not surprisingly, those few were goods that drew on forest products and iron—resources in abundance in the colonies. Shipbuilding, an industry of substantial importance in New England by the late colonial period, was an important example. Some manufactured export goods that drew on abundant colonial resources were restricted by British efforts to limit certain American markets for themselves. Shipbuilding was an activity the British needed and in which they had no comparative advantage (after depleting their own stands of timber, that is). Beginning in 1699, though, and continuing through 1750, a series of laws made it illegal, first, to export colonial wool, woolen yarn, and wool products; then, to export hats made from beaver fur; and finally, in 1750, to export finished iron products (although pig and bar iron were allowed duty-free entry). The overall impact of these restrictions was to limit foreign markets for certain goods and thereby to limit the combined domestic and foreign market.

Again, however, it was the high cost of transportation beyond the seacoast and the tributary river systems that limited the domestic market. The colonists were few in number (although growing rapidly) and widely scattered. Home manufacturing and family self-sufficiency further reduced both the demand for manufactured goods and the money income of potential consumers. Low demand and small market size prevented the specialization of labor that might have reduced costs to levels more nearly equal to those that existed in Britain. Specialization of labor was low within enterprises, and specialization of the enterprises themselves was prevented.

By 1770, the generalizations we have made about colonial manufacturers had become less valid. As the population increased, growing cities and towns provided a local market for small-scale craft-oriented enterprises, and a labor force of skilled craftsmen developed. By 1770, in the more urban areas, a small, locally oriented system of small-scale manufacturers had developed to meet the need for simple manufactures. In the more rural agrarian areas, the most significant form of local manufactures took place within the blacksmith shop, where the simple tools of the farmer were made and repaired.

Skills were transmitted from one generation to the next through the apprentice system. An average manufacturing enterprise was composed of the master employer, a few journeymen working for wages, and a few apprentices learning the trade. Under this system, significant improvements in technology were unlikely.

As we approach 1775 and the American Revolution, the beginnings of larger-size enterprise were occurring in urban areas with their expanding groups of wage earners. By the Revolution, a significant portion of the urban population consisted of these "mechanics," especially in the area of shipbuilding. But we must be careful not to overestimate the relative economic importance of these changes in manufacturing.

After the initial settlement of the coastal areas, some increases in productivity probably were achieved by growth of market demand and by improvements in knowledge gained through experience, which led to greater ability and proficiency in serving developing markets and utilizing local materials. These productivity-increasing factors were small, however, and the manufacturing sector itself was small. Therefore, increases in manufacturing productivity had little impact on the economy as a whole.

COLONIAL COMMERCE

Colonial commerce consisted of exchanges of commodities and services not only within colonies and between colonies but also with Great Britain and—through Britain—with Western Europe.

Intracolonial trade, or trade within a particular colony, grew more slowly than other forms of trade. As indicated earlier, a major reason for the relatively slow growth of internal markets was the cost of overland transportation. The building of roads and canals progressed slowly because the colonies had made only small investments in **social overhead capital,** those forms of capital available for use or consumption by the public. Intracolonial trade was confined to localized activities, such as the milling of grain for farm families in a small market area. The cost of marketing increased rapidly when goods were moved over longer distances. These high transportation costs encouraged relative self-sufficiency in the interiors of the colonies.

Although precise data on intracolonial trade are lacking, we can draw four inferences based on our knowledge of that trade: (a) barriers to integration of resource usage were high, (b) the opportunity costs of self-sufficiency were low, (c) the degree of specialization and division of labor and capital was relatively low, and (d) productivity (output per hour of labor employed) was lower than in other areas of commerce.

Trade between the North American colonies, which we shall call *intercolonial trade,* was more significant.* Intercolonial coastal trade was subject to substantial growth because ocean transportation costs were much lower than overland costs. Deep-water shipping was then, and is even now, the cheapest means of transporting bulky (high weight–price ratio) goods. Many of the goods that moved in intercolonial trade, such as grains and sugar, benefited from this low transportation cost. In this trade, some social overhead capital, such as port facilities, reduced the costs to colonial merchants.

Intercolonial trade was almost exclusively in the hands of colonial merchants. These merchants had a comparative advantage over British merchants and shipping for two primary reasons. First, the need for quick and reliable commercial information is and was essential for rational business decisions. The colonial

---

*Although trade with the West Indies was literally *intercolonial,* we shall treat those exchanges as part of overseas trade and use the term *intercolonial* to refer to exchanges between the North American colonies.

merchants were located close to their markets, and thus had an informational cost advantage over the British merchant and shipper located over 3,000 miles away. Second, the colonial shippers could utilize their smaller, lower-overhead-cost coastal ships more efficiently in the relatively smaller market of the coastal trade, which required frequent stops to discharge and load cargo. The British shipper needed larger ships with larger overhead costs to cross the Atlantic, and thus could not compete costwise in the small-size markets of the coastal trade.

James Shepherd and Samuel Williamson (25) estimated that coastal exports amounted to an annual average of £7,676,000 sterling in the period from 1768 to 1772. Of course, no data exist for gross product for the North American colonies. If, however, we use the range of £20 million to £30 million as representative of the estimates of various scholars, then coastal trade made up about 2 to 4 percent of that product. According to recent studies by David Klingaman (18), coastal trade was growing in the late colonial period; moreover, it was growing in per capita terms, at least as far as Virginia, the most populous of the colonies (after 1730), was concerned.

If we consider that, in spite of high costs, there was a modest amount of trading between colonies by land routes, then the sum of overland and coastal trade probably amounted to not more than 4 to 5 percent of colonial gross product even at the end of the colonial period. However, the cost advantages of coastal trade were such that productivity, related to specialization of resources, was probably growing as the size of the market for coastal trade increased.

Did the North American colonies trade according to the principle of comparative advantage? Basically, the answer is yes. It is clearly yes insofar as the coastal trade between the colonies is concerned. Indeed, the scenario was very similar to the hypothetical one presented in the Review of Economic Concepts later in this chapter. Virginia shipped large quantities of corn to Massachusetts and wheat to New York and other northern colonial areas. In turn, Virginia received shipments from those areas (often reexports) of sugar, rum, molasses, fish, and salt. Where the earnings from these commodity exports (visible items) were inadequate to pay for the imports, the northern colonies earned the difference through services, especially shipping and financial services.

The Overseas Trade

Specialization and comparative-advantage trade tended also to dominate the overseas exchanges of the colonies. The New England colonies exported such things as dried fish, naval stores, and whale oil to Britain and the West Indies, as well as to southern European countries. The southern colonies developed a comparative advantage in certain agricultural exports. Maryland and Virginia primarily exported tobacco, a crop whose demand grew throughout the colonial period. The Carolinas found specialized advantages in two exports, rice and indigo.

The middle colonies (Pennsylvania, Delaware, New Jersey, and New York) specialized in wheat and wheat products, such as biscuits, together with the reexport business (reshipping to the West Indies and England). This is why Philadelphia, and then New York, grew as Boston declined in relative shipping importance.

By the end of the colonial period, both exports and imports were remarkably concentrated according to comparative advantage. Eight commodities accounted for over four-fifths of exports in 1770. In order of importance, these were tobacco, grains and flour, fish, livestock and meat, naval stores, furs and deerskins, indigo, and extracted products.

Manufactured goods dominated the commodity imports from Europe. There was a substantial trade with the West Indies in rum, molasses, and sugar (mostly reexported from the middle colonies to northern and southern colonies). Of course, comparative advantage was dominant in the import pattern, but it was not always a market-determined advantage in either imports or exports. The case of indigo exports is a classic example. Because British textile manufacturers needed indigo to dye their products, the industry was heavily subsidized in the southern colonies and elsewhere in the British Empire. The subsidy shifted the cost advantage in favor of indigo, which made up slightly less than 4 percent of colonial exports in 1770.

Slaves were a major import of the colonies, especially after 1680. Slave importation took place primarily in the southern colonies, but it occurred in the middle and northern colonies as well. The black (mostly slave) population of the colonies grew from about 16,000 in 1690 to about 500,000 at the time of the Revolution.

As with the intercolonial trade, the trade with the West Indies was dominated by colonial shippers and essentially for the same reasons. Colonial shippers, especially in the eighteenth century, were also active in the trade in the Mediterranean and in the slave trade with West Africa.

The colonies benefited from a commodity **trade surplus** (exports greater than imports) with southern Europe; but 75 to 85 percent of their trade was with Britain and represented **trade deficits** (imports greater than exports). And, as Table 2.1 shows, the commodity trade deficit was financed primarily by selling the shipping and other services of the colonists and by the administrative and military expenditures of the British. Overall, as Shepherd and Williamson have shown (25), the colonial trade relationship was remarkably balanced and the net growth of indebtedness by the colonies was quite small.

Money and Trade

A supply of money was needed to accommodate both foreign and intercolonial trade. A commercial British model was probably impractical because of the small size of the market. Since money is anything commonly accepted as a medium of exchange, various commodities, including tobacco, were used for that purpose. Barter had been employed early in the colonial trade, especially in the triangular trade with Britain and the West Indies. Because of their bulkiness, deterioration, and other factors, however, commodities proved to be a high-cost means of financing exchanges, so the colonial merchants turned increasingly to currency and coin.

Table 2.1. Colonial Balance of Payments, 1770 (thousands of pounds sterling)

ITEM	CREDIT	DEBIT
Commodity exports	3023	—
Commodities imports	—	3961
Slave imports	—	108
Imports of indentured servants	—	75
Total balance, visible items		1121
Shipping and other services	845	—
British expenditures on colonial government services	400	—
Total balance, invisible items	1245	
Total balance of payments (visible and invisible items)	124	

SOURCE: Adapted from James F. Shepherd and Gary M. Walton, "Estimates of 'Invisible' Earnings in the Balance of Payments of the British North American Colonies, 1768–1772," *Journal of Economic History*, June 1969; also Ralph Gray and John M. Peterson, *Economic Development of the United States* (Homewood, Ill.: Irwin, 1974).

Even though the volume of commercial transactions was increasing, the growth of the money supply was subject to severe restrictions. The English government restricted the minting of coins and closed down the mint established by Massachusetts. Colonial currency, or paper money, was sometimes issued in such large quantities that both colonial and British merchants refused to accept it at par (face value). The reduced acceptability of currency called into effect **Gresham's law**—(relatively) overvalued or "cheap" money drives out (relatively) undervalued or "dear" money. Merchants tended to hoard the coin and use the paper money, thus further reducing velocity and the growth of the effective money supply. Overall, there were inflationary pressures on colonial prices, especially the prices at which goods were exchanged either at home or abroad in depreciated paper money.

Most students of the colonial period have concluded that although the money supply problems raised the costs of trading (both information and transactions costs), the opportunity cost of creating a commercial banking system in the small colonial market would have been high even if British mercantile policy had permitted or encouraged such a development.

WEALTH AND GROWTH IN THE COLONIES

Some people have viewed the colonies as a frontier society in which wealth was distributed fairly equally. However, the data, including recent important research of Alice Hanson Jones (16, 17), suggest that wealth inequality was substantial and actually increased during the colonial period. James Henretta (14) came to the same conclusion about wealth ownership in Boston, where the propertyless group doubled from 14 to 29 percent of the population between the 1680s and the 1770s. Jones suggests that wealth inequality probably increased in the eighteenth century compared to a century earlier.

Wealth was almost certainly unequally distributed at the outset of the colonial period (reflecting different endowments of land, financial capital, and skills and abilities). Also, there was no governmental policy, such as progressive taxes, designed to reduce inequality of wealth ownership.

In the South, this unequal distribution of income was obvious. By 1770, there were over 500,000 slaves in the colonies, most of them in the South. Plantation slave owners received a substantially larger per capita income than the smaller, family-size farmer in the South. But even in the northern colonies, land was not evenly divided. For example, in Pennsylvania, there were larger than family-size wheat farms in Bucks and Lancaster counties just west of Philadelphia, and in New York, the descendants of the Dutch patroons still held large plots of land originally granted by Holland. By 1770, as we noted, a large group of "mechanics" (wage-earning urban workers) had appeared in the urban areas providing wage labor, especially in the industries centered on shipping and shipbuilding.

Some students of economics believe that a growing inequality of income and wealth are not only inevitable but may even be necessary in the early years of development if savings and investments are to occur on a scale that guarantees on-going economic development.

Growth of the colonial economy was assured by increasing trade and by an eightfold increase in population between 1700 and 1770 (from about 250,000 to just over 2 million). But scholars disagree about the extent of development, or change in per capita income.

George Taylor (29) argues that per capita growth was very slow before 1710, rapid from 1710 to 1775, then slow or zero from 1775 to 1840. He suggests that between 1710 and 1775 per capita output grew from $45 to $90, a substantial increase that, if translated roughly into present-day dollars, amounts to about $500 in 1710 and $1,000 in 1775. These per capita output figures compare favorably with those of all but the very well-developed nations of the 1980s.

Later scholars have questioned Taylor's figures. Robert Gallman (10) believes per capita income may have been as high as $60 as early as 1710. Based on Alice Jones' (16) research of wealth data (developed from probate records, which are among the few good non–export-import data for the period), a figure of $60 to $70 seems reasonable. If so, it appears that slow, steady growth of per capita output occurred in the 1710–1775 period. The growth rate was perhaps 0.5 percent per year, which is significantly high for that period (among the highest in the world), although it is much less than the 2.1 percent annual increases in per capita income that the United States has experienced since the late nineteenth century.

ECONOMIC MOTIVATIONS AND THE COLONIAL MIND

Many people feel intuitively that attitudes toward economic activity seriously affect economic development. People are surely more capable of finding and taking advantage of opportunities for economic development if they are motivated to work hard, eager to try improved techniques, and willing to save and invest capital to increase output. Such people seem better prepared for development than those who are more traditionally oriented, satisfied with what is, and reluctant to try to develop new, more productive methods. But while we understand intuitively the importance of attitudes about economic activity, it is difficult to construct theories about them and their effects on economic development.

What factors molded the American colonists' attitudes toward economic activity? The settlers had been conditioned by the religious doctrines of Luther and Calvin, summarized in the **Weber Thesis** (described in the following section). Also, the political and economic philosophy of John Locke had a profound influence, especially on the Founding Fathers of the United States. Additionally, the colonists were affected by being within a frontier environment. Finally, the southern colonies were basically affected by the institution of slavery in ways that remain the subject of research and intense debate.

Religious Values and Economic Development

Do religious values and practices influence the rate and pattern of economic development? We suspect that a poll of students of economic history would result in a majority answer of yes. Yet after a lengthy period of debate and research on this topic, it still is not clear whether the influence can be identified or, if it can, whether its magnitude can be assessed. Nonetheless, it has seemed to some that the religious values of colonial America were a significant force in creating the foundation for the growth path of the United States.

The Weber Thesis

Max Weber (32), a German sociologist writing in the early twentieth century, concluded that the theology of the sixteenth- and seventeenth-century Reformation period influenced human behavior in ways that were beneficial to economic development. Weber was concerned with the psychological conditioning that resulted from the theological positions of the Protestant reformers, especially Luther and Calvin.

Luther and Calvin continued to maintain the Catholic position that economic effort was an area of personal activity subject to the moral judgments of religious prescriptions. These Protestant reformers considered usury and violations of "just price" (fair price) as improper conduct. They condemned high interest rates and unjust prices (high prices based on short supplies) as exploitive and immoral economic practices.

Both Luther and Calvin placed great importance on the concept of the "calling" (one's earthly occupation) and on the obligation to work hard and diligently. Calvin added that a person is obligated to choose the best "calling" he or she is capable of performing. This ideal was coupled with the belief that, since all wealth belongs to God, each person is God's earthly steward over his or her own share of wealth. One should not spend God's wealth foolishly; frugality and saving are virtues, and each person is required to invest wisely in order to increase God's wealth. This commandment leads to investments oriented toward increases in output.

According to Weber, the Calvinist concept of predestination supports this system of hard work, frugality, saving, and productive investment, and leads to increased output. Calvin said that God ordained at the beginning of time who would be saved and who would be condemned to the fires of hell. There was nothing an individual could do to change that outcome. But there was a way to tell if one was among the elect, that is, those who would be saved. The individual must live the proper life and, even more important, must believe in being saved; any element of doubt about one's own election for salvation was ultimate proof against election. The doctrine of predestination adds an inner discipline to the concept of the "proper life" that includes hard work, rational selection of a calling to maximize income, and frugality and savings so as not to waste God's wealth. All these psychological characteristics are excellently suited to produce a population that strives toward economic development.

A secular manifestation of this Protestant ethic can be found in the sayings of Ben Franklin in *Poor Richard's Almanac;* for example; "A penny saved is a penny earned," "God helps them who help themselves," and "Early to bed and early to rise makes a man healthy, wealthy, and wise." Note that Franklin was a product of Calvinist Boston.

Weber and many other writers emphasize that the Protestant ethic cannot be attributed exclusively to the Puritans of New England. Most of the colonies were settled originally by groups with a strong religious background, and all but the Catholics of Maryland were of Calvinist origin. New York was first settled by the Calvinistic Dutch. In Pennsylvania, the Quaker followers of William Penn and the German Moravians were, at least in attitude, both Calvinist. New Jersey had the Calvinist Swedes, while Virginia had the Scottish Presbyterians—again, Calvinist. Perhaps even the Catholics of Maryland should not be left out, for many of Weber's critics have pointed out that elements of the Protestant ethic emerged in Catholic thought during the sixteenth and seventeenth centuries.

Some writers, including Stuart Bruchey (4), argue that the Protestant ethic was irrelevant to the American colonial economy. These authors stress the conflict between capitalist activity and religious prescriptions forbidding the taking of interest or charging an "unjust price." These critics are right in the sense that religion limited profit-seeking activities dealing with consumers and taking advantage of limited-supply conditions. But with such activities banned as immoral behavior, colonists conditioned by the new theology channeled their efforts into production.

The Philosophy of John Locke

The British economic system was transferred, virtually in toto, to the North American colonies. British statutory and common law included provisions guaranteeing the primacy and transferability of property rights, and these were supported by provisions of contract law. This system of relationships so essential to the evolution of a market economy based on voluntary exchange had its underpinnings in the writings of John Locke, a seventeenth-century English philosopher.

According to Locke, the best method of producing the goods society needs is through private ownership of the tools of production and of output. In a society without government, however, all would war against each other, and the strong would take from the weak. To protect private property, the many should combine, form a social contract, and create a government; thus the main function of government is to protect private property, which is the best institution to ensure economic production.

In the Declaration of Independence, Jefferson paraphrased Locke, who would have said, "Life, liberty and the pursuit of property." The popular ideology of colonial times gave a central place to individual private property rights. But Locke himself was influenced by the Protestant religious ethic, and implicit in his defense of the rights of private property was the obligation to utilize that property for rational investment and production.

The Frontier

From the beginning of settlement in 1607, the frontier nature of the colonies reinforced habits and attitudes that proved conducive to economic development: individual initiative; economic optimism, with its characteristic high level of effort; and a willingness to enter into cooperative effort when necessary.

Figure 2.1.   John Hancock (left) and Samuel Adams, Colonial Merchants and Revolutionary Leaders. (Photos from the National Archives)

Individual effort was needed, wherever the frontier was located during the colonial period, first to survive and then to obtain comforts. This initiative reinforced a sense of individuality and at the same time proved that economic gains could be made through individual effort. Because labor was scarce and raw materials were abundant, labor was conserved, and resources such as trees and fertile soil were used freely in a manner that many today would consider wasteful and ecologically damaging. During the frontier era, however, this manner of using resources saved labor and allowed for rapid increases in output. When the frontier people faced tasks that were too difficult for individual effort, they cooperated to achieve desired ends. Because of the abundant resources of the frontier, economic and social mobility was greater in the colonies than in Europe, and this factor not only retarded the development of an entrenched class structure but may also have contributed to improved individual welfare through relatively high wages.

Slavery and the South

During the colonial period, another factor was introduced that had a special effect for the South, namely, slavery and the plantation system. Settlers in the plantation areas of Maryland, Virginia, the Carolinas, and Georgia were generally conditioned by the same factors that affected the population of the rest of the colonies—the religious work ethic, the philosophy of John Locke, and frontier conditions. However, slavery and the plantation system gave rise to a peculiar set of conditions. The institution of slavery created new social relations and attitudes that tended to affect mobility of resources. Slavery enabled larger units (plantations) to be formed and increased the political, social, and economic influence of the plantation owners. Whites dominated blacks, and one race became set against another.

Figure 2.2.   Patrick Henry. (Photo from the National Archives)

McClelland and the Achieving Society

The first three factors just described—the Weber Thesis, the philosophy of John Locke, and the frontier nature of the colonies—would seem to foster attitudes conducive to economic development. It will be useful here to review a present-day theory concerned with attitudes and economic development developed by David C. McClelland (20), keeping in mind how the conditions just described encouraged the attitudes that McClelland considers beneficial to economic development.

McClelland, who was a psychologist, "invaded" the domain of the economist with his book *The Achieving Society* (1961). He maintained that one specific motive, the need for achievement (n-achievement, or n-ach), is essential for high degrees of entrepreneurship. In brief, n-achievement stimulates entrepreneurship, which in turn stimulates economic development. McClelland feels that differences in degree of n-achievement significantly explain why some groups and countries take advantage of developmental situations while others do not. The important advantage of the n-achievement concept, according to McClelland, is that it can be measured with an index and related to the level of economic activity.

Some characteristics of high n-achievers are the following: They are more interested in a job well done than in the more mundane rewards of money or prestige. They can work in groups as well as alone. They have a rational framework for decision making. Although they are willing to risk failure in seeking achievement, they carefully evaluate realistic probabilities for success by distinguishing factors that are susceptible to control from those that depend on chance. High n-achievers have a greater future time sense. They are willing to forgo immediate gratification to obtain future rewards. They are more inclined to use their own carefully reasoned judgment, after obtaining information about an investment, than to be overwhelmed by the prevailing opinion of others; that is, they are more independent and less susceptible to social pressure. In brief, high n-achievers make rational decisions after careful reasoning on the evidence; they are more independent, more willing to take reasonable risks, more willing to plan ahead and await future rewards, and more concerned with accomplishment than with power.

The American colonists seem to fit McClelland's description of high n-achievers. In part, this may have been due to the factors influencing the self-selection of those who chose to come to the colonies. Perhaps the rigors of immigration and its challenges biased this selection to the more daring, vigorous, healthy, youthful, and so on. Also in part, the preponderance of high n-achievers among the colonists may have been due to the Protestant ethic.

REVIEW OF ECONOMIC CONCEPTS: DEVELOPMENT

A Classical View

The two objectives of rising output per capita and decreasing dualism approximate the process of development. Development results when a nation chooses more future goods; that is, when it saves and invests, creates more capital goods, and increases its capacity to produce, while undergoing the structural change necessary to accommodate this process. The rate at which it develops depends on how large a part of current output is saved and invested and on the power of compound interest. The production possibilities model, however, does not give us the insights we need concerning the underlying causes of development and the factors that constrain it for economies in general and for colonial economies in particular.

A very general and widely accepted view of the causes and limitations of economic development is the **classical view** set forth in one form or another by economists beginning with Adam Smith (1723–1790) in the late eighteenth and early nineteenth centuries. Despite its relative antiquity, the classical view is still valid and applies to all economies, colonial or noncolonial, integrated or dualistic, agricultural or industrial, high-income or low-income.

According to this classical view, intensive growth and economic development are virtually synonymous with productivity growth. Basically, productivity growth is determined by the degree of specialization and the division of labor and capital in production processes. Adam Smith pointed out that as both people and machines took on more and more specialized tasks, their productivity grew very rapidly. Smith observed this growth, for example, in the operation of an eighteenth-century pin factory where the number of pins produced per worker grew very quickly with specialized labor tasks and with specialized machines.

What determines the extent of, or the limits to, specialization and division of labor and capital? According to the classical economists, it is the size of the market. As the size of the market grows, it becomes feasible for people to specialize and to employ specialized kinds of capital. The size of markets depends on both demand and supply. Any of the factors that may cause demand to grow (population and income growth, for instance) or supply to grow (reduced transportation cost, for instance) will increase the size of markets. As Smith (27) noted, "When the market is very small, no person can have any encouragement to dedicate himself entirely to one employment, for want of power to exchange all that surplus part of the produce of his own labor, which is over and above his own consumption, for such parts of the produce of other men's labor as he has occasion for."

Classical economists generally felt that the size of the market depended on the amount or stock of capital and the pattern of institutions. According to Smith, "No regulation of commerce can increase the quantity of industry in any society beyond what its capital can maintain." In other words, greater specialization of labor—a condition for productivity growth—must be preceded by an increased stock of capital. The second factor influencing the size of the market was the pattern of economic institutions and institutional regulations. The classical economists argued that the optimal set of institutions was that which permitted and enforced competition, for that would harness the self-interests of individuals to increase the goods and services available to a society through what Smith referred to as the influence of the "invisible hand."

With the exception of Smith, the classical economists were pessimistic about the ability of economies to continue to experience intensive growth and to develop indefinitely. Most saw an early upper limit to real per capita output, a stationary state, as shown in Figure 2.3. In the classical growth path, growth occurs rapidly at first. Then the rate of growth diminishes, for a variety of reasons, including a limited supply of land, a diminishing growth of productivity of capital, the use of technology from a fixed menu of choices that adds less and less to output, a falling rate of profit, or a population growth that outstrips output gains. Finally these resistances grow strong enough to offset any tendencies to increasing real per capital output, and the economy reaches its stationary state. Among the classical group, only Smith thought this stationary state could occur at a very high level of real output or income.

Comparative Advantage: Why People Trade

When market exchanges occur, it is because buyers and sellers expect to improve their respective positions. A common explanation for this disposition to trade is based on the **principle of comparative advantage.** According to this principle, resources are relatively more productive in some uses than in others. Thus individuals, areas, regions, or nations (including colonies) can have a greater volume of commodities and services for consumption if they specialize in producing those goods in which they have the greatest *relative* efficiency or productivity and then trade some of their output to import goods produced by other areas or nations that are also producing according to their own greatest relative efficiency or productivity. This is true for any individual, nation, or area, even though it may be possible to produce every good it consumes with an **absolute advantage,** that is, using fewer real resources per unit of output than any other person, nation, or area with which it trades.

Assume, for example, in the case of colonies, that both Massachusetts and Virginia could produce grain, make flour, and catch and process fish. According to the principle of comparative advantage, each should specialize in producing the thing(s) in which it is relatively more efficient, or less inefficient. Perhaps Massachusetts should specialize in its fisheries industry, since its soil is relatively poor, and Virginia should specialize in its grain and flour industry, since its soil is relatively rich.

The gains from this trade are illustrated in Figure 2.4, which shows the relationship between the production possibilities curve of each colony before trade and the consumption possibilities curve of each after trade.

The Gains from Trade

Each of the hypothetical production-before-trade (production possibilities) curves in Figure 2.4 represents the various combinations of grain and flour and processed fish that Virginia or Massachusetts could produce at a given time with full employment of resources and use of the best technology. Each is drawn as a straight line to reflect a simplifying assumption of no specialization of resources, or a constant rate of real cost (constant rather than diminishing returns). Notice also that the internal rate of exchange, the rate at which either colony must give up one commodity to get more of the other, is different in the two colonies. In Virginia, the rate of exchange is approximately 1:1 (1 ton of grain and flour for 1 ton of processed fish). In Massachusetts, however, the ratio is about 0.45:1. Massachusetts must give up 0.45 tons of grain and flour to obtain a ton of processed fish. Virginia thus has a comparative advantage (is less inefficient) in producing grain and flour, and Massachusetts has a comparative advantage (is less inefficient) in producing processed fish.

If both colonies specialize and if each exports to the other part of its output of the comparative-advantage good, both can have more goods for consumption (indicated in the consumption-after-trade curves for each colony) than would be available without trade. The rate at which Virginia's grain and flour exchange for Massachusetts' fish depends on the structure of their two markets.

Suppose for the sake of illustration that the exchange rate becomes 0.8:1 (0.8 ton of Virginia grain for 1 ton of Massachusetts fish). Compare Points C and D; if Massachusetts produces only fish (8 tons) but exchanges 4 tons with Virginia, it can obtain 3.2 (4 × 0.8) tons of grain. Thus it can consume 4 tons of fish and 3.2 tons of grain and flour with trade, whereas it could consume only 4 tons of fish and 2 tons of grain and flour without trade (Point C). The additional 1.2 tons of grain and flour is a gain from trade. Likewise, if Virginia produces only grain and flour (10 tons) and, for example, exchanges 5 tons of those commodities with Massachusetts, it can obtain 6.25 tons of fish (5 × 11/8 = 6.25). Thus, with trade, Virginia can consume 5 tons of grain and flour plus 6.25 tons of fish, more than the 5 tons of grain and flour and 2 tons of fish available without trade. Again, the additional 4.25 tons of fish is a gain from trade.

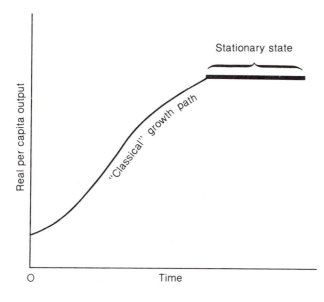

Figure 2.3. A Classical Growth Path.

Although the gains from trade in this example accrue primarily to one colony, Virginia, there are gains to both trading partners. Allowing for increasing costs (concave production-before-trade curves), specialization will not be complete; both trading partners will reach a point at which they will produce some of both products.

Individual Exchanges: The Basis for Such Gains

The essential basis for a market economy is *voluntary* exchange. The primary reason economists conclude that such exchanges make both individuals and societies better off is that individuals (indeed, all resources) are relatively more productive in some activities than others. Thus Joe Jones may be a skilled computer programmer and also an outstanding baseball pitcher. It is almost certain, however, that he is *relatively* better at one than the other. Jane Smith may be a highly skilled attorney as well as a very capable office manager; again, she is *relatively* better at one or the other.

In a market economy, we must have some guide to the relative or comparative advantages in using resources. That guide is relative prices, what individuals or firms will pay for those resources in different uses. If Jones and Smith may choose between salary offers for their labor skills, the uses in which they are relatively more productive will be reflected in higher factor payments. Both individuals will specialize: Jones will accept the higher-valued employment as a pitcher; Smith will accept employment as an attorney. Both will more than cover their *opportunity cost*, the next-most-valued uses of their labor skills.

As a general rule, then, as resources acting on price signals move to their comparative-advantage uses, societies will realize a greater value of output. They will

Figure 2.4.   Hypothetical Production and Consumption Possibilities for Virginia and Massachusetts.

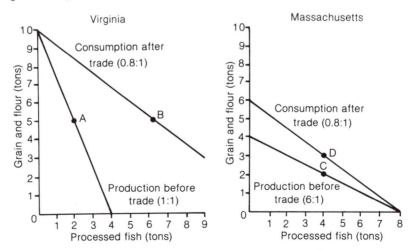

realize through voluntary exchange the benefits of comparative-advantage–based trade and uses of resources.

QUESTIONS

1. Why are the terms of trade so important to an economy?
2. What is the difference between absolute advantage and comparative advantage? What are the sources of the gains from trade that comparative-advantage exchanges make possible?
3. Was the distribution of colonial land ownership relatively even? What were the obstacles to land ownership? How was a labor force provided for the family-size farm? For the commercial farm?
4. What was the main process of capital formation in the family-size farm? What were the main sources of financial capital for the commercial farms?
5. What were the basic factors causing productivity increases in colonial agriculture? Explain.
6. Evaluate the statement: "The totally self-sufficient colonial farm was rare, as was the totally commercial farm."
7. Why was the level of productivity increase so low in colonial manufacturing?
8. Why were the British restrictions on colonial banking and paper money of little burden to the colonial economy?
9. What were the major obstacles to development of internal markets in the North American colonies?
10. Did coastal trade grow during the colonial period? Why?
11. Did the North American colonies engage in comparative-advantage trade? What was the pattern of overseas trade by the colonies?
12. What happened to the trade balance of the colonies in the eighteenth century?
13. What were the problems associated with financing colonial trade? What is Gresham's law? How does it apply to the colonial trade?
14. What changes occurred in the distribution of wealth in the North American colonies? Were any changes in this distribution favorable to economic development? Why?
15. What are the views about the level and rate of growth of per capita income in the colonies?
16. Describe religious and philosophical factors that affected colonial attitudes toward economic development. Which were conducive to economic development? Why? Which were not? Why?

SUGGESTED READINGS

1. Anderson, Terry. "Wealth Estimates for the New England Colonies, 1650–1709." *Explorations in Economic History, 14,* (October 1977).
2. Bidwell, Percy W., and John I. Falconer. *History of Agriculture in the Northern United States, 1620–1860.* Washington, D.C.: Carnegie Institution of Washington, 1925.

3. Bridenbaugh, Carl. *The Colonial Craftsman.* New York: New York University Press, 1950.

4. Bruchey, Stuart. *The Roots of American Economic Growth, 1607–1861.* New York: Harper and Row, 1968. Pp. 23–41, 42–48.

5. Curten, Philip. *The Atlantic Slave Trade: A Census.* Madison: University of Wisconsin Press, 1969.

6. Dorfman, Joseph. *The Economic Mind in American Civilization, 1606–1865.* Vol. 1. New York: Viking, 1959.

7. Ferguson, E. James. "Currency Finance: An Interpretation of Colonial Monetary Practices." In *Issues in American Economic History,* ed. Gerald D. Nash. Lexington, Mass.: Heath, 1972.

8. Foner, Phillip. *History of the Labor Movement in the United States.* Vol. 1. New York: International Publishers, 1947.

9. Galenson, David. "White Servitude and the Growth of Black Slavery in Colonial America." *Journal of Economic History. 41* (March 1981).

10. Gallman, Robert. "The Pace and Pattern of American Economic Growth." In *American Economic Growth,* ed. L. Davis, R. Easterlin, and W. Parker. New York: Harper and Row, 1972.

11. Gray, Lewis C. *History of Agriculture in the Southern States to 1860.* Vol. 1. Washington, D.C.: Carnegie Institute of Washington, 1933.

12. Harper, Lawrence. "The Burden of the Navigation Acts on the Thirteen Colonies." In *United States Economic History,* ed. Harry B. Scheiber. New York: Knopf, 1964.

13. Harris, Marshall. *Origin of the Land Tenure System in the United States.* Ames: University of Iowa, 1953.

14. Henretta, James A. "Economic Development and Social Structure in Colonial Boston." *William and Mary Quarterly 27* (January 1965).

15. Hofstadter, Richard, and Seymour Lipset, eds. *Turner and the Sociology of the Frontier.* New York: Basic Books, 1968.

16. Jones, Alice Hanson. "Wealth Estimates of the New England Colonies about 1770." *Journal of Economic History, 33* (March 1972).

17. Jones, Alice Hanson. "Wealth of a Nation to Be: The American Colonies on the Eve of the Revolution." New York: Columbia University Press, 1980.

18. Klingaman, David C. "Food Surpluses and Deficits in the American Colonies, 1768–1772." *Journal of Economic History, 36* (September 1975).

19. Loehr, Rodney C. "Self-Sufficiency of the Farm." *Agricultural History, 26* (April 1952).

20. McClelland, David C., and David G. Winter. *Motivating Economic Achievement.* New York: Free Press, 1969.

21. Primack, Martin L. "Land Clearing Under Nineteenth-Century Techniques: Some Preliminary Calculations." *Journal of Economic History, 23* (December 1972).

22. Rothenberg, Winifred B. "The Market and Massachussets Farmers, 1750–1855." *Journal of Economic History, 41* (June 1981).

23. Sacks, William. "Agricultural Conditions in the Northern Colonies Before the Revolution." *Journal of Economic History, 13* (Summer 1953).

24. Shepherd, James F., and Gary M. Walton. "Trade, Distribution and Economic Growth in Colonial America." *Journal of Economic History,* (March 1972).

25. Shepherd, James F., and Samuel Williamson. "The Coastal Trade of British North American Colonies, 1768–1772." *Journal of Economic History, 33* (December 1972).

26. Smith, Abbott E. *Colonists in Bondage: White Servitude and Convict Labor in America, 1607–1776.* Chapel Hill: University of North Carolina Press, 1947.

27. Smith, Adam. *An Enquiry into the Nature and Causes of the Wealth of the Nation.* New York: The Modern Library, 1937.

28. Stampp, Kenneth M. *The Peculiar Institution: Slavery in the AnteBellum South.* New York: Alfred A. Knopf, 1956.

29. Taylor, George Rogers. "American Economic Growth Before 1840: An Exploratory Essay." *Journal of Economic History, 25* (December 1964).

30. Tryon, Rolla M. *Household Manufacturers in the United States, 1640–1860.* Chicago, 1917.

31. Turner, Frederick Jackson. *The Frontier in American History.* New York: Holt, Rinehart and Winston, 1962.

32. Weber, Max. *The Protestant Ethic and the Spirit of Capitalism.* New York: Scribner's, 1958.

33. Weiss, Roger W. "The Issue of Paper Money in the American Colonies, 1720–1774." *Journal of Economic History, 30* (December 1970).

Chapter 3 ————————————————————————————

MERCANTILISM, TAXES, AND THE AMERICAN REVOLUTION

In 1763, the French and Indian War (known in Europe as Queen Anne's War) ended. The French no longer constituted a threat to the British colonies in America. Instead of peace, however, conflict raged between the American colonists and the home government of Britain. Disagreements, which eventually led to violence and revolution, surfaced over political theory and philosophy, civil liberties, taxes, and the nature of the relationship between the home government in London and the American colonies.

This chapter will examine the theory of mercantilism to give some insight into British expectations about how a colony should relate to the home country and to analyze the economic effects of such a program on the colonies. What we are searching for is an economic explanation of the Revolution. Among the various aspects of economic policy we will consider are the effects of taxes on the colonies. Were the colonies driven to rebel by excessive taxation? Finally, we will consider the economic impact of the Revolution itself on the colonial economy and society.

GOVERNMENT AND THE COLONIES

The economist must consider the effects of government activities on the economic development of the American colonies on two levels. We must look at both the activities of the government residing within the 13 colonies and, more importantly, the activities (laws and enforcement) of the government in England as they related to the American colonies.

The American Revolution was an outgrowth of conflict between the colonists and the government in England. Can the conflict that ended in revolution be explained in economic terms? Was England exploiting the colonies for the home country's benefit, or was it using mercantilist policy to maximize economic benefits for both the colonial and English economies? Is there a reasonable economic explanation for the American Revolution?

By the beginning of the eighteenth century, the British government had increased its control over the governing of the colonies. In doing so, it had replaced private control by the separate proprietors with royal appointment of governors; it also had reduced the power of the local assemblies. Market economies had developed enough so that the royal governments now had some impact on the economy. Their effects were small but noticeable and were manifested mostly in the area of patronage. There was enough demand for goods for governments to give out some contracts, almost all of which went to the favorites of the governors. In this way, a small group of colonial merchants obtained a somewhat special advantage in economic activity, and a small class of favored merchants had a special interest in preserving royal control over the colonies.

At the same time, the self-governing institutions of the colonies intervened widely, developing their own local mercantilism. They attempted to stimulate desired kinds of enterprises and regulated significant aspects of the economy, at times including prices and interest rates. Some were in conflict between defending royal control out of self-interest rooted in special treatment and defending self-rule and its local mercantilism.

Mercantilism and the American Colonies

Mercantilism was a system of practical European economic policies that was dominant in the seventeenth and eighteenth centuries. Although the recommendations and policies varied from one country to another and from one period of time to another, certain theories provided the common thread binding mercantilist thought and practice in this era.

The basic motivation of mercantilist policy was to maximize the economic power of the nation. To accomplish this, the national government had to become involved in all facets of economic activity. A mercantilist economy was a "managed" economy.

Our focus here is on only one aspect of mercantilism, that concerned with international trade and colony–home country relations. The volume of international trade was regarded as fixed. If France's exports increased, some other country's exports would have to decrease. Thus the aim of a single country was to increase its **favorable balance of trade** (the excess of exports over imports). A country with a favorable balance of trade would receive an inflow of money (gold and silver) in payment for its excess of exports. As its supply of gold and silver increased, so would the wealth and power of the nation.

The accumulation of gold and silver was more important in France than in England, where there was greater concern to maximize output, profits, and employment. Also, the primary emphasis in England was on international trade, whereas France placed greater emphasis on internal affairs.

The function of colonies was to help in this economic objective. Mercantilists viewed the home country and its colonies as one entity, each with a different role to play. The colonies were to provide the raw materials needed by the home country, and thus reduce its need to import such raw materials from the outside. In turn, the colonies would provide a market for the manufactured goods of the home country. In this way, the empire would become more self-sufficient.

During the sixteenth, seventeenth, and eighteenth centuries, the major imperial powers—England, France, Holland, and Spain—developed a mercantile policy aimed at implementing these approaches. Each nation passed laws restricting their colonies' trade with other nations. Subsidies and other forms of help were extended to colonies to facilitate the production of desired raw materials, and at the same time, the colonies were restricted in their right to produce manufactured goods in competition with the home country.

The goal was to create a separate, self-contained economic world within each empire. Economic benefits generated by this interrelationship would arise through specialization of functions and through cooperation between the two parts—not through exploitation of the colonies by the home country. In the British mind, at least, both home country and colonies would benefit economically. A major question for us, then, is: Was English mercantile policy beneficial to the North American colonists?

Beyond the question of the economic effects of mercantilist laws, one must ask whether the colonies were helped or hurt by membership in the British Empire, with all its privileges and burdens. The answer to that question is not simple, and, as is the case with all complex situations, historians disagree on the relative importance of different factors. Some historians condemn the British for blatantly exploiting the colonies (Harper [11] and Aptheker [1], for example), others conclude that the colonies received marked net benefits from their relationship with Britain (Dickerson [6], for example), while still others take an intermediate position (Nettels [15] and Thomas (20) It is difficult to quantify all the complex interrelationships and give a definitive answer. The various elements of British mercantilist policy are summarized in Table 3.1.

An important regulation in the **Navigation Acts** was the restriction that trade within the empire could be carried on only by British ships. Because the colonists were considered citizens of the empire, their ships were not excluded. This policy established a common market of considerable size. The elimination of foreign competition, especially from Dutch and French shipping, was an advantage to colonial shipping interests, although it reduced competition and therefore increased shipping rates for colonial products. By the end of the colonial period, the advantages and disadvantages of the elimination of foreign shipping competition were probably of little importance. The colonists held a cost advantage in the coastal and West Indies trade because of geographic proximity and raw material advantages in the

Table 3.1   Selected Acts of Parliament and the King That Affected the American Colonies.

YEAR	DESCRIPTION
1651 1660 1696	Navigation Acts. Required that ships flying the merchant flag of England must be of English or colonial construction and must be owned and manned by citizens of the British Empire. All enumerated articles exported from the colonies had to be sent to Britain. Also, imports into the colonies coming from Europe and the Far East had to go through Britain. Only British Empire vessels could engage in the colonial British trade.
1699	Woolen Act. Prohibited export of wool and woolen products from the colonies.
1732	Hat Act. Forbade the export of beaver hats from the colonies.
1733	Molasses Act. Was considered the "old sugar act." Among other things, all molasses not produced in the British West Indies was taxed 6 pence per gallon. Considerable smuggling occurred to avoid this law.
1750	Iron Act. Placed restrictions on manufacturing of iron products and encouraged production of pig and bar iron.
1751	Paper Money Act. Regulated the issues of paper money in New England by requiring that provision be made for redemption within five years.
1763	Proclamation of 1763. Created the Indian country west of the Appalachian Mountains and restricted western expansion.
1764	Revenue Act of 1764. Was generally known as the Sugar Act. It was designed in part to pay for British troops employed in America to control the Indians and the conquered French. It amended the 1733 Sugar Act by reducing the tax on foreign-produced molasses to 3 pence per gallon.
1764	Stamp Act. Levied taxes to obtain stamps on official and business documents. Opposition was so well organized and effective that the act was voided by 1766.
1767	Revenue Act of 1767 or the Townshend Act. Levied import duties on glass, paper, paint, and tea imported into the colonies. Resistance by the colonists was strong; the act was repealed in 1770.
1773	Tea Act. Placed import taxes on tea and gave a monopoly on tea to the East India Company by allowing the company to ship tea directly to the colonies, eliminating the cost of shipment to England. Very strong resistance included the Boston Tea Party.
1774	Quebec Act of 1774. Among other things, extended the territory of Quebec to the south, limiting expansion of settlement beyond Pennsylvania.

construction of ships. At this time, transatlantic shipping was dominated by English interests, and here the English held the advantage over the colonists because of their geographic proximity to the European continent. The French and Dutch found it hard to compete in either the coastal or transatlantic trade.

It must be kept in mind that all the colonial powers had similar mercantile regulations. It was illegal for American colonial ships to trade with the colonies of France, Spain, and Holland in the West Indies, although significant amounts of illegal traffic did occur. If the American colonies had been outside the British Empire after 1763, they would have been legally excluded from their lucrative trade with the British West Indies. It must also be kept in mind that the point just made about the cost of being outside the British Empire is separate from the general argument about the cost to the colonists of the Navigation Acts themselves.

Given the political structure of the world trading community, the imperial requirement that only British ships could trade within the empire was a benefit to the pre-Revolutionary colonial economy. The disadvantage to the colonists of higher shipping cost for their exports and imports was not significant because foreign shippers were unable to compete against the comparative advantage of colonial and British shipping.

A second set of regulations within the Navigation Acts had a greater effect on the American colonial economy. These regulations required that colonial exports, enumerated by various Acts of Parliament, should be shipped first to England and that colonial imports should be shipped through England, regardless of their origin. British West Indies trade, however, was exempt from this requirement to use England as the **entrepot** for both imports and exports. Another exemption allowed the colonists to ship agricultural provisions directly to Spain south of Cape Finisterre and in the southern Mediterranean.

For the colonies, the shipping, handling, storage, and middleman costs of both imports and exports were increased by this requirement to ship exports ultimately destined for non–British Europe to Britain and to obtain imports produced on the continent by way of Britain. Furthermore, banning direct trade with the European continent north of Cape Finisterre restricted the area of economic activity of colonial merchants and shippers. Some argue that these restrictions in effect created a monoply by British mercantile interests of colonial trade destined for and originating in continental Europe. Lawrence Harper (11) concludes that the economic costs of these restrictions were substantial: at least $5 million to $7.5 million a year toward the end of the colonial period. This total, he maintains, was greater than federal expenditures per year during Washington's presidency.

Robert Thomas (20) presents a hypothetical example of the burden of this requirement that the enumerated exports of the colonies first be shipped to Britain (Figure 3.1). The price would be P_2, and the quantity Q_2, if there were no restrictions. As Thomas expresses it, "The additional costs borne by enumerated goods upon their reexport has the effect of lowering the prices received by the colonial producer and depressing the quality exported."

In economic terms, the world market prices shown in Figure 3.1 would, in the absence of regulation, be P_2 and exports would be Q_2. The effect of the additional cost of shipment through England is to raise the price to the consumer to P_3. Colonial exports, consequently, are reduced to Q_1; therefore, both consumers and producers suffer from the enumeration of colonial exports whose final destination is not England.

The measure of the burden to the colonial exports is the shaded triangle between P_1 and P_2 (indirect burden of foreign revenue) plus the crosshatched rectangle ($P_2 - P_1 \times Q_1$), the direct burden or revenue loss at the prevailing quantity and price.

Thomas concludes, then, that the requirement to ship enumerated products first to England did lower prices to the colonists and raise prices to the ultimate European consumer. However, he estimates that the burden was modest, with the total burden of British mercantile policy amounting to $905,000 in 1770, or about $.42 per colonist. Gary M. Walton (21) substantially agreed with Thomas's general conclusions but showed that his estimates were about 100 percent too high.

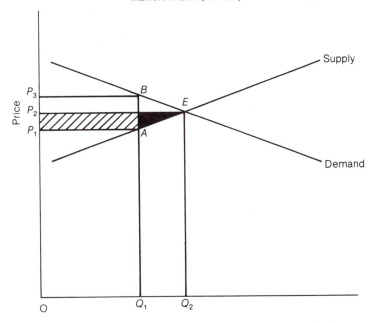

Figure 3.1. Hypothetical Supply and Demand for Colonial Enumerated Product.

Source :   Robert P. Thomas, "A Quantitative Approach to the Study of the Effects of British Imperial Policy upon Colonial Welfare: Some Preliminary Findings," *Journal of Economic History, 25* (December 1965): 622, 623. © Economic History Association.

    Stuart Bruchey (3) also maintains that the additional costs of shipment first to Britain were not as high as Harper estimated. Bruchey points out that merchants in England performed a number of functions that colonial merchants would have had to perform themselves if the use of England had been avoided. These English merchants, for example, graded, repacked, and sorted tobacco and had contacts on the continent from which they obtained necessary information about where, when, and how much to ship. The costs of performing these marketing services must be subtracted from Harper's estimates of additional costs incurred because of the requirement to ship first to Britain. Oliver Dickerson (6) maintains that the decline of total tobacco exports after the Revolution can be explained, at least in part, by the loss of these British marketing services. These kinds of services were performed for other exports from the colonies as well.

    The transatlantic trade had to be carried out by larger ships than the coastal trade, and these larger ships had higher total operating costs. Significant losses of efficiency would result if the storage holds of these ships were not fully used. They had to be able to pick up and deliver cargo to one place or only a few places, and sufficient cargo had to be concentrated at one place so that all cargo space would be used. British ports served as collection points for European cargo and added to it the substantial addition of British exports. In other words, the need to pick up and deliver cargo at specific places in order to operate transatlantic ships most efficiently could have prevented significant direct trade by the colonies with the continent. Tobacco might have been shipped directly to France, but it is unlikely that sufficient return cargo could have been found at prices competitive with British manufacturing prices. The potential gains from direct trade, then, would have been smaller than some have presumed.

Furthermore, if direct trade with the continent of Europe had been permitted, resources of the colonies would have been diverted from existing uses. Were the opportunity costs of direct trade high enough to justify shifting shipping from the coastal and West Indies trade? Transatlantic direct trade would have had to yield higher returns than coastal West Indies trade to make it profitable to move these resources to direct trade. One might ask: Why didn't the colonists build more ships? Under conditions of full employment—and most evidence shows that this was the case—building more ships would have required moving resources out of their uses. If resources had been shifted, then the opportunity costs in those uses would have to be taken into account. These factors seem to justify accepting Walton's lower estimate over that of Thomas.

It seems, then, that the colonies' costs were increased and their economic opportunities restricted by the need to ship enumerated exports to England and to import goods from England, but both the costs and the restricted opportunities were decreased by the following factors: British merchants performed the valuable services of grading, sorting, and packaging; of concentrating export cargo to the colonies; of dispersing import cargo from the colonies; and of maintaining the commercial contacts necessary to time the distribution of cargo from the colonies. Even without the Navigation Acts, the need to concentrate cargo to use the storage space of transatlantic ships efficiently would have led to much trade being concentrated through Britain. Finally, the opportunity cost (the revenue earned in occupations that would have to be given up as resources moved to the activities involved in direct trade) of direct continental trade might not have been much higher than the income earned in indirect trade.

A third set of mercantile laws involved restrictions on colonial industrial production that was in competition with British manufacturing. These restrictions were used against colonial production of such goods as hats, textiles, and iron products. Even Harper admits that manufacturing restrictions had little effect on the colonial economy, which was not suited to the production of manufactured items for sale. Competition with Britain was prevented in the colonies by the scarcity and consequent high costs of labor and capital, the low level of technical skills and knowledge, and the limited size of the colonial market, which reduced the economies of specialization and size. One industry in which the colonies could compete was shipbuilding. Another industry in which they excelled was the production of pig iron, most of it exported to England duty-free. The colonies provided about one-seventh of world pig iron production. The colonists' main advantage in these two areas was an abundance of raw material—wood and iron ore deposits. Whenever opportunities looked profitable, they often violated the restrictions of the mercantile laws.

Other mercantile laws involved bounties and subsidies supporting export sectors of the colonial economy. Bounties and subsidies for the timber industry of northern New England were intended to encourage the export of trees for use in constructing ships for the British navy. Naval stores such as tar and pitch from the pine forests of North Carolina were subsidized. South Carolina and Georgia received subsidies for the growing and exporting of indigo, a dye used in British textiles. Such subsidies increased the cash income of the colonial economy.

In considering the economic effects of the British mercantile system, one must remember that *all* colonial empires were run on the basis of mercantile philosophy. If the American colonies had not been part of a colonial empire, they would have been excluded from legal trade with all of Europe and its colonies. Wouldn't this exclusion have been even more economically damaging than membership in an empire? Perhaps it is less relevant to ask whether one mercantile law or another was a net benefit to the colonial economy than whether membership in the British Empire with all of its obligations and privileges was economically beneficial to the colonial economy.

Taxes and More Taxes?

Every analysis of the events leading up to the American Revolution has stressed the role of taxes levied on the American colonies by Britain. Our interest is in the economic importance of these taxes, not their political and philosophical implications. How heavy was taxation? Why was it imposed?

Statistics from the eighteenth century are subject to question, but even so, the data in Table 3.2 reflect striking differences in taxation. Whatever adjustments one might make to Table 3.2, the conclusion is unchanged. Considering that per capita income was probably higher in the colonies than in Britain, the tax burden on the colonists was relatively low. It was the British, not the colonists, who paid most of the direct costs of the French and Indian War, which ended in 1763 and removed the very real threat of France on the colonial frontier.

Table 3.2. Total Taxes per Capita: Britain and the Colonies, 1765.

	TAXES PER CAPITA
Great Britain	$5.79
Massachusetts	0.22
Pennsylvania	0.22
Maryland	0.22
New York	0.15
Connecticut	0.13
Virginia	0.10

SOURCE: R. R. Palmer, *The Age of Democratic Revolution: A Political History of Europe and America, 1760–1800.* vol. 1: *The Challenge* (Princeton, N.J.: University Press, 1969), p. 155. In Gerald Gunderson, *New Economic History of America* (New York: McGraw-Hill, 1976), p. 89.

The effort to increase colonial taxes, through various tax laws enacted from 1764 to 1775, would have resulted in an increase in revenues to Britain of approximately £120,000, or about £.10 per capita, in the colonies. Only a small fraction of this increase was realized, an amount hardly large enough to justify a charge of massive increase in colonial taxes. The issue was not the size of the tax, for that was indeed moderate, but the manner in which the tax laws were passed. Perhaps also the colonists feared that their tax burden would be raised to that of Great Britain, and this fear may have been an economic factor in the buildup to the Revolution.

Remember, whether taxes are a burden depends on the services that are received in return. If more is paid in taxes than is received in services, taxes may be considered a burden. A British army was maintained in the colonies to protect the settlers from the Indians at least until the 1770s, when the army was increasingly used against the colonists themselves. The cost of maintaining the army in the colonies, almost £370,000 in 1764, was far more than the amount received from taxation. Even more important was the protection afforded by the British navy to the commercial activities of the colonists. The navy provided protection from pirates for colonial ships trading with the West Indies, Africa, and Spain, as well as protection during time of war. The diplomatic strength of the British government was also used to the colonists' advantage; for example, in obtaining from Spain the right for the colonists to use the port of New Orleans. This privilege enabled the colonists to ship western agricultural products down tributaries to the Mississippi River and on to New Orleans and the Gulf of Mexico. The benefits obtained from the British government far exceeded the tax cost to the colonists.

The Sugar Tax of 1764 actually lowered the tax on molasses imported from the French West Indies. After smuggling and laxness in enforcement had reduced the old Sugar Tax of 1733 to a dead letter, the British decided to lower the tax rate on imported molasses, but were determined to enforce the new tax. Since taxes had not been collected on the old act, even the lower rate meant a higher real tax burden and therefore reduced the profits and the prosperity of the smuggling trade with the French West Indies. The British were angered by the colonists' smuggling activities, especially the illegal trade with the enemy during the French and Indian War. Enforcement involved not only catching the smugglers but also convicting them. A jury of colonial peers would not convict. Therefore, smugglers were removed from the jurisdiction of the colonial courts to the admiralty courts, where there was no jury trial. Conflict was stimulated not only by economic motivations but also by contending political philosophies.

Even the infamous Tea Tax of 1773 was moderate; but the outcry, especially from colonial merchants, was huge. The British East India Company was given the right to directly ship tea to the colonies without going through England. This reduced the cost of tea below that of tea smuggled in by colonial merchants. The British East India Company could now undersell colonial merchants.

In the Proclamation of 1763, further westward movement into the frontier was forbidden. Explanations for this prohibition vary from concern to prevent future

Indian wars to the fear that competition with British manufacturing would develop in isolated settlements. Perhaps a more important explanation was that the British wanted to protect the western fur trade for the Hudson Bay Company, operating out of Canada. This restriction alienated western settlers and also those living farther east who were heavily involved in western land speculation inside the prohibited area. It seems that many of the Virginia-Maryland plantation owners were involved in this speculation.

When the advantages of being part of a colonial empire are weighed carefully, it is not at all clear that British economic policy had a net detrimental effect on the colonies. The various costs and benefits are difficult to measure, and the casual interrelationships are complex. The debate about whether membership in the British Empire was a burden to the colonists will not be resolved here, but will continue to fascinate historians and economists.

AN ECONOMIC EXPLANATION FOR THE AMERICAN REVOLUTION?

If it is not at all clear that membership in the British Empire in 1770 was harmful to the colonial economy as a whole, what kind of economic explanation can be offered for the American Revolution?

One explanation is that various aspects of British economic policy had alienated one group of colonists or another, regardless of that policy's overall benefit. What may have been important was the distribution of the burdens of British economic policy among specific groups that held political power. Furthermore, certain groups, especially the wealthier members of colonial society, may have developed expectations about the direction of post-1763 British policy and its impact on their economic position. Consider the following:

1. Both the western pioneer and the eastern land speculator were alienated by the Proclamation of 1763 forbidding western settlement. For example, Patrick Henry may have been thus alienated.

2. Colonial merchants excluded from patronage may have wished either to eliminate special privileges or to replace those obtaining this patronage. John Hancock or Samuel Adams of Boston may have had such motives.

3. Plantation owners may have thought that the monopoly of British merchants in marketing and financing the tobacco crop constituted an unfair burden on Virginia and Maryland. George Washington and Thomas Jefferson may be examples.

4. Colonial merchants, after experiencing the tea tax and privileges granted to the East India Company to their own disadvantage, may have feared further discriminatory legislation that would benefit British capital at the expense of the colonial economy.

5.   Other merchants and shipowners may have felt restive under British restrictions on direct trade outside the empire.

Another explanation, or partial explanation, concerns the expulsion of the French from Canada at the end of the French and Indian Wars. The American colonists had diverged in character and sentiment from the people of Britain. Devoid of many of the social and economic restriction of the Old World and separated from it by 3,000 miles of ocean and months of travel, the frontier produced a unique society with a sense of its own distinctiveness. The existence of the French on the northern frontier presented a threat that tied the colonies to Britain. With the British capture of Canada, both the threat and the dependence were eliminated.

Economic causes were not the only impetus to revolution. Although economic reasons contributed to the conflict, the picture is incomplete without an analysis of differences in philosophical, political, and social conditions between the colonies and Britain. Economic determinism does not work too well in this case because economic factors were only a part of the broader social and political considerations that led to the American Revolution.

THE REVOLUTION AND ITS EFFECTS

The major economic problem of the young United States from the time of the Declaration of Independence (1776) to the adoption of the Constitution (1789) was how to accommodate the American economy to the break with the British Empire. The colonial economy had been dependent on and tied to the rest of the British Empire, not only by the system of mercantile laws and regulations that had grown up over the first 170 years of the colonies' life, but also by a system of economic relationships that, surprisingly, were substantially based on comparative advantage. But the international economic community was primarily based on imperial mercantile relationships: each empire had its own mercantile relationships. Could the young United States achieve both political and economic independence?

The revolutionary bid for economic independence created difficulties. In part, these difficulties involved the sharp increase in the money supply during the Revolution, followed by a reduction in the money supply after independence was achieved in the 1780s. In addition, the break with Britain created problems concerning new sources of exports to replace those lost by withdrawal from the British Empire. These two problems—variations in the supply of money and the need for alternative sources of foreign markets—are important themes affecting economic processes from 1776 to 1789.

THE REVOLUTION AND THE ECONOMY

At the beginning of his excellent history, *The Emergence of a National Economy, 1775–1815,* Curtis Nettels (16) wrote, "During the forty years after 1775 the American people brought forth not only a new nation, but also a national economy. The Revolution began a process of change that modified nearly every phase of American life." By necessity, our treatment of that process will be restricted to two areas: the responses of the American economy to the absence of commercial trade with Britain during the war and the economic effects of efforts to finance the Revolution.

Commercial Independence

Even before declaring political independence from Great Britain, the Continental Congress had made a declaration of economic independence from the British Empire. On October 20, 1774, the First Continental Congress formed the Continental Association and declared a boycott against all British Empire goods. On September 10, 1775, an embargo, or a ban, was declared on exports from America to Britain, the British West Indies, and Ireland. On April 6, 1776, Congress opened American ports to all foreign ships, except those of the citizens of Great Britain. The Congress sent representatives to European countries, especially to France, to negotiate economic assistance.

The British in turn passed the Prohibitory Act of December 22, 1775, which prohibited vessels from trading with the 13 colonies and authorized seizures of vessels that violated the act. Although the British launched a blockade to prevent other nations from trading with the 13 colonies, they had neither the ships nor the bases to make the blockade effective.

Substitutes for British Trade

Before the Revolution, the American colonies were economically bound to Britain. In all practical terms, the British Empire was both their source of manufactured goods and their primary export market. Where would the former colonists get their manufactured goods, and where would they sell their surplus output? The new nation increased commercial trade with European nations other than Britain, expanded domestic manufactures, and tried to meet the demands of the Revolutionary armies. Also, privateering became an important source of money and goods.

At that time, governments often granted commissions making it legal for privately owned sea raiders to capture enemy merchant vessels, sell them, and distribute the proceeds among the owners and the crew. Congress gave commissions to 1,697 privateers, and the state of Massachusetts commissioned an additional 958 vessels. About 10,000 seamen served on these vessels. According to Nettels, the British lost 2,000 vessels, 12,000 sailors, and £18 million, mostly through the actions of the privateers.

These privateers brought in significant quantities of military and civilian supplies for the new nation, plus needed hard currency from selling their prizes in Europe. Substantial losses to British mercantile enterprise resulted in some bankruptcies. Privateering provided employment in American shipbuilding, substitute employment for sailors from fishing, and employment in commerce—all industries that had been severely restricted by the outbreak of the Revolution.

With the stoppage of legal trade with the empire, the Americans were successful in establishing extensive direct trade with other European nations, especially France, Holland, and Spain, and also with their colonies in the West Indies. There was even a roundabout trade with Britain itself. British goods were imported into Holland and reexported to the United States; in payment, American goods were imported into Holland, repacked and relettered, and shipped to Britain. Imports were paid for in part by loans from France, Holland, and Spain, but mostly through exports of U.S. products, especially tobacco. Major imports included all kinds of military supplies, from gunpowder to army uniforms.

Did the Revolution Stimulate the Economy?

Although imports from non-British sources and goods seized by privateers were important, they were not adequate to meet the needs of both the civilian population and the military. These insufficiencies, plus the British blockade, stimulated an increase in demand for the domestic economy's output. Needs of the military severely strained the simple economy of the time.

Agents of the Congress set up a system of procurement throughout the country to provide supplies for the army. These activities not only increased market production but also stimulated improved roads and gave many people experience in organizing economic activity on a large scale.

The colonial economy was essentially a dual economy: a money exchange economy and a nonmoney economy with large amounts of home-produced and -consumed production, or production locally bartered in exchange. On balance, whether or not the Revolution was economically "beneficial" is hard to determine; the answer depends on the time frame within which benefits are measured. The increased needs of the military, American, British, and—toward the end of the war—French, drew more of the nonexchange economy into a money exchange system. The foreign export-oriented sectors of the colonial economy, such as tobacco and indigo, were seriously affected by wartime disruptions of their normal export markets. These disruptions created tendencies that expanded and also contracted money exchange activities.

Thus economic needs created by the Revolution led to a number of significant changes. American merchants learned to trade with the world trading community, not merely with Britain, and these wider contacts were maintained after the war. The new nation gained experience in handling large economic transactions, which included working with larger manufacturing enterprises. Major expansion of foreign trade did not occur until after 1792, and sustained manufacturing expansion did not take place until 1815; but the training and experience in these areas gained during the Revolutionary period were important prerequisites for future development.

Financing the Revolution

Financing the military operations of the war was a vexing problem for the Continental Congress. Various solutions were considered: taxation, issuing paper currency without gold or silver backing, borrowing from the American public through interest-bearing bills of credit, and finally, borrowing from foreign countries. At one time or another, the Continental Congress used each of these four methods to finance the Revolutionary War.

Because the authority to tax resided solely in the states, the Continental Congress lacked a major prerequisite of sovereignty. Although Congress could request funds from the states and could ask the states to approve a tax to be levied and collected by Congress, unanimous approval of all the states was needed to allow Congress to levy a specific tax. As part of a wider effort to reform its finances, the Congress tried to get approval of a 5 percent federal tax on imports. Rhode Island remained the lone holdout, thus preventing implementation of the tax.

Because taxes were never a realistic solution, the Congress early issued paper currency not redeemable in specie. The idea was that if each state would tax and accept the Continental currency, the total amount could be kept within reasonable bounds. However, not only were the states reluctant to tax, but many issued their own paper currency. By 1783, state-issued currency amounted to about $200 million.

The first issue of Continental currency occurred in June 1775 in the amount of $2 million. Because of increased issues and the lack of taxes by the states to withdraw this currency from circulation, the total amount of Continental currency increased to a high point of $191.5 million by 1780. The amounts issued each year were $6 million in 1775, $19 million in 1776, $13 million in 1777, $63.5 million in 1778, and $90 million in 1779.

As the amounts in circulation increased, currency depreciated rapidly in comparison with gold or silver coins. In December 1776, the rate was $1.00 in coin to $1.50 in currency. By the end of 1779, the ratio was 1 to 42.2, and by 1781, it was $1.00 in coin to $147.97 in currency. This depreciation obviously meant that prices, in terms of Continental currency, rose rapidly. Toward the end of the Revolution, people were even reluctant to accept this currency in payment for goods. By 1783, the currency had been removed from circulation, an act accomplished in part by its conversion to long-term debt of the central government and in part by withdrawal through payment of state taxes.

Here we see the workings of the equation of exchange: $MV = PQ$. The supply of money (M) was increasingly rapidly with the successive increases in Continental currency. The velocity of exchange (V), the number of times that supply of money changes hands, probably also increased as, even with slow communications, transportation, and almost nonexistent banking systems, people tried to pass on the rapidly depreciating paper currency. With MV increasing, P (prices) and Q (output) had to increase. Output (Q) increased to some extent as the nonexchange economy experienced some shift to the exchange economy. But the bulk of the impact of increases in *MV* caused increases in prices (*P*). This experience of an uncontrolled increase in the supply of money was matched in American history only by the issuance of Confederate currency during the Civil War.

Early in the Revolution, the Continental Congress tried with little success to sell long-term interest-bearing debt. The lack of sufficient domestic wealth and the uncertainty of the outcome of the Revolution worked against efforts to persuade Americans to lend money to fight the war. Toward the end, after substantial funds lent by France, Holland, and Spain had provided gold and silver to pay interest on domestic loans, these efforts were more successful. The central government, aided by Robert Morris, was able to raise about $11.5 million in domestic loans—a small part of the total required to run the war. Robert Morris, like others, was willing to loan money to the central government once interest payments were made in gold and silver.

A much-needed source of gold and silver came from $7.8 million in foreign loans. Most of the loans were obtained from France ($6.4 million), but private loans were obtained in Holland for $1.3 million, and $174,017 was borrowed from Spain. Most of the proceeds of the loans were spent in Europe for desperately needed military supplies.

Hession and Sardy (12) sum up the results of the financial costs of the Revolution as follows: "In summation, it may be noted that the direct money cost of the Revolution is estimated in specie to have been $135 million. Against this total we may place the federal debt which stood at $42,413,000, and state debts which aggregated $18,271,786. The difference between the total direct costs as stated and the total debts of over $60 million may be considered as paid for by taxation, depreciated paper money, and other sources of revenue." The bulk of this $75 million was paid by people holding depreciating Continental currency. When a farmer was paid in currency for supplies sold to Washington's army, he lost by the amount that the currency depreciated while he had it.

Long-Term Effects of the Revolution

There is no doubt that the inflationary effects of financing the Revolution through the issuance of paper money were substantial. Was the result, though, to retard the long-term development prospects of the United States? While the issuance of paper money greatly diminished the value of currency in comparison with specie, the currency was used to finance real economic transactions, especially the sale of land and other goods contributing to economic growth. In short, the inflationary experience doubtless was redistributive—in favor of debtors and against creditors. At the same time, it does not appear to have harmed the long-term growth prospects of the new nation.

QUESTIONS

1. Describe the main elements of mercantilist theory. How was mercantilism used in the colonial policy of the home country?

2. Describe the chief regulations of British mercantile policy. Did these regulations restrict colonial economic development?

3. What was the role of the West Indies in the economic relationships between the colonies and England? How did British mercantilism affect this role?

4. Were the taxes that the British government tried to levy on the American colonies from 1764 to 1775 an "unjust" burden on the colonial economy?

5. On balance, was membership in the British Empire an economic burden to the American colonies up to 1775?

6. Present your analysis of the economic causes of the American Revolution.

7. What was the special economic situation of New England in regard to the causes of the Revolution?

8. How did the Continental Congress declare economic independence from Britain?

9. In what ways did the American economy adjust to the loss of Britain as a source of manufactured goods and a market for American exports during the Revolution?

10. What were the problems facing the Continental Congress in financing the American Revolution? How did the Congress attempt to meet these problems?

SUGGESTED READINGS

1. Aptheker, Herbert. *The American Revolution, 1763–1783.* New York: International Publishers, 1960. Chaps. 1 and 2.

2. Beer, George L. *British Colonial Policy, 1754–1765.* Gloucester: Peter Smith, 1958.

3. Bruchey, Stuart. *The Roots of American Economic Growth, 1607–1861.* New York: Harper and Row, 1968. Pp. 42–48.

4. Clough, Shepard B. *European Economic History: The Economic Development of Western Civilization.* New York: McGraw-Hill, 1968. Chap. 11.

5. Coleman, D. C., ed. *Revisions in Mercantilism.* London: Methuen, 1969.

6. Dickerson, Oliver M. *The Navigation Acts and the American Revolution.* New York: Barnes, 1963.

7. Ferguson, E. James. *The Power of the Purse: A History of American Public Finance, 1776–1790.* Chapel Hill: University of North Carolina Press, 1961.

8. Gipson, Lawrence H. *The Coming of the Revolution, 1763–1775.* New York: Harper and Row, 1954.

9. Hacker, Louis M. "The First American Revolution." *Columbia University Quarterly,* Part 1. (September 1935). Reprinted in Gerald D. Nash, ed., *Issues in American Economic History.* New York: Heath, 1972.

10. Hammond, Bray. *Banks and Politics in America, from the Revolution to the Civil War.* Princeton, N.J.: Princeton University Press, 1957.

11. Harper, Lawrence A. "Mercantilism and the American Revolution." *Canadian Historical Review,* 23 (March 1942).

12. Hession, Charles H., and Hyman Sardy. *Ascent to Affluence.* Boston: Allyn and Bacon, 1969. Pp. 48–56.

13. McClelland, Peter D. "The Cost to America of British Imperial Policy." *American Economic Review,* 59 (May 1969).

14. Nash, Gerald D., ed. *Issues in American Economic History.* Lexington, Mass.: Heath, 1972. Chap. 7.

15. Nettels, Curtis P. "British Mercantilism and the Economic Development of the Thirteen Colonies." *Journal of Economic History,* 12 (Spring 1952).

16. Nettels, Curtis P. *The Emergence of a National Economy, 1775–1815.* New York: Harper and Row, 1969.

17. Reid, Joseph. "On Navigating the Navigation Acts with Peter O. McClelland: Comment." *American Economic Review,* 10 (December 1920).

18. Reid, Joseph D., Jr. "Economic Burdens: Spark to the American Revolution?" *Journal of Economic History,* 37 (March 1978).

19. Schwertzer, Mary McKinney. "Economic Regulations and the Colonial Economy: The Maryland Tobacco Inspection Act of 1747." *Journal of Economic History,* 40 (September 1980).

20. Thomas, Robert Paul. "A Quantitative Approach to the Study of the Effects of British Imperial Policy upon Colonial Welfare: Some Preliminary Findings." *Journal of Economic History,* 25 (December 1965).

20. Walton, Gary M. "The Burdens of the Navigation Acts; A Reply." *Economic History Review,* 26 (November 1973).

21. Walton, Gary M. "The New Economic History and the Burdens of the Navigation Act." *Economic History Review,* 24 (November 1971).

22. Willis, James F., and Martin L. Primack. *Explorations in Economics.* Redding, Ca.: CAT Publishing Co., 1987. Pp. 144–145, 269–273.

23. Wright, Esmond, ed. *Causes and Consequences of the American Revolution.* New York: Quadrangle, 1966.

Chapter 4

INDEPENDENCE, THE ARTICLES OF CONFEDERATION, AND THE CONSTITUTION

The 1780s

The Revolution has been successful and the Treaty of Paris signed. The 13 former colonies are independent from England and a new nation born, the United States. This new country must now find its place within the world economy. Of course, economic problems appear.

This chapter is concerned with several important historical processes. We will begin by exploring the various economic problems generated by being independent within the world economy of the 1780s. We will also consider how the national government under the Articles of Confederation, as well as the various states, attempted to deal with these problems. In addition, we shall explore the problems generated by the efforts of the national and state governments to confront these economic problems and how these efforts led to a "second revolution"—the formation and adoption of the Constitution. Finally, we will describe the provisions of the Constitution and their implications for the American economy.

Earlier, we emphasized the importance of institutions, including political ones, in the economic development of the American colonies. An important topic of this chapter is the evolution of our political institutions under the Constitution.

THE POSTWAR ECONOMY

Imports After the Revolution

During the Revolution, manufactured goods imported from France and Holland and goods brought in by privateers (from captured British vessels) amounted to a small fraction of the prewar imports from England. Under the protection of the price stimulus created by the British wartime blockade, domestic manufactures increased, and some goods were newly manufactured in North America. This increased output was negligible in amount and variety, however, and products were probably of poor quality. In 1783, inventories of consumer goods were very low in the new nation, and the demand for manufactured imports very high among Americans long deprived of many kinds of manufactured goods.

After the Revolution, British merchants regained their dominance in the American market. French and Dutch merchants could not compete in price, variety, and quality and, perhaps most important, were not willing to extend credit. Furthermore, American merchants preferred to deal with British merchants because of their common language, similarity in culture and customs, renewal of old contracts, and familiarity with business practices and products. From 1784 to 1786, Americans imported almost $7.6 million worth of manufactured goods of all descriptions, from cotton cloth to playing cards. These imports were obtained on credit, and that credit was extended throughout the economy. British exporters sold to American importers on credit; importers sold to wholesalers on credit, who sold to retailers on credit, who finally sold to consumers on credit. The problem was how to pay for all these imports.

Exports After the Revolution

Normally, imports are paid for by the claims to money obtained from exports. In the 1780s, however, the United States had just made its break from the British Empire, and exports suffered during the period of adjustment. From 1784 to 1786, the United States exported goods worth only $1.26 million per year, one-third of its imports for the same time period. In brief, the young country had a substantial **deficit in its balance of trade.** That deficit can be defined simply as the excess of a nation's payments for imports of goods and services over its earnings from the export of goods and services.

In 1763, tobacco exports from Maryland and Virginia had constituted 44 percent of all exports by value from the American colonies. By the end of the Revolution, the Chesapeake area had suffered serious damage. Virginia's labor force was depleted by the loss of 30,000 slaves, mostly through transfer by the British to the West Indies. In comparison to 1774, Virginia's output was 18 percent less in 1783–1784 and 7 percent less in 1784–1785. Loss in output, though, was not the most serious problem; the relatively low prices of 1783 to 1786 were more damaging.

Since the American colonies were no longer in the British Empire, Britain placed a tax of 15 pence per hundredweight on tobacco imported into Britain. This tax decreased the quantity of American tobacco demanded by the British. France, which was the major ultimate market for American tobacco, created the Farmers General (a monopsony, a single buyer) as importing agent for American tobacco in France. Thomas Jefferson maintained that this monopsony purchasing agent forced prices down by 50 percent from 1785 to 1787. However, part of the decrease in price realized by Virginia and Maryland planters was due to the fact that British merchants were no longer performing such functions as repacking, grading, sorting, and managing an efficient flow of tobacco to the European market, as they had before the Revolution.

Another major export crop was rice produced in South Carolina. Because of physical destruction during the Revolution and the loss of possibly as many as 20,000 slaves, rice production fell by 46 percent of the 1770–1773 average during 1783–1786. But despite falling supply, prices received by farmers decreased. Britain placed high import duties on rice imported into the British West Indies and into Britain itself. Harassment by pirates from the Barbary States of North Africa reduced exports of rice into the Mediterranean. Other markets could not be found quickly enough to prevent a collapse of prices between 1783 and 1786.

Prior to the Revolution, naval stores from North Carolina, timber from New England, and indigo from South Carolina received bounties from Britain. With independence, these bounties disappeared. The British maintained a preference for output from their remaining colonies. The French, applying mercantile concepts, also favored their own colonists over America. Export earnings therefore dropped drastically for these products; for naval stores, earnings dropped to less than a third of the prewar level.

Before the Revolution, agricultural products of the northern states, including wheat and flour, animal products, and corn, had been exported to the British West Indies and, under British protection, to Spain and the Mediterranean area. After the Revolution, these sources of foreign exchange were drastically reduced. No longer part of the British Empire, America could not legally trade with the British West Indies. In the Mediterranean, the Barbary States of Algeria, Tripoli, and Morocco demanded tribute from the United States. Congress could neither raise the money for tribute nor finance a navy to protect U.S. ships.

And the story goes on and on: One area after another of export earnings was reduced as the United States had to stand alone. Potential fur exports from the frontier were reduced as Britain refused to vacate the frontier forts. Agricultural exports from the frontier settlements west of the mountains were interfered with as Spain refused to allow the frontiersmen the use of New Orleans, the terminal of the river route to markets. New England found it difficult to compete in sale of ships to Britain as restrictions were placed on U.S. sales after independence. Demand for the output of U.S. fisheries fell off as the French West Indies failed to replace lost markets in England and the British West Indies, and as the Barbary states interfered with shipping to southern Europe.

In brief, the deficit in the U.S. balance of trade during 1784 and 1785 was a direct consequence of severing ties to the mercantile system of Great Britain. The former colonies could not engage in free trade, since every other country had a mercantile relationship with its colonies. Restrictions were placed on U.S. trade with most major areas. The French, for instance, allowed the United States to trade with their colonies in the West Indies, but prohibited the sale of U.S. wheat and flour there. Furthermore, the U.S. government, under the Articles of Confederation, lacked the economic, diplomatic, or military power to force concessions from anyone.

The Depression of 1785–1786

With foreign exchange earned by exports only about one-third the value of imports, the only other source of repayment, specie (gold and silver) exports, was also inadequate to solve the problem without crisis. There were large amounts of gold and silver in the economy in 1782, largely from the proceeds of loans from Holland and France during the Revolution and from spending by French and English troops in the colonies. Nonetheless, after 1783, the drain of gold and silver from the United States to Britain to service this rapidly expanded commercial debt was too great for economic stability. One estimate of the flow of gold and silver to Britain between 1784 and 1786 was $1.6 million, an amount large enough to reduce the supply of money seriously, although not large enough to finance the imbalance of imports over exports. That remaining imbalance was financed primarily by British short-term commercial credit and long-term investments.

This drastic decline in the supply of money had two major economic effects that began to be felt by the end of 1784. First, the reduced supply of money decreased prices. Consider the effects in terms of the equation of exchange: $MV = PQ$. In this period, the supply of money (M) was decreasing while velocity (V) was constant. P, the price level, had to fall, assuming that output (Q) was constant or also falling. Remember that debtors were hurt by a deflation (or decline in prices) because they had to repay their loans with money of higher purchasing power than that which they borrowed. Also, since prices were falling, debtors had to sell more of whatever they produced to earn the dollars needed to pay their debts. Here we see for the first time in American economic history, political conflict between debtor and creditor groups over political policy concerning the supply of money. The second effect of a constricted money supply was the scarcity of actual coin to pay debts. The supply of money became so reduced that in a number of rural areas people were forced out of money exchange relationships. The general effect of this drastic cut in the supply of money was to make it difficult for debtors to pay their debts. These economic effects only applied to the money exchange sectors of the economy. The nonmoney exchange sector, which made up a great deal of the economy, was insulated from these processes.

Since the system of debt relationships was so pervasive, the commercial economy shook like a house of cards. Consumers couldn't pay retailers, who couldn't pay wholesalers, who couldn't pay importers, who couldn't pay British exporters. Not coincidentally, the number of commercial bankruptcies was significant in the United States in 1785 and 1786, and a few prominent ones occurred in England. Nettels (12) provides a number of examples:

Some fairly substantial merchants failed—among them Clement Biddle of Baltimore and Samuel A. Otis of Boston. Other prominent merchants, including George Meade, Haym Solomon, and Robert Morris in Philadelphia, the Purviance brothers in Baltimore, and Jackson and Higginson in Boston found themselves hard pressed for funds. Ruin befell many small inexperienced traders who, unable to collect money from their debtors, lost their assets through forced sales for the benefit of their creditors.

Because the economy was primarily agricultural and because agriculture was still significantly self-sufficient (much of its output and consumption was not within the cash economy), the depression of the mid-1780s was primarily a commercial and financial one. However, the slow recovery of the agricultural export market, and high levels of debt within agriculture in general, caused economic hardship in that whole sector, especially on the part of those producers who were in debt. Exacerbating the situation were high levels of government debt, especially those of the various states, incurred primarily during the Revolution. Any effort of the states to meet their debt obligations only added to the repayment problems of the economy.

THE SEARCH FOR SOLUTIONS

In summary, the economic difficulties facing the young nation resulted from these factors: High import levels from 1783 to 1785 were financed primarily by the extension of credit by British merchants. The inability of the economy to export enough to pay for the high levels of imports caused a flow of specie to Britain, which in turn caused a reduction in the supply of money. This forced prices down. Decreasing prices added to the burdens of repayment by debtors through increasing the purchasing power of the money they paid back and reducing the prices of what they had to sell to earn that money. A need arose for additions to the supply of money, not only to stem falling prices, but also to provide needed means of internal and international payments. Insufficient means of payments to carry on economic transactions were responsible for the increased use of barter in many areas outside the major cities. The result was not only higher transaction costs but also significant commercial failures in the cities.

The search for solutions led to two major conclusions: the United States had to reduce the excess of imports over exports and had to increase its supply of money.

Efforts to Increase Exports

Attempts to increase U.S. exports involved reducing the various economic and political obstacles to trade. These problems could be solved only through international diplomacy. The central government, under the Articles of Confederation, sent various diplomatic missions to a number of countries in an effort to enlarge foreign markets. These missions uniformly failed.

John Adams was sent to England to negotiate both a commercial treaty and an evacuation of the forts held by Britain on American soil. When Adams failed, Congress lacked the power to retaliate against the British. The English thought that the Americans would continue to buy British goods because they were cheaper than domestic manufactures. Congress did not have the funds to pay the remaining prewar commercial debts and reimbursements to the loyalists for seized property, the major points of British contention.

The U.S. mission to the Barbary States of North Africa failed in its efforts to end attacks against American ships in the Mediterranean and thereby to open up trade with southern Europe. Congress had neither the money to buy off the pirates nor the navy to fight them.

American diplomats tried unsuccessfully to gain further commercial access for U.S. exports to the markets of Spain and its colonies and to obtain access through the Mississippi River systems and New Orleans for the shipment of the products of western farmers. Efforts to gain more liberal commercial access to France and French colonial markets also failed.

These diplomatic efforts to increase U.S. exports were unsuccessful, in large measure, because Congress, under the Articles of Confederation, had no powers that could be used in negotiations with foreign governments. These attempts to negotiate only emphasized the need for a stronger union.

Efforts to Decrease Imports

The inability of the central government to reduce through diplomatic means the large deficit in the balance of trade shifted responsibility for solutions to the states. A number of states tried to use tariffs to protect their domestic industries and to reduce imports. During the mid-1780s, New York, Pennsylvania, Rhode Island, Massachusetts and New Hampshire enacted such laws. These experiments only showed that tariff laws, to be effective, had to be instituted by a central government and applied equally to all 13 states.

The tariffs of an individual state could be avoided. Through larger enterprises and the increased use of machinery, industries were able to produce goods for several states, but one state could not provide tariff protection for a market larger than that state. And because tariff protection was completely absent in the South, northern manufacturers could not compete there against British products. Finally, the tariffs of one state could be avoided by shipping the imports into a nearby tariff-free state and across the state border from the adjacent state. For example, New Jersey and Connecticut did not have tariffs. Goods destined for Rhode Island and Massachusetts could be landed in Connecticut and transhipped to these states. Or goods could be landed in New Jersey and transported to New York and Pennsylvania. Some feared that in response to the avoidance of tariffs individual states would begin to raise tariffs against movement of goods from one state to another. Such tariffs would, in effect, destroy what union there was among the states and create 13 independent economies.

Manufacturing in the United States

One alternative to imports was domestic manufacturing. The high cost of U.S. manufactures prevented their effective substitution for British imports. Still, it is informative to look at manufacturing in the United States during this period.

Under the stimulus of the Revolution, and later to counter the depression, a number of enterprises in such industries as metalworking and gun and textile manufacture grew larger than the typical master-journeyman-apprentice firm and produced for a wider market. Some of these firms benefited from state tariffs and were able to survive renewed trade with Britain. These few enterprises and their small output promised little potential for the future, though, because they were operated with low efficiency and high costs. Labor was expensive, capital was scarce, interest rates were high, and technological knowledge was scanty.

Internal markets were small and fragmented by the lack of a unified low-cost transportation system. With such small markets, there was little opportunity for specialization and increases in productivity. In 1786, it seemed unlikely that these conditions would change enough in the near future to enable domestic manufactures to compete with imports.

For all these limitations, the manufacturing development of this period provided an advantage that was indispensable to subsequent industrialization: the larger firms became valuable training grounds for management. By operating on a larger scale, a few firms accumulated personnel with experience in managing labor and in managing the organizational problems of material sources, production, and sale, with the corollary problems of capital supply and technological development. The necessary learning process began during these early years of independence.

The Supply of Money

Between 1784 and 1786, as the excess of imports over exports continued to result in an outflow of gold and silver, a great controversy arose about how to increase the supply of money in the United States. We have already seen how decreases in the money supply reduced prices and output and increased the burden on those in debt. Debtors, who had borrowed money that had low purchasing power had to repay their loans with money that had high purchasing power; meanwhile, they had to accept lower prices for the products they sold. As the supply of money fell, neither individuals nor governments could find enough money to provide for economic transactions, including the payment of debts. The overall financial burden was only increased by any effort to raise taxes to pay the government debt and its interest cost.

The controversy focused on three ways to increase the supply of money and thus prices: (a) currency could be issued by merchant banks, (b) currency could be issued through what were called *land banks,* or (c) state and the national government could print money.

Merchant Banks

By 1786, three **merchant banks** had been chartered by state governments with the power to issue currency backed by specie (gold and silver). One such bank was located in each of three cities: Philadelphia, New York, and Boston. Their ability to expand the supply of money by issuing currency was limited by the public's faith in the banks' ability to pay specie on demand for currency or in the reserves held in the form of specie, and by the amount of demand for specie. The issuance of paper currency was restricted by this factor to some ratio of the amount of specie held by the banks.

Since not everyone who had a bank's currency would want specie at the same time, the bank could have more currency in circulation than specie in the vaults of the bank. In that situation, banks turned to the practice of holding **fractional reserves:** their reserves were equal to only a fraction of their currency in circulation plus demand deposits (checking accounts).

Merchant banks, then, provided a specie-backed money supply in the major commercial centers, in addition to credit facilities for the holding of demand deposits. These banks were extremely conservative in that they extended predominantly short-term credit and generally demanded prompt repayment.

Opposition to these banks was widespread. Some critics charged that they favored only a small group of merchants in the towns where the banks were located. The short-term credit they extended did not help farmers, who needed long-term credit. The currency they issued circulated in the towns where the banks were located and did not benefit the entire state.

Land Banks and State Issuance of Paper Currency

Major opposition to the merchant banks came from the farmers, who needed long-term loans and an increase in the supply of money both to pay debts and taxes and to raise prices. They proposed the establishment of **land banks,** which would issue paper currency backed only by loans on land. South Carolina, New Jersey, New York, and Rhode Island established land banks and issued currency backed by mortgages on land. Georgia, North Carolina, and Pennsylvania issued paper currency, without specie backing, directly through the state governments.

Merchants and creditors strongly opposed this issuance of "unbacked" currency from land banks and state governments. These merchants owed money to British exporters and had to pay in gold or silver. Since they in turn were owed money for products that they sold, they were afraid they would be paid in depreciated currency that could not be used to pay the British merchants. Creditors generally wanted to be paid in hard money (gold and silver), while the debt-ridden farmers wanted inflated currency that would increase prices and their ability to repay their debts. It was the eternal battle between creditors and debtors, in all its economic and political complexity.

The conflict was bitter throughout the 13 states. In Georgia, South Carolina, and North Carolina, paper currency depreciated rapidly. In Pennsylvania, the conflict was extreme and centered around the activity of the Bank of North America in Philadelphia. In Rhode Island, laws were passed to enforce acceptance of the paper currency at par with gold. The conflict that ensued verged on armed clashes. Indeed, New Hampshire did see armed conflict, and there was Shays' Rebellion in Massachusetts.

A Conclusion

By 1787, it seemed obvious to many that the central government under the Articles of Confederation did *not* have the power to deal with the international commercial problems of the United States or to provide a stable monetary system. Also, it was clear to wide segments of the population, not just the creditor groups, that individual states could not by themselves solve the many economic problems created by independence. The young nation needed greater unity to survive not only politically but also economically in a world based on mercantilist policy. Prior to the Revolution, the colonists had been limited by British mercantilism, but they had also been protected by it.

Not until the Napoleonic Wars was this mercantile system weakened and finally destroyed. Only then did the United States gain the opportunity for less restricted trade with the whole world. But before that happened, the new nation had changed its system of government and introduced a new set of political institutions that were extremely favorable to the economic development of the United States.

CONTROVERSY CONTINUES

The traditional view of the period from 1783 to 1789 is that it was one of frustration, if not chaos. As John Fiske, a late-nineteenth-century historian put it, "The business of exchange was thus fast getting into hopeless confusion.—Nobody who had a yard of cloth could tell how much it was worth. But even worse than all this was the swift and certain renewal of bankruptcy which so many states were preparing for themselves...."

Beginning in the 1950s, however, a number of historians began to dissent from the position that the period from 1783 to 1789 was critical in U.S. economic history and that the inadequacies of the political structure contributed to the economic problems. Merrill Jensen (9) viewed the 1780s as a period of "extraordinary economic growth" based on expanding exports, growth of manufacturing, and the recovery of the South. According to Jensen:

> The balance sheet on the federation does show certain positive things—[that] a new nation had cash income from the states; that it had sound credit with Dutch brokers; that it paid most of the interest on the foreign debt and part of the interest on the domestic debt. It can be argued that the Confederation perhaps came as close to making ends match needs as many a twentieth century government....

The majority view, however, seems to be substantiated by the evidence, and Jensen's claim of economic growth lacks widespread support.

One factor that contributed to the recovery of the U.S. economy in the 1780s was the increasingly favorable terms of trade. Remember that a movement toward more favorable terms of trade occurs when the index of export prices increases relative to the index of import prices. A given amount of physical exports then buys more imports. Gordon C. Bjork (2) points out that these relative export-import prices (the terms of trade) were favorable to the United States in the 1780s. In the 1770s, before the Revolution (see column 3 in Table 4.1), the index of the terms of trade averaged in the 70s; in the 1780s, it was mostly in the 90s. Bjork seems to prefer to consider the glass half full rather than half empty; he comments that one should not be surprised that exports were so low in the 1780s, but rather should be pleased that they were as high as they were.

The favorable terms of trade in the 1780s are generally attributed to the increased efficiency of foreign trade that resulted from the freedom the United States now enjoyed. No longer restricted by Britain, Americans could now import from the cheapest source; for example, they could import sugar or molasses from the French West Indies rather than from the British West Indies. However, it should be noted that export prices fell between 1784 and 1789, while import prices remained constant. The terms of trade, although higher than before the Revolution, fell from 112 in 1784 to 88 in 1789.

Bjork, who points out that eighteenth-century statistics should be approached with a great deal of caution, considers his own results preliminary. But although the reliability and representativeness of the data are open to question, the trends they indicate seem reliable.

But even if one accepts the argument that the terms of trade were more favorable after the Revolution than before, the data suggest that the picture we have drawn of political and economic conflict between groups is valid. Despite the more favorable terms of trade, the excess of imports over exports generated a decrease in

Table 4.1.   Import-Export Prices and the Terms of Trade.

	1 *INDEX OF EXPORT PRICES* *(1790 = 100)*	2 *INDEX OF IMPORT PRICES* *(1790 = 100)*	3 *TERMS OF TRADE* *(1) ÷ (2)*
1770	69	110	63
1771	75	104	72
1772	83	102	81
1773	78	109	72
1774	73	108	68
1775	70	109	64
1784	115	103	112
1785	106	101	105
1786	97	101	96
1787	92	101	91
1788	87	99	88
1789	87	99	88
1790	100	100	100

SOURCE: Gordon C. Bjork, "The Weaning of the American Economy: Independence, Market Changes, and Economic Development," *Journal of Economic History*, 24 (December 1964); 554.

the supply of money and falling prices. The controversy continues, but it seems clear that the economic problems of the 1780s, whether a matter of rolling adjustment to the end of war or a critical situation demanding immediate drastic remedies, provided a strong impetus to a complete reevaluation of the political system of the United States. The result was the Constitution of 1789.

A Recap

Under the Articles of Confederation, the United States was independent, but its political processes were incomplete. The adoption of the Constitution was to complete the political transformation of the new country. There were strong economic motivations to revise or scrap the Articles of Confederation. As we have seen, under the Articles, neither the states nor the central government could solve the trade deficit problem or stop the drain on the money supply in the mid-1780s. Thus the major economic problems of the post-Revolution economy stemmed from difficulties in the foreign trade sector.

After the Revolution, the United States imported about three times the value of the goods it exported. The relatively low level of exports meant that much of the value of imports was paid for by exporting gold and silver. The major difficulty in balancing the excess imports through trade was that the United States, as an independent nation, was outside the mercantilist systems of the world trading communities. These communities did not allow trade based on comparative advantage and maintained discriminatory systems favorable to their own colonies. The United States had lost the essentially comparative-advantage trade that the colonies had enjoyed within the protective trading system of the British Empire. Imports remained high as the United States found it very difficult to maintain a self-contained economy without trade (see Figure 4.2).

We have seen what happened to the United States as a result of the outflow of gold and silver: the domestic supply of money declined substantially, prices fell, and debtors unable to pay their debts were forced into bankruptcies. The outcome was the depression of 1785–1786. The individual states could not resolve these problems, and under the Articles of Confederation, Congress could not deal with them successfully.

INADEQUACIES OF THE ARTICLES OF CONFEDERATION

The depression of 1785–1786 seemed to reveal the inadequacies of the American political system under the Articles of Confederation. These inadequacies can be seen within several categories.

First, the central government was not strong enough to negotiate concessions from the major colonial powers, Great Britain, France, and Spain. The Congress had no power to tax or any independent revenue sources, and thus could not build up a treasury for the maintenance of military forces. This lack of power doomed its efforts to obtain favorable trade access to the European countries or their colonies. Comparative-advantage trade could not be achieved through negotiations.

Neither did the central government have the power to control entry of foreign goods (imports) into the United States. The efforts of individual states to impose controls on imports through tariffs proved ineffectual and raised the specter of tariff discrimination between states. The American economy was unable to retreat to a no-trade or less-trade position that would have offered increased self-sufficiency.

The central government could not protect against threats to property and contracts. Examples of these threats include Shays' Rebellion, debt moratorium laws by the states, inflationary monetary policy, and widespread "leveler" sentiment.

Finally, the central government did not have the power to establish and control the money supply and to create a sound credit and banking system.

Monied and commercial groups wanted a revision of the Articles of Confederation that would provide a system capable of protecting property and creating situations where profits could be more easily obtained. They wanted to curtail the power of the debtor classes, who had gained control over state legislatures and, as they saw it, were expropriating property by creating an inflated, unbacked currency.

A new constitutional convention was called in 1787 to formulate changes in the Articles of Confederation. What emerged, of course, was a completely new system of government based on the present Constitution of the United States. Although it appears that the creditor groups controlled this constitutional convention, and that small farm owners and others in society had little representation, many groups in the United States supported the adoption of the Constitution. The Constitution held the promise of improving economic conditions and of creating greater economic stability. In examining the powers granted to the federal government under the new Constitution and how these powers were used in the Federalist program, we must carefully note how property rights were strengthened and a more favorable environment for obtaining property was created.

Obviously, all economic activity takes place within a set of institutions. Institutions define not only specifics—for example, a specific type of banking system that establishes conditions under which money and credit function—but also the ideological system, that system of beliefs about how economic activity *should* take place. The Constitution recommended in 1788 set the basic legal framework within which economic activity has taken place in the United States ever since. It also *ratified* a huge amount of legal powers that were worked out through *state* constitutions and laws.

ECONOMIC CHANGES OF THE CONSTITUTION

The Constitution achieved several economic objectives. It created the political environment necessary for a single free-trade area within the United States. In addition, it made the central government a potentially effective instrument of foreign economic policy. Perhaps most important, it firmly recognized the primacy of property rights and the freedom of individuals to acquire and transfer property.

The Constitution created the potential for a common market area within the United States by granting the following important powers to the federal government. The federal government had the exclusive power to regulate both foreign and interstate trade (trade between states). Interstate and foreign trade would be subject to a single set of uniform laws and a single set of uniform taxes. These regulations prevented individual states from creating barriers to the movement of goods between states and, from the political point of view, created the possibility of one large common market area within the United States. Federal control made possible a unified economic policy toward international trade.

The federal government also acquired the power to define, create, and regulate the supply of money. State governments were prohibited from issuing money directly but were permitted to charter banks that could issue currency. This power enabled the federal government ultimately to create a unified monetary system and to remove the specter of state-issued, unbacked, inflationary currency that haunted the creditor classes.

The federal government had the power to make uniform rules governing naturalization of immigrants. Because immigrants were given greater freedom to choose their place of residence within the United States, the mobility of labor was increased and a unified labor market was made possible for the entire country.

The states were prohibited from enacting laws interfering with the obligations of contract. No state could interfere with the carrying out of contractual obligations, either interstate or intrastate. This guarantee helped to remove barriers between the states and promoted nationwide economic activity.

The federal government became responsible for setting up a single postal service and common standards of weights and measures. Also, the federal government could grant patents and copyrights that applied to the entire country. These last two powers reinforced the prohibition against individual states interfering in economic activity across state lines.

Finally, various powers granted to the federal government under the Constitution made it a more effective instrument for foreign economic policy. The federal government had the power to make treaties; these treaties were the law of the land and took precedence over state law. And, at last, the central government had the power to tax. This power enabled the federal government to control imports and to finance an army and a navy, in addition to a central bureaucracy. The central government now had effective bargaining instruments in foreign negotiations and could exert greater power in international economic relations.

It would be inappropriate to state that these powers are unambiguously net benefits. Many of these powers, as exercised, may either promote *or* retard economic development. In fact, some economists have argued that the use of some of these powers has proved detrimental to economic activity. An example often cited is the rise of public regulation at the end of the nineteenth century. Later in this book, we will consider both the advantages and disadvantages of regulation.

The strengthening of property rights promoted private enterprise. No one could impede the enforcement of private contracts. These provisions were essential for releasing the energies of individuals to pursue personal gain and, as Adam Smith put it, for maximizing the public good through private economic activity.

Beard's Interpretation of the Constitution

What we have set forth is an economic interpretation of the origins of the Constitution: that it grew out of the inability of the Articles of Confederation to deal with the many economic problems generated by independence. The idea of an economic interpretation of the Constitution was first associated with Charles Beard (1) through his path-breaking book, *An Economic Interpretation of the Constitution of the United States.* However, his interpretation differs substantially from the one just given.

As a result of his research, Beard concluded that the framers of the Constitution were motivated by personal self-interest and that the small farmer, the mechanic, and the poorer classes were not represented at the Constitutional Convention of 1788. Beard attributed to the 54 delegates the following distribution of economic interests:

40 held Continental and state debt
24 were money lenders
15 were southern slaveholders
14 were involved in land speculation
11 were involved in manufacturing, commerce, and shipping

Beard maintained that "The overwhelming majority of members, at least five-sixths, were immediately, directly, and personally interested in the outcome of their labors at Philadelphia, and were to a greater or lesser extent economic beneficiaries from the adoption of the Constitution." He concluded that the same interests provided the dynamic element both in formulating the Constitution and in moving its adoption by the various states. He maintained that the leading supporters of the movement to adopt the Constitution were those who had personal property interests embodied primarily in speculation in continental and state debt.

Beard, who broke new ground in the analysis of the motives involved in the formulation and adoption of the Constitution, hoped that his scanty research would encourage further investigation. His hope was realized. Although at first there was widespread agreement with his formulation, in time critics appeared. One of the most compelling of these was Forrest McDonald (10) who published *We the People: The Economic Origins of the Constitution* in 1958.

McDonald maintained that Beard's analysis was an oversimplification because the motivations concerning both formulation and adoption of the Constitution were more complex than Beard realized. He argued also that these motivations varied from one section of the country to another. McDonald concluded that it was not at all apparent that personal property interest represented in ownership of Revolutionary debt was the primary element behind the adoption of the Constitution. Seven of the delegates opposed to the Constitution had more than twice the per capita holdings of Revolutionary debt of those who supported the Constitution.

McDonald found that the most common property interest of the delegates was ownership of agricultural land. Beard had implied that in the campaign over the ratification of the Constitution, farmers were opposed to the Constitution and the holders of Revolutionary debt were in favor of adoption. This contention does not seem to be supported by the facts. The Constitution was easily passed in the primarily agricultural states of Connecticut, New Jersey, Delaware, Maryland, and Georgia. McDonald concluded from his own analysis of the votes on ratification that in some states security holders were a small minority of the supporters of the Constitution; in others, security holders were a larger percentage of those opposed than of those in favor of ratification; in many states, there was no correlation between security holdings and positions on ratification. It seems that as many security holders were opposed to ratification as were for it.

Although Beard's argument has been weakened by the subsequent research that he stimulated, Beard himself is recognized as a pioneer who opened a new territory of study and analysis.

THE FEDERALIST PROGRAM

Although the discussion that follows concentrates on the federal level, one should not overlook the importance of state governments in economic development. When the U.S. Constitution was adopted, state constitutions were already in place, dealing with property rights, corporations, banks, common carriers, and so forth. State programs to stimulate internal development were widespread. However, lack of space restricts the discussion here to the federal level.

Although the Constitution laid down the general framework of political institutions within which economic activity was to take place, how this framework would work in practice depended on the policies of the political parties in control of the government after 1789. The political party that controlled decision making in the formative years of the new government was the Federalist Party. The Federalists maintained control through two administrations of George Washington and one of John Adams; that is, the 12 years from 1789 to 1801. The most important economic spokesman for the Federalists was Alexander Hamilton.

Hamilton's primary concern was to foster the development within the United States of a strong manufacturing sector. His *Report on Manufactures* called for high protective tariffs and used an "infant industries" argument to justify them. That his program as adopted did not achieve this objective was due in large measure to the lack of a comparative advantage in manufacturing rather than to a lack of favorable political policies. The immediate effect of the Hamilton (Federalist) program was to stimulate commercial advancement. In time, when the basic economic conditions for industrial development appeared, the political structure was there to assist it.

The first Federalist measure was the Tariff Act of 1789, a declaration of commercial independence from Britain. Hamilton's *Report on Manufactures* had called for high protective tariffs to shield the infant manufacturing industries of the United States. It also had a strong "mercantilist" flavor, urging a substantial program of internal improvements. The North wanted protection from British imports for its manufacturing industries. The South, basically an importer of manufactured goods, opposed the Tariff Act because tariffs would increase the price of these imports. The comparative advantage of the South was in agricultural exports, primarily tobacco (and later cotton). Because of southern opposition, the tariff passed in 1789 was a compromise and therefore basically moderate. It provided some protection for the North's infant industries, and the proceeds of the tariff provided needed revenues for the Federalist government.

Another measure in the Federalist program was the Tonnage Act of 1789, which raised additional revenues for the federal government and provided aid to the northern shipping interests. Foreign-built and -owned ships had to pay 50 cents a ton on their cargo on entering U.S. ports. United States-built but foreign-owned ships had to pay 30 cents a ton, while domestic-owned and -built ships paid only 6 cents a ton. The difference in tonnage fees gave an advantage to U.S. shipping and also offered inducements to foreign shipping interests to buy vessels manufactured in the United States. Again, opposition came from southern states, especially Georgia and South Carolina. The Tonnage Act increased prices to the South through higher shipping charges.

The intent of the Hamiltonian programs, as mirrored in both the Tariff and Tonnage Acts, was to interfere in the workings of comparative advantage for the benefit of specific interest groups, namely northern manufacturing and shipping.

Hamilton's plan for the public debt was detailed in his *Report on the Public Credit.* He wanted the federal government to assume all the debts of the states and refund the old federal and state debt at face value, issuing new debt at 6 percent interest payable in coin. Hamilton argued that this funding of the old federal and state debt would restore international confidence in both the public and private credit of the United States and would encourage commerce. Because of the restoration of confidence, the new debt would extend, augment, and complement the supply of money and raise prices. Allowing the interest rate on federal debt to decline significantly to 6 percent would lower general interest rates, which would tend to encourage economic growth. Furthermore, the public debt would encourage thrift (savings), growth of capital markets, and attitudes of investing in securities (including corporate securities).

Vigorous opposition to this refunding proposal was led by Thomas Jefferson and was especially strong in the South. The criticisms were based primarily on two arguments. First, many of the original purchasers of both the federal and state Revolutionary debt, those who had actually supported the Revolution financially, had sold their debt at very large discounts. Therefore, the speculators who had purchased this debt would make large gains when the debt was refunded at par (its original issue price). Second, opponents objected that the assumption of state debts by the federal government would increase the power of a remote central government at the expense of the states and home rule.

In the end, Jefferson supported the funding act in exchange for placing the capital on the Potomac River between Virginia and Maryland. Hamilton's *Report on Public Credit* provided the basis for the Funding Act of 1790. This act, however, increased the need for new taxes to pay the interest. One of them was the tax on whiskey, which sparked the Whiskey Rebellion of 1794 in western Pennsylvania. Transportation costs for corn from the western counties of Pennsylvania to their eastern markets was high. Only by reducing the corn to whiskey and increasing its price-weight ratio could the farmers market their corn. The fight between the "revenuers" and the makers of whiskey started early in U.S. history.

Hamilton's 1790 *Report on a National Bank* was embodied in the 1791 act that established the First Bank of the United States with a 20-year federal charter. The bank had $10 million in capital stock, of which $6 million was in securities of the U.S. government. The bank could issue up to $10 million in currency, which was to be acceptable in all payments; that is, currency of the bank was declared **legal tender,** money that by law must be accepted in payment for all debts both public and private. The bank's home office was in Philadelphia; by 1805, it had eight branches throughout the United States.

The bank was conservative, and as a private profit-making enterprise, it was successful. It could keep the issuance of currency by other banks under strong limitations. All currency received in the bank from its customers and the government could quickly be presented to the issuing bank for payment in gold and silver. This practice kept currency close to the holdings of gold and silver by the banks and provided a secure but restricted currency supply. Although the Bank of the United States had the power to restrict currency issues, most observers conclude that it did not do so to its maximum potential. The Bank of the United States made primarily commercial and short-term loans.

Hamilton and other Federalists opposed westward expansion. They argued that the movement to the West drew part of the labor supply from the East, raised eastern wages, and hindered the development of eastern manufacturing. Therefore, to stimulate manufacturing the westward movement had to be slowed. The 1784 act that had required a minimum purchase of 640 acres in the western territories at $1 an acre for cash was changed in 1796, when Congress set a price of $2 an acre. At a cost of $1,280, the minimum purchase was beyond the means of most small farmers.

Economic Effects of the Federalist Program

The immediate result of the Federalist program was a vast increase in the paper wealth of the country through the refunding of old federal and state debt and the capital stock and currency of the Bank of the United States, among others. The in-

Figure 4.1. Alexander Hamilton, Advocate of Manufacturing and Shipping (left), and Thomas Jefferson, Advocate of Farmers and Laborers. (Photos from the National Archives)

creased credit resources and currency for business had a marked inflationary effect. (See the section on the equation of exchange in the Review of Economic Concepts at the end of this chapter.) Prices increased from an index of 78 in March 1789 to 100 by June 1790, a rise of 22 percent in just over one year. The objective of increasing the supply of money and prices had been achieved. But it had been done with a form of money and forms of other debt instruments that were acceptable to foreign creditors and that increased the credit ratings of the American businessman.

Federalist measures succeeded in fostering a lively interest in manufacturing in the northern states. Town societies to promote manufacturing sprang up, and new enterprises were established. Domestic prices rose rapidly as a result of the financial expansion. But because experienced managers, skilled workers, and up-to-date machinery were lacking, domestic manufactures could not compete with imports. When international trade was restored, much domestic industry, even that protected by the tariff of 1789, could not survive. The manufacturing expansion collapsed in 1792.

Hamilton's program primarily benefited the commercial Northeast. The Funding Act and the creation of the Bank of the United States established U.S. international credit, expanded commercial credit domestically, and generated a sounder monetary system. The Tonnage Act fostered northeastern shipping interests. The increased authority of the federal government contributed to the effectiveness of the United States in negotiations with foreign governments.

In summary, the Hamilton program was aimed at interfering with the workings of comparative advantage in international trade, primarily through the Tariff and Funding Acts. Hamilton's intent was to provide protection for northern industries until they became efficient enough to compete with foreign manufacturers. In effect, it was the first industrial program of the United States, with Hamilton attempting to change the comparative-advantage situation over time through government action. One result of this effort was the intensification of conflict between the South, which suffered from higher prices for its imports, and the North, which obtained protection for its industries.

The Republican Opposition

Opposition to the Federalist program on the frontier and among the debt-ridden farmers and laborers, enabled the Republican Party (the Democratic Party of today) to elect Thomas Jefferson in 1802. Led by Jefferson and Madison, the Republicans charged that the Federalists had created inequities that favored manufacturers and speculators in the following ways.

Federalist financial policies had benefited a northeastern area with a seaboard-European nexus and retarded development of the West. The Funding Act had stripped the poor to enrich the wealthy; speculators had made huge capital gains. The Bank of the United States was an engine of monopoly and privilege that concentrated banking capital in the urban, commercial seaboard area. The whiskey tax was cited as another example of discrimination; the tax was used to finance the Funding Act and develop a navy to further commercial diplomacy; but it oppressed the farmers, who could market whiskey more easily than corn. The tariff and the tonnage acts increased prices to the agricultural sectors and favored the commercial, shipping, and manufacturing sectors of the Northeast.

Although these Republican criticisms of Federalist programs were substantially correct, the Federalists had maintained control of the government for 12 years because of the widespread desire for economic and political stability and general economic development in the United States. But the opposition had not been totally unsuccessful during those 12 years; Republicans had been able to moderate much of Hamilton's promanufacturing program, especially in the area of tariffs. However, when Jeffersonian Republicans came to power in 1802, the Hamiltonian program remained basically unchanged.

REVIEW OF ECONOMIC CONCEPTS: THEORY OF MONEY AND PRICES

The Equation of Exchange

The quantity theory of money, based on the equation of exchange, is a simple model that explores the effect of variations of the supply of money on prices and output. The **equation of exchange** is stated as $MV = PQ$. M represents the supply of money, V the velocity of exchange, P the price level, and Q the output in physical terms.

During the Revolution, from 1775 to 1781, large amounts of paper money, un-backed by gold and silver, were issued by the Continental Congress and the various states, supplementing the gold and silver components of the supply of money (M). During the 1780s, the supply of money (M) in the young United States consisted mainly of gold and silver coins. The **velocity of exchange** (V) is the number of times the supply of money changes hands during a particular period of time. The kinds of purchases that cause money to change may be defined in a number of ways. The simplest (and the one used here) is that V, or the changing of money from one person to another, is for final goods and services. Velocity depends on the habits and customs of the people and, perhaps more significantly, on the degree of development of the financial institutions of the economy. Since the financial institutions of the economy were rudimentary and communication was slow between 1775 and 1789, it seems reasonable to assume that velocity (V) was constant. Velocity varies as people respond to unusual circumstances. Velocity can increase when people spend depreciating currency (for example, during the Revolution) more quickly. It can decrease as people hold on to a scarce money supply (1784–1786) and the money supply decreases still further.

If the supply of money increases while velocity is constant, PQ must increase. As long as there are unemployed resources, output (Q) of final goods and services can increase. As the economy approaches full employment, however, prices (P) must increase, and at full employment only prices (P) can increase.

If the supply of money (M) decreases while velocity (V) is constant, prices (P) must decrease, and output (Q) may decrease as well. But the proportion of total output sold within markets was small in the United States from 1775 to 1789 because many products were produced and consumed at home. Thus the main effect of a decrease in the supply of money was to reduce prices.

The Demand for Money

Three basic motives explain why a person desires to hold a certain amount of money at any point in time:

1. The **transactions motive.** Because the receipt of money through wages or gifts is not perfectly timed with the desire to purchase goods, a person must keep some money to pay for all purchases made until the next payday.
2. The **precautionary motive.** People hold money against unforeseen happenings. If an illness should occur, for example, money will be needed to buy medicine and pay the doctor or hospital.
3. The **speculative motive.** Holding money is an advantage when a person encounters an opportunity to make a good investment.

What determines the specific amount of money that a person wishes to hold? The answer includes a number of factors, such as habits and customs, the level of income generated in the economy, the inventory of consumer goods that the individual holds, and the amount of assets that can be converted into money. Although people vary, everyone wishes to hold a certain amount of money. When changes in the supply of money change the amounts that individuals actually hold, people react in ways that restore an equilibrium.

If the supply of money is increased, people find that they hold more money than they want and, as a result, they attempt to convert this money into consumer or investment goods. If such goods are in short supply, prices will increase. However, if the supply of money is decreased, people have less money than they want and, as a result, attempt to increase their holdings of money by reducing purchases of consumer or investment goods. The resulting decrease in demand decreases prices.

Whether we use the equation of exchange or the demand for money as our model, the results are the same. If the economy is at full employment, an increase in the supply of money increases prices, while a decrease in the supply of money decreases prices.

Price Changes: Debtors and Creditors

When prices increase, debtors benefit at the expense of creditors. Since the purchasing power of money decreases as prices increase, debtors borrow money of higher purchasing power when prices are lower and pay back money of lower purchasing power when prices rise. Creditors suffer for the same reason. When prices fall, the reverse occurs. In addition, if no change occurs in the quantity of output, money incomes fall as prices fall, and the debtor has less money income to pay back the loan. (These generalizations ignore the possible effects of changes in price expectations. If borrowers and lenders have anticipated future price changes correctly, prices already reflect those expectations).

Variations in prices create conflict between debtors and creditors about government policies. It is in the debtors' self-interest to encourage policies that are inflationary (that increase prices), but it is in the creditors' self-interest to oppose price-increasing policies.

A MODEL OF IMPORT SUBSTITUTION EFFECTS

Nations trade commodities and services with one another because such trade is to their mutual advantage. When one nation produces those goods in which it has a comparative advantage and imports the goods in which another nation has such an advantage, both countries are better off; each has more to consume than it would have had in the absence of trade.

Now, what happens in an economy that has attained a comparative-advantage trade equilibrium if that equilibrium is severely disrupted by war, a decision to forgo international trade, a change in trading relationships with other nations, or any other set of events?

Figure 4.2, which represents hypothetical production and consumption possibilities of a colony or nation with and without trade, is useful as a means of
visualizing the kinds of relationships set in motion by such a trade disequilibrium.
Shown in Figure 4.2(a) are the domestic production possibilities curve of an agricultural economy and that economy's consumption possibilities curve when it engages
in trade with another nation that has a comparative advantage in producing
manufactured goods. For simplicity's sake, both "curves" are drawn as straight
lines, to reflect an assumption of no specialization of resources and a constant rate
at which one good must be given up in order to produce the other. Let's take Point
R (A_0 of agricultural goods and M_0 of manufactured goods) as a reference point.
Since Point R lies on the economy's production possibilities curve, it is a possible
equilibrium without trade; in fact, we shall suppose (arbitrarily) that R is the initial
equilibrium. At Point R, A_0 of agricultural goods and M_0 of manufactured goods
are available for consumption.

Turning to Figure 4.2(b), Sd is the domestic supply of manufactured goods,
while D is the nation's demand for manufactured goods. Supply (Sd) and demand
are equal at Price P_0. Now what is its gain if the agricultural nation engaged in
bilateral trade with the other nation? Point R', while not unique, illustrates that gain.
By exporting some of the agricultural goods in which it has a comparative advantage to the other nation and importing some of that country's comparative-advantage manufactured goods, our hypothetical nation can reach Point R' on its
consumption possibilities curve. Point R' represents A_0 of agricultural goods and
M_0' of manufactured goods; therefore, there has been a gain from trade. Now look

Figure 4.2. Hypothetical Production-Possibilities and Consumption-Possibilities Curves. Domestic Pricing of Manufactured Goods (with and without imports).

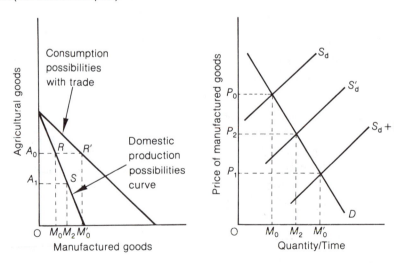

again at Figure 4.2(b). The increase in the supply of manufactured goods through trade ($M_0' - M_0$) causes the supply curve of such goods to increase, to shift to $Sd + f$ (domestic and foreign). As a result, the price of manufactured goods falls to P_1.

What happens now if international trade is disrupted? For example, what happens if war breaks out between the two nations that had been exchanging agricultural and manufactured goods? For simplicity's sake, let us assume that there is a total cessation of trade (no blockade runners or other illegal trade). Initially, the domestic supply of manufactured goods returns to Sd, and the society tends to return to Point R (with A_0 of agricultural goods and M_0 of manufactured goods). But suppose that the society whose imports of manufactured goods have ceased decides to produce more of those goods itself; in other words, it decides it must turn inward and substitute its own products for those it has previously imported.

In turning inward, the nation denied trade is constrained—even at full employment—to the choices along its domestic production possibilities curve. Since we are assuming that the nation wants to produce more manufactured goods (to prosecute the war or for whatever reason), it will move down that curve (to the right of Point R). The higher prices of manufactured goods (such as P_0 with domestically produced supply Sd) will act as incentives to domestic producers or would-be domestic producers to expand or create manufacturing enterprises.

We have been assuming in this chapter that the PP curve was a straight line. Now we will use concave PP curves. Remember, though, that in moving down the now-concave curve, the nation faces an increasingly unfavorable trade-off: it forgoes more and more agricultural goods to get each increment in manufactured goods. The nation may, as the former North American colonies did, successfully create a gunpowder and munitions industry, but that industry will probably produce goods less efficiently than foreign producers.

Let's suppose that ultimately our hypothetical nation reaches Point S, at which it is producing A_1 of agricultural goods and M_2 of manufactured goods. In turn—look at Figure 4.2(b) again—domestic supply of manufactured goods increases to Sd' and price falls to P_2, still far above the price with trade, P_1.

Throughout this discussion, we have assumed a constant demand for manufactured goods. If, as seems likely, that demand increases during the cessation of trade (from new military supplies plus some of the old civilian demand), prices will be greater than they would have been otherwise (above P_2), and the stimulus to manufacturing enterprise will be further enhanced.

Restoration of Trade

Let's suppose now that the war or other event that caused the cessation of trade is ended and that trade is restored on the old terms. Assume that there has been no change in either country's comparative advantage. Equilibrium trading relationships now exist all along the consumption-possibilities-with-trade curve of the nation represented in Figure 4.2(a). In other words, the other country's comparative-advantage (cheaper) manufactured goods can now enter our hypothetical nation. Let us suppose (again, arbitrarily) that Point R' is restored as the consumption possibilities equilibrium. If we assume that there are some minor barriers to complete specialization (in which our hypothetical country would produce only agricultural goods and the other country only manufactured goods), domestic supply becomes Sd and total supply (domestic plus foreign) becomes $Sd + f$. Manufactured goods' prices fall to P_1.

The model shows that nations (or nations and their colonies) can have more to consume if they trade with one another on the basis of comparative advantage. A nation that "turns inward" (creates infant industries) may successfully produce goods that are not in its comparative advantage so long as trade is blocked, as occurred during the Revolution. When trade is restored, however, the price stimulus will be removed, and prices of goods traded on a comparative-advantage basis will fall. Domestic industries created during the hiatus in trade will find themselves at a disadvantage, and some, if not all, will find it unprofitable to continue producing the good(s) that are not in the country's comparative advantage.

QUESTIONS

1. Why were U.S. exports restricted after the Revolution? What were the specific restrictions placed on some major American exports?
2. What caused the depression of 1785–1786? Describe in detail the role of the supply of money in that depression.
3. How did the Continental Congress attempt to expand U.S. exports? Was the attempt successful? Why?
4. How did the state governments attempt to constrict imports? Were they successful? Why?
5. Explain the three means that were available to increase the supply of money in the 1780s. What were the controversies surrounding each approach?
6. If you were a debtor in 1786, which approach to the supply of money would you have favored? Why? If you were a creditor, which one would you have favored? Why?
7. Some authors dissent from the position that the 1780s were a period of economic hardship in the United States. What points do they make to support their argument?
8. What were the major economic difficulties facing the United States in the 1780s? What efforts were made to deal with these problems prior to the adoption of the Constitution of 1789? Were these efforts successful?
9. Why was Congress unable to solve the economic problems of the 1780s under the Articles of Confederation?
10. What is the authors' view of the economic factors that fostered the development of the Constitution?
11. What was Beard's economic interpretation of the Constitution? Do you think he was correct? Why?
12. What economic changes were made possible by the Constitution?

13. What were the main objectives of the Federalist program? How did the Federalists try to implement their goals?

14. What were the main economic effects of the Federalist program? What were the criticisms of this program?

15. Do you favor Hamilton's view or Jefferson's view of economic policy in the early years of the United States? Explain your choice.

SUGGESTED READINGS

1. Beard, Charles A. *An Economic Interpretation of the Constitution of the United States.* New York: Macmillan, 1913.

2. Bjork, Gordon C. "The Weaning of the American Economy: Independence, Market Changes and Economic Development." *Journal of Economic History, 24* (December 1964).

3. Brown, R. E. *Charles Beard and the Constitution.* Princeton, N.J.: Princeton University Press, 1956.

4. Ferguson, E. James. "The Nationalists of 1781–1783 and the Economic Interpretation of the Constitution." *Journal of American History, 56* (1969).

5. Ferguson, E. James. *The Power of the Purse: A History of American Public Finance, 1776–1790.* Chapel Hill: University of North Carolina Press, 1961.

6. Fiske, John. *The Critical Period.* Boston: Houghton Mifflin, 1888. Excerpted and reprinted in Gerald Nash, ed., *Issues in American Economic History.* 2nd ed. Lexington, Mass.: Heath, 1972.

7. Hammond, Bray. *Banks and Politics in America, from the Revolution to the Civil War.* Princeton, N.J.: Princeton University Press, 1957.

8. Hession, Charles H., and Hyman Sardy. *Ascent to Affluence.* Boston: Allyn and Bacon, 1969. Pp. 48–56.

9. Jensen, Merrill E. *The New Nation: A History of the United States During the Confederation, 1787–1789.* New York: Knopf, 1950.

10. McDonald, Forrest. *We the People: The Economic Origins of the Constitution.* Chicago: University of Chicago Press, 1958.

11. Nash, Gerald D., ed. *Issues in American Economic History.* Lexington, Mass.: Heath, 1972. Chap. 7.

12. Nettels, Curtis P. *The Emergence of a National Economy, 1775–1815.* New York: Harper and Row, 1969.

13. Shepherd, J. F., and G. M. Walton. "Economic Change After the American Revolution: Pre- and Post-War Comparisons of Maritime Shipping and Trade." *Explorations in Economic History, 13* (October 1976).

14. Wright, Esmond, ed. *Causes and Consequences of the American Revolution.* New York: Quadrangle, 1966.

Chapter 5 ———————————————————————

THE NAPOLEONIC WARS AND U.S. COMMERCIAL EXPANSION, 1793–1815

In 1790, the prospects for rapid economic development of the American economy seemed dim. However, in the next 25 years, just such a period of expansion occurred. What factors could have caused this dramatic turnabout? The answer, at least from the demand side of the economy, is wars—not ones directly involving the United States, but rather wars in which the United States was a prominent neutral. This factor, together with supply growth and institutional changes favorable to the expansion and integration of a market economy, produced substantial growth.

This chapter continues the economic history from 1790 through the Napoleonic Wars and the U.S. War of 1812 (1812–1815). The single most important economic factor in this period was the very substantial increase in U.S. commodity exports and shipping earnings. Thus the foreign trade sector of the U.S. economy played a crucial role in economic development during these 25 years. The Review of Economic Concepts in this chapter contains a simple model of export-led development that will prove useful in understanding this period.

THE U.S. ECONOMY IN 1790

The classical theory of economic development emphasizes the importance of the size of markets and the level of technology. Market size is the factor limiting specialization and division of labor, and with a given technology, as specialization and division of labor increase, productivity also increases and intensive growth occurs. The size of markets, then, is a determining factor in economic development, and to understand the potential for development in the United States in 1790, we must concentrate on an analysis of the potential for growth of markets.

Douglass C. North (5), in his excellent study *The Economic Growth of the United States 1790–1860,* draws the following conclusion:

> By 1790 the political crises had been resolved and the economy enjoyed a measure of prosperity. Given political stability, an energetic populace, and an abundance of resources, the country's long-run economic growth would appear assured. Yet there was little prospect of rapid growth on the horizon, and available information about the economy from 1789 through 1792 provides incomplete but convincing evidence that the prospects of the economy in the foreseeable future were limited by the size of the domestic market and an inability to expand the foreign market.

In brief, while the Constitution and the economic ideology of the American people created a favorable political, social, and psychological environment for development, potential development was severely limited by the size of internal and foreign markets.

Limits of the Internal Market

Although the population of the United States in 1790 was almost 4 million, and the per capita real income was probably higher than in England, only a small part of the output resulted in market demand. There was no market demand from the almost 700,000 slaves in the South, nor from the 200,000 settlers west of the Appalachian Mountains because the frontier was primarily self-sufficient. The rest of the rural population, 2.8 million, maintained market relationships of varying degrees. However, even the 200,000 people in urban centers produced a significant amount of home manufactures, thus reducing the size of the cash market. Although few people were completely self-sufficient (entirely within the noncash economy), most had varying degrees of self-sufficiency (varying degrees of noncash involvement).

As we have sought to emphasize earlier, the primary factor restricting the spread of the market was the high cost of transportation other than by rivers and by sea. Most agricultural products are high in bulk and low in value; land transportation for such products was restricted to short distances. It is hard, then, to find fault with North's conclusion: "Whatever proportion of the rural population is assumed to have been part of the domestic market, it is impossible to escape the conclusion that this market was small and not heavily concentrated." In other words, the cash economy was small and spread out.

Limits of the Export Market

The restrictions of the export market are, by now, familiar to you. When the United States was part of the British Empire, it received all the economic privileges of mercantilist relationships. After the Revolution, the United States lost its favored treatment from Britain. Indeed, it then faced unfavorable, discriminatory treatment from most Western European countries. Not only was direct trade with the colonies of European countries severely restricted, but there were also limitations in many areas on trade with the home countries themselves. These restrictions included prohibition of trade with certain colonies, prohibition of import of certain goods, import taxes on certain goods, and taxes levied against foreign ships (including U.S. ships) engaged in direct trade with certain countries.

These restrictions on U.S. foreign trade limited its ability to increase exports and restricted the further expansion of the American carrying trade. In 1790, only 58.6 percent of the foreign trade of the United States was carried in U.S. ships.

In 1790, the prospects for rapid economic growth by increases in the size of the market seemed very dim. Internal trade was relatively low and unlikely to increase because of high transportation costs. External trade was limited because of mercantilist trade restrictions employed by the European powers. With such an abundance of land, and with relatively high labor and capital costs in manufacturing, the American economy was at a comparative disadvantage with Europe in manufactured goods.

ECONOMIC EXPANSION, 1793–1815

Now let us examine the experience of the United States from 1793 to 1815. Although prospects for a period of substantial economic development in the United States in 1790 seemed dim, external events changed that picture and helped to initiate just such a period between 1793 and 1815. The leading sectors in this expansion were the shipping and export industries, the latter including both reexports of foreign products and exports of American products. The reexports came primarily from the colonies of the belligerents in the Napoleonic Wars in the West Indies. These exports could not be carried directly from the West Indies colonies to the home country—for example, from French colonies to France—because they would be seized by the English fleet as contraband. Therefore, a legal fiction was created: these exports were carried to U.S. ports and reexported as U.S. goods. The British Essex decision in 1805 sought to restrict neutrals to the trade they had carried before the war. Napoleon's Milan decree destroyed this legal fiction concerning reexports and declared a blockade of Britain. Both, along with the British Orders in Council in 1807, laid U.S. ships carrying reexports from the West Indies open to seizure by the British or French navies.

Every turn in this expansion of the American economy was determined by economic and military policies connected with the intermittent warfare between Britain and France from 1793 to 1812. There was a mild break in this expansion in 1797 when France accelerated its capture of U.S. merchant vessels and there was some talk of peace. There was a sharp break in 1801 and 1802 while an unstable peace existed between France and Britain. Resumption of war in Europe in 1803, however, sparked a renewal of expansion in American trade. In response to seizures of U.S. ships by both Britain and France (528 ships by Britain and 389 by France) under the British Essex decision and Napoleon's Milan decree, President Jefferson, over the violent opposition of the shippers themselves, enforced the **Embargo of December 1807.** That embargo was replaced by the **Nonintercourse Act of 1809,** after which trade slowly resumed with the European continent, excluding Britain. In 1812, a second war between the United States and Great Britain brought an end to the era.

What caused such a large expansion of the carrying trade and of reexports? Mostly the disappearance of many merchant ships of the belligerents, France, Holland, and Spain. During the Napoleonic Wars, the vast colonial trade of Europe was largely placed in the hands of neutrals, and the neutral nation most capable of handling this trade was the United States. Even Britain found it advisable temporarily to open the British West Indies to U.S. ships. The Napoleonic Wars thus substantially, if only temporarily, broke down the mercantilist system that had restricted the ability of the United States to expand its foreign markets. When war gave the United States an opportunity to expand, United States merchants and shippers took full advantage of it.

As the demand for U.S. exports and the services of U.S. ships through the reexport trade increased, prices of exports and fees for U.S. shipping also increased, shifting resources from the noncash economy and from the non–export-oriented cash economy into the export-oriented cash economy. Productivity rose as these resources flowed from lower-productivity activities and as the size of the market in export-oriented activities increased, stimulating specialization and division of labor. This process is illustrated in the Review of Economic Concepts at the end of this chapter.

The Carrying Trade

British-French conflict created an opportunity for U.S. ships to trade with both the colonies and the home countries of the European empires. As a result, from 1790 to 1807 earnings of U.S. ships increased 700 percent. Net earnings (total receipts minus costs) for the carrying trade rose from $5.9 million in 1790 to $42.1 million in 1807 (see Table 5.1). This increase was due, in significant measure, not only to increases in ocean freight rates but also to increased efficiency in the utilization of ships and especially to a doubling in the total tonnage of American shipping.

Another sign of the expansion of American shipping, as the British-French wars drove belligerent merchant vessels from the seas, was the dramatic increase in the use of U.S. ships for transporting U.S. exports and imports. U.S. shipping had carried only about 59 percent of the country's foreign trade in 1790, but this increased to 90 percent by 1807. The increase was concentrated primarily in the Northeast, especially in the three large port cities of Boston, New York, and Philadelphia.

Table 5.1.   Exports, Reexports, Imports, and Earnings of the Carrying Trade (in Millions of Dollars).

YEAR	EXPORTS	REEXPORTS	IMPORTS FOR DOMESTIC USE	NET FREIGHT EARNINGS
1790	20.2	0.3	23.5	5.9
1791	19.0	0.5	30.0	6.2
1792	20.8	1.0	31.5	7.4
1793	26.1	1.8	30.8	11.9
1794	33.0	6.5	29.5	15.5
1795	48.0	8.3	63.0	19.0
1796	67.1	26.3	56.6	21.6
1797	56.9	27.0	50.4	17.1
1798	61.5	33.0	37.6	16.6
1799	78.7	45.5	35.5	24.2
1800	71.0	49.1	44.1	26.2
1801	94.1	46.6	66.7	31.0
1802	72.5	35.8	42.6	18.2
1803	55.8	13.6	52.1	23.7
1804	71.7	36.2	50.8	26.9
1805	95.6	53.8	72.3	29.7
1806	101.5	60.3	76.3	34.6
1807	108.3	59.6	85.1	42.1
1808	22.4	13.0	45.1	23.0
1809	52.2	20.8	40.2	26.2
1810	66.8	24.4	65.0	39.5
1811	61.3	16.0	41.9	40.8
1812	38.5	8.5	70.3	29.6
1813	27.9	2.8	19.3	10.2
1814	6.9	0.1	12.8	2.6
1815	52.6	6.6	78.8	20.6

SOURCE: Douglass C. North, "The United States Balance of Payments, 1790–1860." *Trends in the American Economy in the Nineteenth Century*, Studies in Income and Wealth of the National Bureau of Economic Research, Vol. 24 (Princeton, N.J.: Princeton University Press, 1960), pp. 591–592, 595.

Exports and Reexports

This remarkable increase in the earnings from shipping was accompanied by increases in exports, both exports of American-produced commodities and reexports. **Reexports** were commodities produced outside of the United States, shipped to a U.S. port, temporarily stored in warehouses, and reshipped without being changed in form. Important examples of such reexports were the sugar and molasses produced in the West Indies sugar islands of Britain, France, and Spain. The Napoleonic Wars restricted the ability of vessels from these countries to carry the sugar, leaving the trade primarily to the United States. Also, U.S. merchants' efforts to find new markets resulted in the reexporting of tea from China.

American-produced exports were primarily agricultural commodities, led by southern staples. Cotton, which dominated the expansion of domestic exports, accounted for half of the increase. Next in importance was tobacco, and then general agricultural output from the North, consisting of wheat, flour, and animal products.

From 1790 to the peak year of 1807, total exports rose from $20.2 million to $108.3 million—an impressive fivefold increase (see Table 5.1). Expansion of the reexport trade was the major factor in this increase. Reexports, $0.3 million in 1790, increased to $59.6 million in 1807, while domestic exports rose from $19.9 million to $58.5 million.

Imports, Terms of Trade, and the Balance of Payments

Imports for domestic use increased from $23.5 million in 1790 to $85.1 million in 1807—almost a fourfold increase. Reexports have been separated from the import and export data in Table 5.1 because they increase imports when they come into the United States and increase exports when they leave. When imports for domestic use are compared to exports, we see an import surplus (imports exceeding exports) in every year from 1790 through 1814 except for 1811 and 1813. This commodity import surplus was more than made up by earnings from the carrying trade. For example, in 1807 imports for domestic use were $85.1 million, while exports were $59.6 million, leaving an import surplus of $25.5 million. Earnings of the carrying trade in 1807 were $42.1 million, more than enough to cover that import surplus.

Our earlier analysis of a simple export-led growth model indicated that this surge in export demand should lead to increases in prices. Increased demand for imports would indicate also an increase in import prices. These increases in prices had a marked effect on both imports and exports. A useful measure to compare relative changes in export-import prices is the net barter Terms of Trade index—the index that measures the rate of export prices to import prices. Table 4.1 gives the Terms of Trade index to 1790, and Table 5.2 continues the index to 1815. Using 1790 as 100, the terms of trade fell to under 70 for 1792, rose to a high of 162 in 1798 and 1799, then fell to a low of 93 in 1808. During the period 1792–1807, the terms of trade were favorable to the United States. This means not only that there was substantial expansion in U.S. exports, reexports, and earnings on the carrying trade but also that export prices rose more rapidly than import prices. On the whole, U.S. imports became cheaper relative to U.S. exports.

These "favorable" terms of trade meant that each physical unit of exports could purchase a larger physical amount of imports. The results could lead to such combinations as the following: More imports of consumption goods could be obtained, thus increasing total consumption. Increases in imports of capital goods could be obtained, increasing the productive capacity of the American economy. Finally, resources within the U.S. economy could be shifted into alternative uses, and imports could replace the output lost by this shift. All three possibilities were realized, increasing U.S. per capita income.

Table 5.2.   Index of Export and Import Prices and the Terms of Trade, 1700–1815 (1790 = 100).

YEAR	EXPORTS	IMPORTS	TERMS OF TRADE
1790	100.0	100.0	100.0
1791	85.8	109.8	78.1
1792	81.7	118.8	68.8
1793	97.8	108.4	90.2
1794	103.6	129.2	80.2
1795	153.6	124.3	123.6
1796	172.6	132.8	130.0
1797	174.8	139.9	124.9
1798	207.4	127.6	162.5
1799	220.3	135.5	162.6
1800	145.9	124.6	117.1
1801	154.1	119.9	128.5
1802	131.6	111.8	117.7
1803	132.8	118.0	112.5
1804	147.7	134.7	109.7
1805	156.4	139.5	112.1
1806	142.0	129.8	109.4
1807	136.2	124.7	109.2
1808	115.3	124.3	92.8
1809	116.2	129.1	90.0
1810	128.6	129.8	99.1
1811	128.6	121.1	106.2
1812	127.1	131.7	96.5
1813	126.5	179.7	70.4
1814	127.3	232.3	54.8
1815	182.9	191.3	95.6

SOURCE: Douglass C. North, *The Economic Growth of the United States, 1790–1860* (New York: Norton, 1966), pp. 221, 229.

Internal and Coastal Trade

Internal trade was primarily local, extending out from the seaports into the surrounding areas (their hinterland). Towns farther away were usually connected to the coastal cities by rivers. There was some increase in the geographic as well as economic (demand-supply determined) size of these local markets because of the expansion of turnpikes (roads). But the economic effects of road expansion were minimal, and cost of land transportation was still high.

After 1792, along with the expansion of domestic exports and imports, coastal trade grew rapidly. Trade in the West expanded after New Orleans was opened to U.S. commerce in 1793; New Orleans was closed again, however, in 1802. Finally, in 1803, the Louisiana Purchase by President Jefferson brought New Orleans under U.S. control. Western trade (from Ohio, Kentucky, Tennessee, Indiana, and Illinois) on the Mississippi was primarily one-way down the river. Agricultural products moved downstream on flatboats, and even the flatboats themselves were sold in New Orleans. Most of the goods shipped north were carried on horseback or muleback, which was cheaper than poling upstream.

The Foreign Sector's Impact on the Economy

The leading sectors pacing the rapid economic growth from 1793 to 1807 were domestic exports, reexports, and the carrying trade—all expanded by the opportunities created by British-French conflict. In addition, there were the economic effects from raising export prices and fees for shipping and the economic effects of the favorable terms of trade already mentioned. This expansion had substantial impact on the growth of urban areas. The carrying and reexport trade was primarily concentrated in the Northeast and was strongly mirrored in the growth of the four major port cities of Philadelphia, New York, Boston, and Baltimore. Each of these cities (Table 5.3) doubled in population, and New York and Baltimore almost tripled between 1790 and 1810. Increase in domestic exports was especially strong in the South, where the export of short-staple cotton caused growth in Charleston, South Carolina. Urbanization increased from 5.1 percent of the population in 1790 to 7.3 percent in 1810.

Expanded export activity encouraged growth in what Douglass North (5) called "subsidiary, complementary, and residentiary types of economic activities" and was confined primarily to the Northeast. A **subsidiary industry** is one that is needed so that another industry can function. Most important as a subsidiary industry, one directly created by export activity, was shipbuilding, which more than doubled in terms of merchant ship tonnage. Various shipfitting industries developed around shipbuilding.

Examples of **complementary industries** were commission merchants, brokers, and others who implement trade, marine insurance, banks, and facilities for warehouses and docking. These complementary industries were originally created to service the export sector but, once created, were available to help expand internal trade. Growth in these industries during the period 1790–1812 was substantial and provided a basis for further economic growth after 1815.

Increasing urbanization tied to increased export trade stimulated a variety of locally oriented manufactures and services designed to meet the needs of a growing urban population. Such industries are called **residentiary industries**. The

Table 5.3. Population of the Four Major Cities, 1790–1810.

CITY	1790	1800	1810
Baltimore	13,503	26,114	35,583
Boston	18,038	24,937	33,250
New York	33,131	60,489	96,373
Philadelphia	42,520	69,403	91,874

SOURCE: U.S. Census Bureau, *Compendium of the Seventh Census* (Washington, D.C.: Senate Printer, 1854), p. 192.

widening urban markets exerted pressure to improve local transportation through turnpike construction to bring in needed agricultural supplies for the maintenance of this increased population. Thus this growth stimulated expanding market relationships into the hinterland around the port cities.

AGRICULTURE, 1790–1815

Three distinct agricultural regions appeared in the United States during the years 1790–1815: the North, including New England, New York, Pennsylvania, and New Jersey; the South, including the states along the Atlantic south of Pennsylvania, the middle states of Kentucky and Tennessee, and the "New South" of Arkansas, Alabama, Louisiana, and Mississippi; and the West, including Ohio, Indiana, and Illinois.

The South

As may be seen in Figure 5.1, by 1815, the "Old South," those southern states along the Atlantic, had no discernible frontier because the frontier had moved westward, while the middle states of Kentucky and Tennessee were rapidly reaching that same position. The frontier was a so-called New South, consisting of Louisiana, Mississippi, Arkansas, and Alabama.

A significant shift occurred in the relative importance and location of southern staple crops. Tobacco had shifted from the Virginia-Maryland piedmont to North Carolina, Kentucky, and Tennessee. Soil erosion, a problem common to agriculture in the early development of many nations, was the primary reason for the shift from tobacco to wheat in the piedmont of Virginia and Maryland. Rice was still grown along the coast of Georgia and South Carolina, where ocean tides were used to flood the rice fields. A new staple, sugar, developed along the coast of Louisiana. In the rest of the South, cotton was "king" and had replaced tobacco as the region's most important staple.

Supply Effects: The Cotton Gin. The revolution in textile production in England, starting in the 1760s, greatly increased world demand for raw cotton. In the United States in 1790, a few islands off the Atlantic coast could grow what was called *Sea Island* or *long-staple* cotton, a variety in which removal of cotton seed was simple and required little labor. On the mainland, though, only short-staple cotton could be grown. The labor cost involved in removing short-staple cotton seed was very high and severely limited the spread of cotton cultivation. Eli Whitney, while visiting the South in 1793, invented the cotton gin, which greatly reduced the labor cost of removing the seed from short-staple cotton. This machine was a simple one and so easy to produce that Whitney decided not to bother patenting it. His invention dramatically increased productivity, reduced the cost of cleaning (removing the seed), and made short-staple cotton a very profitable crop. As a result, the crop spread rapidly throughout the South until, by 1815, it was "king."

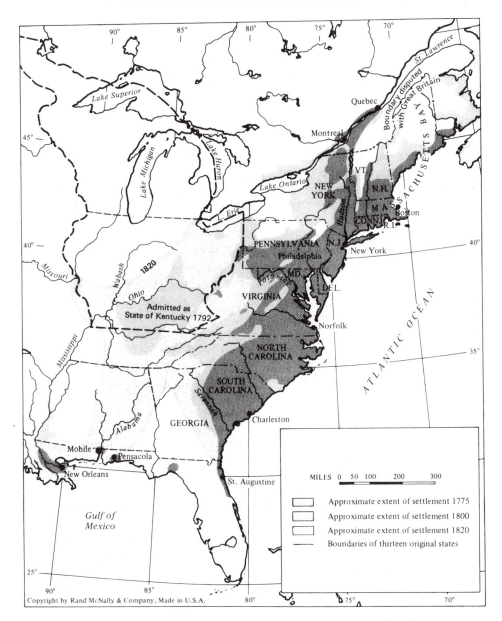

Figure 5.1. Extent of Settlements, 1775–1820.

Source: *Historical Atlas of the World* (New York: Rand McNally, 1988). Copyright © 1988 by Rand McNally and Company, R.L. 88-S-37.

From 1800 to 1860, cotton accounted for more than half the exports from the United States.

The revival of southern staple crops, especially the introduction and expansion of cotton, revalidated the economic advantages of slavery, and that "peculiar institution" showed new vigor. From 1790 to 1810, the rate of growth of the slave population was twice that of the previous 15 years. This growth came primarily from natural increase, not slave importation, as legal importation of slaves was forbidden after 1807. We shall reserve a detailed analysis of the economic importance of slavery for Chapter 9.

The North

In the period from 1790 to 1815, there was little technological change in agriculture and therefore little increase in productivity. Thus the composition of output was largely unchanged. The major exports of the North were still wheat and some animal products. Around the growing urban areas there was increased specialization in dairying and vegetable farming. Dynamic increases in agricultural productivity, though, were yet to come.

After the Revolution, the states renounced their claims to the northwestern territories, which were turned over to the federal government. (Western land policy under the Federalists was discussed in Chapter 4.) States, however, held title to large tracts of unoccupied land within their respective borders. Generally, these were sold in large blocks to speculators, especially in New York. These speculators tried to hold the land until values went up, but the economic difficulties of 1783–1792 bankrupted many of them, including Robert Morris, the "financier" of the Revolution. The interior of New York was not completely settled until the opening of the Erie Canal in the 1820s.

The West

Until 1815, the western frontier consisted of the "Old Northwest" of Ohio, Indiana, and Illinois (see Figure 5.1). As in the East, settlement took place along the river systems, which in the West fed into the Mississippi. With the opening of New Orleans after 1795, western agricultural output, such as wheat, corn, oats, and animal products, traveled downstream by flatboat to New Orleans and from there on to the Northeast and Europe. As mentioned earlier, upstream trade of manufactured consumer products was transported mostly by horses or mules, and transportation costs were much higher than downstream. This transportation problem was the major obstacle to western development. The beginning of a solution was on the scene by 1815 with the appearance of the early steamboats on the Mississippi. Completion of transportation development, however, occurred during the next time period, from 1815 to 1860.

INDUSTRY, 1790–1815

Various stages of industrial development existed side by side in this period. Home manufacture continued at a high level, as rural families still made most of the manufactured items that they used. In addition, the **putting-out system of**

manufactures was being used, primarily in New England in the production of shoes and woolen textiles. A merchant manufacturer would provide raw materials and at times simple tools and machines to workers who, working in their own homes, did one or more operations. The merchant manufacturer would then pick up the finished goods and take them to another worker, who would do the next operation. This continued until the commodity was finished; the merchant would then sell the commodity. The workers, usually farmers and their families, produced these manufactures in their spare time.

There were also the small-scale independent master craftsmen serving limited markets. The major limitation on the size of these small-scale enterprises was the lack of a large market because transportation was so costly. In 1815, firms hiring 15 or more workers were the exception.

Finally, larger enterprises employing power-driven machinery—mostly waterpower, although the steam engine was coming into use—were being formed. As early as the decade of the 1780s, we can see the emergence of what came to be known as the American System of larger automated enterprises. In the mid-1780s, Oliver Evans constructed an automated (waterpower-driven) flour mill near Philadelphia whose nearly continuous production process was to become a hallmark of the astonishing productivity growth in the nineteenth-century American economy. The period of greatest growth in these larger enterprises was from 1807 to 1815, that is, from Jefferson's embargo through the War of 1812. The decline in U.S. international trade after 1807 caused capital to shift in part from trade into manufacturing. But the most important factor in stimulating manu-factures in the United States was the complete prohibition or severe restriction placed on imports of manufactured products, especially from England, by the Embargo of 1807, the Nonintercourse Act of 1809, and finally the War of 1812 itself. Shortages of manufactured imports increased prices, causing resources to shift to manufacturing within the United States.

Larger-Scale Enterprises

Before 1815, the larger firms, called *mills*, produced iron, flour (as in Evan's case), lumber, and textiles. Location was determined by a combination of availability of raw material, waterpower, and centers of demand.

Iron smelting and the production of iron products were widespread because iron deposits were abundant and widespread. Water for power was readily avail-able, and fuel in the form of charcoal was obtained from surrounding forests. Iron smelting was originally located near iron ore deposits. It was not until coal was used as a fuel in the form of coke that the smelting industry became concentrated. Iron was used mostly in small, widely scattered blacksmith shops located near the farmers who used the output of the shops. Because not enough iron was produced to meet the needs of the economy, about one-fourth of the iron used was imported.

Flour mills made notable progress after 1790, and an increased percentage of wheat was exported in the form of flour. Mills catering to the internal market were decentralized, located near the scattered centers of internal demand. Those catering to exports were concentrated around Philadelphia to draw on the wheat produced in fertile Bucks and Lancaster counties of Pennsylvania, and around Richmond to draw on the wheat produced in the Virginia-Maryland piedmont. Waterpower, wheat supplies, and access to the sea were all close by. Larger mills were developed, machinery was improved, and after 1800 steam power was applied. As an example of this developing technology, in 1803 Oliver Evans of Philadelphia built his automated mill, the most advanced flour mill of the day.

Lumber mills were widely scattered since timber was readily available throughout the country and demand was widely scattered. Water, the primary source of power, was abundantly available. Lumber mills catered primarily to the local market.

In 1787, the first cotton textile mill that used the spinning jenny was built in Beverly, Massachusetts. Samuel Slater introduced the water frame, another spinning machine, in 1790. Francis Cabot Lowell of Boston added the power loom for the weaving of cotton cloth to his spinning mills in Waltham, Massachusetts, in 1813. The Embargo of 1807 and the War of 1812 diverted considerable commercial capital to manufacturing, especially to cotton textiles. By 1809, over 5,000 people were employed in cotton mills centered mostly in New England.

The period from 1790 to 1815 was one of stirrings and beginnings rather than one of pervasive changes. Many of the manufacturing beginnings, especially in textiles, were wiped out by renewed importing of British-manufactured products at the end of the War of 1812. But a start had been made. Experience had been gained in handling the many problems of larger-scale production. Managers had learned how to deal with a larger labor force, new technology, the need for larger sources of supply, and the need to sell the larger output. The foundations were laid for more rapid growth after 1815.

BANKING AND FINANCE, 1790–1815

Between 1781 and 1798, 22 banks were established. These were fairly conservative institutions that dealt mainly with mercantile activities involved in foreign trade. Of these banks, 12 were located in New England. From 1798 to 1816, 65 more banks were established. Although these banks were more conservative than those of the post-Jackson period after 1832, they were less conservative than those of the earlier period. More liberal state laws were enacted in regard to bank notes and specie (gold and silver) reserves, and thus the currency in circulation increased. Loans also increased in variety.

The Financial-Economic Program of the Federalists Reviewed

The government of the newly independent United States was faced with serious problems relating to trade and diplomatic relations as well as public finance. The appropriate role of the central government in dealing with these problems was a focus of debate. Early on, the leading exponent of the Federalist position and first secretary of the treasury, Alexander Hamilton, argued for government policies that would promote industry and the investment necessary to transform the United States from an overwhelmingly agricultural nation into one with a manufacturing base.

In the area of public finance, Hamilton argued successfully for the "funding" of the outstanding national debt. This meant calling in the paper money and other forms of indebtedness that had been issued by the previous government and replacing them with interest-bearing notes of the United States. Hamilton clearly believed that this action, together with federal assumption of the debt of the states, would give the moneyed groups in the new nation a stake in its success. The issue of federal debt also greatly enlarged the supply of financial capital and facilitated the growth of larger-scale enterprises.

In 1790, Hamilton proposed the creation of a national bank, the Bank of the United States. Though opposed by agrarian interests who feared centralization of government funds and monopoly control of the monetary system, the bank was chartered for 20 years in 1791. Its primary charge was to deal with the chronic shortage of specie and to act as a central depository for federal government funds.

The First Bank of the United States was also to serve as a regulator of and a check on the state banks in regard to their issue of currency. The federal government would deposit all the state bank notes into the First Bank of the United States, which in turn could present them to the banks for specie payment. Through this practice, the Bank of the United States restrained the issuance of currency by merchant banks. However, one should not overestimate the extent of this practice and its effects on the supply of money. It was not done consistently, and the Bank of the United States did not curtail its own profit-seeking activities to ensure currency restraint in the banking system. In other words, the bank did not act as a central bank in the modern sense. The Jeffersonian Republicans, reflecting the continued opposition of agrarian interests, refused to recharter the First Bank of the United States in 1811. They let the charter lapse in spite of the fact that the bank had helped many state banks out of their financial difficulties.

The third feature of Federalist monetary policy was the creation in 1792 of a United States Mint establishing a bimetallic (silver and gold) standard.

Nonbank Institutions

Under the impact of expanding trade after 1792, insurance companies developed. The first was incorporated in Philadelphia in 1794, and by 1800, 33 active companies were providing investment funds. The activities of the banks and insurance companies were primarily in commerce; only the barest beginning of a noncommercial capital market had been laid by 1815. A sign of this beginning was the creation in the early 1790s of the forerunner of the New York Stock Exchange.

REVIEW OF ECONOMIC CONCEPTS: A SIMPLE MODEL
OF EXPORT-LED DEVELOPMENT

Most economies in the early phase of economic development are tied to foreign trade and its vagaries. To provide a framework for understanding the developmental forces at work in the American economy during the 25 years from 1790 to 1815, we shall build a simple model that shows how foreign trade *may* become a positive influence on that course of development.

Let us make the following assumptions about the economy in question:

1. Two separable economies exist. One is a noncash economy that is generally agricultural and has a low **capital-labor ratio.** The other is a cash economy with a relatively high capital-labor ratio.
2. Because of the disparity in the capital-labor ratios and because larger market sizes permit greater specialization and division of labor and capital, productivity is higher in the cash economy than in the noncash economy and, for the same reasons, higher in the export activities than in the domestic market activities of the cash economy.
3. A significant proportion of the resources of the cash economy is employed in the foreign trade sector to produce commodities and services connected with exports and imports.

Suppose that our hypothetical economy is initially in equilibrium, allocating its resources according to comparative-advantage uses given the tastes and preferences of its citizens. Let us also suppose that the terms of trade are, in some sense, "neutral," equal to 100, which means that export prices (an index) are equal to import prices (an index). We can see this initial relationship in Figure 5.2. With demand for imports D_0 and supply of imports S_0, import prices are P_i. It is apparent that (arbitrarily) $P_e = P_i$ or terms of trade are equal to 100.

Now we want to isolate the effects of changes in the nation's export markets. To do so, we hold demand and supply constant in its import markets. Suppose that initially there is an increase in the demand for that nation's exports of both commodities and services. Perhaps there is an industry in another country that requires more of the export commodity as an input or the invisible items of the nation's trade (its financial services, its merchant fleet services, and the like) are more in demand. If we look at Figure 5.2(a), we see that an increase in export demand to D_1 will bid up export prices to $P_{e'}$. The terms of trade would become $P_{e'} \div P_i$, which *is* greater than $P_e \div P_i$, or greater than 100. Terms of trade have moved "in favor" of the exporting nation. In other words, it takes a smaller quantity of its exports or real resources to buy a particular amount of imports.

Put in another way, the nation's export earnings ($P_{e'} \times Q_{e'}$) have risen (are greater than $P_e \times Q_e$). The additional foreign exchange can be used to import not only consumer goods but also capital, technology, and the like. Or the domestic resource that would have been used to produce the exports necessary to finance a

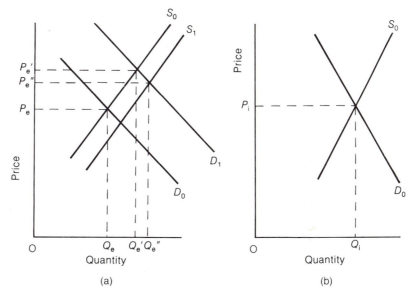

Figure 5.2. Terms of Trade Relationships for a Hypothetical Nation: (a) Exports, (b) Imports.

given level of imports can instead be employed to produce commodities and services for the domestic market.

Since export prices have risen, resource allocation may be changed in two ways. The opportunity cost of using resources (including one's own labor time) in the noncash economy is raised; as a result, resources are bid into the cash economy, where with more capital and a larger market size, productivity is greater. Also, since prices of exports have risen, resources within the cash economy are bid into export industries where, with higher capital-labor ratios and larger market sizes, greater specialization ensues and productivity increases. As productivity rises, output and income per capita rise; development is the result.

To this point, we have seen how a nation may benefit from increases in demand for its exports. Of course, the supply side of its export market may change as well. Let's suppose there is some cost-reducing technological innovation in a principal export industry and that this technology, in turn, results in an increase in the supply of exports. We see this effect in Figure 5.2(a). Export supply increases from S_0 to S_1. As a result, export prices fall from $P_{e'}$ (the price resulting from the demand increase). If supply continues to increase, it will tend back toward P_e if, at that earlier price, resources were being paid for according to their opportunity cost.

What do the price-quantity relationships in Figure 5.2(a) mean to our hypothetical country? They represent its foreign exchange earnings, its command over foreign goods and services. Thus as the combination of demand and supply changes causes $P \times Q$ to grow larger, the nation can import more, not only of consumer goods, but also of financial and physical capital, technological improvements, labor skills in short supply, or whatever is required to expand its leading industries.

Throughout this discussion, we have assumed supply and demand in Figure 5.2(b), our nation's import market, to be constant. This assumption was for convenience, not description. Ultimately, the hypothetical country enjoying the benefits of supply-demand changes in its export market will, and indeed *must*, import more. Almost all countries in an early phase of economic development require imports that are not readily supplied by domestic industry. It must import more because its imports give foreigners claim to its currency, claims that they must have in order to buy exports of the country represented in Figure 5.2.

QUESTIONS

1. How did an increase in exports affect prices and economic development in the United States from 1793 to 1815?

2. Why was it predictable that development would be low in 1790? Was growth likely to occur in the internal market? The external market? Why?

3. In what ways does growth in markets stimulate economic growth?

4. What caused the economy to change after 1792? How did expansion in exports, imports, and shipping affect economic development?

5. Describe the agricultural economy of 1815.

6. Was manufacturing important to the American economy between 1790 and 1815? What was the effect of the cotton gin on that manufacturing development?

7. Could the American economy have grown without the Napoleonic Wars? Explain your answer.

8. What were the major components of the Federalist economic program? On what basis was the opposition to the program founded?

SUGGESTED READINGS

1. Bruchey, Stuart. *The Roots of American Economic Growth, 1607–1861*. New York: Harper and Row, 1965.

2. Clark, V.S. *History of Manufactures in the United States*. 3 vols. New York: McGraw-Hill, 1929.

3. Goodrich, Carter. *The Government and the Economy: 1783–1861*. Indianapolis: Bobbs-Merill, 1967. Esp. Alexander Hamilton, "The Case for a National Bank," pp. 279–297.

4. Nettels, Curtis P. *The Emergence of a National Economy, 1775–1815*. New York: Harper and Row, 1962.

5. North, Douglass C. *The Economic Growth of the United States, 1790–1860*. New York: Norton, 1966. pp. 1–60.

6. North, Douglass C. "The United States Balance of Payments, 1790–1860." *Trends in the American Economy in the Nineteenth Century*. Studies in Income and Wealth of the National Bureau of Economic Research, Vol. 24. Princeton, N.J.: Princeton University Press, 1960.

Chapter 6

THE TRANSPORTATION REVOLUTION AND REGIONAL INTEGRATION

As we saw in earlier chapters, there were major barriers to the growth of the internal market system, first, of the colonies, and then, of the independent American states. Among the most important of such obstacles was the high cost of overland movement of goods and resources over long distances. In the colonial period, consequently, growth and development were tied to coastal trade and, more importantly, to overseas trade. In the early years of independence (1783–1815), this pattern continued.

Many remarkable changes occurred in the American economy between 1815 and 1860. As we shall see, scholars disagree about the cause-and-effect relationships involved in these changes. One disagreement is over the quantitative and qualitative effects of the changing transportation system on the rapid development pace of the nation, especially from 1840 to 1860. Those who have studied the era do agree, however, that a significant set of such effects took place. It is this subject, including those disagreements, that we want to examine in this chapter.

A SIMPLE MODEL OF TRANSPORTATION COSTS AND INTEGRATION

How are transportation costs related to market size, specialization and division of resources, and **economic integration**? Are product and resource markets tied together in such a way that resources are allocated to their most efficient uses? To answer these questions fully, we need first to repeat some assumptions about market behavior. We have assumed that people make market (supply-demand) decisions because they anticipate that those decisions are in their own self-interest, and therefore that market exchanges reflect anticipated mutual advantages to buyers and sellers. Also, suppliers seek their advantage through maximizing profit, the difference between total revenue and total cost (where cost includes an opportunity cost payment to capital and entrepreneurship). Transportation cost is, of course, a part of total cost—often an important part. The higher the transportation cost, the shorter the distance it is profitable to ship goods (or to move resources).

Figure 6.1 depicts the hypothetical effects of transportation costs on three cities: New York, Albany, and Chicago. The arrows connecting them represent the transportation systems existing between them at some particular time, and the dollar figures ($6, $2) above these arrows denote the cost per ton-mile of moving goods between the cities. Below the arrows are numbers (–$3, $1) that represent the unit profit of shipping between the cities. With the existing mode(s) of transportation (perhaps barges or flat-bottom riverboats), it is profitable to ship between New York and Albany ($1). As a consequence, both cities are within the same market system, and whatever economies of specialization exist in that market are available to both. Note, however, that between Albany and Chicago transportation costs ($6) are higher, and unit profit is negative (–$3). As a result, those two cities are not part of the same market system. Indeed, unless Chicago is profitably tied by existing transportation means to other cities (or market areas), it is outside the regional or national market system and is denied whatever economies of specialization are available within that system.

The general, if simple, principle that we are setting forth here is the following: The lower transportation costs are, the greater is the distance over which trade may profitably take place. As this distance increases, resources are bid into market production, market sizes increase, and economies of specialization increase.

COST EXTERNALITIES, PROFITS, AND RENTS

As a new transportation system is introduced or an old one extended or improved, the reduced transportation costs available to firms using that transportation system may become **cost externalities**. Such externalities are reduced average unit costs to firms that result from actions taken outside of those firms. Clearly, the building of a turnpike, canal, or railroad tends to have such effects.

As cost externalities accrue to firms and industries, the profit margin shifts; that is, previously marginal firms with lowered costs now become profitable firms. Of course, over long periods of time, all firms must cover the opportunity costs of using resources, must pay those resources at least what they can earn in alternative

Figure 6.1. Hypothetical Effects of Transportation Costs on Regional Integration.

$$\text{Chicago} \xleftrightarrow{\quad\$6\quad} \text{Albany} \xleftrightarrow{\quad\$2\quad} \text{New York}$$

$$(-\$3) \qquad\qquad (\$1)$$

Figure 6.2.   The Erie Canal, 1825. (Photo from the National Archives)

uses, in order to bid successfully for their use. One such cost is the opportunity cost of **entrepreneurship**: the organizing skill and abilities necessary to combine other resources into producing activities. This payment, the opportunity cost of entrepreneurship, is called **normal profit**.

Lower costs of production and distribution, along with the enlarged markets that are associated with improved transportation systems, tend, however, to produce **economic profits** or **economic rents**: payments to entrepreneurship in excess of what it can earn in alternative uses. Whether such economic profits or rents can be maintained depends primarily on whether the industries in which they exist exhibit free entry. At any rate, to know the total profitability or return on investment in different transportation systems, we must include not only the normal and economic profit of the transportation enterprises themselves but also the profits that accrue to other enterprises as a result of cost externalities.

EARLY TRANSPORTATION

There is no single input or factor whose provision is a sufficient condition for economic development to occur. Among those generally considered necessary, however, are (a) a transportation system that permits tying together of markets and (b) the efficiencies made possible by up-to-date technology and specialization in the uses of resources.

Early forms of overland transportation were rather primitive and high in cost. Throughout its colonial period and up to approximately 1815, the American cash economy was largely confined to the coastal areas, primarily because coastal shipping was much less expensive than land shipping. According to George Taylor (25), it was cheaper to ship grain 300 miles from Northhampton to Boston by water than to ship it 100 miles by road between those two points. Indeed, it cost twice as much to transport grain the first 36 miles by road as to move it 250 miles by deep-water shipment.

References to the transportation "revolution" are misleading if the word *revolution* is associated with "coup d'état." In this chapter, we are examining changes in transportation technology that evolved over at least half a century. The changes occurred in an evolutionary way but combined to produce revolutionary effects.

Roads and Turnpikes

Nothing illustrates better the evolutionary nature of changes in transportation technology than the evolving technology of road building. Throughout the colonial period and even up to the early 1790s, roads were poorly constructed and expensive to maintain. Describing the short trip from Baltimore to Washington, a traveler reported in 1795 that "the roads are so exceedingly bad that a carriage will sometimes sink so deeply as to defy the utmost exertion of the strongest horse to draw it forwards....Bridges built across are equally perilous, being formed of a few loose boards that totter while a carriage passes over them."

Road-building technology began to progress in the 1790s with the construction of turnpikes. Turnpikes, or toll roads, were usually built with rock foundations and were better graded than earlier roads. Because of these improvements, and also because permanent bridges were built along them, the turnpikes were usable throughout the year. These improvements not only made possible heavier horse-drawn loads and faster speeds but also assured year-round supplies of lower-cost commodities and services between the markets thus connected. Like other transportation facilities, the turnpikes had a very high ratio of fixed to variable costs; as the seasonal variations on the use of improved roads were reduced, the costs of their operation fell. Not surprisingly, as costs fell and demand increased with larger, more continuous markets, the most efficient turnpikes were profitable. The Lancaster-Philadelphia Turnpike, completed in 1794, was such a success that Pennsylvania alone chartered 86 turnpike companies during the next 30 years. Few roads were as well built as the Lancaster turnpike, however, and few connected such large commodity and consumer goods markets. One exception was the National Pike, or Cumberland Road, built by the federal government between 1811 and 1838 to connect Maryland and Illinois. East-west travel time and cost were greatly reduced.

A final set of improvements in antebellum road-building technology came along in the 1830s. These were the plank roads called "farmer's railroads" because they were widely used in areas not reached by rail. Constructed of heavy planks tied together by parallel stringers, they permitted horses to pull heavier loads at faster speeds than were possible on the macadamized turnpikes. Although cheaper

Figure 6.3. An Early Turnpike, c. 1830. (Photo from the National Archives)

to construct than first-rate turnpikes ($1,200 to $1,500 per mile versus $5,000 to $7,000 per mile), they were costly to maintain. As with other roads, building them was a capital-intensive activity.

Because of the high price of capital and its high opportunity costs (in terms of returns in agriculture and manufacturing), no true "national system" of roads had been built either by private enterprise or by government even as late as the 1850s. Indeed, further major improvements in American roads were to wait until the twentieth century, when automobiles and trucks created demand and the relative price of capital declined and increased the profitable supply.

A summary point that deserves emphasis is that as early as 1820 the United States had a system of relatively good roads that connected its major cities for north-south travel. That system, together with some east-west roads, continued to evolve in the succeeding three decades but did not lead to significant regional integration or to the building of a national system of integrated internal markets. Again, the main reason quite simply was the relatively high unit cost of shipping goods over those roads with horse-drawn vehicles compared with the unit costs of deep-water (coastal and foreign) shipment.

Steamboats

Early in the nineteenth century, two new transportation systems began to evolve. Both were to have a significant, although unequal, impact on lowering internal transportation costs and integrating the market systems of the United States.

The first commercial application of the steam engine to transportation occurred in 1807 when Robert Fulton's steamboat went from New York to Albany. As Eric Haites and James Mak (8, 10) have shown, steamboat traffic grew very rapidly, particularly on western rivers such as the Ohio and Mississippi. This growth is apparent from Table 6.1. As you can see, the growth of steamboating continued up to the time of the Civil War. Although it declined relative to the railroads in the 1850s, steamboating remained a thriving, growing industry throughout the antebellum period.

What were the great cost advantages of the steamboats? Speed was one: the travel time from New York to Albany was cut from about three days to about eight hours. As a result, firms could ship over long distances and function with less working capital. In addition, steamboats could navigate upstream as well as downstream; upstream travel was uneconomical for the old flatboats.

Mak and Walton have shown that productivity grew rapidly in the steamboat industry. Although most of the productivity increase occurred before 1850, it averaged almost 5 percent a year between 1815 and 1850. Mak and Walton (14) believe that this productivity increase was greater than that of any other form of transportation during any 35-year period of the nineteenth century. Rapid productivity growth, together with substantial competitiveness in the steamboat industry, caused steamboat freight rates to fall greatly. Haites and Mak show, for instance, that in the important trans-Mississippi traffic between Louisville and New Orleans, the per ton rate fell from $20 between 1810 and 1819 to $6 in 1849.

Productivity growth in steamboating was due primarily to improvements in steamboat construction and to greater year-round utilization of the boats. Competitiveness was enhanced through constitutional interpretation. In 1824, in *Gibbons v. Ogden*, the Supreme Court ruled that states could not grant monopoly rights to navigation of their waterways. Interstate commerce, including that by steamboats, became easier to enter now that it fell under the exclusive jurisdiction of the federal government. As we shall see in subsequent chapters, federal control over interstate

Table 6.1.   Tonnage of Steamboats on the Western Rivers of the United States, 1814–1860.

YEARS	NET NEW CONSTRUCTION [a]	AVERAGE TOTAL TONNAGE IN OPERATION
1814–1816	629	1,490
1824–1826	1,599	13,429
1834–1836	6,845	49,504
1844–1846	8,809	97,603
1854–1856	6,296	176,617
1858–1860	-1,516	194,738

[a]Per year, in tons: net represents new construction less depreciation.

SOURCE: Eric Haites and James Mak, "The Decline of Steamboating on the Antebellum Western Rivers: New Evidence and an Alternative Hypothesis," *Explorations in Economic History* (Fall 1973).

commerce has led to reduced competitiveness in some instances; in steamboating, however, there is no doubt that it enhanced competitiveness. Lower rates, greater traffic, and increasing regional integration were the results. It is startling to remember that in 1803 Thomas Jefferson said it would be a thousand years before the area east of the Mississippi could be fully settled. A combination of river steamboats, barge canal traffic, and trans-Appalachian railroad construction reduced that period dramatically, as we shall see.

Canal Building

Only five years after Fulton's first steamboat trip, a new mode of shipping goods over long distances began evolving. Canals, man-made waterways frequently connecting natural bodies of water and employing a series of locks to adjust for differences in level, became popular and were constructed in three waves between 1812 and 1860. Unlike turnpikes and steamboats, which were built with large private investments, the canals were heavily subsidized by state and local governments and, to a much smaller extent, the federal government. Carter Goodrich (5, 6, 7) has estimated that government undertook about 70 percent of total canal expenditures between 1815 and 1860. Private investment was limited, primarily because canals were relatively expensive projects that proposed to push into sparsely settled areas. (The Erie Canal alone represented an investment of more than $10 million.)

Another reason for public participation in canal building was that potential benefits would be reaped by others besides the canal builders. In other words, cost externalities were significant. As an example, the opening of the very successful Erie Canal reduced freight rates from 20 cents to 2 cents per ton-mile. The 134-mile Erie Canal connected Albany on the Hudson River with Buffalo on the Great Lakes. Because of the waterway that now extended from New York to Cleveland and Toledo, shipping costs were reduced dramatically for firms from the eastern seaboard to the Old Northwest.

In terms of our original model, the most successful canals generated economic profits or rents, revenues in excess of costs, through reducing costs and creating cost externalities. Thus, even if a canal was not privately profitable (and, according to Roger Ransom (20, 21, 22), many were not), it might well have been socially beneficial and properly the object of public subsidy.

Ransom, one of the most prolific writers on canals, has estimated the externalities associated with the canal system through estimating economic rents. A wheat farmer in eastern Ohio, for example, earns a rent (economic profit) of $2 a ton because he can ship over the Erie Canal to eastern markets. A farmer farther away—in Indiana, for example—has higher costs and presumably will not transport his wheat to market unless he can cover all his costs. The farmer will not use the canal if the resulting costs cannot be covered out of revenue. If $2 per ton is the maximum rent earned in this activity, then no farmer who cannot at least cover costs will ship his goods over the canal. All who can and who can earn some of the

$2-per-ton rent will engage in market exchange; others, who cannot, will use their resources some other way, including not shipping to market at all but engaging in subsistence agriculture instead.

Ransom's estimates, based on the Ohio and Erie Canal and others, indicate that of the $102 million expended on canals up to 1860, only $31 million was invested successfully in terms of the alternative uses of those resources. Indeed, he believes that other forms of capital investment might have been wiser and that "The role of the canals in contributing toward the economic growth of the United States is far from obvious." Competition from the railroads was a chief cause of declining canal profits during the 1840s and 1850s. According to Ransom, the rate of return on investment in the very successful Ohio and Erie Canal fell from 15.4 percent per annum in 1851 to 2.7 percent between 1854 and 1856. Because of a high ratio of total fixed costs to total variable costs, the canals faced sharply higher average fixed and average total costs as they produced for smaller markets.

A debate continues over whether the canal system encouraged a more specialized use of resources by encouraging interregional trade. Albert Niemi (17) concludes that the canals stimulated regional diversification—production of a wide range of goods—rather than specialization or production of a smaller range of goods. Ransom draws a contrary conclusion, arguing that in both East and West specialization took the form of developing industries specialized to the comparative-advantage uses of resources. The growth of manufacturing along and near canals indicates to Ransom that the agricultural goods moving over the canals were being transformed into semimanufactured and manufactured goods according to comparative advantage. On balance, we believe that the comparative-advantage specialization argument is the more reasonable one.

In summary, the canals appear to have made a significant but mixed contribution to our economic development and to the integration of this country's economic regions. Some, such as the Erie and Ohio, were very successful. Others, such as the Philadelphia and Pittsburgh, were much less successful. What is clear is that by the 1850s the canal era was ending, although a few canals continued to operate profitably. It was the building of railroads in the 1840s and 1850s that virtually brought the canal era to a close.

Railroads

Perhaps no change in transportation technology has occasioned so much research, debate, or disagreement as the railroads. Let us begin with some of the undisputed facts about the railroads before turning to more contentious issues.

Rail transportation, of course, depended on another application of the steam engine. In 1830, the Baltimore and Ohio opened for business. As the data in Table 6.2 indicate, the railway system grew rapidly prior to 1860.

During the 1840s and 1850s, the system was extended across the Appalachian Mountains and then into the present-day Midwest. By 1860, the rails had pushed

Table 6.2. Railway Mileage, 1830–1860.

YEARS	NET ADDITIONS OF TRACK IN MILES	TOTAL MILES OF TRACK AT END OF PERIOD
1830–1839	2,302	2,302
1840–1849	5,063	7,365
1850–1859	21,424	28,789

SOURCE: U.S. Bureau of the Census, *Historical Statistics, Colonial Times to 1957* (Washington, D.C.: U.S. Government Printing Office, 1960).

west to St. Joseph, Missouri, and south to New Orleans (Figure 6.4). Throughout the period, railroad technology improved. Replacing iron-capped wooden rails, the iron rails of the 1840s permitted faster, cheaper movement. Further improvements in boiler locomotive and freight car construction, together with a movement toward

Figure 6.4. Railroads in 1860.

SOURCE: From *Atlas of World History & U.S. Economic History.* © Copyright 1975 and 1970 by Rand McNally & Company, R. L. 88-S-59.

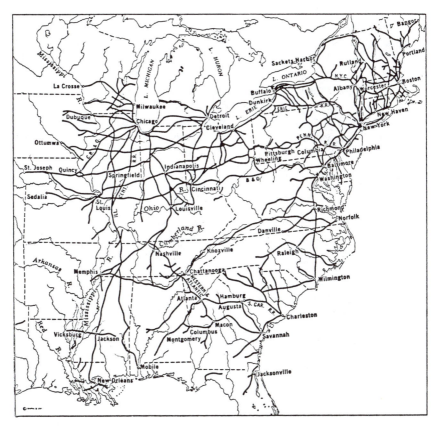

uniform-gauge rails, also lowered transportation costs. We should remember, however, that rail transportation was not cheap. A hundred-mile railway trip cost a month's wages for a typical American in the 1830s, and two to three weeks' wages in the 1850s. Nonetheless, over the period from 1815 to 1860, railways were becoming increasingly price competitive with canals and turnpikes, as can be seen in Table 6.3.

Although railway freight rates came down in the 1850s, even in 1860 canal shipment ($.99 on the Erie Canal) was less expensive per mile than rail shipment ($1.84 on the Erie Railroad). The data also illustrate the great disparity between either canal or rail shipment and shipping goods over the turnpikes ($15.00, even in 1860). Considering the cost disadvantage of railroads in shipping, why did their demand grow so rapidly? The railroads quickly became the major transportation source for moving goods and people because speed and year-round operation meant lowered annual costs to businesses and individuals in spite of the *apparently* high (unit) costs. Robert Fogel (3) points out the major reason. Although the costs of rail transport were reflected in direct payments to railway carriers, that was not true in the case of water carriers. The important costs not covered in the latter industry were cargo losses in transit, transhipment costs, wagon haulage costs from water points to secondary markets not on waterways, capital costs not reflected in water rates, costs caused by the time lost in using a (relatively) slow means of transportation, and the costs of not being able to use the waterways for five months out the year. When these costs are added in, Fogel concludes that the costs of interregional shipments by rail were lower than those by water shipment. In other words, there was a "social savings" attached to the railroads. In addition, productivity grew very rapidly in railroads. Albert Fishlow (1) has shown that productivity throughout the dynamic phase of the railroads (1839–1910) grew almost three times as rapidly as productivity for the economy as a whole. In turn, this growth permitted freight and passenger fares to fall.

Table 6.3.   Average Freight Rate, Different Transportation Forms, 1816, 1853, 1860.

TRANSPORT FORM	1816 (DOLLARS)[a]	1853 (DOLLARS)[a]	1860 (DOLLARS)[a]
Turnpikes	30.00	15.00	15.00
Missouri-Ohio River, upstream	5.80	—	0.37
ErieCanal	—	1.10	0.99
Pennsylvania, Main Line Canal	—	2.40	—
New York Central Railroad	—	3.40	2.06
Pennsylvania Railroad	—	3.50	1.96
Erie Railroad	—	2.40	1.84
Western Lakes, short voyage	—	0.10	—

[a]Dollars or cents per ton-mile.

SOURCE: George Rogers Taylor, *The Transportation Revolution, 1815–1860* (New York: Holt, Rinehart and Winston, 1966).

RAILROADS AND AMERICAN ECONOMIC DEVELOPMENT

Now let us turn to the most controversial arguments surrounding the railroads. What did they contribute to the economic development of the United States, and were they, in fact, indispensable to its pace of development?

Almost no student of American history has sought to dismiss the railroads or to deny their importance. In terms of what may be called the "modern" position on the railroads, there is general agreement that they played a very important role in our history. Leland Jenks (13) strongly argued that position, within the view that economic development occurs fundamentally as the result of **innovation,** the introduction of new products and processes into an economy. Such innovation is the work of entrepreneur-innovators. Jenks says the railroads must be viewed in three phases: as ideas, as construction enterprises, and finally, as sellers of transportation services. He argues, from the economic development framework of Joseph Schumpeter, that productivity-increasing innovations cause economic development. Such innovations occur irregularly or in swarms, and the railroads are a classic example, according to Jenks. As an idea, railroads created economic activity through land speculation, urban relocation, and other activities along their right-of-ways. As construction enterprises, railroads also created direct demand for factors of production, labor, land, and capital. Finally, railroads reduced shipping costs, thereby creating external economies and encouraging the growth of other industries.

Since 1960, the case has been made that railroads were the indispensable leading sector in this country's economic development. Walt Rostow (23) advanced the view that the railroads moved the United States from its "preconditions for growth" into its "takeoff" stage of development. Since the **takeoff** in Rostow's stage theory of development is that great "watershed" or turning point in which development becomes the normal condition for a society, and since Rostow says the railroads between 1843 and 1860 were responsible in the "most direct possible way" for the takeoff, his argument for the indispensability of railroads seems clear.

Important studies of the railroads were made in the 1960s by Albert Fishlow (1) and Robert Fogel (3). As part of his study, Fogel undertook an empirical test of Rostow's takeoff hypothesis. To estimate the effects of the railroads on the "decisive structural change" that Rostow believes took place in the United States between 1840 and 1860, Fogel examined data on changes in the sectoral composition of output. To estimate the "most direct possible" effects of railroad construction during that period, he calculated the direct demand of the railroads for the output of (supposed) major supplying industries, such as iron, coal, and transportation equipment. Fogel concluded that the evidence regarding decisive structural change in the 1840s and 1850s was inconclusive. He believes that if pre-1840 data were available, they would show that there was no abrupt increase in the rate of change in sectoral output after 1840. With respect to the direct demand effects, Fogel concludes that "In the absence of the railroads, demand for manufactured commodities would still have resulted in a 230 percent rise in the output of manufacturing over the years from 1840 to 1859—as opposed to an increase of 240 percent with the railroads." Fogel thus rejects the Rostow argument that ties the American industrial revolution to a 20-year period of railroad building, or to any single industry in any period. Perhaps Fogel has contributed the "bottom line" to the takeoff debate and its bearing on the American industrial revolution in saying, "One should not, however, require a revolution to have the swiftness of a coup d'etat....One need not arbitrarily abstract 18 years out of a continuum to uphold the use of a venerable term."

Is it useful and valid to argue that industrialization requires a leading sector, as Rostow believes and Fogel doubts? If so, were the railroads the leading sector in the American case? The answers remain in doubt. What has become generally apparent is that the impact of the railroads on U.S. economic development must be studied over a time period longer than two decades. Fogel and others have done much work in that direction. In Chapter 12, we shall look at their efforts to measure long-term effects, including those in the post–Civil War era.

INTERNAL IMPROVEMENTS: THE ROLE OF GOVERNMENT

High inland transportation costs, as we have seen, slowed the development of the interior of the United States. Of equal importance was the *perception* that such costs were a serious obstacle to pushing westward and developing the vast areas opened by the Louisiana Purchase of 1803 and subsequent territorial acquisitions.

In view of the widespread perception that internal improvements, especially in transportation, were important for the nation's growth, it is not surprising that a push was made early in the country's history to fully involve the federal government in funding such a system of improvements. In 1807, the U.S. Senate ordered Secretary of the Treasury Albert Gallatin to prepare a plan for "the opening of roads and making [of] canals" to be limited only by the power of Congress. Gallatin's plan, delivered in 1808, called for a system of canals, roads, turnpikes, and communications improvements that would stretch from Massachusetts to Georgia and also inland to create east-west links between the East Coast and the Great Lakes. The plan's cost was estimated at $20 million over a ten-year period. Because these vast areas were thinly populated, Gallatin (probably correctly) thought it would be unprofitable for private entrepreneurs to undertake such a system of improvements. In the secretary's view, however, the external economics of internal improvements to society warranted a major outlay by the federal government.

Almost immediately the plan encountered serious constitutional objections, and consequently, it was never completed by the federal government. Its death knell was sounded in 1830 when Andrew Jackson vetoed a bill to fund the Maysville Road. As Carter Goodrich (5, 6, 7) has shown, it was not so much ideology as sectional rivalry that killed the plan. Failure to agree on which areas would receive the improvements may have been a more significant factor in the defeat of federal funding than arguments about strict construction of the Constitution.

This is not to minimize the role of government in internal improvements during the antebellum period. Goodrich (6) has shown, for example, that most of the Gallatin plan was completed, but with the help of state and local governments. While most of the costs of turnpikes were covered by private investments, other transportation systems were heavily subsidized by government. Harvey Segal (24) has estimated that from 1815 to 1844 the government funded nearly 73 percent of all outlays on canals, and that of the $188 million invested in canals in the entire period 1815–1860, nearly as high a percentage came from government funding.

Government subsidization of railroads, including the land grant program, has been well documented. Contrary to the once-popular view that railway entrepreneurs were men of foresight who undertook high-risk ventures because they had faith in future development, Albert Fishlow (1, 2) has shown that most of the railroads were built to connect existing population centers and markets. Fishlow has also demonstrated that government subsidization of road building varied inversely with profitability; that is, larger government subsidies were required to induce the building of roads with lower profit expectations.

COMMUNICATIONS IMPROVEMENTS

In our model, we dealt with the result of improved transportation in lowering **transactions costs**, expanding the market, creating external economies, and promoting development. In the pre–Civil War era, parallel improvements in an evolving technology of communication were reducing **information costs**, the costs to buyers and sellers of obtaining the price and technical information necessary to make rational choices. Clearly, lowering the average cost of securing the price and other information needed to make effective market decisions increases the supply of goods and thereby the size of markets. Thus lowering information costs also leads to market integration.

Perhaps the most important advance in communications technology in the United States prior to 1860 was the telegraph. Samuel F. B. Morse obtained a grant from Congress in 1843 to establish a line between Baltimore and Washington. The practicality of the telegraph was so obvious by 1860 that 50,000 miles of telegraph lines connected every major city in the country. By 1861, even the West Coast and San Francisco were included. The swiftness and reliability of this communication system greatly reduced the cost of decision making, especially by providing information about market conditions in different parts of the country. Thus the tandem improvement of information flows and reduction of transportation time and cost reinforced each other in tying together or integrating markets.

Other improvements in communication at least deserve mention. The U.S. postal system was greatly expanded, its services improved, and the cost of obtaining information through it reduced over the period from 1816 to 1860. Indeed, between 1791 and 1859, the number of post offices increased from 89 to 27,977, and service miles went from about 800,000 to about 86 million. In 1816, it cost 50 cents to send a two-sheet letter 400 miles. In 1850, a flat rate of 3 cents for all letters was introduced. The cost externalities involved in this communication alone (apart from other social benefits) probably justified large public subsidies.

Finally, in the pre–Civil War era, there was a huge increase in newspaper circulation and readership after the development of the cylinder press in 1846 permitted the mass production of inexpensive newspapers. By 1860, there were 10 million copies of daily, weekly, biweekly, and monthly newspapers in circulation in a nation with a population of about 31.5 million.

SUMMING UP

The period from 1800 to 1860 saw dramatic, although fairly continual, changes and improvements in transportation and communications technology. No single change in that technology, not even the railroad, seems significant enough to explain the rapid pace of development in the United States over that period. Taken together, however, these changes made available very great reductions in transactions and information costs for internal trade and created very large external cost economies to firms. Thus they enhanced the integration of the nation's domestic market system and replaced foreign trade as the major impetus for economic development.

QUESTIONS

1. In general, why were transportation-related transactions costs and communications-related information costs such significant barriers to developing an integrated internal market system in the United States in 1800?
2. How are reductions in transportation costs related to increasing market sizes and market integration?
3. Trace the evolution of road and turnpike technology over the period from 1800 to 1860. Explain why, even at the end of that period, roads and turnpikes did not integrate the regional markets of the United States.
4. What were the major contributions of the steamboats to integrating internal markets and commerce in the United States?
5. What does *Gibbons v. Ogden* illustrate about the relation between the legal structure and constraints on economic development?
6. Why was the canal-building era one of widely mixed successes and failures? In what sense and in what ways did the canals generate cost externalities?
7. Do you think that using the concept of economic rent is an appropriate way to assess the externalities of a transportation system? Why?

8. Do you think the canals encouraged regional specialization or diversification? Why?

9. Trace the evolution of railway technology over the period from 1830 to 1860. What were the effects of these changes on transportation costs in the United States?

10. What is Rostow's argument about the relation between railway building and the American takeoff? What is Fogel's conclusion about the validity of the Rostow argument?

11. What were the major controversies surrounding the role of government in the antebellum period in creating "a system of internal improvements"?

12. What were major communications improvements between 1800 and 1860? What were their effects on information costs and economic integration?

SUGGESTED READINGS

1. Fishlow, Albert. *American Railroads and the Transformation of the Antebellum Economy.* Cambridge, Mass.: Harvard University Press, 1965.

2. Fishlow, Albert. "Internal Transportation," In *American Economic Growth*, ed. Davis, Easterlin, Parker et al., Chap. 13. New York: Harper and Row, 1972.

3. Fogel, Robert W. "Railroads and the 'Take-off' Thesis: The American Case." In *Railroads and American Economic Growth: Essays in Econometric History.* Baltimore: Johns Hopkins University Press, 1964.

4. Fogel, Robert W. "Railroads and American Economic Growth." In *The Reinterpretation of American Economic History,* ed. Robert W. Fogel and Stanley L. Engerman. New York: Harper and Row, 1971.

5. Goodrich, Carter. *Government and the Economy, 1783–1861.* Indianapolis: Bobbs-Merrill, 1967.

6. Goodrich, Carter. *Government Promotion of American Canals and Railroads, 1800–1890.* New York: Columbia University Press, 1960.

7. Goodrich, Carter, Jerome Crammer, Julius Rubin, and Harvey Segal, eds. *Canals and American Economic Development.* New York: Columbia University Press, 1961.

8. Haites, Erik F., and James Mak. "The Decline of Steamboating on the Antebellum Western Rivers: Some New Evidence and an Alternative Hypothesis." *Explorations in Economic History,* 11 (Fall 1973).

9. Haites, Erik F., and James Mak. "Economies of Scale in Western River Steamboating." *Journal of Economic History,* 36 (September 1976).

10. Haites, Erik F., and James Mak. "Ohio and Mississippi River Transportation, 1800–1860." *Explorations in Economic History,* 12 (Winter 1970–1971).

11. Haites, Erik F., and James Mak. *Western River Transportation: The Era of Early Internal Improvement, 1810–1860.* Baltimore and London: Johns Hopkins Press, 1976.

12. Hunter, Louis C. *Steamboats on the Western Rivers.* Cambridge, Mass.: Harvard University Press, 1949.

13. Jenks, Leland. "Railroads as an Economic Force in American Development." *Journal of Economic History,* 4 (March 1944).

14. Mak, James, and Gary Walton. "Steamboats and the Great Productivity Surge in River Transportation." *Journal of Economic History,* 32 (September 1972).

15. McClelland, Peter. "Railroads, American Growth and the New Economic History: A Critique." *Journal of Economic History, 28* (March 1968).

16. Nerlove, Marc. "Railroads and American Economic Growth." *Journal of Economic History, 26* (March 1966).

17. Niemi, Albert W., Jr. "A Further Look at Interregional Canals and Economic Specialization, 1820–1840." *Explorations in Economic History, 7* (Summer 1970).

18. North, Douglass C. *The Economic Growth of the United States, 1790–1860.* New York: Norton, 1966. Chap. 9.

19. Parker, William N. "From Northwest to Midwest: Social Bases of a Regional History." In *Essays in Nineteenth-Century Economic History,* ed. D. C. Klingaman and R. K. Vedder. Athens: Ohio University Press, 1975.

20. Ransom, Roger. "Canals and Development: A Discussion of the Issues." *American Economic Review, 54* (May 1964).

21. Ransom, Roger. "Public Canal Investment and the Opening of the Old Northwest." In *Essays in Nineteenth-Century Economic History,* ed. D. C. Klingaman and R. K. Vedder. Athens: Ohio University Press, 1975.

22. Ransom, Roger. "Social Returns from Public Transport Investment: A Case Study of the Ohio Canal." *Journal of Political Economy, 78* (September–October 1970).

23. Rostow, Walt. W. *The Stages of Economic Growth.* 2d ed. Cambridge: Cambridge University Press, 1971.

24. Segal, Harvey. "Cycles of Canal Construction." In *Canals and American Economic Development,* ed. Carter Goodrich. New York: Columbia University Press, 1961.

25. Taylor, George Rogers. *The Transportation Revolution, 1815–1860.* New York: Holt, Rinehart and Winston, 1966.

Chapter 7

INDUSTRY, FINANCE, AND BUSINESS FLUCTUATIONS, 1815–1860

In Chapter 6 we examined the various effects of transportation innovations from 1815 to 1860. Collectively, these effects have been called the *transportation revolution*. On the one hand, they generated a process of economic integration of the various regions of the United States, and on the other hand, they created the additional market demand needed to encourage regional specialization.

In this chapter, we are going to consider three main areas. First, we will look at the establishment and spread of manufacturing industries as they responded to and reinforced growing markets. Then we will examine the role and evolution of the financial and banking system as it responded to industrial, commercial, and agricultural growth. Finally, we will detail the economic stability and instability that accompanied this growth.

MANUFACTURING INDUSTRY

Evidences of industrial formation in the United States go back at least to the 1790s and the early factories of men such as Samuel Slater and Moses Brown. Textile factories such as that of Francis C. Lowell came somewhat later. In the 45 years from 1815 to 1860, however, the United States experienced a process of sustained industrialization. While some have argued that industrialization is the cause of economic development, that view seems excessive and unsupported by the experience of the United States. As we shall see, a set of factors influenced the rapid economic development of America before the Civil War, and while industrialization was an important member of that set, it was far from influential enough to explain the whole development process.

Let us begin by asking the following question: What were the basic characteristics of the industrial processes that were either begun or expanded in the period from 1815 to 1860? To answer that question we shall look at the creation of the factory system and at its corollary, the specialization of labor and capital, particularly the assembly line and the use of interchangeable parts. In doing so, we shall concentrate on certain industries whose growth and structural change were prominent in the antebellum period, particularly in the phase of rapid development from 1840 to 1860.

The factory system involved a significant change from the home manufacturing system of a much more self-sufficient early America. The hand-driven machines used in the homes were usually simple. The factory system concentrated relatively large, specialized, and expensive power-driven machines in central locations to which a substantial number of laborers were brought. It is worth noting that the factory's specialized functions actually required fewer skills on the part of the laborers and therefore increased the supply of industrial labor by bringing substantial numbers of noncraftsmen into the labor force. In most instances, these new members of the labor force had previously worked at self-sufficient, subsistence-oriented economic activities. In the case of girls and young women, many were working for cash income for the first time. This is an early example of how technological and organizational change may increase labor force participation. Furthermore, the factory system, by increasing the supply of labor, kept wages down, thereby reducing production costs and encouraging investment and industrial growth. Of course, wages for particular types of labor differed widely at any given time, depending on the locational scarcity of the labor. As Table 7.1 shows, the variation could be very great. According to the data, the weekly wage for a given occupation in 1853 was commonly three times as great in San Francisco, where the labor supply was relatively scarce, as in New York, where the labor supply was relatively less scarce. This explanation for *relative* wage differences is valid even if labor was generally scarce in the United States and had been made less scarce in manufacturing by the expansion of the factory system.

The second factor in the growth of manufacturing and the factory system during the period under view was the standardization of manufacturing com-

Table 7.1. Weekly Wages in San Francisco and New York, 1853.

OCCUPATION	SAN FRANCISCO	NEW YORK
Carpenters	$42	$15
Coopers	24–36	12
Bricklayers	48–60	15
Shipwrights	42	18
Shoemakers	24	16
House painters	30	15

Source: Data from John R. Commons, *History of Labor in the United States*, Vol. 1 (New York: Macmillan, 1918), pp. 610–611.

ponents, which permitted the use of interchangeable parts and very great reductions in the cost of producing goods ranging from firearms to clocks. The implementation of interchangeable parts is popularly ascribed to Eli Whitney, although Robert Woodbury (45) has seriously questioned whether so much of the "American System of manufacturing" can be traced to any individual. According to Woodbury, this system was the "culmination of a number of economic, social and technical forces brought to bear on manufacturing by several men of genius, of whom Whitney can only be said to have been *perhaps* one."

Whatever group of individuals may have been responsible is not important here because we are not advancing a "great man" theory of history. Suffice it to say that a collection of entrepreneur-innovators in the period took advantage of the various opportunities for profitable implementation of new products and processes made possible by a variety of favorable growth factors. Continuous production processes, standardized products with interchangeable components, and the formation of factories—all were parts of the American System. An amusing illustration of just how American this system was is contained in the story of a New England clockmaker who, in 1840, devised a method to produce one-day brass clocks with interchangeable parts for less than fifty cents. This was a dramatic reduction in cost from the largely handmade clocks of the time. When the enterprising manufacturer sent a shipment to England and valued them at 50 cents apiece, English custom officials, convinced the clocks were undervalued, exercised their right to buy them for the declared value. The American clockmaker then sent a second, larger batch, which the English also bought up. Presumably delighted with such a growing, low-selling-cost market, the American sent a third, even larger shipment. Finally convinced of the genuineness of the valuation, the British let the third shipment of clocks into the country.

The American System depended on continuous production, interchangeable parts, factories, and non–labor-intensive production processes. Some early attempts at its establishment were unsuccessful; for example, Slater's original textile mill in the 1790s, which was largely based on labor-intensive English counterparts. Even in textiles, which were perhaps America's earliest "growth sector," the first clearly successful factory was not founded until 1814. Ironically, both Slater and Francis C. Lowell, the founder of the 1814 textile factory, got their ideas from copying British machines and organizational practices. By the 1840s, however, it was evident even to the British that continuous production and interchangeable parts had produced a truly American version of the factory system originated in England.

This triumph of the American System was not achieved without opposition. The main opponents were skilled craftsmen, who saw their skills made increasingly superfluous by machine technology, division of labor, and interchangeable parts. They responded with political agitation aimed at restricting immigration and the formation of early labor organizations. Resistance to the new techniques was especially strong among the craftsmen in federal armories. A study of the Harper's Ferry armory has shown that craftsmen there were successful in keeping these techniques out until the Civil War.

The Growth of the Manufacturing Sector

The American System clearly reflected a substantial displacement of home manufactures. The comparative advantage of factories was so great, and the opportunity cost of home manufacture so high, that labor and other resources were bid into the manufacturing sector. There are some significant data problems with determining just how rapidly this happened before 1840. Nonetheless, the very important studies of Robert Martin (see Figure 7.1) provide some insights for the entire period from 1800 to 1860.

While the data in Figure 7.1 do not directly show the decline of home manufactures, we may infer much from them about that subject. Since manufacturing's share of commodity output approximately doubled between 1820 and 1860, that sector's commodity output rose much more rapidly than commodity output in general. Accomplishing this rise required bidding resources into the sector and away from other activities. The available evidence suggests that while some of these resources attracted into manufacturing came from non–market-oriented uses, many of them came from home manufactures.

Figure 7.1 directly shows the percent of the total that manufacturing had in workers, income (at current prices), and real commodity output between 1800 and 1860. Bear in mind that the data before 1840 are fragmentary. Actually, only the 1850 and 1860 censuses provided data comparable to later periods. According to Martin, the share of income originating in manufacturing rose from about 5 percent in 1800 to about 7 1/2 percent in 1820. Also, as the figure indicates, about 7 1/2 per-

Figure 7.1. Rising Importance of Manufacturing. *Note:* Commodity output is treated here as half of GNP.

Source: R. F. Martin, *National Income in the United States, 1799–1938* (National Industrial Conference Board, 1939); and R. E. Gallman, "Commodity Output, 1839–1899," *Trends in the American Economy in the Nineteenth Century,* Conference on Research in Income and Wealth (Princeton, N.J.: Princeton University Press, 1960).

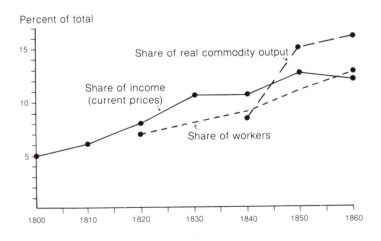

cent of workers were in manufacturing in 1820. By 1860, manufacturing's share of workers had risen to 12 percent and its share of income to slightly less than that.

The problem with respect to interpreting the dramatic post-1840 increase in the share of real commodity output attributable to manufacturing is the paucity of pre-1840 data. If the available data are accepted, that share rose from about 8 percent in 1840 to about 16 percent in 1860. While that is a dramatic increase, the percentage increase in manufacturing's share of income is about the same. In terms of both income and real commodity output, though, manufacturing was increasing its size relative to the rest of the economy.

Some Major Industries

As we have already noted, there is widespread agreement that the textile industry, especially cotton textiles, was the first American manufacturing growth industry to emerge in the nineteenth century. Like many industries, it suffered from some false starts and difficult problems of adaptation. Slater's early effort in the 1790s was not very successful, even though it replaced the spinning jenny with more productive machines, especially Arkwright's water frame and Crompton's mule. Slater had sought to transplant English technology, with its labor-intensive methods, to a labor-scarce America. The cost disadvantage of the American mills served as an incentive to devise an "American technology" suited to the new nation's resource endowments. This incentive became especially strong during the second war with Great Britain.

The Boston Manufacturing Company, established in 1813 by Lowell, was a major response to this cost incentive. Lowell's mill was notable not only for its capitalization ($300,000), which was very large for that day, but also for its integration of production processes, its hiring of young girls rather than children as operators, and for the famous power loom created by Lowell's chief mechanic, Paul Moody. Other American textile producers rapidly adopted the *Waltham Plan*, a system of integrating spinning and weaving power machinery within the same plant.

The most serious problem faced by Lowell and the other cotton manufacturers was finding a supply of labor. Skilled craftsmen, including those being replaced by the new textile machinery, resented working in a factory, and the great wave of Irish immigration had not yet begun. Lowell went to the farmers outside of Boston and convinced many to allow their daughters to work in his factory where they would be housed in dormitories under the strict supervision of house mothers. Their earnings were often used to pay off a mortgage for a father or to send a brother to school or to build up a dowry. As Alexander Field (9) has shown, this system was short-lived, though it contributed an interesting chapter to American labor history.

After the end of the second war with Great Britain, American textile manufacturers found it difficult to compete with the reintroduced British textiles. In reaction, they adopted the cost-cutting Waltham Plan. Also, they pressed Congress for tariff protection. As a result, the Tariff Act of 1816 was passed. Although the effects of this protective tariff were concentrated between 1816 and 1824, the tariff none-theless helped to create a home market for American textiles.

Under these various stimuli, the cotton textile industry grew very rapidly. Research by Robert Zevin (46) has shown just how fast that growth was, as well as its various causes.

The early growth of the textile industry was reflected in a 60-fold increase in value added between 1805 and 1815. Those were the years of the Napoleonic Wars and of the embargo whose influences we have already examined. After the end of the war in 1815, the nation was flooded with British textiles and value added fell from $124,000 in 1815 to $44,000 in 1816. According to Zevin, imports of cloth remained fairly steady after 1826, while domestic production soared.

The relative importance of the cotton goods industry continued to grow through much of the antebellum period. By 1860, it had become the largest manufacturing industry in the United States in terms of value added and the second largest in terms of employment. Those relationships may be seen in Table 7.2.

FACTOR PROPORTIONS AND THE AMERICAN SYSTEM

Many students of nineteenth-century history have sought to explain the peculiar technological choices of American industry. Was the American System based on the abundance of land and scarcity of labor, as English observers of the time believed? Did American employers have to pay relatively high wages to cover the opportunity costs of laborers for whom low-cost (costs of provisions until a first crop) land was a readily available alternative to factory labor? These and related questions have been addressed at length.

Table 7.2.   Ten Leading Manufacturing Industries, 1860.

INDUSTRY	VALUE ADDED (MILLIONS)	EMPLOYEES (THOUSANDS)
1. Cotton goods	$ 54.7	115.0
2. Lumber	53.6	75.6
3. Boots and shoes	49.2	123.0
4. Flour and meal	40.1	27.7
5. Men's clothing	36.7	114.8
6. Iron products	35.7	49.0
7. Machinery	32.6	41.2
8. Woolen goods	25.0	40.6
9. Carriages, wagons, carts	23.7	37.1
10. Leather	22.8	22.7
11. All manufacturing	815.0	1474.0

SOURCE: *Eighth Census of the United States*, Vol. 3 (Washington, D.C.: U.S. Government Printing Office, 1861).

Edwin Rothbarth (29) was the first modern historian to argue that labor scarcity dictated technological choice in America. Sir John Habakkuk (16), however, is most frequently identified with this idea; indeed, it is often called the "Habakkuk thesis." Put simply, the argument is that British workers, having no frontier outlet, were forced to accept lower wages; for this reason, British manufacturers would be expected to adopt labor-intensive techniques.

An Illustration of the Habakkuk Thesis

We can follow the Habakkuk argument in Figure 7.2. Investment (I) is drawn as an inverse function of interest rates. Thus if in America interest rates rose from r_0 to r_1, the quantity demanded of investment would decline from Q_0 to Q_1. But as the new and more productive capital formed by the investment works its way through the economy, productivity in general rises, including the productivity of both capital and labor. The curious result then is that investment demand shifts from I_0 to I_1. At r_1, the end result is that Q_2 of investment capital is demanded, causing a capital broadening, if not deepening. But since there will now be more capital as well as more productive capital employed, labor's productivity will rise and labor's wages will rise as well.

The problem with the Habakkuk thesis is that the recent findings of Alexander Field (8) suggest that British manufacturing was actually *more* capital intensive than that of the United States. American manufacturers had to pay higher wages to cover

Figure 7.2. The Habakkuk Thesis: Investment Demand as a Function of Interest Rates.

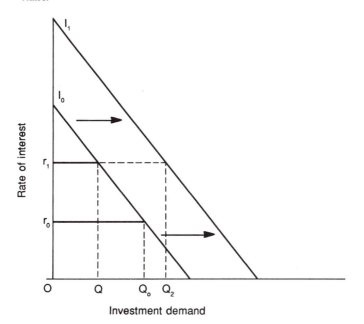

the higher opportunity costs of American labor. To justify paying these wages, however, required higher productivity, which was achieved by using more (complementary) capital (machinery). American industry thus became laborsaving and had high wages and rising productivity relative to its European counterparts.

Going Back to the Old Technology?

Once a society switches to a new technology, can it "reswitch," that is, go back to the old technology? Paul David (3) has argued that, at least in the case of fundamental technological changes, the switch is likely to be permanent. Indeed, once the switch is begun (for example, from individualized hand-crafted products to standardized mass-produced products with interchangeable parts), the entire social, cultural, and political system adjusts to the changes, making any return to the old technology highly unlikely. William Lazonick (22) has provided an interesting application of this idea in his comparison of the British and American cotton spinning industries in the nineteenth century. According to Lazonick, one must take account of both the initial conditions and the background conditions of an industry in order to understand its adaptation to changing technology. In the case of British and American textiles, both sets of conditions differed between the two countries. As Goldin and Sokoloff (14) have shown, American industries—for instance, textiles—that depended heavily on women and minors for labor located in areas such as New England, where farming, the principal alternative employment, provided poor incomes. Covering the opportunity costs of such labor, in other words, made its employment profitable.

Note that the argument is not that reswitching will never occur. As Jonathan Hughes (19) points out, just such reswitching occurred in the 1970s when, with OPEC oil prices soaring, many people switched to woodburning stoves, which had been largely abandoned in the United States earlier in the century.

But Is the Argument Real or Illusory?

Some scholars have pointed out the inherent problems in evaluating the Habakkuk thesis. Peter Temin (33, 34, 35) has argued that there *may* be no clear distinction between British and American nineteenth-century technology. After all, says Temin, the British machines were much longer-lasting and represented much greater capital investment than the flimsier, cheaper American machines. Thus the argument that techniques in America were more capital intensive may simply be wrong, which may help to explain the recent finding of Alexander Field. At the least, the argument may be based on the illusion that all machines are alike if they perform the same economic functions. Still, there is much intuitive appeal to the idea that American innovations were biased in favor of laborsaving. The uses of conveyor belts in milling and slaughtering are only two examples that appeal to intuition. Yet attempts to measure this labor saving by econometric estimation have led to mixed results and any conclusions at this time are highly tentative.

Finally, C. K. Harley has suggested that *relative* abundance or scarcity of skilled labor is the key to what kind of manufacturing techniques are adopted. In

Britain, highly skilled labor was relatively abundant and cheap. Why mechanize when highly skilled labor is a good substitute for capital (machinery)? In the United States, on the other hand, skilled labor was scarce; the machines adopted, therefore, were designed to be operated by relatively unskilled workers. In both cases, firms were simply choosing a cost-minimizing input mix.

Demand-Side Explanations—Were British and Americans Producing the Same Products?

The preceding explanation of the differences between British and American production techniques relies on an effort to identify supply responses that vary according to relative factor endowments and factor prices. Because this effort has, so far, led to no definitive result, it may be useful to consider whether British and American industries were really producing the same products. Should American-made shotguns and British-made shotguns be regarded as the same product? Because of different tastes and preferences and a different distribution of income in the two countries, the answer may well be no. The British product was a high-quality, long-lived, elaborately and individually tooled gun designed to appeal to the English gentry who used it for "sporting" purposes. The American product was a much simpler, more standardized, and shorter-lived gun designed to appeal to the tastes (and incomes) of American farmers and others who used it for more utilitarian purposes. This difference in markets might well prove a more powerful variable than relative factor endowments and prices in explaining the choice of production techniques.

What Caused the Growth of Industry?

Traditionally, much, if not most, of the growth in America's first industrial growth sector was ascribed to technological advance. After all, it was clear that new machines, larger machines, more integrated production processes, more specialized inputs (including a separate, specialized machine goods industry), and the interchangeable parts that expedited maintenance and repair lowered costs and increased supply. The huge increases in production seemed to bear out that kind of analysis.

Robert Zevin (46) posed the question: Since market-clearing (equilibrium) output is determined by supply *and* demand, what part did each play in the growth of the textile industry? Zevin's study is a fascinating exercise that classically illustrates the problems of separating supply and demand changes in the history of an industry's market. The supply growth of the textile industry has been well recorded and was demonstrated in our earlier discussion. Zevin was faced with the problem of estimating the **price elasticity of demand for cotton textiles,** the responsiveness of quantity demanded to changes in their price. This estimate was necessary in order to separate the changes in quantities supplied (primarily the technologically derived output change) from the change in demand. Zevin knew that five factors might have caused a growth in demand and must have done so unless demand was very price elastic. The five demand-changing factors were:

1.   *Population growth,* which was about 3 percent per annum during the period. Of the 16 percent annual growth rate in output, therefore, 3 percent came from population growth and no more than 13 percent from falling cotton prices.

2.   *Tariff protection.* Zevin found that by 1820 the steep tariff had reserved most of the American market for domestic producers.

3.   *Transportation network improvements.* Even without a change in technology, lower transport costs would have reduced retail prices, quantity demanded would have grown, and output would have increased.

4.   *Income growth.* Lack of data for income changes between 1815 and 1820 clouds the question, but Zevin concludes that the growth of income did cause a growth in demand.

5.   *Changes in tastes.* Although it is difficult to separate changes in quantity demanded due to price from changes due to a shift in taste in favor of cotton goods (brighter colors, washable, lighter weight, and so on), there may have been such a shift.

Zevin's rather surprising conclusion is that a large increase in cotton textile output would have occurred because of demand changes even if there had been no improvements in technology. The most important point to remember here is that investors, inventors, and entrepreneur-innovators all look at both sides of a market in making supply decisions. Investment and invention both may be, at least in part, a set of responses to actual or anticipated changes in demand for products or processes.

Noncotton Textiles

Before the 1830s, cloth was a fairly homogeneous product; there was one major category of cotton cloth, another of wool cloth, and so on. With the introduction of power machinery, fabrics could be mixed, short- and long-staple cotton could be combined, even cotton waste could be introduced into the production process. In the 1830s, cotton and hemp were mixed to produce shoddy, a cheap cloth of great durability used for basic clothing, especially that of the slaves. In the 1850s, cotton and flax were mixed to produce a kind of imitation linen.

The wool industry in the United States lagged behind the cotton industry in terms of technological innovation. This may have been partly because of the *expectation* of a slower rate of growth in demand for wool. Nonetheless, innovations in technology (such as the Goulding condenser in 1820s), in automatized cording, in transfer to spinning equipment, and in organization (continuous production) produced cost reductions. Between the 1830s and the 1850s, the price of wool cloth fell by more than 50 percent. Even so, wool lost part of its share of the cloth market to cotton, whose relative price continued to decline.

Power weaving and knitting were applied to the entire cloth industry. By the 1850s, the sewing machine was in widespread use as a device to save on scarce labor. The resulting greatly reduced price of clothing had an interesting real-income effect on Americans. Not only did fewer and fewer American households produce their own clothing (the simple and usually uncolorful homespun), but they also bought more and more diversified clothing. Beginning in the 1830s, rotary printing machinery permitted multicolors, and clothing became more specialized (Sunday-go-to-meeting clothes as opposed to work clothes). Laces and ribbons were factory produced. In all these respects, technological change permitted supply increases. Demand growth and increases in quantity demanded probably diminished toward the end of the period as people became somewhat satiated with new clothing. Falling textile prices tell us that supply was growing more rapidly than demand. The result of the whole process, however, was not only lower prices but also a more colorful and enriched society.

Other Industries

Traditionally, iron and textiles have been viewed as the two key sectors in nineteenth-century industrialization. Two closely related industries, coal and steam engines, are usually included in the complex of sectors considered to have either led or dominated early industrial growth. If this was so, then there is something very peculiar about the early American iron industry. It is true that the industry grew in the 40 or 50 years preceding the Civil War. Total iron output grew 20-fold in that period, or at a rate of about 4 percent per capita.

Yet there is an impression among some that the industry was somehow backward, especially technologically. This pejorative judgment is usually traceable to the fact that Americans continued to use charcoal (wood-derived) rather than coke (made from coal) and the hammer and reheating method rather than the puddling and rolling method (which heated and shaped pig iron without direct contact with the fuel).

At first, it appeared to many investigators that charcoal was preferred because it was cheaper than coke. This turned out not to be true, however, because charcoal production is very labor intensive, and labor was the scarcest factor in America. Around 1830, the English replaced the old bellows with the "hot blast" furnace. The hotter, fuel-saving furnace meant that hard coal (anthracite), which was located in the eastern United States, could be used as a fuel in iron ore production. After 1833, iron ore production in America began more and more to resemble that of Britain.

What accounts for America's "backwardness" in reheating and hammering pig iron? Peter Temin (38) has observed that the United States simply did not have the bituminous coal needed to produce the coke used in the fuel-consuming furnaces that existed prior to the introduction of the hot blast furnace. Also, much of the iron produced in the United States in the early nineteenth century was for stoves, tools, building hardware, and, generally, for items in which iron was not the major component but in which high-quality iron was important. Since wrought (hammered) iron was superior to that produced by puddling, it was reasonable to continue using the old method.

Between 1830 and 1860, however, the new furnaces as well as the growing demand for iron caused a concentration of the industry in the East, particularly in the areas adjoining the Great Lakes. Iron ore locations with anthracite (containing neither gas nor sulfur) were especially plentiful along the Ohio River (such as at Pittsburgh) and other eastern rivers such as the Delaware (for example, above Philadelphia). In sum, it appears that there was a large increase in the demand for iron, especially wrought iron, during the pre–Civil War period. There was only a small increase in supply; that increase, however, prevented larger price increases from occurring.

Sources of Demand for Iron

It is common to associate the demand for iron products before 1860 with the railroads and their major construction phases in the 1840s and 1850s. There is considerable defensibility for this association in the 1850s when, according to Robert Fogel (10), about 22 percent of all domestic crude iron output was consumed by railroad construction and maintenance. Nonetheless, prior to 1850, both stoves and steamboats consumed more iron than did railroads, even if their engines were called "iron horses."

Early urbanization brought forth substantial demand for wrought iron. This was especially the case with "Franklin" stoves, which were great fuel savers compared to fireplaces, and with water and sewer pipe, lamp posts, and many of the other appurtenances of an increasingly urban society. Although it would be many years before America's urban population exceeded its rural population, cities were growing during this period at the fastest *rate* in our history. By 1860, New York had a population in excess of one million, and wrought iron railings had become the major decoration of northern homes.

At least as important as urbanization in the growing demand for iron were successive waves of iron-using transportation innovations. The first of these was the steamboat, whose history we traced earlier. With their huge iron engine blocks, gears, boilers, mountings, and shafts, it is not surprising that far more iron went into steam engines in 1840 than into railways, including locomotives (which, as Fogel has noted, used primarily wooden rails until the 1840s).

Apart from steam engines in transport, Americans did not use the new power source as extensively as the British. After all, New England, clearly the natural manufacturing center of the period, had a comparative advantage in waterpower; both the water wheel and the water turbine illustrated the cheapness of kinetic energy. The fact that steam engines were less widely adapted to industrial uses in the United States than in Britain is not evidence that Americans were technologically backward, but rather, that they were adept at responding to the comparative advantages dictated by their resource endowments.

Railway Demand

If the "iron horse" itself did not create a dominant demand for iron, what about the railway system, especially in its need for iron rails? It appears that even in this overall sense railway demand, although very important, can easily be overstated as a source of the growth of the iron industry. The reasons for this have mainly to do with the timing of railroad building and with the relative disadvantages of American iron makers in supplying iron rails.

The first major wave of railroad building occurred in the mid-1840s. It was not until that time that the railroads, which had experimented with many types of rails, settled on the T-shaped iron rail as their standard. Thus it was not until the mid-1840s that large-scale production of such rails took place in America. Unlike with textile factories, there appear to have been few economies of scale in iron rail production. Indeed, the larger plants were no more productive than smaller ones—they were simply *larger*. Also the quality (especially the durability) of American-made rails left much to be desired. While all iron rails were generally unsuited to long-term use, since they tended to be bent out of shape and periodically had to be reshaped, American iron rails were more prone to bending than those produced by the more mature British industry. In the textile industry, this kind of relative British advantage was quickly overcome. In the iron industry, however, Americans were much slower in overcoming the disadvantage; even by the late 1850s, a significant part of iron rails used in America were imported from Britain.

The Machine Tool Industry

No clearer example exists of classical growth stimuli than the American machine tool industry between 1800 and 1860. Until the early 1800s, mill and factory owners such as Samuel Slater were forced to produce their own tools and machinery. In effect, every mill and factory had a machine and tool shop. As the market grew, however, and the complexity and size of machines increased, separate machine shops began to be established. One of the earliest was set up in 1810 near Philadelphia by David Wilkinson, who had helped Slater build several mills. American machine builders adapted and improved on many English machine tools such as the slide lathe, the milling machine, and gear cutters.

In the process just described, we see strong growth influences at work. As the textile and iron industries grew, the market for machine tools increased, as well as the profitability of establishing independent and specialized firms. As machine shops grew in number and size, they developed inventions, improvements, and innovations. The Blanchard shaper, the turret lathe, the Verier caliper, to name a few, reduced the costs of industries using such tools. Increasing the profitable supply of goods from those industries was a clear growth stimulus.

In sum, the machine tool industry grew out of the firearms industry and had become a major, highly specialized industry by 1860. It served both to create and to transmit technical improvements throughout the American economy, and it enhanced the basic growth industries of the period.

FINANCE

An important corollary of the increasingly exchange-oriented economy whose evolution we have traced from 1815 to 1860 was the development of a financial system, especially a set of institutions to provide the supply of money needed to accommodate market (nonbarter) exchanges. In this area, too, the principle of specialization soon took hold. Until the Revolution, there were no banks in the colonies, but these specialized institutions soon began to develop and paralleled the growth of commerce and industry. The development of banking was anything but smooth, however. There were great national debates over where control of the banking system should lie, as well as broader disputes over the relationship between the banking industry and the American political system. Before getting into those disputes and the history of banking in the period, let us recall briefly why the supply of money is so important a concern to an economy.

The Role(s) of Money

As we have seen, money is any item that is generally accepted in exchange for goods and services. In colonial times, many things ranging from conventional silver coins to unconventional things such as tobacco leaves had served that purpose. Money is necessary for many reasons in an exchange economy. The most important role it plays—whatever form it may take—is that of a medium of exchange. In an economy of increasing specialization, individuals are less and less self-sufficient. They must sell the resources they own and obtain from other people the goods and services they need and want. By the same token, firms, as we have seen, become more and more specialized; they must obtain a more and more varied mix of inputs and sell their increasingly specialized output to other specialized firms as well as final consumers. Money's principal role, then, is to be the common denominator through which the absolute and relative values of all these goods and services may be established, and thus the values at which they exchange for each other.

Imagine the confusion, uncertainty, and high transactions costs in a society in which holders of two commodities must first agree on a third commodity in which to value their own holdings before they can agree on an exchange value for both. What, for example, is the tobacco exchange rate between oxen and wheat? Money is simply the most efficient means to establish such exchange rates.

Money plays other roles as well. Economic development and productivity growth require that there be net investment (current investment greater than current depreciation) in a society. Investment, of course, requires savings. Savings must be priced in order to establish the trade-offs between present consumption and future consumption. Money's role as a store of value fulfills this purpose: it permits individuals and firms to establish the present value of a future stream of (interest) returns on savings and investment.

Finally, money has an important aggregate or overall effect on the economy. Since money is the common denominator that permits setting the individual prices of goods and services, it is not surprising that the supply of money has a direct role to play in establishing overall prices and overall economic activity. We have seen this relationship before in the form of the equation of exchange: $MV = PQ$. Remember that M is the stock of money, V is the income velocity, P is the price level, and Q is the number of (final) goods and services produced. Thus if V and Q are constant, a change in M produces a proportionate change in P. A change in M, in other words, must lead to a changed money gross national product (PQ) or to a lower velocity. A higher PQ does not necessarily reflect more real goods and services; it may simply reflect higher prices for a given amount of real goods and services or may reflect a combination of higher prices and more real goods and services.

Money in the Antebellum Economy

Early in U.S. history, under the urging of Alexander Hamilton, a *bimetallic standard*—one in which the dollar was valued in terms of two metals, gold and silver, and the two metals valued in terms of each other—was established. Since the government ratio between the two metals, the *mint ratio,* was often different from the market valuation of the two, the *market ratio,* problems were created. Whenever the mint ratio overvalued either gold or silver in terms of their market exchange rates, the undervalued metal would be hoarded or shipped abroad for use in foreign trade and the overvalued one would be used in domestic trade. Early in our history, gold was hoarded and silver circulated. Later, after the California gold discovery, the reverse happened because the relative price of gold fell. Although this deprived the nation of the domestic use of some of its specie, it apparently did not create any serious problems.

Banks

The main reason the bimetallic standard had no serious consequences for this country's economy was that coins were not the major form of money in the early nineteenth century. The growth of banks and the various forms of money in the early years of the century can be seen in Table 7.3.

The rapid growth of banking is readily apparent. In the 15-year period 1803–1818, authorized capital stock increased more than 6-fold and notes in circulation increased 12-fold; individual deposits grew more than 7-fold to 1815, though they fell from 1815 to 1818.

Although most early banks maintained large reserves (gold, silver, coins, and certificates), called **high-powered money,** this conservatism declined rapidly. The ratio of specie to deposits and notes fell from 34.7 percent in 1803 to 18.8 percent in 1818.

Table 7.3. Banks in the Early Nineteenth Century, 1803–1818.

YEAR	STATE-CHARTERED BANKS	AUTHORIZED CAPITAL STOCK [a]	NOTES IN CIRCULATION [a, b]	INDIVIDUAL DEPOSITS [a]
1803	53	24,900	1,565	1,522
1806	78	41,340	2,849	2,638
1809	92	45,190	3,804	2,905
1812	143	84,485	6,385	7,248
1815	212	115,232	19,907	11,672
1818	338	160,390	18,072	9,647

[a]Thousands of dollars.

[b]Data available only for the number of banks indicated.

SOURCE: J. Van Fenstermaker, "The Statistics of American Commercial Banking, 1782–1818," *Journal of Economic History* (September 1965).

Banks continued their growth. Although many early banks had been simply extensions or subdivisions of large mercantile operations, by the 1820s, banks were highly specialized separate financial institutions. Their continued growth and influence on the supply of money between 1830 and 1860 may be seen in Table 7.4. Although the banking system was not growing as rapidly as in 1803–1818 period, the number of banks nonetheless tripled from 1834 to 1860, as did bank deposits. Notes more than doubled.

Determining the Supply of Money

In the antebellum period (indeed, as we will see later, up to the early twentieth century), three things determined the American money supply.

Table 7.4. Banks and Bank Money, 1830–1860.

YEAR	NUMBER OF BANKS	DEPOSITS [a]	NOTES [a]
1834	506	102	95
1837	788	190	149
1840	901	120	107
1843	691	78	59
1846	707	125	106
1849	782	121	115
1852	913	182	161
1855	1,307	236	187
1858	1,422	237	155
1860	1,562	310	207

[a] In millions of dollars.

SOURCE: *Historical Statistics, Colonial Times to 1957* (Washington, D.C.: U.S. Department of Commerce).

One was people's preferences for different types of money. If the people wanted to hold specie in gold or silver coins, for example, that reduced the amount of high-powered money or reserves available to the banks and, consequently, the supply of bank money. If people's confidence in banks was threatened, they would convert deposits and notes into specie, reducing the supply of money. This happened several times between 1815 and 1860, and worsened several financial panics.

The second factor affecting the supply of money was the **reserve ratio,** the ratio of reserves to deposits and notes under which banks operated, usually within some form of governmental regulation. The lower the reserve ratio, the greater the ability of banks operating within a fractional reserve system to expand the supply of money (mainly demand deposits)—in other words, the larger the **deposit multiplier.** The fractional reserve principle is based on the idea that not all depositors will show up at the same time to demand specie payment for their notes and deposits. While this assumption was generally warranted, it was severely tested during several financial panics.

Finally, the supply of money was determined by the amount of specie and thereby the amount of high-powered money in the United States. Inflows or outflows of specie—for example, from international trade—could rapidly cause changes in the amount of high-powered money and in the bank-determined money supply.

Organization and Regulation of Banks

By 1800, banks were operating in nearly every state. As can be seen in Tables 7.3 and 7.4, their number, capital, and money supply contribution continued to grow up to 1860. Still, there were problems associated with the growth of the system and its effect on the economy. Widespread mistrust of banks gave rise to recurrent efforts to impose various kinds of controls over the banking system.

Since almost all banks were chartered by the states, ease of entry into banking varied widely from one state to another. So did the controls within which the banks operated. Some states, especially in the old Northwest, at times prohibited banking. Although historians have generally attributed these regional and interstate variations in attitude toward bank chartering and regulation to philosophical differences, Gerald Gunderson (15) believes that it was ultimately the very real differences in need for money and credit to finance development that explained the variations. The West, the area with the greatest need for a highly interest-elastic money supply to profitably finance its growing commercialization of agriculture and its agricultural processing industry, was most liberal in granting charters and generally least rigorous in regulation. According to Gunderson, those states that were already settled and stable, such as Louisiana, were the strictest about chartering and regulations.

Areas that were less strict not only had more banks in proportion to population but also had more problems with redemption of notes. In some states, after

1836, there were so-called wildcat banks; it was said that to redeem their notes, one had to travel to areas habitable only by wildcats. It would be easy to overemphasize this aspect of American banking and to conclude that the whole antebellum era was one of chaos and instability in banking. Such was not the case. While there was considerable variation from one region to another, and even from one bank to another in the same region, the number of banks, at least late in the period, was large enough to offer both individuals and firms banking alternatives. Truly dishonest and corrupt practices by individual banks would have led to a rapid loss of demand for their services.

Nevertheless, there was an early and persistent feeling in the United States that some kind of regulation and control over the banking system was needed. This was deemed necessary to ensure not only a supply of money adequate to finance the growing value of economic transactions but also stability in the supply of that money. An adequate and stable supply of money would prevent wild variations in economic activity and the depressions or panics so feared, as well as an overconcentration of economic power.

Although most of the regulation or control of banking emanated from state and federal activities, one private effort to provide some qualitative control over bank notes was the "Suffolk System," named after the Suffolk Bank of Boston. Because the country (non-Boston) banks' notes were accepted only at discount by merchants (reflecting both the cost of obtaining specie from afar and doubts about specie redeemability), people in Boston used the country notes. This confirms **Gresham's law,** that relatively overvalued money drives out undervalued money. In order to get common acceptability of Boston bank notes and country notes, the Suffolk Bank offered to redeem country notes if the country banks maintained deposits at the Boston bank. Since the country banks would have faced a massive presentation of their notes by the Suffolk bank for specie redemption if they refused, they generally complied. Competition between the Boston banks caused the discount on country notes to fall to zero; the notes were redeemed at par. In a sense, then, the Suffolk Bank was operating like a central bank: maintaining its own reserves, forcing other banks to maintain adequate reserves, and acting as a **clearinghouse** for the notes of other banks. All of these relationships, along with an expanded system of correspondent banking relationships, were to be reintroduced a hundred years later in the Federal Reserve system. The Suffolk System lasted into the 1850s, when clearinghouses in New York, Philadelphia, and other major cities replaced it (21).

Early Central Banking

A central bank is a bankers' bank, one established by government to perform certain functions both for it (fiscal agent and the like) and for private banks (controlling reserve requirements, providing credit to the banks, affecting interest rates, and the like). Of course, accomplishing all these tasks is difficult enough in modern times, when we have advanced information and control mechanisms. Imagine how much more difficult this would have been in the late eighteenth and early nineteenth centuries when there were no typewriters, telephones, or printouts of data on economic activities. It is actually easier for this kind of "central planning" to occur between the most remote village in a poor nation and its capital city in the late 1980s than it was between Washington, D.C., and Boston in 1800.

Nonetheless, central banking (of a sort) was tried in the United States as early as 1791 with the chartering of the First Bank of the United States.* As we saw earlier, the First Bank earned the enmity of other banks and some politically powerful interests. Together with those concerned about the constitutionality of a central bank, these interests defeated a proposal to renew the First Bank's charter in 1811.

For the five years from 1811 to 1816, there was no central bank or federal regulation. As we saw in Tables 7.3 and 7.4, the number of banks rose rapidly during this period. Also, the specie reserves of the banks fell relative to their note issues. In response to a feeling that more central control of the system was needed, Congress in 1816 created the Second Bank of the United States, with a much larger capitalization ($35 million) than its predecessor. Although recent research by Hugh Rockoff (25, 26, 27) and Peter Temin (38) has shown that the Second Bank was generally successful, there were problems in its administration of the money supply.

Much of the Second Bank's later political troubles can probably be traced to its reduction in loans in the western states in 1818 and 1819. When it refused to accept the notes of western banks that did not pay in specie, the Panic of 1819 resulted. One of the western landowners who suffered sharp losses was Andrew Jackson. The so-called Jacksonian fear of central banks was born of, or at least exacerbated by, that experience.

During the 1820s, the Second Bank succeeded in expanding the money supply at a rate consistent with stable prices. The Second Bank's president, the usually able Nicholas Biddle, made a great political mistake, however. Afraid that the bank's charter would not be renewed if Jackson was elected president, Biddle openly campaigned for Henry Clay in 1828. Jackson campaigned and won on a promise to eliminate the Bank of the United States when its charter came up for renewal in 1836. He started to make good on his promise as early as 1832 when he withdrew public deposits from the Second Bank. According to a widely accepted view, the "bank war" between the Jacksonians and the Second Bank's supporters reduced the bank's effectiveness, and the result was a large increase in the money supply and inflation.

As Rockoff (25, 26, 27) and Temin (38) have shown, the money supply (M) and the level of prices (P) did rise, but the reason appears to have been a very large inflow of specie from abroad due to international trade conditions. As Peter Temin has observed, "It would not be misleading to say that the Opium War was more closely connected to the American inflation than the Bank War between Jackson and Biddle."

---

*Neither the First Bank of the United States nor the Second Bank of the United States was a central bank in the sense of being a lender to other commercial banks.

In fact, the United States did not have a true central bank before the Civil War. Given the limitations of the country's metallic standard, it was virtually impossible for a central bank to function. The death of the Second Bank was no great catastrophe; Temin has shown that its demise did not cause the Panic of 1837 or the depression that lasted until 1843. It is generally agreed that the major positive effect of the Second Bank was qualitative; Arthur Fraas (11) has shown that its greatest contribution may well have been to assure interregionally accepted monetary instruments. It probably deserves to be well remembered for this, since these instruments undoubtedly contributed to the growth of interregional trade and the specialization of those regions and the nation's resources we recounted in Chapter 6.

As we said, the federal government began withdrawing from bank regulation as early as 1832 when Jackson stopped depositing government funds in the Bank of the United States and put the funds instead in state banks, which became known as "pet banks." During the 1830s, the funds at least still served as a basis for loan creation and expanded economic activity. In 1840, though, the Independent Treasury Bill was passed, which attempted to eliminate all federal control over commercial credit. Under this act, the U.S. Treasury would not accept bank notes in payment of debts owed the government. Henceforth only specie would be acceptable. The original independent treasury was dropped in 1841, primarily because of opposition from Henry Clay. When it was reinstituted in 1846, however, all federal funds were retained in the U.S. Treasury rather than in banks. The major effect was a withdrawal of specie from circulation whenever the federal government ran a budget surplus, thus further reducing the money supply.

The federal government withdrew entirely from bank regulation between 1832 and 1863. As a result, the number of banks more than doubled and bank deposits more than tripled between 1843 and 1860. It is likely that the ratio of specie to deposits and notes declined and that this created some lack of confidence in the banking system. There are two sides to assess here, however. While it is true that banks with large reserves of high-powered money were viewed with great confidence, they also had a relatively low loan ratio. Yet banks with less high-powered money had less specie, because they had made more loans. In the great majority of cases, those loans were the basis for new and expanded economic enterprises in those areas where rapid economic development was occurring in the United States. In other words, a little less stability, even confidence, in the banking system may have been traded off for more development loans, which the United States and its business community needed. As Hugh Rockoff (25, 26, 27) has shown, free (unregulated) banking may have fostered this country's economic development in an era when a highly interest-elastic supply of money and credit was needed.

Money and Economic Activity

There are great problems in estimating the American money supply in the early antebellum period. The remarkable consistency of the various estimates, however, together with some calculations by Richard Vedder, gives confidence in the relationships between the supply of money, its velocity, the level of prices, and the quantity of output shown in Table 7.5.

As Vedder points out, the seeming price stability between 1799 and 1819 is deceptive. In fact, there was a severe inflation during the War of 1812. Undoubtedly, the money supply (M) grew more rapidly than output (Q). Prices did not rise only because of a reduction in velocity (V). During the most effective period of the Second Bank of the United States, the 1820s, output rose rapidly while the money supply grew slowly. With a steady velocity, prices actually fell. Yet the very rapid growth of the money supply in the 1830s caused inflation, while a decline in velocity in the 1840s caused a fall in prices. When the money stock increased more rapidly than real output in the 1850s, there was inflation. Also, in that period there was a slight increase in velocity (the gold discoveries in California had much to do with the specie increase and money supply increase in the 1850s).

Summing Up

It was conventional for many years for historians to criticize the U.S. banking system before the Civil War. Apart from the "bright periods" of the First and Second Banks of the United States, it was presumed that there was not enough control and regulation to make the system work toward the development ends of the nation. That view is now largely discredited. As Richard Sylla (31) has shown, the fault in the American system of banking before 1860 lay with the incidence of fraud and the number of bank failures rather than with an inadequately elastic supply of money.

It seems, in fact, that the system worked remarkably well, even without the regulatory functions of central banking. This should not be surprising, considering the enormous problems of imposing correct central bank policy in that era.

Table 7.5.   Components of the Equation of Exchange, 1799–1859.

YEAR	MONEY[a]	VELOCITY	PRICES[b]	QUANTITY[c]
1799	29	12.02	113	308
1809	66	7.16	116	408
1819	86	7.75	112	595
1829	120	7.03	86	981
1839	215	7.21	100	1,550
1849	330	5.12	73	2,316
1859	586	5.68	85	3,913

[a] In millions of dollars.

[b] 1839 = 100.

[c] Transactions of final goods and services, in 1839 prices, in millions of dollars.

Note: The estimates of the money stock and prices are reasonably reliable; the estimate of quantity is very tenuous for the pre-1840 period and is based on Paul David's (4) work. The income velocity measure was calculated from the other components and must be viewed as subject to considerable error.

Source: Richard K. Vedder, *The Economy in Historical Perspective* (Belmont, Cal.: Wadsworth, 1976).

ECONOMIC FLUCTUATIONS TO 1865

Fluctuations to 1815

Let's summarize the record of economic fluctuations for the period 1783–1815 that we examined in Chapters 3 and 5. The American economy experienced a recession, or contraction in economic activity, in 1784–1786, primarily stemming from the inability to export enough goods to earn sufficient foreign exchange to pay for the high levels of imports in 1783 and 1784. Only one-third of imports were paid for by earnings on exports. Part of the imports were paid for by a flow of gold and silver to the English exporters, which substantially decreased the supply of money. This decrease in M contributed to a decrease in prices and, to some extent, output. There were increased difficulties in the payment of debts, including the debts owed to English exporters, and there were some commercial bankruptcies.

This recession was primarily a commercial one, especially involving commerce connected with international trade. The large share of noncash production (for home use) cushioned the economy from the recession. However, this recession helped speed up recognition of the weaknesses of the Articles of Confederation and encouraged the formulation and adoption of the Constitution.

From 1792 through 1815, the dominant factor in U.S. economic activity was the long European conflict known as the Napoleonic Wars. These wars created the opportunity for rapid growth in American shipping of both exports and reexports. These sectors expanded until a lull in the fighting in 1798, when trade collapsed. They expanded again from 1799 to 1802. Peace in 1802 and 1803 caused a drastic reduction in U.S. shipping and international commercial activity. With the resumption of war in 1804, our trade expanded again until the Embargo Act of 1807, when trade collapsed because the federal government forbade all trade with Europe in retaliation for British and French seizure of U.S. ships. With the Non-Intercourse Act of 1809 and the removal of the prohibition of trade with France, trade revived to some extent. From 1809 to 1812, there was moderate recovery, but not to pre-1807 levels. Our War of 1812 against Britain caused a further collapse of our international trade until the end of that war in 1815.

It seems apparent that the U.S. record of economic fluctuations for the period from 1782 to 1815 was primarily confined to the international trade sector, involving shipping and commerce. The effects of such fluctuations were minimal on a generally agricultural economy; only those sectors of the economy tied to the international trade sector were affected.

Fluctuations from 1815 to 1865

There was a mild depression in 1815 as trade resumed with the end of the War of 1812 and many of the new, small manufacturing enterprises found they could not compete with British imports. These enterprises had appeared under the protection of trade restrictions against British goods from the time of the Embargo of 1807 through the war.

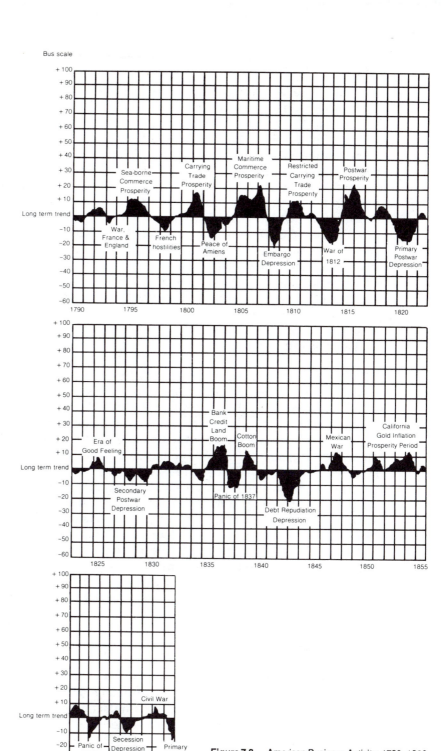

Bus scale

Figure 7.3. American Business Activity, 1790–1860.
SOURCE: Courtesy of AmeriTrust Corporation.

Then there was strong prosperity through the end of 1818. Aggregate demand was high. Exports increased as the restrictions on trade that dated to before the war disappeared. There was a spurt in agricultural exports as the industrial revolution in Britain increased the demand for southern cotton to provide raw materials for the expanding British textile industry. Also, there was a growing demand for general foodstuffs from the North and West to feed the expanding industrial labor force of Britain. Investment increased as high levels of construction were achieved, with increases occurring in shipbuilding, turnpike construction, and canal construction, beginning with the Erie Canal in 1817.

Substantial growth in state banks occurred, which increased the availability of credit to finance the expansion of investment. This increase in banking and credit increased the supply of money, which stimulated output and prices, so that even in manufacturing many of the firms established before 1815 survived the renewal of trade. These grew in size and were joined by new firms as a textile industry became firmly established in the Northeast.

The Panic of 1819

In 1819, there was a banking panic and a downturn in economic activity. Two events originating in Europe and Britain precipitated this contraction. First, Europe had an excellent agricultural harvest in 1818, which reduced demand for United States exports of food crops from the North and West. At the same time, Britain was going through a financial and industrial crisis that sharply reduced its textile industry's demand for cotton. These events underlined the United States' continuing dependence on international trade for its prosperity.

Besides decreasing U.S. exports of agricultural products, the financial crisis in Britain led to a banking panic in the United States when, in response to their own financial difficulties, the British called in large amounts of their American loans. This caused an outflow of gold and sharp reductions in the reserves of urban banks. Some that had insufficient reserves to survive the outflow of gold collapsed. This banking crisis spread to the rural banks outside of the large coastal cities. Prices of agricultural exports dropped sharply as the supply of money was curtailed. The urban economy, so dependent on foreign trade activity and commercial stability, suffered.

The Expansion of 1820–1837

Next, a long period of substantial growth occurred between 1820 and 1837. An important factor in this expansion was the prolonged increase in investment. First, there was a rapid expansion in the small manufacturing sector. There was substantial growth in iron, machinery, shoes, leather, and in textiles, both cotton and woolens. Second, construction activity was high. Between 1816 and 1840, over $125 million was expended on canal construction alone. In 1821, 1,400 tons of steamboats were constructed; in 1837, this had risen to 33,500 tons. There were substantial increases in the construction of sailing vessels, turnpikes, and bridges, including over 3,000 miles of railroads by 1840. As population grew in cities, housing and other forms of urban construction increased.

Consumption within the money economy also increased. Products produced and consumed in the home began to decline in the 1830s as factory-produced products became more available and as the opportunity cost of home manufacture increased. Growing population, both through immigration and natural increase, further raised consumption.

In the 1820s, there was a slow rate of growth in the banking system—from 307 banks in 1820 to 330 by 1830. Also, the growth of the supply of money did not keep pace with output, and prices moved gradually downward. In the 1830s, the number of banks grew more rapidly, especially after the Second Bank of the United States was refused a renewal of its charter. The supply of money increased sharply, and prices rose in the 1830s.

The Banking Crisis of 1837

Growth began to deteriorate in the 1830s, as an increased emphasis on speculative ventures spread throughout the economy. In the westward movement, land speculation became almost universal; both small farmers and large landowners speculated on increases in land values, usually on credit. Manufacturing expanded rapidly, and many new firms were started with insufficient prospects for success. Many canals proved disappointing—profits earned were inadequate because traffic did not live up to expectations. Overall, this speculation was financed by expansion of the banking system and, through it, of the supply of money.

In 1836, the balance of trade turned sharply against the United States as exports fell. In the following year, gold flowed to Britain as British merchants tightened their credit to southern cotton growers. Reserves in the urban coastal banks fell, and a banking crisis developed; but this contraction was restricted to commercial interests in international trade and the banking system.

The economy recovered quickly in 1838 and 1839. The manufacturing sector was still strong, and exports revived. Internal improvements, especially in railroad construction, were strong. Banking reserves grew as British investors increased their purchases of bonds from various state governments.

The Crisis of 1839 and Depression

The revival of 1838 and 1839 was not maintained, however, and a crisis developed at the end of 1839. Credit was again tightened in England, and gold flowed out of the United States, reducing bank reserves and the supply of money. The former Second Bank of the United States, now a Pennsylvania state bank, closed its doors when its speculation in cotton proved disastrous. These factors precipitated a general panic and more bank failures. The overexpansion in manufacturing caused many low-productivity firms to fold. Speculation in land values in the West collapsed, and many rural banks were unable to survive the default on land loans. The result was depression and unemployment that lasted until 1843.

The expansion of the 1820s and 1830s was based on sustained growth of investment with its multiplier effects on income. This growth in income increased the quantity of goods consumed, with consequent increases in induced investment and the positive accelerator, reinforcing the multiplier effect on income. As the expansion began to slow, induced investment declined and a negative accelerator began to contract the economy; there was a decline in aggregate demand and a reverse of the multiplier effect. (If this is confusing, read the Review of Economic Concepts at the end of this chapter.)

The Expansion of 1843–1857

By 1843, the economy had recovered and had entered another long period of expansion, which lasted until 1857. The primary stimuli to that expansion were sustained increases in investment, increases that substantially raised aggregate demand and caused a multiplier effect, expanding income.

Railroad construction played a major role in this increase in investment, a role it was to maintain until the 1890s. In 1840, there were 3,000 miles of track. This had increased to 24,000 miles by 1857. The direct effects on aggregate demand were substantial: employment was provided in the building of the roads, and manufacturing was stimulated to provide materials needed for construction. The indirect effects were perhaps even greater, because transportation costs fell, increasing the opportunities for broadened economic activity. Other forms of investment were also high: factories were built, ships constructed, telegraph lines completed, and urban areas created and expanded, and the westward movement in agriculture continued.

All this required credit and substantial financial facilities. These facilities were provided primarily by expansion in the banking system. Historians have pointed out that part of the banking expansion was provided by "wildcat banks" that had insufficient reserves and, at times, issued fraudulent currency. Despite the confusion of a great variety of currencies of varying reliability, this surge in banking capacity provided (along with foreign investment) the financial capital for expansion.

This expansion in the money supply can also explain the stimulative effects on the growing economy. Increasing supplies of money increased Q (transactions; that is, real output) by increasing demand for investment and consumption. Prices also increased moderately. (See Chapter 4 for a discussion of the equation of exchange. Also check this chapter's Review of Economic Concepts.)

The Crisis of 1857 and Depression

As 1857 approached, a series of factors weakened the economy and precipitated another panic and depression. New investment was discouraged as it became increasingly clear that wide areas of investment, including railroads, had been over-extended and profit expectations on many projects were not being fulfilled. The end of the Crimean War in 1856 decreased demand for U.S. wheat, lowering its price, and also reduced the demand for American shipping. The effects were not felt until 1857.

Adverse events also occurred in the area of finance. In 1858, there was a sharp increase in the demand for credit. This raised interest rates in France and drew British financial capital from the United States to France. The reduced British investment in the United States caused an outflow of gold from the New York banks.

By this time, the securities market in New York was significant and the New York banks had taken to lending their reserves on the call market. People buying securities in the New York stock market would borrow to pay for these securities from the banks; these loans could be called in at any time, forcing the borrowers to sell the securities in the stock market to pay off the loans. Because of the flow of gold to Britain, the reserves of the New York banks were low, and they called in many loans. To pay the loans, investors sold securities on the exchange, and the stock market collapsed. A banking panic developed when some banks could not recapture their loans.

This stock market and banking panic was severe, but short. The resulting disruption in the supply of money and confidence in the banking system contracted demand and output. The depression that ensued lasted until the end of 1859.

The confusion that occurred at the outset of the Civil War caused a contraction in economic activity in the North. This contraction was short because the economy in the North expanded under the impact of increased government expenditures for the military at the start of the Civil War.

REVIEW OF ECONOMIC CONCEPTS: MACRO AND MONETARY MODELS

A Macro Model of Output

To explore the question of economic fluctuations, one must examine what basic factors determine, at a point in time, the level of output and income in an economy. The model to be constructed is a **macro** one, a model concerned with activity on the level of the whole economy—as distinct from a **micro** model, the analysis of the activities of the smaller units in our economy, such as the individual market, consumer, or firm. This macro model can be approached from two directions: (a) analyses of total or aggregate demand and (b) analyses of the effects of variations in the supply of money. By necessity, our treatment will be brief. (For a more complete presentation, consult a text on the principles of economics.)

An Aggregate Demand Model. John Maynard Keynes maintained that the equilibrium level of income and thus output in an economy is determined by its level of effective or aggregate demand.* Five principal factors influence the level of aggregate demand. First, the **consumption function** represents the various quantities that the society is willing and able to consume at differing levels of income. Increases in consumption (a shift upward of the curve) increase aggregate demand, while decreases in consumption (a shift downward of the curve) decrease aggregate demand. The position and shape of the curve are determined by (a) habits, customs, and institutions; (b) the stock of consumer durables; (c) the amount of liquid assets (those easily converted into money) held by the society; and (d) the level of taxes.

Second, the **savings function** represents the various quantities that the society is willing and able to save at differing levels of income. What a society does not consume out of income is either saved or paid in taxes. Therefore, the same factors that determine consumption also determine savings, but in the reverse direction. Increases in savings (shifts upward of the savings function) decrease consumption and thus decrease aggregate demand, while decreases in savings (shifts downward of the savings function) increase consumption and thus increase aggregate demand.

Third, the **investment function** represents the various quantities that the society is willing and able to invest at different levels of income. There are two kinds of investment: autonomous and induced.

Autonomous investment is determined by factors outside the model; that is, it is not affected by income or consumption. The quantity of autonomous investment depends on the interest rate (the cost of investing) and the marginal efficiency of capital (the expected rate of return). Investments will be made as long as the marginal efficiency of capital is equal to or greater than the interest rate. The primary factors determining the marginal efficiency of capital are investors' expectations about future returns and productivity of the investment (technology). The quantity of autonomous investment will increase if (a) the interest rate falls, (b) expectations become more optimistic, or (c) technological change occurs, increasing the productivity of investment. A decrease in the quantity of autonomous investment will occur if the opposite happens.

Induced investment is investment caused by changes in the model, changes in income, and changes in consumption. For now, let us leave induced investment out of the model; we will consider it later.

Fourth, the government expenditure function represents the various quantities of government expenditure that will be made at different levels of income. Such expenditures are obviously determined by governmental decision making. Aggregate demand increases as these expenditures increase and decreases as they decrease.

Fifth, the tax function represents the various quantities that society pays in taxes at different levels of income. Taxes are also determined through governmental decision making. An increase in taxes is paid for in part out of income that would have been spent on consumption; thus consumption and aggregate demand are

---

*Note that this model takes aggregate supply as given. While this is a simplification of reality, it permits us to focus on aggregate demand effects.

decreased by taxation. If taxes decrease, the additional private income is spent in part on consumption; thus consumption and aggregate demand are increased.

In summary, aggregate demand determines the level of income and thus output in the economy. Aggregate demand is made up of consumption, investment, and government expenditures. Increases in savings and taxes decrease aggregate demand, while decreases in savings and taxes increase aggregate demand. Aggregate supply equals consumption plus savings plus taxes.

THE MODEL

Figure 7.4 shows the elements of aggregate demand in a diagram relating income on the horizontal axis and consumption, investment, and government expenditure on the vertical axis. The top line, marked $C + II + G$, represents aggregate demand. The line emanating from the origin divides that quadrant in half (two 45-degree angles) and is called the 45-degree line. The distance from the vertical axis to the 45-degree line is equal to the distance from the horizontal axis to the 45-degree line. The vertical distance to the 45-degree line is equal to income or value of output. The 45-degree line, then, is aggregate supply.

Now for the analysis. The equilibrium income level of the economy (the central tendency of the model) is the level of income that equates aggregate demand and aggregate supply at point B, or Income Level $0A$. Any other level of income

Figure 7.4.   The Determination of Income.

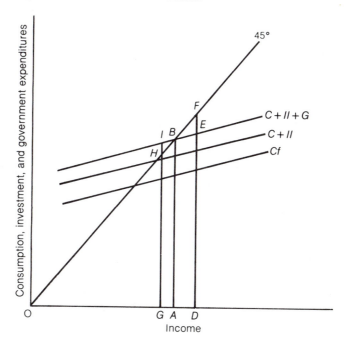

would not be stable and would cause a movement toward Equilibrium Level 0A. At any level of income above the equilibrium (for example, 0D), aggregate supply (DF) exceeds aggregate demand (DE)—more is produced than is demanded. Inventories of business firms therefore become greater by EF than the firms wish, causing them to reduce orders to manufacturers. In turn, these actions reduce output, employment, and income. The level of income shifts to 0A. At any level of income below the equilibrium (for example, 0G), aggregate demand exceeds aggregate supply—more is demanded than is produced. Inventories of business firms decrease below what they have planned as people consume more than was produced for them by IH. To replenish these depleted inventories, firms increase orders to the manufacturers, who in turn increase output, employment, and income. The level of income moves to 0A.

Since the level of income and output is determined by the level of aggregate demand, any change in the latter's components (consumption, investment government expenditure) will change the level of income. In Figure 7.5, we see, though, that this relationship is not a simple one. The increase in aggregate demand (AB) is much smaller than the increase in income (DE). This is known as the **multiplier effect,** or a multiple change in income from any given change in aggregate demand. The size of the multiplier depends on the marginal propensity to consume or save. The **marginal propensity to consume** is the percentage of any change in income

Figure 7.5. The Multiplier.

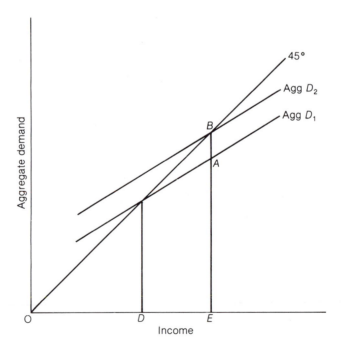

that is spent on consumption. The marginal propensity to consume measures the portion of the income generated by a change in aggregate demand that is returned to demand once again as additional demand. But the main point is that income changes by an amount larger than the original changes in aggregate demand.

Let us assume that the marginal propensity to consume (*MPC*) is one-half, and the government decides to build a post office for $100,000. That $100,000 is an increase in the aggregate demand through an increase in intended investment. Income will increase by $100,000 as this office is built and the people who build it are paid. Now the people who have this additional income will (remember that *MPC* is one-half) save only one-half and will demand more goods and services with the other one-half. Output then will increase by $50,000 as goods and services are produced to satisfy that increased demand. Income increases by another $50,000. People who receive that income also spend one-half of it (*MPC* equals one-half), and output and income increase by $25,000. The process continues until there is virtually no additional demand for output. The point to remember is that income increases by more than the original increase in aggregate demand, the $100,000 for the post office. In this example, the multiplier is two, and income would icrease by $200,000. The multiplier formula is $1/1 - MPC$. Substituting an *MPC* of one-half in the formula gives us $1/1 - 1/2 = 1/ 1/2 = 1 \times 2/1$ or 2.

The last factor to keep in mind about the aggregate demand model is the **accelerator principle.** When induced investment increases, the accelerator is positive, thereby expanding the economy. When induced investment is negative, the accelerator is negative and the economy contracts. Remember that induced investment is induced or caused by changes in the level of income and thus changes in the quantity of consumption. These increases in the quantity consumed increase the need for additional capacity to produce the additional output. These increases in capacity result from induced investment.

But induced investment is not increased simply by increases in total consumption demand, but rather by increases in the *rate* of growth in consumer demand. When the *rate* of growth in consumer demand is increasing, then induced investment is increasing, and the accelerator is positive, thereby expanding the economy. When the rate of growth is constant, induced investment is zero. When the rate of growth in consumer demand is decreasing, induced investment decreases, and the accelerator is negative, resulting in a contraction of the economy. Forces can thus be contracting the economy even when total consumer demand is still expanding.

Summary

In summary, according to the aggregate demand model, the following factors expand the economy:

1. Increases in the consumption function caused by (a) changes in habits and institutions that decrease savings, (b) increases in liquidity (proportion of assets

that could quickly be converted into money), (c) decreases in inventories of consumer-held durables, and (d) decreases in taxes.

2.   Increases in investment, both autonomous and induced. Increases in autonomous investment occur when (a) interest rates decrease, (b) expectations become more optimistic, and (c) technological development occurs. Increases in induced investment occur when the rate of growth in demand increases, creating demand for increases in productive capacity.

3.   Increases in government expenditures. Here we are faced with the fact that government expenditures result from political processes. Variations in such expenditures are not closely related to variations in income. Thus we still take government expenditures as given.

Decreases in the level of income result from the opposite occurring.

Keep in mind that small variations in aggregate demand will cause larger variations in income and output through the functioning and interaction of the multiplier and the accelerator.

A Monetary View

In recent years, a number of economists, including Milton Friedman, have emphasized the role of the supply of money in determining the level of economic activity. These monetarists maintain that money is the *primary* thing that matters, not that it is the only thing that matters. "Keynesians," in contrast, maintain that money is important, but that aggregate demand is also important. Now let's examine how variations in the supply of money affect the level of economic activity.

The model we shall use is the equation of exchange or quantity theory of money already presented in Chapter 4. Let's review it briefly. The equation of exchange is $MV = PQ$. M is the supply of money; V is the velocity of exchange or the number of times M changes hands in a given period of time; P is the price level; and Q is the number of economic transactions in real rather than money terms.

We can distinguish two types of money, M_1 and M_2. M_1 consists of all demand deposits (checking accounts) and all currency and coins in circulation. M_2 is M_1 plus savings accounts and highly liquid (easily converted into money) assets. The velocity of exchange (V) depends on the customs, habits, and so on of the population (how strongly they want to hold on to money), on the degree of efficiency of the financial institutions (how quickly money can be transferred), and on people's expectations about economic activity, including the security of financial institutions.

If there are unemployed resources and the supply of money increases with a velocity that is constant, output or Q tends to increase as more resources are employed. As the economy approaches full employment and the supply of money continues to increase, P or prices also begin to rise. When full employment is reached, only prices will increase (not output) with increase in the supply of money. The reverse of these effects occurs when the supply of money decreases.

QUESTIONS

1. How did the classical economists view the effect of technological change on economic development? Does the experience of the United States in the period from 1815 to 1860 bear out that view? Why or why not?

2. What were the major differences between the factory system and the system of home manufactures? What impact did the factory system have on labor force participation?

3. Why were standardized products and interchangeable parts so critical to the rapid productivity growth of the American System of manufactures?

4. In view of the fact that early American manufacturers got their original ideas from Britain, what was unique about American manufacturing?

5. What happened to manufacturing's share of real commodity output, income, and workers between 1815 and 1860? What is the problem with inferring the relationship between these changes for 1840–1860 and the period from 1800 to 1840?

6. What was the reason for the lack of success of Slater's early textile factory? What changes had to be made to produce a viable American textile factory? When did these changes occur?

7. What was the reaction of American textile producers to imports of British textiles after 1815?

8. What were the five most important manufacturing industries in the United States in 1860? What influences tend ultimately to make an industry such as cotton goods a declining industry in terms of relative importance?

9. According to the study of Robert Zevin, what were the sources of the increased demand for cotton textiles?

10. How does one reconcile the impressionistic sense that the American iron industry was backward before the Civil War with the fact that it was a rapidly growing industry?

11. What were the major sources of demand for iron in the antebellum period? How important was railway demand (both rails and locomotives) to the growth of the iron industry?

12. What caused the development of a successful machine tool industry in the United States after 1800?

13. What is the Habakkuk thesis? What are the problems with specifying the argument and testing it?

14. Why is the money supply so important to a developing economy? What does the equation of exchange tell us about the relation between the money supply and overall economic activity?

15. What was the bimetallic standard? What problems are created when the mint ratio and the market ratio differ significantly?

16. What happened to the number of state-chartered banks, to their authorized capital stock, and to their notes in circulation and individual deposits between 1803 and 1818? What happened to the amount of high-powered money held by such banks? At what rate did the banking system grow from 1834 to 1860?

17. What determined the supply of money and the deposit multiplier in the pre–Civil War period?

18. What seems to have determined the stringency with which states chartered and regulated banks in the antebellum period?

19. Why did the drive to regulate banking gain momentum in the United States? How did the Suffolk Plan illustrate private regulation?

20. Trace the history of the Second Bank of the United States. What ultimately caused its demise? Was it truly a central bank? Why or why not?

21. Why was it difficult to have successful central banking in the antebellum era? What was the major effect of the Second Bank of the United States? What happened to commercial banking after the federal government stopped regulating it?

22. What does the equation of exchange show about the relationship between the supply of money, its velocity, prices, and quantity of output between 1799 and 1859?

23. What was the basic source of fluctuations in the period 1792–1815?

24. What internal factors expanded the economy from 1820 to 1837 and from 1843 to 1857?

25. In comparing the contractions in 1819, 1837, 1839, and 1857, which seemed to be more important, internal factors or factors external to the American economy? Does there seem to have been any change in relative importance between the two factors over time?

SUGGESTED READINGS

1. Bagnall, William R. *Samuel Slater and the Early Development of Cotton Manufacture in the United States.* Middleton: Stewart, 1890.

2. Britto, D. L., and Jeffrey Williamson. "Skilled Labor and 19th Century Anglo-American Managerial Behavior." *Explorations in Economic History 10* (Spring 1973).

3. David, Paul. "Labor Scarcity and the Problem of Technological Practice and Progress in 19th Century America." *Technological Choice: Innovation and Economic Growth.* Cambridge: Cambridge University Press, 1975.

4. David, Paul. "The Growth of Real Product in the United States Before 1840: New Evidence, Controlled Conjectures." *Journal of Economic History, 27* (June 1967).

5. Davis, Lowell, et al. *American Economic Growth.* New York: Harper and Row, 1972. Chaps. 10 and 11.

6. Drummond, Ian. "Labor Scarcity: A Comment." *Journal of Economic History 27* (September 1967).

7. Engerman, Stanley L. "A Note on the Economic Consequences of the Second Bank of the United States." *Journal of Political Economy, 78* (July–August 1974).

8. Field, Alexander. "On the Unimportance of Machinery." *Explorations in Economic History, 22* (October 1985).

9. Field, Alexander. "Sectoral Shift in Antebellum Massachusetts: A Reconsideration." *Explorations in Economic History, 15* (April 1978).

10. Fogel, Robert W. *Railroads and American Economic Growth: Essays in Econometric History.* Baltimore: Johns Hopkins University Press, 1964. Pp. 111–146.

11. Fraas, Arthur. "The Second Bank of the United States: An Instrument for an Interregional Monetary Union." *Journal of Economic History, 34* (June 1974).

12. Gallman, Robert E. "Value Added by Agriculture, Mining and Manufacturing in the United States, 1840–1880." Unpublished doctoral dissertation, University of Pennsylvania, 1956.

13. Gibb, George S. *The Saco-Lowell Shops: Textile Machinery Building in New England, 1813–1849.* Cambridge, Mass.: Harvard University Press, 1950.

14. Goldin, Claudia, and Kenneth Sokoloff. "The Relative Productivity Hypothesis of Industrialization: The American Case, 1820–1850." *The Quarterly Journal of Economics, 119* (August 1984).

15. Gunderson, Gerald. *A New Economic History of America.* New York: McGraw-Hill, 1976.

16. Habakkuk, H. J. *American and British Technology in the Nineteenth Century.* Cambridge; Cambridge University Press, 1962.

17. Hammond, Bray. *Banks and Politics in America.* Princeton, N.J.: Princeton University Press, 1957.

18. Harley, C. K. "Skilled Labor and the Choice of Technique in Edwardian Industry." *Explorations in Economic History, 11* (Summer 1974).

19. Hughes, Jonathan. *The Vital Few,* Chap. 4, "Eli Whitney and American Technology." New York: Oxford University Press, 1973.

20. Hughes, J. R. T., and Nathan Rosenberg. "The United States Business Cycle Before 1860: Some Problems of Interpretation." *Economic History Review, 15* (April 1963).

21. Lake, Wilfred S. "The End of the Suffolk System." *Journal of Economic History, 7* (November 1947).

22. Lazonick, William H. "Production Relations, Labor Productivity and Choice of Technique: British and U.S. Cotton Spinning." *Journal of Economic History, 41* (Spring 1981).

23. North, Douglass C. *The Economic Growth of the United States, 1790–1860.* Englewood Cliffs, N.J.: Prentice Hall, 1961.

24. Redlich, Fritz. *The Molding of American Banking.* New York: Johnson Reprint, 1968.

25. Rockoff, Hugh T. "Money Prices and Banks in the Jacksonian Era." In *The Reinterpretation of American Economic History,* ed. Robert W. Fogel and Stanley L. Engerman. New York: Harper and Row, 1972.

26. Rockhoff, Hugh T. *The Free Banking Era: A Reexamination.* New York: Arno Press, 1975.

27. Rockhoff, Hugh T. "Varieties of Banking and Regional Development in the United States, 1840–1860." *Journal of Economic History, 35* (March 1975).

28. Rosenberg, Nathan. "Anglo-American Wage Differences in the 1860s." *Journal of Economic History, 27* (June 1967).

29. Rothbarth, Edwin. "Causes of Superior Efficiency of USA Industry as Compared to British Industry." *Economic Journal, 56* (September 1946).

30. Smith, Walter B., and Arthur H. Cole. *Fluctuations in American Business, 1790–1860.* Cambridge, Mass.: Harvard University Press, 1935.

31. Sylla, Richard. "American Banking and Growth in the Nineteenth Century: A Partial View of the Terrain." *Explorations in Economic History, 9* (Winter 1971–1972).

32. Taylor, George R. *The Transportation Revolution, 1815–1869.* New York: Holt, Rinehart and Winston, 1951.

33. Temin, Peter. *Iron and Steel in 19th Century America: An Economic Inquiry.* Boston: MIT Press, 1964.

34. Temin, Peter. "Labor Scarcity: A Reply." *Journal of Economic History, 28* (March 1968).

35. Temin, Peter. "Labor Scarcity and the Problem of American Industrial Efficiency in the 1850s." *Journal of Economic History, 26* (September 1966).

36. Temin, Peter. "Labor Scarcity in America." *Journal of Interdisciplinary History, 1* (Winter 1971).

37. Temin, Peter. "The Economic Consequences of the Bank War." *Journal of Political Economy, 76* (March/April 1968).

38. Temin, Peter. *The Jacksonian Economy.* New York: Norton, 1969.

39. Timberlake, Richard. "The Specie Standard and Central Banking in the United States Before 1860." *Journal of Economic History, 21* (September 1961).

40. Uselding, Paul. "Technical Progress in the Springfield Armoury." *Explorations in Economic History, 11* (Spring 1974).

41. Uselding, Paul, and Julia Bruce. "Biased Technical Progress in American Manufacturing, 1839–99." *Explorations in Economic History, 11* (Fall 1973).

42. Van Fenstermaker, J. "The Statistics of American Commercial Banking, 1782–1818." *Journal of Economic History, 25* (September 1965).

43. Ware, Carolyn F. "The Early New England Cotton Manufacture." *American State Papers.* Washington, D.C.: U.S. Government Printing Office, 1931.

44. Williamson, Jeffrey. "Embodiment, Disembodiment, Learning by Doing and Returns to Scale in Nineteenth Century Cotton Textiles." *Journal of Economic History, 32* (September 1972).

45. Woodbury, Robert S. "The Legend of Eli Whitney and Interchangeable Parts." *Technology and Culture, 2* (1960).

46. Zevin, Robert Brooke. "The Growth of Cotton Textile Production After 1815." In *The Reinterpretation of American Economic History,* ed. Robert W. Fogel and Stanley L. Engerman. New York: Harper and Row, 1971.

Chapter 8

REGIONAL INTEGRATION AND SPECIALIZATION TO 1860

The Agrarian West and the Industrial Northeast

In Chapter 6, we examined the process through which transportation changes and the extension of low-cost transportation systems drew more and more of the United States into a single market system. That process undoubtedly meant that an increasing part of the nation's resources, including its labor force, was involved in the cash economy. In turn, more and more people were receiving cash incomes and spending those incomes on goods and services produced for the market. The slave population of the South remained an important exception to this pattern of increasing monetization, as we shall see in Chapter 9.

In this chapter, we are going to explore the particular and, in many respects, very specialized patterns of development that emerged in two of the three great regions of the United States between 1815 and 1860. The patterns that emerged in the Northeast and the West were ones of considerable specialization and involved increasing ties to a national as well as an international system of markets. As we shall see, the regional specialization that evolved was far from complete. Nonetheless, two of the broadest economic themes of the era are production for a *national system* of markets and increasing specialization within that pattern of production.

Classical economists argued that economic growth and development are brought about by expanding markets based on comparative-advantage trade. This trade is made more and more effective by a growing supply based on specialization and division of labor and capital. We shall see clearly the efficacy of this argument in the antebellum experience of the United States.

The South, with its labor system based primarily on black slavery, produced agricultural staples—cotton, tobacco, rice, and sugar—primarily for export outside the region. The West was also agrarian, but based on family-size farms producing a more diversified set of products—wheat, corn, hogs, beef—with the most of its output shipped outside the region, although some processing was done within the region. The Northeast was emerging as the early industrial region. While its agriculture was declining in relative importance, farming was still an important sector of the regional economy. In this chapter we will examine the latter two regions, both in terms of the interrelationships between them and in terms of their peculiar specialized economies. We will examine the South separately in the next chapter.

FOREIGN AND DOMESTIC TRADE

The model we shall employ in this and the succeeding chapter will permit us to focus on trade among all three geographic regions of the United States. We do not seek to slight trade with other nations; rather, we shall take that trade and the factors that determined it as exogenous to (determined outside of) internal trade patterns. While that assumption ignores the interdependence that existed between foreign and domestic trade, particularly their joint effects on market size, it permits us to focus attention on the elements that caused a very rapid growth of internal trade in the 45 years between 1815 and 1860. Indeed, that growth appears to have been even more rapid than the growth in foreign trade.

A Model of Interregional Trade

Basically, we still seek to interpret trade by the Northeast, South, and West in terms of their changing patterns of comparative advantage. In 1815, as we have seen, these regions were very largely independent of one another. Their initial endowments of resources (land, labor, capital, and entrepreneurship) were quite different. The Northeast had the initial advantages of good natural harbors, stands of well-situated timber, and relatively good sources of iron ore and waterpower or kinetic energy. The South was endowed with richer soil and milder climatic conditions and with longer growing seasons. The West had mainly potential resources, primarily in the form of rich soil and timber and furs. As we have seen, the principal constraint on trade both within and between the regions was the lack of low-cost transportation. As that barrier came down, the conditions necessary for specialized comparative-advantage trade between the regions began to fall into place.

When we examined the theory of comparative advantage in Chapter 2, we saw that nations find it to their mutual advantage to exchange goods and services produced on the basis of the comparative advantages of each. Then each nation can have more to consume after trade than before. This is so because trade permits each nation to use fewer resources to produce (or import) the goods it finally consumes. We also saw that increasing opportunity cost tends to cause the degree of specialization to be incomplete. Those same principles can be employed to understand movement of goods, services, and resources within a nation.

Triangular Trade

Successful and growing specialized trade depends on the following:

1. The existence of comparative advantages between the regions.
2. Transportation costs that permit the profitable movement over long distances of the comparative-advantage–produced goods.
3. Growing productivity and incomes that enlarge the size of cash markets.
4. More rapid productivity growth in cash-income activities than in subsistence-income activities (an increase in the opportunity cost of subsistence-oriented economic activities).
5. The existence of a legal, institutional, and social framework that will not only permit but will even encourage the harnessing of the foregoing signals to specialized activities.

   If all these conditions are fulfilled and if three regions exist, what may emerge is a pattern of bilateral trade such as that shown in Figure 8.1, or even triangular flows among the three regions.
   The development scenario suggested in Figure 8.1 is the following: Given the differing initial endowments and conditions indicated in the legend, as transporta-

Figure 8.1. Triangular Trade Between Regions.

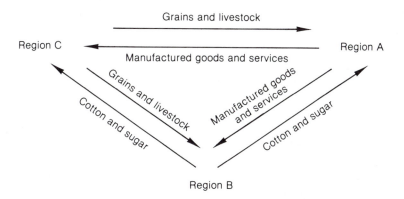

Region A: Waterpower, urban-industrial labor, timber, financial institutions, industrial economies of scale.
Region B: High soil fertility, mild climate, extensive internal river system, agricultural economies of scale.
Region C: High soil fertility, educated farm population, few agricultural economies of scale.

tion costs fall, resources in each region will be reallocated to produce those goods in which each region has its comparative advantage(s). Region A will tend to reallocate resources from agriculture to specialize in producing manufactured goods and financial services for Regions B and C. As new technology develops, whole new manufacturing industries develop, broadening the region's manufacturing base and accentuating its industrial and financial characteristics. As Region A's industries produce for a larger market, Region B will tend to reallocate its largely agricultural resources to specialize in producing a smaller number of agricultural commodities, for example, cotton and sugar. It avails itself in the long run of **internal and external economies of scale**—lowered production costs that will further enhance the industrial comparative advantage of the region. Its comparative advantage increasingly shifts. The economy of Region B tends to become **monocutural;** that is, to specialize in and depend on one or a few basic commodities. Region C tends to reallocate its resources in favor of cash crops that are more diversified than those in Region B. This is because of the lack of economies of scale in Region C.

In our model of a system of markets without institutional or individual barriers, Region A will specialize in manufacturing and will "export" its goods and financial services to Regions B and C. Region B will specialize in a few basic agricultural commodities and will "export" those to Regions A and C. Region C will specialize in the production of a more diversified mix of agricultural goods, such as grains or livestock produced on relatively smaller scales, and will "export" those to Regions A and B.

Incomplete Specialization

Recall that in this model, as in other international trade models of which this is a variant, we assume that as resources are reallocated to different uses, increasing opportunity cost or diminishing marginal productivity is ultimately encountered. Consequently, specialization in each region will be incomplete. The sooner encountered and the stronger the increasing cost is, the less will be the degree of specialization. This will be true even if there are no political or other barriers to interregional trade.

Resource Allocation and Pricing

Specialization within regions requires a means to reallocate resources to their changing most productive uses. For the most part, market signals in the form of relative wage rates, relative rates of return on investment, and other relative prices served that function in the antebellum period. We shall now examine some very fundamental principles that suggest not only how resource prices are determined but also the amount of those resources that are likely to be employed in particular uses.

Resource allocation and pricing, we shall assume, are established through market equilibria. This means that supply and demand are brought into equilibrium by competitive bidding and that resource markets are thereby cleared of shortages or surpluses. In these respects, equilibrium in a labor market, for instance, is similar to equilibrium in a product market. However, a basic difference exists between product markets and resource or factor markets. Demand for a resource such as labor is a **derived demand**—a demand that is brought about by the demand for the product or service that the resource is employed to produce. Thus, in the period under consideration, the demand for slaves on southern cotton plantations was a function of (depended on) the demand for cotton. As the demand for cotton increased, the derived demand for slaves increased.

The supply of a resource will ordinarily conform to the **law of supply**—that is, more will be supplied to the markets at relatively higher prices than at relatively lower prices. Fundamentally, this is because an increase in the price of the resource in a particular use causes that resource to be bid away from other, now relatively less-well-paid uses. These additional amounts of the resource will be successfully obtained by individual firms or regions even if the total supply of that resource, such as slaves, does not change or changes very little with higher prices in the short run.

Demand for a resource will ordinarily conform to the **law of demand**—that is, more will be demanded at (relatively) lower prices than at (relatively) higher prices. This is fundamentally so for several reasons. A firm hires enough of a resource at any given resource price to maximize its profitable use, to make that resource's contribution to the firm's marginal revenue equal to its contribution to marginal cost. For firms buying resources competitively, factor price is a given; thus factor price becomes the **marginal factor cost:** (MFC) the cost of hiring an additional unit of the resource. The rule for most profitable use of a resource, then, is that enough is hired to make that resource's marginal factor cost equal to its contribution to marginal revenue. The latter we call **marginal revenue product** (MRP): the marginal physical product (additional product output of an additional unit of resource) multiplied by the marginal revenue of the firm. We assume that the marginal physical product of any resource ultimately diminishes in the short run or actual production period. Thus the marginal revenue product schedule, the firm's demand curve for labor, slopes downward.

We see in Figure 8.2 how competitive factor prices are determined and, in turn, how individual firms respond to those price signals in bidding resources into particular uses. Figure 8.2(a) represents the determination of a competitive factor price. For the sake of illustration, assume that the marginal factor price (MFC) determined in Figure 8.2(a) is that of a slave, a prime field hand in 1850. The equilibrium price of the slave, P_e, is determined by the competitive bidding (at slave auctions such as in St. Louis) of buyers and sellers. Once established, that price tendency becomes marginal factor cost, the cost of buying an additional slave, to the potential slave owner. Since buying a slave was akin to buying a capital instrument, slave buyers

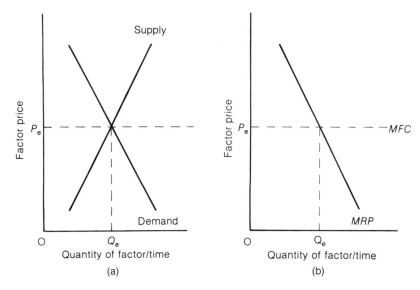

Figure 8.2. Competitive Factor Pricing and Factor Usage by a Single Firm: (a) Competitive Factor Pricing; (b) Factor Use by the Firm.

would calculate the expected net revenue flow from a slave and compare that with alternative forms of investment. Suppose that such a slave is expected to produce $50 of net revenue annually over his lifetime. Ignoring other factors such as aging, if the rate of return on other investments (real estate, crop advances, and the like) is 6 percent, then an individual slave owner will buy slaves at any price up to $833.50, which represents the capitalized value of a 6 percent return on $50; in Figure 8.2(b), the individual slave owner will buy enough slaves to make the competitive price equal to the marginal revenue product (MRP) of such slaves. Remember that the MRP schedule slopes downward because of the assumption of diminishing marginal productivity.

We shall return to the economics of slavery later in the next chapter. Slave prices are used here only as an illustration of factor pricing and the demand for factors by individual firms.

THE EVIDENCE AND THE CONCLUSIONS

In the remaining parts of this chapter, we are going to look at some of the evidence regarding the patterns of development that emerged in the Northeast and the West from 1815 to 1860. We shall see to what extent the trade model we have outlined gives a good approximation to those patterns. Finally, we are going to look at the overall evidence regarding the bilateral and trilateral ties among the three regions to determine how those ties emerged and became increasingly strong; we shall also see to what extent interferences of one sort or another prevented the development of strong three-way trade patterns.

THE WEST

The western United States evolved a pattern of economic organization similar to that of the South in some ways and remarkably different in others. In 1815, little of the area west of the Appalachians and extending to the Kansas and Nebraska territories had been brought into the commercial economy on a regular basis. By 1860, that region had become a major wheat- and corn-growing area, just as the South had become a major cotton-, rice-, tobacco-, and sugarcane-producing area, as the following chapter will elaborate.

The movement westward was, as we have seen, greatly facilitated by improvements in transportation, beginning with steamboats and continuing through the canals and the railroads. That is, the reduced transport costs of western staples increased their supply, not only to the rest of the nation, but also to foreign markets. As Thomas Berry (2) shows, between 1820 and 1860, the amount of manufactured goods midwestern farmers could buy with a given amount of their products more than doubled. According to Douglass North (23), though, the growth and settlement of the West would have been much slower if it had depended primarily on these cost reductions to increase the profitability of supplying western goods to other regional and international markets. In addition, the demand for western wheat and corn grew substantially, beginning as early as the late 1820s. As we see in Figure 8.3, land sales, which probably reflect expectations of future profits, paral-

Figure 8.3. Land Sales in Seven Western States: (Ohio, Illinois, Indiana, Michigan, Iowa, Wisconsin, Missouri), 1815–1860.

Source: Arthur H. Cole. "Cyclical and Seasonal Variations in the Sale of Public Lands, 1816–60," *Review of Economics and Statistics, 9* (1) (January 1927): 50. Reprinted in Douglass C. North, *The Economic Growth of the United States, 1790–1860* (New York: Norton, 1966), p. 137.

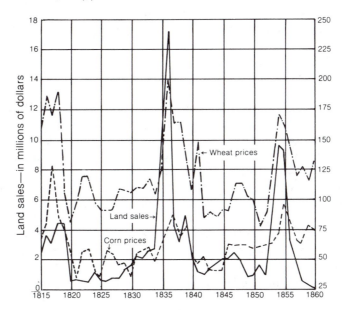

leled the movements of both wheat prices and corn prices. As wheat and corn prices rose, land prices were bid up in an area. This was followed by a longer-term movement farther into the West, with the consequent opening up of new lands and the creation of new capacity, awaiting further increases in the demand for those basic staples. Demand, at least in the East and in Europe, was growing with population and income growth. This, together with increasing urbanization and exogenous factors such as the potato famine in Ireland in the 1840s, was enlarging the market for wheat and corn. The pattern of short-term price increases inducing a movement into new lands was not dissimilar to the pattern of the South.

The Western Pioneers

It is tempting to think of the westward movement in agriculture as creating a way to absorb the increasing flow of immigrants to America. Such a conclusion, however, would seem to ignore the very high costs involved in westward movement. According to Martin Primack (25), a sixth of the entire labor force in the Midwest in the 1850s was employed in clearing land. If a western farm family spent most (perhaps up to 85 percent) of its time in activities relating to current consumption, even if these activities also involved, as in the case of land clearing and fence building, forming capital, then the level of investment required for successful western farming was extraordinarily high. It is therefore unlikely that newly arrived Americans formed the bulk of the western pioneers. Indeed, according to Donald Adams (1), an American factory worker would have had to accumulate average savings for five to ten years to acquire the capital to become an independent farmer.

Thus the pioneers were from the "old stock," to use the phrase of Jonathan Hughes (19). Many were established farmers who took their savings and kept moving westward, often selling a finished or partly finished farm to finance a further movement west.

Differences Between the West and the South

As we have seen, movement into new lands induced by short-term price increases in staples was common to the settlement of the West and the South. There were, however, some basic differences in the economic patterns of the two regions. Land tenancy in the West involved smaller, family-owned farms as compared with the larger, southern cotton plantations. Differences in economies of scale, generally easier entry conditions, and the absence of slavery in western agriculture may have created a western distribution of income less skewed toward upper-income groups than some scholars conclude existed in the South.

Western agriculture was less monocultural (less based on a single crop); not even wheat or corn dominated the West as cotton did the South. As a result, the West, although basically agricultural, developed a broader economic base than the South, including the building of extractive industries for such resources as iron ore, copper, and lead. As North (23) points out, the combination of reduced transportation costs, diversified agriculture, an elastic supply of labor, and a less skewed income distribution created profit possibilities for some intermediate urban industries in the West but not in the South. Industries designed to process agricultural commodities were much more likely to be established in the West than in the South because wheat, corn, and livestock were commodities that were dramatically reduced in weight through intermediate processing. The accompanying reduction in unit transportation costs of interregional trade further enhanced such trade and interregional integration. Urban centers, including Louisville, Cincinnati, Pittsburgh, and St. Louis, grew up either as transportation and distribution entrepots or as centers of manufacturing based on capturing more of the value added in agricultural processing or in transforming agricultural commodities into intermediate or final consumer goods. Louisville became a center for the tobacco and whiskey industries. So did Cincinnati, which added the hog-processing and soap industries. Chicago, of course, became both a transportation center and, later, the center of the meat-packing industry (a development that accelerated with the introduction of refrigerated shipment). Beyond the great river cities, many smaller but growing towns and cities sprang up along the railways in the 1840s and 1850s. These reflected not only land speculation but a demand by farms for the output of residentiary industries (dry goods, seeds, and the like). In the terms of Eugene Genovese (18), the West was pushed more rapidly by its diversification and income distribution into commercial capitalism than was the South. It is not an accident that the first national catalog sales organizations, such as Sears and Roebuck, originated in the Midwest.

Productivity grew rapidly in western farming. As with the South and the cotton gin, this productivity growth was often a result of technological change stimulated by the recognition of profit opportunities. A major case in point in the West is the movement onto the prairies in the 1830s and 1840s. Unlike the forested land left behind, the prairies were frequently covered with thick turf and high grass. Even iron-tipped plows were ineffective in breaking such soils. With a growing demand for wheat and corn and the high price of land further east, though, human ingenuity came to the fore. A series of technological improvements, beginning with the large breaking plows and extending through steel plows, greatly increased output per unit of labor input.

Sometimes there were long lags between the development of a new technology and its widespread implementation. A case in point is the horse-drawn reaper. Though it was developed in the 1830s by Hussey and by McCormick, as late as 1850 not even 1 percent of grain in this country was being cut by reaper; the scythe remained dominant. Yet more than 80,000 reapers were sold in the decade of the 1850s. For many years, the view of historians was that it took the rising grain prices of the 1850s to induce the profitable purchase of this new capital. But Paul David (10), using modern techniques of estimation, concluded that this explanation is insufficient since cutting costs can be profitable even with falling prices. David found that it was primarily the differences in terrain encountered on the open prairies in the 1850s that explained the widespread adoption of the reaper in that decade. This basic conclusion remains valid, although Allan Olmstead (24) has added several qualifications and Lewis Jones (21) has shown that both David and Olmstead may be off in establishing the thresholds of farm size at which reaper use became profitable. As Jones points out, only large, not average-size, farms used reapers even in the 1850s. Therefore, rising grain prices may indeed have quickened the pace of adoption of the new technology.

In general, the terms of trade, according to Thomas Berry (2), moved in favor of the West. Early in the nineteenth century, the cost of floating western goods down the Mississippi was much less than that of bringing goods into the West by horseback. Therefore, transportation innovations, especially steamboats, reduced the costs of bringing goods into the West by far greater amounts than they reduced the costs of bringing western products to market. As Adams (1) showed, this ability of the West to "import" more goods (both capital and consumer goods), with the use of a given amount of its own resources almost certainly enhanced the capital accumulation necessary to expand industry. As compared with the South, western firms and farms benefited disproportionately from two major external economies. The first was the relatively heavy investments in social overhead capital, especially in transportation (rails and canals), storage (warehouses), and the urban facilities necessary to serve an increasingly urban population. The second was the relatively heavy western investments in human capital, especially in education and training. Whether measured in terms of literacy, number of whites in school, or number of libraries, the West led the South by a substantial margin. Because of the many family farms and the growing need for an urban skilled labor force, the marginal revenue productivity of investment in human capital was much greater to westerners than to southerners.

THE NORTHEAST

Industrial Specialization

The great theme between 1815 and 1860 in the New England and Middle Atlantic states (which we shall call the Northeast) was industrialization.

In 1860, the Northeast, with 34 percent of the U.S. population, contained 67 percent of the nation's manufacturing employment. The lack of industrialization in the South and the relatively lesser industrialization of the West are indicated by their smaller percentages of manufacturing employment—13 percent and 20 percent, respectively (see Table 8.1).

It would be a mistake, though, to equate manufacturing with industrialization. The former had thrived in the United States for many years before 1815. A system of home manufactures had particularly characterized isolated towns and communities since colonial times. Industrialization, however, was a combination of two things: (a) the factory system with its interchangeable parts, assembly line,

Table 8.1. Manufacturing Employment by Regions, 1860.

REGION	PERCENT OF TOTAL POPULATION	PERCENT OF MANUFACTURING EMPLOYMENT IN UNITED STATES
East	34	67
West	31	20
South	35	13

SOURCE: Eighth Census of the United States, *Manufacturers of the United States in 1860* (Washington, D.C.: U.S. Government Printing Office, 1865).

and specialization; and (b) the development of production for a national rather than a local or regional market. A national market, necessary to create a demand great enough to exhaust economies of scale, was greatly facilitated by the external economies of improved transportation.

Localized, often home industries (such as the colonial flour mill) are usually tied to a resource subject to diminishing returns, exist primarily because of a particular locational advantage (such as being close to a source of kinetic energy), and generate very small stimuli for the development of other industries. The great industries that developed in the Northeast between 1815 and 1860 did not suffer from these disadvantages.

The first great industry in the Northeast—indeed, the first to produce for a national market—was the cotton textile industry. This industry, using power looms, underwent two dramatic expansions. One occurred in the period of the second war with Britain (1812–1815) and the other after 1817. The growth of the industry can be seen in Table 8.2.

Table 8.2. New England Cotton Industry Output, 1805–1860.

YEAR	YARDS OF CLOTH (000'S)	VALUE ADDED ($000'S) CLOTH
1805	46	2
1810	648	34
1815	2,358	124
1820	13,874	728
1825	69,667	3,658
1830	141,616	7,435
1835	250,773	13,166
1840	323,000	16,958
1845	395,762	20,778
1850	596,867	31,336
1855	634,200	33,296
1860	857,225	45,004

SOURCE: Adapted from Robert B. Zevin, "The Growth of Cotton Textile Production After 1815," in *The Reinterpretation of American Economic History*, ed. Robert W. Fogel and Stanley Engerman (New York: Harper & Row, 1971).

According to Robert Zevin (28), the principal reason for the rapid expansion of the cotton textile industry from 1815 to 1833 was the suitability of mass-produced power-loom cloth (called *sheeting*) to meet the demands of the growing western population. After the mid-1830s, the industry grew at a declining rate, although it was still the most important single commodity-producing industry at the time of the Civil War.

Some other parts of the textile industry expanded rapidly after 1830, though. Woolen textiles grew slowly, because of the competition of cotton textiles. But mixtures of cotton and wool (called *shoddy*) were produced, and the manufacture of lace, silk, linen, and felt was expanded.

The second industry to develop rapidly in the Northeast was the iron industry, heavily concentrated in Pennsylvania. This industry, like textiles (both cotton and woolen) was heavily concentrated in the Northeast. It was slow to adopt the "best" (English) ironmaking technology because the bituminous coal available in the East had a high sulfur content that made coking impossible. Nonetheless, the iron industry grew rapidly, using charcoal (in plentiful supply in Pennsylvania), and achieved significant economies of scale in the 1850s and 1860s. Indeed, the industry probably experienced productivity growth equal to that of other industries of the period.

Secondary and Tertiary Industries

In a real sense, the maxim "Nothing succeeds like success" applies to the Northeast. As the textile and iron industries grew, subsidiary industries grew up around them. The machine goods industry expanded to supply the needs of the textile and iron industries, as well as to supply steamboat engines and, later, the railway industry. In other words, as the scale of established industries grew, this generated external economies for new or would-be industries. Textile factories become more specialized and no longer produced their own machines. A financial industry grew up around the manufacturing industries in the Northeast. Banks, insurance companies, brokerage houses, and stock exchanges all became much more heavily concentrated in the Northeast than in the South or even in the West.

The growth of basic industries, such as iron, and of satellite industries, such as finance, created external economies for consumer goods industries. A good example is the stove industry. Cast-iron stoves were a major consumer good, and the industry, concentrated in New England, produced a value of almost $11 million in 1860. In terms of our model, external economies reduced costs, increased supply, and increased the marginal revenue productivity of labor and other resources. In turn, this increased the derived demand for labor, a stimulus that resulted in greater immigration and urbanization.

Success in a Declining Agriculture: The Northeast

Much of the relative decline of agriculture in the United States during this period could be witnessed in the Northeast. It is well known that the period saw a major decrease in the role of agriculture in that area. Indeed, the Northeast, as we have seen, became a net importer of agricultural foodstuffs and agricultural raw materials. At the same time, even that area of the nation had some significant agricultural success stories. The growth of the factory system and its corollary, urbanization, produced a substantially different set of demands for foodstuffs in the Northeast. Urban families are, of course, much less self-sufficient than their rural counterparts. New York City, with its late 1850s population of over one million, had to be supplied with dairy products and with fresh vegetables and fruits. The high price-to-weight ratios of these products and the lack of refrigerated means of shipment precluded bringing them in from distant areas. As Paul Gates (17) has shown, specialized farms were thriving in the Northeast by the 1830s. According to the records of the period, a surprising variety of fresh fruits and vegetables was available around all urban areas by the 1840s.

Not only was the Northeast shifting from a comparative advantage in agriculture to one in industry and finance, but within agriculture its advantage was in labor- and capital-intensive crops rather than in land-intensive crops. The fundamental reasons for the shift were previously recorded changes in transportation costs. The canals, steamboats, and railroads made possible the relatively inexpensive shipment of commodities with high ratios of weight to price over very long distances. Ultimately, they made possible the shipment of corn, wheat, and other extensively produced crops from the West to the Northeast.

AGRICULTURE—A SUMMING UP

Agriculture in Decline?

To begin, let us see what happened to agriculture's relative share of output in the American economy. As with so many other indices of nineteenth-century economic activity, reliable series date from about 1840. Table 8.3, which is reported by Robert Fogel (14, 15) and based on the work of Robert Gallman (16), provides an overview in constant dollars of the change in percentage distribution of value added in commodity production between 1839 and 1859.

Clearly the relative shares of the sectors in the commodity output of the nation changed dramatically in the last 20 years of the pre–Civil War era. This is espe-

Table 8.3.   Percentage Distribution of Value Added in Commodity Production (Gallman's Constant Dollar Series).

YEAR	AGRICULTURE	MINING	MANUFACTURING	CONSTRUCTION
1839	71.9	0.7	17.4	10.1
1844	68.7	1.0	21.1	9.2
1849	59.7	1.1	29.5	9.8
1854	56.8	1.1	29.2	12.9
1859	55.5	1.2	32.2	11.2

SOURCE: Robert W. Fogel, *Railroads and American Economic Growth: Essays in Econometric History* (Baltimore: Johns Hopkins University Press, 1964).

cially so in the 1839–1849 period, when agriculture's share fell from 71.9 percent to 59.7 percent, while manufacturing's share rose from 17.4 percent to 29.5 percent.

Was agriculture, then, a "declining sector"? In a relative output sense, yes. Two things are apparent in this respect for the entire period from 1800 to 1860. First, agriculture's share declined over the whole period. Assuming proportionality between the percentage of the population engaged in the activities of a sector and that sector's share of commodity output, agriculture probably had declined from about 90 percent in 1800 to about 55 percent in 1860. Correspondingly, manufacturing's share had probably risen from about 5 percent in 1800 to about 33 percent in 1860.

Second, we should not be surprised at these relative sectoral changes because, as we have seen, industrialization was successfully under way in the United States at least by the 1820s. A successful industrial movement implies a change in the relative position of industry if for no other reason than that, to be successful, it must have a great enough productivity edge over agriculture to warrant factor payments that will bid resources out of agriculture. The growth of industrial cities and urban industrial employment reflects that success and that productivity differential.

There is no conflict between viewing agriculture as a declining sector of the U.S. economy before the Civil War and the evidence we will see in Chapter 9 of a productive and profitable plantation agriculture in the South (especially the New South) and an increasingly successful multicrop agriculture in the West. Sectoral decline means merely that agriculture *as a set of national economic activities* was not growing in the value of its output nearly as rapidly as manufacturing was. It does not mean that agricultural productivity was declining.

There are many reasons why we should expect a relative agricultural decline to be associated with the economic development that occurs during a period of industrialization. One of the most important is associated with the **income elasticity of demand**[*]—responsiveness of the demand for agricultural products to changes in income. This elasticity for primary commodities tends to diminish as incomes grow. The demand for secondary and tertiary commodities such as fine clothing and better-quality foods may grow rapidly with income growth (may be income elastic). Demand for other basic agricultural commodities such as coarse clothing and bulky foods, however, may actually decline with income growth (may be income inelastic). The experience of the United States appears to confirm this.

Technological Change in Agriculture and the American System

Technological change, as we have seen in the case of manufacturing, is an important contributor to productivity growth. It shifts the production function of an industry; that is, it makes all inputs more productive. Although the opening up of a highly elastic supply of fertile farmland contributed to the antebellum productivity increase, technical improvements did likewise. Some illustrations will suffice to make the point clear.

[*]See the Review of Economic Concepts in Chapter 11 for a more detailed discussion of this concept.

In the early 1800s, a farmer typically had little physical capital—a few hand tools, an all-purpose plow, hoes, and other simple items of that sort. Given the scarcity of labor, complementary capital that increased the productivity of farm labor was highly desirable, even if its implementation lagged. Improvements in plowing and harvesting equipment are illustrative of the incentives that existed to make improvements in equipment.

Evolutionary changes over several decades in the simple all-purpose plow improved the casting process, reduced breakage, and improved the design and shape of the moldboard. Also, the design of interchangeable parts permitted different plow heads to be used for different purposes. In 1817, Jethro Wood culminated these efforts with the cast-iron plow. At first, wooden plows were cheaper and easier to obtain (iron plows were produced in factories, wooden ones by local craftsmen), but the iron plow became cheaper and dominant even in eastern agriculture by the 1830s. In 1837, John Deere introduced the steel plow, which, with changes in steel technology after the Civil War, was to become dominant in the heavy wet soils of the West.

Improvements on plows gradually removed a seasonal supply bottleneck. However, one problem remained, that of quickly harvesting the mature crop. Wheat and hay, among other grain crops, lose much of their value if not harvested soon after maturity or if allowed to become wet. Here, too, the solution of the problem was an evolutionary process. The horse rake introduced in the 1820s could perform the work of eight to ten men; the revolving hay rake in the mid-1850s was a similar improvement. Also needed were horse-driven machines to cut grain and finally to thresh the crops. The reaper, attributed to Obed Hussy and Cyrus McCormick, greatly increased the speed with which grain crops could be harvested. Because the reaper was not well adapted for the efficient (very near the ground) cutting of grass, a separate hay mower was being developed as well. The superiority of the American machines in this respect was demonstrated at the International Exhibition of 1855. In a contest of reaping and mowing machines, a French machine cut an acre in 71 minutes, an English machine in 66 minutes, and an American machine in 22 minutes.

Down to 1830, most grain in the United States was either threshed by wooden flail or trod on earthen floors by oxen or horses. The grain was separated from the chaff by simply tossing it in the air and letting the wind blow away the chaff. Although the fanning mill was an improvement, experimentation continued to develop a threshing machine. Many were developed, but the most efficient was that of Hiram and John Pitt in 1836. Its relative productivity was demonstrated at the Paris Exhibition of 1855. In that demonstration, six men threshed with flails while four different machines did likewise. The results were as follows:

	Liters of Wheat		*Liters of Wheat*
Six threshers with flails	36		
Threshing machine		Threshing machine	
Belgian	150	English	410
French	250	American	740

There were two amazing demonstrations. The least efficient machine was over four times as productive as six hand threshers, and the product of the American System was three-fourths again as productive as its nearest rival and over 20 times as productive as the six hand threshers. Clearly, this suggests that agriculture's decline was only in relative size; the sector was very vigorous in terms of productivity growth.

The American system of continuous production found its way into agriculture partly in the food-processing industry. The meat-packing industry is illustrative, especially the pork-packing industry centered around Cincinnati and later in Chicago. Hog breeding dramatically changed the quality of swine. With highly specialized meat cutters operating on an automated line, the hogs moved through a highly efficient butchering process. Indeed, it was said that "Everything in the hog was utilized but the oink." In that light, it is not surprising that other related industries soon developed: a lard industry, a hide industry, and a soap industry.

THE NORTHEAST: SUMMING UP

Clearly, the Northeast became the country's manufacturing center, the hub of industrialization, between 1815 and 1860. Probably the greatest factor that permitted this was the growth in the size of the market. Population growth, growing per capita incomes, increasing urbanization and its corollary, reduced self-sufficiency, created ever larger markets for both producer and consumer goods. Combined with falling transportation costs, these factors permitted greater specialization and growth of the sizes of firms and industries. The first such firms (textiles, clothing, shoes, boots, stoves, and the like) to produce for a national United States market were heavily concentrated in the Northeast.

The question remains why the Northeast became the region that enjoyed so many of the benefits of the initial process of industrialization. One explanation often advanced is that the initial (pre-1815) conditions were differentially favorable to the region. Although its soil and climate had never given it a strong comparative advantage in agriculture (with a few exceptions in areas of the Mid-Atlantic states), the Northeast's ready source of waterpower gave it an advantage in manufacturing, at least until steam boilers and electricity freed industries from dependence on kinetic energy. Most of the manufacturing stimulus of the 1790–1815 period (the Napoleonic era) accrued to the Northeast. Earlier, the country's only large-scale nonagricultural industry, shipbuilding, had located by the timber stands of the New England coast. The best seaports were in the region during an era when foreign trade dominated the economy; thus business experience with large-scale enterprises (especially export-import businesses) was concentrated there. In other words, the pattern after 1815 or 1820 merely continued a pattern already established.

In terms of the supply of labor and the marginal revenue productivity of labor, the Northeast attracted most of the arriving immigrants. The region also was the first committed to widespread, if not universal, literacy. The region led the United States in literacy rates, whites in schools, libraries, and the other indices that reflected investment in human capital.

SPECIALIZATION: THE MODEL AND THE EVIDENCE

In an important article written in 1902, Guy Callender (6) set out the argument for the trilateral pattern of trade we saw in Figure 8.1. In that article, he stated that early frontier settlement had little to do with economic development in the sense of specialization and tying together of a nation's resources on the basis of comparative-advantage uses. The reason, according to Callender, was that incomes (especially cash incomes) were low and transportation costs high. He went on to state that two events changed this pattern. "The first was the introduction of the steamboat; the second was the extension of the cotton culture into the Southwest." According to the argument, the "prosperity which [these two things] brought to the whole southern and western population increased their ability to purchase such manufactures as they required and thus provided eastern manufacturers with rapidly expanding markets."

From what we have already seen, the broad outlines of the Callender argument are persuasive. The growth of trade over the Erie Canal, the growth of trade at New Orleans, which in value terms increased 20-fold between 1816 and 1858, the manufacturing growth in the Northeast—all these things testify to the emergence of a national market system in the 45-year period we are studying.

A later (1939) study by Louis Schmidt (26) seriously questioned the extent of the trilateral trade pattern. According to Schmidt, the triangular or circular pattern of internal trade was replaced by a more direct exchange of commodities between the agrarian South and West and the increasingly industrial East. Still, Douglass North (23) argues that the trilateral pattern was important, that the South produced a few staple goods on its plantation while depending on the East for most of its manufactured goods, and finally, that the West had a surplus of grain and livestock to supply the increasing deficits of the South and the East.

The most definitive effort to assess these arguments and measure interregional trade flows has been undertaken by Albert Fishlow (13). He sets out to show that "interregional exchange was a prominent feature of American antebellum development, but not as a result of interdependence among all regions." Fishlow's general results may be seen in Table 8.4.

We can see that between 1839 and 1860 interregional trade grew greatly (from a total gross flow of $178 million in 1839 to $657.1 million in 1860). It appears that what developed, though, was a pattern not of trilateral trade but of bilateral trade. As Fishlow says, "The clear picture that emerges is one of tenuous linkage between

Table 8.4.   Interregional Merchandise Trade Flows (millions of current dollars).

YEAR	ORIGINATING REGION	NORTH	WEST	SOUTH
1839	North	—	19.7	85.6
	West	11.8	—	14.9
		7.1	—	5.5
	South	39.7	6.3	—
		15.1	2.2	—
1844	North	—	25.2	73.2
	West	20.1	—	19.9
		14.5	—	7.6
	South	32.4	6.2	—
		11.6	3.5	—
1849	North	—	41.4	80.0
	West	36.8	—	36.1
		24.2	—	10.5
	South	32.0	8.1	—
		18.9	4.8	—
1853	North	—	94.5	147.1
	West	63.2	—	36.9
		47.9	—	19.2
	South	61.9	17.2	—
		33.0	11.9	—
1857	North	—	163.1	165.7
	West	96.9	—	49.1
		45.8	—	25.5
	South	71.1	13.2	—
		38.0	5.5	—
1860	North	—	164.3	213.8
	West	146.5	—	42.8
		107.6	—	36.4
	South	69.4	20.3	—
		44.6	13.6	—

Note: Uppermost (larger) figure refers to gross flow whether for consumption or reexport; bottom (lower) figure is estimated consumption. In the case of the South-North entry, this is limited to northern purchases of southern cotton and molasses.

Source: Albert A. Fishlow, "Antebellum Interregional Trade Reconsidered," *American Economic Review*, May 1964.

the two regions. To the West, the South was a minor matter for its own demands." In 1860, the North sold $164.3 million to the West and bought $146.5 million from that region. The North sold $213.8 million to the South, and the South sold $69.4 million to the North. Trade between the South and the West was relatively small, however ($20.3 million sold by the South to the West, $42.8 million sold by the West to the South).

Clearly, by 1860, the North was selling its manufactured goods and financial services to both the West and South. In turn, they were selling agricultural goods (and, in the case of the West, some semimanufactured goods) to the North. The weak West-South tie appears to be due to the fact that the South was highly self-sufficient in foodstuffs.[*] Also, the South was, even in 1860, more heavily dependent on foreign markets than was the West. Although Fishlow's data have been challenged by Robert Fogel (14), his basic conclusion about bilateral trade stands. Perhaps, in final comment, it is not surprising that two agricultural regions did not develop strong export ties with each other; rather, those regions sought markets, whether domestic or foreign, in which their produce was an input needed in industry or to sustain an urban interdependent labor force.

QUESTIONS

1. What were two of the broadest economic themes of the period of U.S. development between 1815 and 1860?

2. What determined the basic comparative advantages of the South, the West, and the Northeast?

3. What conditions are necessary for successful and growing specialized trade between regions?

4. According to the three-region model of this chapter, what are the basic economic characteristics of each region?

5. What determines the supply of a resource? Its demand? Why are the general laws of supply and demand observed in resource pricing as well as in product pricing?

6. What were the basic similarities and differences between the patterns of economic development of the South and the West?

7. What roles did short-term and long-term agricultural prices play in the settlement of the West? How did changing geographic conditions in the West beget profit incentive for technological change?

8. What happened to the terms of trade of the West between 1815 and 1860? How did external economies affect those terms?

9. What was the great theme of development in the Northeast between 1815 and 1860? How did manufacturing change into a process of industrialization in the Northeast?

10. What were the major industries in the Northeast in the period from 1815 to 1860? What caused these industries to grow rapidly? How did secondary and tertiary industries become established in the Northeast?

11. What is the explanation for the fact that the Northeast became the first great manufacturing center and industrial region of the United States?

12. What was Guy Callender's argument about trilateral trade among the regions of the United States? What are Albert Fishlow's conclusions about the validity of that argument?

13. What happened to the relative position of agriculture in commodity output in the United States between 1839 and 1850? In what sense does this indicate that agriculture was a declining sector? Why should the decline not be surprising?

[*]Plantation records of the period indicate a high degree of self-sufficiency (foods, basic clothing, and the like) throughout much of the region.

14. What happened to the role of agriculture and the mix of agricultural products in the Northeast between 1815 and 1860? What factors explain these changes?

15. What incentives to technological change existed in American agriculture between 1815 and 1860? What were some of the most notable changes in that technology? What seems to explain the long lags that sometimes occurred in implementing those technological changes?

SUGGESTED READINGS

1. Adams, Donald. "Earnings and Savings in the Early 19th Century." *Explorations in Economic History, 17* (April 1980).

2. Berry, Thomas S. *Western Prices Before 1861: A Study of the Cincinnati Market.* Harvard Economic Studies. Cambridge, Mass.: Harvard University Press, 1943.

3. Bidwell, Percy, and John Falconer. *History of Agriculture in the Northern United States, 1620–1860.* Washington, D.C.: The Carnegie Institution, 1925.

4. Bogue, Allan. "Farming in the Prairie Peninsula 1830–1890." *Journal of Economic History, 1* (March 1963).

5. Bogue, Allan G. *From Prairie to Corn Belt.* Chicago: University of Chicago Press, 1963.

6. Callender, Guy S. "The Early Transportation and Banking Enterprises of the States in Relation to the Growth of Corporations." *Quarterly Journal of Economics* (November 1902).

7. Cole, Arthur H. "Cyclical and Seasonal Variations in the Sale of Public Lands, 1816–1860." *Review of Economics and Statistics, 9,* (January 1927).

8. Danhof, Clarence H. *Change in Agriculture: The Northern United States, 1820–1870.* Cambridge, Mass.: Harvard University Press, 1969.

9. Danhof, Clarence. "Farm Making Costs and the Safety Valve: 1855–1860." In *The Public Lands,* ed. Vernon Carstensen. Madison: University of Wisconsin Press, 1963.

10. David, Paul A. *Technical Choice, Innovation and Economic Growth: Essays on American and British Experience in the Nineteenth Century.* Cambridge: Cambridge University Press, 1975.

11. Eighth Census of the United States. *Manufacturing of the United States in 1860.* Washington, D.C.: U.S. Government Printing Office, 1865.

12. Fishlow, Albert. *American Railroads and the Transformation of the Antebellum Economy.* Cambridge, Mass.: Harvard University Press, 1965.

13. Fishlow, Albert. Antebellum Interregional Trade Reconsidered." *American Economic Review, 54* (May 1964).

14. Fogel, Robert W. "American Interregional Trade in the Nineteenth Century." In *New Views on American Economic Development,* ed. Ralph Andreano. Cambridge, Mass.: Shenckman, 1965.

15. Fogel, Robert W. "Discussion." *American Economic Review, 54* (May 1964).

16. Gallman, Robert. "Self-Sufficiency in the Cotton Economy of the Ante-bellum South", in William Parker (ed). *The Structure of the Cotton Economy of the Ante-bellum South.* Washington: Agriculture History Society, 1970.

17. Gates, Paul. *The Farmer's Age: Agriculture, 1815–1860.* New York: Harper and Row, 1960.

18. Genovese, Eugene D. *The Political Economy of Slavery.* New York: Pantheon Books, 1965.

19. Hughes, Jonathan. *American Economic History.* 2nd ed. Glenview, Ill.: Scott, Foresman, 1987. Chap. 10.

20. Johnson, Emory R. *History of Domestic and Foreign Commerce in the United States.* Washington, D.C.: Carnegie Institution of Washington, 1915.

21. Jones, Lewis. "The Mechanization of Reaping and Mowing in American Agriculture: A Comment." *Journal of Economic History, 37* (June 1977).

22. Merk, Frederich. *History of the Westward Movement.* New York: Alfred Knopf, 1978.

23. North, Douglass C. *The Economic Growth of the United States.* New York: Norton, 1966.

24. Olmstead, Alan. "The Mechanization of Reaping and Mowing in American Agriculture, 1833–70." *Journal of Economic History, 35* (June 1975).

25. Primack, Martin. "Land Clearing Under 19th Century Techniques." *Journal of Economic History, 22* (December 1962).

26. Schmidt, Louis B. "Internal Commerce and the Development of the National Economy Before 1860." *Journal of Political Economy, 47* (December 1939).

27. Stewart, George R. *Ordeal by Hunger: The Story of the Donner Party.* Boston: Houghton Mifflin, 1936.

28. Zevin, Robert. "The Growth of Cotton Textile Production After 1815." In *The Reinterpretation of American Economic History,* ed. Robert W. Fogel and Stanley Engerman. New York: Harper and Row, 1971.

Chapter 9

REGIONAL INTEGRATION AND SPECIALIZATION TO 1860

The Slave South

Why, the reader may well ask, should the South be treated separately from the other two regions? The fundamental answer lies in the institution of slavery, which was unique to the South. As we saw in Chapter 8, the Northeast and the West evolved a set of market institutions based on the advantages of voluntary exchange, not just the exchange of money for goods and services but also the exchange of resources (including labor services) for factor incomes. In the South, however, this system of voluntary exchanges, while widespread, did not extend to slaves, who constituted almost all the black population and about half the labor force of the region.

The full effects of this "peculiar institution," as Kenneth Stampp (40) has dubbed it, have been much researched and widely debated. In view of the institution's importance to the Civil War, which we shall examine in the next chapter, it is important to understand the background as well as the effects of slavery.

SOUTHERN AGRICULTURE

It is probably clear to you that Region B in the model set forth in Chapter 8 comes very close to fitting the basic economic conditions of the South before the Civil War. The South was definitely a region with high soil fertility, mild climate, extensive internal river systems, and a comparative advantage in producing a few agricultural crops. Some students of the South have argued that those crops were also subject to greater economies of scale than existed elsewhere in the United States. However, opposition to that argument has been strongly expressed by some economic historians. Indeed, as Gavin Wright (46) has clearly demonstrated, large-size plantations, a number of which existed in the South, do *not* necessarily imply economies of scale. Nonetheless, southern farms were on average substantially larger than those in the West. Almost 40 percent of farms in the South exceeded 500 acres, while few reached that size in the Midwest (44). From the work of Wright (46) and Metzer (29), it appears that scale economies did exist in southern agriculture, but they were limited not only by the traditional problems of communication and management but also by the problems (costs) of slave discipline.

These general statements are inadequate to set the framework of the antebellum southern economy. An important specification must be added. From an agricultural and economic point of view, there was not truly one South; rather, there were two. The first South was the "Old South," consisting of a belt of states from Virginia through South Carolina and Georgia. These states, among the original colonies, had formed an early pattern of extensive agriculture built primarily around tobacco and rice. Because of the failure to form a pattern of soil conservation, by the second quarter of the nineteenth century soil fertility in the Old South was seriously diminished.

The second South was the "New South," an area encompassing primarily Alabama, Mississippi, Louisiana, Arkansas, and eastern Texas. This area, well served by river transportation systems and enjoying the great fertility of alluvial soils, experienced extremely high yields per acre in cotton and sugar production. Moreover, in the New South, especially in the trans-Mississippi area, there *may* have been significant economies of scale (falling production costs per unit of cotton or sugar with larger-sized plantations) or at least few diseconomies of scale (rising unit costs with larger-sized plantations). Thus, in Mississippi and Louisiana, efficient plantations might consist of several thousand acres, compared to much smaller farms in the rest of the nation.

A caveat is in order here. First, as Wright (46) has noted, cotton was not a very soil-exhaustive crop. Much of the movement of resources from the Old to the New South represented not so much an abandonment of a soil-poor area as an expansion into a soil-rich area in response to a secularly booming cotton market.

SLAVERY: THE PECULIAR INSTITUTION

At the outset of the 45-year period we are examining, most of the South's population and other resources were in the Old South. What mechanisms facilitated the movement of much of that region's resources into the New South? The question cannot be answered without considering slavery and its operations. Slavery had existed since early colonial times. Over time, the "peculiar institution" became concentrated almost exclusively in the South. This happened in part because owners' enforcement of property rights in slaves became more and more costly in northern (and certain border) states whose populations regarded slavery as socially noxious. Some of these states imposed a ban on slavery, a ban that went beyond the constitutional ban on importing further slaves into the United States after 1808.

Figure 9.1. A Southern Mansion, with Slave Quarters in the Foreground. (Photo from the National Archives)

After 1815, then, and in the face of a legally restricted supply, purchases of slaves became a major form of capital investment in the South. Only about 25 percent of the adult male white population owned slaves. Among slaveholders, ownership was concentrated: a fifth of the slave owners had only one slave. Forming the new, large plantations involved moving slaves (and other resources) into the new, more fertile areas of the South.

Was slavery essentially burdensome to the southern economy? Did it hinder resource transfer and the other developmental processes of the region? Few questions in our economic history have been so controversial or so thoroughly researched. Until recent years, the preponderant opinion seemed to be yes. This involved a view of slavery often associated with, among others, Ulrich Phillips, a professor of history at Yale University. In a famous article written in 1905, Phillips (34) argued that slavery was burdensome to the South for a variety of reasons, including the "unwillingness of slaves to work hard" (low marginal productivity) or to reproduce and increase their supply. Most importantly, he argued that, especially after 1815, in the face of an increasingly inelastic (and slowly growing) supply, slave prices rose to reflect large **quasi-rents** (payments due to the relative inelasticity of supply) to slave sellers but that these higher prices did not reflect growing productivity. Phillips believed that a profit squeeze on cotton growers resulted, especially because cotton prices, he thought, were falling. The profit squeeze would have ultimately forced the abandonment of slavery. Slavery, in other words, would have toppled of its own weight. The Civil War, in the Phillips's view, was an unnecessary bloodbath to the extent that it was fought over the issue of slavery.

Beginning especially in the 1930s, various scholars sought to answer the open questions about slavery, including its profitability. Much painstaking examination of plantation records was undertaken. One of the foremost scholars of American agricultural history, Lewis C. Gray (25), concluded that slavery *was* profitable, that slave owners earned rates of return comparable to investment returns elsewhere in the economy. Gray, however, was almost alone in that view. A study in 1929 by Charles Ramsdell (35) had argued that slavery would have become unprofitable because the highly productive lands of the New South, especially in Texas, would have increased the supply of cotton relative to its demand, depressing cotton prices and making the crop unprofitable. Although the Ramsdell argument has been disproved in various ways (especially by showing that the price of cotton was *not* falling over time), it was one of many arguments that caused students of antebellum history to conclude that prior to 1860 slavery was already doomed as an institution.

"MODERN" STUDIES OF AMERICAN SLAVERY

Debates about the profitability of slavery and whether the institution caused the southern economy to stagnate have continued. There have been some notable arguments challenging the orthodox view that slavery was deleterious to the southern economy. An example is contained in *The Peculiar Institution* by Kenneth Stampp (40). In 1958, however, a pathbreaking article, "The Economics of Slavery in the Ante-Bellum South" by Alfred Conrad and John Meyer (5) was published in the *Journal of Political Economy*. In a sense, the "new economic history," employing explicit economic theory and modern quantitative techniques to investigate historical hypotheses, began with this article.

Postulating two production functions, one for the production of slaves, the principal intermediate good, and the other for cotton itself, Conrad and Meyer came to the conclusion that a person purchasing slaves in 1846–1850 could expect, on the basis of recent experience, to earn a rate of return comparable to long-term investments elsewhere in the antebellum economy. Conrad and Meyer found that this was made possible by a well-functioning set of factor markets that transferred slaves from the Old South to the New South, as well as by a well-functioning commodity market for cotton. In other words, slave prices were determined by market forces. Such prices tended to reflect the marginal productivity of slaves, and rising slave prices reflected a growing productivity. The study seems to have laid to rest the Phillips argument about wildly inflated slave prices that reflected conspicuous consumption by planters and the inelastic supplies of slaves.

Although later work by Edward Saraydar (37) reduced the Conrad and Meyer estimates of returns on slaveholding, their basic conclusion still holds: slave buyers in the last half of the 1840s were not, in the main, irrational or given to conspicuous consumption or cavalier reasons for purchasing slaves. Furthermore, a study by

Robert Evans, Jr., (9) broadened the Conrad and Meyer conclusions to the entire period from 1830 to 1860.

Time on the Cross: Slavery, a Rational System?

In 1974, Robert Fogel and Stanley Engerman, two of the best-known "new economic historians," published *Time on the Cross: The Economics of American Negro Slavery* (17), one of the most controversial and widely read modern works in economic history. Among other things, Fogel and Engerman sought to dispel any remaining notions that slavery was an uneconomic or dying institution. They concluded that slave owners were not cavaliers but businessmen concerned about slave productivity. Slaves were relocated primarily from the Old South to the New South, not as individuals, but as families or as entire plantation labor forces, to avoid diminishing their productivity. From a productivity viewpoint, then, it seems unlikely that the slave owner engaged in *widespread* disrupting of slave families and beating of slaves. Such incidents occurred as a matter of discipline, and they have been well recorded in the writings of many, including Booker Washington (45) and Frederick Olmstead (31). But the work of Gutman (26) has confirmed the view that most slave families were headed by *two* adults, and the notion that the practice of disrupting families was widespread has been discredited by historians. Slavery was an economic institution. But was it rational?

Fogel and Engerman's *Time on the Cross* contains many specific profiles of slave prices correlated with particular attributes of slaves. Those attributes include age, sex, and specific skills or disabilities. In the case of each of these profiles, it appears that expectations about relative marginal revenue productivities dictated the demand for slaves and thereby helped determine their prices. Highly skilled slaves such as carpenters and wheelwrights brought prices half again above those for semiskilled slaves. Younger slaves (of productive age) brought higher prices than older slaves, although the prices of skilled slaves peaked at older ages than those of less skilled slaves, reflecting the later payout on investment in their education. All in all, the evidence presented by Fogel and Engerman demonstrates both the workings of an efficient resource market and human capital theory. In many instances, southerners bought slaves, invested in their training, and "rented" them out to others in the obvious expectation that such an investment would yield a higher rate of return than alternative investments.

Reactions to *Time on the Cross*

Fogel and Engerman believed that their study had "contradicted many of the most important propositions in the traditional portrayal of the slave system." Such a fundamental reassessment did not, however, go unanswered. In fact, the outcry over the book has been phenomenal. Traditional historians such as Kenneth Stampp regarded many of the "revisionist" conclusions as exaggerated or simply erroneous. It has also been claimed that *Time on the Cross* ignores the moral issues of slavery as well as the effects of bondage on the productivity of slaves. Stanley Elkins (7), among numerous historians, has argued that slavery destroyed individualism, making slaves almost like concentration camp inmates. Eugene Genovese (23) appears to agree, pointing out how slowly the former slaves adjusted to freedom after the Civil War. The psychic costs imposed by such a system are, of course, ignored in any examination of its economic rationality.

Perhaps the most telling criticisms of the Fogel-Engerman work have come not from historians but from fellow "cliometricians" or new economic historians. A notable and careful analysis is *Reckoning with Slavery* by David, Gutman, Sutch, Temin, and Wright (6). These authors' judgment about slavery is seriously at variance with that of Fogel and Engerman. Indeed, the authors of *Reckoning* conclude that *Time on the Cross* is "simply shot through with egregious errors." David and colleagues corroborate many of the traditional views of slavery as a system that contained irrational behavior and exploited slaves more than Fogel and Engerman acknowledged. If slave exploitation is defined as the ratio of payments to slaves to the competitive wage, then Vedder (44) has calculated this ratio at almost two-thirds, considerably lower than Fogel and Engerman's calculation of about 85 to 90 percent. David et al. suggest that much research remains to be done before it will be possible to draw the kind of fundamental conclusions that *Time on the Cross* purported to draw. Also, the authors of *Reckoning* believe that this reexamination will require a dynamic view of slavery as a *changing* socioeconomic system rather than a static one. There is little doubt that more than a century after the demise of slavery much remains to be heard about it.

Could Slavery Have Continued?

It may be that widespread nineteenth-century and almost universal twentieth-century moral repugnance for an institution that permitted human beings to own other human beings has clouded our view of the economic workings of that institution. If so, has that repugnance also biased our view of the ability of slavery to continue as a means of economic organization? Again, the antebellum South is almost unique as a laboratory in which to explore that question.

It appears that in the absence of the Civil War slavery could have continued for the immediate term beyond 1860 as a viable economic institution. In an important study, Yasukichi Yasuba (47) investigated the impact of expected *future* earnings from slaves, not only to determine the viability of slavery, but also to measure the hopeful view of the future of slave owners. By calculating the cost of producing slaves and comparing that cost from 1820 to 1860 with the market price of such slaves, Yasuba found that slaveowners received a capitalized rent that was never less than 50 percent of the market price of slaves. Generally, also, these rents moved upward during the period. Yasuba's conclusions reinforce and broaden Conrad and Meyer's conclusions and show that not only was the tripling of slave prices between 1815 and 1860 based on increasing marginal revenue productivity but also that in 1860 slave owners had good reason to be sanguine about the immediate future of

Table 9.1.   The Price of Raw Cotton (in cents per pound). Current Price and Real Price.

THREE-YEAR PERIOD	CURRENT PRICE	REAL PRICE[a]
1840–1842	8.7	7.9
1843–1845	6.8	7.4
1846–1848	9.0	8.9
1849–1851	10.7	10.8
1852–1854	10.5	9.3
1855–1857	11.4	8.8
1858–1860	11.8	10.3

[a]Deflated, using the Warren-Pearson Index and with 1850 as the base year.

Source: Adapted from Robert W. Fogel and Stanley L. Engerman, "The Economics of Slavery," in *The Reinterpretation of American Economic History*, ed. Robert W. Fogel and Stanley L. Engerman (New York: Harper & Row, 1971), p. 316.

cotton plantation slavery. These conclusions should not be surprising, since Fogel and Engerman (16) have shown that the demand for cotton was growing more rapidly than its supply in the years preceding the Civil War. We can see the movement of cotton prices in current and real terms in Table 9.1.

The argument by Phillips, Ramsdell, and others that declining cotton prices spelled doom for slavery are not substantiated by the data in Table 9.1. Current cotton prices were rising from 1843 on and, even in real terms, rose in the period just prior to the Civil War. Furthermore, cotton prices never fell back to the lows of the early 1840s (when slavery was considered thriving) in the remaining years before the opening of the Civil War. Although David et al. (6) doubt that cotton prices would have continued to rise and thus validate the profitability of slavery after 1865, the strongest statement that seems sustainable at this point is that slavery *might* have remained an economically viable system in the absence of the Civil War.

SLAVERY AND ECONOMIC DEVELOPMENT

To this point, we have seen that the southern slave economy was viable, able to effectively reallocate slave and nonslave resources to their most efficient uses (as revenue productivity alternatives changed), and apparently hopeful about its future. Two further questions arise, however: If the Civil War had not occurred, might slavery have been abandoned because it retarded the absolute and relative growth of per capita income of the South? And were the rates of saving, investment, and consumer expenditure affected by slavery in such a way that the South's future economic development would have been inhibited by slavery?

Answering the first question requires looking at the per capita income position of the South in the period prior to 1860. Fogel and Engerman (16), expanding on the important work of Richard Easterlin, have provided a clear picture of

Table 9.2.   Per Capita Income by Region 1840 and 1860 (in 1860 prices).

	TOTAL POPULATION		FREE POPULATION	
	1840	1860	1840	1860
National average	$ 96	$128	$109	$144
North	109	141	110	142
Northeast	129	181	130	183
North Central	65	89	66	90
South	74	103	105	150
South Atlantic	66	84	96	124
East South Central	69	89	92	124
West South Central	151	184	218	274

SOURCE: Robert W. Fogel and Stanley L. Engerman, "The Economics of Slavery," in *The Reinterpretation of American Economic History*, ed. Robert W. Fogel and Stanley L. Engerman (New York: Harper & Row, 1971), p. 335.

regional per capita income trends from 1840 to 1860. Those results may be seen in Table 9.2.

The picture that emerges from these data is one of substantial growth in per capita income in both North and South between 1840 and 1860. Nationally, average per capita income grew by one-third in that period. In the North, per capita income for the total population grew by about 30 percent and by slightly more than that amount for the free population. The slight difference reflects the fact that few slaves lived in the North. Clearly, free population per capita income growth within the North was somewhat disproportionate, with the Northeast growing by 41 percent and the North Central states by 36 percent.

In the South, a pace and pattern of per capita income growth arose that virtually eliminates any arguments about slavery causing stagnation. For the total population, per capita income grew by about 40 percent (versus 33 percent in the North); for the free population, the growth was approximately 43 percent. Within the South, for the free population, the pace was faster in the South Atlantic and East South Central areas than in the West South Central. Nonetheless, the New South had a level of income more than twice that of the Old South and almost twice that of the North.

The Development and Continuation of Slavery

From the foregoing, we might conclude that slavery—whatever its social, political, and moral aspects—is capable of being dynamically oriented toward economic growth. Before we end this section, however, let us mention some major reservations that have been expressed concerning slavery's potential effects on development.

Some of the arguments advanced for the ultimate decline of slavery are variants of the "natural limits" arguments about slavery. According to one such variant, slavery would ultimately have become uneconomic because of the rise in slave population relative to the geographic limits of slave plantation land. In its simplest and least acceptable form, this argument supposes that slaves could only be employed in cotton production (although only about 55 to 60 percent were; perhaps 15 to 20 percent were employed in commerce and industry, with the remainder employed as domestic servants) and that slave prices would have declined. In testing this argument, Fogel and Engerman conclude the contrary, that slave prices in 1860 dollars would have risen by 66 percent between 1860 and 1890. Moreover, they conclude that cotton demand increased slightly more rapidly than supply up to 1914, and that the amount of land devoted to cotton doubled between 1860 and 1890 and at least doubled again between 1890 and 1925.

In a subsequent study, Roger Ransom and Richard Sutch (36) question the Fogel and Engerman conclusion. They conclude that cotton prices, especially relative to overall wholesale prices, fell from 1869 to 1877, rose in the 1880s, turned down after 1890, and rose again after 1898. Still, say Ransom and Sutch, the relative instability of cotton prices was not the major developmental problem associated with "King Cotton." Rather, they say, it was the lack of diversification and, even more importantly, the lack of industrialization in the South that was the main negative legacy of the region's great comparative advantage in growing cotton: "There can be little hope for sustained economic growth in an exclusively agricultural society" (36). Admitting that productivity growth in southern agriculture might have led ultimately to industrialization, Ransom and Sutch nonetheless conclude that imperfections in southern capital markets resulted in very high interest rates that discouraged productivity-increasing investments.

A related argument about stagnation of a slave economy is that the terms of trade ultimately turn against a region (or nation) that specializes in the production and export of one or a few basic agricultural staples. As we have seen, the *terms of trade**[*]* (for the South, the ratio of cotton prices to overall wholesale prices) were very changeable. An important form of this argument rests on the **income elasticity of demand** for such staples, the rate at which their demand grows with income growth in the areas or nations to which the staple (cotton, here) is exported. According to a frequent assertion, the income elasticity of demand for the staple export ultimately becomes low relative to the income elasticity of demand of the staple-producing area for the semimanufactured and manufactured goods of the areas with which it trades. According to this argument, the South would have faced a declining cotton price relative to the prices of the goods it "imported" from the North, the West, and abroad. It would have been "squeezed" by having to use more and more of its specialized resources to buy a given amount of imported goods.

Evidence is mixed about the validity of this terms-of-trade argument with respect to twentieth-century economies. The argument is controversial. In the case of the South, its validity is arguable. Prices in the United States generally declined from 1875 to 1900. Relative cotton prices, on the other hand, rose and fell. As indi-

[*]See Chapter 2 for a more detailed discussion of this concept.

cated earlier, the terms of trade probably would have moved in favor of the South at some times and against it at others.

A third stagnation, or antidevelopment, argument links slavery to the slow development, or nondevelopment, of commercial capitalism and its supposed requisite, an urban commercial middle class producing from residentiary industries and selling for cash to a broadly based group of consumers who receive cash income. Eugene Genovese has advanced an argument of this sort about the American South. According to Genovese (22), the income distribution of the South was so skewed (toward upper-income earners in particular and toward whites in general) that there was not sufficient cash demand to cause the widespread development of urban, residentiary industry. Slaves, of course, received little or no cash income. But many white Southerners were outside the cotton plantation economy and also received little cash income.

Genovese says that perceptive critics of slavery made this kind of market-size–economic development argument at the time. He cites Cassius Marcellus Clay, a Kentuckian and outspoken critic of slavery, who said, "Lawyers, merchants, mechanics, laborers, who are your consumers; Robert Wickliffe's two hundred slaves?—Does Mr. Wickliffe lay out as much for himself and two hundred slaves as two hundred freemen do?—a home market cannot exist in a slave state" (22).

Even by Genovese's estimates, however, southern cash expenditures ($125 per person in Mississippi in 1860) were sufficient, according to Fogel and Engerman, to have provided the base for supporting "over fifty cotton textile plants and more than two hundred boot and shoe establishments of Massachusetts size" (17). One wonders whether the South would have availed itself of changing technology and made the rational substitutions of capital for slave labor that occurred in nonslave areas where capital/labor ratios changed in the post–Civil War era. The work of Schmitz and Schaefer (38) seems to suggest that, at least in agriculture, that degree of substitutability under slavery was low.

The skewedness of the southern income distribution is still being debated. It bears repeating that the primary reason the South lagged seriously in industrialization was that its comparative advantage lay strongly in agriculture, especially with "King Cotton." As Douglass North and others have shown, the region did lag badly in **human capital formation,** the investment in education that results in improved human skills or increased marginal physical productivity of labor. According to North, the ratio of pupils to white population in 1840 was 5.72 in slaveholding states compared to 18.41 in nonslaveholding states (30). Illiteracy among whites was 2.13 percent in nonslaveholding states and 7.46 percent in slaveholding states. It has yet to be shown, however, that this impeded productivity growth in the antebellum South or that such improved skills were necessary to expand the output of cotton plantation agriculture. Also, it does not follow that the relatively high rates of return on human capital formation available in twentieth-century societies employing twentieth-century industrial technology were available to a nineteenth-century agricultural society with its own far less complex technology. Indeed, a better anal-

ogy to the antebellum South's experience might be various contemporary agricultural export economies that produce basic commodities; many of these have
probably overinvested in human capital formation in terms of the returns available
on other investments, including physical capital formation.

SLAVERY: A FINAL NOTE

On the basis of the enormous amount of research that has been done on southern
slavery, it appears safe to conclude that slavery is not an economic system with a
built-in self-destruct mechanism. Still, we are entitled to a bit of historical speculation about the *very* long-term viability of such a system. Would the slave South ultimately have begun to create and expand industries built on its agricultural base
(textiles, iron, coal, steel, shoes, and the like)? If so, would this not have created an
urbanization of southern slaves, a need to invest in social overhead capital, and a
need to increase investments in human capital to complement the new physical
capital? Would the enforcement costs of maintaining an urban, better-educated
slave population have ultimately outweighed the benefits of slavery? The research
of Claudia Golden (24) suggests a price-elastic demand in southern urban areas for
slaves. Thus, as slave prices rose, might not an urban South have abandoned slavery
at some point? The answer to all such speculative questions is "Perhaps, perhaps
not." As already indicated, much research remains to be done about the economics
of slavery. At this point in our examination, the bottom line is that southern slavery
was not in, or apparently near, decline at the time of the Civil War. So to the extent
that this nation's greatest conflict was fought over elimination of slavery, that conflict was *not* an unnecessary bloodbath.

QUESTIONS

1. Why was there a "New South" and an "Old South"? How did they differ economically? How did slavery tie the two regions together?
2. Explain the Phillips argument about the ultimate demise of slavery. What were the viewpoints of Lewis Gray and Charles Ramsdell concerning the economics of slavery?
3. What were Conrad and Meyer's conclusions about the profitability of slavery?
4. What do Fogel and Engerman conclude about the rationality of slave prices?
5. What important addition to the study of the economics of slavery did Yasuba contribute?
6. In what respects has *Time on the Cross* been heavily criticized by historians and
   economists?
7. What happened to the price of cotton between 1840 and 1860? What caused this?
8. Did slavery retard the per capita income growth of the South? What are some other possible arguments linking slavery to nondevelopment of the South? Could slavery have
   remained a viable economic system in the United States beyond 1860?

SUGGESTED READINGS

1. Aufhauser, R. Keith. "Slavery and Technological Change." *Journal of Economic History, 34* (March 1974).

2. Bateman, Fred, and Roger Weiss. "Manufacturing in the Antebellum South." *Research in Economic History.* vol. V. Greenwich, Conn: JAI Press, 1976.

3. Blassingame, John. *The Slave Community: Plantation Life in the Antebellum South.* New York: Oxford University Press, 1972.

4. Canarella, Georgio, and John A. Tomaske. "The Optimal Utilization of Slaves." *Journal of Economic History, 35* (September 1975).

5. Conrad, Alfred H., and John R. Meyer. "The Economics of Slavery in the Ante-Bellum South." *Journal of Political Economy, 66* (April 1958).

6. David, Paul A., and Herbert Gutman, Richard Sutch, Richard Temin and Gavin Wright. *Reckoning with Slavery: A Quantitative History of American Slavery.* New York: Oxford University Press, 1978.

7. Elkins, Stanley M. *Slavery: A Problem of American Institutional and Intellectual Life.* New York: Grosset and Dunlap, 1959.

8. Engerman, Stanley, and Eugene Genovese. *Race and Slavery in the Western Hemisphere: Quantitative Studies.* Princeton, N.J.: Princeton University Press, 1978.

9. Evans, Robert, Jr. "The Economics of American Negro Slavery." Universities—National Bureau Committee for Economic Research. *Aspects of Labor Economics.* Princeton, N.J.: Princeton University Press, 1962.

10. "Explaining the Relative Efficiency of Slave Agriculture in the Antebellum South: A Reply." *American Economic Review, 70* (September 1980).

11. Fenoaltea, Stefano. "The Slavery Debate: A Note from the Sidelines." *Explorations in Economic History, 18* (July 1981).

12. Fleisig, Heywood. "Slavery, the Supply of Agricultural Labor and the Industrialization of the South." *Journal of Economic History, 36* (September 1976).

13. Fogel, Robert W. "American Interregional Trade in the Nineteenth Century." In *New Views on American Economic Development,* ed. Ralph Andreano. Cambridge, Mass.: Shenckman, 1965.

14. Fogel, Robert W. "Discussion." *American Economic Review, 54* (May 1964).

15. Fogel, Robert W. *Without Consent or Contract: The Rise and Fall of American Slavery.* New York: W. W. Norton, 1987.

16. Fogel, Robert W., and Stanley L. Engerman, eds. *The Reinterpretation of American Economic History.* New York: Harper and Row, 1971.

17. Fogel, Robert W., and Stanley L. Engerman. *Time on the Cross: The Economics of American Negro Slavery;* and *Time on the Cross: Evidence and Methods: A Supplement.* Boston: Little, Brown, 1974.

18. Fogel, Robert William. "Three Phases of Cliometric Research on Slavery and the Aftermath." *American Economic Review, 65* (May 1975).

19. Fogel, Robert William, and Stanley L. Engerman. "Explaining the Relative Efficiency of Slave Agriculture in the Antebellum South." *American Economic Review, 67* (June, 1977).

20. Gallman, Robert. "Self-Sufficiency in the Cotton Economy of the Antebellum South." *Agricultural History* (January 1970).

21. Genovese, Eugene. *From Rebellion to Revolution. Afro-American Slave Revolts in the Making of the Modern World.* Baton Rouge: Louisiana State University Press, 1979.

22. Genovese, Eugene. *The Political Economy of Slavery.* New York: Pantheon Books, 1965.

23. Genovese, Eugene. *Roll, Jordan, Roll: The World the Slaves Made.* New York: Vintage Books, 1976.

24. Golden, Claudia. *Urban Slavery in the American South.* Chicago: University of Chicago Press, 1978.

25. Gray, Lewis C. *History of Agriculture in the Southern United States to 1860.* Gloucester, Mass.: Peter Smith, 1958.

26. Gutman, Herbert. *The Black Family in Slavery and Freedom.* New York: Pantheon Books, 1976.

27. Hutchinson, William K., and Samuel H. Williamson. "The Self-Sufficiency of the Antebellum South: Estimates of the Food Supply." *Journal of Economic History,* 31 (September 1971).

28. Kotlikoff, Lawrence J., and Sebastian E. Pinera. "The Old South's Stake with Interregional Movement of Slaves, 1850–1860." *Journal of Economic History,* 27 (June 1977).

29. Metzer, Jacob. "Rational Management, Modern Business Practice and Economies of Scale in the Antebellum Plantations." *Explorations in Economic History,* 12 (April 1975).

30. North, Douglass C. *The Economic Growth of the United States.* New York: Norton, 1966.

31. Olmstead, Frederick Law. *The Slave States.* New York: Appleton Century, 1933.

32. Parker, William N., ed. *The Structure of the Cotton Economy of the Antebellum South.* Washington, D.C.: Agriculture History Society, 1970.

33. Passell, Peter. "The Impact of Cotton Land Distribution on the Antebellum Economy." *Journal of Economic History,* 31 (December 1971).

34. Phillips, Ulrich B. "The Economic Cost of Slaveholding in the Cotton Belt." *Political Science Quarterly,* 20 (June 1905).

35. Ramsdell, Charles W. "The Natural Limits of Slavery Expansion." *The Mississippi Valley Historical Review,* 16 (September 1929).

36. Ransom, Roger L., and Richard Sutch. *One Kind of Freedom.* Cambridge: Cambridge University Press, 1977.

37. Saraydar, Edward. "A Note on the Profitability of Antebellum Slavery." *The Southern Economic Journal,* 30 (April 1964).

38. Schmitz, Mark D., and Donald F. Schaefer. "Slavery, Freedom and the Elasticity of Substitution." *Explorations in Economic History,* 15 (July 1978).

39. Stampp, Kenneth. *The Peculiar Institution: Slavery in the Antebellum South.* New York: Knopf, 1956.

40. Steckel, Richard H. "Slave Height Profiles from Coastwise Manifests." *Explorations in Economic History,* 16 (October 1979).

41. Strorolin, Robert S. *Industrial Slavery in the Old South.* New York: Oxford Press, 1970.

42. Sutch, Richard. "The Treatment Received by American Slaves: A Critical Review of the Evidence Presented in *Time on the Cross.*" *Explorations in Economic History,* 12 (October 1975).

43. Thomas, Robert Paul, and Richard Nelson Bean. "The Fishers of Men: The Profits of the Slave Trade." *Journal of Economic History, 34* (December 1974).

44. Vedder, Richard K. "The Slave Exploitation Rate." *Explorations in Economic History, 12,* (October 1975).

45. Washington, Booker T. *Up From Slavery.* New York: Bantam Books, 1963.

46. Wright, Gavin. *The Political Economy of the Cotton South.* New York: Norton, 1978. Esp. Chap. 3.

47. Yasuba, Yasukichi. "The Profitability and Viability of Plantation Slavery in the United States." *The Economic Studies Quarterly, 12* (September 1961).

48. Zepp, Thomas M. "On Returns to Scale and Input Substitutability in Slave Agriculture." *Explorations in Economic History, 13* (April 1976).

49. Zevin, Robert B. "The Growth of Cotton Textile Production After 1815." In *The Reinterpretation of American Economic History,* ed. Robert W. Fogel and Stanley L. Engerman. New York: Harper and Row, 1971.

Chapter 10 ————————————

THE CIVIL WAR—
A WATERSHED?

We began in Chapter 1 by noting that the events recorded by historians can be viewed and interpreted in many ways. No major event better illustrates that than the Civil War. In terms of loss of lives, the war was clearly America's most important military conflict. It also was a series of political events that dramatically changed personal, regional, and national power relationships. The war, in other words, had multiple effects, and both its origins and its effects can be viewed in many ways.

Until the 1920s, it was customary to view the causes of the Civil War largely in political terms. Southern historians often saw the conflict as having been fought over the issue of states' rights and having been initiated through the bungling and miscalculation of southern politicians urged on by abolitionists.[*] Northerners frequently saw the conflict in moral terms as a contest over the institution of slavery. The effects of the Civil War have been the subject of much scholarly research. As we shall see, this research and the debates associated with it are another instance of the argument over how history and historical change should be viewed. Some scholars see the war as a major "shift" factor in causing the transformation of the United States from a rural, agricultural society into an urban and industrial one in which government policy, especially federal policy, plays a major, if not dominant, role. We will begin our investigation by considering some of the effects of war in general from a theoretical point of view.

[*]The pioneering article of Victor S. Clark (3) published in 1918 and cited in the Suggested Readings to this chapter, is an important, although until recently largely neglected, exception.

A MODEL OF SOME ECONOMIC EFFECTS OF WAR

From a conceptual standpoint, the economic effects of war can be divided into the direct effects associated with military actions, especially the destruction of human and nonhuman resources, and the indirect effects on growth, efficiency, and distribution. While it is impossible to hypothesize briefly about all those effects, we can focus on some that are likely to be important.

The direct effects of battle are perhaps the clearest. Destruction of both human capital and physical capital reduces the productive capacity of a nation or region. This diminishes not only the total full-employment output of the society but also average productivity, to the extent that the resources destroyed are among its most productive. Although the physical capital that is destroyed can be replaced, the society still incurs the opportunity cost, the forgone output of goods and services that the capital could have been used to produce. This is a permanent loss.

A second set of microeconomic effects is on the efficiency of resource allocation. War may restrict the ability of a nation to maintain comparative-advantage patterns of trade, those in which it exchanges goods that it produces with relatively few real resources for goods produced with relatively few real resources elsewhere. When this happens, whether because of a blockade or for other reasons, a society necessarily turns inward to produce the goods denied it by trade. Since the destructiveness of war causes productivity to fall, its full-employment output declines. Of course, its output of civilian goods will be reduced in any case as it reallocates resources to the production of war goods.

The macroeconomic (income–employment–price level) effects of war are equally important. The effects of war on prices may be understood in terms of the society's **elasticity of output,** the rate at which output increases as effective demand increases. We can see the importance of this relationship in Figure 10.1.

While the index of output represented on the horizontal axis is difficult to measure statistically, it is conceptually a measure of the real goods and services of an economy. As effective demand increases from Demand' to Demand", there is no increase in the index of prices represented on the horizontal axis; in other words, output is perfectly elastic. The reason for this is that the society is producing more by bringing unemployed resources into use. Let us suppose that at output or aggregate supply level O_f full employment is reached or that bottlenecks further prevent movement toward full-employment of the nation's resources. If demand increases further, say to Demand''', there are no further resources to employ (the elasticity of employment is zero), so all the increased demand must be translated into inflation, an increase in prices from P_0 to P_1.

What might this mean for wartime societies such as the North or South during the Civil War? If such a society begins the war at a condition of full employment (O_f in Figure 10.1) and attempts to bid resources away from private production, and does not finance its wartime expenditures by taxing or otherwise reducing private

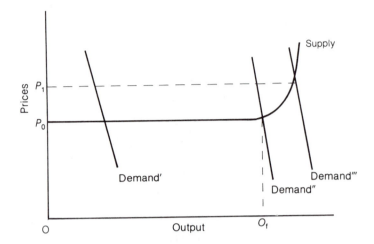

Figure 10.1. Elasticity of Output.

(civilian) expenditure, then the increasing effective demand (fueled by government deficits financed by newly created money) will result in inflation.

What happens to income distribution in these circumstances? If wage growth falls behind growth in price (a form of taxation of wage earners), there may well be an increase in profits (assuming that total real-factor incomes rise) accompanying the decline in real or purchasing-power wages (assuming no change in interest and rent shares). If profits rise, there may be an incentive to entrepreneurs to invest in capital-creating activities. In other words, there may be a heightened incentive to increase the rate of industrial growth.

THE BEARD-HACKER ARGUMENT

Writing in 1927, Charles and Mary Beard referred to the Civil War as the Second American Revolution, which, although it wiped out some economic assets, especially those of the slave-owning aristocracy, "assured the triumph of business enterprise" (2). The Beards went on to say that the capitalists who financed the Union efforts and those who supplied it with war material gained "profits greater than they had ever yet gathered in four years of peace." According to them, these huge profits or masses of capital were used to conquer the continent and exploit the natural resources of the nation. In addition to these direct effects on profits, capital accumulation, and the distribution of wealth, the Beards alleged that the Civil War changed social and political relationships in a way that clearly favored the industrial development of the United States.

The Beards undertook no careful, systematic investigation of the data for the Civil War period. Nonetheless, their conclusions became widely accepted. Arthur

Schlesinger, Jr., referred to the war as having a hothouse effect on the tender industrial growth of America. Harold Faulkner, in a well-known textbook, called the Civil War "terribly important" in our economic development. Writing in 1940, Louis Hacker (12) stated that the war resolved a critical situation, the conflict between the planter capitalist interests of the South and the industrial capitalist interests of the North. According to Hacker, the Union government was free after 1860 to pursue policies favorable to industrial expansion.

The Beards' approach had been to cite specific acts after 1860 that seemed to them to favor industrialization. Among these were the subsidy and land grant programs to the railroads beginning in 1862 and the protective tariff legislation enacted by the Republican-dominated Union Congress. Going beyond that type of casual empiricism, Hacker sought to produce the statistics to show that industry, especially heavy industry, made great strides between 1860 and 1865.

In the 1960s, economic historians began to systematically investigate the effects of the Civil War using recent research techniques and newly available data. One of the most important such efforts was by Thomas Cochran (4) in a 1961 article entitled "Did the Civil War Retard Industrialization?" Taking various indices of economic activity and using data available since 1949, Cochran came to the conclusion that the war actually retarded the country's industrial growth. Cochran cites Robert Gallman's (9) constant-dollar series for value added in manufacturing. That series rose 157 percent from 1839 to 1849, 76 percent from 1849 to 1859, and only 25 percent from 1859 to 1869. According to Cochran, this raises a presumption of slower rather than more rapid growth during the war. Looking behind these aggregate figures, Cochran cites pig iron production (up 17 percent from 1850 to 1855, and 17 percent from 1855 to 1860, but only 1 percent from 1860 to 1865), bituminous coal production (no change in its long-term rate of growth), and the low rate of growth in copper production during the war. Also, railroad track mileage additions declined dramatically during the war, immigration went down, there was an actual decrease in the value of machinery per farm, and the constant-dollar value of loans fell. Cochran concludes that the "Civil War retarded American industrial growth."

In an article subsequent to that of Cochran, Stephen Salsbury (19) points out that Cochran's conclusions rest on a very unquantified, if not unquantifiable, assumption. That assumption is that by 1840 all of the conditions necessary to favor rapid industrial growth were set in the United States. If this assumption is granted, then Cochran's comparisons of the 1840s and 1850s with the Civil War period are fundamentally valid, because the trends of the war period either would continue the industrial growth patterns of the 1840–1860 period or would deviate from those patterns. On the other hand, it appears that what the Beards (and others) were earlier arguing in part was that the Civil War had a major impact on setting those conditions. Salsbury points out that if one looks at the production growth rates of pig iron, bituminous coal, and railway track construction after the war, there is evidence of a postwar boom with rates much above those of the prewar decades. One could then argue that the Civil War was, as the Beards claimed, the catalyst of the conditions for rapid industrial growth.

If conclusions about the direct (production) effects of the Civil War seem to rest on less than universally agreed-on assumptions, what about the indirect effects? Cochran recognizes two kinds of such effects, those that reflected changes in the political and social system produced by the war and those stimulants such as inflation and large federal debt creation resulting directly from the war. Cochran confirms Wesley Mitchell's (18) 1903 conclusion that the rapid wartime inflation brought on by massive printing of greenbacks redistributed incomes from wages (real wages fell) and salaries and interest payments to profits. This action put "savings in the hands of entrepreneurs who would invest in new activities." Also, the inflation reduced the burdens of railroads with large mortgage debts, perhaps encouraging expansion of the railway system. Cochran concludes, however, that these effects have not been shown to be significant in terms of causing postwar growth. Salsbury agrees, but says that until their significance is systematically investigated, we should be wary of concluding that the Civil War retarded industrialization.

Similarly, Salsbury finds room for disagreement with Cochran about the effect of the Civil War on the supply of money and credit and its industrial growth effects. Cochran states that the growth of the banking system between 1800 and 1860 had made credit readily available, and it continued to do so in the North during the war. He says that the war destroyed southern banking and that, even in 1875, 40 percent of banks were outside the new national banking system. From this, Cochran seems to conclude that the war's effects did little or nothing to improve the availability of credit and thereby stimulate investment. Salsbury counters that the evidence Cochran cites neither proves nor disproves the thesis that the war retarded industrial growth. After all, he says, how easy was it to obtain credit before 1860? Was it readily available to finance large-scale ventures? Did this picture change after 1865? If it did, was the change the result of the war? All these questions remain unanswered.

Finally, did the Civil War, as the Beards assert, "enhance the capitalist spirit"? Cochran agrees that it may have, but that this is an argument that is very difficult to evaluate. What legislative and executive measures did the Republicans take? Was there an increase in federal aid to or subsidization of internal improvements (railroad land grants and the like)? Cochran feels that even if one shows such an increase in federal aid, some of it, such as the Union Pacific land grant, was wasteful, that it created uneconomic enterprises or at least enterprises before market demand would have warranted their private creation. Robert Fogel's research indicates that Cochran's assertion about the Union Pacific is probably unwarranted; the line earned an average of 11.6 percent annually on its cost outlays and 29.9 percent social return during the first decade of its operation. (7)

Ultimately, Salsbury concludes, some of these arguments raise issues that are not readily amenable to statistical analysis. For example, did the Civil War place businessmen in undisputed power and thereby enhance the industrialization of this nation? Salsbury says that comparative data on tariffs, land grants, and federal sub-

Table 10.1. Commodity Output per Capita, by Region, 1860–1880.

	NON-SOUTH	COMPOUND RATE OF GROWTH PER YEAR	SOUTH	COMPOUND RATE OF GROWTH PER YEAR
1860	$ 74.8		$77.7	
		0.9%		−4.8%
1870	81.5		47.6	
		2.6%		2.6%
1880	105.8		61.5	

SOURCE: Adapted from Stanley L. Engerman, "The Economic Impact of the Civil War," *Explorations in Economic History, 3* (Spring-Summer 1966).

sidies will help to answer that question. Beyond that, interpretation "based upon nonstatistical, social, political, and psychological analysis" is called for.

Salsbury's conclusion is generally reinforced in a study by Stanley L. Engerman (6), who notes that much research remains to be done. Among other things, little is known about the effect of the conflict on invention, the size of the government budget, or the location of financial markets. Engerman does note that a 1964 conference of economic historians concluded that, apart from commercial banking, the war had not "started or created any significant new patterns of economic institutional change," a conclusion directly contrary to the views of Beard and Hacker.[*] After looking at some specific commodity output figures, Engerman finds the relationships shown in Table 10.1 (based on Gallman's data).

As Engerman notes, per capita commodity output rose much more rapidly in both the non-South and the South in the decade of the 1870s than it had in the war decade. Indeed, per capita output fell greatly between 1860 and 1870 in the South, reflecting not only the direct destruction of labor and capital between 1861 and 1865 but also the productivity effects of freeing the slaves, fragmenting southern landholdings and the like.[†] The fact that per capita output grew much more rapidly in the decade after the Civil War than in the prewar decade is not enough to convince Engerman of the validity of the Beard-Hacker thesis. Indeed, it was not until almost 1885 that the trend value of per capita commodity output extrapolating from the 1840–1860 trend was reached.

Industrial Growth, Summing Up

Following on the research of Cochran, Salsbury, Engerman, and others, few historians today appear ready to fully accept the Beard-Hacker thesis that the Civil War was a great industrial watershed. Yet, because of the data and interpretation

[*]This view appears to overlook the important institutional change of the abolition of slavery.

[†]Engerman notes that the construction of these indices precludes their use to accurately compare the absolute levels of per capita output in both regions. The rates of change in each region are accurate, however.

problems, few also are willing to dismiss the argument entirely in any form (especially in terms of power relationships). As we have noted, much research remains to be done within the limitations of available data (especially the lack of data for the war period itself) before a more definitive judgment can be formed.

Did Particular Industries Benefit from the War?

Future research may shed light on the distributional effects of the war. Although the United States as a whole did not "take off" industrially as a result of the Civil War, the North, as the winner, may have been in a stronger income and savings-investment position vis-à-vis the South. Robert Gallman (9) has calculated that the percent of total personal income received by the South fell from 26 percent in the late 1850s to 15 percent in the late 1870s. The North and West, on the other hand, increased their share of personal income from 70 percent to 78 percent.

Absolute per capita income growth figures also lend some credence to the Beard-Hacker thesis. Between 1840 and 1860, the North grew at a rate of 1.3 percent; between 1860 and 1879, the region grew at 1.75 percent; and from 1880 to 1900, it grew at a rate of 1.9 percent. The percentage of income flowing into capital investment paralleled these changes in northern growth rates.

But what does all this prove? About the only thing indisputable is that there is a good statistical correlation in time between the war period and increasing capital investment, a large part of which occurred in the North. Here we see the age-old problem of correlation and causality. In none of the important Gallman data can one find proof that the war *caused* these changes.

Even when we examine specific industries that might have been affected by the war, the results do little to strengthen the Beard-Hacker argument. As Lee and Passell (16) put it:

> Given the fact that the war placed enormous stresses on an economy already going full tilt, that the services of perhaps one-fifth of the labor force were withdrawn from production, and that normal channels of raw material supply and foreign exchange earnings were broken, it would, in retrospect, be surprising if the war did not *disrupt* [our emphasis] industrial growth.

A few industries enjoyed great growth during the war, especially wool textiles. However, this probably reflected a substitution of wool for the markedly less available cotton. When one looks at other industries such as clothing, boots, iron, and agricultural implements, there is no clear indication of a break with previous (prewar) trends. In an apt characterization of nineteenth- and twentieth-century wars and their effects, Lee and Passell note that "twentieth century wars are fought with iron and petroleum; nineteenth century wars were fought with mules and salt pork." The "spread" effects of a massive conflict today, in other words, might be very different, qualitatively and quantitatively, from those of such a conflict in the 1860s.

The Wage Lag Argument

Research by DiCanio and Mokyr (5) may yet provide some real support for the Beard-Hacker thesis. One indisputable fact is that real average annual wages fell significantly between 1860 and 1865 (16). Specifically, they fell from $363 in 1860 to $261 in 1865. One popular argument is that wages did not keep up with (unanticipated) inflation caused by the war-financing policies of the Union government. As a result, firms' costs fell and profits, the residual after other costs are allocated out of revenue, rose. According to the argument, the profits went to a group of capitalist-entrepreneurs who employed them in favor of industrial investment.

As you probably already suspect, there are problems with evaluating this argument. Wages, according to traditional economic theory, are determined by productivity. Thus the question is: Did the decline in wages reflect a decline in productivity, the drawing off of highly skilled labor into the military with a consequent increase in firms' costs, or were skill levels (productivity) essentially changed with the results outlined in the previous paragraph? Lack of qualitative data on the labor force from 1860 to 1865 makes a detailed answer impossible. If there was a major "drawing off" of labor, that alone should have caused upward wage pressure. To explain the actual wage decline, then, would require showing a truly dramatic decrease in productivity.

Export Disruption and the Wage Lag

Kessel and Alchian (13) have provided an alternative and, to many, a more acceptable explanation of the real-wage decrease. According to them, the explanation for about half the drop lies in the major decline in the terms of trade caused by export disruption. Without southern cotton to sell—which had generated about two-thirds of its prewar export revenues—the North ran a huge trade deficit that had to be financed through devaluing the currency. This, of course, is what many twentieth-century nations have done.

The northern government resorted to the printing press and issued large quantities of greenbacks that were not convertible to specie. The gold and foreign currency value of the dollar fell and commodity import prices rose dramatically. Kessel and Alchian conclude that even if northern wages had been indexed to domestic prices, higher import prices would explain half of the decline in real wages.

The remainder of the real-wage fall, according to Kessel and Alchian, was due to tax increases. Import duties were raised in 1862 and 1864 by a government now unrestricted by southern opposition. Various excise taxes were raised during the war, and in 1864, a 5–6 percent levy on manufactured goods was imposed. According to Kessel and Alchian, about 85 percent of northern revenue came from taxes that affected the real wages of northern laborers. All of this suggests that the wage lag argument, which depends on imperfect labor markets, is unnecessary to explain the decline in real wages.

But DiCanio and Mokyr (5) believe that their research lends real support to the wage lag argument. As Table 10.2 shows, they have identified a wage loss attributable solely to unanticipated inflation that varied between 35.3 and 75.9 percent of the total real-wage loss. The estimates (columns 1 and 2) isolate the effect of unanticipated inflation on real wages from other factors reducing wage purchasing power. Column 4 indicates that inflation explains a major part of the loss (35–76 percent) in each year from 1861 to 1865.

When one looks at the DiCanio-Mokyr estimate of how much of the war was financed through this real-wage loss, the results are less clear. According to Table 10.3 (column 4), unanticipated inflation did play a major role in the wage decline, but only about one-fourth of government expenditures or one-third of the North's war deficit was financed in this manner. Even if one accepts the high estimates of DiCanio-Mokyr, it is questionable that this is a powerful explanation.

At this juncture, it appears that there is some validity to both the export disruption and the wage lag arguments. Taken together, they explain much of what occured in the war period.

Table 10.2. Annual Wage Gap for Average Northern Nonfarm Worker (1860 dollars).

YEAR	LOW ESTIMATE	HIGH ESTIMATE	TOTAL LOSS IN REAL WAGES FROM 1860 (MILLION 1860 $)	LOW ESTIMATE AS % OF TOTAL LOSS
1861	−15.27	−1.86	14.07	—
1862	16.43	31.21	46.49	35.3%
1863	44.92	66.00	59.17	75.9%
1864	53.75	78.14	95.36	56.4%
1865	48.63	85.50	101.91	44.7%
Total	148.46	258.99	317.00	46.8%

SOURCE: Stephen DiCanio and Joel Mokyr, "Inflation and Wage Lag During the Civil War," *Explorations in Economic History, 14* (October 1977), p. 324.

Table 10.3. The Wage Gap as a Means of Financing the Civil War.

YEAR	TOTAL WAGE GAP: LOW ESTIMATE ($ MILLIONS)	TOTAL WAGE GAP: HIGH ESTIMATE ($ MILLIONS)	HIGH ESTIMATE AS % OF FEDERAL EXPENDITURES	HIGH ESTIMATE AS % OF FEDERAL DEFICIT
1861	−31.2	−3.8	—	—
1862	32.5	61.8	16.2	18.2
1863	88.0	129.4	25.7	31.8
1864	107.6	156.4	30.6	46.1
1865	99.9	175.7	26.0	36.9
Total	328.1	523.3	24.5	33.0

SOURCE: Stephen DiCanio and Joel Mokyr, "Inflation and Wage Lag During the Civil War," *Explorations in Economic History, 14* (October 1977), p. 324.

THE SCOPE OF THE WAR

There is at least one sense in which the Civil War was clearly a major watershed. In terms of the degree of involvement of the economies of the North and South, the war marked a dramatic change. Previous wars, even the American Revolution, had not involved all the American people and their land and capital. Although the leaders of both North and South entered the conflict expecting to put forth a greater effort than in any previous war, their expectations were nonetheless too low. In one battle in 1862, that of Antietam, over 23,000 soldiers were killed, more than the entire fatalities in all previous wars fought by the United States. It soon became clear (probably not long after the battle of Bull Run in 1861) that only the total involvement of both economies could raise the men and material necessary to successfully prosecute the war.

Some have asked why the Civil War was so much greater in scope than its predecessors. This was still basically a foot soldier's war. There were few dramatic changes in military technology; an exception was the rifling of gun barrels, which greatly increased the distance and accuracy of rifles and cannon. Ironically, the factor that appears to explain the broadening of the war is lowered transportation cost, the cost of delivering men and material over long distances. The railroads especially reduced the unit costs of such movements and, in a sense, became an external economy of scale to the fighting of the war. Gerald Gunderson (11) has pointed out that after the battle of Chickamauga in Tennessee a large part of the Union's western army was decimated. Within three weeks, however, several thousand troops had been moved over 3,000 miles from the Army of the Potomac to Tennessee and the entire western army resupplied. In no previous war would this have been possible.

Figure 10.2. Abraham Lincoln, President of an Industrial North, and Jefferson Davis, President of an Agricultural South. (Photos from the National Archives)

The South, of course, was systematically denied some of these economies of scale. The Union blockade of southern ports forced the Confederacy to turn to contraband (high-priced goods brought into southern ports, especially to the well-protected port of Wilmington, North Carolina) and to producing goods previously purchased from the North or from Europe. The Union blockade of the Mississippi after 1863 prevented or made very expensive the movement of resources or goods from the Southwest to the Old South. Many ordinary consumer goods became quite scarce; hence consumer goods prices rose dramatically. The South had only one iron works, and its entire output was given over to armaments. Stoves and other consumer goods that used iron became scarce. Ironically, textiles became relatively scarce in both North and South. The South had cotton; even the scorched earth policy of the Union in the latter years of the war did not deprive the region of that. Most of the textile mills, though, were located in the North. There, the lack of the industry's main input resulted in the shutdown of many mills and a virtual depression in several northeastern states. As a result, there was a significant amount of illegal trade involving the sale of southern cotton in exchange for northern goods of various types. This illegal trade went on even in the face of opposition from Union generals, who recognized that it prolonged the ability of the South to continue fighting and was in contradiction to the generals' plan to destroy the economic base on which the South's government rested. Thus at the same time that the Union's army and navy were attempting to strangle the transportation system of the South and destroy its ability to support a large-scale war, the Union was actually importing substantial quantities of southern cotton and paying for those transactions with goods such as bacon, salt, shoes, and clothing that helped to sustain Lee's troops. It is not surprising, then, that the war's outcome was caused not by some ultimate military defeat, but by the success of the war of attrition—ultimately by the inability of the South to produce and distribute the food and clothing necessary to maintain the Army of Virginia around Richmond. Lee's retreat to Appomattox is directly attributable to the desertion of his soldiers in an effort to find such goods.

Northern troops, on the other hand, were among the best fed, clothed, and militarily outfitted in history. The northern transportation system worked so well at resupplying, as Gunderson points out, that the troops frequently discarded blankets at the end of the cold season rather than carry them on marches.

FINANCING THE WAR

Both the North and South were confronted early in the war with the necessity to finance an unprecedentedly large volume of military expenditures. In the South, this proved to be particularly difficult; according to Gunderson, the region's government was forced to find a means to finance purchases equal to more than half of the entire yearly income of the prewar South. Since output almost certainly fell in the South during the war, this was an enormous task. An early effort at property taxation proved very inadequate. Two other principal means of finance were available:

sales of government bonds and the printing of money. Although early issues of southern bonds were oversubscribed, the bonds sold later on only at tremendous discounts. This was especially true as the military fortunes of the South declined, particularly after 1863 and the battle of Gettysburg. In October 1864, only $362 million of the total Confederate government debt of $1,371 million was in the form of bonds, and of that, only $125 million had taken the form of voluntary purchases.

As it found it harder to finance its purchases of goods out of a declining real southern product with either tax or bond revenues, the South turned to the printing press. Eugene Lerner (17) reports that between 1861 and 1864 the stock of money in the (dwindling) Confederacy increased 11-fold. With an increasingly inelastic supply of goods and services as well as a reduced supply, prices rose dramatically—more than 2,800 percent between 1861 and 1864. (Data after 1864 do not exist for the disintegrating Confederacy.) With the value of Confederate currency falling at a rate of 10 percent per month, the velocity of monetary circulation increased and further fueled the inflation.

The high rate of inflation, ascribable in large measure to deficit government spending, was in effect a "tax." By 1864, even this tax was inadequate to finance military purchases. Southern commissary officers turned to simply taking the needed supplies (such as food, fence posts for firewood, horses, and mules). Since the owners were rarely repaid, much less at fair market prices and in currency of constant purchasing power, the practice was virtually one of resource conscription. Ultimately, even conscription, when combined with declining real product (especially once systematic destruction of southern property became Union policy) and a failing transportation and distribution system, became inadequate to provide the resources that would permit the continuation of large-scale warfare.

Early in the war, little was done in the North to raise taxes or adopt other means to finance the war. Ultimately, the North, as we saw earlier, financed its wartime purchases in much the same way as the South, primarily with bond issues, the printing of money (the famous greenbacks), and tariff increases.

In 1861, the Morrill Tariff Act was passed, raising tariffs. The tariff rates were so high, as the Beards note, that the apparent objective of the act was to provide protection for domestic industries rather than to raise revenue. Also, a direct tax of $20 million was levied, along with the nation's first federal income tax—on incomes in excess of $800 per year. These measures failed to raise substantial revenues, however, until late 1864, when rates were raised and internal taxes broadened to cover many commodities. For example, of the $350 million raised by the income tax, only $50 million was raised before the end of the war. Thus most of the financing of the war was done through bond issues (whose value rose with the North's improving military fortunes after the battles of Vicksburg and Gettysburg) and the printing of money.

The National Banking System was established in 1863 (and strengthened in 1864) to facilitate the sale of government bonds as well as the issue of currency (the greenbacks). By taxing state bank currency out of circulation, the Union government gave itself a monopoly of the currency supply in areas under its control. The extent of Union reliance on nontax sources of finances is reflected in the fact that of the $3,300 million spent by the federal government during the war period, only 20 percent came from tax sources.

The results of this financing, however, were quantitatively different from those in the South. Over the period of the war, from 1861 to 1865, prices of northern goods and services rose about 125 percent. This reflected a decreasing elasticity of output. According to Kessel and Alchian (13), average incomes rose only about 90 percent, and private purchasing power fell correspondingly. The reason for the vastly different rates of inflationary tax is that real output probably rose in the North (other than for industries dependent on southern cotton). This is true for all output, even though the supply of civilian goods doubtless declined. In addition, the North continued to engage in comparative advantage legal trade with foreign nations and thus did not have to import high-priced contraband as the South did. Also, both northern bonds and currency did not depreciate as much as those of the Confederacy. In general, then, the North did not suffer from an elasticity of output as low as that in the South. The amount of inflation and decline in northern real incomes (about 15 to 20 percent between 1862 and 1865) necessary to transfer resources from civilian goods to the war effort was therefore smaller. Indeed, the North *appeared* prosperous during the war, with the exception of areas dependent on textile employment, which suffered from at least a partial withdrawal of cotton supplies.

SUMMING UP

Even though there has been a spate of investigations of the Civil War period since 1960, much remains unknown about the period. Because of the absence of five-year data for the period 1861–1865, there are severe limits to how far the quantitative investigations can be pushed. Within these limits, disagreements remain about the "watershed" argument. Little doubt exists that the war left a legacy of destruction and institutional changes that greatly reduced the income position of the South relative to the rest of the nation. Was the destruction of a thriving southern slave agriculture more than offset by a Beard-Hacker effect on future industrial growth? As we have already indicated, there is continued doubt about the Beard-Hacker thesis, but an unwillingness to reject it entirely. Once all the evidence is in, the trade-offs between reduced output growth in one region and whatever enhancement of growth occurred elsewhere *may* give some validity to a very particular version of the argument.

QUESTIONS

1. What were the customary bases for interpreting the Civil War up to 1920? What different interpretation was given to the war by Charles and Mary Beard and restated by Louis Hacker?

2. According to the model set forth in this chapter, how may war directly and indirectly affect the loss of capital and other resources, the efficiency of resource allocation and prices (in terms of the elasticity of output)? What may happen to profits and capital accumulation?

3. What was Thomas Cochran's basic conclusion about the effect of the Civil War on American industrial growth? How did Cochran reach that conclusion?

4. In what respects does Stephen Salsbury disagree with Cochran's conclusions about the effect of the Civil War on U.S. industrial growth? Is the disagreement complete?

5. What data and conceptual problems remain in assessing the industrial impact of the Civil War, especially the indirect effects of that war?

6. What conclusions does Stanley Engerman reach about the economic effects of the Civil War?

7. What happened to the growth of commodity output per capita in the decade of the 1860s and that of the 1870s? What are the interpretations of this in terms of the Beard-Hacker thesis?

8. In what important sense was the Civil War clearly a watershed? What appears to account for the enormous increase in the scope of the war as compared with previous wars?

9. What was the Union's economic strategy with respect to defeating the South? Why did the North continue to trade with the South in spite of that strategy?

10. How was the Civil War financed by the South? The North? Why was the North more successful in its efforts to finance the war?

11. What is the wage lag argument? How do Kessel and Alchian explain the real-wage decline from 1860 to 1865?

SUGGESTED READINGS

1. Andreano, Ralph, ed. *The Economic Impact of the American Civil War.* Cambridge, Mass.: Schenkman, 1967.

2. Beard, Charles A., and Mary R. Beard. *The Rise of American Civilization.* Vol. 2. New York: Macmillan, 1927. Chap. 18.

3. Clark, Victor S. "Manufacturing Development During the Civil War." *Military Historian and Economist, 3* (1918). Reprinted in *The Economic Impact of the American Civil War,* ed. Ralph Andreano. Cambridge, Mass.: Schenkman, 1967.

4. Cochran, Thomas C. "Did the Civil War Retard Industrialization?" *Mississippi Valley Historical Review, 48* (September 1961).

5. DiCanio, Stephen, and Joel Mokyr. "Inflation and Wage Lag During the American Civil War." *Explorations in Economic History, 14* (October 1977).

6. Engerman, Stanley L. "The Economic Impact of the Civil War." *Explorations in Economic History, 2* (Spring-Summer 1966).

7. Fogel, Robert William. *The Union Pacific Railroad: A Case in Premature Enterprise* Baltimore: Johns Hopkins Press, 1960.

8. Friedman, Milton. "Price, Income and Monetary Changes in Three Wartime Periods." *American Economic Association Papers and Proceedings, 42* (May 1952).

9. Gallman, Robert E. "Commodity Output, 1839–1899." In *Conference on Research in Income and Wealth, Trends in the American Economy in the Nineteenth Century*. Princeton, N.J.: Princeton University Press, 1960.

10. Goldin, Claudia, and Frank Lewis. "The Economic Cost of the American Civil War." *Journal of Economic History, 35* (June 1975).

11. Gunderson, Gerald. "The Origin of the American Civil War." *Journal of Economic History, 34* (December 1974).

12. Hacker, Louis M. *The Triumph of American Civilization*. New York: Columbia University Press, 1940. Chap. 24.

13. Kessel, Reuben A., and Arman A. Alchian. "Real Wages in the North During the Civil War: Mitchell's Data Reinterpreted." *Journal of Law and Economics, 2* (October 1959).

14. Keynes, John M. *The General Theory of Employment Interest and Money*. New York: Harcourt Brace Jovanovich, 1935. Chap. 20.

15. Lebergott, Stanley. "Through the Blockade: The Profitability and Extent of Cotton Smuggling, 1861–1865." *Journal of Economic History, 41* (December 1981).

16. Lee, Susan Previant, and Peter Passell. *A New Economic View of American History*. New York: Norton, 1979.

17. Lerner, Eugene M. "Money, Wages and Prices in the Confederacy." *Journal of Political Economy, 62* (February 1955).

18. Mitchell, Wesley Clair. *A History of Greenbacks*. Chicago: University of Chicago Press, 1903.

19. Salsbury, Stephen. "The Effects of the Civil War on American Industrial Development." In *The Economic Impact of the Civil War*, ed. Ralph Andreano. Cambridge, Mass.: Schenkman, 1967.

20. Scheiber, Harry N. "Economic Change in the Civil War Era: An Analysis of Recent Studies." *Civil War History, 2* (December 1965).

21. Sellers, James L. "The Economic Incidence of the Civil War in the South." *Mississippi Valley Historical Review, 14* (September 1927).

22. Studenski, Paul, and Herman Kroose. *Financial History of the United States*. New York: McGraw-Hill, 1952.

23. Williamson, Jeffrey. "Watersheds and Turning Points: Conjectures on the Long Term Impact of Civil War Financing." *Journal of Economic History, 34* (September 1974).

24. Wright, Gavin. *The Political Economy of the Cotton South*. New York: Norton, 1978.

Chapter **11**

AGRICULTURE, 1865–1897

The last third of the nineteenth century was a period of vast change and development in American agriculture, the kind of ferment experienced in few other time periods. The period begins in 1865, at the close of the Civil War, and ends in 1897, at the close of the great depression of 1893, which marked the beginning of 20 years of agricultural prosperity.

Among the elements characterizing this period are the following: The South had to accommodate to the end of slavery and repair widespread wartime destruction. The westward movement rushed across the continent and the frontier disappeared as a geographic line. Technology continued to develop, and the mechanical agricultural revolution persisted into the twentieth century. The federal government accelerated its aid to farmers, but economic problems plagued agriculture (and much of the rest of the economy as well) and farmers devised a number of approaches aimed at resolving these problems.

AGRICULTURE AND SUPPLY AND DEMAND

Before going into the institutional and historical materials dealing with the economic development of U.S. agriculture from 1865 to 1897, it is useful to see how the various supply and demand factors might theoretically have affected agriculture in that period. (Those who feel insecure about supply and demand theory should read the Review of Economic Concepts at the end of this chapter.) First, we shall look at the nature of the demand for agricultural products, then at their supply.

Agriculture and Demand

Agricultural products adhere to the general law of demand: The quantity demanded of an agricultural product increases as its price declines. During the period from 1865 to 1897, the **price elasticity of demand** (a measure of responsiveness of quantity demanded to a change in price for a section of the demand curve) for agricultural products was low compared to that for many other goods; that is, demand for agricultural products was price inelastic (the percentage change in quantity demanded was less than the percentage change in price). Agricultural products are "necessities," are perishable, and have few if any close substitutes; all these factors indicate a price-inelastic demand. Although agricultural products take a significant part of total expenditures, which tends to increase elasticity, this factor was probably not strong enough to offset the other factors. Thus while a particular kind of food may be price elastic, the demand for food in general is price inelastic.

The most important economic implication of price inelasticity is that a given change in supply has a much greater impact on prices than on quantity demanded. In Figure 11.1, the demand curve for agricultural products is presumed to be relatively price inelastic. When supply increases from S_0 to S_1, price declines from A to B, while quantity increases from C to E. *The rate of decline in price is greater than the rate of increase in quantity demanded.* To offset this disproportionate price effect of increases in supply, demand would have to increase (the demand curve shift up).

It is unlikely that tastes or preferences for food in general changed in the second half of the nineteenth century. It was not until the 1950s that medical knowledge of the effects of overeating could have had any effect on decreasing taste and preferences for food, thereby decreasing demand. During the nineteenth century, it may even have been fashionable to exhibit a bit of a "pot" to show one's affluence, a factor that would increase demand.

Figure 11.1.   Inelastic Demand and an Increase in Supply.

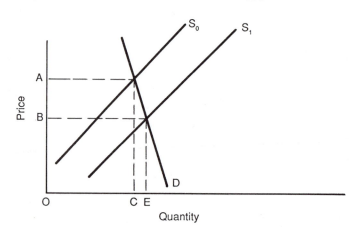

During the second half of the nineteenth century, considerable economic development occurred, and real income on the whole increased. When income increases, demand tends to increase; increased income, then, increased the demand for agricultural products. To measure how much, we need to use the concept of **income elasticity of demand** (which measures the responsiveness of quantity purchased to changes in income). Statistical studies of consumption patterns and income indicate that the demand for agricultural products is income inelastic. In the 1960s, income elasticity of demand for food was about 0.2. To increase the demand for food by 1 percent, income had to increase by 5 percent. It is likely that in the period from 1865 to 1897 income elasticity was higher, although substantially less than 1. In effect, then, increases in real income through economic development meant increases in the demand for food, but these increases were limited by low income elasticities of demand.

Increases in the number of buyers were the dominant factor in increases of demand for food. The population of the United States was growing at a rapid rate from 1865 to 1897, both naturally and from high levels of immigration, which caused domestic demand to grow. World population also was exhibiting high rates of growth, which increased world demand for food.

In brief, price inelasticity of demand for agricultural products caused increases in supply to affect price more than quantity. However, increases in demand occurred, partly because of economic development and consequent increases in incomes, but mostly because of rapid increases in both domestic and international population.

Agriculture and Supply

Now let us look at the nature of the supply of agricultural products. The total supply of food adheres to the law of supply in that, as price rises, quantity supplied increases. **Price elasticity of supply** (which measures the responsiveness of quantity supplied to changes in price for a segment of a supply curve) tends to be highly inelastic—at least in the short run—because of discontinuity in agricultural production. Once wheat or any other field crop is planted, there is little that can be done to increase output until the next planting period. The same applies, although with variations in time involved, for animals and fruits. Therefore, between the beginnings of new production periods, supply elasticity is low, that is, quantities supplied of agricultural products have a limited ability to respond to price variations. In the long run, farmers respond to profit or loss possibilities from the prior period. But these responses may not be appropriate for the present period. This lag increases the probability of error in management decisions and causes greater instability within agriculture.

Changes in supply (shifts of the curve) are influenced by several factors. For one, improvements in technology increase supply. The technological revolution that increased productivity in agriculture started in the United States in the late 1830s and has continued to the present. The record of this increase in productivity is shown in Table 11.1.

Table 11.1. The Number of People One
Farm Worker Could Feed.

YEAR	NUMBER OF PEOPLE
1820	4
1930	10
1950	15
1970	46

SOURCE: James F. Willis and Martin L. Primack,
Explorations in Economics (Boston: Houghton
Mifflin, 1977), p. 434.

Also, in 1865, the frontier had passed the Mississippi River, and land was plentiful and cheap. The price of this resource remained low, and thus did not restrict the increases in supply of agricultural products that occurred in the second half of the nineteenth century.

Perhaps the single most important factor affecting supply was the tremendous increase in the number of farmers and in farm acreage. Table 11.2 shows an increase in the number of farms in the United States from 1.5 million in 1850 to 5.7 million in 1900. Improved farm acreage also showed a remarkable increase, from 114 million acres in 1850 to 416 million in 1900. World supply of agricultural products was expanded by similar increases in farmers and land, particularly in Argentina, Canada, Russia, and Australia.

In addition, because of the large number of farms, it is likely that very substantial conditions of competition existed and that excess demand and excess supply were eliminated, as equilibrium price theory suggests. Farmers could not act together and restrict supply (shift the curve up) to maintain higher prices. **Monopoly power,** the ability of a firm to influence price, *was not* present in agriculture.

Finally, the willingness of farmers to cut production when prices and profits are low depends on their opportunity costs. Opportunity costs represent what farmers could receive in income from the best alternative use of their labor, land, and capital. It seems that farmers' opportunity costs (alternative uses) were indeed

Table 11.2. Farms and Improved Acres of Land (in millions).

YEAR	FARMS	IMPROVED ACRES
1850	1.5	114
1860	2.0	164
1870	2.7	196
1880	4.0	284
1890	4.6	358
1900	5.7	416

SOURCE: U.S. Bureau of the Census, "Agriculture, General Report and Analytical
Tables," *Fourteenth Census of the United States, Taken in the Year 1920,* Vol. 5
(Washington, D.C.: U.S. Government Printing Office, 1922), pp. 38–43.

low. Alternative nonagricultural uses of land, especially in this period, were few (perhaps only hunting) and low in income potential. Although farm machinery was costly, there were few alternative uses of these machines because they were specialized for agricultural production. Even though agricultural labor was highly skilled, it, too, was very specialized and not easily applicable to nonagricultural employment. These low opportunity costs were stronger in the short run than in the long run. Eventually farmers could leave agriculture. Since opportunity costs were so low, prices had to be *very* low for economic forces to impel the movement of resources from agriculture. Of course, nonmonetary factors may have been strong enough to cause such a movement. Many farmers' sons and daughters went to the big city because of the bright lights and excitement.

Some Conclusions

Despite the strong rise in demand caused by increases in real per capita income and growth in the population, the factors increasing supply—technological improvement, cheap land, and increases in the number of farmers—were much stronger. Because of the price inelasticity of demand for agricultural products, more of the effect of relative increases in supply resulted in decreasing prices than in increasing quantity demanded.

THE ROLE OF GOVERNMENT AND TECHNOLOGY

From its founding, the U.S. government has had significant effects on agricultural activity. Before 1860, the price and other terms of sale of federal and state land and land grants to the railroads had a significant impact on the general availability and price of land. Also, in the early 1800s, the patent office was instructed to collect and disseminate improved seeds.

The impact of government policy was even greater after 1860. In 1862, Congress created the Department of Agriculture, which was given cabinet status in 1889. Its function was primarily to study ways of increasing agricultural productivity and to disseminate this information to the farming community. Again in 1862, the Morrell Land Grant Act gave federal land to the individual states for the purpose of setting up agricultural colleges. The Hatch Act of 1887 provided funds for each state to establish experimental stations. By 1897, every state agricultural college had a well-diversified set of offerings in agriculture, an experimental station, and an extension department, which became a vital force in adult education. This accumulation and dissemination of knowledge were prime factors in increasing agricultural productivity and increasing supply.

The Homestead Act

Southern opposition prevented the passage of the Homestead Act until 1862. Essentially, the act gave 160 acres of unappropriated public land to anyone who would live on the land and cultivate it for five years and pay minimal fees. Fred

Shannon (44) described what he called "the hope and the myth" of the Homestead Act as the **safety valve theory.** Free western land given to the poor was to be the "safety valve" that would prevent eastern urban "exploitation" of the American working class. If eastern manufacturers pressed too hard, their workers could go to the frontier and get free land. The seemingly limitless frontier would prevent the United States from becoming like Europe, with its "class distinctions and downtrodden working class." Free land was the safety valve that would keep America free.

In fact, the Homestead Act did not provide this safety valve. For one thing, it did not supply funds to transport eastern workers to the western frontier. For another, it did not supply the draft animals, livestock, or machinery needed to commence farming. Perhaps most important, the act did not provide for the subsistence of the new farm family until its first crop came in. Most urban workers, many of whom earned less than $250 per year, could not possibly save enough to cover these costs of establishing a farm on the western frontier. Furthermore, in the drier parts of the frontier, 160 acres was not enough land to provide a living for a farm family.

Shannon argues that the Homestead Act was not the major element in post–Civil War westward expansion that the myth implies.

> It is true that the number of farms in the United States grew from about 2,000,000 in 1860 to 5,737,000 in 1900, and that the total land in farms rose from 407,213,000 to 838,592,000 acres. It is equally true that not quite 600,000 patents for 80,000,000 acres of homesteads were issued in those same years. In other words, even if all the homesteaders had kept and lived on their holdings, less than a sixth of the new homes and little over a sixth of the acreage would have been on land that came as a gift from the government. Eighty-four out of each hundred new farms had to be achieved either by the subdivision of older holdings or by purchase. Furthermore . . .an astonishing number of homesteaders were merely the hired pawns of land monopolists who took over the land as soon as the final patents were received.

But while the Homestead Act may not have provided a safety valve for the eastern industrial labor force, it may have performed such a function for a portion of the farming community itself. Marginal farmers in the East and Midwest, instead of joining the rural flow to the cities, could more easily move to government lands on the frontier because of the Homestead Act.

TECHNOLOGY AND AGRICULTURAL PRODUCTIVITY

The technological revolution in agriculture began before the Civil War, and many of the basic innovations in agricultural machinery had been made by 1860. Improved iron and steel plows, mowing machinery, grain binders, threshers, and grain planters were invented in the 1840s and 1850s. But while these innovations were developed mostly in the 1840s, it was not until the middle of the 1850s that they were widely used. The traditional explanation for this considerable lag was that it took the high price of wheat and the labor shortage of the 1850s to stimulate greater use of these new innovations. Paul David (11) set out to prove the traditional conclusions. Alan Olmstead (36), criticizing David's research procedures, concluded that the primary factor in the adoption of the innovations was the significant improvement in the machines that was made in the early 1850s. No doubt the debate will continue, but we can say that all three factors—the increased price of wheat, the shortage of labor, and improvements in the machines themselves—contributed to their accelerated use in the 1850s.

In addition, in the North and the West, the Civil War drew off such a large proportion of farm labor for the Union armies that the resulting labor shortage and rising wages further increased the demand for this improved machinery. Mechanized agriculture was firmly established by 1865.

This use of machinery to replace labor was intensified in the period from 1865 to 1897. These machines became stronger, larger, and more efficient. Implements to prepare the soil included the John Deere steel plow (1837), the Oliver chilled-iron plow (1868 and 1877), the addition of a seat for the driver (1864), and the use of wheels (1884), plus multiple or gang plows. The spring tooth harrow (1869) was also an important contribution. These implements could be used to prepare the soil for most field crops.

Drill planters for grains such as wheat and oats were in general use by the 1870s. The corn planter and corn cultivator were perfected by the beginning of the 1880s. Hay mowers, loaders, and forks greatly decreased the labor cost for haymaking. In 1866, Entel perfected the continuous hay baler. The binders and threshers increased productivity in the harvesting of grains.

Table 11.3 compares hand methods to machine methods in the 1890s. The greatest gains were achieved in wheat, oats, and hay. The smallest gains were in cotton, tobacco, and corn. The major problem was that harvesting machinery was very difficult to develop for the latter crops. An efficient corn picker did not appear until the 1920s, and a really effective cotton picker had to await the end of World War II.

Until the invention of an efficient mechanical cotton picker, the size of tenant holdings in the South was limited by the amount the tenant family could pick. On these small farms, the effectiveness of other improved implements was not great enough to justify their costs. Consequently, technical improvement, its adoption, and the resulting increase in productivity were slowest in the South.

In the Northeast, the usefulness of improved implements was reduced not only by small farms but also by the small fields that resulted from irregular, hilly terrain.

The north-central and western prairie states were the ideal setting for improved machinery. On this relatively flat terrain, with larger fields, these machines created economies of scale, and the size of farm that could achieve lowest per unit cost increased substantially. In the 1880s and early 1890s, what were called "bonanza wheat farms" appeared in the wheat belt that extended from North Dakota

Table 11.3.   Hand Methods versus the Machine Methods of the 1890s (per acre).

CROP	TIME WORKED			
	Hand		Machine	
	Hours	Minutes	Hours	Minutes
Wheat	61	5.0	3	19.2
Corn	38	45.0	15	7.8
Oats	66	15.0	7	5.8
Hay: loose	21	5.0	3	56.5
Potatoes	108	55.0	38	00.0
Cotton	167	48.0	78	42.0
Rice: rough	62	5.0	17	2.5
Sugarcane	351	21.0	191	33.0
Tobacco	311	23.0	252	54.6

SOURCE: U.S. Commissioner of Labor, *Thirteenth Annual Report; Hand and Machine Labor*, Vol. 1 (Washington, D.C.: U.S. Government Printing Office. 1899), p. 6.

south to Oklahoma and northern Texas. Tens of thousands of acres of wheat land owned by one person were prepared, seeded, and harvested by gangs of hired labor operating the most modern machinery.

It is important to remember that technological improvement did not advance steadily throughout all American agriculture in this or any other period. Technical change was slow not only in southern tenant agriculture but also in other areas such as dairying. Fred Bateman (3) has shown that productivity growth in dairy farming was very slow in this period.

SOUTHERN AGRICULTURE

The Southern Economy, 1865

By the end of the Civil War, the southern economy was in general collapse. Direct damage was great, especially in the war zones of Virginia, Georgia, and along the Mississippi. An important target of the Union army had been the railroad system. Much of the rolling stock and a substantial amount of track had been destroyed. Southern financial capital was completely destroyed through the issue of large amounts of eventually worthless Confederate currency. The South was now primarily dependent on the North for its financial capital. The small amount of industrial capital was either destroyed by military conflict or worn out because the South could not replace industrial equipment.

Productive potential in agriculture had been seriously reduced. There were substantial decreases in horses, mules, and other farm animals, as well as in acreage and the value of farm buildings. Along the river systems flood-control levees were seriously damaged. The freeing of the slaves presented southern agriculture with the need to create a new labor system. Table 11.4 gives some measures of the depressing effects of the war on southern agriculture. According to Kirkland (26), it took southern agriculture at least ten years after the war to recover to 1860 output levels.

Reconstruction

Kenneth M. Stampp (45) has characterized the traditional view of the southern Reconstruction era, 1865 to 1877, as follows:

> Various historians have called this phase of American history "The Tragic Era," "The Dreadful Decade," "The Age of Hate," and "The Blackout of Honest Government." Reconstruction represented the ultimate shame of the American people, as one historian phrased it, "the nadir of national disgrace." It was the epoch that most Americans wanted to forget.

It was not until the 1930s that this point of view was challenged and a group of revisionist historians appeared. Stampp, a revisionist himself, commented, "The history of an age is seldom simple and clear-cut, seldom without its tragic aspects, seldom without its redeeming virtues."

The radical Republican Reconstruction of the South had three basic aims: first, to guarantee political equality to the blacks of the South; second, to prevent the southern planter aristocracy from regaining political control and thus opposing the Republican Party; and third, to initiate economic development in the South so as to achieve black economic independence.

Under Presidential Reconstruction (1866–1867), southern whites would not allow blacks political or economic equality. The Black Codes of 1866 relegated the black to "a twilight zone between servitude and freedom." Radical Reconstruction, starting in 1867, based its bid for black equality on the Thirteenth, Fourteenth,

Table 11.4. Southern Agriculture, 1860–1870 (in millions).

	1860	1870
Number of Improved Acres		
Southeast	36.6	24.5
South Central	30.5	28.1
Value of Farmland		
Southeast	795.5	443.0
South Central	1,022.8	487.5
Value of Farm Buildings		
Southeast	178.6	127.0
South Central	203.1	142.6

SOURCE: U.S. Bureau of the Census, "Agriculture, General Report and Analytical Tables," *Fourteenth Census of the United States, Taken in the Year 1920*, vol. 5 (Washington, D.C.: U.S. Government Printing Office, 1922), pp. 38–43, 50–55; and Martin L. Primack, *Farm Formed Capital in American Agriculture, 1850 to 1910* (New York: Arno Press, 1977), p. 177.

and Fifteenth Amendments to the Constitution and congressional and military support to state governments dominated by white Republicans and the now-enfranchised ex-slaves.

Republican state governments concentrated on the formation of social overhead capital, economic structures that would create a more favorable overall climate for development. The areas emphasized were primarily railroad construction and the development of educational facilities mainly for the blacks. This same concentration on transportation facilities and education is a major emphasis in developing economies today.

Historians have tended to emphasize the political corruption rampant in the southern state Republican administrations during Reconstruction. Corruption no doubt existed, but corruption was also rampant in other areas of the country. One should not forget the Tweed political ring in New York City nor the Crédit Mobilier scandal in Washington itself.

Radical Reconstruction, on the whole, was a failure. Although the blacks had gained paper equality with the Thirteenth, Fourteenth, and Fifteenth Amendments, the Compromise of 1877 returned the southern state governments to white rule in exchange for southern white support in the electoral college for the election of the Republican Rutherford B. Hayes. The use of white terrorist organizations, such as the night riders and the Ku Klux Klan, and political subterfuge effectively disenfranchised the blacks.

Radical Reconstruction also failed to provide the blacks with an economic alternative to the white cotton economy. Radical Republicans could not bring themselves to implement the "40 acres and a mule" plan that would have given each black family a small farm and the needed livestock and equipment. The Freedman Bureau set up by the federal government at the end of the Civil War to help the ex-slaves was only temporary and provided only limited welfare support. The blacks were forced to accommodate themselves to a market system of labor. Of necessity, they returned to the white cotton economy.

A New Labor System

After the freeing of the slaves, the southern agricultural economy had to devise a new system of labor. Southern landowners first tried to use hired gangs of wage laborers, but, according to Shannon (44), the system was considered unsuccessful because it did not allow landowners enough control over labor. As Ransom and Sutch in *One Kind of Freedom* (39) have shown, there was, in fact, a substantial labor shortage because the former slaves withheld their labor in significant numbers. Absenteeism was high, and competition among landowners for labor during the busy seasons could be considerable.

The final solution adopted by southern landowners was **sharecropping.** The landowner rented land, frequently for a black family to use, and in return received one-half to two-thirds of the crop. The family had direct responsibility, but the landowner had control over what was to be planted. The landowners were no longer responsible for the condition of the ex-slaves; they were concerned only with the growing of a cash crop, and they generally forced their tenants to put all their efforts into growing cotton. Very little homegrown food was produced because it was a drain on land and labor that could be used for cotton (opportunity costs were too high for the landowners).

Since they could grow very little food for themselves, the sharecroppers had to purchase their provisions from the local store, generally on credit. Fred Shannon (44) maintains that abuses of this credit system were substantial and produced what might be called "debt slavery." To enforce this system of sharecropping and debt, most of the southern states passed vagrancy and credit lien laws. People without means of support (without a job or not in sharecropping) could be arrested for vagrancy. Because of racial discrimination, the laws were implemented more vigorously against blacks. Credit extended by the local stores was secured by a lien on the crop produced by the sharecropper. Sharecroppers, in effect, became tied to the land. This system was used also to control poor whites: whites who owned small farms often became entrapped in debt to the local store.

With so much southern financial capital destroyed by the Civil War, the South became more dependent on northern financial capital. For reasons still not entirely understood, the banking system of the antebellum South simply did not reappear after the Civil War. Ransom and Sutch (39) conclude that 90 percent of the southern banking system disappeared after the war. The state banks, saddled with Confederate currency, collapsed. National banks, which required $50,000 capital for chartering, were confined nationwide to urban centers, of which the South had very few. At any rate, local merchants became the source of "commodity

Figure 11.2. Sharecroppers. (Photo from the National Archives)

credit" in the South. According to Ransom and Sutch, they loaned money at rates of 40 to 70 percent per annum; such rates were hardly conducive to investment and growth. Substantial amounts of credit were extended from New York to these local merchants, who in turn extended credit to both plantation owners and their tenants. Cotton, the means of paying the debt, moved back up the chain of debt to New York, as it had before the Civil War. This debt structure forced most of agricultural effort into cotton.

It is an open question whether producing cotton at the high levels of output achieved was based on minimizing opportunity cost. For the sharecropper, devoting some resources to foods grown and consumed on the farm would probably have yielded a higher return. Both the debt and tenant relationships prevented production of homegrown food, however. The landowners, who were also entrapped in this system of debt, had few options as to the use of the land. Perhaps through experimentation and diversification, they could have emerged with a more productive mix of output. But the need to service a large debt may well have pressured southern agriculture into an ever-increasing output of cotton. It is not at all obvious, then, that cotton production minimized opportunity cost.

Figure 11.3 depicts cotton production from 1866 to 1898. Acres grown increased from 6 million in 1866 to 25 million in 1898. It is interesting that this increase in output was accompanied by a fall in prices from about 16 cents a pound in 1869 to a little less than 6 cents a pound in 1898. To repeat, the system of debt and tenancy was substantially responsible for forcing greater effort into cotton as prices fell.

Table 11.5 shows the increase in the number of farms in the South as the process of sharecropping developed. According to Fred Shannon (44), by 1900, five-sixths of black farmers were croppers or tenants and five-eights of the whites farming cotton were croppers. White croppers outnumbered the blacks by five to four.

Shannon in 1945 argued that cotton prices tended to fall from 1865 to 1893. Fogel and Engerman in the early 1970s in *Time on the Cross* disagreed, claiming that cotton prices increased over this period. Ransom and Sutch in the late 1970s in *One Kind of Freedom*, probably the definitive work on the post–Civil War southern agricultural economy, sided with Shannon, arguing that there was a general downward trend in cotton prices in the last third of the nineteenth century.

The price decline in cotton (see Figure 11.3) was due not only to the increase in output of southern cotton stimulated largely by the sharecropper-credit lien sys-

Table 11.5. Number of Farms in the South (in thousands).

	1850	1860	1870	1880	1890	1900
Southeast	242	304	367	637	740	953
South Central	255	327	448	772	849	1199

SOURCE: U.S. Bureau of the Census, "Agriculture, General Report and Analytical Tables," *Fourteenth Census of the United States, Taken in the Year 1920*, vol. 5 (Washington, D.C.: U.S. Government Printing Office, 1922), pp. 38–43.

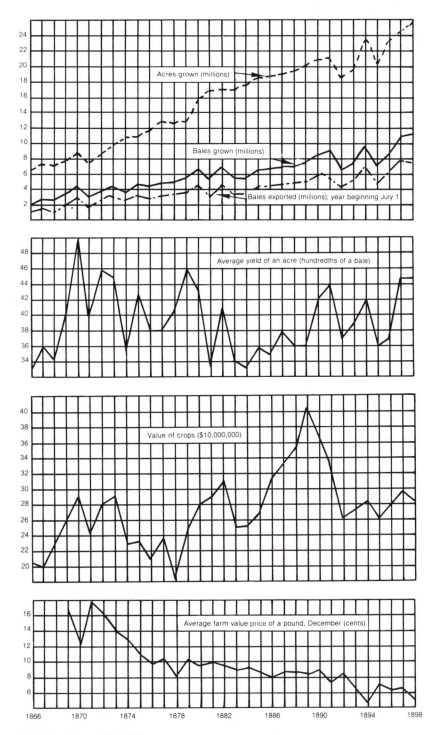

Figure 11.3. Cotton data, 1866–1898.

SOURCE: Fred A. Shannon, *The Farmer's Last Frontier: Agriculture 1860–1897* (New York: Harper & Row, 1945), p. 113.

tem, but also to increased world supply, especially from such places as Egypt and India. England, starved for cotton for its textile mills during the Civil War, had stimulated cotton production in Egypt and India, which became serious competitors. In addition, the rate of growth in textile production in the Northeast and Europe was relatively low after this industry reached maturity around 1870. Prices fell because supply increased very substantially, while demand experienced only a moderate rate of growth.

A further problem facing southern cotton production was the slow development of technology. Abundant and cheap supplies of labor, plus the difficulty of adapting machinery to cotton harvesting, contributed to this near absence of technological improvement in cotton production. Even though output per man-hour rose, the increase was small compared to the national average in agriculture.

Improvement in technology would increase supply and thereby decrease prices, but it would also increase productivity and thus lower costs and perhaps increase profits. While the lack of technological advancement reduced one pressure toward increased supply and lower prices, it also meant the continuation of low levels of productivity and low incomes for cotton growers.

Despite the problems of increased output and falling prices, cotton remained the dominant cash crop in the South. In 1900, the cotton crop was valued at approximately $280 million. The value of the second most important cash crop in the South, tobacco, was only about $40 million. Although his crown was tarnished, his robes ragged, and his house in great disrepair, cotton was still king in the South.

AGRICULTURE IN THE NORTHEAST

The major problem of northeastern agriculture was increased competition from the developing West. The West's higher fertility and greater adaptability of improved machinery, plus declining fertility in the Northeast, increasingly pressured agriculture there. The completion of the railroad network west of the Mississippi provided an efficient transportation system to move western production to the East. The discriminatory system of railroad rates* that at times made long-haul rates lower than short-haul rates often put eastern agriculture under a cost disadvantage.

Urbanization in the Northeast increased the demand for fresh milk and vegetables, and farmers in areas near cities specialized in these products. Railroads, especially after the development of refrigerated cars, greatly extended the agricultural area that could produce milk and vegetables. In regions farther removed from urban areas, the product of the dairy herds went into butter and cheese; factories to process the milk increased substantially in number.

But as western competition took its toll, marginal land and farms were abandoned. Table 11.6 shows that the decade with the highest number of improved

---

*To economists, price discrimination exists for a good when prices of that good vary and the differences are not proportional to cost differences.

Table 11.6. Number of Improved Acres and Farms in the Northeast.

	1850	1860	1870	1880	1890	1900	1910
Number of farms (in thousands)							
New England	168	184	181	207	190	192	189
Mid-Atlantic	328	388	429	498	478	495	479
Total	496	572	610	705	668	687	668
Number of improved acres (in millions)							
New England	11	12	12	13	11	8	7
Mid-Atlantic	23	27	30	34	32	32	30
Total	34	39	42	47	43	40	37

SOURCE: U.S. Bureau of the Census, "Agriculture, General Report and Analytical Tables," *Fourteenth Census of the United States, Taken in the Year 1920,* vol. 5 (Washington, D.C.: U.S. Government Printing Office, 1922), pp. 38–43.

acres in the Northeast was the 1880s (47 million acres). This total declined to 37 million by 1910. The high point in the number of farms—705,000—also was reached in 1880; the number declined to 668,000 by 1910.

Figure 11.4. Agricultural Regions, 1860–1897.

SOURCE: From *History of the American Economy,* Third Edition, p. 300, by Ross M. Robertson. (New York: Harcourt Brace Jovanovich). Copyright © 1973 by Harcourt Brace Jovanovich, Inc. Reprinted by permission of the publisher.

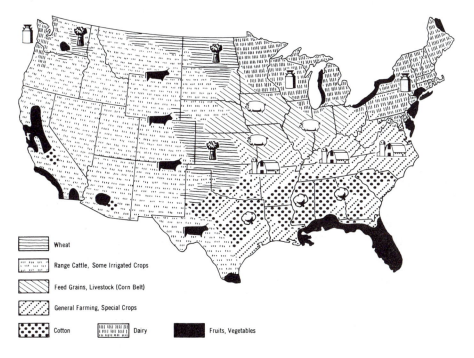

WESTERN AND MIDWESTERN AGRICULTURE

On the basis of agricultural products, the West and Midwest can be divided into three areas: the corn belt, the wheat belt, and the livestock frontier. As Figure 11.4 shows, the corn belt spreads from Ohio through Iowa, the wheat belt lies in the prairie states, and the livestock frontier lies to the west.

The Corn Belt

By 1860, the forested areas of the corn belt in Ohio, Indiana, and Illinois had been settled. After the Civil War, the areas of Iowa, eastern Nebraska, Missouri, southern Michigan, and Minnesota became the frontier and were quickly settled. But the problems found in the prairies were different from those encountered in the forested areas.

By 1870, it took only 1.5 man-days to break an acre of sod in the prairie, while it took 15 to clear an acre of forest land for the plow. This decrease in clearing costs provides an important explanation for the rapid rate of settlement of the prairie. There were, however, severe disadvantages to the prairies. Wood was scarce for housing, farm buildings, and fencing, and the lack of fuel to heat farmers' homes was critical. Buffalo chips (dry dung) and later cow chips were a standard source of fuel, and the sod itself was used to build sod huts. The scarcity of streams and limited rainfall increased the problem of finding an adequate water supply. Locust plagues (the worst in 1874), blizzards, prairie fires, floods, and high temperatures during the summer were serious threats to people, animals, and crops. The vagaries of weather, especially the apparent recurrence of cycles of wet and dry seasons, were also a serious problem. The wet part of the cycle enticed settlement much farther than was justified, and farms were brutally wiped out during the dry part of the cycle. These problems appeared to be greater the farther west toward the Rockies settlement went. In partial recognition of this problem, the government passed the Desert Land Act of 1877, increasing to 600 the number of acres that could be homesteaded in certain regions and selling that land at $1.25 per acre with a requirement that one-third of it be reclaimed by irrigation.

The Wheat Belt

Wheat continued to be the major cash crop on the frontier until it reached the area of minimum rainfall, beyond which the growing of crops was too risky. By 1900, there was a well-defined wheat belt confined by rainfall sufficient for wheat but not great enough for more diversified agriculture. This area started with North Dakota and parts of Montana and then went south through South Dakota, western Kansas, Nebraska, Missouri, Oklahoma, and parts of northern Texas.

California was a leading wheat-producing state until the development of refrigerated cars and irrigation shifted production to fruits and vegetables. Technological change contributes to changing opportunity costs. Refrigeration and irrigation increased the profits that could be obtained from fruits and vegetables, and thus wheat was abandoned for the relatively more profitable alternatives.

The wheat areas in the western prairies had fertile soil and flat topography and were most suited for the use of the improved machinery of the second half of the nineteenth century. In the 1870s, cheap land, high levels of rainfall, completion of railroad transportation, high prices for wheat, and the development of flour-milling machinery for northern-grown spring wheat contributed to the rapid settlement of the northern wheat belt.

The Cattle Frontier

When American agriculture first reached the prairie around 1860, the ranchers and herders outnumbered farmers along the frontier. As farms increased in number, cutting down the amount of free grazing land for the rancher, population pressure increased the price of land and the livestock rancher moved farther west, leaving the land to be used more intensively for crop farming. Eventually, livestock ranching reached areas where rainfall was too low and unpredictable for crop production. By 1900, the cattle belt was established west of the wheat belt and east of the Pacific coastal farming areas.

AGRICULTURAL DISCONTENT

The post–Civil War period, especially after the beginning of the depression of 1873, is known as the "age of agrarian discontent." Along with the creation of millions of new farms, and the bringing into production of hundreds of millions of acres, came a series of problems that vexed great sectors of U.S. agriculture. Many farmers saw these problems under three main categories: the steady fall in farm prices; discriminating practices by the railroads; and unfair practices by agricultural middlemen and food processors.

Agricultural Prices

Figure 11.5 shows that the index of farm prices fell from a high of 161 in 1864 to 72 in 1878 and 1879, then to a low of 56 in 1896. General prices declined from 192 in 1864 to 90 in 1879 and 69 in 1896. Williamson's (51) 1980 study confirms the impressions from Shannon's work that, while prices were falling, the terms of trade for agriculture were improving. The problem was not a deterioration in the terms of trade between farm prices and general prices, for although the relation between the two varied (as shown in Figure 11.5), prices in general fell somewhat more than agricultural prices. But general prices are a poor indicator in this case. Profit mar-

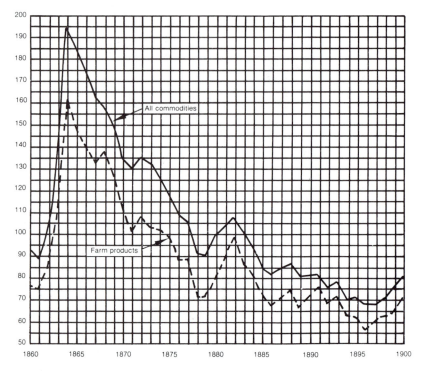

Figure 11.5. Index of Wholesale Prices of Farm Products and All Commodities, 1860–1900.

Source: George F. Warren and Frank A. Pearson, *Gold and Prices* (New York: Wiley, 1935), pp. 30–31; and Fred Shannon, *The Farmer's Last Frontier: Agriculture, 1860–1897* (New York: Harper & Row, 1945), p. 294.

gins narrowed because many more items of cost to farmers failed to fall than the general price index.

Compounding the problem of narrowing and disappearing profit margins was the effect of falling prices on the burden of paying debts. As the West was filled by expanding agricultural settlement, agricultural debt mounted to pay for land, equipment, and livestock as well as for the cost of maintaining new farmers until their land could provide net cash income. As the prices of agricultural products fell and the dollar volume of debt did not decline, more products had to be produced to pay off a given amount of debt. Primack and Willis (38) have shown that this debt burden was indeed significant. If we assume that only the interest on mortgage debt was paid, it would have amounted to 17 percent of the net cash income of mortgaged farms in the United States as a whole, 16 percent in Iowa, and 32 percent in Pennsylvania. These figures become even more significant when nonmortgage debt is included. Even if adjustments downward in interest rates are made to reflect Higgs' conclusion that interest rates were not only falling, but falling faster than prices generally (21), one would still have to conclude that interest and debt repayment were significant users of farm income.

Railroads

The farmers' complaints about the railroads centered in two broad areas: the setting of rates and railroad monopolization of certain middleman functions.

Although farmers complained that general rates were too high, the statistical evidence seems to indicate that railroad rates in general fell at about the same rates as agricultural prices. Rather, the major problem with railroad rates involved rate discrimination. The specific rate for a particular farmer depended on a whole set of competitive forces that varied greatly in kind and intensity from place to place. Competition from other railroads and forms of transportation, such as river, lake, coastal, and canal transportation, created a complex system of shipping costs.

Differences in short-haul and long-haul charges were the subject of a very intense controversy. Often shippers found that charges on goods shipped a longer distance were lower than charges for shorter distances. This apparent price discrimination gave the long-haul shipper a per mile cost advantage over the short-haul shipper. Eastern farmers suffered substantially from this form of discrimination.

Rebates were another form of discrimination that created discontent. If the farming enterprise was large enough, it could pressure the railroads to rebate a portion of the shipping fees. This practice was a serious disadvantage to the smaller farmers.

Farmers in areas where there was considerable competition in transportation had advantages, while those in areas without competition, with perhaps a single railroad, were exposed to the use of monopoly power—the ability of the railroad to dictate price. Even in areas of competition and lower rates, the smaller farmers were at a disadvantage in comparison to the larger ones because they did not have the ability to negotiate rebates.

In the north-central and midwestern prairie states, where wheat was the major crop shipped, railroads tended to branch into grain storage. Farmers often complained that the railroads were forcing them to use these storage facilities at high fees by refusing to ship wheat except from the storage facilities. Higgs maintains that farmers were wrong in their complaints because freight rates tended to fall more rapidly than prices in general. But more important than the truth or falsity of the farmers' claims is that they believed them and acted on that belief.

Agricultural Middlemen

Farmers complained bitterly about the increased monopolization of middleman functions between the farmer and the ultimate consumer. Complaints also were expressed against the combination movement in industries producing goods farmers needed to buy. The middlemen lowered the prices farmers received for their output, and the combinations increased the prices of the things farmers bought.

An example of a middleman organization that lowered the farmers' profits was the milk-marketing trust. The New York Milk Exchange, Ltd., formed around

1882, fixed the prices paid to farmers for milk around the metropolitan New York area. This kept milk prices to the farmers low in sections of the five states that marketed milk in New York. In 1895, it dissolved and was reorganized as the Consolidated Milk Exchange after the courts had concurred that it was fixing prices in violation of the 1890 Sherman Antitrust Act.

Another example is the Illinois Grain Dealers' Association, formed in 1890, with the aim of killing the emerging farmer cooperative grain storage movement. The association pressured railroads and commission merchants in the central city markets to ship or sell wheat only from the association.

Many farmers reacted to these problems by taking direct political action and by developing the agricultural cooperative movement.

Agriculture in the Political Arena, 1865–1897

The effort of many farmers to affect their economic situation by direct political action can be divided by decades into three distinct phases: the 1870s, the 1880s, and the 1890s. In the 1870s, a number of different farm organizations became directly involved in politics and captured a number of state legislatures and governorships with these third-party organizations. The group most numerous was the Grange, and its name was given to a series of legislation sponsored by these farmer parties. Granger laws imposing state regulation of railroads were passed in 1871 in Illinois and Minnesota and in 1874 in Iowa and Wisconsin.

The railroads fought state regulatory laws, but in 1876, in *Munn v. Illinois,* the Supreme Court upheld the right of states to regulate railroads. In 1886 and 1890, the Supreme Court reversed itself. State laws that regulated railroads were held to be invalid under, first, the clause in the Constitution forbidding states to interfere with interstate commerce, and second, under the Fourteenth Amendment due process clause.

In the 1880s, farmers' groups joined with others in launching the national party that came to be called the Greenback Party. It advocated the issuance of unbacked paper currency (greenbacks) to increase the supply of money and to increase prices. These increases in prices would raise profit margins and reduce the burden of debt (how much the farmer would have to produce to pay off a dollar of debt). During the 1880s, farmers' clubs began to coalesce into alliances. By 1890, there were three grand alliances, one in the North, the second in the South, and the third a black farmers' alliance.

In the election of 1890, the farmers' alliances with labor allies gained control of seven state legislatures and elected three U.S. senators and 52 congressmen, mostly from the South. In 1892, in St. Louis, the People's, or Populist, Party was born out of a coalition of farmers, labor unions, and reform organizations. The party's presidential candidate polled 9 percent of the popular vote and received 22 electoral votes.

The Populist Party platform called for regulation of railroads and other monopolies, low tariffs to reduce monopoly power, free coinage of silver and issuance of greenbacks to increase the money supply and prices, a subtreasury plan that would scatter the national treasury across the country and enable it to issue very-low-interest loans to farmers, and a plan to have the government buy up farm surpluses to keep farm prices higher.

By 1900, it was obvious that the farmers' efforts at third-party politics had failed. The Interstate Commerce Commission (1887) and the Sherman Antitrust Act of 1890 had been rendered impotent by the Supreme Court, which undercut federal efforts to regulate railroads and monopolies. Between 1900 and 1914, a number of acts were passed, including the Hepburn Act of 1906, that not only reversed the ineffectuality of the ICC but firmly established it as a regulatory agency. But that story is for a later chapter.

By 1900, general prosperity had returned, and farm prices and incomes began to climb. Farmer discontent evaporated under the pleasant wave of prosperity.

Farmers' Cooperative Movement

A U.S. Department of Agriculture bulletin reported that in 1907 there were about 85,000 farmer cooperatives (business enterprises, other than farms, owned by groups of farmers and operated for mutual benefit) affecting over 3 million farmers, half the farmers in the United States. Despite these seemingly impressive figures, the farmer cooperative movement had achieved only limited success by 1907.

About 72,000 of these cooperatives involved irrigation, telephone, or insurance services. These forms of cooperation were necessary if farmers were to get such services at all, or at rates the average farmer could afford. These forms of cooperation were in areas in which private enterprise did not provide the needed services. Most of the 3 million co-op farmer members went no further in their cooperation than this.

Fred Shannon (44) summarizes his view of the position of the rest of the farmers' co-op movement as follows:

> The stores, marketing associations, and elevators comprised about all the rest of the businesses of any economic significance and these totaled less than seven thousand by 1907, or possibly half as many a decade earlier. It was along these lines that the greatest growth occurred after 1907. If there were a thousand cooperative elevators by the end of the century, they may have benefited a hundred thousand grain growers. But as long as the farmers had no control over the exchanges, and did little if anything to limit their crops to the visible market—as long as the industrial worker was so poorly paid that he could not eat his fill—the saving on marketing costs often was not enough to do more for the farmer than allow him to break even. Much the same might be said for the marketing associations and stores. They were all very nice in their way, but they did not go far enough.

The farmers' co-ops had to overcome many problems, including a lack of skilled management. It took time to acquire knowledge about running cooperatives. Because financial capital was always in short supply, most co-ops operated without reserves against hard times. By charging less, and thus encouraging privately owned competitors to enter price wars, the co-ops prevented the accumulation of desperately needed reserves. Toward the end of the century, the co-ops adopted the Rochdale principles, which included the idea of providing services or goods at the prevailing market price and giving dividends based on patronage at the end of the year. Another problem that plagued many co-ops was the lack of membership loyalty. As economists would expect, when a private competitor offered a lower price, many members would forsake the co-ops. Overall, the most important question was how the co-ops could compete for resources against privately owned and often large economic units in the marketplace.

Eventually, in the twentieth century, farmers' cooperatives carved out a place for themselves in the market economy of the United States. They performed important functions for the farming community, but they did not provide the benefits that many of their founders had envisioned. It was not until the depression of the 1930s and the New Deal that the federal government intervened heavily in the agricultural marketplace in an attempt to raise farm incomes. But again, that is a story for a later chapter.

CONCLUSIONS

The supply of agricultural products of all types increased at an astonishing rate in the United States from 1865 to 1897. This increase in supply was caused by increases in farmland and farmers, and by productivity growth resulting from acceleration of the technological revolution in farm machinery. Although demand also increased, the greater increase in supply caused prices to decline.

The farming sector was thus plagued by problems, and efforts to solve them resulted in institutional changes. One of these changes was the southern labor system in which tenant-debt bondage replaced slavery. But the farmers' efforts also produced changes in politics and political parties and a farm cooperative movement.

In studying agriculture, or any other sector of the economy, one must always be aware of the forces affecting the market. But these forces are not simply technical or theoretical factors that give rise to quantifiable costs. They are also social, political, ideological, philosophical, and historical. One must understand both economic and social causes, as well as the economic and social consequences of particular choices made in response to economic situations.

REVIEW OF ECONOMIC CONCEPTS: DEMAND, SUPPLY, EQUILIBRIUM PRICE, AND ELASTICITY

Demand

The main points about the theory of demand are the following:

1. Demand is not a specific price-quantity relationship, but rather a schedule of the various quantities that buyers are *willing* and *able* to buy at various prices during a particular time period.

2. The demand schedule is constructed under the assumption that, except for price and quantity, all factors affecting demand are constant.

3. When the market demand schedule is diagrammed, the resulting demand curve slopes down, to the right. In other words, the law of demand states that price and quantity are inversely related. Check D_0 in Figure 11.6.

4. When factors other than price and quantity change, the demand curve shifts, changing all prices and quantities. The factors that may shift the demand curve are: (a) changes in tastes and preferences, (b) changes in money incomes, (c) changes in the prices of other goods, (d) changes in price expectations of buyers, and (e) changes in the number of buyers.

5. Again referring to Figure 11.6, observe that when demand increases, the demand curve shifts up from D_0 to D_1. When demand decreases, the demand curve shifts down from D_0 to D_2.

Supply

The main points about the theory of supply are the following:

1. Supply is not a specific price-quantity relationship, but rather a schedule of the various quantities that sellers are *willing* and *able* to sell at various prices during a particular time period.

2. The supply schedule is constructed under the assumption that except for price and quantity, all factors affecting supply are constant.

3. When the market supply schedule is diagrammed, the resulting supply curve slopes up, to the right. In other words, the law of supply states that price and quantity are directly related. Check S_0 in Figure 11.7.

Figure 11.6. Demand.

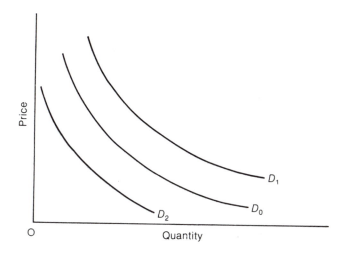

4. When factors other than price and quantity change, the supply curve shifts. The factors that can shift the supply curve are: (a) changes in technology, (b) changes in the prices of the factors of production used, (c) changes in the prices of other commodities using the same factors of production, (d) changes in price expectations of sellers, and (e) changes in the number of sellers.

5. Referring to Figure 11.7, observe that when supply increases, the supply curve shifts down from S_0 to S_1. When supply decreases, the supply curve shifts up from S_0 to S_2.

Equilibrium Price

The main points of the theory of equilibrium pricing are the following:

1. The equilibrium, or market-clearing price and quantity, are established where quantity supplied and quantity demanded are equal. In Figure 11.8, equilibrium occurs at Price A and Quantity B.

2. If price is above the equilibrium price (A), say at price C, the quantity supplied is G, but the quantity demanded is F. There is an excess supply (surplus) of FG, and sellers compete with one another, driving price C down toward price A.

3. If price is below the equilibrium price (A), say at price E, the quantity supplied is F, but the quantity demanded is G. An excess demand (shortage) of FG causes buyers to compete with one another, driving price up toward A.

4. The model assumes that there is competition, that no buyer or seller can influence price.

Elasticity

The concept of price elasticity of demand analyzes the demand curve from a new direction. The law of demand simply noted the general negative slope of the

Figure 11.7. Supply.

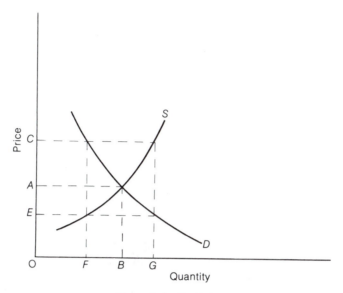

Figure 11.8. Equilibrium.

demand curve, that as price declined, quantity demanded increased. Elasticity deals with the question of the *rate* at which quantity changes as price varies. **Price elasticity of demand** is a measure of the responsiveness of quantity demanded to changes in price along a given portion of a demand curve. In very simple terms, if quantity responds little to a given change in price, demand is **inelastic;** if it responds by a lot, demand is **elastic.** If the response of quantity is proportionate to the change in price, demand is **unit elastic.**

More precisely: If the percentage change in quantity demanded is greater than the percentage change in price, demand is elastic. If the percentage change in quantity demanded is less than the percentage change in price, demand is inelastic. If the percentage change in quantity demanded is equal to the percentage change in price, demand is unit elastic. Specific values for elasticity can be obtained by using the following formula:

$$E = \frac{(Q_1 - Q_2)/(Q_1 + Q_2)}{(P_1 - P_2)/(P_1 + P_2)}$$

E is the **elasticity coefficient,** Q_1 is beginning quantity, Q_2 is ending quantity, P_1 is beginning price, and P_2 is ending price. If E is greater than 1, demand is elastic. If E is less than 1, demand is inelastic. If E is equal to 1, demand is unit elastic. (Ignore the negative sign in the result for it has no economic significance.)

Figure 11.9 is a simple illustration of the concept of elasticity. Beginning price for both D_1 and D_2 is B and ending price is A. For demand curve D_1, beginning quantity is C and ending quantity is E. For demand curve D_2, beginning quantity

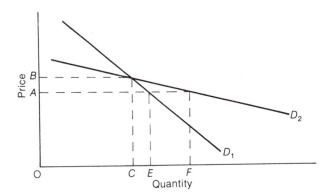

Figure 11.9. Elasticity.

is C and ending quantity is F. For the same change in price, from B to A, D_2 experiences a much greater increase in quantity demanded (C to F) than D_1 (only C to E). Demand curve D_2 is more elastic than D_1 in the price range B to A. We do not know by how much or whether either curve is elastic, inelastic, or unitary because we do not have numerical values and both "curves," as straight lines, have continuously varying elasticities.

What are the factors that make the demand for a good more elastic or less elastic?

1. *Perishability (inelastic) or durability (elastic).* New purchases can more easily be postponed for durable goods than for perishable goods; hence a consumer can respond more readily to changes in the prices of durable goods.

2. *Necessity (inelastic) or luxury (elastic).* Luxury goods may be regarded as those whose consumption can be postponed, while purchase of a necessity cannot. Thus quantity demanded of luxury goods varies more with price than quantity demanded of necessities.

3. *Number of close substitutes.* The larger the number of close substitutes for a good, the more easily one can respond to changes in its price, and the more elastic is its demand.

4. *Percentage of total income.* The larger the percentage of a consumer's income that is spent on a particular commodity, the more the consumer is aware of and affected by a change in price, and thus the more elastic is the consumer's demand for that commodity.

In brief, then, factors that contribute to an inelastic demand are perishability, necessity, small number of substitutes, and a small percentage of total income. The factors that contribute to an elastic demand are durability, luxury, large number of close substitutes, and a large percentage of total income.

The concept of elasticity can be applied to situations other than price and demand. Two further examples are of interest. **Price elasticity of supply** measures the responsiveness of quantity supplied to changes in price. **Income elasticity of demand** measures the responsiveness of quantity purchased to changes in money income.

QUESTIONS

1. Give examples drawn from agriculture of factors that can affect demand. Do the same for supply.
2. How does each of your example factors affect equilibrium price?
3. How does elasticity affect the agricultural market?
4. Was Radical Reconstruction in the South after the Civil War a failure? Why or why not?
5. What was the new labor system created to replace slavery? Did it increase or decrease economic flexibility? Why?
6. Describe various government policies that affected agriculture after 1860. How did they affect agriculture? Were they good policies? Why or why not?
7. What were the problems of applying the new agricultural technology to the post–Civil War South? The Northeast? The prairies? Was the new technology beneficial to the farmers? Why or why not?
8. What were some major economic problems facing the post–Civil War farmers in the Northeast?
9. What were major advantages and disadvantages of farming in the corn belt? The wheat belt? The livestock frontier?
10. What were the major problems causing the farmers' discontent after 1870? How did farmers attempt to deal with them? Were they successful? Why or why not?

SUGGESTED READINGS

1. Aldrich, Mark. "Flexible Exchange Rates, Northern Expansion, and the Market for Southern Cotton, 1866–1879." *Journal of Economic History, 33* (June 1973).
2. Arrington, Leonard. *Great Basin Kingdom.* Cambridge, Mass.: Harvard University Press, 1958.
3. Bateman, Fred. "Improvements in American Dairy Farming, 1850–1910." *Journal of Economic History, 23* (June 1968).
4. Bogue, Allan G. *From Prairie to Corn Belt.* Chicago: University of Chicago Press, 1963.
5. Bogue, Allan G. *Money at Interest: The Farm Mortgage on the Middle Border.* Ithaca, N.Y.: Cornell University Press, 1955.
6. Bogue, Allan, and Margaret Bogue. "Profits and the Frontier Speculator." *Journal of Economic History, 17* (March 1957).
7. Bowman, John. "An Economic Analysis of Midwestern Farmland Values and Farmland Income, 1890 to 1900." *Yale Economic Essays,* (Fall 1965).
8. Bowman, John D., and Richard H. Keehn. "Agricultural Terms of Trade in Four Midwestern States, 1870–1900." *Journal of Economic History, 34* (September 1974).

9. Brown, William W., and Morgan O. Reynolds. "Debt Peonage Re-examined." *Journal of Economic History*, 33 (September 1973).

10. Coelho, Phillip, and James Shepherd. "Differences in Regional Prices: The United States, 1851–1880." *Journal of Economic History*, 34 (September 1974).

11. David, Paul. "The Mechanization of Reaping in the Antebellum Midwest." In *Technical Choice. Innovation and Economic Growth*. Cambridge: Cambridge University Press, 1975.

12. DeCanio, Stephan. "Cotton 'Overproduction' in Late Nineteenth Century Southern Agriculture." *Journal of Economic History*, 33 (September 1973).

13. DeCanio, Stephen. "Productivity and Income Distribution in the Post-Bellum South." *Journal of Economic History*, 34 (June 1974).

14. Farmer, Hallie. "The Economic Background of Frontier Populism." *The Mississippi Valley Historical Review*, 10 (March 1924).

15. Fite, Gilbert. *The Farmers' Frontier, 1865–1900*. New York: Holt, Rinehart and Winston, 1966.

16. Griliches, Zvi. "Hybrid Corn and the Economics of Innovations." *Science*, 132 (July 29, 1960).

17. Harley, C. Knick. "Western Settlement and the Price of Wheat, 1872–1913." *Journal of Economic History*, 38 (December 1978).

18. Hayter, Earl. *The Troubled Farmer, 1850–1900*. DeKalb: Northern Illinois University Press, 1970.

19. Hicks, John D. *The Populist Revolt*. Minneapolis: University of Minnesota Press, 1931.

20. Higgs, Robert. *Competition and Coercion: Blacks in the American Economy, 1865–1914*. New York: Cambridge University Press, 1977.

21. Higgs, Robert. "Patterns of Farm Rental in the Georgia Cotton Belt, 1880–1900." *Journal of Economic History*, 34 (June 1974).

22. Higgs, Robert. "Race, Tenure and Resource Allocation in Southern Agriculture, 1910." *Journal of Economic History*, 33 (March 1973).

23. Higgs, Robert. *The Transformation of the American Economy, 1865–1914: An Essay in Interpretation*. New York: John Wiley & Sons, 1971.

24. Hughes, Jonathan. *The Governmental Habit*. New York: Basic Books, 1977.

25. Jones, Lewis. "The Mechanization of Reaping and Mowing in American Agriculture, 1833–1870." *Journal of Economic History*, 37 (June 1977).

26. Kirkland, Edward C. *Industry Comes of Age: Business, Labor, and Public Policy, 1860–1897*. New York: Holt, Rinehart and Winston, 1961.

27. Kolko, Gabriel. *Railroads and Regulation. 1877–1916*. Princeton, N.J.: Princeton University Press, 1965.

28. McGuire, Robert A. "Economic Causes of Late Nineteenth Century Agrarian Unrest." *Journal of Economic History*, 41 (December 1981).

29. McGuire, Robert A., and Robert Higgs. "Cotton, Corn, and Risk in the Nineteenth Century: Another View." *Explorations in Economic History*, 14 (April 1979).

30. McGuire, Robert A., and Robert Higgs. "A Portfolio Analysis of Crop Diversification and Risk in the Cotton South." *Explorations in Economic History*, 17 (October 1980).

31. Mandle, Jay R. "The Plantation States as a Sub-Region of the Post-Bellum South." *Journal of Economic History*, 34 (September 1974).

32. Martin, Albro. *Enterprise Denied.* New York: Columbia University Press, 1971.

33. Mayhew, Anne. "A Reappraisal of the Causes of Farm Protest in the United States, 1870–1900." *Journal of Economic History, 32* (June 1972).

34. Merk, Frederick. *History of the Westward Movement.* New York: Alfred Knopf, 1978.

35. Miller, George H. *Railroads and the Granger Laws.* Madison: University of Wisconsin Press, 1971.

36. Olmstead, Alan. "The Mechanization of Reaping and Mowing in American Agriculture, 1833–1870." *Journal of Economic History, 35* (June 1975).

37. Parker, William. "Agriculture." In *American Economic Growth,* ed. Lance E. Davis et al. New York: Harper and Row, 1972.

38. Primack, Martin L., and James Willis. "Debt and Tenancy in American Agriculture." Unpublished paper.

39. Ransom, Roger, and Richard Sutch. *One Kind of Freedom: The Economic Consequences of Emancipation.* New York: Cambridge University Press, 1977.

40. Ransom, Roger, and Richard Sutch. "The Impact of the Civil War and of Emancipation on Southern Agriculture." *Explorations in Economic History, 12* (January 1975).

41. Rasmussen, Wayne D. "The Impact of Technological Change on American Agriculture, 1862–1962." *Journal of Economic History, 22* (December 1962).

42. Reid, Joseph D., Jr. "Sharecropping as an Understandable Market Response—The Post-Bellum South." *Journal of Economic History, 33* (March 1973).

43. Sellers, James L. "The Economic Incidence of the Civil War in the South." *Mississippi Valley Historical Review, 14* (September 1927).

44. Shannon, Fred A. *The Farmer's Last Frontier: Agriculture 1860–1897.* New York: Harper and Row, 1945.

45. Stampp, Kenneth M. *The Era of Reconstruction, 1867–1877.* New York: Harper and Row, 1945.

46. Sutch, Richard, and Roger Ransom. "Debt Peonage in the Cotton South after the Civil War." *Journal of Economic History, 32* (September 1972).

47. Swieranga, Robert. *Pioneers and Profits.* Ames: Iowa University Press, 1968.

48. Temin, Peter. "The Post-Bellum Recovery of the South and the Cost of the Civil War." *Journal of Economic History, 36* (December 1976).

49. Turner, Frederick Jackson. *The Frontier in American History.* New York: Henry Holt, 1921.

50. Walton, Gary, James Shepherd, and Douglass North, eds. *Explorations in Economic History, 16,* (January 1979). The entire issue is given over to papers on the Reconstruction South by Claudia Goldin, Joseph Reid, Peter Temin, Roger Ransom, Richard Sutch, and Gavin Wright.

51. Williamson, Jeffrey G. "Greasing the Wheels of Sputtering Export Engines: Midwestern Grains and American Export Growth." *Journal of Economic History, 17* (July 1980).

52. Winters, Donald L. "Tenancy as an Economic Institution: The Growth and Distribution of Agricultural Tenancy in Iowa, 1850–1900." *Journal of Economic History, 37* (June 1974).

53. Woodward, C. Vann. *The Strange Career of Jim Crow.* New York: Oxford University Press, 1966.

54. Wright, Gavin. "Cotton Competition and the Post-Bellum Recovery of the American South." *Journal of Economic History*, 34 (September 1974).

55. Wright, Gavin. *Old South: Revolutions in the Southern Economy.* New York: Basic Books, 1986.

56. Wright, Gavin, and Howard Kunreuther. "Cotton, Corn, and Risk in the Nineteenth Century." *Journal of Economic History*, 35 (September 1975).

Chapter **12**

TRANSPORTATION, INDUSTRY, AND LABOR, 1865–1897

As we saw in Chapter 10, the Civil War took place following a half century of industrial expansion. The last third of the nineteenth century saw a continuation of this expansion, stimulated by the completion of a national transportation network, especially the railroads. Accompanying, and perhaps created by, this industrial expansion was the establishment and growth of national labor unions. But this expansion of the economy was not uniform or proportional in all sectors: some sectors led and pulled along others. The leaders were the railroads, iron and steel manufacturing, and related activities. In this chapter, then, we shall start out with an analysis of the record of railroads, of industry generally, and of labor unions in the 1865–1897 period. The chapter ends with a review and analysis of business fluctuations from 1865 to 1897.

THE RAILROADS

A sector that led the economy and was a primary factor in stimulating the economic development of the United States in the second half of the nineteenth century was the railway industry. In 1865, there were 35,000 miles of railway track; by 1900, there were over 242,000 miles of track. In 1860, railway construction had just begun to cross the Mississippi River. By 1897, there were five transcontinental railroads.

Table 12.1 shows another measure of the expansion of railroads after the Civil War. Per capita freight on railroads increased from 78 ton-miles in 1859 to 1,861 ton-miles in 1900, a 2,500 percent increase.

Table 12.1. Railroad Freight Volume, 1859–1900.

YEAR	TOTAL FREIGHT VOLUME (1,000,000 TON-MILES)	FREIGHT VOLUME PER CAPITA (TON-MILES)
1859	2,400	78
1882	39,302	744
1890	79,193	1,256
1900	141,597	1,861

SOURCE: Richard K. Vedder, *The American Economy in Historical Perspective* (Belmont, Cal.: Wadsworth, 1976). p. 152.

Economic stimulus can be divided into three kinds: primary or direct, secondary, and tertiary. The effects of railroad development on the economy were enormous. The primary or direct effects were in actual construction of the roads, which involved wages paid to the labor employed in construction and the facilities and services needed to maintain that labor.

The secondary effects included the stimulus to those industries that provided the materials used in construction. Two industries were of special importance in this context. Perhaps the more important was the iron and steel industry. It provided the iron and steel for the hundreds of thousands of miles of track and for the many bridges needed to cross rivers and mountains. The other major industry was the railway equipment industry, suppliers of the needed locomotives and railroad cars.

These two industries provide an excellent example of what Albert Hirschman meant by backward linkages. Hirschman, in *The Strategy of Economic Development* (28), maintained not only that historic growth was unbalanced but also that the best approach for rapid development was to unbalance investment in some deliberate, predesigned way. He pointed out that economic activities have both **forward** and **backward linkages.** These linkages and linkage effects are not just input-output relations (forming a demand-supply stimulus); they also establish the probability of the linkage activity or industry. The construction of the railroads clearly pointed to increased demand for the output of railroad equipment and steel ties. At first the demand was substantially filled by imports, but in time domestic development met the linkage needs. These linkage relationships increased the probability of profits large enough to justify the creation of such new domestic facilities.

Railways provided the stimulus for the expansion of plant and equipment to produce steel and rolling stock. The increased level of demand for output also permitted the use of the most up-to-date technology.

Tertiary effects included the general stimulus to the economy as a more efficient transportation system was created. Transportation costs fell. Isolated localized markets were integrated into larger market areas. Competition between regions increased. Demand for individual firms' output increased, permitting efficiencies of larger scale and more up-to-date technology.

These tertiary effects can be interpreted as forward linkages. Transportation facilities created the opportunities for firms to find sources of supplies from outside their immediate geographic areas, and new firms found wider markets for their products.

Railroad development was a classic example of Schumpeter's **innovation** theory. Joseph Schumpeter also developed a theory of unbalanced growth—first in his 1911 book, *Theory of Economic Development*, and later, more fully, in *Business Cycles* (54). To Schumpeter, the process of development is discontinuous. Economies are disturbed from stable, no-development conditions by the introduction of one or more innovations (a new product, process, machine, or market). When such innovations occur, the expectation of profit induces banks to lend funds to entrepreneur-innovators in the field. With these funds, resources are bid into the new activities and away from other possible uses. Schumpeter maintains that the required investment in new plant and equipment is made mainly by new firms under the leadership of "new men." The creation of new leadership becomes the basis of capitalist dynamics.

The first successful innovators obtain monopoly profit. But imitators quickly appear, eager to share in the profitability of the new innovation. Clusters of development occur, expanding the economy. The innovation forces old industry to adapt to the changing pattern of economic conditions.

Eventually the innovation is fully developed, and the required new facilities are completed. Output pours forth from the completed facilities. Investment drops down to replacement level. Or overinvestment may occur, and capacity may exceed demand for the output. New investment falls, and the economy contracts until the excess capacity is worked off. The economy arrives at a new stable position, but at a higher level of development.

Schumpeter feels that the "first innovators" pushed railroads to new areas and were followed by imitators who created clusters of investment. New railroads and new leaders emerged in the process. The total effects of these actions went far beyond the direct effects of railroad construction and operation. Existing industries had to adapt to the new situation as a comprehensive railroad system created opportunities for the development of new firms.

Was railroad expansion after the Civil War as significant in nineteenth-century development as many economic historians believe? Robert Fogel, among others, does not think so. In *Railroads and American Economic Growth* (17), Fogel states that the fact that prior to the Civil War about 50 percent of the U.S. output of pig iron went into rails is diminished substantially when imports and reuse of old rails are considered. The railroads' impact on coal mining was minimal, because wood was the widely used fuel. Further, the widespread use of wood for bridges and railway cars did little for iron demand. Moreover, Williamson's (68) research has further reduced the statistical importance of the impact of the railroads on GNP. After 1865, domestic steel production expanded rapidly, and imports of all kinds of steel and iron products decreased steadily, including rail and locomotive imports. As the forests were cleared and wood became less easily available, coal use increased, especially in the East. As the new steel technology (Bessemer's process, for example) became more widespread, steel decreased in cost and was used more widely in construction.

There is no doubt that Fogel's analysis has substantially reduced estimates of the significance of railroad expansion on the growth of national income. Even so, railroad growth from 1865 to 1897 was perhaps the most important single factor in the general expansion over those years.

Railroad Construction and Finance

Railroad construction was not only an important factor in total income growth and general economic activity, but it also played an important role in the financial world. In 1860, the value of stocks and bonds of U.S. railroads was $1.8 billion; by 1897, their value had risen to over $10 billion. However, after the Civil War, only token issues of railroad stock were publicly offered, and the main instrument used to raise capital was debt (bonds). To give some idea of the importance of railroad financing, the federal debt in 1897 was only $1.2 billion.

The problems of estimating the financial needs and the business expected for railroads were considerable. There was little foreknowledge of the ultimate costs of construction because there was usually a long lapse between the beginning of construction and completion, and the conditions under which plans were made could change totally by completion time. Because the railroads were often developmental (they often were built in undeveloped areas, creating stimulus for development), it was very hard to estimate how much traffic a railroad line would get once it was operational.

The railroad **construction companies** were incorporated separately from the railroads they were to build. Their primary function was to raise capital and then to construct the railroad. Most often, however, the construction company received the railroad company's stocks for nothing and received the bonds at a discount. To many promoters, the impetus for railroad construction was not the potential profits of the completed railroads themselves, but rather the profits on the construction company.

There were two main disadvantages to using the construction company form of financing. First, it substantially increased the possibilities for speculation and manipulation of railroad securities, which could seriously weaken the future financial stability of the railroad. Second, the use of bonds as the main means of obtaining capital divorced those who provided the capital (the bondholders) from those who owned the railroad (the stockholders), thus increasing the chances of management irresponsibility.

The most famous of the construction companies was the Crédit Mobilier, the company that constructed the Union Pacific. The Crédit Mobilier was the center of a huge scandal during the Grant administration. Senators, congressmen, cabinet members, and even President Grant's brother were accused of selling political influence to the Crédit Mobilier. Some have estimated that a profit on the cost of construction of the Union Pacific Railroad as high as 80 to 100 percent was obtained by those who controlled the Crédit Mobilier.

There were three sources of capital for railroad financing: federal, state, or local government; foreign investment; and domestic, private capital. Before 1860, funds from the federal government were less important than those that railroads received from state and local governments, but included tariff remission, government surveys, and materials (wood) from public lands. State and local governments contributed to the financing of the railroads in a number of ways. They gave the railroads almost 50 million acres of land—local rights-of-way, plus land within cities and towns for stations and rail yards. They also granted tax concessions to railroads, guaranteed railroad bond issues, and purchased railway bonds themselves. The future growth, and at times the very existence, of a town depended on whether a railroad came through the town. Towns, public bodies, and private individuals therefore vied with one another offering incentives to attract railroads.

After 1860, the federal government became more involved in financially aiding the railroads. Over 130 million acres of land, valued at over $500 million, were granted to various railroads after 1860. The federal government lent the railroads about $64 million, and by 1900, the unpaid interest on these loans amounted to $114 million. Aid by local governments in the form of donations, loans, guarantees, and subscriptions to securities issues after 1860 was estimated to be about $87 million.

Aid from the various levels of government probably approached $1 billion by 1900, about one-tenth of the total capital investment in U.S. railroads. Despite the substantial financial contribution of the various levels of government, however, the dominant opinion in the United States was that the railroads should be under the sole control of private interests.

Foreign investment in U.S. railroads was very substantial. In 1869, $243 million of railroad bonds were held by foreigners, and by 1900, this had risen to $3.1 billion, most of it held by British citizens. About 25 percent of railroad stock was also held by foreigners. This interest by foreign investors was, on the whole, a progressive element as they led the outcry against mismanagement.

Stock and therefore management control were highly concentrated. Even western and southern railroads were controlled by the "eastern money interests," either as stockholders or as financial underwriters. Private domestic capital accounted for about 60 percent of the financial requirements of U.S. railroads.

The average return on railway bonds in 1869 was 6 percent; on stocks, 7 percent. This rate steadily declined, so that by 1900 average bond and stock returns were only 3.5 percent. The point is not that railroad bond and stock yields were so much less than could be obtained from other economic activities, but rather that railroad fortunes, on the whole, were not earned through railroad operations—they were earned through railroad construction, promotion, and manipulation.

Rate or Pricing Policy

Rate making, or price setting for railroad service, involved a complex system of price discrimination. The practice of discrimination in prices was not simply between different types of goods shipped, but also between shippers, distances, and roads. One factor increasing the intensity of this discrimination was the very strong system of rate warfare. The early monopoly of certain routes disappeared quickly when parallel railway lines were constructed. Also, in relevant geographic areas, alternative forms of transportation on oceans, lakes, and rivers affected rates. Alternative systems of transportation and parallel railway lines were especially competitive in the Northeast and North-Central states.

After the Civil War, rate wars became frequent, climaxing in 1877. Opposition to this rate cutting came from both stockholders and shippers. Some shippers preferred predictable rates rather than uncertain, even if sometimes lower, rates. As a result, the railroads intensified their efforts to reduce competition.

Various methods were used to reduce competition between the railroads. Railroads sometimes both entered into the production of goods to be shipped and also became the shippers, as in the anthracite coal region of eastern Pennsylvania, where the Reading Railroad owned a large number of coal mines and dominated the transportation of coal out of the region. A second method involved special contracts with individual shippers to use only one road; rebates were given as inducements. Such contracts were made only with larger shippers, which placed smaller shippers at a cost disadvantage through higher transportation rates. Shippers might form shipping associations; but the railroads could also organize. The two associations then would bargain over rebates to be made and would apportion the freight among the various railroads.

Often these arrangements were used as devices to discriminate against nonmembers of the shippers' organization. A famous example was John D. Rockefeller's Southern Improvement Association, set up in 1871–1872, which practiced severe discrimination against nonmembers. The association was dispersed under the pressure of an oil shipment strike by nonmembers out of Titusville, Pennsylvania, in 1872. Another example was a livestock shippers' association west of Buffalo in 1875.

A more direct way to reduce competition was for the railroads to engage in **pooling**. Railroads maintained themselves as separate companies, but all cooperated together in pools and jointly decided important market questions. The first railroad pool was established in 1870 by railroads carrying traffic west from Chicago. The two primary issues these pools decided were the freight rate structure and the territory or share of total business to go to each railroad.

The pooling arrangement, like all cartel agreements, was a difficult anticompetitive structure to maintain. Pools had to set up a complex system of regulations to fix rates and shares of the market, regulations that required a bureaucracy, with all its attendant difficulties. Each road constantly jockeyed within the pooling arrangement to improve its position with respect to the rest of the industry. Individual roads also were not above cheating on the pooling arrangements when it was to their advantage, especially under the pressure of declining demand during depressions or business contractions. Perhaps most importantly, pooling, according to English common law, was a conspiracy in restraint of trade and therefore illegal. Since the pooling "contracts" were contracts to commit illegal acts, these arrangements could not be enforced in the courts.

One way of avoiding the problems of pooling and of still reducing competition was through **consolidation,** that is, combining a number of smaller railroads into one large railroad company. Some consolidation occurred prior to 1897. Jay Gould had built a railroad empire in the Southwest and the western Great Lakes region. Commodore Vanderbilt had combined the New York Central, the Erie, and the Michigan Central into the most important railway line in the Northeast. However, by 1897, the United States had only experienced the beginnings of railroad consolidation; its heights were reached in the period from 1897 to 1910.

Railroad Legislation

The basic but by no means the only complaint against railroad policies was the discrimination in rates between shippers. This discrimination took two forms. First, there were the **short-haul versus long-haul rates.** Often rates for a short haul, or short distances, were higher than for a long haul; or when short haul rates were lower, they were not so by an amount proportionate to the relative distances traveled. This form of discrimination could prove disastrous to farm enterprises in unfavorable locations. The second problem was the favorable rates obtained by certain shippers through drawbacks (refunds), special contracts granting favorable rates, and rebates. Small shippers were often put at a serious disadvantage by these practices.

At first, the legislative reaction to these practices occurred at state levels. In the 1870s and 1880s, a number of states passed what were generally called **Granger laws** to regulate railroads either through legislative committees or through separate commissions. The railroads fought back, and part of this fight was carried on in the courts. In 1876, however, the U.S. Supreme Court upheld state regulation of railroads in the case of *Munn* v. *Illinois.* Then, in 1886, in *Wabash, St. Louis and Pacific Railway* v. *Illinois,* the U.S. Supreme Court reversed itself by declaring that the states could not regulate interstate trade. The climax came in 1890 when the Court held that under the Fourteenth Amendment the states could not regulate the railroads because this would deprive railroad owners of their property without due process of law. In effect, state regulation of railroads was now dead. The battle shifted to the federal level.

In 1887, Congress passed the Interstate Commerce Act establishing the Interstate Commerce Commission (ICC), whose primary function was to regulate the railroads. Support for the act came from three main sources: eastern shippers, who wanted an end to the various forms of discrimination; some parts of the railway industry itself, in the hope that national regulation would substitute for competitive anarchy; and investors, especially in England, who wanted an end to mismanagement in operation and fraud in the sale of securities. In addition, a role was played by farmer organizations seeking increased regulation.

The ICC, however, chose to rely on competition and prohibited the pooling wanted by some in the railroad industry. The ICC did attack discriminatory practices by prohibiting rebates and insisting that long-haul rates be higher than short-haul rates. For a time, the railroads cooperated, hoping that the ICC could solve their competitive problems. Eventually, however, the industry opposed the ICC and went to the courts in an effort to diminish its authority.

In 1897, the Supreme Court held that the Interstate Commerce Act did not give the ICC the right to set rates, and thus destroyed its power to control discriminatory rate setting. By 1897, the ICC had abandoned its opposition to pooling and had begun to experiment with pools. The Supreme Court reacted by judging these pools illegal under the Sherman Antitrust Act of 1890. Now the ICC was powerless. But more legislation was soon to come.

INDUSTRY

As we saw in Chapter 10, doubt remains about the argument that the Civil War was an "industrial watershed," freeing the forces of industrial capitalism to propel the United States from a prosperous agricultural nation to world industrial leadership. Whatever the final outcome of the debate about historical discontinuity, however, the period from 1860 to 1900 was truly impressive in terms of American industrial expansion. In 1860, the United States was the world's second most important manufacturing economy, led only by England. By 1900, however, the United States was the undisputed leader, contributing over 30 percent of the world's manufacturing output. An indicator of this phenomenal growth is the manufacturing output index, which was 7.5 in 1863 and 53.0 in 1897, a sevenfold increase. Also, the real output per worker in U.S. manufacturing increased from $223 in the period 1860–1873 to $632 in the period 1912–1916. Real wages increased about 50 percent from 1860 to 1890. Agriculture was the dominant U.S. industry in 1850, with 60 percent of the labor force employed in that sector. By 1910, however, employment in agriculture had fallen to 30 percent, a percentage equal to that of industry.

This growth in manufacturing was achieved through the establishment of the factory system of production. Edward Kirkland (37) defines the factory system as one where the "raw materials were converted into finished goods by consecutive harmonious processes carried along by a central power." Decisive in the spread of the factory into differing industries was the invention of critical machines or methods. For example, the perfection of the refrigerator car for the transportation of fresh meat was necessary to expand the market, increasing the optimum scale of operation in the meat-packing industry to create the factory system of organization there.

But the factory was as much a managerial as a technological problem. Scientific management pioneered by Frederick Taylor in the 1880s, was developed to rationalize the internal flow of processes to increase productivity. Management had to learn to organize the procurement of large supplies of raw materials, organize and discipline the larger amounts of labor necessary, rationalize the flow of productive processes, and find markets for the increased output. An excellent example of an early pioneer was Francis Cabot Lowell in the textile industry near Boston around 1815.

Iron and Steel

A series of innovations revolutionized the steel industry and made it one of the most important industries in the development of American manufacturing. In 1867, only 1.6 *thousand* tons of steel were produced; by 1897, output had grown to the phenomenal figure of 7.2 *million* tons annually.

In 1856, Henry Bessemer in England developed the forced-air process that bears his name, and greatly reduced the costs of producing steel. At around the same time, Kelly in the United States developed similar processes. Martin and Siemens perfected the open hearth method, which gave the steel maker more control over the quality of the finished product. Now, much like the baker making a cake, the steel producer could add different ingredients and make steel to specifications. In the 1870s, steel makers began to use a limestone lining in their furnaces, a practice that allowed them to employ iron ore containing phosphorus. Previously these ores had made very poor-quality steel.

These innovations made raw materials more useful, increased productivity, and, of course, greatly reduced the costs of producing steel. The innovations also increased the optimum size of the steel mill. By 1897, the steel industry had become "big business," and the output of workers employed in operating blast furnaces increased 30 times between 1850 and 1914.

This revolution in steel production had substantial backward and forward linkages. The expansion caused by the technological changes forced a conversion from charcoal to coke and caused the development of the soft coal industry in western Pennsylvania, West Virginia, Ohio, Kentucky, Tennessee, and other places. Other backward linkages led to the development of the Mesabi iron ore field in the peninsula of Michigan. As the cost of steel fell under the technological explosion, forward linkages appeared. Steel and iron could now be used not only in the railroad industry but also in other forms of construction and for consumer products. In total output, stoves became as important as rails. Obviously, the iron and steel industries were stimulated by developments in other fields—railroads, for instance—but in turn they provided the stimulus for other forms of development.

Electricity

While Europeans were more important in developing the scientific principles of electricity, it was primarily Americans who innovated its practical application. The first applications revolutionized communications, with the subsequent economic impact of quickened business communication and reduced information cost. In 1837, Morse invented the telegraph, and in 1876, Bell invented the telephone.

Electricity was applied to lighting homes and businesses by Edison, and the first commercial operation of electric lights was in New York in 1881. Another application of the use of electricity as a source of power was the electrification of street railways by Sprague in 1887. Before electricity could be used widely as a source of power, however, the cost of transporting it over long distances had to be reduced. Westinghouse in the early 1890s solved that problem with the perfection of alternating current.

The use of electricity as a source of power to compete with steam and waterpower was just beginning in 1897. The basic innovations had been made, though it was not until after 1900 that electricity became the dominant power source in the United States.

Water and Steam

As late as the 1870s, waterpower was still as cheap as steam power, and in 1870, about half of the power generated to run the machines of the United States came from waterpower. The main advantage of steam power was its mobility (it was not stopped by lack of water or by winter ice). Parsons in 1884 invented the steam turbine, greatly increasing the amount and efficiency of steam-power generation, and by 1899, waterpower was providing only one-seventh of the total power needs of the United States. In 1900, Westinghouse coupled the steam turbine to the electric generator to produce electricity.

Government Aid to Manufacturing

Direct government financial aid to manufacturing was small, especially when compared to aid given to the railroad system. The federal government provided very little venture capital; aid from local and state governments was somewhat more plentiful. A number of local governments gave manufacturers land for factory sites and control over waterpower. Sometimes state and local governments granted exemptions from taxes. Overall, however, direct government aid was unimportant to manufacturing, although it may have been significant for specific enterprises.

More important than direct (transfer) payments was government protection of U.S. manufacturing through the use of tariffs. These taxes raised the prices of imports and thus increased potential profits in the United States industries so protected. Prior to the Civil War, tariffs levied by the United States were moderate, in large measure because of the opposition of southern legislators, whose region depended on exports of cotton and imports of manufactured and semimanufactured goods. During the Civil War, high tariffs were imposed, partly to help finance the northern war effort. (With the South now unrepresented in Congress, this was relatively easy to do.) Some higher tariffs were also due to political pressure from particular industries. There was no general reduction of these higher tariffs immediately after the war, nor under the Tariff Acts of 1883, 1890, and 1894. The Dingley Tariff of 1897 raised tariffs to all-time highs for a broad range of goods.

The major rationale for these high tariffs was the infant-industry argument—that new industries needed tariff protection until they were developed enough to withstand world competition. But the industries benefiting from the Dingley Tariff of 1897 were not, on the whole, infant industries. The rates from that tariff act seemed to reflect economic need by infant firms less than the political influence of representatives of particular industries.

The federal government's patent system also gave substantial assistance to many firms. A patent granted by the federal government conveyed exclusive monopoly rights to the inventor of a product or process for 16 years, with the possibility of renewal for another 16 years. In 1860, 4,363 patents were granted; in 1879, 22,098 were granted. This growth in patents granted not only reflects the tremendous increase in the pace of technological development but also provides a crude measure of the importance of the patent system as an aid to industry. These exclusive rights to produce certain products or to use certain processes gave the patent holders **monopoly power,** the ability to influence price, and allowed the favored firms to increase prices and at least potentially to obtain **economic profits** (a profit larger than necessary to keep the firm producing).

The Monopolization Movement

The post–Civil War period saw the beginnings of the combination movement in U.S. industry. The aim of this movement was to reduce competition and increase control of prices through the use of various organizational devices. The first organizational device used to reduce competition was the pool.

Pools.   A pool, as we saw earlier, is created when a number of firms in the same industry get together and jointly decide on prices, shares of the market, and other conditions of the industry. Each firm maintains its own separate legal independence. As described earlier, pools were pioneered in the United States by sections of the railroad industry and by John D. Rockefeller in the oil industry. Thus the producers of railroad ties formed a pool in 1887, established production quotas for each firm, and, in consultation with officials of the chief railroads, stabilized prices. The limitations of pooling discussed earlier in this chapter with respect to railroads apply generally to manufacturing.

Trusts.   The next form of monopoly organization employed was the trust. Firms in an industry would turn over their common stock to a board of trustees and would receive trust certificates in return. Since only the trust had voting stock in the individual companies, it could control them, even though each firm remained a legally separate entity. The trustees did not control the formerly competing firms in any managerial or detailed way. The idea was to get each firm's independent management to do what the pool could not legally get them to do—adopt noncompetitive strategies.

In 1882, John D. Rockefeller established the Standard Oil of Ohio trust. In 1892, the General Electric Company trust was formed for firms in the electric light industry. The core organization of the American Telephone and Telegraph Company (AT&T) had formed a trust comprised of firms in the telephone industry by 1899. Of course, many other trusts were formed in other industries.

The primary defect of the trust form, from industry's point of view, was that it was specifically declared illegal by the Sherman Antitrust Act of 1890 and as William Letwin (40) has shown, may well have been unlawful under English common law.

Holding Companies.   A **holding company** is one formed for the purpose of buying stock in other companies. This device was used for controlling major segments of particular industries through controlling their voting common stock. The holding companies were not deemed to violate the Sherman Antitrust Act, perhaps because they were not named in the act. While the trust involved only loose coordination of its member firms, the holding company imposed a centralized, integrated management on its subsidiary companies. Centralized supermanagement became the order of the day.

In the 1890s, John D. Rockefeller converted the Standard Oil trust into a holding company, with Standard Oil of New Jersey as the basic parent company. At the beginning of the 1900s, AT&T was also converted into a holding company.

Consolidations.   Around 1897, another device of the movement toward monopolization was the consolidation form. Consolidation required combining a number of independent firms into one large corporation, unlike the pool, the trust, and the holding company, wherein the individual companies maintained their separate legal existence. The high point of consolidation came at the turn of the twentieth century—but that story will be told in Chapter 14.

THE LABOR MOVEMENT

The concept of workers in the same craft or industry organizing into an association or union seems to stem from three sources. The first is probably as old as manufacturing itself and was embodied in the guild organizations of the Middle Ages, whereby workers in the same craft or trade bonded together for mutual comfort, both economic and social. These guilds were carried over into the craft unions of the nineteenth century. The second source, it is argued by many, were the emerging large-scale often monopolistic firms, of the post–Civil War period in the United States. Many have concluded that workers felt these large firms could only be challenged by a consolidated labor movement. The third source stemmed from rapid technological change. With the development of new processes and machinery and the adoption of the factory system, many skills and trades were eliminated and people who had been employed in them experienced decreases in income and standards of living. Such workers were affected not only economically but also socially and psychologically.

Although the movement toward the organization of labor unions began before 1860, it was during the period from 1865 to 1897 that labor unions became firmly established on the American scene. Even so, in 1880, less than 1 percent of the labor force belonged to unions.

In this period, two basic policy approaches concerning the direction of the labor movement were often in conflict. The first approach, reformism, aimed at either eliminating or controlling the wage system and corporate capitalism. This approach relied on the use of direct political action to achieve reform. The second approach was simple, straightforward trade unionism, which recognized and accepted the wage system and corporate capitalism, but demanded an increased share of income and greater job security for workers. Although conflicting theories about which approach would be more effective continued into the twentieth century, it was apparent by 1897 that straightforward trade unionism was the path the labor movement had decided on.

The Early Years

The lack of a unified transportation system before the Civil War kept markets scattered and contributed to the local or regional nature of the labor movement prior to 1860. The impetus for national organizations came from the establishment of national markets. A taste of what was to come after the Civil War was the founding in 1859 of the first successful national union, the typography union in the printing industry.

The first effort at an organization of national unions, the National Labor Union, was founded in 1866 and centered its brief life on a campaign for an eight-hour day. Its organizational nature contributed to its demise in 1872—its trade union members were in constant conflict with its independent reformist members over the issues of women, blacks, and direct political action.

The Knights of Labor

The Knights of Labor was founded in Philadelphia in 1869 by Uriah S. Stephens. Stephens kept the order secret and control highly centralized. In 1879, when Terrence W. Powderly became Grand Master, secrecy was abandoned, and as a result the organization began to grow. The local unit was the assembly, of which there were two kinds: a **trade assembly,** with all members belonging to the same craft or occupation; and a **mixed assembly,** with members from a variety of different occupations. Self-interest separated the two forms as the trade assemblies became more concerned with obtaining direct benefits for their members through trade union activities.

In 1884, a group of trade assemblies in the railroad industry conducted successful strikes on the Kansas Pacific and other railroads. Thereafter, membership in the Knights of Labor rapidly expanded from 52,000 in 1884 to a peak of 700,000 in 1886. Attempting to repeat the successes of 1884, the trade assemblies in railroading struck the Southwestern Railroad in 1886. The strike failed, and as it crumbled, violence occurred. Partly as a result, membership in the Knights of Labor fell to 100,000 by 1890, and the organization had all but disappeared by 1900.

Many other factors contributed to the rapid decline of the Knights, including the general incompetence of Terrence Powderly and the continuing internal conflict between him and others who aspired to take over the Knights. Powderly had set the course of the order in two directions—toward establishing producer cooperatives to avoid the wage system, and toward exerting political pressure on Congress to obtain more favorable laws for workers. The cooperatives failed because of incompetent management and insufficient capital. The Knights' political agitation also failed to generate any noteworthy political gains.

Powderly was opposed to the use of the strike as a labor weapon on the grounds that it signified acceptance of the wage system, and he withheld the support of the national organization for the strike activities of the trade assemblies. The numerical strength of the Knights was in the mixed assemblies, where trade union activities were not of much interest. After the formation of the American Federation of Labor in 1886, the trade assemblies left the Knights.

The strikes of trade assemblies in the railroads of the Midwest in 1886 and 1887 degenerated into violence as the strikers were losing. Large segments of the press blamed the Knights for this violence, causing bad public relations. This was ironic since the national organization was opposed to strikes.

Defections from the Knights were massive by the end of the 1880s. As stated earlier, the Knights of Labor were no longer an important force in the American labor movement by 1900; dominance had shifted to the American Federation of Labor.

The American Federation of Labor

The American Federation of Labor (AFL), a federation of national trade unions, was founded in 1886 under the leadership of Samuel Gompers of the Cigar Makers Unions.

The basic philosophy of Gompers was stamped on the AFL. In brief, this philosophy was called **trade unionism.** The only concern of the union was to be the welfare of its members; that is, efforts would center on wages, hours of labor, and the various conditions of work. No political or reformist agitation was to be engaged in by the union; the union would not affiliate in any way with any particular political party. The aim was to help labor's friends and punish its enemies through the ballot box, not through direct involvement in politics.

Another basic principle of Gompers' labor philosophy was a reliance on **craft unionism.** A union would represent workers in a particular trade or craft—not an entire industry. This concentration on craft rather than industry gave advantages to small groups of highly skilled workers in organizing unions and bargaining with employers. However, such craft concentration led to the neglect of masses of unskilled and semiskilled workers and contributed to labor's inability to effectively organize important major industries, such as steel, until the late 1930s.

This "craft versus industry" approach introduced a major conflict within the labor movement. Eugene V. Debs, later to run several times for U.S. president under the Socialist banner, organized the National Railway Union in the early 1890s as an industrial union. Soon after its formation the NRU tried to assist the workers of the Pullman strike by boycotting trains with Pullman cars. But after intervention by the courts and federal troops, the strike and boycott failed and the NRU collapsed.

By 1897, the only existing **industrial union** (a union drawing its members from an entire industry) was the newly reconstructed United Mine Workers' Union. Further efforts at industrial unionism were made, but widespread success did not come until the late 1930s.

The final principle of Gompers' trade unionism was complete opposition to **dual unionism.** There was to be only one union in each craft or industry. As rivals to the AFL appeared in the twentieth century, however, dual unionism and its attendant conflicts became a reality.

Nineteenth-century data on membership in the various labor organizations are scanty and open to question. Most of the numbers were probably inflated. Table 12.2 contains estimates of membership in labor unions and of this membership as a percentage of total employment. The data show growth in numbers in the 1880s and 1890s as the American Federation of Labor and the Railroad Brotherhoods became firmly established. But the percentage of the total labor force who were union members remained under the 1870 figure of 5 percent.

Consequences of Trade Unionism

The trade unionism of the AFL was a retreat from the opposition to the factory-corporate market system represented by the Knights of Labor. The AFL accepted

Table 12.2. Membership in Labor Unions and Percentage of the Total Labor Force.

YEAR	UNION MEMBERSHIP (THOUSANDS)	PERCENT OF TOTAL LABOR FORCE
1870	300	5.0
1880	200	2.3
1890	400	3.2
1900	868	4.8

SOURCE: *Historical Statistics of the United States* (1960), pp. 72–73, 98; J. G. Royback, *A History of American Labor* (New York, 1959), pp. 104, 118, 156, 163; L. Wolman, *The Growth of American Trade Unions* (New York, 1924), p. 21; Philip S. Bogwell and G. E. Mingoy, *Britain and America: A Study of Economic Change 1850–1939* (New York, 1970), p. 207.

the legitimacy of the wage system, technological change, factories, and corporate capitalism. The AFL seemed to be saying that it wanted a full piece of the pie for workers; workers wanted their share of "the action."

To get that share, the AFL concentrated on a select group of highly skilled workers organized in crafts where the union could more easily control the supply of labor. As a result, mass production industries were neglected because of the economic strength of the individual firms and the semiskilled nature of the employees. The AFL also neglected the immigrant workers, on the grounds that they could not be organized; in fact, the AFL was strongly opposed to the U.S. policy of unrestricted immigration. Members of the AFL saw the immigrant as a competitor, not as a fellow worker. The AFL also neglected the organization of black workers and women workers.

The AFL was an unimportant force in politics and had a minimal effect on legislation. The union developed a deeply pessimistic view of government relationships with unions; often governments became more the enemy than did employers. Gompers, in the nineteenth century, wanted government to leave unions alone.

Socialists and other left-wing groups within the AFL provided the only challenge to Gompers and his program. In 1894, the Socialists confronted Gompers on the issue of the AFL presidency and challenged his program. Although the threat to the program was defeated, Gompers lost the presidency for two years. The next challenges came from rival organizations—the program was not challenged again from within the AFL until the 1930s.

Tactics of the AFL

The AFL's basic goal was to obtain union recognition and a contract with the employer that set wages, hours of work, and other conditions of employment. If it proved impossible to achieve recognition and a contract through negotiations, then the union would use its ultimate weapon—the strike. Outside of the highly skilled crafts, where the union had control over the supply of labor, it was very difficult to win a strike. In the second half of the nineteenth century, use of the strike was reserved mostly for resisting a cut in wages and to sue for union recognition.

A technique used with the strike was picketing, aimed at "persuading" workers or customers not to enter the premises of the struck firm. In many instances, persuasion became intimidation.

The boycott was another important union weapon. In a **primary boycott,** the striking union urged people not to buy from the struck firm. In a **secondary boycott,** the union urged people not to buy from another firm that did business with the struck firm.

At times, out of desperation because a strike was failing, a union would resort to violence. This violence took the form of physical intimidation of nonstriking workers and damage to the productive facilities of the firm.

Weapons of the Employer

The **lockout** was the employer's equivalent to the union's strike. It was often used to crush developing union organizations. The great Homestead Steel strike of 1892 was, in effect, a lockout, as the owners closed the mills in an effort to destroy the union.

Another important weapon of employers was the **yellow-dog contract.** Workers, on being hired, were required to sign a contract stating that they were not members of a union and would quit if they did join one. These were called yellow-dog contracts because supposedly only a "yellow dog" would sign one. The contracts were used to get court injunctions against union-organizing activity on the grounds that the union's organizer was encouraging workers to violate their contracts.

An especially effective weapon against unions was the use of the **blacklist.** Union leaders, organizers, members, and any other category of worker that it would be "undesirable" to employ were put on a so-called blacklist distributed to all employers. A blacklisted worker found great difficulty in obtaining employment.

When a strike occurred, the employer could and did hire thugs and often had them deputized by the local police to break up the strike. Strikebreakers, often using violence, broke up picket lines and physically intimidated union members. In the case of the Homestead Steel strike, a pitched battle took place between the strikers and strikebreakers brought in by the Pinkerton Detective Agency. The union beat off the strikebreakers after 12 people had died.

The Pinkerton Detective Agency enjoyed a brisk business in providing what were called "company spies" to infiltrate the ranks of the union and report to the employer on union plans and the names of prominent union members. Perhaps the most famous use of a company spy was the agent who infiltrated the Molly McGuires, a labor terrorist group in the Pennsylvania coal fields in the 1880s, and gained evidence needed to convict the leaders of murder. In 1935, firms paid $80 million a year to 230 detective agencies to provide 40,000 company spies; or so it is estimated.

The employer firms very often owned the houses that the workers lived in, and individuals who irritated the employer or workers who struck could be evicted from these homes. When the unions struck at the Pullman plant in 1894, one of the first acts of Pullman's managers was to evict the striking workers from the company homes.

In this period, the unions maintained that government at all levels often interfered on the side of the employers. The courts rarely decided in favor of the unions. In fact, the courts prohibited a wide variety of activities by unions and were a very strong deterrent to the unions' ability to effectively organize. The use of the yellow-dog contract to enjoin unions against organizing activity was an especially serious problem. Also, the federal courts often invoked the Sherman Antitrust Act to prohibit union activity, holding that such activities restrained trade.

The use of local and state police, the national guard, and even federal troops in labor-management disputes was condemned by the unions. Unions charged that these forces were used to end strikes by breaking up picket lines, intimidating strikers, and jailing strike leaders. The trade unions called state police the American Cossacks. Often local police forces deputized people who worked for and were paid by the employers. During the Pullman boycott of 1894, called by the United Railway Union led by Eugene V. Debs in support of the striking Pullman workers, federal troops were called in, obstensibly to protect the U.S. mail being transported by railroads. The unions charged that the troops went far beyond protecting the mails; and were considered by many unionists to be a prime factor in defeating the boycott, thus causing the collapse of the United Railway Union.

A Conclusion

In the period 1865 to 1897, except in the skilled crafts, union power was slight, especially when compared to the economic and political strength of employers. It is quite surprising, then, that union membership grew to the point where the American Federation of Labor and the various railroad brotherhoods were firmly established. The struggle was a bitter one; violence was practiced on both sides. The history of the early labor movement in the United States involved more violence than that of any other labor movement in the world.

ECONOMIC FLUCTUATIONS, 1865–1897

A Brief Recap

On analyzing economic fluctuations from 1815 to 1865, two observations can be made. On the one hand, the American economy was very much influenced by economic conditions in Europe, especially in Britain. Variations in the demand for American exports, as well as financial decisions originating in the British economy, had substantial impact on the United States economy. On the other hand, as the American economy developed and became larger during these 50 years, internal factors affecting aggregate demand and the supply of money played an increasingly important role. As late as 1860, the stability of the U.S. economy was still dependent on European economic conditions, but that dependence was weakening.

The Expansion to 1873

Many warned that the economy would severely contract after the Civil War. However, the economy expanded until 1873, with only two mild recessions. The long war, which forced the economy to concentrate on meeting the needs of the army, caused postponement of considerable amounts of demand in the civilian economy. Thus, after the war, construction both of housing and of the railroads was high, and capital goods production for industry was also high. In addition, high levels of investments were obtained in the newly developing petroleum industry. The processes developed by Bessemer, Siemens, Martin, and others had revolutionized steel production, increasing investment in that new technology. Finally, the economy continued to be stimulated by large government expenditures as bounties, pensions, and back pay were paid to the returning soldiers. Settlement of over $700 million in war-related contracts took four years to pay.

Once again, expansion occurred as aggregate demand, consumption, investment, and government expenditures increased, causing a multiple increase in income. (In turn, a positive accelerator reinforced the expansion.)

The Depression of 1873

By 1872, it was becoming apparent that the expansion was weakening, especially as railroad construction had pushed lines into areas that could not yet provide sufficient earnings. A general contraction of the economy was held off by a wave of speculation and optimism in the now fully developed New York stock market.

In September 1873, a stock market crash and a banking panic were triggered by the failure of Jay Cooke and Company (the great marketeers of Union bonds during the Civil War). There had been much speculation in railroad securities, which were the backbone of the issues sold in the stock market. First the market collapsed. Then the collapse spread to the urban banks, and a general banking panic ensued. The earlier overexpansion, especially in railroad construction now produced a decrease in investment and a depression in the economy. The slowdown in investment caused a decline in aggregate demand and a multiple decrease in income. In turn, induced investment declined, and a negative accelerator further reduced income and output. The economy's recovery was weak until 1878.

The Expansion of 1878–1883 and Depression Again

Under the stimulus of increased railroad construction as well as immigration and urban construction, the economy expanded after 1878. This expansion remained vigorous until the end of 1882, when a slow contraction set in. Again railroad construction overexpanded, and the resulting low earnings on a number of lines caused a slow-up in railroad construction.

In May of 1884, a stock market and banking panic again signaled a sharp downturn in the economy and a depression. Once again, the depression was protracted, and new expansion did not become vigorous until 1886. Once again, both aggregate demand and aggregate supply growth expanded the economy, then, as this growth slowed and declines occurred, a negative accelerator and multiplier caused contractions in the economy.

The Expansion of 1886–1892 and the Depression of 1893

The expansion of 1886–1892 was not as vigorous as that of 1878–1882. Railroads still paced the expansion, but their rate of growth had declined. By 1892, railroad expansion had begun to fall off again. In 1892, the import surplus (imports exceeding exports) substantially widened, and there was an outflow of gold, weakening the reserves of the New York banks. In February 1893, there was, once again, a stock market and banking panic and collapse. The ensuing depression lasted until 1897. As before, the multiplier-accelerator sequences expanded and then contracted the economy.

General Observations

In regard to economic fluctuations, the period from 1865 to 1897 had a number of important characteristics. The most frightening and dramatic aspects of the depressions of 1873, 1883, and 1893 were the coupling of stock market collapses with banking and monetary crises. These depressions began with the collapse of security prices on the stock exchange and with a number of bank closings.

Stock market health and the banking system were linked through the call market for securities. Banks would make call loans on securities; that is, payment could be demanded at any time, and the securities could be sold to pay off the loan. New York bank reserves were heavily committed to the call market; also, deposits of banks outside of New York in the New York banks were heavily involved in the call market. It was the only way that interest could be earned on these funds and that they could also be made immediately available.

Any weakness in either the stock market or the banks could be transmitted to the other. If the banks experienced a drain on their reserves through either a flow of gold to Europe to cover an import surplus or a withdrawal of deposits by rural banks to meet adverse agricultural situations, they might well call in their loans. This meant selling large amounts of securities in the stock market, causing securities prices to fall. In turn, the banks would call in more loans to protect themselves against falling securities prices, causing more securities to be sold, further decreasing prices in the stock market. The cycle would escalate until a stock market panic resulted. Securities prices could fall so rapidly that banks might not recover the full value of their loans; the losses they suffered often resulted in bank closings. However, the original stimulus might come from a decline in prices on the stock market, causing banks to call in loans to protect themselves, and so on down the slide.

The second and equally troublesome aspect of economic instability in this last third of the nineteenth century was the length of the depressions that followed the panics. These periods of business stagnation lasted four to five years (1873–1878, 1882–1885, and 1893–1897). Periods of prosperity were shorter than before the Civil War; the recovery of 1878 lasted until 1882, the less-certain expansion of 1886 lasted until 1892.

The third point to remember is that the record of instability was closely correlated to the pace of railroad building. The nature of the railroad industry and its effects on the economy were especially destabilizing. The cost of constructing a railroad was very high, and the length of time from the start of construction to completion was considerable. By the time a line was completed, the favorable expectations for certain areas, on which the decision to build had been based, might have dissipated; economic conditions might have changed considerably. Or, since the rail lines were developmental in nature, in that many areas along the lines were not yet settled and developed, expectations about their earnings potential may have been too high to begin with. Earnings might prove less than anticipated, and further expansion, for a time, would be discouraged.

Railroad construction also had an impact on industries such as steel and railroad equipment. Changes in the rate of construction functioned with an accelerator impact on the need for increased capacity for those industries supplying materials for construction. Thus decreases in the rate of growth in railroad construction introduced a strong negative accelerator effect on broad sectors of the economy.

The fourth characteristic of this last third of the nineteenth century was the long-term decline in prices. Using 1873 for a base price index of 100, the price index in 1890 was 78, a 22 percent decline; and in 1896, it was 71, a further decrease of 7 percent. Looking at the equation of exchange ($MV = PQ$), we see some of the reason for the decline in prices. Output (Q) was increasing, owing to increases in productivity and resources (population, investment, and so forth). The supply of money (M) was not increasing fast enough to prevent a fall in prices (P). The fall in prices was not proportional throughout the economy—for some industries and firms, cost fell more slowly than the prices of what was sold, and profits were squeezed as a result. Some income receivers found that the prices of their resources (labor, land, and so forth) fell more rapidly than the prices of what they bought. As a result, their real demand was reduced. In this way, the fall in prices may have created potentially unstable economic conditions.

In addition, government policy seemed to work in a perverse manner; that is, it tended to reinforce contractive forces in the economy. Federal fiscal policy (government expenditures and taxes) tended to be contractive. The aim of the federal government was to reduce the national debt incurred during the Civil War. To achieve this, the government generated a budget surplus. Taxes tended to be high, thus reducing consumption. Expenditures tended to be low, thus reducing aggregate demand and the level of income.

More importantly, the federal government engaged in a deliberate policy of restricting the growth of the money supply. In order to alleviate the confusion of a multiplicity of different currencies and to have a more uniform form of currency stemming from the newly created national banks, the federal government in 1866 taxed out of circulation currency issued by state banks.

Moreover, the federal government firmly committed itself to a return to the gold standard. Beginning in 1866, it began to contract the supply of Civil War–issued greenbacks (they were not backed by gold). By 1879, the remaining greenbacks in circulation were being exchanged at par for gold.

Finally, the federal government severely restricted the coinage of silver. From 1873 to 1878, no silver was coined. The government then limited the coinage of silver. This effectively eliminated the use of silver as a method of increasing the supply of money.

There was substantial political opposition to these restrictive money supply policies. The Greenback Party, which had called for increased issues of unbacked currency in the 1870s, was replaced by parties demanding the free coinage of silver in the 1880s and 1890s, especially the short-lived Populist Party and the Democratic Party under the leadership of William Jennings Bryan.

Another problem relating to the supply of money was the inability to expand national bank currency during financial crises. In fact, the opposite tended to occur—a restriction of the currency supply, which tended to decrease prices further. According to the National Bank Act of 1864, the supply of national bank currency had to be backed 100 percent by federal government bonds. When a contraction occurred, interest rates fell, and as interest rates fell, the sale price of bonds increased. Banks, now holding government bonds priced higher in the market, tended to sell them to realize the profit. As they sold the bonds, they had to decrease their currency issues. The result was a decrease in the supply of money, decreased prices, and contracting pressures on the economy.

Some historians have argued that an additional factor explaining the recurrent security market crisis was the action of the so-called robber barons in the railroad securities market. Rampant use of railroads for the short-run immediate gains of promoters left railroads financially weak; ruthless speculation and manipulation of railroad securities by such "barons" as Vanderbilt, Gould, Fisk, Huntington, and Stanford eroded the confidence and security of railroad securities and left the whole stock market unsettled.

The term "robber baron" has been severely criticized in more recent research. While it is not our intent to review that debate, it is true that the most extreme elements of Mathew Josephson's *The Robber Barons* (36) have been discredited. These barons look less and less like predators at the strategic heights of the American economy and (as Louis Galambos has suggested) more and more like businessmen trying to make profits, both from productive enterprise and from the exercise of monopoly power, whichever was available.(19)

The point is that there was significant manipulation of railroad securities and property and that it substantially weakened the financial soundness of many railroads and at times undermined the workings of the stock exchange. Some examples are the Credit Mobilier scandal of the Grant administration concerning the construction of the Union Pacific; the stock market fight between Vanderbilt (controlling the Long Island Central) and Gould (controlling the New York Central) for control over railroad transportation out of New York City in the early 1870s; and, at the beginning of the twentieth century, the fight between Harriman and Morgan for control of the Northern Pacific.

ONE MORE COMMENT

Beyond doubt, an important factor in the economic development of the United States from 1865 to 1897 was the rapid growth and final completion of the railroad network. This network helped to create one large free-trade economy from coast to coast, breaking down the transportation barriers that had previously restricted economic expansion. It also provided direct economic stimulus through its demand for labor and materials in its construction and operation. It is also true that the uneven pace of railroad development increased economic instability in the American economy.

But institutional changes were also important. The factory system became the dominant form of organizing the processes of production under the impact of expanding demand and developing technology. By 1897, the United States had become an industrial society. In the process, various forms of business organization developed in a rush to reduce competition and raise profits. The pool, trust, holding company, and combining of several firms into one firm (consolidation) strongly contributed to the rise of "bigness" in industry. Largely because of this trend, the government began to experiment with intervention; for example, in the form of the Interstate Commerce Act of 1887 and the Sherman Antitrust Act of 1890. A further response to the economic forces of the time was the establishment of a national labor union movement as workers attempted to gain a larger share of the benefits of the economic changes. These unions aimed to monopolize the supply of labor and raise wages.

QUESTIONS

1. In what ways did the growth of railroads in the second half of the nineteenth century affect the economic growth of the United States?
2. What were the advantages, disadvantages, and functions of the railroad construction company? Do you think this was a useful institution in the construction of the railroad system?
3. What were the ways in which railroads attempted to reduce competition in the last third of the nineteenth century? Why was the pool so unsatisfactory a way to reduce competition?
4. What were the two forms of rate discrimination that were strongly opposed by many railroad shippers? Why did they oppose them?
5. How did the courts frustrate the workings of the Interstate Commerce Commission? The workings of the state laws regulating railroads?
6. What economic conditions had to exist in order for the factory system to be established?
7. What was the series of innovations that transformed the iron and steel industry in the second half of the nineteenth century?
8. What were the major innovations in the field of electricity and power in the second half of the nineteenth century?
9. Do you think government aid to manufacturing was important to the growth of manufacturing in the second half of the nineteenth century?
10. Describe the various forms of organization that were used to reduce competition, pointing out their advantages and disadvantages.

11. What new conditions did workers face in the nineteenth century that may have contributed to the drive toward unionization?

12. What were the principal factors causing the rapid decline of the Knights of Labor after 1886?

13. Outline the major elements of Samuel Gompers' trade union philosophy.

14. What were the consequences of Gompers' trade union philosophy?

15. What were the primary weapons of the labor unions?

16. What were the weapons used by employers in labor disputes?

17. List the periods of expansion and the periods of contraction in the U.S. economy from 1865 through 1897.

18. What four major characteristics of economic instability in the last third of the nineteenth century are listed in the text?

19. How were banking and stock market panics linked in the period from 1873 to 1897?

20. In what ways did railroad construction during 1865–1897 increase economic instability?

21. What factors contributed to the long-term decline in prices from 1865 to 1897?

SUGGESTED READINGS

1. Anderson, Terry L., and P. J. Hill. *The Birth of a Transfer Society*. Stanford, Cal.: Hoover Institution Press, 1980.

2. Asher, Ephraim. "Industrial Efficiency and Biased Technical Change in American and British Manufacturing: The Case of Textiles in the Nineteenth Century." *Journal of Economic History, 32* (June 1972).

3. Barnett, Paul. *Business Cycle Theory in the United States, 1860–1900*. Chicago: University of Chicago Press, 1941.

4. Cantor, Milton, ed. *Black Labor in America*. Westport, Conn.: Negro Universities Press, 1970.

5. Carlson, Leonard A. "Labor Supply, the Acquisition of Skills, and the Location of Southern Textile Mills, 1880–1900." *Journal of Economic History, 41* (March 1981).

6. Chandler, Alfred D. *The Railroads: The Nation's First Big Business*. New York: Harcourt, Brace & World, 1965.

7. Chandler, Alfred D., Jr. *The Visible Hand: The Managerial Revolution in American Business*. Cambridge, Mass.: Harvard University Press, 1977.

8. Clark, Victor S. *History of Manufacturers in the United States*. Vol. 2: 1860–1893. Washington, D.C.: Carnegie Institution, 1929.

9. Cochran, Thomas C. *Railroad Leaders, 1845–1890*. Cambridge, Mass.: Harvard University Press, 1953.

10. David, Paul. "Transport Innovation and Economic Growth: Professor Fogel on and off the Rails." *Economic History Review*, 2nd ser., *32* (December 1969).

11. Dubofsky, Melvyn. *Industrialism and the American Worker, 1865–1920,* New York: Crowell, 1975.

12. Engerman, Stanley L. "Some Economic Issues Relating to Railroad Subsidies and the Evaluation of Land Grants." *Journal of Economic History, 32* (June 1972).

13. Feller, Irwin. "The Urban Location of United States Invention, 1860–1910." *Explorations in Economic History, 8* (Spring 1971).

14. Fishlow, Albert. "Internal Transportation." In *American Economic Growth,* ed. Lance E. Davis et al. New York: Harper and Row, 1972.

15. Floud, R. C. "The Adolescence of American Engineering Competition, 1860–1900." *Economic History Review, 37* (February 1974).

16. Fogel, Robert W. "Notes on the Social Saving Controversy." *Journal of Economic History, 39* (March 1979).

17. Fogel, Robert W. *Railroads and American Economic Growth.* Baltimore: Johns Hopkins University Press, 1964.

18. Fogel, Robert W. *The Union Pacific Railroad: A Case of Premature Enterprise.* Baltimore: Johns Hopkins University Press, 1965.

19. Galambos, Louis. *The Public Image of Big Business in America, 1880–1940.* Baltimore: Johns Hopkins University Press, 1975.

20. Gates, Paul W. "The Railroad Land Grant Legend." *Journal of Economic History, 14* (Spring 1954).

21. Grodinsky, Julius. *Transcontinental Railway Strategy.* Philadelphia: University of Pennsylvania Press, 1962.

22. Habakkuk, H. J. *American and British Technology in the Nineteenth Century.* Cambridge: Cambridge University Press, 1967.

23. Hacker, Louis M. *The World of Andrew Carnegie, 1865–1901.* Philadelphia: Lippincott, 1968.

24. Harbeson, Robert. "Railroads and Regulations, 1877–1916: Conspiracy or Public Interest." *Journal of Economic History, 27* (June 1967).

25. Henry, Robert S. "The Railroad Land Grant Legend in American History Texts." *The Mississippi Valley Historical Review, 32* (September 1945).

26. Higgs, Robert. *Transformation of the American Economy, 1865–1914.* New York: Wiley, 1971.

27. Hidy, Ralph, and Muriel Hidy. *Pioneering in Big Business: A History of the Standard Oil Company of New Jersey, 1882–1911.* New York: Harper and Row, 1955.

28. Hirschman, Albert. *The Strategy of Economic Development.* New Haven, Conn.: Yale University Press, 1960.

29. Hughes, Jonathan. *The Governmental Habit: Economic Controls from Colonial Times to the Present.* New York: Basic Books, 1977.

30. Hughes, Jonathan. *The Vital Few: American Economic Progress and Its Protagonists.* New York: Oxford University Press, 1986.

31. Hurst, James Willard. *The Legitimacy of the Business Corporation in the United States, 1780–1970.* Charlottesville: University Press of Virginia, 1970.

32. James, John. *Money and Capital Markets in Postbellum America.* Princeton, N.J.: Princeton University Press, 1978.

33. James, John A. "The Development of a National Money Market, 1893–1911." *Journal of Economic History, 33* (December 1973).

34. James, John A. "Public Debt Policy and Nineteenth Century Economic Growth." *Explorations in Economic History, 21* (April 1984).

35. Jenks, Leland. "Railroads as an Economic Force in American Development." *Journal of Economic History, 4* (May 1944).

36. Josephson, Matthew. *The Robber Barons.* New York: Harcourt Brace Jovanovich, 1962.

37. Kirkland, Edward Chase. *Industry Comes of Age: Business, Labor, and Public Policy.* New York: Holt, Rinehart and Winston, 1961.

38. Kolko, Gabriel. *Railroads and Regulation, 1877–1916.* Princeton, N.J.: Princeton University Press, 1965.

39. Lebergott, Stanley. "The American Labor Force." In *American Economic Growth,* ed. L. E. Davis et al. New York: Harper and Row, 1972.

40. Letwin, William. *Law and Economic Policy in America: The Evolution of the Sherman Antitrust Act.* New York: Random House, 1965.

41. Lindsy, Almont. *The Pullman Strike.* Chicago: University of Chicago Press, 1942.

42. Martin, Albro. *James J. Hill and the Opening of the Northwest.* New York: Oxford University Press, 1976.

43. Martin, David. "1853: The End of Bimetallism in the United States." *Journal of Economic History, 33* (December 1973).

44. Mercer, Lloyd. "Land Grants to American Railroads: Social Cost or Social Benefit?" *Business History Review, 43* (Summer 1969).

45. Mercer, Lloyd. "Building Ahead of Demand: Some Evidence for the Land Grant Railroads." *Journal of Economic History, 34* (June 1974).

46. Miller, Arthur Selwyn. *The Supreme Court and American Capitalism.* New York: The Free Press, 1972.

47. Mulligan, William H., Jr. "Mechanization and Work in the American Shoe Industry: Lynn, Massachusetts, 1852–1883." *Journal of Economic History, 41* (March 1981).

48. Nerlove, Marc. "Railroads and American Economic Growth." *Journal of Economic History, 26* (March 1966).

49. Passer, Harold C. *The Electrical Manufacturers, 1875–1900.* Cambridge, Mass.: Harvard University Press, 1953.

50. Porter, Glenn. *The Rise of Big Business, 1860–1910.* New York: Crowell, 1973.

51. Pred, A. R. *The Spatial Dynamics of U.S. Urban-Industrial Growth, 1800–1914.* Cambridge, Mass.: MIT Press, 1966.

52. Reed, L. S. *The Labor Philosophy of Samuel Gompers.* New York: Columbia University Press, 1930.

53. Rosenberg, Nathan. "American Technology: Imported or Indigenous?" *American Economic Review, 67* (February 1977).

54. Schumpeter, Joseph A. *Business Cycles.* New York: McGraw-Hill, 1964.

55. Smolensky, Eugene. "Industrialization and Urban Growth." In *American Economic Growth,* ed. L. E. Davis et al. New York: Harper and Row, 1972.

56. Spencer, Austin H. "Relative Downward Industrial Price Flexibility, 1870–1921." *Explorations in Economic History, 14* (January 1977).

57. Stover, John F. *American Railroads.* Chicago: University of Chicago Press, 1961.

58. Stover, John F. *The Railroads of the South, 1865–1900: A Study in Finance and Control.* Chapel Hill: University of North Carolina Press, 1955.

59. Sylla, Richard. "American Banking and Growth in the Nineteenth Century: A Partial View of the Terrain." *Explorations in Economic History, 9* (Winter 1971–1972).

60. Temin, Peter. *Iron and Steel in Nineteenth-Century America.* Cambridge, Mass.: MIT Press, 1964.

61. Temin, Peter. "Manufacturing." In *American Economic Growth,* ed. L. E. Davis et al. New York: Harper and Row, 1972.

62. Ulen, Thomas. "Railroad Cartels Before 1887: The Effectiveness of Private Enforcement of Collusion." In *Research in Economic History.* Greenwich, Conn.: JAI Press, forthcoming.

63. Uselding, Paul, and Bruce Juba. "Biased Technical Progress in American Manufacturing." *Explorations in Economic History, 11* (Fall 1973).

64. Vatter, Harold G. *The Drive to Industrial Maturity: The U.S. Economy 1860–1914.* Westport, Conn.: Greenwood, 1975.

65. Ware, Norman. *The Labor Movement in the United States, 1860–1895.* New York: Vintage Books, 1964.

66. Weiher, Kenneth. "The Cotton Industry and Southern Urbanization, 1880–1930." *Explorations in Economic History, 14* (April 1977).

67. West, Robert Craig. *Banking Reform and the Federal Reserve, 1863–1923.* Ithaca, N.Y.: Cornell University Press, 1977.

68. Williamson, Jeffrey. "The Railroads and Midwestern Development, 1870–1940: A General Equilibrium History." *In Essays in Nineteenth Century Economic History,* ed. David C. Klingamen and Richard K. Vedder. Athens: Ohio University Press, 1975.

69. Williamson, Jeffrey G. *Late Nineteenth-Century American Development: A General Equilibrium History.* Cambridge: Cambridge University Press, 1974.

Chapter 13 —————————————————

AGRICULTURE, INDUSTRY, AND TRANSPORTATION, 1897–1920

The depression of 1893 was over by 1897, and America's economy entered a new era. Prosperity was the order of the day as the economy continued its growth. Agriculture, troubled and dissenting for the previous 30 years, now enjoyed unprecedented prosperity. The seemingly limitless frontier had been occupied, and technology continued to advance as the internal combustion engine and the tractor began to replace the horse. Manufacturing development persisted as the United States became the world's leading industrial society. This growth was increasingly accompanied by the formation of larger and larger enterprises. Partially in response to this quickening of the combination movement in industry, the labor movement increased union organization, and the federal government strengthened and expanded the regulation of business.

First, we will look at the progress of agriculture and industry from 1897 to 1920. Then we will briefly discuss transportation changes in the same period. Finally, for those who wish to review the concept of economies of scale or what economic and technical factors affect the size of firms, a simple model is included in the Review of Economic Concepts at the end of the chapter. In the next chapter, we will examine the combination movement in business enterprises, the strengthening and expansion of government regulation, and the expansion of organized labor in the period from 1897 to 1919. Chapter 15 will be concerned with the United States in the international economy during this same period.

AGRICULTURAL PROSPERITY

1897–1914

The end of the depression in 1897 marked the beginning of a period of agricultural prosperity that lasted, with only a brief interruption, more than 20 years. Agricultural prices and farm incomes not only were high but were high relative to prices and incomes in the other sectors of the economy. The prices of what farmers sold rose much more rapidly than the prices of what they bought, both for production and for their own consumption. The terms of trade turned sharply in favor of the agricultural sector. In fact, farmers have ever since used this period as the ideal for relative incomes and prices between agriculture and the remainder of the economy. The period was, in an expression used by many farm organizations, the "Golden Age" of American agriculture, a description reflected in the agricultural statistics in Table 13.1.

The reasons for this prosperity can be found in the farmers' supply and demand conditions. The rate of increase in the supply of agricultural products dropped drastically as the frontier finally became fully settled. The rate of growth of new lands and of the creation and bringing into production of new farms dropped sharply after 1900. The rate of growth in major crops also fell; in wheat production, there was even a decrease in acreage from 1900 to 1910. The productivity of the fairly constant number of farm laborers (11 million in 1900, 1910, and also 1920) increased.

While farm supply experienced a decrease in its rate of growth, farm demand continued its rapid increase. World population, as well as that of the United States, continued to grow. Importantly, domestic demand increased as immigration swelled and as people moved primarily into industrial, urban areas. Total U.S. population grew from 76 million in 1900 to over 106 million by 1920. From 1901 to

Table 13.1.   Selected Agricultural Statistics, 1890–1920.

	1890	*1900*	*1910*	*1920*
Number of farms (thousands)	4,565	5,737	6,406	6,518
Acres in farms (millions)	623	838	879	956
Acres in corn (millions)	75	95	102	101
Acres in wheat (millions)	37	49	46	62
Farm laborers (millions)	9.9	10.9	11.6	11.4
Number of tractors (thousands)	—	—	1	256
Number of horses (thousands)	153	170	192	198
Value of land (millions of dollars)	—	13,048	28,469	54,825
Value of mortgages (millions of dollars)	—	—	3,207	8,449

Source: U.S. Department of Commerce, *Historical Statistics of the United States, Colonial Times to 1970,* Part 1 (Washington, D.C.: U.S. Government Printing Office, 1975), pp. 449–525.

1910, almost 9 million immigrants arrived in the United States. Primarily because of the war, this dropped to about 6 million for the period from 1911 to 1920. Also, both domestic and foreign demand grew as economic development increased real incomes in Europe and the United States.

This relatively more rapid increase in demand than in supply caused agricultural prices to rise. The index of farm wholesale prices (1926 = 100) was 50 in 1900 and had risen to 74 in 1910, an increase of almost 50 percent. The general wholesale price index increased by only 25 percent, or half the percentage increase in agriculture during the same period. In addition to higher incomes and more favorable terms of trade (agricultural purchasing power), agricultural prosperity was expanded by a decrease in the real debt burden due to the increases in agricultural prices.

1914–1920

The surge of prosperity in agriculture continued unchecked until the recessions of 1913 and September 1914. Then, in 1915, foreign demand for agricultural products as well as for all forms of U.S. output increased among the belligerents of World War I, especially the Allies. Prosperity returned to agriculture as farm prices again began to increase.

Farmers strove to keep up with the wartime demand. Mechanization increased to replace the labor that was being drawn to the urban industrial areas and into the armed forces.

During this time, tractors became firmly established. The use of tractors had two expansionary effects on output for the market. The tractor was faster and more powerful than the horse, and thus increased labor productivity; also, each horse displaced released two acres of land to produce food for humans rather than for horses.

The drive to raise output increased the demand for land. With the exhaustion of the frontier by 1900, this increased demand could not be satisfied by bringing additional land into production, except for less productive land. Consequently, the increased demand for land resulted in competetive bidding for a less and less elastic supply of land, resulting in the higher land values seen in Table 13.1. As farmers strove to buy more land, total mortgage values rose. The value of land in agriculture increased dramatically, from $28.4 billion in 1910 to over $57 billion in 1920. At the time, higher mortgages seemed justified to farmers because of the existing higher prices for agricultural products. However, the higher mortgages and expanded agricultural supply were to create problems in the 1920s.

These conditions of high agricultural output, prices, and incomes were maintained by the entrance of the United States into the war in 1917. After the war and through 1920, these conditions were maintained by the high levels of foreign demand for U.S. agricultural products resulting from the wartime devastation of wide areas of Europe.

Along with the prosperity of agriculture, other trends established in the second half of the nineteenth century continued from 1897 through 1920. Governments provided agricultural education and research through the state land grant colleges and universities, experimental stations, and county agents. The expanded activities of the Department of Agriculture contributed significantly to increased productivity.

Increased mechanization, especially the tractor, improvements in livestock and crop varieties, development of superior fertilizers, and chemical sprays continued to increase agricultural productivity. In 1900, 108 man-hours were required to produce 100 bushels of wheat. This dropped to 87 hours by 1920. For corn, the drop was from 147 man-hours per 100 bushels to 113 man-hours. These improvements stemmed from government activities, from the provision by private enterprise of resources to agriculture, and from the agricultural sector itself.

Regional specialization continued: the South concentrated on cotton, and production of wheat, cattle, animal products, and mixed farming each continued in the regions where they had been established by 1900. Moreover, local areas increased specialization in vegetable and fruit raising and in dairying. Technological change, especially in refrigerated forms of transportation, continued to facilitate this form of specialization as it became possible to transport perishable products over longer distances.

These 20 years of prosperity, however, left a legacy of problems for farmers in the 1920s. High mortgages and higher output bedeviled the farmers as demand moved to more normal levels and prices fell.

MANUFACTURING

Manufacturing continued its impressive expansion in the two decades from 1897 to 1920. As shown by Table 13.2, real output more than doubled, while the number of workers in manufacturing very nearly doubled. The money value of products increased almost 600 percent, while money wages increased almost 500 percent. Thus the increase in productivity was not entirely passed on to workers; as a result, profit margins increased. These impressive gains were matched and at times exceeded in earlier time periods, but in this period there was also strong inflation, especially in the price increases from 1914 to 1919. What must be kept in mind about this period is its tremendous contribution to economic development: industrial output increased twice as fast as the total population.

Although the process is more complex and controversial than our brief presentation can allow for, moderate inflation can encourage economic development. As rising prices encourage business expectations of future higher profit, this, in turn, can encourage higher investments to create the facilities to produce the output expected to earn higher profits. Of course, this process could occur only because product prices were expected to increase more rapidly than costs.

Table 13.2. Index of Manufacturing Production.

CENSUS YEAR	PRODUCTION INDEX (1899 = 100)
1899	100
1904	122
1909	159
1914	169
1919	214

Source: Edmund E. Day and Thomas Woodlief, *The Growth of Manufactures, 1899–1923*, U.S. Bureau of the Census, Census Monograph VIII (Washington, D.C.: U.S. Government Printing Office), 1928, pp. 32–33.

Manufacturing increased its importance relative to agriculture. In 1900, agriculture and manufacturing employed equal percentages of the total labor force—30 percent. By 1920, however, agriculture employed only 25 percent of the labor force, while manufacturing's share had grown to 42 percent.

Causes of the Expansion

On the whole, the same factors that caused expansion in earlier periods fueled the expansion of 1897–1920. Some of these factors were technological change and accompanying increases in productivity, a labor force expanding through high immigration and natural increase, and rapidly increasing demand, due in part to expanding population and real income. Note also that the period began with the stimulus of the Spanish-American War of 1898 and closed with the end of World War I. A number of new industries also appeared during this time. The most important was probably the automobile industry, while the most glamorous was the motion picture industry.

The factory system continued to spread, encroaching on both home and small handicraft production. The factory system penetrated the garment industry, utilizing the sewing machine, reducing the number of tailors and dressmakers making clothes to order, and also reducing the making of clothes in the home by the family. The labor force increased as immigrants, especially from eastern and southern Europe, flocked to U.S. cities. This was especially true in the 1904–1909 period. Perhaps equally important was the increase in labor skills and improved management. Frederick W. Taylor's ideas on scientific management, that is, the application of scientific analyses of management and labor to production processes, developed in the 1880s, gained further adherents. Increased attention was paid to the flow of work. These studies and attitudes were especially important in the development of assembly lines and other mass production techniques.

Continuing advances in technology increased productivity in a wide range of industries. Two developments of special importance, which will be treated in greater detail a little further on, were expansion in the use of electricity and mass production and assembly-line techniques.

Changes in international trade also provided stimulus to manufacturing expansion. The proportion of U.S. exports that were agricultural products decreased, and the proportion that were semifinished and finished manufactured products increased substantially. In the period from 1896 to 1900, 21 percent of U.S. exports were finished nonagricultural goods. By 1917, this had increased to 44 percent.

Characteristics of the Expansion

Of prime importance was the continuation of the high levels of production of investment goods (capital equipment needed for further production). It averaged about 20 percent of the value of output during the 1897–1920 period. Frederick Mills (42) estimates that from 1901 to 1913 capital equipment increased at a rate of 5 percent per year, while consumption goods increased at an average of only 2.6 percent per year.

Processing of agricultural and forest products became relatively less important as the growth of manufacturing that used minerals as raw materials increased. Textiles, furniture, and grain processing grew more slowly than iron and steel, chemicals, and petroleum processing and the manufacture of automobiles.

A very important characteristic of manufacturing expansion from 1897 to 1919 was the continuation of the tendency toward larger firms. Faulkner (18) shows that the average manufacturing establishment increased from an average value of output of $13,429 in 1869 to $215,157 in 1919, and from an average number of wage earners of 9.34 in 1869 to 20.49 in 1899 and 31.36 in 1919.

In addition to this increase in the average size of firms, the largest firms statistically dominated wide sections of manufacturing. In 1919, those firms producing over $1.2 million in output, while composing only 3.6 percent of all firms, produced more than 67 percent of the total value of output and employed 56 percent of the workers.

There were two basic reasons for this increase in firm size. First, by combining into larger firms, businesses might reduce their competition, increase their prices, and raise their profits. (The combination movement is reviewed in the next chapter.) Second, the economies of scale created by the vast technological changes of the era encouraged larger establishments to obtain cost savings.

Increased economies of scale became available to firms for a number of reasons related to both costs and the sizes of their markets. From the demand side there were increases in the size of markets that created opportunities to utilize improved production techniques and specialization. World and domestic population increased. (A major reason for this were increases in real income as the United States and Western Europe continued to develop economically.) From the supply side, there were technological improvements in communications and transportation. The technology of the time, such as assembly-line mass production techniques, required larger machines and facilities, and higher levels of output were needed to fully utilize these new techniques. Also, the growing use of Taylor's scientific management techniques introduced methods that postponed increases in average costs (diseconomies of scale) that might otherwise have appeared as the increased size of firms created communication problems. Finally, the relatively faster rate of growth in industries requiring larger scale to reach minimum average cost (iron and steel, automobiles, and petroleum, for example) increased the average size of enterprises. Note that some of these economies of scale increased the average *size* of each plant; technological change, for instance, required larger facilities. Other economies of scale, such as increases in the size of markets, improvements in communication, and improvements in management, expanded the size of the firms by increasing the *number* of plants.

Technology continued to improve in nearly all industries. In 1900, each worker in the steel industry, for example, produced an average of 85 tons of steel; by 1920, this average had risen to 114 tons. From 1900 to 1914, a 76 percent increase in the volume (not dollar value) of manufactured goods was achieved with only a 36 percent increase in the number of workers.

Although there were some geographic shifts of manufacturing, the Northeast maintained its dominance in that sector. According to Keebe and Danhof (30), the share of manufacturing wage earners in New England and the Middle Atlantic states dropped from 52.2 to 46.5 percent between 1899 and 1910. The East North-Central states gained, as their percentage went from 22.8 to 26.3. The rest of the gains were in the West. The West South-Central, Mountain, and Pacific states increased from 5.9 to 9.1 percent. These increases, although small in total, were a clear indication of future trends in the United States.

Electric Power

By 1897, the pioneering giants in the generation and utilization of electric power (Edison, Westinghouse, Parsons, Thomas, and Tesla) had brought the industry to the point where electricity could be carried cheaply over long distances and also be easily applied as a source of power. Faulkner (18) comments that "The fundamental inventions were made before 1897, and the great fruition of a century of research came after the first World War. The two decades under study [1897–1919] appear to be chiefly a period of extension, application, and improvement."

The total available horsepower per worker in industry increased, according to Harry Jerome (28), from 2.11 in 1899 to 3.24 in 1919; and from 1909 to 1919, the increases were even higher in agriculture and mining. In 1899, only 5 percent of all power used in manufacturing came from electric motors; by 1919, this had risen to 55 percent, and by 1925, it was 73 percent.

The advantages of electricity were numerous. Once electricity could be cheaply transported over long distances, the plant was freed from the necessity to locate near a source of power. For instance, plants using waterpower had had to locate near streams, and those dependent on steam power needed a cheap nearby source of coal. Now industry could locate anywhere.

Especially for light industries, it was cheaper to use electricity than steam or water because the latter forms of power required that each firm build its own power plant. And electricity was much more convenient because the portable electric motor could be used for portable machine tools. Electricity provided more uniform speeds of machinery that could be controlled in ways that permitted finer variations of speed.

Assembly-Line Production

Assembly-line production, or what many call **mass production,** is one of the best-known technological innovations of the first two decades of the twentieth century. Henry Ford, became famous as one of its early exponents. The process, depending on standardization, interchangeability of parts, and systems of material flows logically arranged to facilitate product assembly, continued the **American System.**

These production concepts as we know had their origins in the early nineteenth century. A prominent example of their earlier use was Eli Whitney's assembly of guns for the military in the very early nineteenth century. Standardization of parts required sufficient improvements in the machine tool industry so that identical parts could be produced. The development of high-speed carbon tool steel at the turn of the twentieth century was one of the more important of the very many advances in machine tools that made the making of standard parts practical. Taylor's scientific management method advocated systematic management analyses of the work flow, which strongly encouraged assembly-line techniques. The adaptability of electricity to portable tools used along the assembly line was an important contribution. Finally, in order to justify mass production techniques, there had to be sufficient demand for the output. By 1900, domestic plus foreign demand had reached that level in many industries.

Figure 13.1. An Early Light Bulb, and Early Telephone Service. (Photos from the National Archives)

By 1913, Ford had shifted from stationary assembly to moving assembly in the production of Ford automobiles. Now, instead of hand-carrying the parts to the waiting workers, a system of motor-powered conveyors delivered the work at a preset speed. Assembly-line production reduced costs. Ford's Model T fell in price from $950 in 1909 to $490 in 1914, mostly because of the assembly line and interchangeable parts.

Conditions of Wage Earners: 1897–1914

Several factors changed the conditions of wage earners in the period 1897–1914. For example, unionization of labor was expanding, both in numbers and in industries organized—but more on this in the next chapter.

Large-scale immigration continued until 1914. The total immigration to the United States from 1897 to 1914 was over 14 million people. These immigrants were primarily from southern and Eastern Europe, were mostly unskilled, and concentrated in urban areas of the United States. They experienced difficulty adjusting to the culture and language of the United States, and were for varying periods of time isolated from the general society.

Also, there was an accelerated movement of women into the labor force. In 1890, women were only 14 percent of the total labor force. This increased to over 20 percent by 1920 under the impact of labor shortages during World War I. Increased urbanization reduced female work requirements in the home (smaller apartments, no farm chores or such things as canning and food preserving), and mores were changing to allow a more favorable view of the participation of women in the labor force. No doubt an important factor was the economic pressure forcing women to supplement family incomes, especially immigrant and black women. But many working women were young and single, and their wages were their sole financial support.

Finally, blacks began to move out of agriculture into industry, and from the South into northern urban areas. This movement into northern industry was accelerated as labor shortages after 1914 imposed costs on those who would practice discrimination in employment.

The unions were especially hostile to the influx of immigrants, women, and blacks and exerted pressure for anti-immigration regulations. Besides the racial, ethnic, and sexist prejudice that existed among many union members and leaders, unions considered these groups hard to organize.

It should also be noted that there was a sharp reduction in this period in the use of child labor. In 1910, 18 percent of the labor force was under 16 years of age; this had fallen to 9 percent by 1920.

The statistics indicate that real incomes of hired laborers rose little from 1897 to 1914. Wage rates rose about 16 percent to 1914, while prices rose 39 percent. The wages of unionized and skilled workers tended to increase more rapidly. The real-wage index for manufacturing—that is, how much can be bought by the total wages earned—increased from 98 in 1897 to only 103 in 1914. That increase came about because of decreases in unemployment, both full- and part-time, as well as because of the increase in wage rates. In manufacturing, the wage earner's share of the net product dropped from 45 percent in 1889 to 40 percent in 1909.

Although wage earners saw some improvement in their real income, Hunter (27), for one, considers that income inadequate for the support of many employee families. He has estimated that in 1910 the minimum poverty-level income (income necessary to maintain health) for a family of four in an urban area was $640 to $800. In 1909, the average family income for those engaged in manufacturing was $721.

Hours worked per week declined somewhat between 1897 and 1914. In 1897, the 10-hour day and the six-day week were prevalent in most industries. The average work week was 59 hours. This had declined to 55 hours by 1914.

Figure 13.2. Eugene V. Debs, Union Leader, Socialist, and Presidential Candidate. (Photo from the National Archives)

1914–1920

Wage earners made economic gains under the impact of full employment, as war orders started to flow in from the Allies after 1914, as the U.S. economy converted to military production after 1917, and as the leaders of the labor movement gained important positions in the planning structure of the wartime federal government.

Hours worked per week fell for both union and nonunion workers. Average weekly hours for all manufacturing labor declined from 55.2 in 1914 to 51 in 1920, and union manufacturing labor fell from 48.8 hours per week in 1914 to 48.7 in 1920. Average annual earnings for all labor rose from $627 in 1914 to $1,407 in 1920, a 224 percent increase. Hourly wages for all labor in manufacturing rose by 231 percent; union labor's increase was a little over 200 percent. These gains must be put in perspective: there was a 200 percent increase in the consumer price index from 1914 to 1920.

TRANSPORTATION

Railroads

The heyday of the railroads was over. This form of transportation reached its maximum growth and actually began to decline in the period 1897–1920. The year of highest railroad construction in U.S. history was 1906, when 6,262 miles of new track were laid. After 1906, additional miles built declined; and after 1917, more track was abandoned than built. In addition, the rate of growth in tonnage shipped decreased by 60 percent from 1906 to 1916, and the rate of growth in passenger mileage dropped by at least two-thirds.

Railroading was now a mature industry. It had already expanded into its most profitable market areas. In fact, it had overexpanded, establishing some marginal lines that were eventually abandoned as unprofitable. The slowdown in expansion and the eventual contraction of total track mileage were precipitated by competition from the automobile as well as from the trucking industry. Private automobiles competed for passenger traffic, and trucks competed for cargo shipment. The competition intensified after 1920. The test of the ability of private enterprise–controlled railroads to service the needs of the economy came during World War I. The federal government concluded that they had failed, and took over the running of the railroads in December 1917, claiming that private operation was not capable of meeting the transportation needs of the war economy. There is still considerable controversy about whether government takeover was necessary and whether in 1919, when the railroads were restored to private ownership, they were in as good a condition as when received.

By 1917, government regulation of the railroads had gone quite far, with a series of new laws that greatly strengthened the original 1887 Interstate Commerce Act. A detailed discussion of that regulation including its effects on the condition of American railways is reserved for the next chapter.

Urban Transportation

By the 1880s, street rail cars had appeared in urban areas, providing a method of transportation within cities. At first these cars were drawn by horses over rails laid down on city streets. In the early 1890s, however, electricity was applied, greatly increasing the speed of travel. Eventually, streetcar lines were established throughout major cities. These street railroads also established suburban routes, greatly widening the commuting range for cities and for the first time making suburban structures possible, with all their advantages and problems.

Automobiles

There was rapid development of the automobile following its invention in 1895. In that year, there were only 4 autos in the entire United States; but by 1916, there were over 5 million. Capital invested in production facilities for autos reached $1 billion by 1919. The rate of growth would be even greater in the 1920s. The early period, prior to 1910, was one during which inventions necessary to produce a practical and relatively cheap means of private transportation were developed. Such inventions included the brake, air cushion tires, windshield wipers, and safety glass.

The combination movement appeared here too. Between 1903 and 1926, as many as 181 firms had produced cars. Of these, 44 were still in production in 1926, and significant price competition still existed. But the Ford Motor Company held 45 percent of automobile production in 1914; General Motors was formed in 1908; and the future pattern of long-term consolidation into a small number of firms was becoming apparent.

The automobile had a tremendous impact on the U.S. economy. Ford's pioneering application of interchangeable parts and assembly-line production not only was used eventually in the entire auto industry but also served as an example for the rest of manufacturing. The auto expanded commuting distance for the cities and intensified the suburban shift in population. It helped break down rural isolation, providing a more efficient transport for farmers to get to each other and to town. It stimulated, more after 1920 than before, other industries, especially the petroleum industry, to greater growth. And, of course, it established the automobile culture, with all its costs and benefits.

Water Transportation

The water transportation industry suffered mixed conditions. Coastal and Great Lakes transportation was expanding, while ocean, canal, and river transportation was contracting. The basic underlying factors causing these relative movements depended on competitive and opportunity cost relationships.

America's comparative advantage in the coastal trade had persisted since colonial days, and coastal shipping continued to grow vigorously in the hands of

Americans. This trade had reached almost 4 million tons by 1897 and climbed to over 6 million tons by 1917.

Great Lakes transportation was equally prosperous. Long distances covered by large ships gave this form of transportation cost advantages over the railroads. In 1900, lake shipping of one bushel of wheat from Chicago to New York cost only half of railroad shipping. The advantage was intensified by a system of canals that linked the Great Lakes; for example, the Sault Ste. Marie Canal, between Lake Huron and Lake Superior, and the Welland Canal, between Lake Ontario and Lake Erie.

Active competition served to maintain high levels of efficiency and keep rates low. Railroads, while owning some lines—the New York Central owned Western Transit Company, for example—could not control enough of the fleet to affect market conditions. Faulkner (18) points out that "By 1910 the Great Lakes fleet was larger than that of any foreign nation except Great Britain and Germany."

The major product moving east was wheat, in part from Canada, and iron ore from the Mesabi range in Michigan. Important return cargoes were soft and hard coal.

Transoceanic foreign trade, however, had reached its low point, with American registry falling to under three-quarters of a million tons by 1898. In 1901, only 8 percent of U.S. trade was carried in U.S. ships. U.S. ownership of transoceanic vessels fell after the Civil War because (a) profits in shipping were not high enough to justify the opportunity costs of drawing resources from internal development, and (b) foreign governments gave much higher subsidies to shipping than the United States did.

This created a special problem for the United States when World War I began. There were insufficient U.S. ships to carry the cargo no longer carried by British and German ships, so the U.S. government established the Emergency Fleet Corporation in 1917 to build merchant vessels. However, it was not until after the armistice that the first ship was actually completed. Still, the government decided to complete its program of ship construction, and this sharply expanded the U.S. merchant fleet by 1920.

Canal and river transport not connected to the Great Lakes route steadily declined under the impact of railroad competition. The most successful of the canals, the Erie, saw its tonnage fall from 4.6 million tons in 1880 to 2.4 million tons by 1906. One factor causing contraction in the use of the canals was widespread purchase of canals by railroads—by 1909, railroads owned almost one-third of total mileage—and their subsequent almost universal (some charged, deliberate) neglect of the canals.

SUMMARY

The period 1897–1919 was one of general prosperity spurred by high levels of domestic and international demand. This was especially so between 1897 to 1907 and during World War I. Included in agricultural and industrial expansion was the uninterrupted development of improved technology. By 1897, agricultural machinery had been generally adapted to horsepower, and by 1919, the horse was being replaced by the internal combustion engine. Industry was now widely using electricity for power and was experimenting with the economies of interchangeable parts and mass production. Technological transformations (including those in communications) increased the available economies of scale. Supported by increasing levels of demand, the most efficient sizes of enterprises increased.

In transportation, the railroad reached maturity and began to lose, first, relative importance, and subsequently, absolute size. The new transportation miracle, the internal combustion engine, utilized in autos, trucks, and buses, was by 1919 beginning to capture the transportation market.

By 1919, an industrial, urban component was firmly entrenched as the most dynamic and dominant feature of American society.

REVIEW OF ECONOMIC CONCEPTS: ECONOMIES OF SCALE

Two important time periods that economists use are the short run and the long run. In the **short-run time period,** production of goods and services takes place as some factors of production are used in varying amounts. At least one factor input is fixed in outlay to the individual firm and provides a limiting factor in the firm's ability to respond to changing conditions. Often the limiting resource is fixed plant size.

In the long run, all factors of production for the individual firm can vary, including plant size. In the **long-run** (or planning) **period,** the firm can choose from an array of different possible plant sizes (the size of the individual plant can vary as well as the number of plants). Each plant size represents a different **scale of operation.**

Figure 13.3 is a long-run average cost curve for an individual firm. Since the scale of the firm can vary in the long run, Figure 13.3 depicts the long-run average cost ($LRAC$)) curve as an **envelope curve,** one that encloses or envelops a series of possible scales or short-run average cost ($SRAC$) curves. From Output 0 to Output A, average costs are declining as scale increases ($SRAC_1$ through $SRAC_3$). This condition is called **economies of scale** or **increasing returns to scale.** From Output A to Output B, average costs are constant as scale increases ($SRAC_4$ and $SRAC_5$). This is called **constant returns to scale.** After Output B, average costs increase as scale increases ($SRAC_6$ through $SRAC_{10}$). This is called **diseconomies of scale** or **decreasing returns to scale.**

In drawing the long-run average cost curve, we are assuming a few things— for example, that technology is a fixed menu of choices. If technology improved, the entire $LRAC$ curve would shift down. Also, we assume that the firm is small and thus cannot affect the economic environment outside itself. Lastly, because of

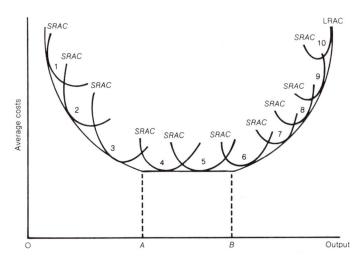

Figure 13.3. Long-Run Average Cost Curve of a Firm.

the preceding assumption, prices of factor inputs are constant as the output of the firm varies.

There are a number of factors that will cause economies or increasing returns to scale. First, a certain minimum output may be necessary before the most improved technology can be used. A hypothetical example in the clothing industry will illustrate. The first scale in Figure 13.3, $SRAC_1$, may represent a scale so small, for example, that it doesn't pay to buy sewing machines, for example, so clothes are sewn by hand. In Scale $SRAC_2$, output is large enough to justify the use of machines for sewing. Second, as output increases, people and machines can be used more fully; that is, they are indivisible or cannot be subdivided below a certain minimum size. In Scale $SRAC_2$, output is large enough to justify the use of the sewing machine but not large enough to use it full-time. In Scale $SRAC_3$, output is large enough to utilize the machines full-time, increasing output without a comparable increase in costs (no need for additional machines). Finally, as output increases, people and machines can become more specialized. At Scale $SRAC_3$, output is only large enough to employ small numbers of workers, each having to do the whole garment. At Scale $SRAC_4$, more workers are hired, each doing a different part of the garment. Productivity (output per worker) increases as less time is lost going from one job to another, as the worker learns a smaller number of operations better, and as the actual aptitude of the worker can be better fitted to the job. Also, at Scale $SRAC_4$, output is large enough to justify the use of special attachments or special machines such as a button sewer.

In brief, economies of scale occur because (a) better technological choices can be used with a larger scale; (b) capital and labor can be used more fully as output increases (they are indivisible or cannot be subdivided below a certain minimum size); and (c) advantages of labor and machine specialization can be realized as output increases. At some point those advantages are used up and constant returns to scale occur.

Diseconomies, or decreasing returns to scale, occur because of management problems causing inefficiencies as scale goes beyond some point; in Figure 13.3, beyond $SRAC_6$. As scale becomes larger, problems of communication between the various segments of the enterprise become more complicated and difficult. Inefficiencies appear as miscommunication becomes more frequent and as information and communication costs rise.

Remember that changes in technology shift the long-run average cost curve. This occurs in the historic time period, one longer than the long run. These changes may intensify the economies to scale and may increase the economic advantage of larger firms. The development of assembly-line techniques, especially in the automobile industry, is of this kind. These changes may, however, reduce the economies obtained from increased scale. The development of small portable electric motors increased the flexibility of applying or using energy, reduced the need for large furnaces and fixtures for steam energy, and consequently reduced the optimum scale or size of firms. Improvements in communications such as the telephone increased the speed and efficiency of communication and thereby slowed down the development of diseconomies of scale due to management inefficiency or discommunication with large scale.

It is important to understand that the level of demand—in other words, the size of the market—must be large enough to enable the firms to move down the long-run average cost curve. In Figure 13.3, demand must enable the firm to move to the scale represented by $SRAC_4$ to take advantage of all economies of scale. There are many activities that may increase demand. Improvements in transportation and the elimination of barriers to larger geographic markets, improvements in communications and lowering of consumer information costs, increases in population and increases in money income from resources growth—all facilitate increases in demand and permit exhausting economies of scale and, thereby, result in larger enterprises.

QUESTIONS

1. List the various factors that lead to larger-size economic enterprises.
2. What were the primary factors increasing agricultural demand from 1897 to 1920? What were the factors increasing agricultural supply? Why did agricultural prices increase?
3. What conditions were being created in 1914 to 1920 in agriculture that would become problems after 1920?
4. What factors cited in the text contributed to the expansion of industry from 1897 to 1920?
5. List and comment briefly on the characteristics of the expansion of manufacturing noted in the text.

6. What were the advantages to industry in the use of electricity? What problems in the use of electricity had to be overcome before it could be widely used as a source of power?

7. What were the various factors that encouraged the development of assembly-line techniques?

8. What were the major factors affecting the conditions of wage labor from 1897 to 1920? Were there significant differences between 1897–1914 and 1914–1920? Why?

9. What were the major characteristics of the railroad industry from 1897 to 1920?

10. What were the economic effects of street railway development in the period?

11. Which forms of water transportation were expanding and which forms were contracting from 1897 to 1920? Why?

SUGGESTED READINGS

1. Atack, Jeremy. "Industrial Structure and the Emergence of the Modern Industrial Corporation." *Explorations in Economic History*, 22 (January 1985).

2. Barger, Harold. *The Transportation Industries, 1889–1946*. New York: National Bureau of Economic Research, 1957.

3. Barger, Harold, and H. H. Landsberg. *American Agriculture, 1899–1939: A Study of Output, Employment and Productivity*. New York: National Bureau of Economic Research, 1942.

4. Bateman, Fred. "Improvements in American Dairy Farming, 1850–1910." *Journal of Economic History*, 23 (June 1968).

5. Brody, David. *Steelworkers in America*. Cambridge, Mass.: Harvard University Press, 1960.

6. Cain, Louis P., and Donald G. Paterson. "Factor Biases and Technical Change in Manufacturing: The American System, 1850–1919." *Journal of Economic History*, 41 (June 1981).

7. Chandler, Alfred D., Jr. *The Visible Hand: The Managerial Revolution in American Business*. Cambridge, Mass.: Harvard University Press, 1977.

8. Clark, V. S. *History of Manufactures in the United States, 1607–1914*. 2 vols. Washington, D.C.: Carnegie Institution, 1928.

9. Cochran, Thomas C. *Railroad Leaders, 1845–1890: The Business Mind in Action*. Cambridge, Mass: Harvard University Press, 1953.

10. David, Paul. "Transportation Innovation and Economic Growth: Professor Fogel on and off the Rails." *Economic History Review*, 2nd ser., 32 (December 1969).

11. Day, Edmund E., and Thomas Woodlief, *The Growth of Manufacturers, 1899–1923*. U.S. Bureau of the Census, Census Monograph VIII. Washington, D.C.: U.S. Government Printing Office, 1928.

12. DuBoff, Richard B. "The Introduction of Electric Power in American Manufacturing." *Economic History Review*, 20 (December 1967).

13. Dunlevy, James A., and Henry A. Gemery. "Economic Opportunity and the Responses of the 'Old' and 'New' Migrants to the United States." *Journal of Economic History*, 38 (December 1978).

14. Easterlin, Richard. "Population." In *American Economic Growth: An Economist's History of the United States,* ed. Lance E. Davis et al. New York: Harper and Row, 1972.

15. Easterlin, Richard. *Population, Labor Force, and Long Swings in Economic Growth: The American Experience.* New York: Columbia University Press, 1968.

16. Engerman, Stanley L. "Some Economic Issues Relating to Railroad Subsidies and the Evaluation of Land Grants." *Journal of Economic History, 34* (June 1974).

17. Erickson, Charlotte. *American Industry and the European Immigrant, 1860–1885.* New York: Russell and Russell, 1967.

18. Faulkner, H. U. *The Decline of Laissez-Faire.* New York: Holt, Rinehart and Winston, 1961.

19. Fishlow, Albert. "Internal Transportation." In *Economic Growth: An Economist's History of the United States,* ed. Lance E. Davis, et al. New York: Harper and Row, 1972.

20. Galloway, Lowell, and Richard Vedder. "The Increasing Urbanization Thesis: Did 'New Immigrants' to the United States Have a Particular Fondness for Urban Life?" *Explorations in Economic History, 8* (Spring 1971).

21. Haydon, Boyd, and Gary Walton. "The Social Savings from 19th Century Rail Passenger Services." *Explorations in Economic History, 9* (Spring 1972).

22. Higgs, Robert. "Landless by Law: Japanese Immigrants in California Agriculture to 1941." *Journal of Economic History, 38* (March 1978).

23. Higgs, Robert. "Race, Skills and Earnings: American Immigrants in 1909." *Journal of Economic History, 31* (September 1971).

24. Higgs, Robert. *The Transformation of the American Economy, 1861–1914: An Essay in Interpretation.* New York: John Wiley and Sons, 1971.

25. Hughes, Jonathan. *The Vital Few.* New York: Oxford University Press, 1973.

26. Hughes, Jonathan. *The Governmental Habit: Economic Controls from Colonial Times to the Present.* New York: Basic Books, 1977.

27. Hunter, Robert. *Poverty,* ed. Peter d'A. Jones. New York: Harper and Row, 1965.

28. Jerome, Harry. *Mechanization in Industry.* New York: National Bureau of Economic Research, 1942.

29. Kahan, Arcadius. "Economic Opportunities and Some Pilgrims' Progress: Jewish Immigrants from Eastern Europe in the U.S., 1890–1914." *Journal of Economic History, 38* (March 1978).

30. Keebe, Harold D., and Ralph H. Danhof. *Changes in Distribution of Manufacturing Wage Earners, 1899–1939.* U.S. Bureau of the Census. Washington, D.C.: Government Printing Office, 1942.

31. Knick, Harley C. "Western Settlement and the Price of Wheat, 1872–1913." *Journal of Economic History, 38* (December 1978).

32. Kolko, Gabriel. *Railroads and Regulation, 1887–1916.* Princeton, N.J.: Princeton University Press, 1965.

33. Kuznets, Simon, and Ernest Rubin. *Immigration and the Foreign Born.* New York: National Bureau of Economic Research, 1954.

34. Lebergott, Stanley. "The American Labor Force." In *American Economic Growth,* ed. L. E. Davis et al. New York: Harper and Row, 1972.

35. Lebergott, Stanley. "United States Transport Advance and Externalities." *Journal of Economic History, 26* (December 1966).

36. MacAvoy, Paul. *The Economic Effects of Regulation.* Cambridge, Mass.: MIT Press, 1965.

37. McClelland, Peter D. "Railroads, American Growth and the New Economic History: A Critique." *Journal of Economic History, 28* (March 1968).

38. McGraw, Thomas. "Regulation in America, A Review Article." *Business History Review, 49* (Summer 1975).

39. Martin, Albro. *Enterprise Denied: Origins of the Decline of American Railroads, 1897–1917.* New York: Columbia University Press, 1971.

40. Mercer, Lloyd. "Building Ahead of Demand: Some Evidence of the Land Grant Railroads." *Journal of Economic History, 34* (June 1974).

41. Mercer, Lloyd. "Land Grants to American Railroads: Social Cost or Social Benefit." *Business History Review, 43* (Summer 1969).

42. Mills, Frederick C. *Economic Tendencies in the United States.* New York: National Bureau of Economic Research, 1932.

43. Neal, Larry, and Paul Uselding. "Immigration, A Neglected Source of U.S. Economic Growth, 1790–1913." *Oxford Economic Papers,* 2nd ser., *24* (March 1972).

44. Nevins, Allan. *Ford: The Times, the Man, the Company.* Vol. 1. New York: Scribner's, 1954.

45. Pred, A. R. *The Spatial Dynamics of U.S. Urban-Industrial Growth, 1800–1914.* Cambridge, Mass.: MIT Press, 1966.

46. Ripley, W. Z. *Railroads: Rates and Regulations.* New York: Longmans, Green, 1912.

47. Rosenberg, Nathan. "American Technology: Imported or Indigenous?" *American Economic Review, 67* (February 1977).

48. Smolensky, Eugene. "Industrialization and Urban Growth." In *American Economic Growth,* ed. L. E. Davis et al. New York: Harper and Row, 1972.

49. Temin, Peter. "Manufacturing." In *American Economic Growth,* ed. L. E. Davis et al. New York: Harper and Row, 1972.

50. Uselding, Paul, and Bruce Juba. "Biased Technical Progress in American Manufacturing." *Explorations in Economic History, 11* (Fall 1973).

51. Weiher, Kenneth. "The Cotton Industry and Southern Urbanization, 1880–1930." *Explorations in Economic History, 14* (April 1977).

52. Williamson, Jeffrey G. "Migration to the New World: Long-Term Influences and Impact." *Explorations in Economic History, 11* (Summer 1974).

53. Williamson, Jeffrey G. *Late Nineteenth Century American Development: A General Equilibrium History.* New York: Cambridge University Press, 1974.

54. Woolf, Arthur G. "Electricity, Productivity, and Labor Savings: American Manufacturing, 1900–1929." *Explorations in Economic History, 21* (April 1984).

Chapter 14

1897–1919 :
THE DECLINE
OF COMPETITION?

The prominent economic historian Harold Faulkner (6) characterized the period 1897–1919 as one in which significant decreases in competition occurred in the American economy. Indeed, Faulkner called his history of this period *The Decline of Laissez-Faire* to point up his conviction that, especially from 1897 through World War I, the classic competitive markets in which government exerted little economic influence had been seriously eroded. He maintained that this competitive economy was replaced by one in which monopoly power, the ability to influence market price, was widely used in the market and in which government regulation became a significant factor. This movement toward attempted monopolization and government regulation preceded 1897 and continued after 1919, but during those years, according to Faulkner, the decline of a competitive economy was most pronounced.

A major weakness of Faulkner's position is that the competitive economy that he assumed prevailed before 1897 may not have existed, especially prior to the completion of the transportation network. As we have seen, high-cost transportation systems resulted in isolated markets. Firms within these markets were small, but market size was also small, so such firms could hold considerable market power. It could be argued that the completion of the railway system in 1897 broke down these barriers, increased the size of markets, and, by creating a national market, increased competition. Further development of automobiles and the trucking industry led to market integration and growth, diminishing the market authority of individual firms. Nonetheless, there was a widespread perception, heightened by the activities of the "muckrakers," that market power by large firms was growing during this period and constituted a threat not only to the welfare of consumers but also to the representativeness of the nation's political system.

A second weakness of Faulkner's argument lies in his failure to precisely define the scope of the market within which competition and its decline is measured. Faulkner seems to utilize an *intra*-industry measure based upon the (declining) number of firms in certain industries (such as the number of firms in the steel industry). Some recent studies in industrial organization suggest that *inter*-industry measures relating competitiveness among products of different industries may be more appropriate (for example, the competitiveness of steel, concrete, aluminum, and similar products in the building materials industry.)

According to Faulkner, however, a decline in competition occurred from three sources: the combination movement contributing to the creation of larger-size firms, the increases in unions and union membership, and the continued extension of government regulation. In this chapter, we will look at the combination movement in manufacturing and transportation, anti-trust legislation, the creation of the Federal Reserve Bank, government regulation through the Interstate Commerce Commission, and the further development of unions. At the end of the chapter, to round out our understanding of economic growth in the period, we will describe and trace the cause of business fluctuations from 1897 to 1920.

THE COMBINATION MOVEMENT

Industry and Transportation

Although the increase in the size and perceived power of business enterprises preceded 1897, it was during the years 1897 through 1920 that the increase in large business organizations was most marked. Specifically, the combination movement started in the late 1870s, gathered momentum in the 1880s and early 1890s, and reached a climax from 1897 to 1904. This process of creating large business entities then slowed, but it revived again in the 1920s.

Up to 1904, the combination movement was concentrated in railroads, heavy industry, and raw materials extraction. From 1904 to 1920, combinations were concentrated more in public utilities and the new industries (autos, motion pictures, and certain chemicals), and in the 1920s, the major industries concerned were retailing and banking. For example, U.S. Steel was formed in 1901, General Motors in 1908 (and then reorganized in 1916), Paramount Studios in 1916, and Alcoa and Union Carbide both in 1917. By 1903, there were total assets of $6 billion in industrial combinations and $20 billion in combinations of public service industries (including railroads). In the railroad industry by 1910, 80 percent of total railroad track was organized into only six financial groups.

As described earlier, the first of these larger business enterprises were created through pools in the 1870s and 1880s. Trusts were formed in the 1880s. The Interstate Commerce Act of 1887 and the Sherman Antitrust Act of 1890 made pools and trusts specifically illegal. After 1897, the methods used to effect combinations became the holding company and the consolidation. (See Chapter 12 for a more detailed discussion of these methods.)

Consolidations were carried out partly through promoters, who organized the formation of the new corporations. It was essential that some of the promoters be connected to investment banks. Also, it was useful if some of the promoters came from the industry to be combined. Promoters had to get options to buy the assets of all the individual companies to be consolidated into the larger corporation. Another requisite was that the promoters form an underwriting syndicate to market the new corporate securities in order to obtain funds to purchase these assets. Profits from this underwriting function were often high. Finally, the promoters would form the new corporation. The owners of the assets in the formerly independent companies would often receive preferred stock, while the promoters would frequently receive common stock.

For example, U.S. Steel Corporation was formed as a consolidation in 1901. J. P. Morgan was the financial promoter, while Judge Elbert Gary managed the huge consolidation. Total capitalization was about $1.4 billion, with about $400 million in bonds, $500 million in preferred stock, and about $500 million in common stock. The actual market value of the assets that went into the new corporation was $700 million at the time of the consolidation. Profits in the still expanding steel industry were high enough to meet the interest charges on the bonds, dividends on the preferred stock, and dividends on common stock for every year between 1901 and 1929 except two. The underwriting syndicate formed by the promoters received $62.5 million in fees.

Combinations in the railway industry were equally spectacular. These consolidations were accompanied by bankers' control. The movement started with the depression of 1893, when one-fourth of the total track mileage belonged to roads that went into receivership. Railroad lines were bought up, and the two leading investment banking houses, J. P. Morgan & Company and Kuhn and Loeb, invested heavily.

Reasons for Combinations

In examining the characteristics that tended to encourage combinations and the creation of larger business firms, it is important to distinguish between two types of factors. First, there were the factors that increased economies of scale, both in terms of increased size of individual plants and in terms of the sizes of enterprises. Costs were reduced with increased output, and the economy as a whole benefited. The second type of factor encouraged larger size in order to decrease competition. So although the motivation for increased size was always greater opportunities for profits, these could be obtained either by economies of scale and lower costs or by reduced competition and higher prices.

Changes in technology in this period tended to encourage the increase in size of firms. First, mechanical innovation led to higher fixed costs in plant and equipment, such as in steel and oil refining. In the second half of the nineteenth century, the shift from water to steam power required an enlargement in power-generating facilities.

By 1900, a technological revolution in transportation and in communications, connected to the completion of railroad and telephone networks, broke down locally isolated markets and created a national market for many products. This expanded market increased demand, so that economies of scale could be utilized and increases in scale toward the optimum size could take place. An expanded market also required an enlarged structure of distribution, another factor tending to increase the size of firms.

Taylor's development of the concepts and techniques of scientific management introduced methods to deal more efficiently with the problems of managing larger-scale enterprises. Scientific management techniques contributed to increased economies of scale. Furthermore, the techniques of financing large enterprises developed with the increased sophistication of securities markets and the rise of investment banking. The use of these techniques was predicated on the application to manufacturing of the corporate structure pioneered in large measure in the railway industry.

Government itself contributed to the rise of large firms. Since the Civil War, tariffs had remained high, reaching their highest level with the Dingley Tariff of 1897. Taxes on imports raised the prices of foreign goods and reduced the effectiveness of foreign competition.

The patent system also encouraged the formation of monopolies by giving one producer exclusive control over a new invention for 16 years, with the possibility of renewal of the patent for another 16 years. The United Shoe Machinery Company, for instance, maintained a monopoly through the control in 1900 of over 6,000 patents. The agreement of Westinghouse and General Electric in the 1890s to share patents gave these two companies substantial monopoly power in the electrical equipment industry.

The social benefit claimed for patents is that exclusive use of inventions and thus monopoly profits encourages research and causes the rate of technological improvement to remain high. Society thereby experiences a more rapid rate of productivity increase and the introduction of new and improved products. The loss of competition is the negative factor that reduces these benefits. The controversy over whether patents provide a net benefit to society is still going on, with little prospect of any immediate resolution.

In brief, the combination movement, the creation of large firms, was at its height at the turn of the century. The profit motive for the creation of these large firms had three basic components: (a) to take advantage of potential economies of scale in order to reduce costs; (b) to reduce competition, raise prices, and thus increase profits; and finally, (c) to obtain profits for the promoters and underwriters out of the very act of creating the new corporation.

The Opposition

Opposition to the combination movement was considerable, although singularly unsuccessful in stemming its progress. There were many criticisms of these new giant firms. The first, but not the least, was that they reduced competition and increased prices to the consumer.

Increased size by itself may not create monopoly power (the ability to influence price), since there are various restraints on the use of monopoly power. As we have seen, these restraints include lack of control over the quantities demanded by consumers, competition within the same industry and from other industries producing substitutes, threat of entry of new firms to take advantage of higher profits, and possible adverse public and government reaction. Furthermore, increased monopoly power must be actually exercised to be effective.

Still, competition may have been reduced, and in some instances, unfair and perhaps illegal methods of competition were applied to smaller businesses. For example, it was once widely held (and some still hold the view) that Rockefeller's Standard Oil Company eliminated competition by lowering prices below costs in local markets to drive out small local firms, while keeping prices higher in the rest of the country. However, McGee (22) (among others) concludes that there is neither historical evidence nor theoretical analysis to support this belief in Standard Oil's predatory pricing. McGee's view has been challenged, particularly by Frederic Scherer (28). At any rate, Rockefeller's attempt to monopolize the petroleum industry was halted by a successful antitrust suit, and in 1911, Standard Oil was broken up into 34 separate companies (26).

It has also been charged that the combinations reduced economic opportunities and caused a decline in the number of small firms in many industries. Fewer small businesses and greater concentration of wealth may have reduced social mobility in the United States. But insofar as these larger-scale firms stemmed from increases in optimum size of the enterprise, they were more efficient than smaller firms. So smaller firms may make for greater social mobility, but at the cost of reduced efficiency.

LABOR UNIONS

Labor and Labor Organizations

As firms grew in size and concentration occurred in basic industries between the late 1880s and World War I, a transformation took place in the position of individual workers. In 1880, fewer than 1 percent of the labor force belonged to unions. We were primarily a nation of individual farmers and shopkeepers. Jonathan Hughes (12) reports that in a population of over 50 million, there were almost 3 million independently owned farms and 750,000 small businesses. In the period from 1880 to 1914, we went from being a population almost three-fourths rural to one that was 55 to 60 percent urban.

It is no surprise, then, that in the period we are examining in this chapter an increasingly urban labor force, employed by larger and larger enterprises where management was often dissociated from ownership, sought to organize itself. This organizing was done not only to bargain for wages and working conditions, but also to vest in labor, as a factor of production, the status of legal property rights long associated with other factors of production. The path to the creation of national unions was fraught with difficulties, however, for labor unions had long been viewed as conspiracies. The tools of modern unions, including strikes and secondary boycotts, were only partially established in the period under view in this chapter.

Union History, 1897–1909

The "great advance" of 1897 to 1904 saw total union membership rise from 447,000 to 2 million, more than a 400 percent increase in seven years. The American Federation of Labor (AFL) was the major beneficiary of this expansion, increasing from 265,000 members to 1,676,000, more than a 600 percent increase. Much of this expansion was concentrated in the skilled occupations of the building trades, a stronghold of AFL craft unions from the beginning. The coal-mining industry experienced a revival of union organizing with the successful founding of the United Mine Workers (UMW) toward the end of the nineteenth century. Though against Gompers' craft union principle, the UMW became the first industry-wide union to join the AFL. There was no practical way to organize it along craft lines.

The prime factors in this union growth were the prosperity and low unemployment of the time. In the face of this union growth employers staged a counteroffensive. A number of employers' organizations were active in this period. The most famous was the National Association of Manufacturers. Others were the Citizens Alliance, the Citizens Industrial Association, and the American Anti-Boycott Association. Their main objectives were opposition to the closed shop (a firm where only union members could be hired) and to the boycott. Not only did these organizations try to influence public opinion; but at times they also provided financial help to those in conflict with unions.

Other factors besides this counteroffensive by employers slowed the growth of unions. The depression of 1907 reduced the demand for labor, increasing unemployment and making it more difficult for labor to pressure management for recognition. High unemployment made union membership less attractive to workers as well. Internal friction and outside rivalry distracted union attention. And finally, adverse public opinion plagued unions, which were associated in many people's minds with violence and radicalism.

In 1905, the governor of Idaho was assassinated and Big Bill Haywood and other leaders of the Western Federation of Miners were charged with the murder; however, Clarence Darrow obtained an acquittal. In 1910, the *Los Angeles Times* building was bombed, and the McNamara brothers, leaders of the International Association of Bridge and Structural Iron Workers (which was striking against the *Los Angeles Times*), were charged with the act. Darrow again came to defend these labor leaders, but the brothers confessed. These and other acts of violence charged against the unions generated unfavorable public reaction.

A series of court decisions unfavorable to organized labor caused the unions to view the courts as a major enemy. The following two examples are illustrative. In 1902, the United Hatters staged a strike and boycott against a Connecticut firm. They were charged with violating the Sherman Antitrust Act and were sued for damages. The union lost the case; in addition, the homes of some union members were attached. In 1907, a federal lower court issued a sweeping injunction against an AFL boycott of a St. Louis stove company. The union tried to test the injunction's validity before the U.S. Supreme Court, but the Court refused to review. The use of the injunction became an even more crippling antiunion weapon in the 1920s.

Within the AFL, the socialists actively opposed the conservative attitude of the federation toward the unskilled, immigrants, women, and blacks. This internal dissension, while persistent, failed to change the policies of the AFL during that time. It is somewhat ironic that throughout this period participation rates of (mainly white) women in the labor force were increasing sharply. This increasing economic participation, together with the resulting accumulation of property rights, led to the passage of the Nineteenth Amendment to the Constitution in 1920 granting women the right to vote. What is perhaps most importantly illustrated here is that property rights and political rights tend to go hand-in-hand (8).

The Industrial Workers of the World

Competition to the AFL appeared with the formation of the Industrial Workers of the World (IWW) in 1905. The IWW was formed primarily of four groups: the Western Federation of Miners, the Socialist Party of Eugene V. Debs, the Socialist Labor Party of Daniel De Leon, and a large group of radical unionists. This peculiar combination of socialists, syndicalists, and anarchists thought a revolutionary class struggle could be achieved through industrial unionism.

The IWW was mainly an outgrowth of union conditions in the West. It was produced by the violent oppression of the frontier mining and lumber camps (5). Western strikes involved the most bitter and violent labor warfare in American, if not world, labor history. The IWW attracted primarily unskilled and migratory workers, although the union was never more than 60,000 to 70,000 strong.

The IWW led a series of strikes started by unorganized, unskilled workers who were neglected by the AFL. In 1912, at Lawrence, Massachusetts, and again in 1913, at Paterson, New Jersey, textile workers struck for higher pay and better working conditions. In both cases, the workers were inexperienced at running a strike, and after the AFL refused to help, they asked the IWW to provide leadership. At Wheatland, California, in 1913, the migrant workers in the hop fields struck and asked for IWW help. After a bitter strike, this first effort at a union of migrant fieldworkers failed.

The IWW was widely condemned. It was anticapitalistic, and thus engendered general public hostility. It was a rival of the AFL (10) and that organization did whatever it could to counter the IWW. In 1907, the Western Federation of Miners left the IWW, and at about the same time the IWW ousted De Leon and his Socialist Labor Party. But what eventually destroyed the IWW was its opposition to U.S. involvement in World War I. Partially as a result of this opposition and its radical anticapitalist philosophy, the IWW became a prime target of Attorney General A. Mitchell Palmer who, in response to the mass hysteria in reaction to the Russian Revolution, arrested and imprisoned thousands of IWW members.

1910–1917

By 1917, union membership had increased to over 3 million. The increase came about primarily in four industries: transportation (mainly railroads), the building trades (the traditional stronghold of the AFL), mining (primarily in coal), and the clothing industry (newly organized).

The United Mine Workers extended their base from western Pennsylvania and Ohio into West Virginia; in the strike of 1912, they expanded their membership into the anthracite coal fields of eastern Pennsylvania. Their strike in the Colorado coal fields in 1913–1914, which failed, was one of the most bitter in U.S. labor history. The striking miners were evicted from the company houses, and they set up a tent city at Ludlow, Colorado. National guard units, plus guards from the mines, surrounded the tent city one morning and fired into it, killing several men, 2 women, and 11 children. John D. Rockefeller, who owned the mines, still refused to deal with the union.

In 1909, the International Ladies' Garment Workers Union (ILGWU) declared a general strike in the women's garment industry in New York. Two immigrant groups, the Eastern European Jews and the Italians, provided the bulk of the workers in the industry. Together, they forged an effective coalition that won the strike and firmly established the ILGWU. In 1910, Sidney Hillman successfully led another union, the United Garment Workers (UGW), in the Chicago strike against Hart, Shaffner, and Marx, the largest men's clothing firm in the country. This established the UGW in the men's clothing industry. With these two sections of the garment industry successfully organized, immigrants became an active force in the U.S. labor movement. These two unions strengthened the industrial unionist approach within the AFL.

After World War I broke out, the Allies relied heavily on the U.S. economy for supplies of all sorts. Between January 1915 and the entry of the United States into the war in 1917, the Allies spent over $5 billion in the United States. This stimulus, plus increased spending on the army and navy as the United States prepared for entry into the war, expanded the economy to full employment, shortages, and rising prices.

World War I, 1917–1920

Samuel Gompers, the president of the AFL, fully supported the war effort and cooperated with it wherever possible. President Wilson, to assure labor union support, placed union representatives on the various planning committees set up to plan for a more efficient allocation of the nation's scarce resources for war production.

Labor benefited from these arrangements. Favorable conditions were written into many government contracts in return for no-strike pledges by labor. Cost-of-living clauses and favorable work conditions were easily obtained as business profits soared during the war. In this more benevolent atmosphere, union membership rose from 3 million in 1917 to over 5 million by 1920.

With the end of the war, both unions and employers were in strong positions, as full employment and increased membership filled union treasuries and high wartime profits made businesses financially prosperous. Unions, however, were dissatisfied with the progress they had made during the war. From 1914 to 1919, average annual earnings of the employed had increased 87 percent, but their purchasing power had increased only 5 percent. Business had no desire to continue the labor-management cooperation imposed during the war. Thus the years 1919–1920 saw management-labor confrontation.

Strikes increased rapidly in 1919. The most spectacular was the 1919 Steel Strike, the first effort made since the Homestead Strike of 1892 to organize the steel industry. Despite a massive effort, the strike failed, but as a result of the strike, public pressure brought an end (several years later) to the 12-hour day, seven-day week that had prevailed in much of the industry. Other notable strikes took place in the men's clothing industry, in railroads (by the newly organized shop crafts), and in soft coal mining.

But the unions still had basic weaknesses. First, they had not penetrated the primary manufacturing industries, especially steel and automobiles. The obstacles of large, powerful corporations and the unions' own craft orientation were difficult to overcome. Second, the Bolshevik Revolution and the reaction to it by the U.S. Justice Department, the press, and major sections of the American public created a very negative attitude toward anything that seemed to be opposed to American capitalism. This led to vigorous antiunion activity. The unions started the decade of the 1920s with public sentiment against them.

Arguably, the most important accomplishment of those seeking to achieve as a property right the right to organize labor was exemption from the antitrust laws. In a case (*Loewe v. Lawler*) heard in 1908, the Supreme Court ruled that unions fit the meaning of the phrase "combinations in restraint of trade," as used in the Sherman Act (12). After intense lobbying, the Clayton Act was passed, which exempted unions from the antitrust laws on the economically dubious grounds that labor is not an item of commerce and is therefore not a fit subject for federal regulation. We say "economically dubious" because the rents of labor unions—their ability to obtain wages higher that those of nonunion workers—are based on their ability to restrict entry into labor markets. This ability would be vastly diminished, if not eliminated, by widespread application of the antitrust laws to their formation and activities.

GOVERNMENT INTERVENTION

When Harold Faulkner (6) said that "the decline of laissez-faire" was the main characteristic of the period from 1897 to 1917, he was not simply referring to the rise of the large corporation or the establishment of national unionism. He was also referring to the developing commitment of the federal government to intervene in markets, even to interfere directly in certain kinds of business activities and industries. By 1920, government regulation of various areas of economic activity had become an established fixture of the economic scene.

In this section on government intervention, we will first examine railway regulation, especially the continued development of the Interstate Commerce Commission. Then we will look at the development and use of antitrust legislation. Finally, we will consider the creation of the Federal Reserve System as an illustration of intervention in financial markets.

Railroad Regulation

The foundation of federal regulation of railroads was laid with the Interstate Commerce Commission Act of 1887, creating the Interstate Commerce Commission (ICC). For the first few years, the ICC had the cooperation of the railroad companies, who hoped that the Commission would alleviate what they considered to be the major problem in the industry; too much competition. However, the ICC tried to maintain, if not encourage, competition, so after 1890, the railroad companies opposed the Commission's actions and looked to combinations as the device through which to control competition. The conflict between the ICC and the railroads was fought out in the courts, where the Commission lost.

By 1900, the U.S. Supreme Court had, in effect, nullified the Interstate Commerce Commission Act. Between 1887 and 1905, 16 decisions were handed down by the Court on the act, 15 of them in favor of the railroads. The federal courts refused to accept the findings of the ICC as valid. In 1897, the Supreme Court ruled that the ICC could not set rates, concluding that the 1887 act did not give the ICC that power. This undercut the ICC's power to eliminate rate discrimination.

In response to the crippling rulings of the Court, the ICC attempted at first, with limited success, to use the Sherman Antitrust Act as a legal basis to control discriminatory railroad practices. Then an effort was made to strengthen the ICC. The Expediting Act of 1903 established that ICC and antitrust suits in the courts would be given preference over other cases. This substantially increased the speed with which ICC cases were decided. The Elkins Act of 1903 forbade the giving of rebates, eliminating that form of discrimination. The Hepburn Act of 1906, which increased the size of the ICC and its budget, greatly strengthened the Commission by explicitly requiring it to establish rates on railroads, pipelines, and terminal facilities. The Mann-Elkins Act of 1910 introduced two important provisions. New rates issued by the ICC were to remain in force for at least ten months if the railroads chose to challenge them in the courts. Prior to this act, the rates were not in force until the question was decided in the courts. The act also stated that charges for shipment must be higher for longer distances. This definitely resolved the short-haul versus long-haul problem that had been an important motive for the original act establishing the Interstate Commerce Commission.

By 1920, railway regulation had been firmly established. The courts had recognized the authority of the ICC to set rates, and the obvious forms of discrimination—rebates and short-haul rates higher than long-haul rates—had been declared illegal. However, the ICC still lacked the power to regulate the financial structure of the railroads. That is why, according to Kolko (16) and Faulkner (6), the Commission could not stop the mismanagement and corruption that had put many of the roads under substantial financial strain. Actually, by the time the ICC was strengthened, much of the damage had already been done, and the age of the railroad magnates and financiers was mostly over. Practical railroaders were mainly in control.

Kolko and Faulkner argue that by 1920 regulators were still trying to foster competition in an industry that should have been considered a monopoly. They say that instead of relying on competitive forces to establish prices, the ICC should have been more vigorous in deciding price policy.

Figure 14.1. Theodore Roosevelt, the "Trustbuster." (Photo from the National Archives)

Some opponents of that view maintain that there are very substantial competitive forces in transportation, if not specifically in railroading, and that railroading is not an example of a natural monopoly. They maintain that government regulation inhibited the functioning of a competitive market and created inefficient allocation of resources, higher costs, and higher prices. They further maintain that, especially after 1920, the auto, truck, bus, and later the airplane, coupled with water transportation, would have assured a sufficiently competitive market to prevent the abuses of the past.

Robert Harbeson's (11) opinion was that the ICC eventually carried out the plans of the railroad industry by helping to lessen competition through eliminating much of the price cutting. He finds it interesting that the official rates of the ICC were very similar to those set by an informal railroad cartel. But while Harbeson argues that the ICC was "captured" by the railroad industry, scholars such as Albro Martin (21) argue that if it was captured, it was captured by consumers of railway services. By refusing to grant rate increases, the ICC caused rates of return to fall to levels at which the system could neither be maintained adequately nor modernized. That is at least partly why it functioned so poorly during the war that it was taken over by the federal government in 1917.

Antitrust Legislation

By the late 1880s, there was increasing pressure to enact laws against efforts aimed at monopolizing markets. Although, as William Letwin (18) has shown, common law drawn from Britain recognized the illegality of monopolies unsanctioned by specific acts of government, it was thought necessary to formalize the opposition to monopoly in a legislative act, so Congress passed the Sherman Antitrust Act of 1890. As Senator Sherman remarked, failure to act would mean that the nation would find itself with a "trust for every production and a master to fix the price of every necessity of life" (9).

Almost from the outset there were problems with the Sherman Act. The act did deal clearly with explicit collusion and treated as unlawful per se such acts as price-fixing conspiracies and efforts to "rig" markets. Since 1890, there have been over a thousand prosecutions under Section 1, which says that "Every contract, combination...or conspiracy, in restraint of trade or commerce among the several States, or with foreign nations, is hereby declared to be illegal." The defense by firms that their actions were "reasonable" was disallowed by the courts as early as 1897 in *U.S.* v. *Trans-Missouri Freight Association* (9).

Section 2 of the act states:

> Every person who shall monopolize, or attempt to monopolize, or combine or conspire with any other person or persons, to monopolize any part of the trade or commerce...shall be deemed guilty of a misdemeanor....

Alas, this provision is anything but crystal clear. What is the difference between creating a monopoly and monopolizing trade or commerce? Is intent required? Shall market share or dominance by a firm of an industry be considered evidence of monopolization? If so, what about firms that achieve such dominance simply through better management or other activities that it may be socially unwise to restrict? In the century since the passage of the Sherman Act, much judicial interpretation has been devoted to spelling out a "rule of reason" to be used in answering such questions.

Antitrust Enforcement

Antitrust legal actions increased during Theodore Roosevelt's administration, with 25 indictments under the Sherman Act from 1901 to 1908. The most famous of these was the Northern Securities Case of 1904. This company had succeeded in gaining control of all railroad transportation in the entire Northwest. Although the government won the case, the victory had little practical result. The government could think of no effective way to break up the Northern Securities Company, so the Hill-Morgan group maintained ownership of the company and control of the railway system in the Northwest.

During William Howard Taft's administration (1908–1912), there were 43 indictments under the Sherman Act. The American Tobacco Case was an important example. A combine created by James B. Duke, American Tobacco controlled as much as 93 percent of the tobacco industry by the turn of the century. The antitrust action charged that predatory tactics had been used to achieve this market dominance. The Supreme Court agreed in 1911 and ordered the dissolution of the combine. However, it was not clear that substantially greater competition existed in the oligopolistic market that ensued (9).

As with regulation of the railroads, legislation was passed to strengthen antitrust activity. The Expediting Act of 1903 also applied to antitrust cases and substantially speeded up the handling of these cases in the courts. In the same year, the U.S. Department of Justice received a $500,000 appropriation to set up a special branch and to create a special staff to handle antitrust cases.

Because there were so many difficulties interpreting Section 2 of the Sherman Act, Congress passed the Clayton Act in 1914, seeking to plug loopholes dealing with mergers and other *potentially* anticompetitive activities. This act specifically forbade discrimination in pricing and exclusive selling or leasing contracts; both had often been used as weapons to lessen competition. Also forbidden was the use of interlocking directorates and holding companies for the purpose of reducing competition. (**Interlocking directorates** existed when the same people appeared on the boards of directors of a number of different corporations in the same or closely related industry; these governing bodies could more easily formulate policies to reduce competition in the industry.) Finally, the Clayton Act exempted labor unions and farmer cooperatives from government antitrust actions.

In 1914, Congress also passed the Federal Trade Commission Act. The commission set up under this act was responsible for defining and preventing "unfair" competition in commerce. It was given the power to investigate, issue cease-and-desist orders, go to court, and enforce court decrees.

Antitrust: Success or Failure?

Harold U. Faulkner (6) concluded that the antitrust legislation was a failure by 1917. He maintained that the legislation was meant to restore competition in a "changing economic order" that was no longer meant for competition. Faulkner argued that if monopoly by large firms was to be controlled, a different approach would have to be used. Even after 1903, when within the U.S. Justice Department a small staff and budget were earmarked for antitrust activities, antitrust prosecutors did not have resources at their disposal equal to those of the large corporations. Even when cases were won by the Justice Department, the government had difficulties obtaining and evaluating data, and had no clear guidelines for breaking up trusts; it often recommended fines that were too small to be a deterrent. The vigor of enforcement varied according to the interest and initiative of the incumbent U.S. president; it was fairly vigorous in the period 1901 to 1917 and very weak in the 1920s. Furthermore, the effectiveness of enforcement was sharply affected by the shifting point of view of the U.S. Supreme Court. Faulkner concludes that by 1914 it was already too late to take this kind of action because in many industries the large corporations were already formed and little competition remained.

Other economists, such as Yale Brozen (2), concur on the failure of antitrust legislation but approach the problem from a very different direction. Their argument is that government regulation replaced the workings of the marketplace with bureaucratic decision making. Under these conditions, the allocative function of the market was disrupted, inefficiencies in the allocation of resources occured, and the combination of goods produced was not the one that consumers preferred.

Which is worse—economic inefficiency and threats to liberty induced by bureaucracy, or economic inefficiency and threats to liberty induced by manipulation of the market and the influencing of the political process by large firms? Or indeed, were these the only two alternatives? Was the U.S. economy still vibrantly competitive, making constant adjustments to changing technology and economic conditions? Extensive historical research and endless theoretical debate have led to very few areas of broad agreement. The debate continues to rage.

What is undisputed is that by the end of this period there were large economically powerful firms and large union organizations and the government had taken large steps into regulation. Whatever the consequences, large special-interest groups and government economic involvement were a continuing part of the U.S. economic scene.

The Federal Reserve Act of 1913

Economic activism by the federal government grew partly out of the perceived decline in competition and partly out of concerns about America's financial markets, particularly its banking industry. In the Panic of 1907, national banks came close to suspending payment, that is, refusing to redeem bank notes for specie. Interest rates on call money (loans that could be called in at any time) reached 125 percent in 1907! The weaknesses of the national banking system had been evident for decades. Only the intervention of a group of private investment bankers headed by J. P. Morgan, who, according to Robert West (34), acted much like central bankers, had averted a financial collapse. So even a nation that remembered the economic and political problems associated with the Second Bank of the United States had to move toward a federally created central banking system. The National Monetary Commission, known as the Aldrich Commission for its chairman, Senator Nelson Aldrich, was created in 1908. In 1911, the commission produced a plan for a National Reserve Association with the United States divided into 15 districts. Modified by the Democrats in 1912, the proposal became the Federal Reserve Act and was signed into law by Woodrow Wilson in 1913.

In the report of 1911, the Aldrich Commission had condemned the following conditions: There was no adequate national clearing system for checks. The supply of currency was not elastic; that is, it could not readily vary in response to the needs of the banking system. Finally, and perhaps most importantly, the individual commercial banks had no lender of last resort available in case of financial crisis.

The Federal Reserve Act established the Federal Reserve System and to varying degrees, met these inadequacies in the banking sector. But the nation's deep-seated reluctance to establish one central bank, a philosophy dominant in American banking since Jackson vetoed the rechartering of the Second Bank of the United States in 1832, was mirrored in the act. Instead of establishing 1 bank, the act established 12 banks, one in each of 12 districts. Instead of making it mandatory that all commercial banks belong to the system, the act required only national banks to join, with membership optional for state banks. By 1917, only 37 state banks had joined.

Despite this reluctance, the Federal Reserve System was vested with political authority in a Board of Governors appointed by the president and confirmed by the Senate. As such, it had sufficient power to eventually become an instrument of control over the commercial banking process of the United States. The control increased with experience and with further legislation that enhanced the powers of the "Fed."

Although there is much controversy about *how* the Federal Reserve System should behave and how effective it has been, there seems to be little dissent that some kind of "Fed" was needed to regulate the supply of money and to serve as a lender of last resort to protect the banking system. In its early years, however, the Fed had little impact on the supply of money and displayed no predilection for deliberate changes in monetary conditions and liquidity to counteract business cycles. Nonetheless, Elmus Wicker (35) has argued that the Fed accidentally moved to increase the money supply in 1920–1921 and did reduce the severity of that economic downturn.

ECONOMIC INSTABILITY, 1897–1920

Overall, this period was one of growth in the American economy. Not only did firms and labor organizations increase in size, but market sizes grew as many factors, including immigration, caused demand to increase. Still, it was uneven growth punctuated by a sharp contraction in 1907.

Expansion, 1897–1907

The recovery from the depression of 1893–1897 was caused by a combination of very favorable demand and monetary factors. Furthermore, international factors were also favorable. Europe recovered faster than the United States from the depression of 1893, which generally increased the demand for U.S. exports. In addition, in 1897, there was a drought in France and there were floods in Austria, the Balkans, and Russia, which more than doubled U.S. wheat exports.

Railroads, many of them in bankruptcy during the depression, recovered sufficiently by 1897 to engage in much-needed repairs, plus a resurgence of new construction. New construction averaged 3,400 miles of track a year from 1897 to 1902. This expansion increased the demand for iron and steel, railroad cars and locomotives, and new bridges and terminal facilities. Obviously, the multiplier and accelerator effects were substantial.

With the resumption of prosperity and increases in employment opportunities, large-scale immigration resumed, supplying labor for the urban manufacturing centers. As a result, urbanization, with its construction activity, expanded. Finally, the Spanish-American War began in 1898, increasing government expenditures, especially for the U.S. Navy. As a result, steel, munitions, and shipbuilding expanded.

Besides these expansions in aggregate demand, there were expansionary monetary developments. The very favorable balance of trade in 1896 brought in $122 million in gold, which went into the reserves of the banks. Gold strikes in the Yukon in Alaska and in South Africa doubled world gold production after 1896. An increased world supply of gold increased the supply of money, increased prices, and expanded demand.

With this renewal of prosperity, profits rose, there was a glut of investment funds in the market, and financial speculation followed. In the spring of 1901, speculation in the stock market went rampant. The climax was reached on May 9, 1901, with the fight for control of the Northern Pacific Railroad between Morgan and Harriman. Both bought at high prices as much Northern Pacific stock as they could. Some brokers sold stock they didn't have, hoping to buy the stock at lower prices for later delivery. On May 9, it seemed that more stock was sold than existed. In six hours, the stock price went from 160 to over 1,000. However, a truce was called, and a panic was avoided.

Again in 1903, speculation and stock prices rose and the stock market panicked; but this "rich man's panic" had little effect on the rest of the economy.

Panic and Depression of 1907

Speculation and stock manipulation contributed to the stock market Panic of 1907. This panic spread from the stock market to the banks, with a number of bank failures. The depression that followed was acute and lasted into 1911.

The economy recovered in 1912 but lapsed again in 1913. Recovery had started by the beginning of 1914, but the economy contracted again as war began in September 1914. By the middle of 1915, however, the U.S. economy was booming, because the United States was the primary country capable of filling the production needs of the belligerents. The demand for U.S. exports by the warring nations of Europe, especially the Allies, tremendously stimulated the U.S. economy. These large export surpluses of the United States were paid for at first by the liquidation of large amounts of European-held investments in the United States. Later in the war, especially after the entry of the United States on the side of the Allies, large loans were extended by the United States to the Allies. By the end of the war, the United States had shifted from a **net debtor nation** (Americans owed foreigners more than they owed us) to a **net creditor nation** (foreigners owed Americans more than we owed them) a position it was to hold until the late 1980s.

A number of reasons have been offered to explain the fits and starts of the U.S. economy from 1907 to 1914. One important explanation is the inefficient and inelastic credit system existing under the national bank system. A serious deficiency was the lack of a central bank that could lend to the banking system during crises so as to shore up reserves and expand the ability to lend. Also, the existing tie between currency and government debt restricted the ability to expand the currency supply during crises. Both were serious inadequacies of the national bank system. The efforts to deal with these problems resulted in the overhaul of the banking system with the Federal Reserve Act of 1913. This was the last attempt to resolve the problems and misery generated by a sharp recession (the Panic of 1907) through reforming the monetary system and creating a new kind of currency (Federal Reserve notes). The depression of 1920–1921 was too brief for such monetary restructuring. By the 1930s, there was a widespread perception that "tinkering" with the monetary system was a hopelessly inadequate and often ill-timed device for averting recessions and depressions.

In explaining the depression that followed the Panic of 1907, some charged that promoters and financiers had overloaded railroads and the recently created large corporations with such a high ratio of debt to total assets that they impaired the efficient working of these firms. It was also charged that of the firms created through the combination movement, those large enough to greatly influence prices were reluctant to lower prices after 1907 in the face of weakened demand. This use of monopoly power (control over price) restricted the stimulating effects of price declines that usually occur after or during recessions.

Because wages barely kept up with rising prices, some concluded that increases in productivity (technological change and so forth) increased profit mar-

Figure 14.2. Northern Factories. (Photo from the National Archives)

gins, not consumption. As a result, consumption was restricted more than investment expanded, and aggregate demand grew less than it might have.

Others argued that during the first decade of the twentieth century the an-
tibusiness articles written by muckrakers, government committees investigating
business practices, and higher levels of antitrust action aimed against monopolizing practices caused a loss of confidence by investors and thus a decrease in the
willingness to invest.

What all this indicates is that business cycle theory was far from adequate
then, or even now. The quantitative importance of each issue is strongly debated.
The presentation here is not made for the purpose of entering into the debate about
the significance of the "robber baron" thesis of Josephson (14) or the decline-of-
competition thesis of Faulkner (6). That these factors were even present is still
moot. If they were, whether they were sufficiently strong to cause the instability
between 1907 and 1914 is unknown. A more probable explanation lies in the slow-
ing down of a long-term expansion (1897–1907) and the resulting negative accelerator effects.

REVIEW OF ECONOMIC CONCEPTS: THE WELFARE
EFFECTS OF MONOPOLY

In this section, we shall compare the welfare effects of monopoly industries with
those of competitive industries. Though the comparison can be made between

competition and any extent of monopoly (monopolistic competition, oligopoly, or pure monopoly), the comparison here will be between polar extremes: pure monopoly at one end of the market spectrum and pure competition at the other.

Let us make clear at the outset what is involved in this theoretical comparison. The fundamental difference between pure monopoly (a single-firm industry in which prices can and must be set by the firm) and pure competition (a multifirm industry in which individual firms have no influence over price) is that substantial barriers to entry exist in the former and are absent in the latter. If we use for comparison an industry in which costs do not dictate a single firm (natural monopoly or monopoly created by an always falling long-run average cost condition), it seems likely that monopoly will lead to output restrictions and to higher prices as compared with competition. Let us see, though, what the argument entails in this comparison.

Short Run: Competition versus Monopoly

In Figure 14.3, we see a comparison between short-run output and prices under pure competition and pure monopoly. The market demand curve to either industry is D and the marginal revenue curve for a single-firm monopoly appropriate to D is MR. The short-run supply curve of either a competitive industry or a monopoly industry is SS. This is the monopolists' marginal cost curve and, as well, equal to the aggregated (sum of marginal costs) supply of competitive firms. In a competitive market, equilibrium pricing will occur at that level that equates the quantity supplied (on the MC curve) with the quantity demanded (on D). Thus a competitive industry will produce Qc and competitive firms will each sell at Pc, the equilibrium price. The price-setting monopolist facing downward sloping D and MR, on the other hand, will equate MC and MR (where SS cuts MR) and produce Qm, setting a market-clearing price of Pm (where a vertical from Qm cuts D).

Note that the competitive firm acts on a price equal to marginal cost. This is an important relationship. Price indicates the value that consumers place on the last unit purchased. Marginal cost measures the opportunity cost (what society gives up in other goods not produced) of that last unit purchased. When the two are equal, the value of the unit to the consumer is equal to its cost to society. With prices providing the needed signals for activities, this situation means the economy enjoys allocative efficiency, that resources are allocated to produce that combination of goods consumers prefer.

For the monopoly firm, price is above marginal cost. Thus consumers place a higher value on the last unit produced by the monopolist than the cost to society through the loss of alternative goods not produced. In effect, the consumer, in terms of other goods, prefers the good produced by the monopolist more than the goods that could have been produced by the resources used by the monopoly firm. As less of the good is produced than society prefers, there is a misallocation of resources because firms are not producing that combination of goods consumers prefer. Allocative inefficiency, then, is an additional loss attributable to monopoly.

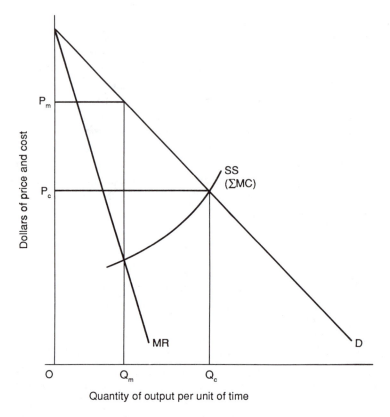

Figure 14.3.   Pure Competition Versus Pure Monopoly in the Short Run.

Long Run: Competition versus Monopoly

Now it is time to look at the assumption that costs are the same in the two market situations. In the long run, a larger-size monopoly firm may use a technology involving larger scale than that employed by individual firms in a competitive industry. The situation may be the one depicted in Figure 14.4. If a monopoly situation existed, the short-run average cost curve would be *SRACm* at quantity *Qm* and cost *Cm*. If the market were subdivided among enough firms to create a competitive situation, the size of the firm might be too small to take advantage of economies of scale. The short-run average cost curve might be at *SRACc*, and average costs would be much higher at *Cc*. The previously listed disadvantages to society for a monopoly firm may be compensated for by the economies of scale and lower cost obtained with the larger-size firm. But if the size of the monopoly firm exceeds the optimum, *SRACm* in Figure 14.4, added size results without economies of scale. Finally, these cost advantages through economies of scale are not necessarily passed on to consumers through lower prices. Because of barriers to entry, these gains might remain with the monopolist through increased profits.

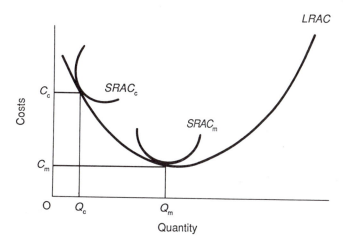

Figure 14.4. Pure Competition Versus Monopoly in the Long Run.

Another problem that makes comparing competitive and monopoly firms complex is the question of technology. First, which firm will more rapidly adopt already perfected technology? Second, which firm will more rapidly develop new technology? The answers to both questions are not simple.

It is generally accepted that the competitive firm, selling at the same price as all other firms in the industry, will rapidly adopt already perfected technology in order to keep its costs as low as those of other firms. For the monopoly firm, pressures to increase efficiency from other firms are substantially less, and thus pressures to adopt new technology are less. There is a "but" to be added here: "But" if the improved technology leads to increased size (increased size of plants and/or number of plants) and if, to achieve optimum size, the competitive firm had to move from *SRACc* in Figure 14.4 to *SRACm*, it would become a monopoly firm.

The question of which firm would more rapidly develop new technology is also not simple. Some innovations require extensive research facilities, large staffs, and considerable financing. Competitive firms may not be able to afford such research. For example, in the second half of the nineteenth century research in steel or petroleum or electrical power generation would have been beyond the means of competitive firms. However, this does not mean, especially 100 years ago, that with larger size, more research and more technological development would have taken place.

At the time, much of the development of technology *was* taking place in small firms, and individual inventors were making the inventions. Bell and the development of the telephone he invented is one example; barbed wire, invented by a farmer in the Midwest, is another. Furthermore, a great many productivity innovations came from small changes most often made by people close to the production line. The larger the firm, the more communication obstacles there are to prevent this kind of innovation. Furthermore, in the twentieth century, research increasingly became publicly financed by the government and nonprofit organizations.

These qualifications notwithstanding, we must note that there are welfare losses from monopoly even in the long run. The monopolist in Figure 14.4, even if operating *SRACm* and producing *Qm*, will set a price above *MC*. As in the short run, consumers would prefer an increase in output in terms of the value they place on other goods and services. We see this in Figure 14.4. The monopolist maximizes profit by producing *Qm* and exhausts the economies of scale by using plant *SRACm*. But price will still be set at a level greater than marginal cost.

Constraints on Monopoly Pricing

In Josephson's *The Robber Barons*, one gets the impression that the "captains of industry" who controlled those large monopolistic firms operated without restraint. As with a number of other concepts associated with the "robber barons," this one has been seriously questioned. Restraints on firms stem from a number of sources.

First, while the monopoly firm has significant control over price, the nature of demand (the shape and position of the curve) determines the quantity bought at each price. The firm may set price but not quantity demanded. It does not have control over both.

Second, the monopoly is restrained by competition—if not from within the industry, then at least from industries producing substitutes.

Third, as profits become higher through the use of monopoly power, the gains to be made by new firms penetrating the industry increase. Firms have an incentive to work vigorously to overcome barriers to entry.

Finally, monopolies are very visible and must be aware of the potential reaction of the public and the government. This was especially true after passage of the Interstate Commerce Act in 1887 and the Sherman Antitrust Act in 1890.

In brief, in looking at the problems caused by the exercise of monopoly power, one must distinguish between increases in size in response to increased economies of scale and increases generated for the purposes of exercising monopoly power. The first benefit the entire economy, through lowered costs and increases in efficiency. The second benefit the monopolistic firm at the expense of the economy, through higher profits achieved by increased prices and possibly decreases in efficiency and high costs. In addition, one must add the net effects of the development and utilization of technology.

The problems generated by the existence of monopoly power go beyond the simple economic ones of distribution of resources and income and questions of efficiency. They are also social, political, and philosophical.

QUESTIONS

1. How was the typical consolidation formed in the 1897–1904 period?
2. List the various reasons for the formation of large firms in the period 1897–1920. Which of these reasons were beneficial to society in general?

3. What is Faulkner's argument about the period 1897–1919? What are the weaknesses of his argument?

4. What were the arguments in opposition to the creation of large-scale monopolistic firms?

5. What are the different views concerning the success or failure of transportation regulation by the ICC?

6. "The Sherman Act of 1890 is clear in some of its aspects and has been the source of great uncertainty and interpretation in other respects." *Explain.*

7. Describe the various acts that attempted to strengthen antitrust legislation between 1900 and 1920.

8. Evaluate antitrust legislation and enforcement during the period. Was it successful? Why or why not?

9. What conditions seem to have given rise to the Federal Reserve Act of 1913? Did the act create a central bank?

10. Why was labor union growth rapid from 1897 to 1904 and slower from 1905 to 1909? What seems to account for union growth in size and strength throughout the period?

11. Describe the basic characteristics of the Industrial Workers of the World. What was the source of its conflict with the AFL?

12. In what major industries did unions expand their membership between 1910 and 1917?

13. Describe the strengths and weaknesses of organized labor in 1920. What may have been the greatest accomplishment of unions between 1897 and 1920?

14. What various factors caused a recovery and then expansion in the economy from 1897 to 1907?

15. What are the various explanations for the fits and starts of the U.S. economy from 1907 to 1914?

SUGGESTED READINGS

1. Attack, Jeremy. "Industrial Structure and the Emergence of the Modern Industrial Corporation." *Explorations in Economic History,* 22 (January 1985).

2. Brozen, Yale. "Antitrust Witch Hunt." *National Review,* November 24, 1978.

3. Chandler, Alfred D., and Galambos, Louis. "The Development of Large-Scale Economic Organizations in Modern America." *Journal of Economic History, 30* (March 1970).

4. Cochran, Thomas C. *Railroad Leaders, 1845–1890: The Business Mind in Action.* Cambridge, Mass.: Harvard University Press, 1951.

5. Dubofsky, Melvyn. "The Origins of Western Working Class Radicalism." In *The American Labor Movement,* ed. David Brody. New York: Harper and Row, 1971.

6. Faulkner, Harold U. *The Decline of Laissez-Faire, 1897–1917.* New York: Holt, Rinehart and Winston, 1961.

7. Friedman, Milton, and Anna J. Schwartz. *A Monetary History of the United States 1867–1960.* Princeton, N.J.: Princeton University Press, 1963.

8. Goldin, Claudia, "Female Labor Force Participation: The Origin of Black and White Differences, 1870 and 1880." *Journal of Economic History,* Vol. 37 (March 1980).

9. Greer, Douglas F. *Industrial Organization and Public Policy,* 2nd ed. New York: Macmillan, 1984.

10. Grob, Gerald N. "Knights of Labor versus American Federation of Labor." In *The American Labor Movements,* ed. David Brody. New York: Harper and Row, 1971.

11. Harbeson, Robert. "Railroads and Regulations, 1877–1916: Conspiracy or Public Interest?" *Journal of Economic History, 27* (June 1967).

12. Hughes, Jonathan. *American Economic History,* 2nd ed. Glenview, Ill.: Scott, Foresman, 1987.

13. Hughes, Jonathan. *The Governmental Habit.* New York: Basic Books, 1977.

14. Josephson, Matthew. *The Robber Barons: The Great American Capitalists, 1861–1901.* New York: Harcourt Brace Jovanovich, 1934.

15. Klehamer, Benjamin. "Potential Competition and the American Antitrust Legislation of 1914." *Business History Review, 38* (1964).

16. Kolko, Gabriel. *Railroads and Regulation, 1877–1916.* Princeton, N.J.: Princeton University Press, 1965.

17. Lebergott, Stanley. "The American Labor Force." In *American Economic Growth,* ed. Lance E. Davis et al. New York: Harper and Row, 1972.

18. Letwin, William. *Law and Economic Policy in America: The Evolution of the Sherman Antitrust Act.* New York: Random House, 1965.

19. Lipset, Seymour. "Trade Unionism and the American Social Order." In *The American Labor Movement,* ed. David Brody. New York: Harper and Row, 1971.

20. MacAvoy, Paul. *The Economic Effects of Regulation.* Cambridge, Mass.: MIT Press, 1965.

21. Martin, Albro. *Enterprise Denied.* New York: Columbia University Press, 1971.

22. McGee, John S. "Predatory Price Cutting: The Standard Oil (N.J.) Case." *Journal of Law and Economics, 137* (1958).

23. McGraw, Thomas R. "Regulation in America: A Review Article." *Business History Review, 49* (1975).

24. Millis, H. A., and R. E. Montgomery. *Organized Labor.* New York: McGraw-Hill, 1945.

25. Nelson, R. *Merger Movements in American Industry, 1895–1956.* Princeton, N.J.: Princeton University Press, 1959.

26. Pratt, Joseph A. "The Petroleum Industry in Transition: Antitrust and the Decline of Monopoly Control in Oil. *Journal of Economic History, 40* (December 1980).

27. Rayback, Joseph G. *History of American Labor.* New York: Macmillan, 1959.

28. Scherer, F. M. *Industrial Market Structure and Economic Performance.* Chicago: Rand McNally, 1970.

29. Soule, George. *Prosperity Decade: From War to Depression. 1917–1929.* New York: Harper and Row, 1947.

30. Thorelli, Hans B. *The Federal Anti-Trust Policy: Organization of an American Tradition.* Baltimore: Johns Hopkins University Press, 1955.

31. Ulen, Thomas. "The Market for Regulation: The I.C.C. from 1887 to 1920." *American Economic Review, 70* (May 1980).

32. Ulen, Thomas. "Railroad Cartels Before 1887: The Effectiveness of Private Enforcement of Collusion." In *Research in Economic History.* Greenwich, Conn.: JAI Press, 1987.

33. Ulman, L. "American Trade Unionism, Past and Present." In *American Economic History*, ed. Seymour E. Harris. Berkeley: University of California Press, 1961.

34. West, Robert Craig. *Banking Reform and the Federal Reserve, 1863–1923*. Ithaca, N.Y.: Cornell University Press, 1977.

35. Wicker, Elmus. *Federal Reserve Policy, 1917–1933*. New York: Random House, 1966.

Chapter 15

THE UNITED STATES IN THE INTERNATIONAL ARENA

In 1790, the United States was economically dependent on Europe, especially England. By 1920, it had the most powerful economy, in terms of both production and finance, in the world. In 1790, the United States was dependent on foreign investment—again, especially from England—to pay for a large share of its imports and encourage economic growth. It was a net debtor nation, owing more to other countries than was owed to it. By 1920, the United States was a net creditor nation, with investments in other countries far greater in value than these other countries had in the United States.

In 1790, the United States was bordered by the Mississippi River on the West. By 1920, the United States stretched westward from the Atlantic to the Pacific, south to Mexico, and north to Canada. In addition, the United States had gained direct control of territories outside its continental boundaries, such as Alaska, Hawaii, the Philippines, territory in the Caribbean, and islands in the Pacific. Despite its territorial expansion, however, the United States was still inexperienced in the ways of world economic leadership in the 1920s.

International influences on American economic development between 1850 and 1920 cannot be entirely summarized or analyzed in terms of trading data or even the dramatic scope of the nation's geopolitical expansion. Especially after 1865, an immigration movement of unprecedented proportions occurred. This movement not only changed the size and composition of the American labor force but also had major effects on wages, income distribution, and investment, and thus the pace and pattern of the entire economy.

In this chapter, we will review the role of the United States in world economic affairs to 1920. The reader will find it helpful to know something about the concepts involved in the balance of payments. For that reason, we have included at the end of the chapter a Review of Economic Concepts concerning balance of payments principles.

THE BALANCE OF PAYMENTS FROM 1850 TO 1920

The period 1850–1920 saw dramatic changes in the balance of payments as the United States continued to develop into a mature industrial society. There were changes in the growth and composition (both as to products and countries) of the various balance of payments accounts. The balances of the individual accounts changed as the United States shifted from being a net importer of products and capital to being a net exporter of both. Table 15.1 will be used as a basis for much of our discussion of the period through 1913. (Because of the special effects of World War I, the period from 1914 to 1920 will be discussed later separately.)

Imports and Exports

The international trade of the United States was not only increasing dramatically in this period, it was increasing more rapidly than the total of world trade. In 1850, the United States' share of world trade was about 10 percent; by 1913, that share had risen to about 15 percent. The change is even more dramatic when one looks at the U.S. share of the world's exports of manufactured goods, which increased from 2.8 percent in 1880 to 12.6 percent in 1913.

Not only did U.S. trade increase, both absolutely and relatively in terms of world trade, but the composition of that trade as to both products (see Table 15.2) and countries involved also changed. These changes reflected the long-term continuation of industrialization.

As shown in Table 15.2, the dominant place held in U.S. exports by raw materials, primarily cotton (column I) gave way first to foodstuffs, including manufactured foodstuffs (wheat, flour, processed meats—columns II and III) in the 1870s and 1880s. They, in turn, surrendered first place to manufactured goods,

Table 15.1.   U.S. Balance of Payments, 1850–1913 (millions of dollars).

	1850	1870	1876	1900	1913
1. Imports	195	449	470	854	1829
2. Exports	153	413	562	1395	2600
3. Balance of merchandise account	−42	−36	+92	+537	+771
4. Balance of invisible items	+4	−97	−134	−265	−604
5. Balance of long-term capital account	+29	+97	+42	−271	+87
6. Balance of current account and gold (+ credits, − debits)	+9	+36	0	+1	−70

SOURCE: *Historical Statistics of the United States; Trends in the American Economy in the Nineteenth Century* (Princeton, N.J.: National Bureau of Economic Research, 1960), pp. 699–705.

Table 15.2. Percent Composition of U.S. Exports and Imports, 1851–1910.

	I RAW MATERIALS	II NONMANU- FACTURED FOODSTUFFS	III MANUFAC- TURED FOODSTUFFS	IV SEMIMANU- FACTURED GOODS	V FINISHED GOODS MANUFACTURES
Exports					
1851–1860	61.7	6.6	15.4	4.0	12.3
1876–1880	32.2	23.9	24.4	4.6	14.9
1896–1900	26.1	18.9	24.0	9.6	21.4
1906–1910	31.7	8.9	18.1	14.2	27.1
Imports					
1851–1860	9.6	11.7	15.4	12.5	50.8
1876–1880	18.6	18.2	21.5	12.4	29.3
1896–1900	29.5	15.1	15.9	13.3	26.2
1906–1910	34.6	11.0	11.8	17.8	24.8

SOURCE: U.S. Department of Commerce, Bureau of the Census, *Historical Statistics of the United States, Colonial times to 1970*, Part 2 (Washington, D.C.: U.S. Government Printing Office, 1975), pp. 889–890.

both semifinished and finished (columns IV and V) by 1910. Imports also showed the effects of U.S. industrialization: imports of raw materials and semimanufactured goods increased to provide needed materials for the finished goods manufactures that were later exported, and imports of finished goods manufactures declined by 1910 to less than half the 1851–1860 percentage level.

Of all U.S. exports, 75 percent went to Europe in 1860; this had fallen to 68 percent by 1906–1910. The share of exports going to Canada rose from 7 to 10 percent in the same period, and those going to Asia rose from 2.4 to 5.5 percent. In 1860, 60 percent of U.S. imports came from Europe; this had fallen to 51 percent by 1906–1910. The share of U.S. imports coming from Asia and South America increased in the same period.

Starting in 1876 (and except for 1887–1889 and 1893), significant credit balances in the **merchandise account** became the rule. These **credit** balances meant that exports from the United States exceeded imports into the United States. This was a favorable balance of trade: U.S. residents were obtaining claims to foreign currencies in greater amounts than foreigners were obtaining claims to dollars. This reversed the long-term condition of imports exceeding exports, which as a rule had generated a **debit** balance prior to 1876.

Invisible Items

Table 15.1 shows an increasing debit balance in the **invisible items accounts** between 1870 and 1913. Invisible items represent a number of different accounts that, together with the merchandise account (imports and exports of goods), make up what is called the *current account*. They include tourist expenditures; transportation and insurance fees; the flow of dividends, profits, and interest on foreign investments; and transfer payments. The single most important reason for this outflow of funds from the American economy was to pay the profits, dividends, and interest on foreign investment in the United States. This outflow of funds increased as foreign investments made in the United States rose from approximately $1.5 billion in 1870 to about $6.3 billion in 1913.

The second reason for the growing debit balance in invisible items stemmed from a substantial shift after the Civil War from the carrying of U.S. exports and imports by U.S.-owned ocean vessels to carrying by foreign, especially British, vessels. As more U.S. goods were shipped on foreign vessels, transportation fees paid to nonresidents increased.

Another reason for these debit balances was increased tourism by Americans in Europe. After the Civil War, the expanding U.S. upper- and upper-middle-income groups began to seek the "higher culture" of Europe. Expenditures they made in Europe put claims to dollars in the hands of nonresidents, resulting in debits in the U.S. invisible items account.

Finally, European immigration into the United States increased markedly between 1880 and 1914. Many immigrants sent funds back to their original countries to bring their relatives to the United States, or sent funds back to help support their families still in Europe, or returned to Europe themselves, taking their American savings with them. These **unilateral transfers** went to nonresidents (the immigrant who returned to the old country became a nonresident), and were debits, or outflows, of claims to U.S. dollars.

The Current Account

By 1876, the U.S. economy had achieved an export surplus in its merchandise account (imports and exports). These credit balances in the balance of trade became large enough by 1881 to offset the growing debit balances in invisible items. The **current account** is the sum of the merchandise and invisible items accounts, lines 3 and 4 in Table 15.1. Credit balances in the current account were modest until 1896, and then became much larger, a factor that reduced the U.S. dependence on foreign inflows of capital to balance overall payments accounts.

Capital Movements

Except for the period from 1897 to 1905, annual foreign investment in the United States exceeded U.S. investment in foreign countries from 1850 up to 1914. The **long-term capital account** held a credit balance, except for the years 1897 to 1905, when there were debit balances ranging from $23 million in 1897 to $245 million in 1901. A credit balance in the long-term capital account meant that nonresidents (mostly English) had invested more in the United States than U.S. residents had invested in other countries. This caused an inflow of foreign exchange into the United States. By the end of the nineteenth century, credit balances in the current account reflected the fact that the United States had become a source of international capital.

Until the start of World War I in Europe in 1914, the United States remained a **net debtor nation** (there was more total foreign investment in the United States than U.S. residents had invested in other countries). The U.S. net debt position was $75 million in 1803, $1.5 billion in 1869, $2.7 billion in 1897, and $3.7 billion by 1914. Almost all of this net debt was with Europe. One-half of the net debt was held by English residents, and one-half was in railroad stocks and bonds.

Despite its net debtor position, the United States had made substantial amounts of foreign investment of its own by 1914. These foreign investments totaled $2.6 billion in 1914, up from $634 million in 1897. More than half of the investments were in the two closest neighbors of the United States: over $860 million in Canada and $850 million in Mexico.

In Canada, a great deal of the U.S. investment was attracted to the manufacture of products for sale in the Canadian market. High Canadian tariffs encouraged the effort to "jump the tariff walls" by direct investment. But a substantial amount of investment also went into raw materials, especially lumber and minerals, items needed for the growing manufacturing sector of the United States. In 1914, U.S. investment in Canada was only one-half the amount of English investment there. By the 1920s, though, U.S. investment exceeded that of the English.

In Mexico, "the Peace of Porfirio Díaz" created a favorable environment for foreign investment until the Madero revolution of 1911. Afterward, nationalistic sentiment seriously threatened foreign investment. From 1897 to 1914, an average of $40 million a year from the United States flowed into investments in Mexican railroads, mining, oil, agricultural properties, and public utilities.

After Cuban independence, U.S. investment rose rapidly in that country, from $50 million in 1897 to $200 million in 1914. After 1914, foreign investment in Cuba was largely monopolized by Americans. In Central America, about one-third of the $93 million invested by U.S. residents by 1914 was in the fruit industry. Investments in South America by U.S. citizens rose from $38 million in 1897 to about $366 million in 1914. Of this, about two-thirds was in mining. Investment in oil in South America developed later, after 1916.

The Asian market proved small for the United States. Exports to Asia in 1897 accounted for only 4 percent of U.S. total exports; this had grown merely to 6 percent by 1914. The United States was a latecomer on the China scene, arriving after the European powers and Japan had carved up that country into their own spheres of influence. The **open door policy** (that everyone should be equally able to trade and invest throughout China) advocated by the United States was largely ignored. Deep poverty by most Asian populations contributed to the relatively low level of demand for U.S. products and investment. U.S. investments in all of Asia grew from $23 million in 1897 to $235 million by 1914, but most of this growth occurred in Japan.

After 1914

In 1914, the United States was a net debtor nation by $3.7 billion. With the advent of World War I, however, U.S. exports expanded rapidly. By April of 1917, over $3 billion of U.S. securities held by Europeans had been sold to U.S. residents in partial payment for these purchases. In addition, $2,263 million in loans to the Allied countries were made, plus $45 million to Germany and $365 million to neutrals. By the end of 1918, the United States had become a **net creditor nation** by about $7 billion, that is, nonresidents owed American residents $7 billion more than Americans owed them.

A fundamental shift had occurred in the structure of international finance. The United States had now become the strongest financial power in the world. It is likely that the United States would have achieved that status eventually, even had there been no World War I, for there was a long-term historical trend to relative increases in exports and foreign investment by U.S. residents. But the war catapulted the nation into that position in just a few years. The big issues to be answered in the next chapter are: How would the world adjust to this fundamental shift? And how would the United States adjust to its new responsibilities?

Summary

From 1790 to 1876, the United States was a **young debtor nation.** Its import surplus (a debit balance in the merchandise account) was paid for by substantial inflows of long-term capital (a credit balance in the long-term capital account). This inflow not only paid for the excess of imports over exports but also led to increased productivity from the capital goods (machines, factories, and so forth) created by investments. The resulting greater output permitted the increased exports needed to pay the interest, dividends, and profits earned by foreign investors.

Between 1876 and 1914, the United States became a **mature debtor nation,** as its export surplus grew large enough to pay for the outflows of dividends, profits, and interest in the invisible items account created by foreign investments. The nation became less and less dependent on foreign investment to balance its payments.

After 1914, because of the outbreak of World War I in Europe, the United States became a **young creditor nation.** Export surpluses were now large enough to provide funds for significant amounts of foreign investments by Americans in other countries. In terms of the balance of payments, a young creditor nation is one that generates a credit balance in the merchandise account that provides the foreign exchange for debit balances in the long-term capital account.

TARIFFS

American tariff policy is an important factor to review in this consideration of the United States and the international economy. Tariffs are taxes on imports that raise the prices of these imports. As import prices increase, competing domestic goods acquire a greater competitive advantage. But this is not a net gain, because governmental interference in international relative prices raises domestic prices and causes a less efficient allocation of resources. Exports may be adversely affected also, as when other countries retaliate and raise their tariffs against U.S. goods, causing a decreased demand for U.S. exports.

Before the Civil War, American tariffs were moderate and imposed essentially for revenue. Opposition, in large measure from the agricultural South, which was a primary importer of manufactured goods, kept tariff rates from becoming significantly protectionist. In fact, tariff rates were on the decline after 1832.

After 1860, with the South out of the Congress and with the Civil War creating a need for large amounts of revenue, this low-tariff trend was reversed. From 20 percent in 1860, average tariff rates had risen to 47 percent by 1864. After the war, these "temporary" rates became permanent, and high protectionist rates became the policy of the federal government.

The Dingley Tariff of 1897 pushed tariffs to the highest rates in U.S. history, an act that triggered retaliatory rate increases against U.S. products, especially by England and Canada. The next tariff passed was the Payne-Aldrich Tariff of 1909. Faulkner (9) concludes that there was no essential difference between the two tariffs—that perhaps the Payne-Aldrich Tariff was a little less aggressively protectionist but reflected even more obvious logrolling, with those groups with more political influence obtaining the greatest benefits.

The Democratic Party made these high tariffs a campaign issue in the congressional elections of 1910. Although the party made enough congressional gains to pass a lower tariff bill, President Taft (a Republican) vetoed it. In 1913, the Underwood Tariff reduced tariff rates, but the tariff structure of the United States was still basically protectionist.

What arguments can be made in favor of these relatively high tariff rates? Some said that tariff protection was needed to protect American labor against cheap foreign labor, but this hardly seems a valid argument considering the unrestricted, and very high, immigration into the United States from 1880 to 1914 by this selfsame "cheap foreign labor." Besides, U.S. labor was paid on the basis of its productivity, and achieved higher productivity and wages because of higher skills and larger amounts of capital invested per worker.

High tariffs certainly reduced imports. However, the United States was not suffering from any chronic balance-of-payments problems that would have required higher tariffs to counter. Furthermore, the United States was moving steadily toward a mature debtor position. Thus the balance of payments seems to have created little reason to decrease imports.

Some also argued that high tariffs would foster United States manufacturing. No doubt some industries were begun under tariff protection and needed that protection to develop. But that cannot be said about industry in general. By 1900, manufacturing in the United States was firmly established in conditions very favorable to the American producer. The sector had a large domestic market, with ready access to supplies of materials, large amounts of capital, and a rapidly developing system of technological innovation.

Finally, some argued that high tariffs were needed to obtain revenue for the federal government. Tariff revenues did provide a significant portion (at least 50 percent) of total federal government receipts after the Civil War. But these receipts produced a federal government budgetary surplus through most of the period from 1870 to 1914. In addition, tariffs frequently are a regressive form of taxes, falling more heavily on lower-income groups, which raises a serious question of equity.

Against whatever gains one could rationalize from high protective tariffs, there were distinct disadvantages. Interference in comparative-advantage trade reduced efficiency in the allocation of resources and increased prices. High tariffs also provoked retaliation by other governments, which increased their tariffs against U.S. exports, thereby reducing U.S. output and employment in export industries. Finally, tariffs, by reducing foreign competition, may have encouraged combinations in the United States by monopolistic producers and enabled them to set higher prices.

TERRITORIAL EXPANSION

Expanding international relations carried over to geographic or territorial expansion. Prior to 1897, the territorial expansion of the United States was primarily internal. The basic aim was to reach from the Atlantic to the Pacific. As may be seen in Figure 15.1, land was obtained either by purchase, such as the Louisiana Purchase in 1803 and the purchase of Florida in 1821; or by conflict—Texas was admitted into the Union in 1845 after the Texas Revolution and the Mexican-American War resulted in the cession of California and the Southwest; or by negotiation, such as the Oregon Territory in 1846. In addition to the territories included in the continental United States, Alaska was purchased in 1867.

The territories added after 1897 were not obtained for direct colonization or other purposes. They were primarily acquired for strategic purposes. One objective was to obtain enough naval coaling stations to maintain a two-ocean navy. Thus the United States acquired the Philippines and Samoa as part of the Pacific fueling system. In addition, these countries provided overseas access to the Asian markets.

Another economic (and political) objective was to obtain a protected canal route across the Isthmus of Panama. The U.S. acquisition of Puerto Rico, a naval base in Cuba, the Virgin Islands, and the Canal Zone itself all contributed to satisfying this objective.

The case of the Hawaiian Islands was substantially different. The United States took over these islands mostly by accident. According to Faulkner (9), the McKinley Tariff of 1890 increased the tariff duties on imported sugar to help the Louisiana sugar producers. The American sugar producers in Hawaii

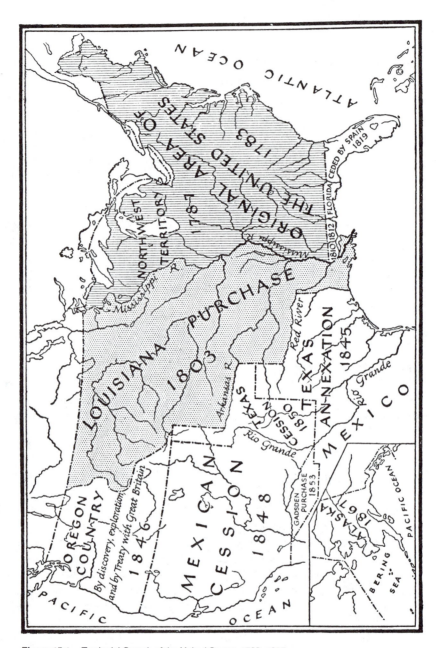

Figure 15.1. Territorial Growth of the United States, 1783–1867.

Source: Excerpted from *The Beards' New Basic History of the United States* by Charles A. Beard and Mary R. Beard. Copyright © 1944, 1960, 1968 by Doubleday, a division of Bantam, Doubleday, Dell Publishing Group, Inc. Reprinted by permission of the publisher.

Figure 15.2.   Construction of the Panama Canal. (Photo from the National Archives)

wanted to take advantage of the new tariff by making Hawaii a part of the United States, so they organized a revolt against the native Hawaiian government. They lost. To stop the Hawaiian queen from executing the American rebels, the commander of the U.S. naval squadron at Hawaii "reluctantly" placed the islands under the protection of the United States. In the end, the U.S. sugar growers achieved their objective. Few people in the United States were unhappy with the annexation of Hawaii in 1898. The islands were dominated by American economic interests, and the Hawaiian harbors were important during the 1898 war with Spain. Furthermore, there was growing fear of Japan's intentions toward the islands.

IMMIGRATION AND THE AMERICAN ECONOMY

The post–Civil War era saw an enormous flood of European migration to America. The reasons for this greatly expanded movement are not difficult to find. European farming was in decline. Not only could European farms no longer support a growing population, but relatively cheap American agricultural exports were significantly eroding the market for domestic farm goods throughout that continent. Ironically, the huge stream of immigrants, by increasing labor supplies in the United States, kept wage costs in American export industries low and further enhanced those industries' comparative advantage over their European counterparts.

The second economic factor accelerating the flow of migrants from Europe was the falling cost of transatlantic travel. The major cost to the immigrants was their opportunity costs (forgone earnings in European employment), and that cost apparently fell with declining marginal productivity in European agriculture. Indeed, Jonathan Hughes (12) has argued that this opportunity cost was "probably negative," particularly for the immigrants from Eastern Europe. Direct costs, especially transportation costs, fell after the Civil War. Steamships made the voyage from Europe to the American East Coast in a week; sailing ships had required up to three months.

The scope of this migration to America may be seen in Table 15.3. Both the scope and composition of this migrant flow are worth noting. Notice that in the 50 years between 1865 and 1915 more than 39 million Europeans immigrated to the United States. To put that in perspective, bear in mind that the total population of the United States in the early 1900s was about 90 million. For a more contemporary slant, imagine that two-thirds of the entire population of the United Kingdom or France or West Germany decided to migrate to a single overseas nation whose population was perhaps twice the size of the migrant flow! Though the comparison neglects the differences between population as a stock and as a flow, you can nonetheless appreciate the kind of impact this might have on the "receiving" economy and society.

The second striking factor visible in Table 15.3 is the change in the geographic origin of the immigrants. From 1865 to 1890, about 93 percent of European immigrants came from the United Kingdom and Northwest Europe and Germany and Central Europe. Although migrants from those areas increased in number after 1890, about 25 percent of the immigrants in the 25 years preceding 1915 came from Russia and East Europe and Italy and Southern Europe.

The point is that not only was immigration adding to the stock of human capital in the United States, but its contribution was changing with the changing

Table 15.3.   European Immigration to the United States by Place of Origin (000s), 1865–1915.

	UNITED KINGDOM AND NORTHWEST EUROPE	GERMANY AND CENTRAL EUROPE	RUSSIA AND EAST EUROPE	ITALY AND SOUTHERN EUROPE	TOTAL EUROPEAN IMMIGRATION
1865–1890	5,532	3,304	262	409	9,507
1890–1915	8,010	4,692	3,258	4,141	29,608
Total (1865–1915)					39,115

Source: U.S. Department of Commerce, Bureau of the Census, *Historical Statistics of the United States, Colonial Times to 1970*, Part 2 (Washington D.C.: U.S. Government Printing Office, 1975), pp. 33–34.

skills and backgrounds of the immigrants. One thing that did not alter over the entire period, however, was that European immigration steadily reduced the percentage of the nonwhite population of the United States.

Immigration-Induced Economic Changes

It is impossible to assay here the entire set of influences that this immigration flow had on the American economy. Several of the major effects, however, deserve mention. The effects on output and income were unquestionably large. By lowering the costs of production, immigrant labor doubtless increased the total supply of goods and services and raised the growth of gross national product beyond that which can be explained by entrepreneurial innovation, formation of capital, or other sources of growth. This is true even though it is likely that unrestricted immigration altered the production input mix in favor of labor intensity, the result of which may have been to retard capital formation.

The second major effect of immigration was a corollary of the first, the effect on wages and the factor distribution of income. American union leaders, many of them immigrants themselves, had argued for years that "unbridled" immigration was retarding the wage gains of workers. The (ultimately successful) political position of many unions was that immigration restrictions were necessary to assure the economic progress of working people in America. Though a normative judgment on that position is beyond the scope of this book, the unions appear to have been substantially correct about the factual results of unrestricted immigration. According to Stanley Lebergott (19), average earnings from nonfarm workers (in 1914 dollars) rose by about 52 percent between 1860 and 1914. Then, at first by exigencies of war (1914) and later by legislation (1920s), restrictions on immigration were put in place. Between 1914 and 1929, Lebergott calculates that real wages of nonfarm workers rose by 29 percent, almost two-thirds of the entire growth that took place in the preceding 44 years. Once this more rapid wage growth occurred, mechanization—substitution of capital for labor—increased. As a result, output per man-hour grew by 72 percent between 1919 and 1929.

As a final consideration, what happened to the immigrants in the decades after their arrival in America? E. P. Hutchinson (14) studied this question, drawing on data from 1910, when immigration reached its maximum. Using the percent of the foreign-born in the American labor force as the base (=100), Hutchinson calculated the percent of the foreign-born (the first generation) and those of foreign stock (the subsequent generation) working in several occupations in 1910. The results can be seen in Table 15.4.

Occupations such as accountants, lawyers, and teachers contained relatively few foreign-born people. Contrarily, occupations such as domestics, charwomen, and transport laborers contained relatively large numbers of the foreign-born. Even if some of the immigrants possessed the skills required for the professions, they could not immediately make a lateral move into the American labor force. As Jonathan Hughes so aptly put it, "Russian Jews who were engineers

Table 15.4. Occupation Concentration in 1910
(Overall concentration = 100)

	FOREIGN-BORN	FOREIGN STOCK
All occupations	100	100
Accountants	62	131
Engineers	47	104
Lawyers	25	102
Physicians and dentists	45	86
Teachers	39	75
Domestics	173	87
Charwomen, porters	208	104
Janitors	168	102
Construction laborers	169	84
Transport laborers	224	58

SOURCE: E. P. Hutchinson, *Immigrants and Their Children, 1850–1950*
(Chicago: University of Chicago Press, 1956).

drove taxis on their arrival, Vietnamese lawyers became cooks, etc." Then and now there are lags in assimilation.

However, the lags were not long. Note the startling change in the participation rates of those of foreign stock. Accountants, engineers, and lawyers all contained more people of foreign stock than those of foreign stock constituted of the total labor force! In one generation, there was dramatic upward mobility. No wonder that the United States has been characterized as the "land of opportunity."

Altogether, the Hutchinson study, along with that by Neal and Uselding (23), validates the view of the United States as a *relatively* open society, willing to enrich its stock of human capital by encouraging immigration and drawing upon the skills of all its citizens, including those of foreign stock. This view still holds, despite the questions raised in recent years about the upward mobility of Hispanic immigrants.

Immigration and Long-Term Growth

What were the relationships between these great immigration tides, which ebbed and flowed between 1850 and 1920, and the long-term growth trends of the American economy? Although occasionally the immigrants were "pushed" out of Europe, especially European Russia, by political and economic events (pogroms, crop failures, etc.), migrants generally were "pulled" to the United States by an economic lure. We should expect, then, that the tide of migrants would rise during long-term upswings of the American economy and ebb during downswings.

There is, in fact, a remarkable correspondence between the peaks of immigration flows (1873, 1882, 1892, 1903, 1907, 1910) and the upswings in business cycle activity in America. Wherever this correlation seems weak, particularly in some of the years between 1898 and 1910, it seems that the "push" effects we just referred to more than offset the reverse pull influences. In summary, the data suggest that, other things being equal (especially political conditions and relevant economic conditions in Europe), immigrants did react to reports and expectations of employment conditions as they varied with American business cycles.

Kuznets Cycles

Simon Kuznets (16), one of the most distinguished American economists, has argued that there are long swings of 16 to 18 years in the American economy (now known as Kuznets cycles), and has strongly suggested that immigration was not only tied to these waves, but strongly reinforced them. The long-term upswings in the United States were 1844–1861, 1862–1877, 1879–1897, and 1898–1914. Kuznets argues that it was the perception and expectation of *secular* trends in the U.S. economy that triggered emigration from Europe. He tells how the factors were interrelated, beginning with the growth of per capita consumer goods in the initial phase of the upswing:

> The long swings in additions to per capita flow of goods to consumers resulted, with some lag, in long swings, first in the net immigration balance and then in the natural increase, yielding swings in total population growth. The latter then induced, again with some lag, similar swings in population-sensitive long swings in "other" capital goods to consumers. The swing in the net migration balance, and in natural increase, and so on." (16)

An Atlantic Economy? The Thomas Model

Some scholars have seen the Atlantic Ocean, at least in some periods, as a lake freely crossed by all on its periphery, not only with their bodies, but also with their capital. The Welsh economist Brinley Thomas (27) has argued this with great persuasiveness. According to Thomas, the U.S. upswings were accentuated by the free flow of Europeans and their capital. When the United States was growing relative to Europe, the human and financial movement increased and added to the pace of the American economy. In turn, when the U.S. economy lagged, European capital (and Europeans) stayed home. The Atlantic economy, then, moved in *inversely* related Kuznets long waves, even if the shorter-term business cycles exhibited nearly the same patterns on both sides of the "lake."

These free movements, according to Thomas, had major structural effects. When the tide of immigration rose, investment in the United States was relatively labor-using (more labor per unit of investment). For Thomas, this resulted in a "widening" of capital. When the tide of immigration ebbed, investment in the United States became relatively laborsaving (less labor per unit of investment) in a process Thomas calls the "deepening" of capital.

According to Thomas, all the factors necessary to this grand transatlantic rhythm were in place before 1920. Unrestricted immigration to the United States, the currency convertibility of the gold standard, and the relative occupational mobility of the American "melting pot" society permitted, even encouraged, this intricate tying of long-term growth rates on both sides of the Atlantic. As Jonathan Hughes (12) has put it, "Before it was disrupted by World War I, subsequent immigration restriction in the 1920s, as well as the shattering of the international gold standard and its institutions, the Atlantic was truly a European-American lake."

SUMMARY

A number of observations can be made about the U.S. economy and the international economic setting before 1920. Perhaps the most important is that, as the U.S. economy developed and matured into the largest industrial complex in the world, the center of economic power shifted. No longer did the U.S. economy depend on the tempo of economic activities and financial decisions in Europe, especially Britain. Even more, the dependence was being reversed. Europe was now to react, perhaps in the ways suggested by the Thomas model, to the actions of the new economic giant, the United States.

A second point deserves notice. Until 1897, U.S. investors and entrepreneurs were primarily occupied with utilizing the economic opportunities of the continental United States. In addition to U.S. investment and enterprise, significant infusions of European capital and enterprise were productively utilized. By 1897, however, U.S. enterprise began to vigorously seek opportunities for profit beyond U.S. borders. Foreign investments by U.S. citizens rose rapidly to exploit foreign profit-making opportunities. The U.S. government, too, went beyond the boundaries of the United States, as more territory was acquired to satisfy the strategic needs of two-ocean trade.

An additional point to consider concerns the fundamental shift in international economic power that resulted from World War I. Not only did the United States shift from being a net debtor to being a net creditor, but this shift resulted in a $7 billion net credit position. The large size of these credits would put a severe strain on the ability of the European debtors to meet their debt obligations. In addition, it put the United States under an obligation to create conditions to enable those countries to pay or meet their debts, an obligation the United States met poorly in the 1920s.

Finally, we must remember the various and considerable influences of immigration. The gigantic, undulating waves of immigrants had, as we have seen, a major influence not only on the pace but also on the pattern or structure of the American economy. Immigration and continued European capital flows had influences on the United States that were both short-term and long-term in the cyclical sense. They had much to do with augmenting the stock of human capital and with the nature and pace of investment.

World War I also caused significant shifts in international markets. Europe lost markets heavily in North and South America and in Asia to the United States and the emerging economy of Japan. The loss of these markets compounded European postwar economic adjustments. The drama begun in 1914 continued long after the war was over. The international economic strategy the United States would use after the war, however, was already clearly defined by 1914. High protective tariffs with a tendency toward increases (except for the Underwood Tariff of 1913) were the policy of the U.S. government after 1860. To allow for repayment of loans and to increase export markets in the 1920s, the United States would have had to increase its own imports, largely by lowering tariffs. Instead, the high tariff policy was continued.

REVIEW OF ECONOMIC CONCEPTS: THE BALANCE OF PAYMENTS

The **balance of payments** is an accounting summary of all economic transactions between the residents of one country and the residents of all other countries during a given time period. It is important to point out, first, that the balance of payments accounts are summaries of transactions and do not contain a record of each individual transaction. In that sense, they are like balance sheet items in accounting, not like journal entries. Second, the accounts reflect transactions between residents, not citizens, of countries. The important thing is where people are living or residing. Finally, the balance of payments is for a specific time period—usually one year—and only includes transactions of that time period; it is not cumulative.

The balance of payments is set up in a T-account, or double-entry system: for every transaction, two equal and offsetting entries are made, a credit and a debit. Therefore, if all the debits are added up and all the credits are added up, they will be equal; thus the balance of payments always balances.

Credits are all economic transactions that create an immediate obligation for a nonresident to pay a resident. Debits are all economic transactions that create an immediate obligation for a resident to pay a nonresident. Thus credits create inflows of payments (foreign exchange) and debits create outflows of payments (foreign exchange).

We can also define debits and credits in the balance of payments accounts from another point of view. Credits are all economic transactions that increase the demand for dollars in a foreign exchange market as nonresidents seek dollars to pay residents or increase the supply of foreign exchange, as nonresidents offer their own monies to obtain dollars to pay residents. Debits increase the demand for foreign monies, as residents seek foreign exchange to pay nonresidents or increase the supply of dollars to obtain foreign monies to pay nonresidents.

The Major Accounts of the Balance of Payments

Figure 15.3 is a schematic presentation of the balance of payments accounts most relevant to the period through 1920. The first major account is the current account, which is divided into two major subaccounts, the merchandise account and services or invisible items. The merchandise account consists of exports (credits) and imports (debits). Invisible items consist of a number of different accounts: first, services, including fees for transportation and insurance; second, expenditures of tourists in other countries; third, payments of profits, dividends, and interest on prior foreign investment; fourth, funds spent in other countries to maintain military forces and diplomatic missions; and finally, transfers not requiring repayment, such as immigrants sending money back to families in the old country.

The second major account is the short-term capital account. It consists of changes in demand deposits (checking accounts) and short-term debt (debt that matures in less than one year).

The third major account is the long-term capital account. This account records foreign investment—nonresidents investing in the United States or U.S. residents investing in other countries—in the form of purchase of corporate stock or equity instruments, purchase of corporate debt or bonds, or direct investment in noncorporate forms.

The last major account is the gold account. Exports or outflows of gold are credits, and imports or inflows of gold are debits. The official reserve transaction account includes all transfers that result in the balance.

Balance of Payments Deficit

Since debits always equal credits, by the nature of the way the accounts are set up, the balance of payments always balances. But the various accounts *individually* need not balance. There are stable sets of balances between the accounts, and there are unstable ones. The stable balances can be maintained for extended periods or can contain self-correcting mechanisms. A debit balance in the merchandise account (imports exceeding exports) can remain stable as foreign investment flows into the economy. Credit balances in the long-term capital account, as capital is formed, increase the productive capacity of the economy. Eventually output increases, and this import balance can be reversed.

Figure 15.3. Major Accounts in the Balance of Payments.

  I. Current Account
     A. Merchandise Account
     B. Invisible Items
 II. Short-Term Capital Account
III. Long-Term Capital Account
 IV. Official Reserve Transactions Account

Deficits in the balance of payments occur when these balances in the individual accounts are potentially not stable. Credit balances in the short-term capital account (bank balances), as well as credit balances in the gold account, are considered potentially unstable. Increases of bank balances by nonresidents cannot be maintained indefinitely, because if those nonresidents cannot use their balance to buy the output of the U.S. economy or to obtain investments, they will wish to use these funds in their own economies. Prior to the 1930s, this would result in a withdrawal of gold. Since gold was the main reserve of the banking system in the nineteenth and early twentieth centuries, the loss of gold would have reduced both credit activities of the banking system and the supply of money. The level of general economic activity could then be affected. However, according to gold standard theorists, these changes in the supply of money would change prices so as to introduce self-correcting activities.

QUESTIONS

1. What changes occurred in the current account of the United States from 1850 to 1913? Which of these changes attest to the growing industrial nature of the American economy? Why do they do so?
2. Trace the changes in the long-term capital account of the United States from 1850 to 1920. Did these changes indicate an increasing or a decreasing dependency of the U.S. economy on Europe? Why?
3. In what countries and industries was U.S. investment to 1914 primarily concentrated? Why do you think this was so?
4. What fundamental change occurred during World War I in regard to the U.S. balance of payments? Why was this change important?
5. Evaluate the arguments made in favor of high tariffs.
6. What are the disadvantages of tariffs?
7. What were the basic economic motives for territorial expansion of the United States? First, within the continental United States? Second, outside the continental United States?
8. What factors in the United States as well as in Europe created the massive immigration to the United States between 1850 and 1914?
9. What changes took place in the geographic origin of European immigrants after 1890?
10. Of the many economic changes in the United States induced by immigration after 1865, which do you think were the most important?
11. Were the unions right in their oft-stated argument about the effects of unrestricted immigration on wages and the distribution of factor income?
12. What were the short-term and longer-term relationships between European immigration and economic growth in the United States between 1865 and 1920?
13. What are the Kuznets and Thomas arguments with respect to the relationship between transatlantic immigration and capital flows and the long-term growth of Europe and the United States?
14. What were the four points made about the United States and the international economy in the summary to the chapter?

SUGGESTED READINGS

1. Aghevli, Bijan B. "The Balance of Payments and Money Supply Under the Gold Standard Regime: U.S., 1879–1914." *American Economic Review, 65* (March 1975).

2. Ashworth, William A. *A Short History of the International Economy, 1850–1950.* New York: Longmans Green, 1952.

3. Baack, Bennett D., and Edward John Ray. "Tariff Policy and Comparative Advantage in the Iron and Steel Industry, 1870–1929." *Explorations in Economic History, 11* (Fall 1973).

4. Baack, Bennett D., and Edward John Ray. "The Political Economy of Tariff Policy: A Case Study of the United States." *Explorations in Economic History, 20* (January 1983).

5. Bagwell, Philip S., and G. E. Mingay. *Britain and America 1850–1939: A Study of Economic Change.* New York: Praeger, 1970. Esp. Chaps. 4 and 9.

6. Bullock, Charles J., John H. Williams, and Rufus S. Tucker. "The Balance of Trade of the United States." *Review of Economic Statistics, 1* (1919).

7. Easterlin, Richard. *Population, Labor Force, and Long Swings in Economic Growth: The American Experience.* New York: Columbia University Press, 1968.

8. Erickson, Charlotte. *American Industry and the European Immigrant, 1860–1885.* New York: Russell and Russell, 1967.

9. Faulkner, Harold U. *The Decline of Laissez-Faire, 1897–1917.* New York: Holt, Rinehart and Winston, 1951. Esp. Chaps. 3 and 4.

10. Feis, Herbert. *Europe, the World's Banker, 1870–1914.* New York: Norton, 1965 ed.

11. Hawke, G. R. "The United States Tariff and Industrial Protection in the Late Nineteenth Century." *Economic History Review, 27* (February 1975).

12. Hughes, Jonathan. *American Economic History.* Glenview, Ill.: Scott, Foresman, 1987.

13. Hughes, Jonathan. *Industrialization and Economic History: Theses and Conjectures.* New York: McGraw-Hill, 1970.

14. Hutchinson, E. P. *Immigrants and Their Children, 1850–1950.* Chicago: University of Chicago Press, 1956.

15. Jenks, Jeremiah, and Jeff Lauch. *The Immigration Problem.* New York: Funk and Wagnalls, 1926.

16. Kuznets, Simon. "Long Swings in the Growth of Population and in Related Economic Variables." *Proceedings of the American Philosophical Society, 102* (February 1958).

17. Kuznets, Simon, and Ernest Rubin. *Immigration and the Foreign Born.* New York: National Bureau of Economic Record, 1954.

18. La Feber, Walter. *The New Empire: An Interpretation of American Expansion, 1860–1898.* Ithaca, N.Y.: Cornell University Press, 1963.

19. Lebergott, Stanley. *The Americans: An Economic Record.* New York: Norton, 1984. Esp. Chap. 26.

20. Lebergott, Stanley. "The Returns to U.S. Imperialism, 1890–1929." *Journal of Economic History, 40* (June 1980).

21. Lipsey, Robert. "Foreign Trade." In *American Economic Growth: An Economist's History of the United States,* ed. Lance E. Davis et al. New York: Harper and Row, 1972.

22. National Bureau of Economic Research. *Historical Statistics of the United States: Trends in the American Economy in the Nineteenth Century.* Princeton, N.J.: Princeton University Press, 1960. Pp. 699–705.

23. Neal, Larry, and Paul Uselding. "Immigration, A Neglected Source of U.S. Economic Growth, 1790–1913." In *Oxford Economic Papers,* 2nd ser., vol. 24 (March 1972).

24. Novak, David, and Matthew Simon. "Commercial Responses to the American Export Invasion, 1871–1914." *Explorations in Economic History, 3* (1966).

25. Taussig, Frank W. *The Tariff History of the United States.* New York: Putnam's Sons, 1932.

26. Taylor, Phillip. *The Distant Magnet: European Immigration to the United States.* London: Eyre and Spottiswood, 1971.

27. Thomas, Brinley. *Migration and Economic Growth.* Cambridge: Cambridge University Press, 1953.

28. United States Department of Commerce. *Long-Term Economic Growth, 1860–1970.* 1974.

29. Williamson, Jeffrey G. *American Growth and the Balance of Payments.* Chapel Hill: University of North Carolina Press, 1964.

30. Williamson, Jeffrey G. *Late Nineteenth Century American Development: A General Equilibrium History.* New York: Cambridge University Press, 1964.

Chapter 16

THE PROSPERITY
OF THE 1920s

An "era of normalcy," it was called, but the decade of the 1920s was a dramatic time in the economic history of the United States. With an economy that generally boomed, the 1920s became synonymous with the idea of prosperity. Indeed, George Soule titled his excellent economic history of this period *Prosperity Decade* (32). Leading this expansion was the automobile; the American people began their rush to a life on four wheels. At the same time, the United States had become the most powerful financial power in the world, and Americans had their first taste of being world economic leaders. Ironically, though, this was the same decade that started with the depression of 1921 and ended with the stock market crash of 1929. Although not the beginning, the crash was the first dramatic sign of the international economic disaster known as the Great Depression of the 1930s.

THE BEGINNING

After a brief pause during the conversion to civilian production, the U.S. economy after World War I continued to expand. The reasons for this are fairly simple and involve both demand and supply factors. Government expenditures were still relatively high in 1919, owing especially to bonus and discharge pay to the armed forces and the decision to complete the construction of merchant vessels under the Emergency Fleet Corporation. Exports were high, because agricultural and industrial products were needed by Europeans to tide them over until their countries' war damages could be repaired. Consumer demand was also high, because purchases had been postponed in 1917 and 1918 when resources were mobilized for the war effort. Purchasing power to pay for the increased demand came from high levels of savings, both in saving banks and through government bonds (Liberty Bonds) accumulated during the war. On the supply side, investment, both in residential construction and in industrial plants and equipment, was high because such investment had been postponed during the war. Also, the supply of money continued to increase.

Under the impact of this expanding demand and lagging supply growth, inflation increased, which created the usual wave of speculation in inventories. Business firms bought goods not only to make a "regular" profit on their economic functions (retailing, for instance) but also to profit from the expected increase in prices between the time they bought the goods and the time they sold them. Thus, in 1920, inventories increased beyond the normal needs of business. Apparently price increases exceeded the interest cost of holding inventories. This not only further increased demand but also made the economy more subject to cyclical swings.

The speculative expansion of inventories increased the rate of growth in demand for manufacturers of consumer goods. This resulted in increased investment, because new plants and equipment were needed to manufacture the additional goods, producing a positive accelerator effect and thus expanding the economy. Later, as the speculative buying of inventories slowed down, the demand for investment in additional production capacity also decreased, and this negative accelerator effect contracted the economy.

Government expenditures decreased toward the end of 1920 because military expenditures fell, construction under the Emergency Fleet Corporation had been completed, and war contracts were no longer in effect. Exports declined as Europe completed its reconstruction. Also of considerable importance, the inventory bubble had burst by the end of 1920. In late 1920, the U.S. economy contracted, and a severe, although short, depression took place during 1921.

Some charged that the Federal Reserve System was responsible for the collapse of the inventory speculation because it ordered the banks under its regulation to cease making loans to finance such inventories. It seems likely, though, that this action had little effect on the outcome. Every wave of speculation must end because (among other things) any hesitation in price increases brings a crash as people, acting with changed expectations, rush to get out from under the fall. In any case, excess inventory accumulations probably contributed to the severity of the depression. Seen in a demand framework, as income levels fell because of declines in total demand, firms had larger inventories than they wished. Consequently, they cut orders to their suppliers, which, in turn, decreased output, employment, and income. In 1920, inventories were swollen because of speculation. When inventory accumulation declined, income fell even more than it would have without the speculation.

The contraction in 1921 was severe. Constant GNP fell by about 6 percent, and unemployment rose to about 12 percent, with almost half a million workers unemployed. By the end of 1921, the index of industrial production had dropped almost 18 percent from its September 1919 high. A major characteristic of the contraction was the sharp drop in prices. The wholesale price index fell from 227 in 1920 to 150 in 1921 (1913 = 100). Industrial prices decreased somewhat less than the average, while raw material prices decreased more than the average.

Agricultural prices declined almost to their prewar levels. This relatively greater decline in agricultural prices stemmed from several factors. Agriculture was highly competitive, and farmers, individually or collectively, could not reduce supply enough to stem the fall in prices. Also, war and immediate postwar demand had encouraged farmers to expand output, which, by 1921, created excess supply. Furthermore, with the end of the war and renewed freedom of shipping, foreign supplies (for example, from Argentina and Australia) could reach the European markets. Finally, war reconstruction had advanced to the point where European demand for imported food fell.

THE PROSPEROUS TWENTIES—1922–1929

However sharp the downturn of 1921, it was short-lived. Basic demand for consumer goods and investment remained sound, and the U.S. economy renewed its expansion at the beginning of 1922. This expansion continued throughout the 1920s into 1929, with only a mild interruption in 1924 and an even milder one in 1927. Current GNP increased from $69.5 billion in 1921 to $103.1 billion in 1929. Unemployment dropped from 11.7 percent in 1921 to 3.2 percent in 1929. The price level itself fell very moderately, from 53.6 (1967 = 100) in 1921 to 51.3 in 1929.

General Business Conditions in the 1920s

The dynamics of a private enterprise economy are driven not only by changes in the level of demand but also by supply changes. The latter both affect and are affected by general business conditions. As an introduction to the Roaring Twenties, it is instructive, therefore, to see what general business conditions were after 1921. Table 16.1 presents selected data on general business conditions between 1921 and 1930.

If the number of firms is a rough measure of favorable expectations, the "business climate" was favorable; the number of firms rose from 1921 through 1929. Failure rates of firms rose in 1922, but fell in 1923 and thereafter remained fairly constant until 1930. Average liability in failures declined after 1923 and even in 1930 was below the 1923 level. The prime interest rate declined from 6.62 percent in 1921 to 5.07 percent in 1923, and remained below 5 percent through 1928; importantly, the prime was positive in a "real" sense, that is, above the rate of price increase. Interestingly, the data suggest that the "mania" for stock purchases through much of the decade was founded in rationality, even on the part of risk-averse investors; the yield on industrial stocks was often above that on corporate bonds! In the case of U.S. government bonds, this was so in every year between 1921 and 1930. Such yields, when combined with the expectation of capital gains,

Table 16.1. Selected Data on General Business Conditions, 1921–1930.

YEAR	BUSINESS FIRMS (000s)	FAILURES PER 1,000 FIRMS	AVERAGE LIABILITY OF FAILURES ($1,000)
1921	1,927	102	31.9
1922	1,983	120	26.4
1923	1,996	93	28.8
1924	2,047	100	26.4
1925	2,113	100	20.9
1926	2,158	101	18.8
1927	2,172	106	22.5
1928	2,199	109	20.5
1929	2,213	104	21.1
1930	2,183	122	25.4

YEAR	CORPORATE AA BOND YIELDS	INDUSTRIALS STOCK YIELDS	PRIME RATE
1921	5.97	5.84	6.62
1922	5.10	5.37	4.52
1923	5.12	5.40	5.07
1924	5.00	5.25	3.98
1925	4.88	4.75	4.02
1926	4.73	5.24	4.34
1927	4.57	4.72	4.11
1928	4.55	3.82	4.85
1929	4.73	3.65	5.85
1930	4.55	4.45	3.59

SOURCE: U.S. Department of Commerce, Bureau of the Census, *Historical Statistics of the United States, Colonial Times to 1970*, 1960 ser. (Washington, D.C.: U.S. Government Printing Office, 1975).

explain why the stock market was attractive to increasing numbers of investors throughout the decade.

The Automobile

In 1920, 26 percent of households owned automobiles; by 1930, that percentage had risen to 60 percent. Rapid growth in automobile production was probably the single most important factor in the 1920s expansion. The direct and indirect effects of the widespread use of the auto had an enormous impact on the U.S. economy of that decade. The industry performed the same kind of leading-sector role that railroad construction had played from 1865 to 1893. As in the 1865–1893 period, one could see the 1920s period in terms of Hirschman's unbalanced growth concept with forward linkages (the creation of the service station industry and increased road building) and backward linkages (stimulus to the industries that provide the materials used to construct cars, such as steel and rubber). Also, the Schumpeter innovation-imitation model suggests some useful ways to explore the role of the auto industry in the expansion of the 1920s.

Although the auto was first used around 1895, its period of greatest growth was the 1920s. In 1921, 1.5 million passenger cars were produced and about 10.5 million motor vehicles were registered in the United States. By 1929, these figures had increased 300 percent, to 4.5 million passenger cars produced and 26.7 million registered motor vehicles, 23 million of which were passenger cars. In 1929, almost 13 percent of the value of all manufactures was automobiles, and over 7 percent of all manufacturing sector wage earners were employed in making cars.

The growth in the number of cars produced obviously had a major direct impact on the U.S. economy, reflected in total demand and thus in aggregate income. It also had substantial impact on the output of industries that provided materials to build the cars. It was the largest single source of demand for many industries—for example, plate glass and rubber—and used 15 percent of the nation's total steel production. In petroleum refining, it caused the substantial shift to gasoline production that revolutionized the industry.

This rapid increase in consumer demand and thus in induced investment caused high levels of demand for plant and equipment, not only in the auto industry but also in those industries that provided the materials to construct the cars. As the rate of growth in consumer demand increased, there was additional need for plant and equipment (induced investment) to meet the increased demand.

While it is certain that increased real income during the 1920s brought about increased demand, and improvements in the auto made the car even more attractive, the following two factors seemed most responsible for the expansion in demand. The first was an innovative method of financing auto purchases. The introduction and subsequent widespread use of time-payment plans or installment credit made the sale of cars to those of only moderate income possible, since it was difficult for such consumers to save the full purchase price. By 1925, over 68 percent of the dollar purchase amount of new cars was "on time," although this dropped to about 58 percent by 1928. The second factor was helped by the first and also by decreases in price as productivity increased and competition remained strong; that factor was the large **primary demand** that existed in the early 1920s because many people had not yet bought their first car. Although automobile output increased by a total of 19 percent in 1929, most of the increase was at the beginning of the year; output began to fall by the middle of the year, several months before the stock market crash. As Stanley Lebergott (16) has observed, this was a "period of two markets, the mass market and the stock market."

It is hard to estimate the total impact of the auto industry on the American economy. Its growth encouraged state and local governments to expand road construction, and even the federal government began to lay plans for a national network of interstate highways. It created a new service industry, the retailing of gasoline. As more families took to four wheels, the automobile encouraged movement away from urban areas to the suburbs and the establishment of the commuting life.

An effect of the auto that even now has not been adequately assessed is its impact on the competitiveness of the economy. Especially in its retailing activities, these effects appear to have substantially lessened monopolistic and oligopolistic pricing. By providing increasing numbers of consumers with alternatives to monopolistic prices, the automobile, from the early 1920s, may have contributed to increasing competition and downward pressure on prices. As Stanley Lebergott (16) has observed, "Leland and Ford and Durrant intensified business competition, and thereby productivity, more than all the free market economists and antitrust legislators in history."

Autos and the trucks competed seriously for passenger and freight demand with the railroads, a factor that contributed to the problems of the already troubled railway industry. Automobile use also restricted trolley systems to city cores; many were abandoned or torn up in this period.

Other Durable Goods Industries

A number of other durable goods industries also had surges of growth in the 1920s. These industries, including radios, refrigerators, washing machines, and other electrical appliances, experienced increased demand for the finished products, causing increases in induced investment and a positive accelerator effect as plant and equipment expanded to provide additional capacity. Furthermore, as these products increased in quantity, the rising demand for the electricity needed for their use caused construction of new and expanded electrical power facilities. Similarly, greater use of radios increased the demand for radio stations. Estimates of the extent of this increase in demand are startling. According to Lebergott (16), the percent of households with electricity almost doubled (from 35 to 68 percent) between 1920 and 1930. Similarly, the percent with washing machines tripled from 8 to 24 percent in that period. Households with inside flush toilets more than doubled (from 20 to 51 percent) during the decade.

These increased demands stemmed from rising real income or purchasing power; lower prices for electricity, reflecting its more efficient production; and decreases in the share of total expenditures for food because food prices remained low after the 1921 depression. Of equal importance was the application of consumer installment credit, developed for autos but also used for other consumer durables. There are no estimates of the distribution between autos and other consumer durables of total consumer credit. Total installment credit grew from $4.7 billion in 1925, to an estimated $7.1 billion in 1929. By 1929, it is estimated that 15 percent of all consumer purchases of nonfood items was on credit.

The rapid rise in consumer credit obviously stimulated demand by making possible a higher level of consumption. But mortgaging future income introduced an additional element of instability into business activity. As long as incomes were climbing and people were optimistic, the process of expansion could continue. But if incomes leveled off or declined or if people became insecure about their economic future, retrenchment in consumer purchases would more readily take place,

Figure 16.1. A "Modern" Kitchen of the 1920s. (Photo from the National Archives)

because people had to pay off debts already accumulated, and debt repayment reduced funds available for new consumption.

The Construction Industry

During World War I, resources were channeled from civilian into military production at the same time that incomes and profits remained high. Personal and business savings substantially increased in the process. After the war, families and businesses rushed to make up the postponed demand for residential housing and business construction. The growing use of cars increased the demand for roads, and construction of roads at all three government levels increased. Thus demand for construction survived the depression of 1921 and accelerated during the 1920s.

Building construction in 120 cities increased by almost 300 percent between 1919 and 1925. In 1926, total construction peaked at $12.6 billion, of which $5.4 billion was residential. Government construction of roads increased steadily throughout the 1920s, and by 1929 road construction constituted 8 percent of industry total. Residential construction peaked in dollar value in 1926, and then began to fall. Business construction took up the slack for a while, but by the end of 1927, it too began to fall.

Productivity Gains

So far we have seen that the U.S. economic expansion from 1922 to 1929 was supported by high levels of demand for consumer goods, especially consumer durables; by high levels of demand for investment; and by construction in all three categories: residential, business, and government (primarily road building). Perhaps equally important was the sustained growth in productivity, both labor productivity (output per unit of labor) and capital productivity (output per unit of capital).

Some rough indicators of this rise in productivity are represented in the following data. The index of manufacturing production rose from 100 in 1921 to 188 in 1929; it was 124 in 1920. Real gross national product per capita rose from $375 (in 1913 dollars) in 1921 to $500 in 1929. Real gross product per man-hour rose 28 percent from 1920 to 1929. Productivity of labor increased about 2.2 percent per year from 1919 to 1929. In manufacturing, it rose at the astonishing rate of 5.6 percent per year during that period.

As Joseph Schumpeter (31) observed in 1946, the major features of the 1920s are explained by a rapid growth in output and an "unparalleled development in industrial efficiency."

Four main developments brought about these productivity gains, especially as they related to manufacturing. The first was the final general adaptation of electricity to production processes. The use of electric power spread widely as refinements were made in electricity-generating steam turbine engines and electric motors. The second factor was the widespread application of the concepts of assembly-line and mass production techniques. Automatic feeding devices, conveying systems, and more widespread mechanization, especially that powered by electricity, increased productivity, not only in the automobile industry, but also in such industries as glass, rubber tires and tubes, and cigarette making. The third factor was the accelerating application of science to production processes. This was especially true in the chemical industry; for example, in rayon production and in the production of gasoline. Many larger-scale firms established special research divisions where the application of scientific knowledge to production was systematically explored. Finally, the 1920s witnessed a continuing application of Frederick Taylor's theories of scientific management; through new management techniques, many producers obtained increases in output without expanding plant size.

Lessons learned during wartime mobilization about how to expand production without expanding plant size were applied. The drastic reduction of immigration due to the war and the restrictive immigration laws passed during the early 1920s gave added incentive to increase labor productivity, especially that of less skilled labor.

These factors were all interrelated; changes in one area created opportunities for improvements in productivity in others. For example, refinements in the generation and use of electricity in electric motors greatly facilitated the spread of assembly-line techniques. This, in turn, encouraged the development of new management techniques, while expanding consumer demand made it possible to sell the increased output that resulted. As output and market sizes grew, specialization could be extended by the establishment of special divisions for production, accounting, and sales.

Who benefited from this increased productivity? The answer to this question could help explain the expansion of the 1920s and perhaps the subsequent depression of the 1930s. The benefits of increased productivity may go to consumers, to wage earners, or to business firms. They may go to consumers, for example, via a decrease in prices, to wage earners via increases in real wages, and to business firms via an increase in their rate of profit.

The consumer price index fell only slightly between 1921 and 1929; thus the gains from increased productivity did not go primarily to consumers. We know that average real income of employees increased by about 30 percent in the 1920s, but not all of this can be attributed to passing on productivity gains to employees through higher wages. High average levels of employment after 1921, the availability of overtime, and the slight fall in prices, as well as higher productivity, contributed as well to higher real income. When George Soule (32) compared this 30 percent increase in real income to the 40 percent increase in productivity from 1919 to 1928, he concluded, "Business did not fully share its productivity gains with wage earners and consumers by a combination of wage increases and price reduction."

These apparently increasing profit margins during the expansion of the 1920s tended to keep investment levels high. Firms experiencing high and expanding total profits and profit margins were very optimistic about the prospects of continued profits and thus inclined to continue their high levels of investment. This is not, however, to advance the frequently stated argument that "underconsumption" arising from an income stream redistributed against households was responsible for the ultimate end of the decade-long prosperity. The evidence we have shown of rapidly rising ownership of consumer goods, together with the expansion of housing, is simply inconsistent with the underconsumption argument. Industries producing consumer goods grew just as strongly in the period from 1925 to 1929 as they had in the preceding five years.

FALTERING SECTORS IN A GROWING ECONOMY

But not all sectors of the economy experienced the benefits of the prosperity decade. A number of significant sectors in fact experienced economic difficulties. These included agriculture, coal mining, textiles, (especially in New England), and the railway industry. In addition, situations were developing in the area of international economic relationships that were to intensify the 1930s contraction.

A Faltering Agriculture

From 1897 to 1920, American agriculture, as we have seen, experienced prosperity. The depression of 1921 caused this prosperity to collapse, and agriculture was unable to recover to predepression conditions. The Great Depression of the 1930s dealt U.S. agriculture a further staggering blow. While much of the rest of the economy was celebrating the Roaring Twenties, agriculture was going through a dress rehearsal for the Great Depression of the 1930s.

One measure of this distress is found in the concept of **parity.** Parity is a measure developed by the U.S. Department of Agriculture to express the purchasing power of farm products. It compares an index of farm prices to an index of the prices of what farmers buy. In 1921, with the period 1910–1914 equal to 100, the parity index fell to 80; in other words, each dollar of agricultural output in 1921 only brought 80 percent of what it did in 1910–1914. At no time in the 1920s did parity reach 100; it touched a high point of 95 in 1925 (see line 11 in Table 16.2). Parity has been criticized, however, as the sole measure of relative purchasing power between the agricultural and nonagricultural sectors. Relative purchasing power also depends on relative changes in technology, and thus changes in productivity.

The problem was in part due to a greater fall in farm prices in 1921 than in nonfarm prices. Farm prices fell from an index of 83 in 1920 to 49 in 1921. Prices of what farmers consumed fell from 71 to 51, and prices of items they used for production fell from 68 to 45 (see Table 16.2).

Agriculture had expanded output during the war, partly because of the high levels of exports. After the war, the value of these exports sharply declined. From July 1919 to July 1920, agricultural exports were $3.8 billion. Exports fell to $1.9 billion during the period from July 1921 to July 1922; the annual value of exports remained below the 1920 figure all through the decade. A number of factors contributed to this collapse, including a shortage of foreign exchange in Europe, European countries' protection of their own agricultural sectors, the renewal of worldwide exports in competition with the United States, and expanded U.S. capacity left from the high levels of war demand. Although U.S. domestic demand did increase in the 1920s because of higher incomes, that increase was not enough to offset declining exports.

Agricultural losses were further emphasized by the decline in the value of farm property. Since farmers tended to put their savings into their land, this decline was especially burdensome. The value of agricultural property fell from $78 billion in 1920 to $56 billion in 1927. In 1921, the value of agricultural property was 57 percent of its 1910–1914 value. The value had dropped to 35 percent by 1928, which, if computed on a constant purchasing power basis, was an additional 20 percent below the prewar figure. Moreover, the index of gross farm income (1910–1914 = 100) for 1920 was 209 and fell all the way to 39 in 1921. While it rose again, it was still only 82 in 1929.

Table 16.2. Important Statistics of the 1920s.

	1920	1921	1922	1923	1924	1925	1926	1927	1928	1929
1. Current GNP (in billions of $)	91.5	69.5	74.1	85.1	84.7	93.1	97.0	94.9	97.0	103.1
2. Percent unemployment of civilian labor force	5.2	11.7	6.7	2.4	5.0	3.2	1.9	3.3	4.2	3.2
3. Consumer price index (1967 = 100)	60.0	53.6	50.2	51.1	51.2	52.5	53.0	52.0	51.3	51.3
4. Production of passenger cars (in millions)	1.9	1.5	2.3	3.6	3.2	3.7	3.7	2.9	3.8	4.5
5. Registered motor vehicles (in millions)	9.2	10.5	12.3	15.1	17.6	20.1	22.2	23.3	24.7	26.7
6. Percent of the value of manufacturing in the auto industry										13
7. Percent of manufacturing wage earners in the auto industry										7
8. Consumer debt (in billions of $)	3.0	3.0	3.2	3.7	4.0	4.7	5.2	5.3	6.3	7.1
9. Value of new construction (in billions of $)	6.7	6.4	8.0	9.7	10.8	12.0	12.6	12.4	12.0	11.2
10. Index of manufacturing production (1921 = 100)	124	100	124	148	140	156	164	164	172	188
11. Agricultural parity (1910–1914 = 100)	99	80	87	89	89	95	91	88	91	92
12. Index of farm prices (1967 = 100)	83	49	52	56	56	61	51	55	58	58
13. Index of prices of what farmers consume (1967 = 100)	71	51	48	48	48	50	49	48	48	48
14. Index of prices of what farmers buy for production (1967 = 100)	68	45	44	48	49	51	49	49	52	51
15. Value of agricultural exports (in billions of $)	3.9	2.6	1.9	1.8	1.9	2.3	1.9	1.9	1.8	1.8
16. Value of farm property (in billions of $)	78.4	71.4	62.0	60.1	58.5	57.4	57.4	56.4	56.7	57.7

17. Gross farm income (1910–1914 = 100)	209	139	146	160	169	180	174	174	189	182
18. Agricultural bankruptcy rate as percent of all farms	8.7				18	18	18			9
19. Farm tenancy as percent of all farms	38									42
20. Sales of bituminous coal (in millions of short tons)	569	416	422	565	484	520	573	518	501	535
21. Employment in bituminous coal mining (in thousands)	639	664	688	705	620	588	594	594	522	503
22. Capital investment in railroads (in billions of $)	19.8	20.3	20.6	21.4	22.2	23.2	23.8	24.5	24.9	25.5
23. Railroad passenger revenue (in billions of $)	1.3	1.2	1.1	1.2	1.1	1.1	1.0	1.0	.9	.9
24. Railroad freight revenue (in billions of $)	4.4	4.0	4.1	4.7	4.4	4.6	4.9	4.7	4.8	4.9
25. Railroad employment (in millions)	2.0	1.7	1.7	1.9	1.8	1.8	1.8	1.8	1.7	1.7
26. Value of textile production (in billions of $)				3.9						3.6
27. Index of physical output of textiles (1929 = 100)		64		83		86		92		100
28. Members of organized labor (in millions)	5.0	4.8	4.0	3.6	3.5	3.5	3.5	3.5	3.5	3.5

SOURCE: U.S. Department of Commerce, Bureau of the Census, *Historical Statistics of the United States, Colonial Times to 1970* (Washington, D.C.: U.S. Government Printing Office, 1975).

But the major calamity resulted from the high level of farm mortgages accumulated during the war through efforts by farmers to obtain more land for expansion. With the fall in prices in 1921, farmers had to produce more in order to meet payments on the high mortgages. Many were unable to do so; as a result, the bankruptcy rate increased from 1.7 percent of all farms in 1920 to almost 18 percent in 1924–1926, declining afterward to almost 9 percent in 1929 (see Table 16.2).

Farm tenancy increased as farmers forced from ownership took to renting land in order to continue farming. Tenancy, from being the traditional method for farmers to climb the ladder to farm ownership, became the ladder down which increasing numbers descended to become farm laborers and then moved out of agriculture. Farm tenancy increased from 38 percent of all farms in 1920 to 42 percent in 1930 (see Table 16.2).

As in manufacturing, farmers strove to increase their productivity to counter the lower, post-1920 prices. During the 1920s, the move to internal combustion machines, especially tractors and more efficient combines, continued. Productivity increased by about 26 percent for the decade. The more efficient farmers gained, but the high level of competition and the release of even more acres to output as the shift from horses continued both tended to restrain a general recovery from low prices.

As in the Populist revolt of the 1890s, farmers turned to the government for help. The major piece of farm legislation in the 1920s was the Agricultural Marketing Act of 1929. After vetoing, for the second time, the McNarey-Haugen bill (an effort to establish a two-price system—a higher domestic price and a lower foreign price for agricultural products), President Hoover agreed to the formation of the Federal Farm Board with an appropriation of half a billion dollars. The board would loan to cooperatives so that they could buy and store surplus agricultural products to restrict supply and raise prices. During periods of shortages, these supplies could be sold and prices could be stabilized.

The story of the Farm Board's failure is best told in the next chapter. Though farm intervention programs since World War II cast doubt on it, the board might have been successful in more normal times. But the advent of the depression of the 1930s, with its falling agricultural prices, plus the inability of the board to control agricultural production doomed this effort at controlling the agricultural market. By mid-1932, the Federal Farm Board had lost $354 million, without stemming the further collapse of the agricultural economy.

Coal Mining

Another industry that failed to share the blessings of prosperity was coal mining, especially bituminous or soft coal. Bituminous coal sales in 1920 reached 569 million short tons. Except for 1926, though, sales were below the 1920 figure throughout the 1920s. Prices fell from $3.75 a short ton in 1920 to $1.78 in 1929. Employment dropped from 639,000 in 1920 to 502,800 in 1929. Jobs shrank from 2.6 percent of the national total in 1920 to 1.2 percent in 1929.

The reasons for this disastrous record were many. During the war, demand was high and supplies relatively short. Substantial expansion occurred. With the 1921 collapse, however, the industry, because of its highly competitive nature based on ease of entry (the low cost of opening a mine) and because there were many small-scale individual firms, could not easily reduce output. Thus the industry suffered from chronic oversupply. Although competition from electricity and oil was beginning to be felt, coal was still the country's primary source of energy. But demand was inelastic; the already low prices and the relatively fixed relationship between output and the technical requirements for coal reduced any stimulating effects of falling prices.

A major problem was the slow and painful process of moving resources out of coal mining. The less efficient mines could be left idle, providing standby capacity for peak periods of demand, but the miners themselves were slow to move out of mining because they lacked local employment alternatives and were tremendously reluctant to leave localities they had lived in for generations. This, of course, is often a problem with declining industries.

The Railroads

The relative position of the railroads had already begun to decline with the decrease in total track mileage beginning in 1916. The statistical evidence of the 1920s clearly shows further weakening. While capital investments rose substantially, from $19.8 billion in 1920 to $25.5 billion in 1929, passenger revenue declined from $1.3 billion to $0.9 billion (passenger miles dropped from 47 million in 1920 to 34 million in 1927), and freight revenue rose barely enough to offset the decline in passenger revenue. High investment, with its accompanying increases in productivity, caused a decline in employment from 2 million in 1920 to 1.7 million in 1929.

Two reasons are generally given for this stagnation and relative decline in the economic position of the railroads. Competition from new modes of transportation began to make serious inroads into demand for railroad services. The explosion in the number of automobiles and trucks, coupled with a substantial increase in roads, reduced railway passenger demand and restricted the growth in freight revenues. Some people charge that this competition was unfair, in that the government subsidized autos and trucks through the construction of roads, which were not directly paid for by the road users. But the same government subsidy charge could have been made against railroads, in the 1800s, by canal owners. Highway user taxes, in the form of tolls and gasoline taxes, did not come into real use until after the 1920s.

Another major reason that has been advanced by many for the railroads' decline is the failure of the Interstate Commerce Commission to imaginatively and efficiently regulate railroads so as to maintain their competitive position. The Hoogenbooms (11), in their book *A History of the ICC,* maintain that the ICC was a very significant factor in the stagnation of railroads in the 1920s.

The Transportation Act of 1920, the Esch-Cummins Act, made major revisions in the power of the ICC and changed its basic objective as well. The act mandated that the Commission set rates so as to give a "fair return upon the aggregate value of the railroad property"; thus the Commission's responsibility was shifted from protecting the public from railroad discrimination to seeing that the railroads got a "fair return" on their investment.

Furthermore, it was recognized that increased efficiency was needed to assure such a fair return. The act required that the Commission work out and implement a national plan to combine the railroads into from 20 to 35 railway networks. Further, the act included a recapture clause. Half of any road's net income over 6 percent would be turned into a fund that could be used for loans to weaker roads. One must wonder about the economic logic of the recapture clause since it tended to penalize efficiency and reward inefficiency.

The Commission failed in many significant ways to carry out the major provisions of the act. Because of its own reluctance to implement the recapture clause, and under pressure from the stronger railroads, it asked Congress in 1930 to eliminate the recapture clause provision. Also, it was not until the end of 1929, almost ten years after the act was passed, that the Commission formulated a tentative scheme for consolidating railroads into 21 networks. Even then, very few consolidations, none of them significant, were put through. In 1940, Congress finally relieved the Commission of this responsibility.

The Hoogenbooms conclude that the timidity of the commissioners, the lack of strong leadership, the growing bureaucratic power of the ICC staff, and the complex and conflicting pressures of railroads and shippers caused the commission's failure to act effectively. It took the easy way out and opted for the maintenance of the status quo at a time when change was essential to improve or even to maintain the railroads' competitive position.

New England Textiles

The textile industry also did not share in the prosperity of the 1920s. The value of output of both cotton and woolen textiles declined from its peak in 1923 of $3.9 billion to $3.6 billion in 1929. This decline was due solely to falling prices, because the index of physical output increased from 64 in 1921 to 100 in 1929. Thus increases in productivity occurred as better machines and methods were introduced. Also, there was an increase in the work week, so that the greater output was achieved with a 2 percent reduction of the labor force.

Like agriculture and coal mining, the textile industry was an old, established industry that was characterized by intense competition. Its age of rapid growth had long passed. Demand for textiles was probably price and income inelastic (clothing was a necessity). The effects, then, of changes in supply would more strongly affect prices than quantity (see Figure 16.2). In addition, demand declined because of changes in fashions that substantially reduced the amount of cloth per dress.

In Figure 16.2, demand is relatively inelastic. Where supply increases from S_0 to S_1, price falls from $0B$ to $0A$. This fall in price is much larger than the increase in quantity that takes place from C to E.

Compounding the problem of general stagnation was the marked shift of textile production into the noncoal Appalachian South. Textile mills were created in North Carolina, Virginia, and Georgia in response to their cheaper labor costs, both as to wages and regulation of hours of work. Most of the 39 percent increase in wage earners in that region in the 1920s was due to textile employment. Only the

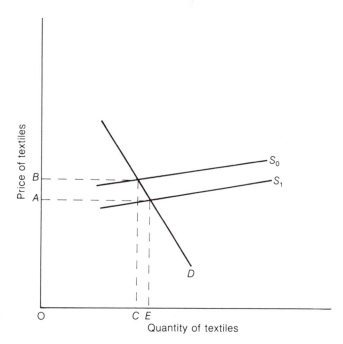

Figure 16-2. Elasticity and
Quantity Demanded.

northern mills with exceptionally good management, or those with special advantages, escaped the effects of the move south.

The United States as a World Creditor

Fundamental changes had occurred during the war and as a result of the Peace Treaty of 1919. The shift of the United States from a net debtor to a net creditor position, and the large amounts of the war debts owed the United States plus the impossibly high levels of reparations to several countries demanded from a defeated Germany, required fundamental changes in the international economy. The adjustments made in financing international economic transactions during the 1920s seemed, on the surface, to keep international activity stable; the yearly reparations payments by Germany were scaled down, especially after the Dawes Plan of 1924, but by the end of the decade, it was apparent that this stability could easily be shaken.

Table 16.3 shows that for 1919 private net assets (what U.S. residents were owed minus what U.S. residents owed others) were almost $3 billion in the United States' favor. This was in addition to the $9.6 billion in net debt owed to the U.S. government. The net government debt was primarily war debts owed by the Allies. At the same time, the Allies (excluding the United States) demanded reparation payments from Germany. The Reparations Commission in 1921 set these payments at $375 million a year from 1921 to 1925 and afterward at $900 million

Table 16.3.   America's International Balance Sheet (billions of dollars).

	1914	1919	1929
Assets (private account)			
Securities	.9	2.6	7.9
Direct investments	2.6	3.9	7.6
Short-term credits	—	.5	1.6
Total	3.5	7.0	17.1
Liabilities			
Securities	5.4	1.6	4.3
Direct investments	1.3	.9	1.4
Sequestrated properties and securities	—	.7	.2
Short-term credits	.5	.8	3.1
Total	7.2	4.0	9.0
Net assets privately held	−3.7	3.0	8.1
Intergovernmental debts			
To U.S. government	—	10.0	11.7
By U.S. government	—	.4	—
Net assets on government account		9.6	11.7
Total net assets on private and government account	−3.7	12.6	19.8

SOURCE: Cleona Lewis, *America's Stake in International Investments.* (Washington, D.C.: Brookings Institution). 1938, pp. 447–450.

a year. If these debts were to be repaid, a profound change would have to take place in international economic relations.

One way in which these loans might have been paid back was for the debtor countries to increase their exports of goods and services to the creditor country (here, the United States). In effect, then, the United States would have needed to increase imports of goods and services from its former allies in order for the latter to be able to pay off their war debts. Instead, the United States increased its already high tariffs. The Emergency Tariff of 1921 and the Fordney-McCumber Tariff Act of 1922 pushed tariffs to all-time highs on a wide variety of imports. The United States did not decrease its exports to reduce this drain of European foreign exchange. The U.S. invisible items account continued to show a credit balance, further drawing foreign exchange from Europe as the flow of dividends, profits, and interest from U.S. foreign investment more than offset U.S. tourist expenditures in Europe. The Allies followed a similar policy with Germany, and as a result, that nation could not generate a large enough surplus to meet its reparation payments in 1922.

Another way in which these war debts and reparations might have been dealt with was to cancel them. England perceived the seriousness of the international money problems by 1921, and it was willing to cancel both reparations from Germany and the substantial debt owed to England by the other European Allies if, in turn, the United States would cancel the war debts owed by England to it. Instead, the U.S. government demanded payment. A more sensible arrangement was made under the Dawes Plan in 1924. But this happened only after Germany had defaulted on reparations, France had taken over the industrial Ruhr area in Germany, and Germany's hyperinflation in 1922–1923 had made its assets worthless in fixed money values.

As a result of the Dawes Plan, reparations payments were scaled down. Further negotiations between the former Allies and the United States reduced the interest rate on war debts from 5 to 3 percent. In effect, they reduced, for example, the debt by 30 percent for England and over 80 percent for Italy. But war debt and reparation payments still had to be made. In addition to government debt relations, the private net credit position of the United States required payments of interest, profit, and dividends that could not be made while the United States remained in a credit position in the balance of payments merchandise account.

The answer was largely found through foreign investment by the United States. The private net creditor position increased from the $3 billion position in 1919 to over $8 billion in 1929 (see Table 16.3). Although direct investment increased from $3.9 to $7.6 billion, securities bought by Americans increased even more—from $2.6 to $7.9 billion. Private investment, mostly in Germany and, because of the multilateral nature of international trade, in Latin America, provided the foreign exchange for Germany to pay reparations to the European Allies, which in turn provided them with the exchange to pay the U.S. government on their war debts. In effect, then, there was no net reduction of international debts with the United States but rather a shift from government debt relationships to private investments and to private means of international payments.

These creditor-debtor relationships would not have threatened stability so much if they had resulted in increased productive facilities that could provide the surplus to repay the investments. But George Soule (32) concludes that many of the securities investments "were not used for productive purposes or were made to countries that would have difficulty in making repayments if the flow of new capital would stop, since they could not be expected to develop an export surplus. Germany was in this category." Furthermore, Soule charges that American investment companies were more interested in the profits from floating these loans than in their repayment.

Direct investment had a better record in regard to the security of the investments. Most of the direct investments were undertaken by the larger corporations with international business relations and were used to provide sources of raw materials and semifinished goods for U.S. production or to jump the tariff walls of many countries. These investments showed ample evidence of potential profitability. Soule concludes, however, that a sizable minority even of direct investments were of doubtful profitability.

In brief, the problem caused by the war debts and reparations repayments might have been resolved either by cancellation or by increases in exports from the debtor countries to the creditor countries. Neither alternative was allowed to operate to the point of resolving the questions with stability. Instead, the U.S. government encouraged increases in foreign investment by its citizens to provide the foreign exchange needed. Some of this investment, especially in securities, had poor prospects of being repaid. A circular pattern was created as private investment from the United States provided the foreign exchange for the European Allies to pay war debts to the U.S. government. Rather than reducing the overall levels of debt, government debt relationships were converted into private debt. The process could only continue if private U.S. investors continued their foreign investment at ever-increasing rates to cover war debt and reparations repayments plus the servicing of a growing private investment. But if private U.S. foreign investment decreased, the process would not only collapse but would also seriously impair private international means of payments.

Investments in foreign securities began to fall by the middle of 1928, as the unprofitability of many of the investments became apparent and as U.S. corporate securities increased in price on Wall Street. The decrease was hidden by increases in foreign direct investment. With the contraction in June 1929 and the stock market crash in the following October, U.S. foreign investments declined sharply, as did imports from Europe. Not only did the circular system of capital movements evaporate, but the international means of private payments were also seriously impaired.

There are some parallels between the "debt crisis" of the 1920s and the debt crisis of the 1980s. Again, private investors are being urged to continue loans that are based retrospectively on unprofitable activities. Again, debtor nations are unable to earn the export income to service the debt, much less repay it. Occasionally, it appears, history does indeed repeat itself!

THE DECLINE OF ORGANIZED LABOR

Labor union success since the founding of the American Federation of Labor (AFL) in 1886, at least in terms of the number of union members, was impressive up to 1920. Although this increase in union members had proceeded in fits and starts, numbers rose from 0.3 million in 1870–1872 to 0.9 million in 1900, to a high point of 5 million in 1920, as estimated by Leo Wolman(35). Of these 5 million, about 4 million were members of the American Federation of Labor.

With the onset of the 1920s, the upward trend was sharply reversed. By 1929, total union membership had declined to 3.5 million, with only 3 million in the AFL. While most of this drop came early in the decade—by 1923, only 3.6 million members remained in unions—there was hardly a year in the 1920s that did not see a decline in union membership.

The largest gains in union membership had occurred during the war, as full employment and government production planning created a favorable environment for union expansion. After the war, these industries saw the largest contraction in union membership as output and employment fell. But traditional strongholds of unionization also had trouble maintaining membership.

The United Mine Workers were especially hard hit as stagnant demand, overproduction, and strong antiunion activity by employers reduced UMW membership. The Textile Union was also hard hit, as productive capacity moved from the Northeast, a stronghold of unionism, to the Southeast, where public sentiment against unions was very strong.

There were a number of reasons for this decline. One of the more important was the unsympathetic and basically antiunion position of the U.S. courts in general and the U.S. Supreme Court in particular. When the Republicans returned to power with the election of President Harding in 1920, the Senate confirmed former president Taft as chief justice of the Supreme Court. Taft was a strong opponent of unions, and his leadership intensified the antiunion attitude of the Court in the 1920s. Even before 1920, however, a number of decisions adverse to unions had been made. Two examples of substantial importance were the Danbury Hat case of 1908 and *Hitchman Coal and Coke v. Mitchell* in 1917. In the first case, the Supreme Court ruled that the individual members of the union were liable without limit for monetary damages resulting from the actions of their union officials. In the Hitchman case, the Supreme Court enjoined the United Mine Workers from attempting to organize workers who had signed a "yellow-dog contract" (a pledge by the workers not to join a union).

The Taft Court ruled consistently against unions in the 1920s. Two areas of special difficulty for unions were the use of the injunction to abridge union activities and the Court's interpretations and use of antitrust legislation to condemn as illegal many actions of unions. Irving Bernstein (1) in *The Lean Years* points out that "At the end of the twenties the leading students of labor law were in accord that the marriage of the labor injunction with the yellow-dog contract was a peril to the survival of trade unionism in the United States." In the decade of the 1920s, 921 injunctions limiting union activities were issued by federal and state courts, half of the total injunctions of that kind issued between 1845 and 1930. By 1929, a union had to presume that an injunction would be issued if it called a strike.

Despite the seeming exemption of unions from antitrust legislation in the Clayton Act of 1914, the Taft Court in the 1920s used the Sherman Act of 1890 to judge such actions as strikes, picketing, and boycotts as illegal restraints of trade. Taft found that the Clayton Act only stated that unions in themselves were not a conspiracy; their *actions* could still be judged as conspiratorial. Besides restricting union activities, these rulings laid unions open to monetary damages and the possibility of criminal prosecution. Bernstein (1) summarized his conclusion about the courts in the 1920s thus: "The law recognized the equal freedom of the employers to destroy labor organizations and to deny the rights of employees to join trade unions."

Another important factor in the decline of labor unionism in the 1920s was the antiunion activities of employers. One strong weapon, of course, was the yellow-dog contract. Another was the use of the **company union,** an organization only for employees of the particular firm that was dominated by company officials. The trade unions' attitude toward these organizations is mirrored in the words of an old union song: "The Hatmakers union is a no-good union. It's a company union for the boss."

The spread of welfare capitalism in the 1920s, including efforts to get employees to buy stock in the firms where they worked, undermined union loyalty and enhanced company loyalty. Major companies had programs providing full medical care, educational projects, encouragement to workers to own their own homes, stock sharing, and, especially, forms of group insurance and pensions. Although humanitarian motives were involved, Scheiber and his associates (30) conclude that the main motivations were antiunion.

Equally important in weakening unions in the 1920s was the severe antiunion feeling among the general public. The Bolshevik Revolution, which occurred in Russia in 1917, and other revolutions and revolts in Europe in 1919, especially in Germany and Hungary, created in the United States an atmosphere of fear of the "Red Menace." The wave of strikes in 1919 and 1920 convinced many that unions were somehow un-American. These strikes, generally made to resist declines in wages, often failed. For example, the Railroad Strike of 1919, the Steel Strike of 1919, and the coal miners' strike of 1920 all terminated unfavorably for the unions. In 1919, there were nine major industrial strikes, and more than 4 million workers were on strike.

Adding to these problems were some basic flaws in the union camp itself. The craft orientation of the AFL continued to limit the ability of organized labor to unionize the major mass production industries such as steel, autos, and petroleum refining. In addition, Samuel Gompers, an organizational genius who had dominated the AFL since its founding in 1886, died in the early 1920s. The new leadership was far less competent and appeared cautious for the trying conditions facing labor unions in the 1920s.

THE BEGINNING OF THE END

A detailed analysis of the causes and the sequence of events of the Great Depression of the 1930s must await the next chapter. But the foundations of that human and social catastrophe started in 1929. The two main supports of the 1920s expansion—construction and manufacturing, especially of that major consumer durable, automobiles—were contracting output by June 1929. Foreign investment also was contracting in 1929.

The value of construction reached its high point, over $17 billion, in 1928, and declined to a little over $16 billion in 1929. George Soule (32) comments about the auto industry: "The final burst of prosperity in 1929 brought a gain of 19 percent, but output began to fall off several months before the stock market crash. The index of industrial production reached a high of 188 (1913 = 100) in June of 1929 and began to fall."

The signs were there. The sustained investment that accumulated productive capital from 1923 to 1929 was now approaching a point of producing more than consumers would buy. The weakening of output in construction, autos, and manufacturing in general was added to the near-decade-long weaknesses in coal mining, agriculture, textiles, and railroads. Some significant contraction was imminent. But no one seemed to notice. A wave of speculative expansion on the stock exchanges maintained optimism and diverted attention from the growing signs of economic difficulty.

Wall Street, 1929

The 1920s are an excellent example of speculative tendencies in the American people. The decade opened with speculation in normal business inventories. That bubble broke when prices fell with the depression of 1920–1921. In 1925, there was the Florida land speculation, as people bought land in Florida at rapidly increasing prices. Here, too, values collapsed in the end, and many lost their investments. In late 1928 through October 1929, broad sections of stocks listed on the New York Stock Exchange increased rapidly in price. On October 24, 1929, these prices collapsed, and the great stock market crash of 1929 entered history.

Figure 16.3. Wall Street of the 1920s. Photo from the National Archives)

Many trace the origins of the boom in stock prices to the Federal Reserve's efforts to support the faltering English pound in 1928 by reducing interest rates in the United States. These lower interest rates and the greater availability of credit increased the demand for stocks on the call market of the stock exchanges; that is, where stocks were purchased on margin, or through the borrowing of significant portions of their purchase price. This higher demand increased stock prices, and these rises in prices caused people to expand their demand in anticipation of even further price increases. Thus the process snowballed.

By September 1929, stocks had reached a very high price-earnings ratio. Also, the call rate for money borrowed to finance stock purchases rose sharply. Additionally, the premium for purchasing industrial stocks (over less risky municipal bonds) had fallen substantially. A contraction in the economy had already started with the decrease in construction in 1928 and the decrease in manufacturing in June of 1929.

The conjunction of these factors occurred on October 24. High stock prices could no longer be maintained and the market crumbled. The collapse was intensified because of the high proportion of securities purchased on margin, and, when prices collapsed, the selling of these securities to protect lenders.

Briefly, the stock market collapse intensified the already developing contraction in a number of ways. First, the stock market had always been an important measure of what the public thought was the state of the economy. Thus when stock prices rose in the first three quarters of 1929, people felt very optimistic. The gathering signs of a contraction were ignored, and consumption and investment demand were probably higher than would have existed without the stock market expansion. After the crash and the collapse of stock prices, the public became discouraged about prospects for high levels of economic activity. This pessimism probably caused lower levels of consumption and investment.

Also, the prime economic function of the stock exchanges was to facilitate the issuance of new stock to raise financial capital needed by corporations to expand productive capacity. With the collapse of stock prices, obtaining new financial capital became difficult and costly. No doubt this contributed to the decline in investment and added to the decrease in aggregate economic activity.

In addition, the crash dried up the flow of U.S. financial capital to Germany that had been funding the circular flow of reparations payments from Germany to the former Allies, that in turn flowed back to the United States as war debt repayments. If the circular flow had been confined to payments between governments, little economic damage would have resulted; but unfortunately the payments had been intertwined with private means of international payments, and these private payments were seriously impaired. The results weakened the international exchange system and decreased international trade, further decreasing worldwide demand and thus output, income, and employment.

Finally, the decline in stock prices reduced the financial wealth of stockholders. Being now "poorer," these investors tended to decrease their consumption.

CONCLUSION

Were the 1920s a period of prosperity built on a bed of quicksand, or were they a decade of new beginnings, a predecessor of the modern era that was to blossom after 1945 and the end of World War II? The question has not yet been resolved.

On the one hand, W. Elliot Brownlee, in *Dynamics of Ascent* (2), titles his chapter on the 1920s "The 1920s: A Glimpse of Modernity." He states:

> To understand the economy during the 1920s, we should view it, not as a sick decade, full of foreshadowings of the depression to follow, but as a period that bears a strong resemblance to the best years of the post–World War II era in its rising standards of living, sustained high employment, stable prices, and strong market for articles of mass consumption. Despite our retrospective awareness that a major depression was to follow, the prosperity was unprecedented and was sustained from 1922 through much of 1929, with only modest pauses in 1924 and 1927.

On the other hand, Scheiber, Vatter, and Faulkner, in *American Economic History* (30), title their chapter on the 1920s "The Great Illusion." They state:

> Not all economists of the era were willing to grant unreservedly that this decade was a period of prosperity. Prosperity, if such it was, was exceedingly uneven, for it did not include all sections or all groups. Coal mining, cotton manufacturing, shipbuilding, the shoe and leather business, the railroads, and particularly agriculture were stagnant or declining. The Middle Atlantic, East-North-Central, and Pacific states seemed prosperous; but New England, which suffered from the textile depression, and the South, the agricultural areas of the Middle West, and the mountain sections, which suffered from the virtual failure of farm output to grow, did not participate greatly in the economic boom. Even in the most prosperous of these years, there was considerable unemployment, due in part to technological improvements. Indeed, it is a striking fact that manufacturing employment was constant from 1919 to 1929, despite a strong rise in the index of manufacturing production.
>
> These were not the only sour notes in the paean of self-congratulatory praise. Some students were quick to point out that, notwithstanding the increase in profits, in wages, and in the consumption of consumers' goods, practically no progress was being made in solving the problems of unemployment or of economic and old-age security. Moreover, the move for gambling and speculation was a warning signal to the experienced economic navigator.

However, the debate should not be oversimplified as optimism versus pessimism. One must integrate both positions because both give insight into the economic nature of that decade and into the future—the Great Depression of the 1930s and also the expansion of the post-1945 period.

QUESTIONS

1. What factors expanded the economy from the end of World War I to the end of 1920?
2. What factors contributed to the depression of 1921? Did inventory speculation play a role?

3. Why did agricultural prices fall more than industrial prices during the depression of 1921?

4. As well as we can measure them, were general business conditions in the 1920s favorable or unfavorable?

5. What were the various ways in which expanded auto production and use affected the economy in the 1920s?

6. Explain the major factors that expanded the demand for consumer durables other than autos in the 1920s.

7. What factors contributed to the high levels of demand for construction during the 1920s?

8. How were the productivity gains of the 1920s distributed among business, labor, and consumers? Was this distribution favorable to the expansion of the 1920s? Why?

9. Why did agriculture fail to share in the general prosperity of the 1920s?

10. In your view, was the legislative relief given to agriculture in 1929 a wise move? Why or why not?

11. Why did coal mining fail to share in the general prosperity of the 1920s?

12. What were the factors that restricted the growth of output in the railroad industry in the 1920s? What was expected of the Transportation Act of 1920? Was it achieved? Why?

13. In what ways might reparation payments and war debts be paid off? What was the way chosen in the 1920s? Was this a wise method of payment? Why?

14. A number of factors contributed to the contraction in union membership in the 1920s. What were they?

15. In what ways did the stock market crash in October 1929 intensify the contraction of 1929?

16. Take either position, that of Brownlee or that of Scheiber, Vatter, and Faulkner, as to the essence of the 1920s, and defend it. May both positions be valid?

SUGGESTED READINGS

1. Bernstein, Irving. *The Lean Years: A History of the American Worker, 1920–1933.* Boston: Houghton Mifflin, 1960.

2. Brownlee, W. Elliott. *Dynamics of Ascent.* New York: Knopf, 1974. Esp. Chap. 12.

3. Chandler, Alfred D., Jr. *Strategy and Structure: Chapters in the History of American Industrial Enterprise.* Cambridge, Mass.: MIT Press, 1962.

4. Cochrane, Thomas C. *The American Business System, 1900–1955.* Cambridge, Mass.: Harvard University Press, 1965.

5. Feis, Herbert. *The Diplomacy of the Dollar, 1919–1932.* Baltimore: Johns Hopkins University Press, 1965.

6. Friedman, Milton, and Anna J. Schwartz. *A Monetary History of the United States, 1867–1960.* Princeton, N.J.: Princeton University Press, 1963.

7. Galbraith, John Kenneth. *The Great Crash.* Boston: Houghton Mifflin, 1955.

8. George, P. J., and E. H. Oksanen. "Saturation in the Automobile Market in the Late Twenties: Some Further Results." *Explorations in Economic History, 11* (Fall 1973).

9. Gordon, Robert A. *Economic Instability and Growth: The American Record.* New York: Harper and Row, 1974.

10. Holt, Charles. "Who Benefited from the Prosperity of the Twenties?" *Explorations in Economic History, 14* (July 1977).

11. Hoogenboom, Ari, and Oliver Hoogenboom. *A History of the ICC from Panacea to Palliative.* New York: Norton, 1976. Esp. Chap. 3.

12. Hughes, Jonathan. *American Economic History.* Glenview, Ill.: 2nd. ed. Scott, Foresman, 1987. Esp. Chap. 24.

13. Johnson, Thomas. "Postwar Optimism and the Rural Financial Crisis of the 1920s." *Explorations in Economic History, 11* (Winter 1973–1974).

14. Keller, Robert. "Factor Income Distribution in the United States During the 1920s: A Reexamination of Fact and Theory." *Journal of Economic History, 33* (March 1973).

15. Lampman, Robert. *The Share of Top Wealth Holders in National Wealth, 1922–1956.* Princeton, N.J.: Princeton University Press, 1967.

16. Lebergott, Stanley. *The Americans: An Economic Record.* New York: Norton, 1984.

17. Lebergott, Stanley. *The American Economy.* Princeton: Princeton University Press, 1976.

18. Leuchtenbury, W. E. *The Perils of Prosperity, 1914–1932.* Chicago: University of Chicago Press, 1958.

19. Lewis, Cleona. *America's Stake in International Investments.* Washington, D.C.: Brookings Institution, 1938.

20. Lewis, W. Arthur. *Economic Survey, 1919–1939.* London: Allen and Unwin, 1949.

21. Lorant, John H. "Technological Change in American Manufacturing During the 1920s." *Journal of Economic History, 27* (June 1967).

22. Mercer, Lloyd J., and W. Douglas Morgan. "Alternative Interpretations of Market Saturation: Evaluations for the Automobile Market in the Late Twenties." *Explorations in Economic History, 9* (Spring 1972).

23. Mercer, Lloyd, and W. Douglas Morgan. "Housing Surplus in the 1920s: Another Evaluation." *Explorations in Economic History, 10* (Spring 1973).

24. Perleman, Selig, and Philip Taft. *History of Labor in the United States, 1896–1932.* New York: Macmillan, 1935. Esp. Chaps. 37–44.

25. Pilgrim, John D. "The Upper Turning Point in 1920: A Reappraisal." *Explorations in Economic History, 11* (Spring 1979).

26. Potter, James. *The American Economy Between the World Wars.* New York: Macmillan, 1974.

27. Rae, John B. *The American Automobile: A Brief History.* Chicago: University of Chicago Press, 1965. Esp. Chaps. 6 and 7.

28. Roose, K. D. "The Production Ceiling and the Turning Point of 1920." *American Economic Review, 48* (June 1958).

29. Rothbard, Murry. *America's Great Depression.* Kansas City, Kan.: Sheed and Ward, 1972.

30. Scheiber, Harry N., Harold G. Vatter, and Harold A. Faulkner. *American Economic History.* New York: Harper and Row, 1976. Esp. Chap. 21.

31. Schumpeter, J. A. "The Decade of the Twenties." *American Economic Review,* supplement (May 1946).

32. Soule, George. *Prosperity Decade: From War to Depression, 1917–1929*. New York: Holt, Rinehart and Winston, 1947.

33. U.S. Department of Commerce, Bureau of the Census. *Historical Statistics of the United States, Colonial Times to 1970*. Washington, D.C.: U.S. Government Printing Office, 1975.

34. Williamson, Jeffrey, and Peter Lindert. *American Inequality: A Macroeconomic History*. New York: Academic Press, 1981.

35. Wolman, Leo. *The Growth of American Trade Unions, 1880–1923*. New York: National Bureau of Economic Research, 1924.

Chapter 17

THE GREAT DEPRESSION
OF THE 1930s

The end of the "prosperity decade" of the 1920s was the prelude to the unparalleled economic disaster of the 1930s. Never before in U.S. history had the economy suffered such a severe and prolonged depression. Never before had it taken so long to recover to former levels of output.

The causes of the depression as well as its severity and length remain subjects of great controversy. We shall survey both the facts and the controversies in this chapter.

THE DECLINE: A STATISTICAL OVERVIEW

The gross national product (value of all final goods and services produced annually) fell from a high of $104.4 billion in 1929 to a low of $55.6 billion in 1933 (Table 17.1). Even when the data are adjusted for the fall in prices, real output declined by about 25 percent (Table 17.2). It was not until 1937 (Table 17.2) that the economy recovered to its 1929 level of output. Unemployment rose from 3.2 percent of the labor force in 1929 to a high of almost 25 percent in 1933 (Table 17.3). In addition, almost another 25 percent of the labor force was only partially employed in 1933. Unemployment was still about 10 percent when the United States entered World War II on December 7, 1941.

Net private domestic investment, which is especially important in providing increases in capacity and therefore the ability to increase output, was particularly hard hit. In 1929, it stood at $8.3 billion (Table 17.1). By 1933, it had dropped to minus $5.6 billion. Note that the economy for seven of the years in this decade had negative net investment, it was not even replacing worn-out capital equipment.

Table 17.1. Current GNP and Selected Components, 1929–1939 (billions of dollars).

	GROSS NATIONAL PRODUCT	NET CONSUMPTION	INVESTMENT	CONSTRUCTION
1929	$104.4	$79.0	$8.3	$8.7
1930	90.4	69.9	2.1	8.7
1931	75.8	60.5	−2.2	6.4
1932	58.0	48.6	−6.3	3.5
1933	55.6	45.8	−5.6	2.9
1934	65.1	51.3	−3.6	3.7
1935	72.2	55.7	−0.4	4.2
1936	82.5	61.9	1.4	6.5
1937	90.4	66.5	4.6	7.0
1938	84.7	63.9	−6.6	7.0
1939	90.5	66.8	−4.0	8.2

SOURCE: U.S. Department of Commerce, Bureau of the Census, *Historical Statistics of the United States, Colonial Times to 1970* (Washington, D.C.: U.S. Government Printing Office, 1975).

Table 17.2. Real GNP and Selected Components, 1929–1939 (billions of 1929 dollars).

	CONSUMPTION	GROSS INVESTMENT	CONSTRUCTION	GROSS NATIONAL PRODUCT
1929	79.0	16.2	8.7	104.4
1930	74.7	10.5	6.4	95.1
1931	72.2	6.8	4.5	89.5
1932	66.0	0.8	2.4	76.4
1933	64.6	0.3	1.9	74.4
1934	68.0	1.8	2.0	80.8
1935	72.3	8.8	2.8	91.4
1936	79.7	9.3	3.9	100.9
1937	82.6	14.6	4.6	109.1
1938	81.3	6.8	4.1	103.2
1939	85.9	9.9	4.9	111.0

SOURCE: U.S. Department of Commerce, Bureau of the Census, *Historical Statistics of the United States, Colonial Times to 1970* (Washington, D.C.: U.S. Government Printing Office, 1975).

THE CAUSES

Insufficient Demand?

As we saw in the preceding chapter, the economy had started to contract before the stock market crash of October 1929. By June 1929, demand for autos and general manufactured goods had begun to decline. The index of manufacturing production reached 188 in June and then began to fall. Primary demand

Table 17.3. Unemployment and Consumer Prices, 1929–1939 (1929 = 100).

	UNEMPLOYMENT RATE	GNP PRICE DEFLATOR
1929	3.2	100
1930	8.7	96
1931	15.9	85
1932	23.6	77
1933	25.2	75
1934	22.0	80
1935	20.3	79
1936	17.0	82
1937	14.3	83
1938	19.1	83
1939	17.2	82

Source: U.S. Department of Commerce, Bureau of the Census, *Historical Statistics of the United States, Colonial Times to 1970* (Washington, D.C.: U.S. Government Printing Office, 1975).

on the part of those who had not purchased autos and other consumer durables had been temporarily satisfied. Replacement demand, or **secondary demand,** had not yet reached levels that could sustain overall demand.

These decreases in consumer demand created a negative accelerator effect as induced investment (facilities needed to expand output to meet expanding demand) fell. Thus contraction in investment involved not only the auto and other consumer durable industries but also the various industries that provided materials for their production, such as steel and other metals, rubber, glass, and textiles.

Residential construction, the second major prop to the prosperity of the 1920s, had begun to crumble before 1929. The industry had been saturated by 1926, although business construction continued to expand the total of all construction until the middle of 1927. By June 1929, both of these segments of construction had substantial excess capacity.

Rising profits and profit margins were beneficial during the 1920s, maintaining optimism and encouraging continued investment. But as demand began to decrease after June 1929, these increased profit margins may have become a liability to the general economy. There was insufficient purchasing power to buy the increased output. Put in "Keynesian" terms, the large savings caused by the widening of the profit margins reduced consumption demand. As investment fell, aggregate demand, income, and output also fell.

Monetary Explanations?

Though there are many economists who disagree with the Friedman-Schwartz monetarist explanation of the depression, most believe that monetary forces, at the least, aggravated the contraction of 1929–1933 and helped turn it into our most severe depression. Monetarist explanations for the length and severity of the Great

Depression were far from demolished by Temin's (49) influential study which emphasized the role of changes in consumer demand. Indeed, Thomas Mayer (32), among others, has provided a skillful and forceful rebuttal to the Temin argument. Among other things, Mayer argues that *real* interests rates—the difference between nominal rates and the expected changes in prices—may have been rising even though nominal rates were constant or even falling. Thus an ill-timed monetary contraction could be a major factor in explaining the sharpening contraction of the economy. Mayer also argues that Temin's explanation of the contraction as deriving from unexplained changes in consumer demand rests on highly questionable empirical grounds, and that even if Temin proves to be right, the Fed might still be a major "villain" because it surely could have used the tools of monetary policy aggressively to offset the decline in consumer spending.

The question is not so much whether real or monetary forces drove the economy downward in the 1930s. No single approach has yet provided a clean, simple, single-factor explanation. All models, except very simple, early "Keynesian" ones and the latest ones involving rational expectations (which deny government policy any power because its actions are fully anticipated), assign monetary policy a role in affecting aggregate economic activity. The debate, in other words, continues.

Still, the decline and weakening of the economy in 1929–1930 might have been nothing more than the precursor to another of the recessions or sharp but relatively brief depressions that we have seen characterized that U.S. economic history up to this point. Nobel Laureate Paul Samuelson (41) noted about the period from mid-1929 to late 1930: "The contraction, though severe, had been a garden variety recession, unmarred by banking difficulties, runs on the banks, or the like." What, then, led to the "non-inevitable avalanche of bank failures, debt suspension . . . deflation and depression?" (40) What, indeed, turned a garden variety recession into a wrenching experience that would color the views of Americans regarding their economy into the 1980s?

The Stock Market Crash of 1929—
Back to the Beginnings

Starting in 1928, there was an accelerated increase in prices of corporate securities on the New York Stock Exchange. *The New York Times* industrial averages increased from 245 at the beginning of 1928 to 452 on September 3, 1929. These price increases, although based primarily on an expectation of further price increases, became much too high to be justified by current earnings. A collapse of the price expectations and of stock prices was inevitable. On October 24, 1929, the stock market declined by over 30 points on *The New York Times* index, but this was only a preview of the future. The market continued to fall until it reached a *New York Times* industrial average of 58 on July 8, 1933.

Keep in mind that although the contraction in the economy began before the stock market decline, the crash seriously aggravated the developing depression.

Perhaps its most important effect was psychological. Many people used the relative state of the stock market as an indicator of the health of the general economy. The disastrous decline of corporate securities prices created more strongly pessimistic expectations about the future of the economy than conditions warranted, further reducing investment and accelerating the contraction.

Another effect of the crash was to further decrease the availability of investment funds for capital formation. A major function of the stock exchanges was to reduce the costs to corporations of raising financial capital, and this function evaporated with the progressive collapse of the stock market. But since much corporate investment apparently came from retained earnings, the significance of this effect is questionable.

An additional factor in the crash was the international means of payments and foreign trade. Remember from Chapter 16 that the United States had become a net creditor nation, in part by making war loans to the Allies. To avoid having to cancel these debts or to increase imports to provide the foreign exchange for countries to pay the debts, the U.S. government encouraged its private citizens to invest in foreign countries. This was especially true of Germany, which desperately needed to obtain foreign exchange to pay reparations to the Allies, who in turn used the exchange to repay their war debts to the United States.

This circular system was encountering difficulties before the crash. U.S. foreign investment had already begun to fall by the start of 1929, and the collapse of the stock exchanges caused foreign investment to virtually disappear. The circular flow evaporated as Germany ceased reparation payments. The adverse effect of this on world and U.S. economic activity stemmed from the intertwining of the circular system with the international private means of payments. As these payments became significantly impaired, international trade and investments contracted, decreasing U.S. and world output.

Wealth effects also resulted from the collapse of stock prices. A reduction of financial wealth in this manner on the one hand reduces purchasing power, forcing decreases in consumption, and on the other hand makes stockholders feel poorer and encourages them to cut back on consumption. Many writers minimize the indirect effect of the crash on consumption. Those who actually suffered losses were a minority of the population, even a minority of the middle class. But whatever the magnitude of the effect, it was to contract consumer demand.

Finally, the collapse of the stock market seriously undermined the financial security of broad sections of the banking system, especially the New York banks. Before the crash, call market loans amounted to over $8 billion; more than half of this came from banks. The share of call loans held by banks increased during the crash—banks were forced to replace funds nonbanks withdrew as the panic developed, to try to prevent total collapse. At times stock prices fell so fast that banks could not cover their loans by sales of securities. The margins on call loans were as low as 10 percent (that is, the purchaser of the security paid only 10 percent, and the bank lent 90 percent). Despite the high interest rate (10 percent) on the call market, the collapse caused significant losses to a number of banks.

The Banking Crises of 1930–1933

Starting in 1930, the crisis-ridden U.S. banking system gave the deepening recession an additional series of blows. The first banking crisis occurred in November and December 1930, when bank failures increased in the agricultural states of Missouri, Indiana, Iowa, Arkansas, and North Carolina. These, plus the failure of the Bank of the United States of New York, caused people to increase their holdings of currency and to reduce deposits. Some banks were not able to withstand the withdrawals.

Did such monetary shocks cause the movement from recession to depression? As we have seen, Friedman and Schwartz (12) have argued that this was so.

Peter Temin (49) describes the monetary hypothesis about the great contraction of 1929 to 1933 in these terms: "The assumption is that the banking panics turned a short depression into a sustained decline in national income." If variations in the supply of money were more important than variations in aggregate demand in causing the depression, then these banking panics must have been independent of contractions in aggregate demand. The banking panics in 1930 were the first, and thus the most crucial. According to Temin, falling agricultural prices and deepening depression in farm areas were the primary causes for these failures. Thus the bank failures were caused by the developing depression; they were not the cause *of* the depression, as suggested by Friedman and Schwartz.

Schwartz (44) has more recently responded that there was still "resilience of the economy" after the first banking panics, and that "adjustment of the economy was aborted by a second round of banking failures compounded by the Federal Reserve's reaction to gold losses in the Autumn of 1931." According to Schwartz, an open market purchase program in April 1932 produced positive results: prices moved upward and output grew. With the end of the program, though, impetus ended, rumors abounded of imminent bank failures, and runs on the institutions continued until 1933 and the "bank holiday." "Destroy a banking system and the real economy will grind to a halt," says Schwartz. There were "equilibrating forces" at work in the economy, as witnessed by "interludes during the contraction when real output increased." Monetary policy was the major flaw; "different policies would have resulted in different behavior."

The late 1930 panic resulted in the failure of banks that held $600 million, or 3 percent of the U.S. supply of money. In March 1931, the second banking panic took place. Bank failures continued, the worst wave occurring in 1933. When President Franklin D. Roosevelt took office, he declared a bank holiday, closing all banks.

Perhaps the most devastating effect of this almost-three-year wave of bank failures was the decrease in the supply of money—a reduction of about one-third from 1929 to 1933 (Table 17.4). Part of this decrease came from the failure of banks, for when closed, their deposits were no longer available to serve as part of the supply of money. Also, as bankers came to anticipate panic withdrawals of deposits in the form of currency, they reduced their lending, both for new loans and for loan renewal, in order to increase their reserves or

Table 17.4. M_1 Supply of Money (Currency in Circulation and Demand Deposits), 1929–1939 (billions of dollars).

YEAR	M_1 MONEY	YEAR	M_1 MONEY
1929	26.4	1935	25.5
1930	25.4	1936	29.2
1931	23.6	1937	30.3
1932	20.6	1938	30.0
1933	19.4	1939	33.6
1934	21.5		

SOURCE: M. Friedman and A. J. Schwartz, *A Monetary History of the United States, 1867–1960* (Princeton, N.J.: Princeton University Press, 1963), Table A-1, pp. 709–716.

liquidity. This contraction of loans not only reduced deposits created through lending, and thus the supply of money; equally important, it reduced the availability of credit for investment as well as for consumption. Finally, the economic contraction itself caused a decline in the amount of borrowing, both from a pessimistic public and from a pessimistic banking system, again reducing the supply of money. The effect was to decrease the level of economic activity and to deepen the depression.

We know from the equation of exchange ($MV = PQ$) that a decrease in the supply of money (M) and a decrease in velocity (V) will decrease prices (P) and also output (Q.) And, in fact, prices declined by 24 percent from 1929 to 1933, and real output fell by about 25 percent in the same period.

But the widespread failure of banks also had aggregate demand effects. First, large amounts of people's deposits became valueless as banks failed, which had a depressing effect on consumer demand. Second, these failures created a depressed psychological outlook, as the banking system and the whole economy seemed on the verge of total collapse. Consequently, postponable consumption and investment were deferred.

International Trade

Devastating as the statistics were for declines in domestic output and employment, the collapse of international trade, which can be seen in Table 17.5, was even more dramatic. U.S. exports fell from $5.2 billion in 1929 to $1.6 billion in 1932. U.S. imports experienced a similarly drastic decline during the same period, from $4.4 billion to $1.3 billion. Growing depression in European countries decreased their demand for U.S. exports, depressing U.S. output and employment.

The collapse of U.S. foreign investment after the stock market crash in 1929 partly explains the decrease in U.S. exports, since some of these dollars had been used to finance the export surplus from the United States. Generally, however, falling demand due to the developing depression in both the United States and the rest of the world accounts for a great deal of the decline in inter-

Table 17.5.   U.S. Exports and Imports (millions of dollars).

YEAR	EXPORTS	IMPORTS
1929	$5241	$4399
1930	3843	3061
1931	2424	2091
1932	1611	1323

SOURCE: U.S. Department of Commerce, Bureau of the Census, *Historical Statistics of the United States, Colonial Times to 1970* (Washington, D.C.: U.S. Government Printing Office, 1975).

national trade. Making matters even worse was the Smoot-Hawley Tariff of 1930, which raised U.S. tariffs and touched off a wave of retaliatory protectionism in Europe.

Further aggravating the situation were developing difficulties in the international financial markets. As we have already noted, the cessation of foreign investment with the collapse of the New York Stock Exchange dried up sources of foreign exchange for German payments of reparations. In 1931, Germany defaulted on reparation payments. Although President Hoover arranged for temporary suspension of reparation and war debt payments, tightening credit in England forced many Austrian and German banks to close, and caused those countries to abandon the gold standard. Britain abandoned the gold standard soon after, and the United States followed suit in 1933. The multinational payments system collapsed as nations jockeyed for favored positions through **"beggar thy neighbor" policies,"** programs designed to increase domestic employment through increasing exports while decreasing imports.

In the United States, this effort to "export depression" came to fruition with the previously mentioned Smoot-Hawley Tariff of 1930. Faced with the highest tariff rates in U.S. history, other countries reacted with tariff barriers of their own, which ensured a major fall in the volume of international trade. This decline not only had adverse effects on aggregate demand but also introduced serious distortions into resource allocation, which caused a reduction in productivity.

While few would argue that rising tariffs and subsequent declines in trade *caused* the Great Depression, most students of the era agree that its intensity was aggravated significantly by trade wars. As Karl Brunner (6) observes in the epilogue to the best recent collection of work on this period that "this effect [adjustments of exchange rates and increasing protectionism] did not initiate the Great Depression. It did not operate as an initiating causal impulse but worked as a reinforcing deflationary condition on the ongoing process."

A Recap

The forces leading to depression apparently began building in mid-1929 with reductions in manufacturing output, construction, and investment in plant and equipment. Aggravating forces, both domestic and foreign, turned what might have been a "garden variety" recession into a deepening and, ultimately, unprecedented depression. Beyond the stock market crash of October 1929, these forces included widespread bank failures, a sharp decline in the supply of money, major reductions in the volume of international trade, and disruptions in the international payments system.

Arguments continue about whether monetary or real forces were the principal cause of the unparalleled decline from 1929 to 1933. Many economists have concentrated on the independent decline in aggregate demand, especially consumption spending, as the major causative explanation. Monetarists, including Friedman and Schwartz (13) in their classic *Monetary History of the United States,* argue that decline in the money supply, beginning with an incorrect and ill-timed Federal Reserve policy, was the major cause. Peter Temin (49) has tested the Friedman-Schwartz argument and concluded that it cannot be supported. He concludes that demand changes, importantly in consumption spending, drove the economy downward and that monetary forces were merely adjustments to these changes in real factors. Many economists think that no model yet advanced provides a complete explanation for what happened in the period 1929–1933.

THE HOOVER YEARS, 1929–1933

Contrary to the popular view of the politically ill-fated Hoover administration of 1928 to 1932, the president actively sought to improve the country's economic condition. As we shall see in the ensuing discussion, Hoover tried using moral suasion, or jawboning, and fiscal policy to achieve economic objectives. He also made substantial changes in U.S. economic structure, and tried to effect an improvement in international economic conditions. Could Hoover have done a better job of holding back the depression and inducing a recovery? Or was Hoover a victim of history, a man in the presidency at the wrong time? Is it possible, as rational expectationists would argue, that no change in government policy would have prevented the disaster?

Moral Suasion, or Can One
Talk an Economy into Prosperity?

President Hoover called a number of conferences of manufacturing and financial leaders, especially in 1929 and 1930, to consider the problems of the evolving depression. He asked for and received pledges from these business leaders that they would hold the line on wages, employment, and investment. He called for firms to resist the temptation, given the fall in demand, to cut wages or decrease employment. He called for increases in investment rather than cuts.

Murray Rothbard (40) concludes that these attempts by the president did indeed restrict the fall in wages and employment. However, Rothbard, writing from

Figure 17-1. Herbert Hoover Worked to Improve Economic Conditions. (Photo from the National Archives)

an "Austrian" point of view, claims that this was a grievous error because it prevented the market from causing necessary liquidations of marginal enterprises. In his view, eliminating inefficient enterprises would have reallocated resources to more productive uses.

Ironically, in light of the monetarist arguments we have considered, Rothbard thinks that both the president and the Fed were *too* activist in this period, that the Fed bought too many government securities (its holdings increased from $511 million in 1929 to $2.4 billion in 1932). The nominal money supply fell too little, not too much, says Rothbard, thereby reducing the fall in prices and the creation of the price earnings ratios that would have energized investment and a more rapid recovery. While relatively few economists have entirely embraced this explanation, it remains a logical counterpoint to both monetarist and neo-Keynesian arguments.

At any rate, Hoover's jawboning did not cause a revival of favorable economic conditions. People became tired of continually hearing that recovery was around the corner. Many concluded that jawboning was all Hoover could do, and became more pessimistic as a result.

Hoover's Fiscal Policy

President Hoover's first response to the contraction at the end of 1929 was to increase government spending and cut taxes. He also encouraged local and state governments to increase their expenditures. In 1930 and 1931, he increased federal public works expenditures. The **full-employment budget** is a statement of federal government revenues and expenditures that contrasts actual revenues and expenditures with those that would exist at full employment. In 1929, there was a full-employment surplus of $1 billion. This fell to a full-employment deficit of $3 billion in 1931, a substantial deficit that was not duplicated until 1936.

In 1932, President Hoover reversed fiscal policy and asked Congress for a tax increase, which was granted and was embodied in the Revenue Act of 1932. This act increased taxes by one-third, the highest peacetime tax increase in U.S. history. The increase in taxes reduced demand and worked to contract the U.S. economy. Why did Hoover perform such a turnabout?

Reasons given vary. Some argue—Scheiber, Vatter, and Faulkner (42), for instance—that the large (for that time) deficits in the federal budget in 1930 and 1931 were simply too much for a president raised in a world of "sound" fiscal policy and that Hoover's conservatism prevented him from using the more "radical" programs the occasion demanded. Others are more understanding of economic predicaments of the time. W. Elliot Brownlee (5), for example—argues that Hoover was concerned that the federal government would have to finance its deficit by borrowing in capital markets in competition with private investors. A question still exists whether this concern was valid. Also, Hoover thought a move toward a balanced budget would discourage the export of gold and strengthen the international gold standard, thus encouraging a recovery of international trade.

Overall, we must conclude that in the early period of the depression, from 1929 to 1931, federal fiscal policy was expansionary (though obviously not expansionary enough to stop the depression). In 1932 and 1933, however, federal fiscal policy sharply reduced aggregate demand, doing more harm than any possible good that may have resulted from the encouragement of domestic investment and international trade.

Changes in Economic Structure

Activism by the Hoover administration was not confined to fiscal affairs. Early on, the government intervened in various sectors of the economy. One of the first was agriculture.

The Federal Farm Board was set up by the Agricultural Marketing Act of June 1929 and given $500 million to stabilize farm prices at some acceptable level (the law did not specify what the acceptable level was). Worsening recession precipitated sharp declines in agricultural prices, which the board tried to stem by purchasing grains and cotton. Except for a few temporary successes in 1930, the board had lost $354 million by the summer of 1932 without achieving much of significance. The severe demand-decreasing effect of the depression and the inability of the board to control supply doomed its efforts at price stabilization. Much of the cotton and wheat bought with the fund was given away or sold at a loss, without accomplishing the board's objective. In this failure, we see a harbinger of agricultural problems that continued into the 1980s.

The major structural change initiated by the Hoover administration was the creation of the Reconstruction Finance Corporation (RFC) in January of 1932. By July 1932, the RFC had capital and a borrowing ability of almost $4 billion. Empowered to lend to various corporations, cooperatives, and states, and to public and private agencies, the RFC had lent over $3 billion by the time Roosevelt took office in March 1933. About 80 percent of this went to railroads and, especially, banks, providing the liquidity needed to keep many banks solvent.

The Roosevelt administration continued the RFC and also used it as a major instrument to foster recovery. Its lending ability was increased, and its activities were shifted significantly from the support of banks to a wider range of lending. This was especially true after the bank holiday of March 1933.

Hoover and the International Economy

Hoover maintained from the beginning that economic recovery in the United States required recovery in the rest of the world, and much of his policy was formulated around that concept. In 1931, he initiated a temporary halt to reparation and war debt payments. As we have seen, some argue that his tax increase in 1932 was intended to reduce the federal budget deficit and discourage the withdrawal of gold, which was undermining confidence in the international gold standard.

What confounds this interpretation of Hoover's policies, however, was his signing of the Smoot-Hawley Tariff of 1930. This tariff initiated a wave of retaliation by European countries and a marked shift away from trade based on comparative advantage. Thus Hoover's international economic policies were contradictory in the end, and on balance probably contracted both the U.S. economy and that of the rest of the world.

The Federal Reserve System Under Hoover

As we have seen, the Federal Reserve System was established in 1913 to stabilize the country's banking system and to influence the supply of money and interest rates. However, by monetarist interpretation or any other, the Federal Reserve did not perform its functions very well from 1929 through 1933.

From October 1929 to October 1931, the Federal Reserve—especially the New York bank—followed an easy money policy, purchasing $160 million of government securities in October 1929 and reducing the **rediscount rate** (the rate charged banks for borrowing from the Fed) until it was at a low of 1.5 percent in May 1931. Then, from October 1931 to February 1932, the Fed tightened credit, selling government securities and increasing the rediscount rate. These actions were taken in response to Britain's abandonment of the gold standard in September 1931 and to the consequent outflow of gold from the United States. Between April and August 1932, the Fed purchased $1 billion of government securities. The New York bank eased credit in February and June of 1932.

Figure 17.2   Franklin D. Roosevelt, Architect of the New Deal. (Photo in the National Archives)

Unfortunately, the rest of the Fed did not follow suit. When gold began to flow out of the banks after November 1932, as speculators presumed Roosevelt would abandon gold, the Federal Reserve banks again contracted the reserves of the banking system.

The record indicates that the Fed seemed more concerned with the international gold problem than with internal U.S. economic stability. When the Fed did engage in easy money policies, they were not consistently followed but were pushed primarily by the New York bank. Also, the amount of action by the Fed was probably far less than the amount needed, especially in **open market operations** (the buying and selling of government securities). When the Fed contracted credit, it put heavy burdens on the banking system, burdens the system was not prepared to carry. The action, or inaction, of the Federal Reserve must be given a substantial portion of the blame for the more than one-third reduction in the U.S. supply of money from October 1929 through March 1933 and for the negative economic consequences.

The Federal Reserve did not cause all the contraction of the money supply, however. Banks themselves substantially decreased the supply of credit, out of deep pessimism about repayment. At the same time, decreases in loan demand were heavy because businesspeople viewed the potential profitability of new investment pessimistically. Both these actions decreased the size of money supply as both new and renewed loans fell. It is doubtful that further increases in reserves and decreases in interest rates by the Fed would have substantially changed the situation.

Temin (49) shows that the first bank panic, in 1930, centered in the agricultural Midwest and South and originated in the deepening depression and its effects on profits in agriculture. This started a wave and then, over time, recurring waves of distrust of banks and heavy withdrawals of deposits. This, in turn, led to both a large decrease in the money supply and waves of bank closings. Anticipating the withdrawals, banks fought to become more liquid by reducing lending and converting existing loans into reserves. But many banks had become financially unsound, not necessarily because they had made unsound loans in the 1920s but rather because many loans that were sound under conditions of prosperity in the 1920s became unsound under the press of the deepening depression. The withdrawals became too much for the weakened conditions of the banks. Some see a parallel with the increasing number of unsound and nonperforming loans in agriculture and abroad by banks in the 1980s.

Perhaps the Fed could have saved more banks by increasing overall liquidity more than it did. Lending to banks by the RFC did contribute to easing the liquidity problem. We must not forget, though, that falling incomes and rising bankruptcies, coupled with bank losses due to their involvement in the call market of the collapsed stock exchange and to their large holdings of real estate mortgages in a drastically declining real estate market, would have left the banking system shaky no matter what the Fed did.

RECOVERY AND DEPRESSION AGAIN: ROOSEVELT
AND THE NEW DEAL

In March 1933, President Roosevelt took office and initiated what became known as the New Deal. The intent of the new administration was to initiate a recovery from the disastrous decline of 1929 to 1933, to rectify what were perceived as structural weaknesses in economic institutions that had aggravated the contraction, and to create a more equitable balance between the various sectors in the economy. These three elements were so often intertwined that they are difficult to separate.

Roosevelt's New Deal has been seen as primarily concerned with saving the private enterprise society of the United States, not as out to make a revolution. It had no coherent plan, however, tending to "assault" each sector separately, often with little concern for (or knowledge of) how actions in one sector affected the other sectors.

The Economic Record

After Roosevelt's inauguration in March 1933, the economy began to recover. From $55.6 billion in 1933, current GNP rose to $90.4 billion in 1937. From May 1937 to June 1938, the economy contracted once again, with current GNP falling to $84.7 billion in 1938, but recovering in 1939 to $90.5 billion (Table 17.1). **Current GNP** includes the effects of changing prices and thus is not the best measure of economic performance. **Real GNP** takes out the effects of price changes. Since prices fell after 1929, real output computed in 1929 prices would be higher than the current GNP figures. The record of recovery seems better when viewed in real GNP computed with 1929 prices (Table 17.2). Real GNP fell from the high of $104 billion in 1929 to $74.4 billion in 1933, and then rose to $109.1 billion in 1937, somewhat higher than in 1929. The recession of 1937–1938 brought real GNP down to $103.2 billion in 1938, but the economy recovered to $111 billion in 1939.

While the record of real GNP shows that under the Roosevelt administration the economy had recovered to predepression real output by 1939, the record for unemployment is decidedly not as good (Table 17.3). Unemployment had climbed to 25 percent by 1933, declining to 14.3 percent by 1937. During the recession of 1937–1938, unemployment rose again, to 19.1 percent; it then fell in 1939 to 17.2 percent.

If one wished to look at the record optimistically ("the glass is half full"), one would say that ten years after the beginning of the depression in 1929, real output had recovered to predepression levels and unemployment had fallen by one-fourth. If one wished to be pessimistic ("the glass is half empty"), one would say that after ten years of depression the economy had only just managed to recover to 1929 real output. Unemployment, however, remained at the very high level of over 17 percent, and the economy had to wait for World War II and the huge increases in war-related expenditures to achieve full employment.

It needs to be noted, however, that many people found employment in the 1930s *outside* the private sector. Some economists, puzzled by the long-term high rates of private unemployment reflected in the data shown in Table 17.3, have wondered what the multiplicity of public employment programs in the period did to affect these data. For the answers, we are indebted to Michael Darby (11), who provided the corrections shown in Table 17.6.

Several conclusions may be drawn from Darby's corrections. The New Deal, which budgeted almost 20 percent of federal outlays for unemployment programs, did have a significant effect on overall unemployment. Clearly, the private sector, for reasons that remain arguable, was able to create through investment a demand for labor that left unprecedented and continuing high levels of people un-

Table 17.6. Percentage of Labor Force Unemployed.

YEAR	PRIVATE UNEMPLOYMENT	DARBY CORRECTION	PERCENTAGE POINT REDUCTION
1933	25.2	20.9	4.3
1934	22.0	16.2	5.8
1935	20.3	14.4	5.9
1936	17.0	10.0	7.0
1937	14.3	9.2	5.1
1938	19.1	12.5	6.6
1939	17.2	11.3	5.9

Source: U.S. Department of Commerce, Bureau of the Census, *Historical Statistics of the United States: 1960 Series* (Washington, D.C.: U.S. Government Printing Office, 1975), p. D46; Michael Darby, "Three and a Half Million U.S. Employees Have Been Mislaid: Or an Explanation of Unemployment, 1934–41," *Journal of Political Economy, 84* (February 1976).

Table 17.7. Government Fiscal Operations, 1929–1939 (billions of dollars).

	TOTAL GOVERNMENT DEBT	FEDERAL RECEIPTS	FEDERAL EXPENDITURES	FEDERAL DEFICITS	STATE AND LOCAL DEFICITS AND SURPLUSES
1929	16.9	3.9	3.1	+0.7	—
1930	16.2	4.1	3.3	+0.7	—
1931	16.8	3.1	3.6	−0.5	—
1932	20.8	1.9	4.7	−2.7	—
1933	23.6	2.0	4.6	−2.5	−0.2
1934	28.5	3.0	6.6	−3.6	−2.3
1935	30.6	3.7	6.5	−2.9	+1.5
1936	34.4	4.0	8.4	−4.4	−1.0
1937	37.3	5.0	7.7	−2.8	+1.5
1938	39.4	5.6	6.7	−1.2	+0.7
1939	41.9	5.0	8.8	−3.9	−1.3

Source: U.S. Department of Commerce, Bureau of the Census, *Historical Statistics of the United States, Colonial Times to 1970* (Washington, D.C.: U.S. Government Printing Office, 1975).

employed. Make-work programs by government, however, did not push the economy toward full employment. Even in the recovery year of 1937, the combined labor demand of the private sector and the federal government (Civilian Conservation Corps, Works Progress Administration, Public Works Administration, etc.) left more than 9 percent of the American labor force unemployed. As Jonathan Hughes (24) has observed, "even with the New Deal's direct federal employment effort, the 1930s constituted a period of disaster-level unemployment."

Fiscal Policy

The "New Economics" of John Maynard Keynes (27) practically revolutionized traditional viewpoints about government expenditures and taxes. In *The General Theory of Employment, Interest, and Money,* published in 1936, Keynes advocated using government expenditure and budget deficits and surpluses to manage aggregate demand in the ways and amounts that would create jobs and decrease unemployment with stable price levels. Keynes' views, however, had relatively little influence on U.S. government policies in the 1930s. Although some American economists embraced the "Keynesian" framework and, particularly in the case of Alvin Hansen (22), sought to popularize it as an approach to economic stability, it was only years later that this began to happen.

Both the Hoover and Roosevelt administrations adhered to traditional conservative concerns for a balanced budget. During the presidential campaign of 1932, Roosevelt continually attacked the deficits of the Hoover administration that had been created by falling tax receipts under the impact of the depression's falling incomes. Indeed, Roosevelt campaigned on a pledge to balance the budget. Again during the 1936 campaign, Roosevelt promised a return to a balanced budget. This concern with budgetary deficits prevented the government from generating enough demand to more vigorously counteract unemployment.

Table 17.3 shows that the federal deficit increased from $2.7 billion in 1932 to $4.4 billion in 1936. At this point, Roosevelt attempted to reverse the trend, and deficits fell to a low of $1.2 billion in 1938. Roosevelt's failure to pursue deficit financing is generally considered to be a major cause of the sharp contraction that occurred in 1937–1938. The administration then reversed itself, and the federal deficit rose in 1939 to $3.9 billion, which was still less than the deficit of 1936. Friedman (12) dissents from the position that fiscal policy reversal was to blame for the 1937 contraction and argues instead that incorrect decisions and timing on the part of the Fed in regard to the money supply were the major causes. Virtually everyone agrees that, whatever the mix of ill-timed fiscal and monetary policy decisions in 1937, their negative effect on the economy was reinforced by the withholding of Social Security taxes from the paychecks of employed workers. This significant reduction in purchasing power had the short-term effect of reducing consumer demand.

The fiscal policies of the states were generally contractive, with substantial surpluses generated in 1935, 1937, and 1938. When the fiscal policies of all

Figure 17.3. John Maynard Keynes, Founder of the "New Economics." (Photo from the National Archives)

levels of government are considered together, in 1931 and 1936, combined fiscal efforts were clearly more expansionary than in 1929. The expansionary efforts of combined fiscal policy in 1930, 1932, and 1939 were mild. In 1933, 1937, and 1938, combined fiscal policy was substantially less expansionary than in 1929. To quote E. Cary Brown (4), "In brief, then, it took the massive expenditures forced on the nation by the Second World War to realize the full potentialities of fiscal policy. Until then, the record fails to show its effective use as a recovery measure."

A view was built up among many historians and economists in the 1940s and 1950s that the spending programs of the New Deal, including those for direct employment, had markedly reduced the severity of the depression. Brown's 1956 study (4) dealt this view a crushing blow. Indeed, Brown concluded that "Fiscal policy, then, seems to have been an unsuccessful recovery device in the thirties—not because it did not work but because it was not tried."

In a 1973 article, Larry Peppers (36) recalculated the estimates of fiscal drag in Brown's study and concluded that not only was the New Deal not activist in its use of fiscal policy but that, indeed, the fairly small deficits of the period were equivalent to fiscal surpluses at full-employment levels of income. At this point, Franklin Roosevelt looks like anything but a Keynesian.

Monetary Policy

The story of monetary policy is more complicated than simply the Federal Reserve's policy concerning the supply of money. It also involves policy concerning the value of the dollar in terms of gold, and institutional changes in the Federal Reserve System and the banking system as a whole. The institutional changes will be discussed further on.

Monetary policy on the part of the Federal Reserve was expansionary from 1933 to 1937. In addition to the normal expansionary actions of purchases of government securities by the Fed and lower discount rates, the federal government greatly increased its holdings of gold and silver. This resulted from executive orders of March and April 1933 forbidding the exportation of gold, the executive order of October 1933 resuming the gold standard, and the Gold Reserve and Silver Purchasing Acts, both of 1934.

The resumption of the gold standard was accompanied by substantial changes. The price of gold increased from $20.67 per ounce in October 1933 to $35 per ounce in January 1934. Also, gold itself could only be purchased for international transactions. The first factor, a price increase for gold, devalued the dollar, but retaliatory devaluation by the major international trading countries kept exchange rates relatively constant. The second factor reduced the ability to speculate on possible future changes in the gold content of the dollar. This protected the domestic and foreign money markets from the effects of such speculation.

The increase in U.S. government holdings of gold and silver coming from these actions increased the supply of money. The decrease in the gold content of the dollar and the increase in the supply of money were aimed at increasing prices. This inflationary policy was successful to some extent, as the index of prices (1929 = 100) rose from a low of 75 in 1933 to 83 in 1937 (Table 17.4).

Having said that, it is crucial to note that serious questions remain about both the amount and the timing of Federal Reserve actions. Although the Fed reported in the mid-1930s that it was following a "liberal policy of open market purchases," its idea of liberalism seemed unrelated to the enormity of the economic disaster going on around it. A Nobel Laureate, James Tobin (50), has concluded that "The Fed's failure to undertake an aggressive policy of open market purchases seems incredible." Many students of the period think that the worst example of the Fed's ill-timed decisions is to be found in 1937. At just the moment when the Fed might have been expected to reinforce the private recovery and offset the fiscal drag of budget surplus and (Social Security–based) tax increases, it chose instead (with 14 percent unemployment) to fight possible inflation by reducing the money supply.

Recap

Federal fiscal policy was mildly expansive from 1933 to 1937. Deficits in the federal budget occurred as expenditures rose faster than depression-restrained taxes. The administration reversed itself in 1937 and sought to reduce the deficits, perhaps precipitating the recession of 1937–1938. In any event, fiscal policy, if it did not precipitate, certainly increased the severity of the contraction.

Monetary policy, including policy concerning gold and silver, was more expansive than fiscal policy in the period of 1933 to 1937. The supply of money rose from $19.4 billion in 1933 to $30.3 billion in 1937 (Table 17.5). The reversal of monetary policy in 1937 and the cutting of the supply contributed to the contraction of 1937–1938.

In sum, recent studies have concluded that fiscal policy was not even tried as an expansionary device in the 1930s. The idea that New Deal government expenditure programs had a major ameliorating effect on the depression has been largely demolished. Indeed, only in 1930 and 1931, under the Hoover administration, was fiscal policy basically expansionary. Most students of the period are no less critical of the timing and quantity of the monetary policy exercised by the Federal Reserve Board. To view the 1930s as a hothouse in which the ideas of Keynesianism, or even activist aggregate government policy in general, were widely tried is to misread the period.

INSTITUTIONAL CHANGES

Of greater importance perhaps than the monetary and fiscal policies of the Roosevelt administration were the widespread changes in the institutional structure of many sectors of the economy. These changes were not a part of an overall plan on the part of the administration, but rather a piecemeal attack on the problems of the economy. They stemmed from the desire to revive the economy, to rectify what the administration perceived to be problems in various sectors of the economy, and to "balance" the structures and benefits of the economy. In short, while leaving the structure of private enterprise in place as the major device for investment and job creation, the New Deal sought, often in unpredictable ways, to change the "rules of the game" under which private individuals acted in the economy.

Industry and the NRA

The administration's direct efforts to revive industry were embodied in the National Industrial Recovery Act of 1933 (NIRA), which set up the National Recovery Administration (NRA). The traditional government policy in regard to industry had been to encourage competition. Traditionally, our legal system, derived from English common law, and special antitrust legislation, such as the Sherman Act of 1890, the Clayton Act of 1914, and the Federal Trade Commission Act of 1914, had made it illegal for companies to collude with a view to setting the various conditions of the market such as prices and market shares. The NIRA was a complete about-face.

The act sought to enforce cooperation in industry by establishing associations of producers in each industry who, together with representatives from the government (from the NRA) and, where present, from organized labor, were to set up a code of fair practices for that industry. These industrial codes were issued over the president's signature and had the force of law. Roosevelt's aim was "the elimination of practical methods and practices which have not only harassed honest business but also contributed to the ills of labor."

Competition had failed, so now industrial self-regulation would reduce overproduction, raise prices, and increase wages and profits. The act gave labor the right to organize and to be represented in drawing up an industry's codes. The public was to be protected by open hearings and the government's representatives.

Bernard Bellush (1) charges that in practice many industries were dominated by the larger companies. Where organized labor already existed, its representatives may have been effective in protecting its workers' interests. But most industries were not organized or represented by labor unions, and Bellush says that labor was not adequately protected in most codes, and that even those codes with labor protection were consistently violated.

Charges were continually made at the time that the larger firms were dominating the industries and that the codes favored them over the smaller firms. In all this, the consumer was ignored. The intent of the act was to reduce output and increase prices. The interest of consumers, supposedly looked after by the government's representatives, was never of prime concern.

A more telling criticism of the NRA was its profoundly unsettling effects on the private investment climate. By changing prices and the composition of output around in unpredictable ways, as well as by promising unpredictable reforms, the NRA clearly increased uncertainty and retarded the private investment, particularly long-term investment, that might have fostered a stronger recovery. As Stanley Lebergott (30) observes, this is a judgment concurred in by economists as diverse as Joseph Schumpeter, a brilliant critic but also unabashed supporter of private enterprise capitalism, and Robert Aaron Gordon, a distinguished liberal Keynesian.

A flood of complaints moved the administration to appoint the National Recovery Review Board. But before it could exercise oversight, the U.S. Supreme Court, in the 1935 Schechter case, declared the NIRA unconstitutional on the grounds that it was an improper use of the interstate commerce power and improper usurpation of legislative power by the administration.

Agriculture and Government Regulation

As we have seen, the Federal Farm Board created in 1929 was incapable of stemming the fall in prices of agricultural products up to 1933 because it lacked an essential power, the ability to reduce agricultural supply. The primary intent of the Roosevelt administration's agricultural policy also was to increase prices.

The First Agricultural Adjustment Act of 1933 aimed at reducing supplies and raising farm incomes by increasing prices. This was to be accomplished by use of acreage allotments to reduce the plantings of specific crops, by government payments to withdraw land from use, by government purchase and destruction of crops and animals, and by more efficient marketing of agricultural products. The program was financed by taxes on the processing of agricultural products. Thus the public was to pay through higher prices and higher taxes for a program of dubious merit that ignored the nutritional problems of a nation with enormously high unemployment rates. In one famous incident, 6 million pigs were slaughtered and buried in 1933 in an effort to cut pork supplies.

Other problems plagued the program. Output in 1933 was not much less than in 1932 because good weather, concentration of allotments on the most productive land, increased use of fertilizers, and violations of acreage restrictions maintained production levels. Higher domestic prices tended to increase agricultural imports and to decrease agricultural exports.

But parity prices increased from 55 in 1933 to 73 in 1936. **Parity** measures the purchasing power of agricultural products in terms of their purchasing power in a base period. At this time, the base period was 1910 to 1914. A rise from 55 to 73 in parity meant that agricultural prices increased more rapidly than the prices of things farmers bought.

After the First Agricultural Adjustment Act was declared unconstitutional in *United States v. Butler* (1936) as an improper use of the taxing power, the Soil Conservation and Domestic Allotment Act of 1936 was passed as a stop-gap measure that appropriated $500 million to get farmers to put land into sod for soil conservation purposes. Then the Second Agricultural Adjustment Act (AAA) of 1938 set up the machinery that has endured with various modifications for over 50 years. The government aimed at parity pricing to increase the purchasing power of agricultural products. If two-thirds of the growers of a crop agreed, quotas would be set. A price would be set, and if prices dropped below that level, farmers could sell to the government at the set price. If output went beyond quotas, acreage allotment would be decreased, reducing the land for future plantings.

The AAA of 1938 firmly implanted parity pricing and acreage controls in U.S. agriculture. Competition was replaced by the decisions of the U.S. Department of Agriculture. Consumers suffered, as they had to pay in two ways, through higher prices and higher taxes. The economy, in addition, had to bear the costs of resource distortions or misallocation.

Another area of legislative activity important to agriculture was credit. For decades, farmers had complained that their credit needs were neglected by the banking system. Acts such as the Farm Credit Act of 1933 and the various agricultural acts of 1934 concerned with mortgages brought the federal government directly into the area of agricultural credit.

Banking and Finance

We have already seen that recurrent waves of bank panics from 1930 to 1933 were an important factor in deepening the depression. The supply of money (Table 17.5) dropped from $26.4 billion in 1929 to a low of $19.4 billion in 1933, forcing prices down (Table 17.4) from an index of 100 in 1929 to a low of 75 in 1933. The great stock market crash in October 1929 was followed by a continued, jerky decline in stock prices that brought *The New York Times* industrial average of corporate stock prices from its high of 452 on September 3, 1929, to 58 on July 8, 1932. These experiences led people to advocate basic institutional changes. The Roosevelt administration moved quickly.

Immediately on taking office, Roosevelt declared a bank holiday on March 9, 1933, closing the banks for a week. All banks were audited; half were allowed to reopen without supervision, one-fourth reopened under various degrees of supervision, and one-fourth were considered too shaky to reopen at all. This massive surgery restored the public's confidence in the banking system and stopped runs on banks and waves of currency withdrawals.

A number of acts were passed that changed the institutional structure of banking and credit. These included the Emergency Bank Act of 1933, the Bank Acts of 1933 and of 1935, the Gold Reserve Act of 1934, and the Home Owners Loan Acts of 1932 and 1933. The most important features of these acts were the following:

1. The Federal Deposit Insurance Corporation (FDIC) was created to insure deposits against bank failures. Once depositors were assured that they would be able to recover their deposits if a bank failed, the main reason for runs on banks was nullified. Confidence returned and currency flowed back into the banking system.

2. The structure of policy-making of the Federal Reserve was centralized as the powers of the Board of Governors were increased. No longer could individual Federal Reserve banks refuse to go along with board policy. The action unified Federal Reserve economic policy-making. This creation of a single monetary policy for the United States was not without its costs and brings to mind the saying that "When they are right, they are very, very right; when they are wrong, they are horrid."

3. The power of the president to vary the gold content of the dollar was confirmed, and, with the Silver Purchase Act of 1934, the treasury increased purchases of silver and its use in the nation's supply of currency. Devaluation and increased use of silver were part of the administration's strategy to increase prices. This inflationary strategy was only partially successful.

4. The powers of the Reconstruction Finance Corporation (created under Hoover) were extended and increased. In addition to lending to banks, railroads, and power companies, the agency began to lend to industrial companies.

5. The Hoover program of guaranteeing loans to homeowners was extended. These guarantees were taken over by the Federal Housing Administration (FHA). The effort was to stabilize the real estate market and reduce foreclosures on homes.

With the Sale of Securities Act of 1933 and the Securities and Exchange Commission (SEC) Act of 1934, the administration turned its attention to the stock exchanges. They were now to be regulated by the Securities and Exchange Commission, and corporations were required to file with the SEC information concerning the securities they issued and were held liable for misinformation.

Similar reforms were made concerning the various commodity exchanges with the establishment of the Commodity Exchange Commission through the Commodity Exchange Act of 1936.

Social Legislation

The Hoover administration refused to involve the federal government in direct relief to the unemployed. Instead, it put the entire burden of supporting the millions without jobs on private charitable agencies and state and local governments, a responsibility far too great for them to handle. With continued criticism and great reluctance, the New Deal early entered into providing federal relief to the massive numbers of destitute people in American society.

From 1933 to 1936, the Federal Emergency Relief Administration dispensed about $3 billion for direct relief. The Public Works Administration (PWA), set up under the NIRA in 1933, spent over $4 billion by 1941 to employ workers on public works projects. In 1935, the Works Projects Administration (WPA) was set up to coordinate public works programs. From 1935 to 1942, the WPA spent over $13 billion on public interest construction projects. It employed at one time or another 8.5 million people; the most employed at any one time was 3.8 million.

The Civilian Conservation Corps was established in 1933 to provide employment for young men, who were taken out of the cities and employed on useful projects concerned with conservation in the parks and forests of the country. Hundreds of thousands of young men were helped in this way.

A modest start in the area of public housing was made with the Wagner-Stingall Housing Act of 1937. The aim was slum clearance and low-cost housing. But by 1940, only 150,000 homes had been built, which was a modest amount, if one accepts the president's comment that one-third of the American people were poorly housed.

The Fair Labor Standards Act of 1938 set a maximum workweek standard of 40 hours by 1940, and set a minimum wage that would increase from 25 cents to 40 cents per hour over seven years. Many categories of labor were excluded, however, including agricultural workers. This form of intervention in labor markets remains controversial to this day. Some see it as not only distorting labor markets but also as retarding job formation, causing capital substitution for labor, and even enhancing economic discrimination.

The best-known New Deal social legislation is the Social Security Act of 1935. With it, the United States finally followed the example of other developed nations, such as Germany and Great Britain, in providing its workers with a national retirement program. The retirement portion was constructed as a compulsory "insurance" program, with contributions from both the employee and the employer. The act also provided for unemployment "insurance" to be paid by federal taxes on payrolls. There were many criticisms of the program, including those directed at its actuarial unsoundness.

First, it did not immediately benefit—perhaps it even harmed—the recovery. While those benefits under the program that would increase purchasing power were slow in coming because it took time for people to qualify, the increase in taxes was immediate and restricted disposable income.

Second, coverage was restricted primarily to workers in industry and commerce. It took many years of effort to expand coverage to the majority of the population.

Third, taxes to fund the program were highly regressive, falling more heavily on lower-income groups. This introduced questions about equity in taxation that have not yet been resolved. (Questions of equity must be answered not only with regard to the incidence of taxation but also with regard to the distribution of the benefits of government expenditures.)

Fourth, payments under the act, especially payments to retired persons, were low and many found it hard to survive on Social Security payments alone.

Organized Labor

Irving Bernstein (3) in his excellent history of the labor movement in the 1930s, *Turbulent Years*, concluded:

> The most important development that took place was the dramatic increase in the size of the labor movement. If one uses the National Bureau of Economic Research series, constructed by Leo Wolman and Leo Troy on conservative criteria, the membership of American unions (excluding Canadian members) rose from 2,805,000 in 1933 to 8,410,000 in 1941. This constituted an almost exact tripling in size. Perhaps even more significant, for the first time in the history of the nation unions enrolled a substantial fraction of those at work; by 1941, 23 percent of nonagricultural employment. Further, the prospect at the close of this period was that rapid growth, both in absolute numbers and in the share of employment, would continue for at least the duration of the war.

This expansion was accompanied by radical changes in the structure of the labor movement and in the national environment itself. Favorable public opinion concerning the problems of labor unions was mirrored by the revolution in labor legislation. Also, the principles of the American Federation of Labor as formulated by its founder, Samuel Gompers, were substantially altered.

Three prounion legislative acts reversed the basically antiunion legislative and court situation. The Norris-LaGuardia Act of 1932, passed under the Hoover administration, rendered yellow-dog contracts unenforceable in the courts. Courts could no longer issue an injunction against union activities on the grounds that workers had signed contracts with the firm stating they would not join a union. This act seriously reduced judicial power to restrict union practices and thus aided union organizing.

Section 7(a) of the 1933 NIRA, stated that employees have the "right to organize and bargain collectively through representatives of their own choosing and shall be free from interference, restraint, or coercion of employers of labor, or their agents, in the designation of such representation or in self-organization." Labor representatives were to sit on the NRA boards of each industry, and the codes of each industry were to protect worker and union rights.

The third piece of legislation was the National Labor Relations Act of 1935, also known as the Wagner Act. It set up the National Labor Relations Board (NLRB), which was to enforce the act. The board was to draw up a list of fair employment practices, binding on both labor and management, and also was to oversee elections within firms to determine which collective bargaining organization would represent the workers. Finally, employers were forbidden to interfere with employees' rights to bargain collectively or to discriminate against union members as to tenure and employment and were required to bargain in good faith.

Although these laws were prolabor, it was the actions of the unions themselves that caused the expansion of the labor movement. First, the Wagner Act was not effective until April 1937. Charges of widespread violation of 7(a) and of the labor section of the NRA codes were frequently made. Insofar as this was true, it reduced the effectiveness of Section 7(a). Challenges to the NLRA were immediately made in the courts and the constitutionality of the act was not finally upheld until April 1937. Only then could the board function. Unions had broken out of their decline by April 1936, however, and by 1937 had increased their membership by 1.5 million. The point to keep in mind is that these acts only created a more favorable environment for membership growth; they were not the cause of the advances.

In 1933, union membership had reached its lowest point since 1920. Then, partly in response to Section 7(a), partly in response to the promises of the New Deal, new organizational drives were made. These were led by the three industrial unions in the AFL—the United Mine Workers under John L. Lewis, the Amalgamated Clothing Workers Union under Sidney Hillman, and the International Ladies Garment Workers Union under David Dubinsky. Their success in their own industries greatly strengthened the industrial union wing of the AFL. In 1935, these three industrial unions, along with a number of smaller ones, under the leadership of John L. Lewis, formed, first within the AFL, the Committee on Industrial Organization to organize labor on an industry basis.

They set up organizing committees in both the steel and auto industries. In 1937, violent strikes in the auto industry resulted in establishment of a union throughout the industry except for the Ford Motor Company. The violent opposition of Ford ended in 1941. In steel, the United States Steel Corporation reversed its historic antiunion policy, recognized the union, and signed a contract with it in 1937. Several important steel firms did not go along with U.S. Steel, and what was called "little steel" (such companies as Republic and Bethlehem) was not organized until 1942.

Conflict arose between the parent AFL and the committee. At the core of the conflict was craft versus industry unionism. The heart of the AFL was still the craft unions, such as the carpenters and the machinists. They saw the committee as a threat to growth in their membership and to their power in the AFL. The AFL executive committee ordered the Committee on Industrial Organization to dissolve and to place the newly organized members into their respective craft unions, not industrial unions. When the committee refused to do so, and the unions within it were expelled from the AFL. The expelled unions established a rival organization, the Congress of Industrial Organizations (CIO) in 1938.

With the formation of the CIO, the AFL in self-defense launched an aggressive organizing effort. In the process, it came to realize that its craft orientation was a considerable hindrance, so it, too, shifted to an industrial form of organization. While the craft unions remained a powerful factor in the AFL, the nearly 75-year conflict of craft versus industry was decided in favor of industrial unionism.

With the establishment of the CIO in 1938, the fear of Samuel Gompers about dual unionism (two unions in the same industry or craft) was realized. As Irving Bernstein (3) termed it, "civil war" broke out in the labor movement. The jurisdictional strike, one in which the workers strike to force the employer to recognize one union rather than another, occurred with increasing frequency after 1938. But this rivalry, as already noted, forced the AFL itself into active organizing. By 1941, the CIO was firmly established, but the AFL maintained its commanding lead in the labor movement. Although the CIO claimed 5 million members in 1941, Bernstein accepts Troy's (51) estimate of an actual membership of 2,654,000; Troy's figure for the AFL was 5,179,000.

Political neutrality, another favored principle of Samuel Gompers, was undermined in the 1930s. Unions increasingly had an urban industrial base. Politically, Roosevelt made urban labor an important part of the Democratic coalition and the CIO became firmly committed to the Democratic Party. The AFL refused to endorse a presidential candidate until 1952.

Of greatest importance in assessing the changes in labor markets under the New Deal is the fact that the state became an active participant in establishing wage agreements. Employers were no longer free to choose whether to negotiate with representatives of their employees. Wage *floors* were established, and remain a feature of both interstate and intrastate commerce. Hours of work were subject to a maximum. As Jonathan Hughes (24) has noted, "Old time capitalists like Henry Ford were stupefied by these changes." Still in force today, some of these changes remain controversial.

THE NEW DEAL: AN EVALUATION

As with most questions in economic history, an evaluation of the effects of the New Deal on American economic life is open to controversy and debate. But the following points seem to be consistent with the preceding analysis.

Neither New Deal fiscal nor monetary policy was actively and consistently employed to push recovery and shorten the depression. This conclusion especially applies to fiscal policy, although at times (especially in 1937) the direction and timing of monetary policy was absolutely perverse and procyclical.

The New Deal's policy on gold and international exchange insulated the domestic economy from the possible disruptions of changes in international demand for gold. Thus monetary policy became more free to deal with domestic monetary policies. However, these actions accentuated international tendencies toward trade restrictions and a "beggar thy neighbor" policy that hampered recovery of international trade. And, as we have seen, even with greater latitude to concentrate on domestic economic growth and stability, the Fed did little to consistently push toward accomplishing those objectives.

The inflationary aspects of the gold policy were only partially successful, with prices increasing more slowly than the devaluation of the dollar. Whether the price increases were beneficial to business enterprise through increased profit margins is an open question. But they did increase the burden on consumers since the domestic purchasing power of the dollar fell.

Numerous changes were made in economic institutions. The Federal Reserve System was now a more centralized instrument of monetary policy. The establishment of the Federal Deposit Insurance Corporation, which insured bank deposits, met a serious deficiency in the banking system. It made the likelihood of runs on banks, and thus bank failures, more remote, so the security of the banking system was substantially increased. The Securities and Exchange Commission now regulated securities exchanges and provided rules for giving required information by issuers of securities.

The efforts to stimulate industry through the NIRA and its attempted establishment of industrial cooperation through association failed. The failure was not simply due to the declaration of unconstitutionality by the courts. By the time that happened, the unwillingness of large firms, small firms, and labor unions to cooperate and share whatever revenue benefits would accrue from cooperation had eliminated much of the effectiveness of the act. The resulting increase in prices put an additional burden on the consumer. To the extent that the act was effective, it reduced competition and thereby lowered the competitive incentive to increase output.

The agricultural program, embodied in the Agricultural Adjustment Acts of 1933 and 1938, among other places, achieved moderate success in raising farm incomes. Even more important, the programs decisively set the federal government on a course of persistent and increasing involvement in the most competitive industry of the economy. The decisions of the administration became a significant factor in determining the level of farm incomes. But the nature of this involvement produced a triple burden on the general population: high prices to consumers originating from the price supports, the taxes needed to fund the support program, and finally, the distortions in allocation of resources.

Social welfare programs, such as the WPA and the CCC, and federal financial support for state and local welfare programs provided incomes for the unemployed and lowered the rate of unemployment. Even the New Deal programs were not large enough to eliminate unemployment, and insufficient thought was given to their structure. But the New Deal established the precedent of federal involvement in direct aid to the unemployed.

The Social Security program was initiated with the Social Security Act of 1935. The effect of Social Security on the depression was contractive. Recipients of Social Security during the period were few because of the need to qualify by working the necessary period of time and by the narrowness of the coverage, but taxes were collected from present incomes, reducing buying power.

Labor legislation, such as the Norris-LaGuardia Act of 1932, Section 7(a) of the NIRA of 1933, and the National Labor Relations Act of 1935, revolutionized the legislative position of organized labor. These acts reduced the use of the injunction and recognized the right of workers to organize, making it mandatory for management to bargain in good faith with unions. However, they introduced further monopoly power into the labor markets. Although this legislation was a substantial boon to union expansion, vigorous union organizing in the favorable public atmosphere of the depression was more important in explaining union growth.

Some contemporaries and students of the period have charged that the New Deal was bent on destroying American capitalism. This does not appear to have been the intent, and it certainly was not the accomplishment, of the New Deal. Still, the role of the federal government, which had participated significantly in the private market economy from its inception, increased both qualitatively and quantitatively in the 1930s, and the New Deal firmly established what has been called a **mixed-market economy.** Federal government expenditures and taxes rose to a level that made them a significant factor in the economy.

Federal regulation was expanded and became a decisive factor in a number of sectors of the economy. The New Deal's legacy, for good or for ill or for both, is the era of the mixed-market economy, the era of big government. In the 1980s, this legacy became the subject of intense debate and reexamination.

QUESTIONS

1. What explanations have been offered for the enormous contraction of the economy from 1929 to 1933? Distinguish between basic causes and aggravating factors.
2. An important monetary explanation for the contraction of 1929–1933 has been offered by Milton Friedman and Anna Schwartz. That explanation was rejected by Peter Temin.

Recently, the monetarist explanation has been defended by Thomas Mayer. Explain and evaluate these monetary and real-force arguments.

3. Does any single explanation for the contraction of 1929–1933 seem adequate at this point? Why or why not?

4. In what ways did the stock market decline of 1929–1933 contribute to the economic contraction of the 1930s?

5. How did the banking panics of 1930 to 1933 affect the economy?

6. Evaluate the effects on the contraction of the Hoover administration's fiscal and monetary policies.

7. Did Hoover help or hinder the international economy during 1929 to 1933? What role did international trade and financial crises play in the great contraction?

8. What were the strengths and weaknesses of Hoover's policy in regard to the depression?

9. What is the Austrian (Rothbard) explanation for the great contraction of 1929–1933?

10. What were the basic objectives of the New Deal?

11. Evaluate the Roosevelt administration's fiscal and monetary policies from 1933 to 1939. Was the New Deal "Keynesian"?

12. What effect, according to Michael Darby, did New Deal direct employment policies have on the rate of unemployment in the 1930s? What were the major programs under these policies?

13. How did the New Deal attempt to reflate or raise prices through the NRA?

14. What basic changes occurred in agricultural policy under the New Deal?

15. What changes in labor markets occurred under the New Deal?

SUGGESTED READINGS

1. Bellush, Bernard. *The Failure of the NRA.* New York: Norton, 1975.

2. Berkiowitz, Edward, and Kim McQuaid. *Creating the Welfare State.* New York: Praeger, 1980.

3. Bernstein, Irving. *Turbulent Years.* Boston: Houghton Mifflin, 1970.

4. Brown, E. Cary. "Fiscal Policies in the Thirties: A Reappraisal." *American Economic Review,* 46 (December 1956).

5. Brownlee, W. Elliot. *Dynamics of Ascent.* New York: Knopf, 1974.

6. Brunner, Karl, ed. *The Great Depression Revisited.* Boston: Martinus Nijhoff, 1981.

7. Cagan, Phillip. "Comments." In *The Great Depression Revisited,* ed. Karl Brunner. Boston: Martinus Nijhoff, 1981.

8. Chandler, Lester V. *America's Greatest Depression, 1929–1941.* New York: Harper and Row, 1970.

9. Chandler, Lester V. *American Monetary Policy, 1928–1941.* New York: Harper and Row, 1971.

10. Cox, Charles C. "Monopoly Explanations of the Great Depression and Public Policies Toward Business." In *The Great Depression Revisited,* ed. Karl Brunner. Boston: Martinus Nijhoff, 1981.

11. Darby, Michael. "Three and a Half Million U.S. Employees Have Been Mislaid: Or an Explanation of Unemployment, 1934–41." *Journal of Political Economy, 84* (February 1976).

12. Friedman, Milton, and Anna J. Schwartz. *The Great Contraction, 1929–1933.* Princeton, N.J.: Princeton University Press, 1956.

13. Friedman, Milton, and Anna J. Schwartz. *A Monetary History of the United States, 1867–1960.* Princeton, N.J.: Princeton University Press, 1963.

14. Gagliardo, Dominic. *American Social Insurance.* New York: Harper, 1949.

15. Galbraith, John Kenneth. *The Great Crash, 1929.* Boston: Houghton Mifflin, 1954.

16. Gandolfi, Arthur. "Stability of Demand for Money During the Great Contraction, 1929–1933." *Journal of Political Economy, 82* (September/October 1974).

17. Gandolfi, Arthur, and James Lothian. "Review of 'Did Monetary Forces Cause the Great Depression.' " *Journal of Money, Credit and Banking, 9.* (December 1977).

18. Gordon, Robert A. *Economic Instability and Growth: The American Record.* New York: Harper and Row, 1974.

19. Gordon, Robert J., and James Wilcox. "Monetarist Interpretations of the Great Depression: An Evaluation and Critique." In *The Great Depression Revisited,* ed. Karl Brunner. Boston: Martinus Nijhoff, 1981.

20. Gramm, William. "The Real Balance Effect in the Great Depression." *Journal of Economic History, 22* (June 1972).

21. Green, George D. "The Ideological Origins of the Revolution in American Financial Policies." In *The Great Depression Revisited,* ed. Karl Brunner. Boston: Martinus Nijhoff, 1981.

22. Hansen, Alvin. *Fiscal Policy and Business Cycles.* New York: Norton, 1941.

23. Hawley, Ellis W. *The New Deal and the Problem of Monopoly: A Study in Economic Ambivalence.* Princeton, N.J.: Princeton University Press, 1966.

24. Hughes, Jonathan R. *American Economic History.* Glenview, Ill.: Scott, Foresman, 1981.

25. Hughes, Jonathan R. *The Governmental Habit.* New York: Basic Books, 1977.

26. Hughes, Jonathan. *The Vital Few.* New York: Oxford University Press, 1973.

27. Keynes, John M. *The General Theory of Employment, Interest and Money.* New York: Harcourt Brace Jovanovich, 1936.

28. Kindleberger, Charles. *The World in Depression, 1929–1939.* Berkeley: University of California Press, 1973.

29. Kirkwood, John. "The Great Depression: A Structural Analysis." *Journal of Money, Credit and Banking, 4* (November 1972).

30. Lebergott, Stanley. *The Americans: An Economic Record.* New York: Norton, 1983.

31. Mayer, Thomas. "Consumption in the Great Depression." *Journal of Political Economy, 86* (December 1978).

32. Mayer, Thomas. "Money and the Great Depression: A Critique of Professor Temin's Thesis." *Explorations in Economic History, 15* (April 1978).

33. Meltzer, Allen. "Money and Other Explorations of the Great Depression." *Journal of Monetary Economics, 2* (October 1976).

34. Mitchell, Broadus. *Depression Decade: From New Era Through New Deal, 1932–1940.* New York: Harper and Row, 1969.

35. Nash, Gerald D. "Herbert Hoover and the Origins of the Reconstruction Finance Corporation." *Mississippi Valley Historical Review, 46* (December 1959).
36. Peppers, L. C. "Full Employment Surplus Analysis and Structural Change: The 1930s." *Explorations in Economic History, 10* No. 2 (Winter 1973).
37. Ransom, Roger. *Coping with Capitalism.* Englewood Cliffs, N.J.: Prentice Hall, 1981.
38. Reading, Don C. "New Deal Activity and the States, 1933–1939." *Journal of Economic History, 33* (December 1973).
39. Romasco, A. U. *The Poverty of Abundance: Hoover, the Nation, the Depression.* New York: Oxford University Press, 1965.
40. Rothbard, Murray. *America's Great Depression.* Kansas City, Kan.: Sheed and Ward, 1972.
41. Samuelson, Paul, and Milton Friedman. "Banking and the Great Depression." *Journal of Portfolio Management* (Fall 1979).
42. Scheiber, Harry N., Harold G. Vatter, and Harold Underwood Faulkner. *American Economic History.* New York: Harper and Row, 1976.
43. Schemter, Joseph. "The Present World Depression: A Tentative Diagnosis." *American Economic Review, 21* (1931).
44. Schwartz, Anna J. "Understanding 1929–1933." In *The Great Depression Revisited,* ed. Karl Brunner. Boston: Martinus Nijhoff, 1981.
45. Schwartz, J. A. *The Interregnum of Despair: Hoover, Congress and the Depression.* Urbana: University of Illinois Press, 1970.
46. Smithies, Arthur. "The American Economy in the Thirties." *American Economic Review, 55* (June 1965).
47. Sobel, Robert. *The Big Board: A History of the New York Stock Market.* New York: Free Press, 1965. Chap. 13.
48. Sweezy, Alan R. "The Keynesians and Government Policy, 1933–1939." *American Economic Review, 42* (May 1972).
49. Temin, Peter. *Did Monetary Forces Cause the Great Depression?* New York: Norton, 1976.
50. Tobin, James. "The Monetary Interpretation of History." *American Economic Review, 55* (June 1965).
51. Troy, Leo. "Trade Union Membership, 1897–1962." Occasional Paper 92. New York: National Bureau of Economic Research, 1965.
52. Wallis, John Joseph, and Daniel K. Benjamin. "Public Relief and Private Employment in the Great Depression." *Journal of Economic History, 41* (March 1981).
53. Walton, Gary M., ed. *Regulatory Change in an Atmosphere of Crisis: Current Implications of the Roosevelt Years.* New York: Academic Press, 1979.
54. Warren, Harris G. *Herbert Hoover and the Great Depression.* New York: Oxford University Press, 1959.
55. Weinstein, Michael. "Some Macroeconomic Impacts of the National Industrial Recovery Act, 1933–1935." In *The Great Depression Revisited,* ed. Karl Brunner. Boston: Martinus Nijhoff, 1981.
56. Wolman, Leo. "Concentration of Union Membership." *Proceedings.* Industrial Relations Research Association, 1952.
57. Wright, Gavin. "The Political Economy of New Deal Spending: An Econometric Analysis." *Review of Economics and Statistics, 56* (February 1974).

Chapter 18

THE 1940s AND 1950s

At least from a macroeconomic perspective, the economic history of the two decades after 1940 falls conveniently into four periods. The war years from 1940 through 1945 witnessed a dramatic recovery of the American economy under the impact of expanded wartime demand. This expansion continued in the immediate postwar period from 1946 to 1949, when delayed demand as well as delayed investment and supply from a depression and war-starved domestic economy was supplemented by the demand created by the reconstruction of war-ravaged Europe.

The recovery from the mild recession of 1949 was accelerated by both military and consumer demand after the outbreak of the Korean conflict in 1951, and the economy expanded until 1954. There was a mild recession in 1954 at the conclusion of the Korean conflict, followed by a surge in the demand for consumer durables in 1955, and in 1956 and 1957 by an increased demand for producer durables. The sharp contraction in 1958 was followed by a quick but weak recovery in 1959.

These 20 years experienced the continuation of a number of factors. With the end of World War II, the large foreign investments typical of the period from 1900 to 1929 were resumed, and by 1950, the multinational firm had made its appearance. The expansion of unionization that commenced in the middle of the 1930s depression continued into the 1950s. The expanded role of the federal government, stimulated by the New Deal and furthered during World War II, continued through the 1950s.

But there were also changes in economic patterns. After the war, urbanization, which had been so much a part of post–Civil War development, slowed as people took to the road and the flight to the suburbs became a flood. While the percentage of total employment in agriculture continued its historic decline, the percentage in manufacturing also began to decline as the service industries became increasingly important. The pre–World War II period saw no recurrent and severe contractions of the economy such as the depressions of 1929–1933, 1921, and 1907. After the war, the economy went through three mild recessions, in 1949, 1954, and 1958. The concern for unemployment characteristic of the 1930s was replaced by a concern for inflation as the postwar inflation of 1946 to 1949 continued through the 1950s.

If this introduction seems to focus almost entirely on a demand-side explanation of the macroeconomy, it is not meant to ignore or minimize supply-side influences. During the period from 1942 through 1945, however, savings and investment activities were largely chaneled into war finance. As Table 18.1 indicates, gross investment after 1941 declined to levels comparable to those of the late depression years. Much of the supply of savings went into the financing of the federal deficits, which reached a high of $53.8 billion in 1943. In this respect, the huge military expenditures reflected in Table 18.1 forced the Congress and the Roosevelt administration to choose between current (tax-based) financing of government expenditures and deficit financing of those expenditures. During World War II, the latter clearly won and established at least a short-term precedent that had been resisted throughout the 1930s. That precedent was to create a debate both about the role of government and the mode of financing its activities that has continued up to the late 1980s. The latter decade

Table 18.1. Economic Statistics, 1940–1945 (billions of dollars).

YEAR	GNP	CONSUMPTION	GROSS INVESTMENT	FEDERAL EXPENDITURES FOR GOODS AND SERVICES Military	Other
1940	99.7	70.8	13.1	2.2	3.8
1941	124.5	80.6	17.9	13.8	3.1
1942	157.9	88.5	9.8	49.4	2.5
1943	191.6	99.3	5.7	79.7	1.4
1944	210.1	108.3	7.1	87.4	1.6
1945	211.9	119.7	10.6	73.5	.7

YEAR	FEDERAL DEFICIT	UNEMPLOYMENT CONSUMER PRICE INDEX (1957–1959 = 100)	NATIONAL LABOR FORCE	DEBT
1940	−2.7	48.8	14.6	50.7
1941	−4.8	51.3	9.9	57.5
1942	−19.4	56.8	4.7	79.2
1943	−53.8	60.3	1.9	142.6
1944	−46.1	61.3	1.2	204.1
1945	−45.0	62.7	1.9	260.1

SOURCE: U.S. Department of Commerce, Bureau of the Census, *Historical Statistics of the United States, Colonial Times to 1970* (Washington, D.C.: U.S. Government Printing Office, 1975).

has seen efforts to cap government expenditures through such restraints as the Graham-Rudman Act and a much-debated proposed constitutional amendment requiring annually balanced federal budgets.

WORLD WAR II, 1940–1945

Prewar Years

War broke out in Europe in September 1939, and the recovery of the American economy accelerated. Americans, remembering the inflation of World War I, increased consumption demand in anticipation of price increases. Exports swelled from $3.1 billion in 1939 to $5.2 billion in 1941 as the Allies increased purchases in the United States, and shipments under Lend-Lease (the lending or leasing of material to the Allies) burgeoned after January 1941. In addition, the federal government increased its own expenditures, primarily on the military, from $6 million in 1940 to almost $17 billion in 1941 (see Table 18.1).

These increases in total demand generated multiplier effects as the higher expenditures increased payrolls and purchasing power and further raised consumer demand. In addition, the increased government and consumer demand stimulated a greater need for facilities and induced investment. The economy expanded, and GNP increased from $90.5 billion in 1939 to $124.5 billion in 1941. Because depression-related high unemployment and unused facilities permitted an elastic aggregate supply, the consumer price index increased by only 5 percent in 1940–1941 (see Table 18.1).

The War Years, 1942–1945

The United States entered the war on December 8, 1941, and the economy shifted onto a war footing. Federal government expenditures increased sharply, growing from $17 billion in 1941 to $52 billion in 1942, $81 billion in 1943, $89 billion in 1944, and, as the war approached its end, $74 billion in 1945. Under the pressure of war, nonmilitary expenditures decreased from $3 billion in 1941 to $0.7 billion in 1945. As government demand expanded, GNP grew from $124.5 billion in 1941 to $212 billion in 1945.

At the beginning of 1942, expansion was facilitated by a 10 percent unemployment rate and by large amounts of excess plant and equipment. By September 1942, the economy had achieved full employment. The unemployment rate continued to decline, to a low of 1.2 percent in 1944, a level unattained since and one explained almost entirely by **frictional unemployment** or the unemployment associated with those moving from one job to another. Resources continued to be shifted into war production. People worked overtime, and many who would normally not have been part of the labor force went to work for the war effort. This expansion of the labor force included fabled "Rosie the Riveter" and many others like her who now entered paid employment and contributed substantially to the war effort.

The opportunity cost of the war soon became apparent. While consumption increased moderately, many forms of consumer goods were not produced; for example, the auto industry shifted completely to tanks, trucks, jeeps, and airplanes. Shortages in a wide variety of consumer durable goods appeared by the end of 1942. Unessential forms of investment goods were sacrificed as these resources were shifted to war production. Gross investment fell from nearly $18 billion in 1941 to a low of $5.7 billion in 1943. Rationing and shortages induced by price controls would ordinarily be expected to lead to black markets and a widespread "underground economy." While such illicit activities did occur, the war enjoyed popular support and its opportunity costs to consumers were borne with surprising equanimity. Of course, it is worth noting that the supply of many nondurable consumer goods actually rose during the war. Although nylon stockings, sugar, rubber tires, and gasoline were in short supply, it was hardly a period of acute austerity.

Economic planning was employed on a much more extensive scale than for World War I. Such agencies as the War Production Board and the Office of Emer-

Figure 18.1.   Wartime Production, "Rosie the Riveter." (Photo from the National Archives).

gency Management established a system of priorities for a wide range of raw materials, semifinished goods, and transportation. As a result, resources were channeled with reasonable efficiency into war-related uses. Widespread support for the war contributed to the high levels of cooperation between management and labor. Strikes were both illegal and uncommon.

The shift of resources from civilian uses into the war effort, together with the system of price controls, caused excess demand for consumption goods to mount. Despite wage controls, increases in civilian purchasing power as full employment returned caused serious problems in allocating, equitably and with a minimum of inflation, short supplies of certain goods already referred to. As Hugh Rockoff (18) has observed, there almost certainly were implicit price increases as both the variety and quality of goods among which consumers could choose declined.

Beginning in 1942, the Office of Price Administration (OPA), established by the Stabilization Act of 1942, set prices, wages, and rents. It also set up a system of rationing for many of the basic civilian goods, including sugar, butter, tires, and gasoline. As noted before, black markets appeared, especially in gasoline and tires, but their quantitative importance was probably small.

The government could have used taxation to reduce the growing purchasing power generated through the economic expansion. Although new taxes were added and receipts of taxes did grow, tax receipts accounted for only about 50 percent of the increased government expenditures. The other half reflected government deficits, which totaled $190 billion between 1941 and 1945. Savings grew rapidly, as people voluntarily curtailed their consumption to help the war effort; they also found their choices of goods restricted, and were concerned about a possible return of unemployment after the war.

An important factor in the war against inflation was the sale of war bonds to individuals and banks. The sales greatly increased bank reserves (the money supply grew by almost two and a half times between 1941 and 1945) and created a potential liquidity that had the capacity to fuel an expansion of demand after World War II. Also, these bond sales, while increasing the financial assets of the people, absorbed large amounts of purchasing power. A heroine of this war against inflation was Kate Smith, who, singing "God Bless America," encouraged the sale of millions of dollars in bonds.

On the whole, the effort to control inflation was a remarkable success. Prices increased by the moderate amount of about 4 percent per year during 1942 through 1945. This statistic understates the true impact of inflation, however, since it does not take into account the already noted decreases in quality that undoubtedly took place. Still, all in all, inflation was moderate, probably because of price controls, rationing, and savings. These programs were largely successful because of the patriotic cooperation of the substantial portion of the American people. Obviously, increase in savings was encouraged also by the unavailability of consumer goods.

THE POSTWAR ECONOMY, 1946–1949

The Record

Much to the surprise of some economists, the conversion from a war economy, one in which government expenditures used as much as 50 percent of total output, was quick and was accomplished with little unemployment. Remembering the post-war depression of 1921 and the disastrous 1930s depression, many were concerned about a return to conditions of substantial unemployment. Instead, GNP rose from $208.5 billion in 1946 to over $257 billion in 1948, and unemployment remained below 4 percent. This expansion, however was accompanied by a surge in prices as the consumer price index increased from 68 in 1945 to almost 84 in 1948—an increase of almost 24 percent in three years (see Table 18.2).

In late 1948, the expansion began to weaken, and the economy experienced its first postwar contraction. When compared to past experience, however, (such as 1907, 1921, 1929–1933, and 1937–1938), this recession was mild indeed. The GNP declined from $257.6 billion in 1948 to only $256.5 billion in 1949, and unemployment increased to 5.9 percent. Prices decreased slightly. By the beginning of 1950, the economy was recovering.

The Causes of Expansion

A major cause of the postwar expansion was the surge in consumer demand, especially for durables, which had been very low through 16 years of depression and war. By 1946, consumers had a small stock of durable goods, and the

Table 18.2. Economic Statistics, 1946–1949 (billions of dollars).

YEAR	GNP	CONSUMPTION	GROSS INVESTMENT	FEDERAL EXPENDITURES FOR GOODS AND SERVICES	
				Military	Other
1946	208.5	143.4	30.6	14.7	2.5
1947	231.3	160.7	34.0	9.1	3.5
1948	257.6	173.6	46.0	10.7	5.8
1949	256.5	176.8	35.7	13.3	6.8

YEAR	FEDERAL DEFICIT	CONSUMER PRICE INDEX (1957–1958 = 100)	UNEMPLOYMENT	FEDERAL DEBT	NET EXPORTS
1946	−18.2	68.0	3.9	271.0	+6.7
1947	+6.6	77.8	3.9	257.1	+10.1
1948	+8.9	83.8	3.8	252.0	+5.7
1949	+1.0	83.0	5.9	252.6	+5.3

SOURCE: U.S. Department of Commerce, Bureau of the Census, *Historical Statistics of the United States, Colonial Times to 1970* (Washington, D.C.: U.S. Government Printing Office, 1975).

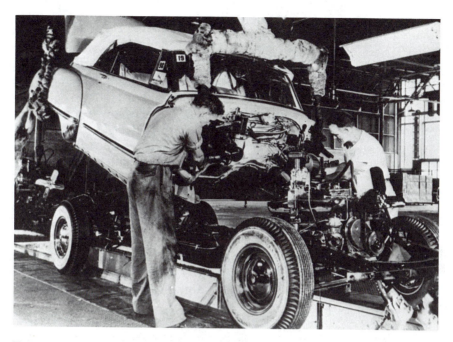

Figure 18.2. Postwar Production, Meeting Pent-up Demand. (Photo from the National Archives)

initial postwar output of these goods seemed incapable of meeting the very large demand. From the supply side, investment in plant and equipment had been abnormally low during these same years, and there were now large orders for new plant and equipment to replace that which had become technologically obsolete and also to increase capacity in view of the expected high levels of consumer demand.

The financing of this increased supply-demand activity came from a variety of sources. Much came from liquid assets accumulated during the war in the form of savings and war bonds. Also, profits accumulated during the war had substantially increased retained earnings of corporations, which were used for investment expansion. In addition, both consumer and business borrowings rose rapidly after the war. Finally, in 1946, Congress forced substantial tax cuts for both individuals and businesses on a reluctant President Truman, who, like Franklin Roosevelt, was no Keynesian.

Residential construction also revived and surged ahead as the housing shortage that had developed during the war became critical. Construction of housing for nondefense and nonmilitary purposes had ceased during the war. This, coupled with the low levels of construction during the 1930s, had caused a severe shortage. A rise in births during the 1940s (the beginning of the so-called baby boom) had increased population by 19 million. A renewal of the shift to the suburbs that had started in the 1920s further increased the demand for housing.

Residential construction built almost 5 million new units between 1946 and the end of 1950.

Though most of this expansion was financed from borrowing and the liquid assets accumulated by individuals during the war, the government also contributed. Under the G.I. Bill of 1944, the government guaranteed mortgages for veterans. In 1946 and again in the Housing Act of 1949, the federal government committed itself to building subsidized housing for low-income groups under the responsibility of the Federal Housing Authority.

An additional stimulus to aggregate demand came from increased exports as war-ravaged Europe and Asia relied on U.S. productive capacity to assist them until they could recover. Under the United Nations Relief and Rehabilitation Agency (UNRRA), primarily financed by the United States, supplies flowed into the devastated areas to provide for the hungry and the destitute. When the "cold war" between the Soviet Union and the United States began to intensify in 1949, U.S. aid became more directly politically motivated. The Marshall Plan was launched to strengthen the internal productive capacity and financial structure of a number of European countries in order to reduce the possibility of communist success. Eventually, under the plan, almost $9 billion was channeled into such countries as Greece, Italy, France, and West Germany. Most of these funds were used to buy exports from the United States.

While the U.S. government, having learned from the reparation–war debt experience of the 1920s, used primarily governmental unilateral transfers or foreign aid to support desired foreign economies, private foreign investors from the United States were also active after World War II. In 1946, foreign investments began to increase, primarily in Europe, but also in the various less developed countries. Unlike the 1920s, these were mainly direct investments in productive capacity. The investments, especially those in Europe, were increasingly made in manufacturing industries. In the less developed countries, investments in raw materials were still important, but more and more concentration was placed on processing materials and on manufacturing.

This process of foreign investment had begun before World War II. In time, the steady increase in direct foreign investment in manufacturing and processing created **multinational firms.** These are firms with worldwide economic facilities for processing, manufacturing, and sales.

The development of multinational firms was, in large measure, a response to the growth of world markets. Improved communications lowered information costs; improved transportation and technological development, especially of computers, increased economies of scale. These factors allowed firms to increase their size without incurring diseconomies of scale. However, the multinationals generated concern in part because their global nature gave them such flexibility that it was thought no one country would be able to exercise control over their activities.

In summary, funds provided to other countries by U.S. government transfers and foreign investment and exports to the United States financed a U.S. export surplus in the amounts of $6.7 billion in 1946 and $5.3 billion in 1949. These net exports increased total demand in the United States and contributed to the expansion.

Government Economic Policy

With the end of the war, the Republican-dominated Congress moved quickly to liquidate wartime spending, taxes, and controls. Government expenditures and taxes were cut substantially. Given the inflation that occurred, these cuts were not contractive enough despite the appearance of government surpluses in 1948 of $8.9 billion. Truman, concerned that inflation in 1946 would get out of hand, pushed for the extension of OPA and price controls. Congress, however, allowed the act to expire in 1946, thus removing federal controls over prices, wages, and rents. While government actions were not designed explicitly to counter business fluctuations, fiscal policy played a contractive role, although not enough to prevent inflation.

Congress passed the G.I. Bill in 1944, which gave veterans the right to $20 a week for 52 weeks after discharge; the right to a guaranteed mortgage loan on the purchase of a house; and the right to subsidy payments on attending an approved educational institution. The G.I. Bill had many ramifications, but in terms of its effect on total demand, it was definitely expansionary.

In 1946, the Employment Act was passed. It created the Council of Economic Advisers to advise the president on economic matters and created the Joint Committee on the Economic Report of the President to give Congress a committee specializing in economic matters. Also, it stated that the federal government should work to achieve "maximum employment, production and purchasing power." This act committed the government to formulating and executing stabilization policies, though not to achieving full employment.

The Union Movement

Unions continued to increase in membership, from 7.3 million in 1940 to 14.7 million in 1949. But after the war, union pressures for higher wages and widespread strikes met a hostile reaction from the public and Congress. The Taft-Hartley Act of 1947 was meant to restore balance to a situation seen as too favorable to unions. A number of provisions unfavorable to unions were included. These included prohibition of secondary boycotts, jurisdictional strikes, excessive union fees, featherbedding, and closed shops. Furthermore, unions were required to give 60 days' notice of intent to strike and required also to bargain in good faith for 30 days. The president could declare a strike a threat to the national interest and obtain a court injunction delaying the strike for 90 days. The honeymoon that the revitalized union movement had enjoyed during the 1930s with a sympathetic public and Congress was over.

1949 and Recession

Toward the end of 1948, the ability to supply began to catch up with the high levels of postwar demand. The growth rate of demand started to level off. Inventories began to pile up, and induced investment started to slide as demand for expansion of facilities decreased. Investment dropped sharply from $46 billion in 1948 to $35.7 billion in 1949. Increases in consumption and government expenditure were not enough to offset this decline. GNP dropped slightly (by about $1 billion), and unemployment rose from 3.8 percent to 5.9 percent. Prices also dropped, by about 1 percent.

By the end of 1949, the economy was beginning to recover from this mild first recession after the war. Consumption and residential construction were still expanding, as were government expenditures for goods and services, especially military goods. Almost as if by accident, the tax cut in 1948 prior to the contraction sustained consumer purchasing power.

THE KOREAN WAR EXPANSION, 1950–1954

The Record

By the beginning of 1950, the economy was recovering from its first postwar recession. The outbreak of the Korean conflict in June of 1950 further accelerated this expansion, and the economy moved forward rapidly. GNP increased from $285 billion in 1950 to $365 billion in 1953. As a result of this expansion, unemployment fell from 5.3 to 2.9 percent. But also under the stimulus of expanding demand, prices rose from an index of 84 in 1950 to 93 in 1953 (see Table 18.3).

In 1953, the Korean War ended, and federal expenditures, especially military expenditures, declined. In the absence of offsetting investment expenditures, the economy entered its second postwar recession. This, too, was mild, although unemployment climbed to 5.5 percent in 1954.

Causes of the Expansion

During the 1949 recession, consumer demand for durable goods and residential construction was still strong because of the privations of the 1930s depression and the war years. Residential construction was stimulated as interest rates declined under the impact of general falling demand in 1949. The recovery began by early 1950.

After the Korean War broke out in June 1950, aggregate demand surged. Part of the increase in consumption and investment was in anticipation of a renewal of inflation and the reestablishment of wartime controls. A second surge was prompted by increases in government expenditures for goods and services. On the

Table 18.3. Economic Statistics, 1950–1954 (billions of dollars).

YEAR	GNP	CONSUMPTION	GROSS INVESTMENT	GOVERNMENT EXPENDITURES	FEDERAL EXPENDITURES FOR GOODS AND SERVICES	
					Military	Other
1950	285	191	54	38	14	4
1951	328	206	59	60	34	4
1952	346	217	52	75	46	6
1953	365	230	53	82	49	8
1954	365	237	52	74	41	6

YEAR	FEDERAL DEFICITS	CONSUMER PRICES (1957–1958 = 100)	FEDERAL DEBT	NET EXPORTS	UNEMPLOYMENT
1950	−2.2	84	256.9	+1.1	5.3
1951	+7.6	91	255.3	+3.0	3.3
1952	0.0	93	259.1	+2.6	3.0
1953	−5.3	93	266.0	+1.4	2.9
1954	−1.2	94	270.8	+2.5	5.5

SOURCE: U.S. Department of Commerce, Bureau of the Census, *Historical Statistics of the United States, Colonial Times to 1970* (Washington, D.C.: U.S. Government Printing Office, 1975).

federal level, an expanded military sector boosted expenditures from $14 billion in 1950 to $49 billion in 1953. State and local government expenditures also contributed to the expansion under the impact of continued shifts of population to suburbia and the increase in educational expenditures as the baby boom continued into the 1950s.

Given the relative inelasticity of supply, this increase in demand was greater than the ability of the economy to fill it without increases in prices. Inflation returned in 1950. The government responded with controls over prices, but the legislation that gave the president the power to set prices was allowed to lapse in 1952.

The 1954 Recession

With the end of the Korean War in 1953, federal expenditures, mostly in the area of military expenditures, were cut by $10 billion. This decrease should have caused a severe contraction, but because fiscal and monetary policy were used stimulatively, it resulted in only a mild recession. As government expenditures were cut, taxes were also decreased, shifting demand from government to civilian sources. At the same time, the Federal Reserve engaged in an easy money policy, increasing bank reserves and reducing interest rates. An increasing supply of money and falling interest rates stimulated borrowing for consumption, investment, and state and local expenditures based on borrowing.

AGAIN BOOM AND RECESSION, 1955–1959

The economy was recovering by the end of 1954. Stimulated by a boom in demand for consumer durables, the economy surged ahead in 1955. Record highs were made in the production of autos as well as of other consumer durables. As this boom collapsed, the slack was taken up by expansion in producer durables. The economy continued to expand until late 1957. But inflation revived along with the expansion.

The low levels of demand for consumer durables and a declining level of investment demand toward the end of 1957 slowed down the expansion. Efforts by the Eisenhower administration to counter the persistent inflation triggered the third and most severe postwar recession, that of 1957–1958. The administration moved to reduce the deficit in the federal budget, and the Federal Reserve contracted the supply of money and raised interest rates. The economy contracted. The federal budget deficit increased to almost $13 billion in 1959. Unemployment rose to almost 7 percent, the highest rate since the beginning of 1942. But for the first time prices increased during a contraction. The economy recovered quickly and began to expand by the end of 1958 (see Table 18.4).

WHAT'S NEW? THE GOVERNMENT SECTOR

Regulation

Most historians presume that direct federal government regulation of the business sector started with the Interstate Commerce Act of 1887 and its establishment of

Table 18.4. Economic Statistics, 1955–1959 (billions of dollars).

YEAR	GNP	CONSUMPTION	GROSS INVESTMENT	GOVERNMENT EXPENDITURES	FEDERAL EXPENDITURES FOR GOODS AND SERVICES	
					Military	Other
1955	398	254	67	75	39	6
1956	419	267	70	78	40	5
1957	441	281	68	86	44	5
1958	447	290	61	95	46	8
1959	484	311	75	97	46	8

YEAR	FEDERAL DEFICITS	CONSUMER PRICES (1957–1958 = 100)	FEDERAL DEBT	NET EXPORTS	UNEMPLOYMENT
1955	−3.0	93	274.4	+2.9	4.4
1956	+4.1	94	272.8	+4.6	4.1
1957	+3.2	98	272.4	+6.3	4.3
1958	−2.9	102	279.7	+3.4	6.8
1959	−12.9	104	287.8	+1.2	5.5

SOURCE: U.S. Department of Commerce, Bureau of the Census, *Historical Statistics of the United States, Colonial Times to 1970* (Washington, D.C.: U.S. Government Printing Office, 1975).

the Interstate Commerce Commission to regulate the railway industry. In 1890, the Sherman Antitrust Act began a series of antitrust laws. Government regulation was furthered in the pre–World War I period of 1900 to 1915 with acts strengthening the ICC and antitrust administration, the Pure Food and Drug Act (1906), the Federal Trade Commission Act (1914), the Clayton (antitrust) Act (1914), and the establishment of the Federal Reserve System (1914). This push toward business regulation was expanded in the 1930s, mostly under the New Deal programs of President Roosevelt. In the 1940s and 1950s, regulation continued to expand outside of war planning, especially in the areas of agriculture and transportation.

Agriculture and the Federal Government

After the abortive efforts of the Federal Farm Board (1929–1932) to increase farm incomes by purchasing and storing agricultural surpluses, Congress passed a series of acts aimed at increasing farm incomes. These included the Agricultural Adjustment Act of 1934, the Soil Conservation Act of 1936, and the Agricultural Adjustment Administration of 1938. Seen as a program, the aim of this legislation was to increase agricultural prices by destroying substantial amounts of output (1934) and by withdrawing land from production (the Soil Conservation Act of 1936). Finally, the program sought to have the government, through the Commodity Credit Corporation, buy surpluses of products and store them in order to increase prices by reducing agricultural supplies.

By 1941, the idea of government manipulation of agriculture prices to achieve parity between prices of agricultural products and prices paid by farmers for goods purchased was firmly implanted in the thinking of government policymakers. During the war, high demand for agricultural products seemed to resolve the problem of farm income. But policymakers were worried about a renewal of relatively low farm incomes after the war. For that reason, legislation was passed guaranteeing 80 percent of parity to agricultural prices for two years after the war ended.

After 1945, high levels of demand for food from a war-ravaged Europe and a prosperous America maintained high farm incomes. Still, political pressure by the farm lobby secured the federal government's continuing commitment to farm incomes based on parity (high farm prices). The device used was loans from the Commodity Credit Corporation to farmers on their products. If prices rose above the prices lent, the products were sold and the loans paid. If not, the CCC would take possession of the products for storage.

Under Truman, Agricultural Secretary Brannon tried to change this system of price supports to one of direct payments to farmers. This would minimize the cost of market intervention and allow supply and demand to freely fluctuate, reducing ultimate costs to consumers-taxpayers. Partly because direct payment seemed too much like welfare, this proposal was defeated.

In the early 1950s, agricultural prices started to weaken and the CCC parity–surplus storage system evolved to that point began to function. Efforts to reduce surpluses by reducing acreage had little effect because farmers withdrew their best land from production and increased output on the remaining land. Toward the end of the Eisenhower administration, Secretary Ezra T. Benson introduced the soil bank program that paid farmers to withdraw land from crop production. By the end of the 1950s, stored surpluses were reaching scandalous proportions. In 1950–1954, the average number of bushels held by the CCC for wheat was 382 million and for corn 324 million. This had grown to 1,195 million bushels of wheat, and 1,286 million bushels of corn by 1960. In short, attempts to intervene in agricultural markets seemed to achieve little in terms of stabilizing income or meeting government parity goals. Achievements in that regard were not only modest but also accomplished at high costs, both in terms of administrative costs and loss of efficiency in resource allocation.

Transportation and Regulation

As we already know, regulation of the railway industry started at the federal level with the creation of the Interstate Commerce Commission in 1887. At first the Commission tried to control abuses in the railroad industry by stimulating competition. By 1900, it had changed its emphasis to fixing the prices of railway services. The Transportation Act of 1920 shifted the Commission's emphasis again: it was now supposed to regulate so as to generate acceptable rates of return in the industry. Congress had recognized that railway investment, based on rates of return generated by ICC price regulation, had fallen greatly. This recognition was hastened by the fact that during World War I railway plant and equipment proved to be in such poor condition that a government takeover for 26 months was required to facilitate movements of material and soldiers. Thus the Transportation Act mandated the Commission to study both efficiency and profits.

This shift from a policy of protecting the consumer from monopoly pricing to one of concern for acceptable profits by the railroads was a dramatic change that dominated ICC policy through the 1930s, 1940s, and 1950s. Nonetheless, the railroad industry declined throughout this period. In the 1920s, the railroads had barely managed to hold their own in an expanding economy against the emerging competition from trucks for freight and autos for passenger traffic. The depression of the 1930s was especially harmful to the railroads. Even in a recovering economy after 1933, railroad activity continued to contract. The mushrooming growth of the trucking industry was especially serious competition.

In response to what some saw as chaotic growth in trucking, the Motor Carriers Act of 1935 placed common and contract carriers under Interstate Commerce Commission regulation. The act became Part II of the Interstate Commerce Act. Again, the ICC was charged with maintaining acceptable profits, now in both the railroad and the trucking industry.

By 1960, only one-third of all trucking was regulated. The growth of private carriers was stimulated by rate setting to protect the least efficient regulated firm and by entry restrictions.

By the Transportation Act of 1940, common water carriers involved in interstate commerce on rivers, lakes, and canals within the United States were also placed under the control of the ICC; this became Part III of the ICC Act. Because of the rise of private lines and numerous exemptions, however, only 10 percent of inland water traffic actually came under ICC control.

Now the ICC had to set prices and regulations for three competing forms of transportation: railroads, trucks, and inland waterway transportation. The Commission was charged with obtaining acceptable rates of return for the firms. Some critics have charged that the ICC actually hindered efficiency and fostered higher costs and prices.

Despite this regulatory support, the railroad industry continued to decline after 1945. Increasing amounts of coal, iron ore, and wheat were shipped by lake, and shipping of steel and other bulk manufactured materials to the coasts declined as imports of these goods increased. Also, high-value low-bulk production was increasingly being carried by trucks. In addition, the automobile and airplane greatly reduced railroad passenger traffic.

From its early days, air transportation received subsidies from the federal government, including those contained in establishing airports and air traffic control systems. In 1938, the Civil Aeronautics Act established the Civil Aeronautics Board (CAB) and the Civil Aeronautics Administration (CAA). The CAB set rates, issued permits to fly assigned routes, and established safety rules. The CAA enforced safety rules and promoted air traffic. The charge to the CAB was to achieve, through rate setting and other regulation, acceptable rates of return for the airlines in such a way so as to promote air transportation.

By 1960, regulation of transportation by the ICC and the CAB was clearly oriented to the firm and the industry, not to the consumer. Indeed, some critics argued that the government had created a regulated cartel in each industry and that firms had responded to the prohibition against price competition by engaging in other cost-increasing forms of competition that distorted resource allocation without generating monopoly profits. By legislative mandate, the prime concern of the ICC and CAB in establishing pricing and other forms of regulation was the profitability of the regulated firms. Many have concluded that in carrying out this charge the ICC and CAB supported less efficient firms and distorted industrial activity to the point where neither consumers nor firms gained from their activities.

As we shall see in the next chapter, federal regulation of industries reached its zenith in the 1960s and 1970s, when it was extended to product labeling and safety, civil rights, consumer disclosure, and environmental impact, among other spheres. The Occupational Health and Safety Act of 1970 created the Occupational Safety and Health Administration (OSHA) with broad powers to mandate and enforce job safety standards. All of this finally led to a searching reexamination of the personal and economic effects of government regulation. As much as anything else, such regulation has been linked to declining productivity. One distinguished industrialist, David Packard, has argued that government regulation conceivably is the most important single factor in the decrease in productivity in the United States.

Automatic Stabilizers

The three postwar recessions, in 1949, 1954, and 1958, were relatively mild, especially when compared to the economic disasters involved in the depressions of 1907, 1921, 1929–1933, and 1937–1938. One explanation for the relative mildness of these business fluctuations is the appearance of a number of **automatic stabilizers,** factors that tend to dampen business fluctuations without conscious decision making. Two points must be kept in mind about these stabilizers. First, they were not created to function as stabilizers, and second, they were not strong enough to eliminate fluctuations.

One stabilizer is government expenditures in the form of transfer payments. Unemployment compensation, welfare payments, Social Security, veterans' payments, and business subsidies, especially to agriculture, tend to increase automatically during a contraction. The increase in expenditures enlarges purchasing power, countering the contraction. During a period of expansion and inflationary pressure, such expenditures decline, inhibiting the rate of demand increase and reducing inflationary pressures. The strength of this stabilizer increased as transfer payments grew from 4 percent of personal income in 1940 to 6.6 percent in 1950 to 7.1 percent in 1960.

A second stabilizer is the progressive federal personal income tax. As unemployment develops with a contraction, personal income falls, along with aver-age effective tax rates. Thus the effective overall tax rate falls, lessening the impact of the contraction on disposable income and consumption. During inflationary periods, money incomes increase and incomes move into higher tax brackets, lessening the expansion of disposable income and consumption growth. This effect, though stabilizing, eventually created strong resistance from taxpayer groups, who saw their real incomes falling in the inflation of the late 1970s and early 1980s at the same time that their after-tax incomes were being reduced by movement to higher marginal tax rates as a result of increases in their nominal incomes. Support developed for indexing—tying marginal tax rates to changes in real income—and that is reflected in the federal tax legislation of the 1980s. We will say more about these matters in the last chapter.

Federal income taxes increased in importance from 1940 to 1960. In 1940, federal income taxes were only 15 percent of federal tax receipts. In 1950, they were 38 percent, and by 1960, they were 44 percent. Payment of federal income taxes averaged 1.4 percent of personal income in 1940 and 10 percent in 1960.

In 1929, government expenditures for goods and services were about 9 percent of GNP. By 1960, this had grown to about 25 percent. Because government expenditures are more stable than investment, total demand became more stable, lessening business fluctuations. Of course, this increase in the share of

GNP taken by government has had many other consequences, including the deficit financing associated with much of that expenditure. Concern that this deficit financing was negatively affecting interest rates and crowding private investors out of the financial markets was to lead in the 1970s and 1980s to advocacy of balanced budgets (the Graham-Rudman legislation). Of course, budgets can be balanced with gov-ernments taking a larger or smaller share of GNP, so government expenditure remains a relatively stable component of GNP.

Inflation

When World War II ended, as we have said, many people were concerned about a possible revival of the high unemployment rates of the 1930s. As an example of this concern, toward the end of the war the company making Pabst Blue Ribbon beer had sponsored an essay contest for economists on the question of how 50 million civilian jobs could be obtained after the war. This concern over unemployment quickly gave way to worries about persistent long-term inflation. The price index (1957–1958 = 100), which was 48.8 in 1940, increased to 84 in 1950 and to 104 in 1959. Prices over these 20 years rose by more than 100 percent.

The Military-Industrial Complex

President Eisenhower in 1961, during his last address to the people of the United States, warned about the dangers of what he called the *military-industrial complex,* or the cooperation between the Defense Department and a collection of major corporations that provide materials for the military. He was concerned that this combination of economic and political power would be difficult to control by the civilian political leadership.

Of course, military expenditures for goods and services reached a high point toward the end of the war in 1945, with $73.5 billion expended, or 34 percent of GNP. These declined after the war until a rearmament program began with the start of the cold war in 1948. The Korean War in 1950 gave a further boost to military expenditures, which declined again at the end of that war in 1953. In 1955, military expenditures again increased. By 1959, such expenditures for goods and services stood at $46 billion, almost 10 percent of GNP.

It is true that military expenditures constituted a substantial share of total federal expenditures for goods and services, and they were a significant share of total GNP. It also seems that these expenditures played a role in business fluctuations, their increase aiding in the recovery from the recession of 1949 and their decrease impacting the contraction of 1954. However, military expenditures have not been shown to be the primary factor in explaining the expansions and contractions of the U.S. economy from 1945 to 1959. These variations were the result of many factors, only one of which was variations in military expenditures.

The Distribution of Income and Poverty

Table 18.5 shows that there was little change in the share of total income going to the lowest 40 percent of income receivers between 1941 and 1962. However, the middle income receivers (the third and fourth fifths in the table) did increase their shares somewhat from 1941 to 1957, at the expense of the top fifth income receivers.

The word "poor" is defined here within the context of the United States experience and involves *relative* income shares. Those who fall within the lowest 40 percent of income receivers are arbitrarily designated as "poor," although not all of these people would be considered poor in the absolute sense. As we have seen from Table 18.5, income redistribution from the production of goods and services did not increase this group's relative shares. Income improvement for the poor came from the growing total incomes created by economic growth and from transfer payments for unemployment compensation, Social Security, and growing welfare systems. Alan Blinder (3), examining a longer and slightly different postwar period, 1952 to 1977, found that the share of the top 5 percent of family incomes fell but that the share of the lowest 2 percent rose only slightly. As he observes, "the central stylized fact about income inequality has been its constancy." Clearly, the view of many neo-classical economists that economic growth is a powerful engine for solving or ameliorating economic problems is borne out by U.S. economic experience since 1946. However, it remains to be seen whether greater income equality will also result from that growth process.

John K. Galbraith (8), in his best-seller *The Affluent Society* (1958), sounded a note of concern that was to be taken up loudly by others in the 1960s. He maintained that public needs, including income redistribution to the poor, had increasingly been neglected in people's concern with their own private consumption needs.

The Balance of Payments

From 1945 through the rest of the 1940s and 1950s, the United States experienced large deficits to be financed in its balance of payments (see the Review of Economic

Table 18.5. Percentage of Income Received by U.S. Families and Individuals, 1941–1962.

INCOME BANK	1941	1947	1957	1962
Lowest fifth	4	4	4	3
Second fifth	10	11	11	11
Third fifth	15	17	18	17
Fourth fifth	22	24	25	25
Highest fifth	49	46	43	44

Source: U.S. Department of Commerce, Bureau of the Census, *Historical Statistics of the United States, Colonial Times to 1957* (Washington, D.C.: U.S. Government Printing Office, 1960), p. 166; Herman P. Miller, *Income Distribution in the United States* (Washington, D.C.: U.S. Government Printing Office, 1966), p. 21.

Concepts in Chapter 15). U.S. earnings of foreign exchange came primarily from two sources: the favorable balance of trade, with exports exceeding imports; and the flow of dividends, interest, and profits from U.S. foreign investments. This second source was a growing one, as U.S. residents continued to make foreign investments after the war.

However, these earnings were not high enough to provide the foreign exchange needed to finance other foreign transactions. These transactions were primarily in four categories. First, as peace returned, American tourists spent increasing amounts in other countries. Second, the United States became the "policeman" of the world, and spent significant sums abroad to maintain its military forces. Third, for political and perhaps also for humanitarian reasons, the U.S. government provided large sums to rehabilitate and strengthen the economies of many countries. At first, under the Marshall Plan, these funds went primarily to the war-ravaged developed economies of Europe and Japan, those that would provide allies against Russia in the cold war. Later in the 1950s, this aid went increasingly to less developed economies. Finally, with the end of the war, the location of American foreign investments changed. Such investments increasingly went to developed countries rather than underdeveloped countries, and more went into facilities for commodity production than into the production of raw materials.

Since the demand for foreign exchange exceeded what our trade surplus could supply, a balance of payments deficit developed. To finance that deficit, nonresidents accumulated claims to U.S. dollars and a small but steady trickle of gold was exported.

For most of the period, this deficit, with its nonresident accumulation of dollars and gold, was desired and was actually a goal of government policy. At the end of the war, the economic future of the noncommunist European economies was very uncertain. Much of their physical capital had been destroyed. Financially, there were few monetary reserves. The accumulation of dollars and gold through the U.S. deficits solved this problem of lack of reserves and greatly strengthened these noncommunist economies.

However, by the mid-1950s, this **dollar gap** or shortage had been solved. In fact, the gap had become a surplus. But the U.S. economy did not seem to be able to reverse its deficit position in the balance of payments.

A SUMMARY

The economic expansion of the 1940s and 1950s was marred by only three mild contractions, in 1949, 1954, and (the most severe) in 1958. This 20-year period (even excluding the war years of 1941–1945) was one of long-term increases in income and sustained employment that rivals, if not exceeds, the period of 1897 to 1914 and the "prosperity decade" of 1922 to 1929.

High levels of consumption demand, fueled by the privations of the 1930s and the postponed demand of the war years, were led by demand for consumer durables. The move to the suburbs, the housing shortages caused by depression and war, and government subsidizing of middle-class housing through veterans' benefits and FHA loan guarantees stimulated high levels of residential construction. Investment demand for construction of plant and for equipment was fueled by induced investment (the need for facilities to meet increased consumption demand), replacement investment (replacing worn-out and technologically obsolete plant and equipment, resulting from low levels of investment during the depression and war), and autonomous investment (technological changes occurring from 1945 to 1959). High levels of government expenditures from rearmament, highway construction, and income redistribution through increased transfer payments were significant additional sources of demand.

But there were persistent problems that continued to plague the economy. The concern about a possible return of massive unemployment after the war was replaced by 1959 with growing concern about inflation. Income distribution concerned many, though that concern grew in the 1960s. The lowest 40 percent of income receivers did not increase their share of total cash income. The poor gained from economic growth and growing transfer payments, but the problem of poverty remained. A balance-of-payments deficit created after the war to strengthen noncommunist economies (the dollar gap) remained by the end of the 1950s after the dollar gap had been met.

Expansion continued into the 1960s and 1970s. But old problems remained, and new problems were to appear. A key, if controversial, feature of the postwar period was the change in the relationship between government and business. Increasingly, government seemed to believe that private economic processes could not be relied upon to provide an adequate quality of life and security for the citizenry. As a result, regulatory activity was extended to many major economic activities, including, at one time or another, prices, health and safety, and consumer information. A regulatory bureaucracy was created that became so extensive and intrusive that its effects were to occasion a searching reexamination of regulatory costs and benefits in the late 1970s.

QUESTIONS

1. What were the factors that caused the expansions of 1940–1948, 1950–1953, and 1955–1957?
2. What were the factors that caused the contractions of 1949, 1954, and 1958?
3. How did the automatic stabilizers contribute to the relatively mild contractions that occurred from 1940 to 1959?
4. What were the problems that plagued the U.S. economy from 1940 to 1959?
5. Evaluate the performance of the U.S. economy from 1940 to 1959, stressing both its strong points and its weaknesses.
6. What seems to have occasioned the growth of government regulation after World War II? What were some of the major forms of this regulation?

SUGGESTED READINGS

1. Anderson, Terry, and P. J. Hill. *The Birth of a Transfer Society*. Stanford, Ca.: Hoover Institution Press, 1980.

2. Bernstein, Irving. "The Growth of American Unions, 1945–60." *Labor History, 2* (Spring 1961).

3. Blinder, Alan S. "The Level and Distribution of Economic Well-Being." In *The American Economy in Transition*, ed. Martin Feldstein. Chicago: National Bureau of Economic Research, 1980.

4. Blyth, C. A. *American Business Cycles, 1945–50*. London: Allen & Unwin, 1968.

5. Craf, John R. *A Survey of the American Economy, 1940–1946*. New York: North River Press, 1947.

6. Feldstein, Martin. *The American Economy in Transition*. Chicago: National Bureau of Economic Research, 1980.

7. Friedman, Milton, and Anna J. Schwartz. *A Monetary History of the United States, 1867–1960*. Princeton, N.J.: Princeton University Press, 1963.

8. Galbraith, John Kenneth. *The Affluent Society*. Boston: Houghton Mifflin, 1958.

9. Galbraith, J. K. *A Life in Our Times*. Boston: Houghton Mifflin, 1981.

10. Gilder, George. *Wealth and Poverty*. New York: Basic Books, 1981.

11. Gordon, Robert A. *Economic Instability and Growth: The American Record*. New York: Harper and Row, 1974.

12. Graham, Otis, Jr. *Toward a Planned Society: From Roosevelt to Nixon*. New York: Oxford University Press, 1976.

13. Hamberg, Daniel. "The Recession of 1948–49 in the United States." *Economic Journal, 62* (March 1962).

14. Higgs, Robert. *Crisis and Leviathan: Critical Issues in the Emergence of the Mixed Economy*. New York: Oxford University Press, 1986.

15. Kolko, Gabriel. *Wealth and Power in America*. New York: Praeger, 1962.

16. Lebergott, Stanley. *The American Economy: Income, Wealth and Want*. Princeton, N.J.: Princeton University Press, 1976.

17. Miller, Herman P. *Income Distribution in the United States*. Washington, D.C.: U.S. Government Printing Office, 1966.

18. Rockoff, Hugh. *Drastic Measures: A History of Wage and Price Controls in the United States*. New York: Cambridge University Press, 1984.

19. Rockoff, Hugh. "Indirect Price Increases and Real Wages During World War II." *Explorations in Economic History, 15* (October 1978).

20. Soltow, Lee. "Evidence on Income Inequality in the United States 1866–1965." *Journal of Economic History, 29* (June 1969).

21. Soltow, Lee. "Income Inequality in the United States from 1790 to 1860." *Journal of Economic History, 9* (Fall 1971.)

22. Vatter, Harold G. *The U.S. Economy in the 1950s*. New York: Norton, 1963.

Chapter 19 —————————————

THE 1960s AND THE 1970s

We are just now beginning to develop a historical perspective on this period in our recent past. For that reason, it is advisable to exercise caution in attempting to discern within it historical turning points in our economic development. Still, it is possible to make at least a tentative assessment of this period that was often marked by both domestic and international turbulence.

At the outset we will take a macroeconomic view of the two decades, with the primary focus on variations in output, employment, and prices as well as the distribution of income. We shall also offer some indications of the causes of these variations. In the second part of the chapter, we will look at some of the more significant new and continuing problems of the economy and assay some of the more important structural changes that occurred during the period.

A MACRO VIEW OF THE 1960s

Slow Growth and Low Inflation, 1960–1964

The decade opened in 1960–1961 with the mildest of the four postwar recessions. Declines in investment and slow growth in consumption and government expenditures kept the advance of GNP in 1961 to $14 billion. In 1961, unemployment rose to almost 7 percent. Some economists have argued that the main cause of the recession was the extended strike in the steel industry in 1960.

The economy expanded more vigorously in 1962, but the rate of growth in real terms remained low, averaging less than 3 percent per year from 1962 through 1964. Although this rate was near the long-term average for the post–Civil War economy, it became a matter of concern when compared to the two-digit real growth rates in such countries as West Germany and Japan and the more than 5 percent rate in the Soviet Union. Also, this slow growth was mirrored in unemployment rates above 5 percent, rates that many considered too high for the health of the economy. The one redeeming feature of this sluggishness was the low rate of inflation, which averaged only a little more than 1 percent per year from 1960 to 1961 (see Table 19.1).

Income Distribution

Partly as a result of the higher unemployment rates, there was increasing concern about income distribution and poverty. It was not that family incomes were fall-

Table 19.1. Economic Statistics, 1960–1969 (billions of dollars).

YEAR	GNP	CONSUMPTION	GROSS INVESTMENT	GOVERNMENT EXPENDITURES FOR GOODS AND SERVICES	
				Federal Defense	Federal Other
1960	504	325	75	45	9
1961	520	335	72	48	10
1962	560	355	83	52	12
1963	591	375	87	51	14
1964	632	401	94	50	15
1965	685	433	108	50	17
1966	750	466	121	61	17
1967	794	492	117	72	18
1968	864	536	126	78	21
1969	930	580	139	78	20

YEAR	STATE AND LOCAL EXPENDITURE	GOVERNMENT TRANSFER PAYMENTS	FEDERAL DEFICIT	CONSUMER PRICE INDEX (1967 = 100)	UNEMPLOYMENT (PERCENT OF CIVILIAN LABOR FORCE)
1960	46	28.5	+0.3	89	5.5
1961	50	32.4	−3.4	90	6.7
1962	54	33.3	−7.1	91	5.5
1963	58	35.3	−4.8	92	5.7
1964	64	36.7	−5.9	93	5.2
1965	70	39.9	−1.6	95	4.5
1966	79	44.1	−3.8	97	3.8
1967	89	51.8	−8.7	100	3.8
1968	101	59.6	−25.2	104	3.6
1969	111	65.8	+3.2	110	3.5

SOURCE: U.S. Department of Commerce, Bureau of the Census. *Historical Statistics of the United States: Colonial Times to 1970* (Washington, D.C.: U.S. Government Printing Office, 1975).

ing or that a growing percentage of American families were becoming impoverished; on the contrary, economic growth since 1950 had raised many incomes substantially. Income distribution effects can be seen in Table 19.2.

Note that the income measures in Table 19.2 are constant (1977) dollars. Current-dollar figures would greatly overstate the effect of growth because inflation (the consumer price index grew from 89 in 1960 to 181.5 in 1977; see Tables 19.1 and 19.3) raised the nominal incomes of almost all Americans and caused a near disappearance in the period of those earning less than $3,000.

Even in constant dollars, though, the engine of growth had major effects in dramatically reducing the percentage of families with incomes below $5,000. In 1960, the start of the period with which this chapter is concerned, more than 17 percent of families earned less than $5,000; by 1977, this percentage had declined by almost half to slightly more than 9 percent. Equally startling is the percentage of families with incomes over $12,000: They increased from 44.2 percent in 1960 to 64.4 percent in 1977. This progress clearly benefited not only whites but also large numbers of black and other minority families, more than half of whom earned less than $5,000 in 1950 and less than a quarter of whom received such low incomes in 1977. Many in these groups were also becoming middle-class and upper-income recipients by 1977; those with incomes above $12,000 increased from 6.4 percent in 1950 to 44.8 percent in 1977.

Still, growth and transfer payments clearly did not eliminate poverty. Indeed, as Stanley Lebergott (12) has argued, it may be that the American economy generates both growth and poverty through its social processes. Those who are elderly, divorced, the single-parent heads of households, and the like inevitably have less income than others and tend to grow in numbers (though not necessarily as a percent of the population) as economic growth occurs. Even in 1977, more than 31 percent of black families and 22.7 percent of Hispanic families had incomes below the official poverty level.

Table 19.2. Distribution of Family Incomes (constant 1977 dollars).

YEAR	$3,000 AND UNDER	$3,000– $4,999	$5,000– $5,,999	$6,000– $6,999	$7,000– $9,999	$10,000– $11,999	$12,000– $24,999	$25,000 AND ABOVE
1950	14.3	10.3	7.3	7.1	23.8	19.7	16.6	0.8
1960	8.6	8.5	4.1	4.7	15.0	14.8	36.8	7.4
1970	4.3	5.7	3.2	3.5	11.0	7.9	46.3	18.2
1977	3.6	5.7	3.5	3.7	10.9	7.2	42.0	22.4
			BLACK AND MINORITY INCOMES					
1950	33.8	19.3	10.9	9.0	17.1	3.6	5.4	1.0
1977	9.6	13.2	6.3	6.1	14.2	7.9	34.0	10.8

SOURCE: *Statistical Abstract of the United States, 1979* (Washington, D.C.: U.S. Government Printing Office, 1979).

the convertibility of gold (limiting it to foreign central banks), and pressures on the dollar caused more gold to flow out of the U.S. economy. This reduction in gold convertibility moved the U.S. economy further away from a convertible gold standard.

Although the 1960s experienced the longest sustained expansion of the U.S. economy in history (1961–1969), it also ended with serious problems. Inflation had returned and was rising. Balance-of-payments problems were deepening. Indeed, they had become a major problem. The war on poverty had collapsed. In addition, poverty became increasingly concentrated in urban areas, contributing to the crisis of the inner city. In part, urban financial problems, which were approaching crisis proportions, were caused by the influx of the poor into the cities and the simultaneous flight of the middle class and industry to the suburbs.

The performance of economic policy recommended by the economics profession was mixed. The tax cut of 1965 and the tightening of credit by the Federal Reserve in 1966 were considered to have been successful on the whole. But the tax increase of 1968 was a failure in stabilizing unemployment and inflation.

INSTABILITY IN THE 1970s

The Recession of 1970–1971

The long-term expansion of the 1960s ended with the recession of 1970–1971. The rising inflation of 1969 eventually discouraged consumption and investment; the decline in investment after the extended expansion caused a fall in real GNP. Unemployment rose to 4.9 percent in 1970 and to almost 6 percent in 1971.

The experience of the 1958 recession was repeated, only worse. The rise in unemployment was accompanied by inflation. The price index increased from 110 (1967 = 100) in 1969 to 116 in 1970 and to 121 in 1971.

Both the unemployment and inflation rates were widely deemed unacceptable. But an effort to reduce one seemed to require policies that would tend to increase the other. Some economists were beginning to talk of a "crisis in government policy." John Kenneth Galbraith (3, 4) labeled the phenomenon of rising unemployment coupled with inflation a "crisis in stabilization policy." He argued that functional finance fiscal policies and monetary policies based on "Keynesian" analysis could not deal with both conditions at the same time. Efforts to reduce unemployment would at the least prevent prices from falling. He called for mandatory price and wage controls to control inflation.

In early 1971, Congress voted President Nixon the authority to impose wage and price controls. While some have argued that this was more a dare than a serious intention, if dare it was, Nixon accepted it. On August 15, 1971, the president issued what has been called his "New Economic Policy." This policy, indeed radical for its time, was to attack all three problems of the economy at once: unemployment, inflation, and the balance-of-payments deficits.

To deal with unemployment, Nixon proposed a number of tax cuts especially aimed at stimulating investment. To combat inflation, he utilized the powers conferred on him by the recent legislation and imposed a 90-day wage and price freeze, to be followed by a series of phases with various degrees of controls. The controls would end with a voluntary program in late 1973 and 1974 when the enabling legislation expired. To attack the balance-of-payments deficits, he imposed a 10 percent increase in tariffs on imported automobiles and abandoned the gold standard completely by **floating the dollar** in the international exchange markets. The aim was to let market forces determine exchange rates of the dollar against other currencies. With a deficit, the dollar would **depreciate** (more dollars would be needed to buy a given amount of foreign exchange), and consequently, the foreign price of U.S. exports would decrease while the domestic price of imports would increase. The resulting increase in exports and decrease in imports would help to alleviate the payments problem.

It is unclear whether Nixon's wage-price controls were a success or a failure; more research is needed. The controls have many critics. Some charge that they were unnecessary because the rate of growth of prices was beginning to decrease before August 15, 1971. Others have concluded that the administration of the controls was inadequate and influenced by pressure groups and that serious mistakes were made. There have been arguments that, as the controls were removed, prices and wages increased to "catch up" and that part of the inflation of 1973 and 1974 was caused by firms and unions trying to make up for postponed increases.

But the freeze and early controls may have broken the cycle of price increase expectations that lead to anticipatory demand and price increases. In effect, then, the freeze may have "cooled" the inflationary surge started in the late 1960s. Clearly, during the three months of Phase I, there was virtually no increase in consumer prices; and during Phase II, there was only a 3.4 percent price rise over a 17-month period.

Expansion and Decline, 1972–1974

The economy resumed its expansion before the end of 1971 (see Table 19.3). But unemployment fell only slowly with this advance, remaining at an average level of almost 5 percent in 1973. While the inflationary rate cooled in 1972, it began to increase toward the end of that year. A prime stimulant of the increase was the sharp rise in food prices, primarily the result of a billion-dollar purchase of wheat for immediate delivery by the Soviet Union, plus a disastrous loss of the anchovy catch off Peru, which increased the prices of feed grains and flour. The depreciation of the dollar by 10 percent in 1973 further increased foreign demand for relatively cheaper U.S. agricultural exports. Another stunning blow to world and U.S. inflation was the increase in crude oil prices by OPEC (Organization of Petroleum Exporting Countries) in late 1973.

As inflation accelerated in 1973, the Federal Reserve moved to severely restrict excess reserves in order to increase interest rates and to reduce lending.

These monetary actions were designed to reduce the money supply and prices. The Fed, however, proved unsuccessful in controlling prices despite increases in the prime bank rate to over 12 percent and, for a time, the drying up of excess reserves to such an extent that *The Wall Street Journal* wrote about the possibility of a liquidity crisis in the banking system.

Inflation continued to increase in 1974, but at the same time unemployment also began to increase and real output to decline. The recession of 1974 was the most severe contraction the economy had faced since the 1930s. Real GNP declined by about 3 percent. Unemployment reached a high of 9.2 percent. Aggravating the contraction and inflicting additional harm, though, was inflation, which topped 12 percent in 1974. The term applied to this situation of high inflation and high unemployment occurring at the same time was **stagflation.**

Recovery, 1975–1979

Under the impact of high unemployment and low levels of demand, as well as an easing of oil prices, the inflationary rate declined, in some months of 1976 to lows of 4 to 5 percent (on an annual basis). Unemployment rates fell from a high of 8.5 percent in 1975 to 5.8 percent in 1979. While the economy was growing, though, it became apparent that it was growing at a slower and slower rate. By 1980, the economy clearly was entering a recession with declining per capita GNP and rising unemployment.

Stabilization Controversies

As we have seen, the idea of using government budget surpluses and deficits as active contracyclical tools achieved considerable *academic* popularity after World War II. Not, however, until the Kennedy-Johnson years did it receive sufficient political support to be tested as public policy. There had been, of course, budget deficits and occasional surpluses earlier, but they were more the result than the cause of cyclical variations in tax revenues and expenditure programs. To some extent in earlier postwar recessions (1958 and 1970–1971), but especially in the recession of 1974, economic stabilization policies encountered a new situation—one of simultaneously rising unemployment and prices. Traditional fiscal and monetary policies could not deal with both at the same time; whenever policymakers tried to deal with one, the policies pursued tended to aggravate the other. If unemployment and inflation were both at unacceptable levels (as, for example, in 1974, when unemployment was 9.2 percent and inflation was over 12 percent), the worsening of either one made an already high level of the other even more unacceptable. In addition, both inflation and unemployment seemed to be becoming more resistant to control. There was increasing concern that stagflation had become built into the structure of the American economy.

Various explanations were advanced for this phenomenon of stagflation. In part, it might derive from sources external to the American economy, and therefore not be susceptible to control by U.S. policymakers. An outstanding example is OPEC's 400 percent increase in oil prices at the end of 1973. Also, structural changes such as growing monopolization might be causing price increase higher than productivity growth or higher than would occur under competitive conditions. Examples are cost-push inflation generated by unions and administered price inflation from firms that increase prices on finished products by restricting supply. Unemployment might be caused by shifts in demand for different kinds of labor through changes in demand for products (anthracite coal to oil, for example) or changes in technology (such as automation eliminating the need for unskilled labor). Another factor proposed to explain stagflation is inflation induced by the federal government through high deficits, increasing demand above the ability of the economy to supply at stable prices, and through price-increasing regulation by such agencies as the Department of Agriculture and the Interstate Commerce Commission.

Concern began to grow among both economists and policymakers that traditional "Keynesian" remedies, operating largely from the demand side of the economy, would be inadequate to deal with stagflation. This crisis in economic theory and policy gave rise to the supply side arguments that were to have such a substantial influence in the 1980s.

International Trade and the American Economy

A key change in the American economy in these two decades was the rapidly growing importance of international trade and finance. Indeed, this sector resumed an importance it had not enjoyed since before World War I. Exports, for example, grew more than 11-fold between 1960 and 1980, while the GNP grew more than 5-fold. By the 1970s, net exports (exports minus imports) had become negative for the first time in decades. These relationships can be seen in Table 19.4. By the 1970s, balance-of-payments problems were persistent and troublesome. Deficits to be financed were not new; indeed, they had started at the end of the war as government aid was extended to a war-ravaged world.

Table 19.4.   U.S. International Merchandise Transactions, 1960–1980 (millions of dollars).

YEAR	EXPORTS	IMPORTS	NET
1960	19,650	−14,758	4,892
1965	26,461	−21,510	4,951
1970	42,469	39,666	2,603
1975	107,088	98,185	8,903
1980	224,269	240,749	−25,480

SOURCE: *Economic Report of the President* (Washington, D.C.: U.S. Government Printing Office, 1986).

By the early 1970s, it had become clear that trade policy changes were required. As part of his New Economic Policy of August 1971, President Nixon abandoned an already greatly restricted gold standard and floated the dollar. Since then, the exchange rate of the dollar has either floated, determined by market demand, or has been stabilized by market activities of either the United States or foreign governments or both.

In terms of the balance-of-payments accounts itself, the major problems lay in the inability of the United States to earn enough in the merchandise or commodity account (exports versus imports), and in receipts of dividends, profits, and interest from prior foreign investment, to provide foreign exchange for other transactions in the current account plus the steady debit balance in long-term capital. The situation worsened during the 1970s because of a tendency to increase imports relative to exports. In the 1960s, the balance between imports and exports was, for the decade, a credit balance of $40.8 billion. From 1970 to 1980, this had become a debit balance of 129.3 billion.

Because of U.S. inability to earn enough foreign exchange to pay for debit balances in both the current and the long-term capital account, nonresidents have continued to accumulate short-term assets in the United States. These assets are concentrated in four groups: Japan, West Germany, holdings by OPEC countries, and claims to dollars held in Europe (so-called *Eurodollars*). Critics have referred to this as the "selling of America."

The increase in imports was concentrated in two areas: oil and manufactured and semimanufactured goods, principally from Japan and Western Europe, but increasingly from newly industrializing nations such as Korea, Taiwan, Singapore, and Brazil.

By the mid-1970s, the decline in the export-import position of the United States had reignited the old debate about trade policy. The International Trade Commission of the United States received an increasing number of complaints about unfair trade restrictions imposed by other countries. The threat of trade wars, almost forgotten during the era of the General Agreement for Tariffs and Trade (GATT), awakened memories of the 1930s.

Pollution and Health and Safety

The economic growth of the United States has been accompanied by substantial disregard for the future supplies of many resources and a lack of concern for the externality effects of production and consumption on the environment within which we live. The virtual mining of the soil (continuous cropping without replacing losses in soil nutrients) in agriculture through most of the nineteenth century and the overcutting of many areas of timberland are prime examples of this disregard of future resources. Pollution of air, rivers, lakes, and oceans through consumption and industrial production are costs that were largely ignored until recently.

Economic analysis suggests that wasteful uses of natural resources may have been rational early in our history when labor was the scarce resource and land or timber the abundant one. Also, as long as the environment could absorb the pollution and "clean itself," clean air and water were free goods, and the use of the environment as a free dumping ground for production and consumption waste could be tolerated. Therefore, the calls for conservation—for example, the conservation movement during the presidency of Theodore Roosevelt in the early twentieth century—went largely unheeded.

By the 1960s, the problems of pollution and scarcity of material resources could no longer be avoided. A rash of books, articles, and organizations concerned with pollution and scarce resources began to appear, predicting that unless economic growth itself was curtailed, pollution would intensify to the point of threatening human existence on this planet. The Club of Rome sponsored a study by Meadows and others (14), called *The Limits of Economic Growth*, that predicted the exhaustion of nonreproducible resources such as oil by the year 2000 and resultant worldwide poverty if economic growth was not immediately curtailed.

Most economists are confident that pollution can be controlled by government regulation, or even by the market itself, without reducing economic growth. In fact, the Club of Rome, in a more recent study, has revised its predictions in a more optimistic direction. Many people argue that economic growth is needed to provide the resources to reduce pollution. Also, many economists maintain that (a) technological change caused by high prices of scarce resources will encourage new technology that conserves the scarce resource or new technology that substitutes new resources for the old; and/or (b) the functioning of the market, in which high prices for scarce resources reduce the quantity demanded of that resource, will encourage the use of lower-priced, more abundant resource substitutes. Either or both of these outcomes may solve the problem of reduced supplies of nonreproducible resources.

Beginning in the 1960s, a series of legislative acts at the federal and state level substantially expanded government responsibility in the areas of pollution control and health and safety. Included in these acts was the establishment of the federal Environmental Protection Agency (EPA) and the Occupational Safety and Health Administration (OSHA). Many criticisms have been directed at these programs. Some feel that they are too weak to reduce pollution significantly and protect health and safety. Others charge that the programs are choked in administrative red tape, increase costs of production, and sacrifice needed jobs in communities when facilities are closed because of the higher cost of pollution control or because projects are refused permission to operate on environmental or health and safety grounds. A more telling criticism has been expressed by Stanley Lebergott (12), who points up the irrational pattern of expenditures by these agencies. Both the EPA and OSHA have as their primary objective the saving of human lives. Yet the EPA, for example, has spent $112,000 to save a human life through cleaning up drinking water systems and

$70,700,000 to save a life through controlling coke ovens. It takes little imagination to see how a reallocation of funds could save far more lives for the same total outlay.

Lest we be accused of imbalance concerning this effort to internalize the externalities of supply activities, we note that some interventions have been entirely creditable. For instance, a major pollution-health problem, automobile emissions, was dramatically reduced by government intervention. Between 1963 and 1970, hydrocarbon emissions fell by 75 percent and carbon monoxide emissions by 66 percent. Nevertheless, the question remains: What is the optimal level of intervention by agencies such as the EPA and OSHA?

Poverty

We have already noted that President Johnson's war on poverty ended not with a bang but a fizzle. The official end came with the breakup of the Economic Opportunity Administration in 1973 and the transfer of its few remaining programs to other agencies. At the beginning of the program, about 20 percent of all U.S. families and individuals were defined as living in poverty. By 1977, this had dropped to about 12 percent, but the decrease was primarily due to economic growth.

Poverty was still concentrated disproportionately among "disadvantaged" minorities (blacks, Native Americans, Chicanos, and Puerto Ricans), families headed by women, and the aged. Also, it was increasingly concentrated in urban areas. But, perhaps most disturbing of all, second- and third-generation welfare recipients were becoming more and more common.

The optimism of the 1960s passed. The public increasingly felt that eliminating poverty was a hopeless task. No one seemed satisfied with the existing welfare programs; in fact, many assessed them as not only failing to eliminate poverty, but perhaps as being an important factor in perpetuating it. Yet no one appeared to be able to come up with an acceptable alternative.

The Federal Bureaucracy

The federal bureaucracy grew slowly in the nineteenth century, reaching 95,000 employees by 1900. In the next 30 years, however, growth quickened, reaching 565,000 employees by 1930. With the coming of the depression and the advent of the mixed economy (one in which the federal government plays a substantial role), the federal bureaucracy expanded at a rapid rate: to 996,000 employees in 1940, 1.93 million in 1950, 2.27 million in 1960, and 2.73 million in 1977.

This bureaucracy entered almost every phase of economic activity. There are departments dealing with agriculture, commerce, labor, housing, health, education, and welfare. There are the major regulatory agencies, such as the Interstate

Commerce Commission, Federal Trade Commission, Securities and Exchange Commission, Food and Drug Administration, Federal Communications Commission and the Environmental Protection Agency. One must not forget the Defense Department and, of course, the Internal Revenue Service. There is little that society does in the United States that is not in some way or another touched by the federal bureaucracy.

Our purpose here is not to comment on the desirability of government bureaucracy but rather to ask some questions that have grown out of our historical experience with that bureaucracy: Whose interests are served by the bureaucracy? And who controls it?

There are three possible areas of bureaucratic interest. First, the interest of the society as a whole may be the prime motivating factor. The bureaucracy may try to juggle the conflicting interests of the various segments of the society to come up with actions that in some way benefit the whole of society.

Second are the interests of the particular segments of the economy for which particular bureaucrats are responsible. The Department of Agriculture is concerned about the interests of farmers; the Department of Labor is concerned about labor's interests; and so on. In other words, each agency becomes the spokesman for the particular group in its charge. Schultz and Dam (16) have called this the Balkanization of government.

John K. Galbraith (3, 4), in his books *The New Industrial State* (1966) and *Economics and the Public Purpose* (1973), has argued that the corporations and governments are really run by interlocking committees of experts. These technocrats are necessary because the problems and size of the activities are too complex for anyone but experts. An important point in his argument is that these experts operate on the basis of their own self-interest, which is to maintain control and expand that control. While there are disagreements about the specifics of Galbraith's theory, that the bureaucracy is motivated, at least to some degree, by its own self-interest is more generally accepted.

Serious questions have been raised about whether Congress and the president, who have the immediate "watchdog" function over this bureaucracy, can, or even desire to, control it. An even more pertinent question is: Can the voting citizen adequately "watchdog" the "watchdogs"?

And finally, the ultimate question is: Will the bureaucracy (federal, state, or local) prove flexible enough to meet the nation's problems as we approach the end of the twentieth century?

By the 1970s, the answers to these questions were largely negative. In the late 1970s, the country witnessed the beginning of a partial retreat from bureaucratic regulation. President Carter, on the advice of Alfred Kahn, an economist who was chairman of the Civil Aeronautics Board, sought and received from Congress legislation to deregulate the airline industry in all but safety areas (13). That impetus to deregulate was to grow under the Reagan administration. But more about that in the last chapter.

Industrial Organization—Competition
and the U.S. Economy

In our look at the history of the U.S. economy, we have touched on the development of monopoly power through the creation of large-scale business firms, unions, and big government. Since World War II, two additional forms of business organization have appeared that make the problem of measuring the amount of monopoly power that exists and the means by which it is exercised in the marketplace more difficult and complex. These forms are the conglomerate and the multinational firm. The latter, of course, is an extension of the growing role of international trade in the U.S. economy to which we referred earlier.

Historically, large enterprises were formed through vertical and horizontal integration within the same industry. When it was formed, U.S. Steel included coal mines, coke works, iron mines, steel mills, and plants working the steel into different forms. This was an example of **vertical integration,** or one firm controlling the various stages of production in one industry. As it grew, General Motors absorbed automobile plants making different brands of cars. This is **horizontal integration,** or one firm controlling several plants at the same stage of production.

A **conglomerate** is a single organization that produces goods or services in a variety of different industries. LTV is a conglomerate that owns operating divisions in such diverse industries as electronics, aerospace, electrical wire, steel, stereo equipment, and meat packing. The conglomerate makes antitrust regulation more difficult since it creates the possibility of informal, noncompetitive arrangements between industries.

The multinational firm, as noted in an earlier chapter, is one that gains a significant portion of its assets and income from facilities outside its home country. The operation of multinationals is truly worldwide, not only because they market products all over the world, but also because they draw raw materials and semi-finished products from a network of their facilities in many countries and because their manufacturing plants are located in many different countries. Some examples of multinational firms based in the United States are Exxon, Standard Oil, Ford, and General Motors. Examples of those based in foreign countries are Royal Dutch Shell, Mitsubushi, Nestle's, Krupp, and Volkswagen.

In recent decades, some economists and policymakers have viewed multinational firms as potential sources of monopolization, but this may not be the case. In fact, these firms, particularly under conditions of relatively free trade, may permit a larger measure of contestability in markets, even those that seem monopolized by conventional static measures. The freeing of trade after 1945 almost certainly increased the latitude of large firms to move both resources and products, thereby facilitating market entry and competitiveness. This factor, along with falling information costs and transactions costs from technological change, almost certainly has enhanced competitiveness. In the 1980s, we have seen added to this list of competition-enhancing changes the takeover threats against firms whose management behaves as though it is insulated from competitive market pressures. William Shepherd (17) has concluded that between 1958 and 1980, competition increased significantly in the American economy. While not spread evenly throughout the economy, this growth in competition appears to have resulted from (a) imports and the effects of freer trade, (b) deregulation, especially trucks, airlines, and banking, and (c) the effects of antitrust action.

Structural Change: The Service Economy and the Role of Women

As Jonathan Hughes (8) has pointed out, the classical school of economics forecast a movement of societies to industrialization, to be followed by a secular decline in capital formation because of diminishing long-run returns to capital and because of market behavior. Thus a maturing economy would ultimately result in increasing numbers of underemployed or unemployed industrial workers.

Two important forces that were either unanticipated or underestimated by the classical economists have created a development scenario in industrial economies that is quite different from what they expected. One force was technological change, which, as we have seen, raised the productivity of all factors of production and, via factor complementarities, created a pace of growth far faster, more open-ended, and more enduring than foreseen. The stationary state, with all its implications for human welfare, proved an illusion in industrial societies.

The second force unanticipated or discounted by classical scholars was the structural or sectoral transformation of industrial economies associated with long-term economic development.

Economies can be divided in terms of economic activities into three basic sectoral activities: *primary sector* activities, or those in agriculture, fishing, forestry, and mining; *secondary sector* activities, or those involved in raw materials processing and in manufacturing; and *tertiary sector* activities, or those involved in the services and professions. Classical economists did not anticipate the changing structure of demand in the form of tertiary activities that has accompanied industrial development.

We can see the results of this sectoral reallocation of the American labor force in Table 19.5. The startling overall conclusion to be derived from the data in Table 19.5 is that there has been a dramatic decline in the relative demand for labor in agriculture (almost 38 percent of the labor force in 1900, less than 3 percent of the labor force in 1981) and a dramatic relative increase in the demand for technical, professional, managerial, clerical, and sales labor (13 percent of the labor force in 1900, almost 47 percent of the labor force in 1981).

The growth of the tertiary (service) sector of the economy, reflected in Columns VI, VII, VIII, IX, and XI, is a near total reversal of the pattern in 1900. Two things are especially worth noting about this changed pattern. First, a large part

Table 19.5 Employment of the American Labor Force by Sectors, 1900–1981 (millions of workers).

YEAR	TOTAL CIVILIAN LABOR FORCE	I FARMERS AND FARM MANAGERS	II FARM LABORERS AND FOREMEN	III CRAFTSMEN FOREMEN, ETC.	IV OPERATIVES AND KINDRED WORKERS	V LABORERS (EXCLUDING AGRICULTURAL AND MINING)
1900	29.0	5.8	5.1	3.1	3.7	3.7
1920	42.2	6.4	4.9	5.5	6.6	4.9
1940	51.7	5.3	3.6	6.2	9.5	4.9
1960	64.7	2.5	1.4	9.0	11.3	3.2
1981	100.4	1.5	1.3	12.7	10.5	4.6
Percentage change, 1900–1981	246.2	−74.1	−74.5	309.6	183.8	24.3

YEAR	VI PROFESSIONAL TECHNICAL AND KINDRED WORKERS	VII MANAGERS, OFFICIALS, PROPRIETERS (EXCLUDING AGRICULTURE)	VIII CLERICAL AND KINDRED WORKERS	IX SALES WORKERS	X PRIVATE HOUSEHOLD WORKERS	XI SERVICE WORKERS (EXCLUDING HOUSEHOLDS)
1900	1.2	1.7	0.9	1.3	1.6	1.0
1920	2.3	2.3	3.4	2.1	1.4	1.9
1940	3.9	3.9	5.0	3.4	2.4	3.7
1960	7.0	7.0	9.1	4.6	1.7	6.8
1981	16.4	16.4	18.6	6.4	1.0	12.4
Percentage change 1900–1981	1268.7	576.5	1,996.7	393.3	−37.4	1,140.0

SOURCE: *Historical Statistics, 1960*, Ser. D. *1978 Census of Population Statistical Abstract, 1982–1983* (Washington, D.C.: U.S. Government Printing Office, 1983).

of this dramatic change has occurred since World War II, and especially since 1950. Second, the huge increase in productivity in agriculture and manufacturing made possible the real income flows (+400 percent from 1900 to 1981) and changed patterns of demand that gave rise to the service economy. It is no wonder that by the 1960s there were increasing references to the United States as a "postindustrial" society.

The Service Economy and the Participation of Women

There is a strong association between the growth of the tertiary sector and the rising rate of labor force participation by women, and the association appears to be more than merely statistical. Jonathan Hughes (8) reports that in 1900 only 18 percent of the wage-earning labor force consisted of women. In the most recent (1980) census, that percentage exceeded 37 percent. By 1984, more than half of all women over 18 were wage earners, and 85 percent were employed in the service economy.

As Claudia Goldin (5) has pointed out, even in the late nineteenth century women constituted about a third of the factory labor force. The development of laborsaving devices in the home (appliances, convenience foods, and the like) and cultural changes (for example, the feminist movement) made possible an enlarged supply of female labor to markets. For what are probably cultural reasons, women have always been underrepresented in skilled crafts and management; but the rising labor demand of the tertiary sector has provided jobs to accommodate the increasing supply of female workers at wage rates higher than would otherwise have occurred.

The Service Economy and the Participation of
Minority Groups

The 1960s and 1970s saw major legislative and administrative efforts to reduce wage and job discrimination in American labor markets. Some areas, such as the skilled crafts, that blacks and other minority group members might have moved into and upward from were long closed to them by various factors, including strong union resistance. It is not surprising, then, that the growth of the service economy represented in the expansion of the tertiary sector provided most of the expanded employment opportunities for minorities. As a kind of implicit measure of mobility within the sector, between 1960 and 1980 black and other minority employment in blue-collar and service worker jobs declined, while there was a dramatic growth in employment of those groups in white-collar jobs. Barring a "reindustrialization" of America or a relapse into practices of discrimination, it may well be that continued expansion of the tertiary sector offers the best hope for continued absorption of minority workers into jobs of higher and higher productivity.

QUESTIONS

1. What were the significant features of U.S. economic fluctuations in the 1960–1964 period? The 1965–1969 period?
2. Do you think the accepted recommendations of certain advisory economists for economic stabilization in the 1960s were successful? Explain your conclusion.
3. Between 1960 and 1980, what were the main changes in the distribution of income in the United States?
4. Given the concern about poverty in the United States, what happened to black and minority incomes between 1950 and 1977? In view of this, why has poverty not been virtually eliminated?
5. In view of the long economic expansion of 1961–1969, what economic problems were present at the end of the 1960s?
6. Briefly describe the main characteristics of economic fluctuations in the 1970s.
7. What was Nixon's New Economic Policy? Was it "successful"?
8. In the recessions of 1970–1971 and 1974, there was much talk of a crisis of economic policy. What did this mean?
9. What were the major trends in the trading relationships between the United States and other nations in the 1960s and 1970s? What was the climate of these relationships as America entered the 1980s?
10. The 1960s and 1970s saw a dramatic increase in government regulation in many areas. What gave rise to this trend and what criticisms have been made of this regulatory effort?
11. What were the major changes in business organizations in the 1960s and 1970s? What criticisms have been made of these changes? Do the criticisms seem valid?
12. What have been the major sectoral changes in the American economy since 1900?
13. What are some of the major implications for the growth of the service economy, including those for women and minority group members?

SUGGESTED READINGS

1. Chiswick, Carmel V. "The Elasticity of Substitution Revisited: The Effects of Secular Changes in Labor Force Structure." *Journal of Labor Economics, 3* (Fall 1985).
2. Freeman, Richard B. "The Evolution of the American Labor Market." *The American Economy in Transition,* ed. Martin Feldstein. Chicago: University of Chicago Press, 1980.
3. Galbraith, John K. *Economics and the Public Purpose.* Boston: Houghton Mifflin, 1973.
4. Galbraith, John K. *The New Industrial State.* 2nd ed. Boston: Houghton Mifflin, 1972.
5. Goldin, Claudia. "The Work and Wages of Single Women, 1870 to 1920." *Journal of Economic History, 40* (March 1980).
6. Harrington, Michael. *The Other America.* New York: Macmillan, 1962.
7. Haveman, Robert H. *The Economics of the Public Sector.* New York: Wiley, 1976.
8. Hughes, Jonathan. *American Economic History.* 2nd ed. Glenview, Ill.: Scott Foresman, 1987.

9. Jarret, Henry, ed. *Environmental Quality in a Growing Economy.* Baltimore: Johns Hopkins University Press, 1970.

10. Johnson, Arthur W. *The American Economy: An Historical Introduction to the Problems of the 1970s.* New York: Free Press, 1974.

11. Kessler-Harris, Alice. *Out to Work: A History of Wage Earning Women in the United States.* New York: Oxford University Press, 1982.

12. Lebergott, Stanley. *The Americans: An Economic Record.* New York: Norton, 1984.

13. McGraw, Thomas K. *Prophets of Regulation.* Cambridge, Mass.: Harvard University Press, 1986.

14. Meadows, Donella H., et al. *The Limits to Growth.* New York: Universe, 1972.

15. Ratella, Elyce J. "Women's Labor Force Participation and the Decline of the Family Economy in the United States." *Explorations in Economic History, 17* (April 1980).

16. Schultz, George, and Dam, Kenneth W. *Economic Policy Beyond the Headlines.* New York: Norton, 1977.

17. Shepherd, William. "Causes of Increased Competition in the U.S. Economy, 1939–1980." *Review of Economics and Statistics, 64* (November 1982).

18. Ward, Barbara, et al., eds. *The Widening Gap: Development in the 1970s.* New York: Columbia University Press, 1971.

19. Will, Robert E., and Harold Vatter, eds. *Poverty in Affluence.* 2nd ed. New York: Harcourt Brace Jovanovich, 1970.

Chapter 20

THE 1980s AND BEYOND

Will the United States reindustrialize? If so, will we revert to the priorities in using our resources that existed in an earlier post–Civil War period? What is likely to happen to our savings rate, now the lowest among industrial nations? To reindustrialize—or for other reasons—will we make institutional changes, including changes in taxation? What of our seeming inability to establish a "reasonable" relationship between federal expenditures and tax revenues? Would doing so require fundamental changes in our governmental system? What of our relationships, both economic and political, with other nations? Will a nation that refers to major areas of its economy as a "rust belt" revert to protectionism and forget the trade war experience of the 1930s?

It is tempting in preparing an economic history text to exclude the immediate period in which it is written because it is "not yet history." We have resisted that temptation because the 1980s have generated such controversies as well as continuations of historical trends that ending this book at 1980 would seem excessively abrupt. We will, therefore, take a brief and highly tentative look at the present decade; we shall even venture a few speculative comments about the dimension that has come to be known as "the future as history."

A MACROECONOMIC OVERVIEW, 1980–1985

As America entered the 1980s, its economy was perceived to be performing poorly both in absolute terms and in terms of post–Civil War trends of growth. We can see some evidence of this in Table 20.1.

Table 20.1. Selected Macroeconomic Data: U.S. Economy, 1980–1985 (billions of 1982 dollars, unless otherwise indicated).

YEAR	GNP	CONSUMPTION	GROSS INVESTMENT	NET EXPORTS	GOVERNMENT PURCHASES
1980	3,187	2,000	509	57	621
1981	3,249	2,024	546	49	630
1982	3,166	2,051	447	26	642
1983	3,278	2,146	503	−19	648
1984	3,492	2,240	661	−85	676
1985	3,574	2,313	651	−105	715

YEAR	FEDERAL DEFICIT (CURRENT DOLLARS)	CONSUMER PRICE INDEX (1967 = 100)	UNEMPLOYMENT AS % OF CIVILIAN LABOR FORCE	NATIONAL DEBT (CURRENT DOLLARS)
1980	−74	247	7.1	914
1981	−79	272	7.6	1,004
1982	−128	289	9.7	1,147
1983	−208	298	9.6	1,382
1984	−185	311	7.5	1,577
1985	−212	322	7.1	1,827

SOURCE: *Economic Report of the President* (Washington, D.C.: U.S. Government Printing Office, 1986).

Perhaps the most noteworthy element of the data is that real GNP—and in view of a rising population, real per capita GNP—was falling as the nation entered the 1980s. GNP fell from 1979 to 1980 ($3,192 to $3,187 billion), grew very slowly from 1980 to 1981, and fell again from 1981 to 1982. Although consumption expenditure rose slowly through this period, gross investment fell, net exports approached zero, and government spending increased very slowly. Along with this alternately sluggish and declining economy was a very substantial increase in unemployment, which peaked in December 1982 at 10.7 percent of the civilian labor force. This rising and ultimately double-digit rate of unemployment was accompanied early in the period by double-digit inflation, which, as measured by the rate of change in the consumer price index, was slightly more than 10 percent between 1980 and 1981.

By 1983, the economy began to grow again, as shown in the GNP, consumption, gross investment, and government purchase data. The weakening position of American exports, reflected in the rapidly growing negative net exports (exports minus imports) was a drag on this growth and a source of increasing concern, about which we shall say more later. Inflation declined greatly after 1981, averaging about 3 percent per annum beginning in 1983. The unemployment rate proved to be more sluggish, remaining high (although below double-digit figures) until

1984, when it fell to 7.1 percent. A growing real GNP (6.5 percent in 1984, 5.5 percent in 1985) seemed unable to push unemployment rates down to the levels of previous decades. As late as 1979, the unemployment rate had been 5.8 percent. This led some economists to speculate that there had been an increase in the *natural rate of unemployment*—by one common definition, the percent of the labor force unable to find employment at existing wage rates. Nonetheless, the American economy did enjoy a substantial recovery after the decline of the early 1980s and by 1988, the unemployment rate had fallen to 5.4 percent. Indeed, the fact that the labor force in the 1970s and 1980s grew almost twice as fast as the general population (implying a rising rate of labor force participation) suggests that the economy created jobs at a very rapid rate. Between 1970 and 1985, the population grew by about 17 percent, whereas the labor force grew by almost 40 percent. These facts may well suggest in large measure why the unemployment rate remained relatively high by post–World War II standards.

Problem Areas: Macro-Micro

If "sticky" unemployment rates are at least partly explicable by greater participation in the labor force, what troublesome economic problems seemed to stand out in the mid- to late 1980s? At least two are revealed by the data in Table 20.1.

The dramatic decline in net exports seems to many to represent a future as well as a present problem far greater than simply financing an imbalance on the country's current trade account. Although some believe that the growing imbalance derives from the "overvalued" dollar of the early to mid-1980s, the gap between exports and inports declined little as the dollar fell against other currencies in 1985 and 1986. While some think that this is simply a problem of lagged adjustments in international trade, others believe that it reflects fundamental problems within the American economy. Still other explanations suggest that the failure of exports to rise was due to the very uneven pattern of exchange rate changes or the acceptance of falling profit rates by exporters to the United States. While the dollar fell sharply against some major currencies (the Japanese yen and many European currencies), it fell little if at all against those of other major trading partners, including Canada and Mexico, (second and fifth, respectively, among America's trading partners). The second major problem revealed by the data in Table 20.1 is the dramatic growth in the federal debt, which doubled between 1980 and 1985. Debt growth was tied to the financing of federal deficits, which totaled $886 billion between 1980 and 1985.

Debt Problems

The doubling of the national debt in current dollars between 1980 and 1985 was without parallel in the peacetime history of the United States. The financing of a significant part of that debt occurred through sales to foreign buyers, and by late 1986, the United States had surpassed Brazil, Mexico, and other major debtors as the greatest international debtor nation. This federal debt accumulation was received by economists and noneconomists alike with concern in at least two major dimensions. The first was in financing the debt. Fear was expressed that either private investors would be "crowded out" of capital markets or that a net increase in the supply of private and public securities would cause rising interest rates and a return to the capital market conditions of the late 1970s and early 1980s. As this revision is undertaken, neither of these fears seems to have been realized, largely because of the previously mentioned foreign capital inflows into the United States and because of a disposition of the Federal Reserve to expand the money supply in view of continuing excess capacity in American industry.

Nonetheless, this unparalleled debt accumulation has been seen by many to portend a second serious problem—the inability of the nation to legislate and fund governmental programs in a manner and at a pace that balances, in some periods of time, government spending with government revenues. The Graham-Rudman-Hollings legislation of 1985 was an attempt to impose expenditure limits to deal with this problem. Although criticized widely as limiting the stabilization role of government, as being difficult if not impossible to achieve because of the inaccuracy of revenue-expenditure projections, and as constitutionally defective in its mode of implementation, the ideas underlying Graham-Rudman and the recognition of the politico-economic system that gave rise to it seem to have achieved widespread, if often grudging, acceptance. The problem seems unlikely to disappear in the foreseeable future, and we venture to guess that automaticity in the balancing of the federal budgets will continue to be a major element in the debates about political economy. If nothing else, the awarding of the Noble Prize in Economic Science to James Buchanan in 1986 for his work in public choice theory and its efforts to extend the calculus of private decision making to public activities suggests that economists may be giving greater emphasis to the relations between political and economic systems as we approach the 1990s. A significant part of the budget problem derives from the entitlement programs that have proved intractable to expenditure reductions.

Falling Productivity Growth: Problem or Illusion?

The weakened export position of the United States has been laid by some to a decline in productivity growth in American industry. But although there has been some decline in productivity growth measures, Michael Darby (5) has shown that once proper adjustments are made in labor force data to account for changes in age, sex, immigration, and education, there was no change in long-term trend productivity growth in the United States between 1900 and 1979. As Jonathan Hughes (9) observes about declines in the conventional measure of output per unit of factor input, "But not to worry, it will pass."

The "Rust Belt" Syndrome

There is reason to worry about the declining competitiveness of certain basic U.S. industries that became so apparent in the 1980s: autos, steel, shoes, textiles, and even such "high-tech" industries as computers and computer chips. At least in the case of certain old-line industries such as automobiles, steel, machine tools and parts, and construction equipment, it began to appear that changing comparative advantage along with other factors had caused some U.S. industries to become less and less able to compete in both domestic and international markets (13). Illustrative of this change is the steel industry, whose share of world output fell from almost half in the early 1950s to about 15 percent in the early 1980s. A new term, "rust belt," was coined to denote those areas of the country, particularly in the Midwest, where many plants were closing (2). Why had all this happened? Responsibility was cast widely, sometimes on labor-management relations that produced relatively high-cost structures for U.S. firms, sometimes on unimaginative short-term-horizon management that had been cushioned in oligopolistic industries. Also, allegations were made of "unfair" trading practices such as dumping, export subsidization, and nontariff barriers by Japan and other U.S. trading partners.

To an objective observer, all this might seem to be a continuation of patterns evidenced earlier in our nation's history. Throughout, we have witnessed growing industries that matured and ultimately declined as the result of various factors, including changes in technology and consumer tastes and preferences. In earlier chapters, we saw this happen to cotton, textiles, iron railways, and other industries. Are the recent declines in steel, autos, machine parts, textiles, shoes, and other U.S. industries no more than evidences of temporary market disequilibria, signals to reallocate the nation's growing resources to new, more productive uses? Is this what we will see in the next 10 to 20 years? Or are these phenomena more long-lived, structural in nature, and part of a transition to a service-based economy with slower long-term growth prospects? Only time will tell. Both scenarios have their forecasting advocates as the United States approaches the end of the twentieth century.

POLITICAL ECONOMY IN THE LATE TWENTIETH CENTURY

As we saw in earlier chapters, public-private sector relationships have been subject to great variations during our nation's history. At times, special interest groups have sought protection, even direct subsidization, from government. At other times, groups, sometimes even those representing the same interests, have opposed government intervention, especially industrial regulation. In perhaps no period of U.S. history have these contradictory strands been more evident than in the period since the 1960s. As Thomas McCraw (12) has observed, the conflict between concern for efficiency and safety in areas such as pollution and health and safety

> presented a most peculiar spectacle. In an ironic historical example of the ways in which ideas can move policymakers in opposite directions, significant deregulation had been instituted for such industries as airlines, trucking, railroads, financial markets and telecommunications. At the same time, additional social and environmental regulation had become firmly embedded in the structure of state and federal governments. . . .

What, then, does the ambivalent experience of our post–Civil War history suggest about the future role of government as an economic regulator and protector? The safe assumption is that both pushes for regulation and deregulation will continue. As technology changes, natural monopolies may disappear, as happened through dramatic changes in microwave communication to long-distance communication in the 1970s. When private firms and consumers are perceived to incorrectly internalize cost and benefit externalities, there will, contrarily, be pushes for broadened regulation. Thus the future promises neither more regulation nor more deregulation. Instead, it seems likely there will be a changing structure of both.

Equity: An Ever-Present Concern

As we have seen in recent chapters, income distribution since World War II has been notable for its constancy, although transfer payments and productivity growth raised the incomes of the lowest (less than $5,000 annually) groups. What, though, of the distribution of wealth, held in the form of stocks, real estate, equity bonds, and other assets? A study by Weicher and Wachter (16) in late 1986 concluded that wealth inequality increased between 1977 and 1983, but that the changes were based largely on age and education rather than on race or how families are constituted. Older families (heads of households over 55) and households whose heads had some college education increased their net worth relative to younger and less well educated heads of housedholds. Interestingly for public policy, the study concluded that black households, though having relatively little net worth, increased that wealth during the period more rapidly than white households. However, the net worth of Hispanic households declined slightly. There was evidence, according to the study, that households headed by females, an increasing phenomenon in the 1970s and 1980s, increased their wealth in the period studied.

Findings such as these may allay some concerns about the creation of a perpetual "underclass" in America based on race and household composition. Overall concerns about equity and the competing claims for transfer payments and other income and wealth redistribution sources seem less likely to diminish in the future.

SUMMARY

The 1980s have presented the American economy with some continuing problems as well as some problems that are perceived to be new in nature or emphasis. Among the latter are the "rust belt" with its politico-economic consequences, the unparalleled federal debt accumulation, and the simultaneous occurrence of double-digit inflation and unemployment. Debates about protectionism and government regulation are clearly continuations of historical problems. Concerns for equity, though conditioned by recent evidence about wealth accumulation, are part of a debate as old as the republic. Projecting the future from the past is hazardous and uncertain, but the evidence of the 1980s presented in this chapter suggests that economic debates of the late 1980s and the 1990s may well center on protectionism, federal debt, public regulation, and equity.

QUESTIONS

1. What conditions characterized the macroeconomic performance of the American economy in the early 1980s?
2. Although GNP grew between 1983 and 1987, what were the continuing macroeconomic problems of the United States during that period?
3. At what rate did the economy grow between 1970 and 1985? What was the corresponding rate of growth of the labor force? How may these two rates be reflected in unemployment rates in the late 1980s?
4. What has happened to the foreign trade position of the United States in the 1980s? What seem to be the explanations for this change from historical trade relationships?
5. What is the evidence regarding productivity growth in the American economy in the 1980s? If this is a change from historical trends, does it seem to be temporary or long-term?
6. What seem to be the reasons for the creation of the "rust belt" in the United States in the 1970s and 1980s?
7. What happened to the size of the federal debt in the 1980s? What problems are seen to be associated with that accumulation of public debt?
8. Describe the ambivalent tendencies regarding the protective and regulatory role of government in the American economy in the 1980s?
9. What apparently happened to the distribution of wealth (net assests) in the United States in the late 1970s and in the 1980s? If there has been a redistribution, in whose favor has it occurred? Do changes in that distribution seem to you to portend problems for the future?
10. Judging from what happened in the American economy in the 1970s and 1980s, what do you think are the likely major economic issues for the United States in the 1990s?

SUGGESTED READINGS

1. Anderson, Terry, and P. J. Hill. *The Birth of a Transfer Society*. Stanford, Cal.: Hoover Institution Press, 1980.

2. Bluestone, Barry, and Bennett Harrison. *The Deindustrialization of America: Plant Closings, Community Abandonments and the Dismantling of Basic Industry*. New York: Basic Books, 1982.

3. Branson, William H. "Trends in United States International Trade and Investment Since World War II." In *The American Economy in Transition*, ed. Martin Feldstein. Chicago: University of Chicago Press, 1980.

4. Buchanan, James, and Richard Wagner. *Democracy in Deficit*. New York: Academic Press, 1977.

5. Darby, Michael R "The U.S. Productivity Slowdown: A Case of Statistical Myopia." *The American Economic Review*, 74 (June 1984).

6. Easterlin, Richard. "Why Isn't Everyone Developed?" *The Journal of Economic History*, 41 (March 1981).

7. Friedman, Benjamin. "Postwar Macroeconomic Performance." In *The American Economy in Transition*, ed. Martin Feldstein. Chicago: University of Chicago Press, 1980.

8. Gilder, George. *Wealth and Poverty*. New York: Basic Books, 1981.

9. Hughes, Jonathan. *American Economic History*. 2nd ed. Glenview, Ill.: Scott Foresman, 1986. Esp. chap. 31 and 32.

10. Hughes, Jonathan. *The Governmental Habit: Economic Controls From Colonial Times to the Present*. New York: Basic Books, 1977.

11. Janowitz, Morris. *Social Control of the Welfare State*. Chicago: University of Chicago Press. 1976.

12. McCraw, Thomas K. *Prophets of Regulation*. Cambridge, Mass.: Belknap Press, 1984.

13. McKenzie, Richard B. *Fugitive Industry: The Economics and Politics of Deindustrialization*. San Francisco: Pacific Institute, 1982.

14. Mogaziner, Ira C., and Robert B. Reich. *The Decline and Rise of the American Economy*. New York: Harcourt Brace Jovanovich, 1982.

15. Olson, Mancur. `The Logic of Collective Action: Public Goods and the Theory of Groups*. Cambridge, Mass.: Harvard University Press, 1971.

16. Weicher, John, and Susan Wachter. *Distribution of Wealth in the United States, 1977 to 1983*. Washington, D.C. American Enterprise Institute, 1986.

17. Weidenbaum, Murray. *Business, Government and the Public*. Englewood Cliffs, N.J.: Prentice Hall, 1977.

GLOSSARY

Absolute advantage The advantage that occurs when a nation or area is more efficient in producing a good or all goods than any other nation from which it might import that good or those goods.

Accelerator principle The principle that as the rate of growth of consumer and industrial demand increases, the need for additional facilities increases and induced investment increases. These increases create a positive accelerator and the economy expands. The reverse occurs where the rate of growth of consumer demand declines.

Aggregate production function The function showing the factors that determine changes in output.

American System The term given to the system of standardized products, continuous production, and interchangeable parts begun in the early nineteenth century.

Assembly-line production, or **mass production** A process depending on the standardization and thus interchangeability of parts and the development of a system or systems of flow of materials logically arranged so as to facilitate assembly of the product.

Automatic stabilizers Factors in the economy that tend to dampen business fluctuations without conscious decision-making.

Autonomous investment Investment determined by factors other than changes in income or consumption.

Backward linkages Effects of input-output relationships or demand-supply stimuli from one economic activity to probable economic activities that existed in prior stages of production. For example, expansion of steel production through technological change increases the probability of developing coal and iron deposits.

Balance of payments A summary accounting statement of all economic transactions between the residents of a country and the residents of all other countries during a given time period.

"Beggar thy neighbor" policy Policy of international trade restriction on the part of a country aimed at increasing exports relative to imports.

Blacklist A list distributed to employers of workers considered "undesirable" for employment. Used against union members.

Capital-labor ratio The number of dollars of capital (invested in machines, buildings, and so on) used per unit of labor.

Ceteris paribus assumption The assumption that all factors but one are held constant in order to observe the effects of changes in the one allowed to vary.

Classical view A view of economic development set forth in various forms during the late eighteenth and early to mid-nineteenth centuries by the classical economists, beginning with Adam Smith. Economic development is regarded as productivity growth, which is obtained through specialization and division of labor and capital, which in turn depend on the size of the market, the stock of capital, and economic institutions.

Clearinghouse A means by which the notes of different banks are cleared through some central bank or institution.

Company union A union whose membership consists only of the employees of a particular firm and that is dominated by that firm's officials.

Competition The market form in which no buyer or seller is able to influence price by his or her own actions. Competition requires the following conditions: absence of collusion, flexible prices, and free entry and exit.

Complementary industries Industries that serve a number of different industries, although they may have been created to service only one.

Conglomerate The combining of firms that produce in different industries.

Consolidation Forming one larger company out of a number of smaller companies.

Constant returns to scale The return when long-run average costs are constant as scale (short-run average cost curves) increase.

Construction companies Separately incorporated firms whose primary function was to raise financial capital and construct the railroads.

Consumption function A function representing the various quantities that a society is willing and able to consume at different levels of income.

Cost externalities Reductions in the average costs of a firm that result from actions taken outside the firm.

Craft unionism Union representation of workers by trade or craft rather than by industry.

Credit All transactions in the balance of payments accounts that generate an immediate obligation for a nonresident to pay a resident. Or, all transactions that increase foreign demand for dollars or increase the supply of foreign monies in the foreign exchange market; for example, an export.

Cross-sectional data Data that show the occurrence of a particular event in different activities at the same point in time or over the same span of time.

Current account The sum of the balance of payments merchandise and invisible items accounts.

Current GNP Total value of annual output of final goods and services; it includes the effects of price changes. It is not the best measure of economic performance of the economy.

Data The records of economic events. In a broad sense, the word *data* refers to all events or happenings that are observed and recorded, not simply those that are quantified.

Debit All transactions in the balance of payments accounts that generate an immediate obligation for a resident to pay a nonresident. Or, all transactions that increase foreign supply of dollars or increase the demand for foreign monies in the foreign exchange market; for example, an import.

Decreasing returns to scale See **Diseconomies of scale.**

Deficit in the balance of payments A deficit that results when a country is unable to obtain enough foreign exchange from its sale of goods and services or from long-term investment to pay for what its citizens purchase from other economies.

Demand A schedule that indicates the quantity of a good that will be purchased at each of a set of prices in a particular time period.

Deposit multiplier The increase in money supply possible under a fractional reserve banking system given the reserve requirement and the amount of excess reserves in the banking system.

Depreciate A currency depreciates when it buys less of a foreign currency per unit of the domestic currency.

Derived demand Demand for a resource that is brought about by the demand for a product or service produced by that resource.

Diseconomies of scale, or decreasing returns to scale The return when long-run average costs are increasing as scale (short-run average cost curves) increases.

Dollar gap Shortage in international reserves in Western European countries and Japan that existed between 1945 and 1955.

Dual unionism More than one union existing for a single craft or industry.

Economic determinism In the pure sense, the view that economic history is a progression of events in which people act almost exclusively on the basis of their economic self-interest or through adjusting to the changing economic reality.

Economic development The long-term process through which per capita output grows and structural change occurs as well.

Economic fluctuations Variations in the level of economic activity, primarily variations in output, employment, and prices. It is considered a more appropriate term than *business cycles,* or *business fluctuations.*

Economic institutions The organizational means through which economic decisions are made and implemented.

Economic integration The tying together of product and resource markets in such a way that resources are allocated to their most efficient uses.

Economic interpretation Employing economic theory and methodology to assay economic causes and consequences of events.

Economic profit (rent) A payment to a factor of production greater than that necessary to bid for its use or greater than its opportunity costs.

Economic rent See **Economic profit.**

Economies of scale, or Increasing returns to scale The returns accruing as the long-run average cost curve slopes down as successive short-run average total cost curves, each showing a larger scale of operation, result in lower average costs.

Elastic demand The relationship that exists when the quantity responds greatly to a given change in price, or when the percentage change in quantity demanded is greater than the percentage change in price, or when the elasticity coefficient is greater than 1.

Elasticity coefficient A number indicating the degree of responsiveness of quantities to something else; as, for example, the price elasticity of demand represented by the following formula:

$$\frac{Q_1 - Q_2}{Q_1 + Q_2} \div \frac{P_1 - P_2}{P_1 + P_2}$$

Q_1 is beginning quantity, Q_2 is ending quantity, P_1 is beginning price, and P_2 is ending price. (Ignore the minus sign in the results.)

Elasticity of demand The ratio is between the rate at which the quantity demanded of a product changes as its price changes.

Elasticity of output The rate at which output increases as effective demand increases.

Embargo of December 1807 On the basis of an action of Congress, President Jefferson forbade the import or export of goods from and to Britain and France in retaliation for their seizure of U.S. commercial vessels from 1792 to 1807.

Empty lands Those lands in which a new economy (rather than the evolution from an old economic order) evolves.

Entrepot trade Trade that enters a country and then is transhipped to another country without being changed in form.

Entrepreneurship The function of organizing resources in such a way that economic production occurs.

Envelope curve The long-run average cost curve as it encloses or envelops an array of short-run average total cost curves, each representing a particular scale of operation.

Equation of exchange A definitional relationship that shows that $MV = PQ$, where M is the stock of money, V is the income velocity of money, P is the price level, and Q is the number of final goods and services.

Equilibrium price Also a market-clearing price. The central price tendency of a market or the price that tends to eliminate both gluts and shortages.

Extensive growth The growth that occurs as more resources are used to produce an output unchanged in composition or techniques of production.

Favorable balance of trade When exports exceed imports or there is a credit balance in the merchandise account.

Floating the dollar A policy that allowed the exchange rate of the dollar for foreign monies to fluctuate depending on supply-and-demand conditions without government interference.

Forward linkages Effects of input-output relationships or demand-supply stimuli from one economic activity to probable economic activities closer to the ultimate user of the activity. For example, wheat production provides raw materials that could be used in flour milling.

Fractional reserves In colonial times, refers to the need of a merchant bank to keep reserves in the form of gold or silver that are a fraction (less than 100 percent) of the currency in circulation. This is based on the principle that depositors will not come into the bank and demand gold or silver for the currency in an amount equal to total deposits.

Frictional Unemployment The rate of unemployment associated with those moving from one job to another.

Full-employment budget The expenditures of the federal government, compared to taxes that would have been received if there had been full employment.

Granger laws State laws passed in the 1870s and 1880s to regulate railroads.

Gresham's law The rule that relatively overvalued money drives relatively undervalued money out of circulation.

High-powered money The reserves of banks, consisting of gold, silver, coins, and certificates to specie, that could be readily loaned.

Holding company A company formed for the purpose of buying stock in other companies and thereby controlling those other companies.

Horizontal integration The combining of firms that produce at the same stage of production in the same industry.

Human capital formation The investment in education that results in improved human skills and increased marginal physical productivity.

Income effect The effect on the quantity demanded of a good caused by the change in purchasing power resulting from a change in the price of that good.

Income elasticity of demand The rate at which the demand for a product changes in relation to the rate at which income changes.

Increasing returns to scale See **Economies of scale.**

Induced investment Investment induced or caused by changes in income and consumption. When the rate of increase in consumer demand is increasing, induced investment increases.

Industrial union A union that draws its members from a specific industry rather than from a specific trade or craft.

Inelastic demand The relationship that exists when the quantity demanded responds little to a given change in price, or when the percentage change in quantity demanded is less than the percentage change in price, or when the elasticity coefficient is less than 1.

Information costs The costs to buyers and sellers of obtaining the price and technical information necessary to make rational choices.

Innovation According to Schumpeter, innovation means new products, new processes, new machines, or even new markets that open up new opportunities for profits.

Intensive growth The growth that involves increased productivity and involves a changed composition of output and techniques of production.

Interlocking directorates Situations in which the same people appear on the boards of directors of a number of different corporations in the same industry; policies could then be more easily formulated in these several corporations that would eliminate competition and substitute cooperation.

Internal and external economies of scale Lowered unit costs of production associated with larger-scale activity. Such lowered costs are internal if they result from increased scale by the individual firm; they are external if they result from actions taken outside of the individual firm.

Interpretation The final product of economic history, the result of drawing historical conclusions by testing hypotheses within the framework of theory.

Investment function A function representing the various quantities that the society is willing and able to invest at different levels of income.

Invisible items account A major subaccount within the current account of the balance of payments. It contains primarily services such as expenditures by tourists; transportation; insurance fees; dividends, profits, and interest on foreign investments; and transfer payments.

Land banks Established by a number of states in the 1780s, these banks issued paper currency backed only by loans on land.

Law of demand The hypothesis that consumers will buy more of a good at (relatively) lower prices than at (relatively) higher prices.

Law of diminishing returns Also known as the law of increasing opportunity cost. The idea that in reallocating resources to produce one good, a society must ultimately give up more and more of another good.

Law of supply The hypothesis that firms will supply more of a good at (relatively) higher prices that at (relatively) lower prices.

Leading sector theories Theories that hypothesize the existence of a sector or sectors of the economy that create effects on intensive growth and development through supply and demand effects that spread through the rest of the economy.

Legal tender Money that according to law must be accepted in payment for all debts, public and private.

Lockout The employer's equivalent of the strike. Occurs when the employer locks the door of the plant and does not allow workers to work.

Longer planning horizon A longer investment planning time.

Long-run time period A period of time long enough so that all factors of production used by the individual firm can vary, including plant size.

Long-term capital account A balance-of-payments account containing all entries in the balance of payments concerning long-term investments (the purchase of stock or bonds or direct investments) by residents in other countries or nonresidents in this country.

Macro model One concerned with economic activity on the level of the whole economy.

Marginal factor cost The cost of hiring an additional unit of a resource.

Marginal propensity to consume The percent or portion of any change in income that becomes personal consumption expenditure rather than savings or tax payments.

Marginal propensity to import The amount of increased income spent on imported goods.

Marginal revenue product The change in total revenue associated with hiring an additional unit of a resource. It is determined by multiplying the marginal physical product of the resource by the marginal revenue of the firm.

Mass production See **Assembly-line production.**

Mature debtor nation A nation that has a credit balance in the balance-of-payments merchandise account. This, in turn, provides the foreign exchange to pay for the debit balance in dividends, interest, and profits resulting from outflows of income earned by prior foreign investment in the nation's economy.

Mercantilism A system of practical economic policy, dominant in the seventeenth and eighteenth centuries, giving rise to "managed" economies with extensive government involvement. Each government aimed to maximize the economic power of the nation by creating a favorable balance of trade resulting in an inflow of gold.

Merchandise account A major subaccount within the current account of the balance of payments. It reflects the exports and imports of goods.

Merchant banks of the 1780s Banks chartered by state governments with the power to issue currency backed by gold and silver. Their loans were primarily commercial.

Micro model The analysis of the activities of the smaller units in the economy such as the individual market or consumer or firm.

Mixed assemblies A local unit of organization in the Knights of Labor consisting of union members from a variety of occupations.

Mixed-market economy Combination of important federal expenditures and taxes in the economy and regulation of sections of the economy to make the federal government an important factor in the market economy.

Model See **Theory.**

Monocultural In reference to a region, monoculturalism is specialization in producing one or a very few basic commodities.

Monopoly power The ability of a seller to directly influence price by varying supply in the market.

Multinational firm A firm with economic facilities for supply, processing, manufacturing, and sales that are worldwide.

Multiplier effect A multiple change in income from any given change in aggregate demand. The size of the multiplier depends on the marginal propensity to consume or save.

Navigation Acts A series of acts by which the British Parliament regulated trade during the colonial period. Among other regulations, the acts restricted trade within the empire to ships of the British Empire and enumerated exports that had to be shipped directly to Britain, regardless of their ultimate destination.

Net creditor nation A nation that has more investment in other countries than foreigners have in that country.

Net debtor nation A nation that has more investment by foreigners in its economy than its residents have in other countries.

Nonintercourse Act of 1809 Act of Congress that allowed trade with Britain or France if they stopped seizure of U.S. ships. In 1809, trade was allowed to resume with France.

Normal profit A payment to entrepreneurship equal to its opportunity costs.

Open door policy A policy advocated by the United States in the late nineteenth century to allow all countries to trade and invest throughout China.

Open market operations The buying or selling of government securities by the Federal Reserve in the open market for the purpose of affecting reserves and thus the ability to lend of the commercial banking system. When the Fed buys securities, it increases bank reserves. When the Fed sells securities, it decreases reserves.

Opportunity cost The amount of one good given up in order to produce more of another.

Parity A measure to express the purchasing power of farm products. It compares an index of farm prices to an index of the prices of what farmers buy.

Pooling Firms jointly deciding prices, shares of market, and other conditions of the market, as a method of reducing competition between firms.

Precautionary motive for holding money Holding money for protection against unforeseen happenings that require spending.

Price elasticity of demand A measure of the responsiveness of quantity demanded to changes in price along a given demand curve.

Price elasticity of supply A measure of the responsiveness of quantity supplied to changes in price along a given supply curve.

Primary boycott When a striking union urges people not to buy from the firm against which the union is striking.

Primary demand The initial demand for a product stemming from those who had never before bought the product.

Principle of comparative advantage The advantage that a nation or area derives from specializing in producing those goods in which it is relatively more efficient and, importing from other nations the goods that they produce with relatively greater efficiency.

Production function The input-output combinations of an economy, an industry, or a firm.

Production function of the staple The function that shows the relationship between resource input and staple product output.

Production possibilities curve A diagrammatic presentation of a production possibilities function.

Production possibilities function A relationship that shows the various combinations of output that the full employment of a nation's resources (land, labor, capital, and entrepreneurship), using the best current technology, can produce.

Putting-out system of manufactures Home industries using materials supplied by merchant manufacturers. The merchant would then pick up these finished or semifinished products from the workers' homes and pay them.

Quasi-rents Payments to a resource owner due to the inelasticity of supply of that resource.

Real GNP Total value of annual output of final goods and services that has been adjusted for changes in prices so that it measures only changes in output of goods and services. It is a better measure of economic performance than is current GNP.

Rediscount rate The interest rate charged banks by the Federal Reserve for borrowing from the Fed.

Reexports Foreign imports that are exported again without any change in form.

Regressive taxes The tax rate decreases as taxable income increases.

Reserve ratio The ratio of bank reserves to deposits and notes; this reserve indicates the amount of specie that banks chose to or were forced to maintain in relation to their loans and note issue.

Residentiary industries Industries that provide goods and services needed by residents of a particular area.

Safety valve theory The assumption that in the nineteenth century the free or nearly free land on the frontier would provide an alternative to eastern industrial employment and would limit the ability of industrial employers to "exploit or oppress" the American working class.

Savings function The various quantities that a society is willing and able to save at different levels of income.

Scale of operation A firm's operations when utilizing a particular size of plant or number of plants.

Secondary boycott When a striking union urges people not to buy from another firm that does business with the firm against which the union is striking.

Secondary demand Replacement demand for a product, or, for example, by those who bought a second car to replace an original car.

Sharecropping A system of tenancy in which the renter pays the landlord a certain percentage of his crop for the use of the land.

Short-haul versus long-haul rates Often discrimination in railroad rates occurred when rates for short hauls (distances) were either higher than for longer hauls or were higher per mile, giving a price advantage to those shipping over longer distances.

Short-run time period A period of time short enough so that at least one factor of production is fixed in amount for the individual firm. Often the limiting factor is fixed plant size; that is, fixed floor space.

Social overhead capital Forms of capital available for use or consumption by the public (such as roads, canals, railroads, and educational facilities).

Speculative motive for holding money Holding money in order to make investments when opportunities arise.

Stagflation A condition of high unemployment and high inflation at the same time.

Subsidiary industries Industries needed to allow another industry to function. In the leading sector of 1792–1815, foreign trade, shipbuilding and shipfitting were subsidiary.

Substitution effect The amount by which consumers tend to substitute a good when its price is falling, for other, now relatively more expensive goods (as implied by the law of demand).

Supply A schedule of the various quantities that sellers are willing and able to sell at various prices during a given time.

Takeoff In the economic development theory of Walt Rostow, the stage in which economic development becomes the normal and ongoing condition of society.

Terms of trade The ratio of export prices received to import prices paid (stated in the form of indices).

Theory A set of formal relationships between forces of factors, or a model, or an analogy to, or a simplification of, the complex reality of a period.

Time series data Data that show the occurrence of a particular kind of event at different points in time.

Trade assembly A local unit of organization in the Knights of Labor consisting only of union members from the same craft or occupation.

Trade deficit A deficit that occurs when imports exceed exports.

Trade surplus A surplus that occurs when exports exceed imports.

Trade unionism A philosophy of union organization in which the concentration is primarily on gaining benefits for union members in terms of increased wages, reduced hours of work, and other conditions of employment; avoids direct political involvement.

Transactions costs The costs of effecting exchanges between buyers and sellers.

Transactions motive for holding money Holding money to buy things between paydays.

Trust A form of business organization in which firms in an industry turn over their common stock to a trust company and receive in return trust certificates. As a result, the trust company controls each individual firm.

Unilateral transfers Funds transfers arising when nonresidents receive funds that they are not obligated, now or in the future, to pay back, either in money or goods and services. An example is an immigrant's savings of U.S. dollars that he takes with him when he moves back to his original homeland.

Unit elastic demand The condition that exists when quantity demanded changes proportionately with a given change in price; or the percentage change in quantity is equal to the percentage change in price; or the elasticity coefficient is equal to 1.

Velocity of exchange (V) The number of times the supply of money changes hands in a given time period. The assumption here is that the spending of money is only for final goods and services.

Vertical integration The combining of firms that produce at different stages of production within a single industry.

Visible items of trade Commodities, such as tobacco, that can be exchanged in trade.

Waltham Plan A system of integrating spinning and weaving equipment within the same plant; introduced in Waltham, Massachusetts.

Weber Thesis The argument of Max Weber that Protestant theological ideas of the Reformation period influenced the behavior of people in ways that were beneficial to rapid economic development. Weber said that psychological conditioning was induced by the theological positions of religious leaders, especially Luther and Calvin.

Yellow-dog contract A contract with an employer wherein a worker agrees not to join a union. Often used as the basis for a court injunction against a union's organizing activities.

Young creditor nation A nation that has a credit balance in the balance-of-payments merchandise account that provides the foreign exchange to permit long-term capital investment in other countries; it has a debit balance in the long-term capital account.

Young debtor nation A nation that has a debit balance in the balance-of-payments merchandise account, paid for by credit balances in the long-term capital account.

INDEX